You the Writer
Writing, Reading, Thinking

Hans P. Guth

Santa Clara University

Gabriele L. Rico

San Jose State University

Houghton Mifflin Company

Boston   New York

SPONSORING EDITOR: Jayne M. Fargnoli

SENIOR ASSOCIATE EDITOR: Linda M. Bieze

EDITORIAL ASSISTANT: Terri Teleen

SENIOR PROJECT EDITOR: Janet Edmonds

SENIOR PRODUCTION/DESIGN COORDINATOR: Jill Haber

SENIOR MANUFACTURING COORDINATOR: Marie Barnes

SENIOR MARKETING MANAGER: Nancy Lyman

COVER DESIGN: Mark Caleb

Acknowledgments

Maya Angelou, "Step Forward in the Car, Please" from *I Know Why the Caged Bird Sings.* Copyright © 1969 by Maya Angelou. Reprinted by permission of Random House, Inc.

Norman Atkins, "The Cost of Living Clean" from *Rolling Stone,* May 5, 1994, by Straight Arrow Publishers Company, L.P. 1994. All Rights Reserved. Reprinted by permission.

Toni Cade Bambara, "The Lesson" from *Gorilla, My Love.* Copyright © 1972 by Toni Cade Bambara. Reprinted by permission of Random House, Inc.

Donald Barthelme, "The School." Copyright © 1976 by Donald Barthelme. Reprinted by permission of The Wylie Agency, Inc.

Acknowledgments continue on p. 608, which constitutes an extension of the copyright page.

Printed in the U.S.A.

Library of Congress Catalog Card Number: 96-76950

Student Text ISBN: 0-395-68635-0
Examination Copy ISBN: 0-395-84395-2

123456789-CS-01 00 99 98 97

BRIEF CONTENTS

CONTENTS

Writing is a struggle against silence. **CARLOS FUENTES**

To the Instructor

How do writing teachers help students discover their potential as writers? What kind of writing course will help our students overcome any negative expectations, help them discover their resources, and build their competence and confidence? What will arouse their curiosity; what will bring their native intelligence, mother wit, and idealism into play? We have designed *You the Writer* as a textbook for courses that help students discover writing as a central medium of communication in our world, as a tool of learning and self-discovery, and as a many-faceted means of interacting with others.

Much classroom exploration, much listening to students, much dialoguing with colleagues, and much sifting of professional publication — inspiring or depressing — go into the preparation of this kind of book. We have aimed at a consensus of what is most promising or productive in current classroom practice and the burgeoning field of composition studies. We have proceeded on the assumption that underlying our profession's discussions about multiculturalism, patriarchy, or an exploitative hiring system is a shared commitment.

Here is some of the thinking that has guided us in writing this book:

Writing: The Core of the Curriculum   Writing is at the core of the student's education. An educated person uses written language effectively for his or her own purposes. Most work today involves written language: résumés, memos, manuals, guidelines, reports, promotional brochures, proposals, and evaluations. Much of our thinking about our social and political culture is shaped by writers who write with authority about today's world. Computer writing, e-mail, and electronic networking are multiplying the numbers of those who think, work, and interact through the medium of the written word.

Validating Student Writing   The credo of writing teachers is that students have resources of intelligence, imagination, and curiosity not tapped by routine procedures. Although we serve our students as mentors, editors, or evaluators, our aim is to teach them to use language effectively in the service of their own agendas. We want them to become self-motivated, self-directed, and self-critical. This text recognizes no artificial separation between professional writing and student writing. Students are capable of writing with commitment and imagination, using writing for self-expression, communication, and persuasion.

Learning by Writing   Students learn from increasingly more challenging writing and reading. Grappling with first-hand experience and observation, processing information, integrating a range of material, guiding choices, weighing the pro and con, appealing to readers' values — these are things good writers do. These are things at which first-rate writers excel. These dimensions of writing are not self-contained or mutually exclusive modes; they are dimensions of the student's personal and academic growth. They are capabilities that students study and practice so that written communication will serve them well.

Thinking/Writing Strategies   In this book, we highlight the thinking that gives writing shape and direction. Writing on the computer has shortened the distance between letting ideas take shape and putting them into words — between thinking and writing. The challenge for the instructor is not to teach thinking/writing strategies as formulaic think schemes but to involve students in issues where the writer's strategy arises from the writing situation, where it proves the logical way of thinking the subject through.

The Workshop Format   In classes with a workshop format, students and instructors explore, discuss, and respond to work in progress. *You the Writer* again and again models for students how a paper takes shape — what motivates writing, where writers turn for material, how they focus it and pull it into shape, how they revise and rethink in response to peer criticism and instructor's comments. Students share in hands-on discussion of other writers' work. They learn from the example and feedback of their peers. They participate in collaborative projects.

Integrating Whole and Part   In *You the Writer,* we have decided not to present first a rhetoric of the whole and then a rhetoric of parts, leaving to the teacher the often frustrating task of integrating the two. Where do macro-rhetorical and micro-rhetorical concerns intersect? When or where in a course would a teacher work best with words, sentences, or paragraphs? The "Writer's Tools" sections in this text are optional, and they may be used independently in accordance with the instructor's estimate of the needs of a class. However, they appear in the text where they are most organically related to the writing tasks at hand.

Acknowledgments   We owe a large debt to the linguists and compositionists who succeeded in reversing the negativism of much composition teaching and to the many members of the writing movement who have maintained their enthusiasm for the teaching of writing in hard times. We have especially enjoyed networking with colleagues at the annual CCCC's conference, at the annual Young Rhetoricians' Conference in Monterey, and at many meetings and workshops around the country.

Among those who have helped us with this book, we owe a special debt to Brian McLaughlin for his competent and conscientious research and to Karen Harrington for her invaluable editorial work. The quick intelligence, lively imagination, and youthful idealism of our students have been our main sources of inspiration. We are grateful to the many students who have given us permission to use or adapt their writing. We want to thank especially Michael Bravo, Neema Buruku, Amy Casey, Megan Chang, Richard Childers, Megan Clemens, Ben Domingue, Simone Eppich, Alisa Garni, Jeff Griffis, Jensen Jeung, Luis Lorenzano, Kerry Morris, Chris Navarro, James Perry, Melanie Phung, Brady Rasmussen, Von Reyes, Hugo Rodriguez, Arnulfo Sanchez, Tara Sheedy, Francia Stephens, Lisa Tankersley, Craig Waters, and Emily Waters.

We also wish to thank the reviewers who read and advised us on the various drafts of this book: Kathleen Bell, University of Central Florida; Leonard Engel, Quinnipiac College; William Gilbert, California State University–Long Beach; Larry Hawes, Aiken Technical

College; Mark Rollins, Ohio University; Joanne Stoddick, University of Massachusetts–Boston; Heidemarie Weidner, Tennessee Technical University; Irwin Weiser, Purdue University; and Mark Withrow, Columbia College.

Hans P. Guth
Gabriele L. Rico

Orientation:
Why Writing Matters

When something is important enough, we put it in writing. Writing is everywhere around us. It ranges from a letter to the campus daily or a magazine article on single-parent families to a new book about the emerging economic powers of the Pacific Rim or an entry on the Russian revolution in an online encyclopedia. Computers have greatly increased the numbers of those sharing information and ideas through written communication. Computer writing, e-mail, and electronic networking are multiplying the numbers of those who think, work, and interact through the medium of the written word.

Why is writing important to you personally? Writing confidently and effectively is a survival skill in the modern world. It will work for you as a student, as a person, as a job seeker, and as a participating citizen. Consider areas like the following:

Writing as a Student   Many courses require written work that shows what you know and how you think. In many classes, you will be writing to show how well you use your reading, work up material from relevant sources, and lay out material. Your writing will show how good you are at grasping information and ideas and making them accessible to others. As a member of the campus community, you may be contributing to group mailings, newsletters, or circulars. Working for a cause, you may help write copy for posters or letters to potential supporters.

Writing for Self-discovery   In a writing course, you may discover writing as a means of understanding who and what you are. You may have a chance to think through influences that have shaped your personality or changed the course of your life. Much writing is self-expression, self-examination, self-revelation. It feeds the "hunger of memory," often finding a large audience among readers wanting to learn more about others and themselves.

1

Writing at Work   You will encounter writing everywhere in the world of work. Most work today involves written language. Typically, you start with your résumé and letter of application. As a new hire, you are exposed to manuals and guidelines for the newcomer. You discover the flow of memos, specifications, reports, promotional brochures, or customer complaints that make up the working day. Co-workers script sales presentations or fundraising proposals. Supervisors prepare reviews of employees' performance. Committees work on guidelines on harassment or establish policies for mainstreaming people with disabilities.

Joining the Public Dialogue   Writing serves as a medium for the discussion of public issues. It looms large in the language of politics. Often what has a lasting impact is preserved in the minutes of a meeting, in a reporter's article, or in a petition summing up grievances. The written word carries weight: A well-argued letter of support may help save the job of a city council member facing a recall election. A poison pen letter may jeopardize a career.

How can you make the most of instruction in writing? Obviously, your expectations will be shaped by your previous experiences, good or bad. Also, writers, like everybody else, learn as much by trial and error or by watching others as they do from teachers or mentors. However, a writing course gives you a chance to think seriously about yourself as a writer. It will ask you to do some concentrated work in writing and to make the best use of opportunities for feedback and revision. Expectations like the following will help you make the best use of the opportunities a writing course offers:

• *Think of writing as a creative process.*   A successful paper is the result of a process — going from tentative first ideas and promising material to a finished piece of writing. Ideally, you start by clarifying in your own mind what you are trying to do. What issue are you trying to deal with, or what need are you trying to fill? Who are your readers, and what will your writing do for them? Where will you turn for material? How much informal research will you do — talking to classmates, interviewing insiders, reading *Time* or *Ms.* magazine? What strategy will you work out for laying out your material? What opportunity will you have to rethink and revise in response to feedback from your instructor and from your peers?

• *Be prepared to take on different writing tasks.*   Ideally, you will take on gradually more challenging tasks and apply what you have learned from earlier assignments. Here are tasks you may be asked to perform:

> Share with your readers what you have learned from personal experience about the single-parent family or about women in the world of work.
>
> Help your readers understand how something works and how they can make it work for them.
>
> Help your readers make choices — between places to live, among careers, or between lifestyles.
>
> On debatable subjects from gun control to immigration, show how a reasonable person might arrive at a balanced conclusion.
>
> Enlist support for a cause.

• *Think of writing as an opportunity to learn.* Many questions worth writing about are open questions. Have men come to accept women as full partners in police work? Are retraining programs for workers training them for jobs that don't exist? What can be done to help women heading single-parent families profit from a more equitable wage structure? You will often be motivated to write when you need to rethink an issue. You may listen to old solutions for a familiar problem — and decide that changing situations have made them obsolete. When a tradition is being challenged, deciding what was valuable and what needs to be updated may take serious thought.

• *Be prepared to work in a workshop setting.* In a workshop setting, you come to class prepared to work with other student writers. You join others in studying and discussing professional work, learning from others' questions and insights. Sharing in class discussion of options for writing, you can make sure that writing topics are meaningful for you, that you can see them in context. You share your own writing, and profit from feedback from your peers and from your instructor. Many writing classes today take a piece of writing through several rewrites, with opportunities for discussion of work in progress.

• *Be prepared to participate in collaboration.* You may have opportunities to join in the give-and-take of group projects. Working with others, you learn how to organize group work, how to farm out tasks, and how to pool results. You may also learn something about group dynamics from possible personality conflicts and their resolution. Make it a habit to volunteer — collaborating, for instance, on a class publication assembling the best work of the class.

In a writing course, *you* are the writer. Obviously, you will try to profit from feedback and advice. But at the same time you learn to trust your own observation and experience. Sooner or later you need to rely on your own reading and viewing. You draw your own conclusions and organize your own thinking. You learn to make writing serve your own purposes — to make others see your side, to enlist support, to make your input count.

I only have twenty-six letters of the alphabet. I don't have color or music. I must use my craft to make the reader see the colors and hear the sounds. **TONI MORRISON**

1

You the Writer

Writing as a Creative Process

How do writers write? How do they move from a blank screen or page to writing that they are willing to share with others? Every paper is different. Every writing task poses a different challenge. You cannot expect a computer program to lead you in a straight line from input to a structured piece of writing. However, as you put a paper together, you will find yourself doing things that for every writer are part of the day's work. You will try to do justice to major dimensions of the writing process. These intermesh, so that different tasks may go on at the same time. If you tend to be a perfectionist, you may start rewriting as soon as you finish writing your first paragraph or two, working on them till they come closer to what you want to say. If you tend to prevaricate, you may still be shifting things around while doing your final editing.

This preview chapter will ask you to take a look at what effective writers do. It will suggest procedures that are likely to produce good results. It may suggest ways to get a project moving forward again when you feel bogged down.

Discovering Your Purpose

What axe you have to grind is very important — and you have to take it into account as you structure your argument.

SUSAN JACOBY

What are you trying to do? What problem are you going to explore? What misunderstanding are you going to correct? What information are you going to lay out for your reader?

Ideally, your reading, class discussion, or your own interest leads you to a topic that makes you say: "On this I have something to say. On this I am something of an expert. On this I want to be heard." For instance, people often write best when they have a point to prove or a misunderstanding to correct. They may be trying to correct a stereotype that has gotten in their way: the inscrutable Oriental, the dumb blonde, the insensitive male, the black natural athlete, the abusive police officer, the emotionally absent father. A young woman from a Mormon family wrote a strong paper correcting an impression of Mormons as glum moralists bent on spoiling other people's fun. Talking back to the stereotype, she stressed the warmth of family relations in her background, the good times during family outings or reunions.

Good writing has a purpose. Here are some of the purposes that, alone or in combination, may make you want to write. You may want to

- tell your story
- come to terms with the past
- clarify a difficult concept
- analyze a confusing situation
- correct misinformation
- register a grievance
- pay tribute
- sound a warning
- expose abuses
- give advice
- enlist support
- promote a policy
- clear someone's name
- build morale

WRITING WORKSHOP I

Exploring the Issues

Which of the following questions mean anything to you? Do any of them strike a chord? Do you have strong feelings about one of these possible topics one way or the other? Choose *one*: Explain why your choice is a live topic for you.

• Is the talk about sensitive, caring males mostly media hype — or do you see a movement in this direction? (What sensitive males do you know personally? Do sensitive males in movies or TV shows seem true to life?)

• Is it true, as some surveys claim, that the next generation may be *more* rather than less prejudiced or racist than their elders? (Are we backsliding rather than making progress?)

• Why is the divorce rate among young couples as high as it is? (What dooms many unions that people enter into with love and the best intentions?)

• Why do women earn less than men? (Are we any closer than in the past to equal pay for equal work? Are we moving closer to equal pay for comparable work?)

• Has courtship become a minefield for young people? (Is it true that young males today feel defensive, afraid to be accused of harassment while dating or in a relationship?)

• Have you or has someone you know well ever felt hurt by a damaging stereotype? (Have you felt unfairly judged as a member of a group to which you belong — ethnic, religious, social, or the like?)

SAMPLE STUDENT RESPONSE: The topic concerning sensitive, caring males interests me because I know several males in my life that fit this description. I consider my stepfather, Joe, to fit the image of a sensitive male; he is the one in our family who is always going out of his way to help others. For instance, when my sister was bedridden with a broken back, he was the person who took care of her. Moreover, he is open with his feelings — he does not hesitate to show concern when someone is upset. Ironically, upon first meeting Joe you might not expect him to have a sensitive side. He is an ex-homicide detective, and he has very conservative political views. I do not really believe there is much media hype about males becoming more sensitive. Recently I read an article about husbands who stayed home with their children while their wives went off to work, but the journalist knew she was writing about exceptions. Perhaps there is more public awareness of men being allowed to be more nurturing, and this makes them feel less embarrassed to express their nurturing sides.

WRITING WORKSHOP 2

Talking Back to the Stereotype

Prepare for an oral presentation or panel discussion focused on stereotypes. Be prepared to help correct a misunderstanding, set the record straight, or talk back to a stereotype that concerns you personally. Be prepared to show what the misunderstanding or the stereotype is. Think of ways to correct or refute the misunderstanding. (Before and during the presentation, take notes that might provide the basis for a paper.)

Targeting Your Audience

Who is your audience? **Discourse communities** are groups of people who talk to one another and speak one another's language. They share a similar background and have similar agendas. In writing for people in your group, you can invoke shared memories and common allegiances. Often, however, your challenge will be to reach out to readers who do *not* already share your grievances and aspirations.

The Mythical General Reader   Much writing assumes an educated reader concerned about issues facing us in our world. Educated readers want you to respect their intelligence. By and large, they recognize assumptions of modern science, names and events in modern history, and major social or political issues. (Even so you will do well to include capsule definitions or capsule descriptions in your writing as reminders.) They will resent being condescended to; they do not like to be manipulated. They are likely to frown on blatant personal attacks — like attack ads during political campaigns.

The Target Audience   You may be targeting a campus community agitated by a spate of carjackings and attempted rapes. Or you may aim mainly at women concerned about unequal pay and glass ceilings in the workplace. Or you may target angry white males objecting to preferential hiring for minorities. In writing for a specific target audience, you would keep considerations like the following in mind:

  • A teachers' group will understand references to budget crunch, teacher burnout, ballooning class sizes, and schools where the roof leaks and gangs fight it out in the parking lot.

• People who are on mailing lists for listener-supported radio or television are likely to love classical music and distrust media hype. They are likely to support the theater groups, local concert series, and public libraries that keep cities from becoming spiritual wastelands.

• Law enforcement officials, suburbanites, and small-business owners are likely to feel that there is too much sympathy for the accused, the suspect, or the defendant and to question law enforcement methods.

The Lay Audience Much writing is done by the expert or insider for people in need of information or explanations. Writers earn their keep when they initiate a lay audience into a demanding or technical subject. What does the outsider, the newcomer, the novice need to know? How do you help fellow students browse the Internet? How do you explain to a person not mechanically inclined the role computers play in the running of a late-model car?

The In-Group Audience Many writers are most comfortable with an audience of like-minded readers, sharing a similar agenda or commitments. How hard could it be to get members of a business club to denounce bureaucrats and regulations? How much would it take to get students to object to cuts in student loans? However, the real challenge for a writer is to take on a reluctant or hostile audience. What does it take to convince members of the chamber of commerce to vote for new taxes? How would you convince gun lovers to support new registration requirements for handguns?

You can tell that your fellow students are becoming more audience-conscious when they make comments like the following:

COMMENTS ON AUDIENCE: I covered a key aspect of the current welfare debate, but I knew a completely unaware reader would not have enough background to follow the paper.
In the current political climate, I realized my readers would be skeptical of programs designed to rehabilitate juvenile offenders, so I made sure to concede some points to the other side.
I knew the readers would include "angry white males," so I tried to cushion the blows.
Talking to minority students impressed on me that if you or people in your community have been brutalized by police you are going to be suspicious of law enforcement.

WRITING WORKSHOP 3

The Audience Profile

Working alone or with a group, prepare an audience profile for one of the following populations or a similar group. What knowledge about the target audience could help a vote-getter, recruiter, promoter, or fundraiser reach its members effectively? (If time allows, help your group develop the strategy — survey, questionnaire, interviews, study of media sources — for gathering helpful information.) Choose a group like the following:

- black male college students
- single mothers
- angry white males
- Asian Americans or Latinos on campus
- untenured or part-time faculty
- subscribers to listener-supported radio or television
- the unemployed in your community
- nonvoters
- small-business owners near the campus

Exploring Your Subject

I do think that part of the innate talent of being a writer is a natural curiosity or instinct. I work on remembering. I don't have a particularly steel-trap mind, so I have to discipline myself to remember details that help to tell a story: someone's clothes, the way people express themselves.

GRETEL EHRLICH

Where do you turn for material? Early in a writing project, you go through a stage of exploration — of looking, reading, talking. You jot down reminders to yourself, copying quotable quotes, or perhaps excerpting key statistics. Habits like the following will help:

 • *Draw on firsthand observation.* Learn to trust your eyes and ears. Your writing will have a more authentic ring if you can relate ideas and theories to what you have observed with your own eyes. Effective writers recall in vivid detail scenes, people, and events from the past. They often are willing to go into the field to take a firsthand look at what is happening now.

• *Read with the writer's eye.* Writers tend to have an eye out for potentially useful material. They are often compulsive notetakers. They may highlight or underline passages in their reading; they are likely to collect clippings. They tab key sections in a book; they photocopy key pages from books and magazines. The more serious you become about your writing, the more you will earmark, store, and retrieve potentially useful information and commentary on subjects of interest to you.

• *Join in the dialogue.* Listen with an attentive ear to what people say and how they say it. Try to talk to insiders, eyewitnesses, people in the know. If you can, prepare questions for an informal interview.

To help you generate promising material, try out prewriting techniques like the following and adapt them to your own purposes:

Brainstorming When you **brainstorm**, your mind is conducting a quick search of the memory banks of your brain. Let one idea lead to another. Jot down anything that comes to mind as you think about a key word or a central issue — whether the homeless, affirmative action, or backlash politics. Jog your memory for incidents, impressions, headlines, slogans, overheard remarks. Include any questions that arise or tentative ideas. At this stage, don't sort out or censor the material. You are trying to work up a fund of possibly useful material.

Some writers jot down key words and phrases; others jot down finished and half-finished sentences. The following are brainstorming notes for a paper on the current backlash against large-scale immigration. What happened when the writer decided: "Think immigration"?

BRAINSTORMING: **Don't Give Me Your Huddled Poor**

Kennedy: *A Nation of Immigrants*
Little Saigon
Korean merchants in South Central
menial jobs for illegals — stoop labor, garbage
Pakistani doctor in emergency room
other side: turned back at Ellis Island
ban on Asians (check dates?)
Chinese boat people intercepted by Coast Guard
Immigration Service raids sweatshops
proof of citizenship required for jobs
entry fee at Mexican border
proposed electrified fence (how many thousand miles?)

governor blames deficit on welfare for illegals
health care denied to illegals
poet from India writes about "dotbusters"
fear of jobs lost to illegal immigrants

WRITING WORKSHOP 4

Brainstorming Your Topic

Here is a set of brainstorming notes for a paper on the macho male. What is promising about these notes? What kind of paper do these notes make you expect? How far along is the writer toward writing a substantial paper likely to make her readers think? Jot down a similar set of brainstorming notes for one of the following: volunteers, violence, sexual harassment, affirmative action, hate speech, jocks. Try to include concrete images, actual incidents, specifics from your reading or viewing.

BRAINSTORMING: **Muy Macho**

Macho: big, muscular, unfeeling, rough — harsh, moves to kill. (Sylvester Stallone: I hate what he promotes.) Negative impression. Hard craggy faces with mean eyes that bore holes in you.

Men who have to prove themselves through acts of violence.

The man who is disconnected from his feelings, insensitive to women's needs — cannot express himself in a feeling manner.

The word has negative connotations for me because I work part-time in a bar. I am forever seeing these perfectly tanned types who come on to a woman.

When I was a child, *macho* meant a strong male type who could take care of me — paternal, warmth in eyes. John Wayne: gruff, yet you could feel secure knowing that someone like him was around. Jimmy Stewart: that twinkle of warmth in the old movies.

Crude, huge — the body, not the heart — tendency to violence always close to the surface. Craggy face. Bloodshed excites them.

Arnold Schwarzenegger muscles, gross.

Tend to dominate in relationships — desire for control. "Me Tarzan, you Jane."

Clustering   **Clustering** makes lines of association branch out from a core meaning or core issue. A network of thoughts and images takes shape that charts memories and associations inspired by the stimulus term at the core of the cluster. You may want to think of clustering as brainstorming-plus: Even while it calls up images and ideas from your mental memory banks, it activates the pattern-making capacity of the brain. More so than other free-association techniques, clustering helps people give shape to their thoughts and feelings. A pattern — or configuration — takes shape that helps the writer organize a passage, a paper, or a script for a speech. The following cluster maps thoughts and associations that thinking about the symbolic meaning of flowers brought to one writer's mind:

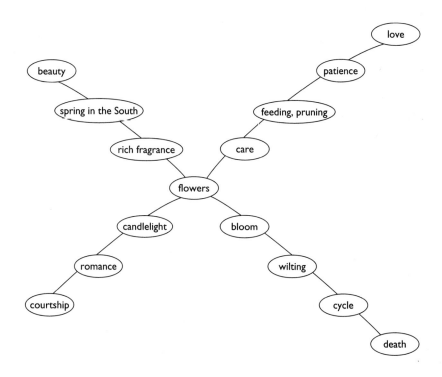

This cluster does more than take inventory of a rich range of images and associations. It already points up a central double meaning in the symbolism of flowers. On the one hand, flowers are symbols of life-affirming values, of beauty and love. On the other hand, the short life span of flowers and their quick wilting point to the transient quality of life — reminding us of death. This polar opposition might help the writer organize a paper on the central paradox in the symbolic meaning of flowers. More elaborate clusters keep sprouting branches or pushing out lines of association until they seem to map out a whole paper.

WRITING WORKSHOP 5

Clustering Your Core Concept

What kind of paper do you see taking shape as you study the following cluster? How do you think the writer might proceed? What would be major areas covered? What do you think would be the overall point? Cluster the same term on which you did a brainstorming exercise or another term like *immigration, prejudice, violence, guns,* or *censorship.*

Discovery Frames   You may want to try sets of questions that help you explore a topic. Such **discovery frames** help you generate ideas. They set up a program for checking out relevant material, guiding your exploratory reading and listening. To work up material on a current issue, you will often be able to adapt a set of questions like the following:

• *What is the issue?*   What is at stake? What striking event, example, or statistic could dramatize the issue for your readers?

• *What is your personal connection with the issue?*   Where has it touched on your own experience? What difference does it make to your own life or the lives of people close to you?

• *How are the media dealing with the issue?* What are striking recent examples of media coverage? Where has the issue come up in articles, editorials, documentaries, talk shows, movies, or cartoons? Is there a common thread?

• *What popular misconceptions or prejudices cloud the issue?* Is there a lack of reliable information? Does the issue raise questions that challenge traditional ways of thinking?

• *What do the experts say?* Who are the authorities on this subject; who are the insiders? Do they agree, or are they divided?

• *What does the future hold?* Where do current trends point? What are some of the alternatives? It the outlook promising or discouraging?

Here is a discovery frame focused on a current trend. Like other discovery frames, this one already provides a rough framework for a paper. It moves from surface impressions to a look at background facts and underlying causes.

DISCOVERY FRAME: **The Fitness Craze**

1. *Surface Symptoms:* Where do you see signs of the fitness craze? What signs of it do you see in your neighborhood or on campus? What role does it play in advertising and more generally in the media? (Do you see runners in the streets? Are you aware of special events — Saturday morning races, local marathons, bicycle competitions? Do you see ads for exercise bikes, rowing machines, running shoes? Are new health clubs opening in your community?)
2. *A Closer Look:* Are you a participant or merely an observer? How did you become personally involved? Have close friends or family members gone in for bodybuilding, weight lifting, or aerobics? How has it changed their lives? Do they propagandize others? What do they say?
3. *Background Facts:* Do you read articles about health and fitness? Do you encounter statistics on the benefits of different kinds of exercise or activity? What do experts say on topics like stress reduction, weight control, or the prevention of heart disease?
4. *Deeper Causes:* Why is keeping in shape a major goal of today's young people? What ideals or values in our culture drive people toward more awareness of their bodies and their health? Do we have a cult of youth and of looks in our society?
5. *Second Thoughts:* Have you seen any signs of a backlash against the fitness cult? Have you read warnings about the dangers of excessive or inappropriate exercise? Do you know people who have become disillusioned about their pursuit of health and fitness?

WRITING WORKSHOP 6

Filling in Your Discovery Frame

Use or adapt the discovery frame you have just studied for a topic that you have previously used for prewriting or another topic of your choice. (For instance, choose volunteers, violence, sexual harassment, affirmative action, hate speech, jocks, immigration, prejudice, violence, guns, or censorship.) Fill in one or two paragraphs of material under each heading in your discovery frame.

Interviewing   You will often pick up information or ideas relevant to your topic by listening to casual conversation or to a formal talk. However, you may decide to use **interviewing** as a way to get the inside story and interesting sidelights on a topic. Often a paper will profit from your questioning people with insider's knowledge or relevant experience.

Some interviewers put people at ease — showing interest in and respect for their lives, opinions, or callings. Others are more aggressive, goading people into revealing what they would normally keep to themselves. Whatever your personal style, think ahead about what you would like to find out. Make a tentative list of questions to ask. However, be prepared to be flexible, following up interesting hints and leads. You may want to go from safe or friendly questions to more probing ones, as did the student who interviewed a police officer:

INTERVIEWER'S QUESTIONS:
How does one become a police officer?
Why did you decide to become one?
What is the daily routine on the job?
What about the job surprised you?
What has been your most dangerous experience?
What do you think of how the media portray the police?
What movie or TV program gives the truest or fairest picture?
How do you react to charges of harassment or police brutality?
What do you think helps or hinders you most in your job?

Be an attentive listener, and use written notes. Or tape the interview. If you plan to publish the interview, it is courteous and cautious to let the person see a first draft. People dislike being misquoted. Here are some excerpts from a productive interview:

SAMPLE INTERVIEW: **Woman Engineer**

Q: What is your background and what or who inspired you to become an engineer?

A: After high school graduation I began college as a pre-med student. During the summers, I held jobs in electronics and mechanical assembly that had to do with lasers. The summer jobs extended over two years, and I switched to an engineering major. . . .

Q: In advanced science or mathematics courses in college, did you find that you were the only female or just one of a few?

A: No, actually in the engineering classes about a third of all the classes had women in them. These women included majors in general engineering, mechanical engineering, industrial engineering, and civil engineering.

Q: Have you had to overcome any specific obstacles in reaching your goal to become an engineer? Has anyone ever turned you down for a job because of doubts that you could do the job?

A: No, actually I find that most women engineers in my field find the opposite. Some people might call it reverse discrimination because there are not very many women engineers around, so for many companies it is a feather in their cap to get a woman on their staff.

Q: Why is that?

A: Equal opportunity requires a number of minorities and women on the staff, and women engineers are considered a minority. As for obstacles, there are a number I have seen. I don't know that they have been obstacles because I have found ways to get around them. One of the obstacles is the older male engineers who make you feel that you have to work twice as hard as your male counterparts to prove that you know what you are doing. With the younger engineers, closer to my age, I find there is more acceptance because they have gone to school with women students, so they don't have the same bias.

Q: Otherwise, were you readily accepted in your company?

A: Sometimes you have a very curious relationship with other women you work with. For the most part, I think the technical women have no problem because they are in the same position. However, I remember going out to lunch with a group of women, and we were all laughing and kidding around. The next day someone came up to me and apologized. She said, "I am really sorry. I didn't know you were an engineer." I was really shocked because I don't consider anyone "just a secretary.". . .

Q: Do you have any advice you would like to give to up-and-coming women engineers?

A: Yes. Don't be put off by any of the old stigmas and the old realities. For women in a male-dominated field, there are some definite obstacles. You cannot pretend that we have all been liberated and everything is equal and everybody accepts you for what you can do. I say go in with your eyes open and accept some of the realities. I don't think it helps to be really militant about it and point out to everyone that you are a woman. They can see that when you walk through the door. The idea is to go in and show what you can do.

WRITING WORKSHOP 7

Interviewing the Insider

Interview someone who has a special interest in an issue you are concerned about. Find someone with relevant experience or training — someone who is in a position to know. Prepare pointed questions for the person to answer. Record the most fruitful parts of the interview. Use a question-and-answer format.

WRITING WORKSHOP 8

Applying Prewriting Techniques

Explore an issue of special interest to you that is currently much in the news. The issue might be domestic violence, local regulation of handguns, or women's share of varsity teams. Prepare a set of notes that represent a range of prewriting techniques:

• Do *brainstorming* or *clustering* to mobilize what you already know.

• Sample current *media coverage* of the issue. Select three or four quotes from newscasts, newspapers, or newsmagazines. Introduce them with a credit tag identifying the source, briefly summing up the credentials or qualifications of the person you are quoting.

• *Interview* someone who has a special interest in an issue you are concerned about or is in a position to know. Prepare pointed questions for the person to answer. Record the most fruitful parts of the interview.

Working on a Draft

There is excitement in the very act of composition. Some of you know this at first hand — a deep satisfaction when the thing begins to take shape.

CATHERINE DRINKER BOWEN

What is going to be your strategy? Even as you collect material, you will be sorting it out, identifying tentative categories or areas of concern. You push toward a key idea, or thesis. You draw up a working outline to guide you in writing a first draft — adjusting or refining your outline as you go along. You start writing major chunks of the paper — or else you start at the beginning and push ahead to the end. This is the kind of thinking that will help you organize your first draft:

Focusing   Ask yourself: "What question am I really trying to answer? What am I trying to do for my audience?" For instance, no short piece of writing can probe everything wrong with our schools — from absenteeism and short attention spans through overcrowded classrooms and burnt-out teachers to falling down buildings or drugs and violence. Try to focus on a limited question on which you can bring evidence to bear or on which you can examine detailed testimony. Try to sum up in your own mind what question about your school or about schools you expect your paper to answer.

- Should your campus adopt a speech code banning racial, ethnic, or sexual slurs?
- Should public schools accept free materials — hardware, software, television programs that include advertising — from corporations?
- Should taxpayers' money be used to help fund religious schools?

Pushing toward a Thesis   Much of the thinking that goes into a paper goes into formulating the answer (or answers) to the basic question you raise. In a well-worked-out paper, the answer to your central question provides the **thesis** of your paper. The thesis is a statement, often early in your paper, that sums up the central claim you are making. It signals to the reader: "This is what I am trying to prove; this is what my paper is all about."

As you explore your material, start thinking about a **trial thesis** and ask yourself: "Is this what I want to say? Is this what I have learned? Is this something that I have the material to support?" Each of the following thesis statements makes an assertion. The writer is taking a stand:

TRIAL THESIS: Speech codes on campus reflect our growing awareness that verbal abuse can be as damaging as physical abuse.

TRIAL THESIS: Potential dropouts need to discover that education means exploration and discovery and not just being told.

Your thesis will often be tentative at first, and it will often need adjustment as you go on. It may have to be scaled down or refocused. For instance, you may be exploring the effect of broken homes on young people's emotional lives and their own prospects for developing lasting family ties. You may at first have shared the common assumption that people from split families tend to be suspicious of commitment. Their own relationships are likely to be at risk, likely to flounder. However, as you talk to a number of people who witnessed their parents' divorce, you may become aware of a strong countertrend. Your thesis will then sum up what you have learned:

TRIAL THESIS: People from broken homes do not always remain shell-shocked and suspicious of close ties; they often know the value of what they have lost and work harder than others at making relationships last.

For readers eager to get to the point, you may decide to put your thesis statement at the end of a brief **introduction** that dramatizes the issue. Try to phrase a lively, intriguing **title** that already hints at your central message. Then use your introduction to lead up to your main point. A striking example or a provocative quotation often serves to bring the issue into focus. Here is a brief introduction that heads directly for the writer's thesis:

INTRODUCTION: **O Say Can You See**

Businesses selling flags, large and small, are doing fine. Citizens turn out in large numbers for Fourth-of-July parades. High school students again participate in patriotic essay contests sponsored by service organizations. ROTC programs, once shunned on campuses, are making a comeback, and we again hear the "left-face" and "right-face" of the drill sergeant outside classroom buildings. *Patriotism has come back into style, with a difference.*

Such a thesis is a promise to the reader. After reading this introduction, your readers would expect your paper to provide follow-up on two parts of the implied agenda: They will need evidence from your experience, reading, or viewing that patriotism is indeed back in style. And they will expect you to document how the new patriotism is different from the "my-country-right-or-wrong" patriotism of the past (or of people living in the past).

Often a strong **conclusion** will reinforce (not just repeat) the central thesis. The conclusion may show the application of the thesis to a wider area or its significance for the future. Many writers save a striking example or clinching quotation for last. Remember that no law requires you to use the traditional **thesis-first** strategy. Some writers prefer to leave the issue open for much of an article or chapter, exploring it together with the reader. They finally lead into a well-earned thesis with a "Therefore, we must conclude . . ." or words to that effect.

Using a Working Outline   While pushing toward a thesis, you will at the same time start laying out the material that supports it. Often a thesis, like the one about the new patriotism, will carry with it a nutshell outline of the paper. Many writers work with a simple **scratch outline** early in the project. Perhaps you have read that goddesses representing fertility and the bounty of the earth may have played a central role in the earliest prehistoric religions. Thinking about a paper on the subject, you might draw up a rough scheme like the following:

SCRATCH OUTLINE: twilight of the male gods
earth goddesses rediscovered
Ishtar (Babylonian)
Demeter (Greek)
other?

Many writers gradually make such rough schemes more specific, developing a more detailed itinerary for the paper to follow. To get a better sense of what belongs where, they use **working outlines** with headings and subheadings (and sometimes subsubheadings). Suppose you have been annoyed by the many local, state, and federal regulations that tell citizens what they may and may not do. Your first rough working outline might look like this:

WORKING OUTLINE: Unnecessary regulation
— helmet laws
— restrictions on snowmobiles
— restrictions on dirt bikes
— no-smoking codes
Necessary regulation
— health codes for food handlers
— testing of new drugs
— additives in food

Such an outline helps you map your paper — and it makes you see where you might want to change your itinerary. On further reading, you might change your mind about the need for some of the regulations you thought petty or superfluous. You might decide that you need a third category: debatable regulations. Here is a more fully worked out, revised version of your outline:

REVISED OUTLINE: **Toward a (De)Regulated Society**
I. Clearly necessary regulation
   A. Traffic laws
   B. Health codes for food handlers
   C. Testing of new drugs
II. Clearly unwanted regulation
   A. Job restrictions because of sex
   B. Job restrictions because of age
III. Debatable regulation
   A. Compulsory airbags
   B. Helmet laws
   C. Restrictions on dirt bikes and snowmobiles

Writing a Draft   Many writers do a rough first draft by writing a paragraph or two for each item in a working outline. They do not brood over a difficult part but push on and come back to the trouble spot later. For other writers, writing the first draft is a matter of splicing together material from their notes, arranging it in some sort of meaningful order. As you move ahead, remember a familiar refrain: Do not just state your points — follow them up; develop them. If you raise a question, show that you have given the answer some thought. If you make an accusation, line up evidence.

For writers with a track record, it becomes second nature to fill in the "for example." They do not just say "Scientists have shown us how human the apes are." They follow through:

> *Scientists have shown us how human the apes are.* When two gorillas quarrel, they stare at each other till one of them gives in and shifts his eyes away. Chimps make rough tools from twigs and use them to get at food. They greet each other with kisses and cuddles. Apes have been taught sign language, using it to ask for drink or express pain.

WRITING WORKSHOP 9

From Notes to Draft

Study the following materials. How did the student writer move from her notes to a first draft?

PREWRITING NOTES: **The Airhead Stereotype**

Arrival of the Amazons: Current TV shows and movies are full of women who kick attackers in the groin and administer karate chops to losers. Rapist gunned down by tough broad in the parking lot.

In the wasteland of reruns, the old media stereotypes persist? Blonde airhead in tight sweater works for radio station in the heartland. Diane in *Cheers* was smart and had a college education. However, in many episodes, she was shown to be arrogant and presumptuous. (Note: Although educated, she worked year after year in a bar.)

Myself as victim of the stereotype: unsolicited advice to put up my hair in a bun, use no makeup, wear glasses. Student commenting on my "Barbie Doll" voice while working on a group project. Instructor's negative comments on oral report.

Women as well as men think in terms of the stereotype: At least men have the excuse of being conditioned to react in sexual terms to women who sound and act "feminine." Unfair focus on appearance: Brunettes more likely to be taken seriously?

Norman Mailer on Marilyn Monroe : "She was not the dark contract of the passionate brunette depths that speak of blood, vows taken for life, and the furies of vengeance. . . . No, Marilyn suggested sex might be difficult or dangerous with others, but ice cream with her" (*Marilyn*, p. 15). "So we think of Marilyn who was every man's love affair . . . who was blonde and beautiful and had a sweet little rinky-dink of a voice . . . which carried such ripe overtones of erotic excitement and yet was the voice of a little child" (pp. 15–16).

 Science note: Pitch of voice is determined by size of the larynx and how tightly the muscles in it are stretched. Voiceprints are individual like fingerprints; can be used for identification.

How did the student writer funnel the material from these prewriting notes into her paper? How did she use her materials? How did she organize them and why? On what overall strategy did she decide? What thesis emerged from her exploration of the subject? (Where does she state it? How well does the rest of the paper support it?) Reconstruct the working outline the writer might have used in writing her draft.

FIRST DRAFT: **Dream Girls**

 The stereotype killed Marilyn Monroe. She became, as Norman Mailer says in *Marilyn*, "every man's love affair," blonde and beautiful and "with the voice of a little child." She "suggested sex might be difficult or dangerous with others, but ice cream with her." Marilyn lived a role for the public that her inner self couldn't be, and she died of an overdose.

 Today, we may think that, as the ad says, "you have come a long way." In current movies and television shows, the blonde heroine kicks her male attackers in the groin and administers karate chops to three hoodlums with ski masks attacking her in the alley. The politically correct tough broad is more than a match for her wimpy male adversaries. However, the wasteland of reruns is a better gauge of what has shaped the daydreams of today's "adult" male. The stereotype of the dumb blonde is cut deep into the minds of men, bosses, those in power, and even other females. (Blonde joke: "Do blondes have more fun?" "Yes, but they can't remember with whom.") A blonde with good looks and a soft voice has a harder climb to the top than her dark-haired sisters.

 Hollywood created the stereotype of the blonde airhead and television perpetuated it. In one show, canceled at first because it offended women's groups but then brought back, a blonde dream girl in tight sweaters and plastic gloves delighted the two men who hired her as a maid. The role of Diane in *Cheers* was at first coveted by actresses because Diane was college-educated and had some depth of character. In the end, Diane was a fool. She had an education that made her arrogant and presumptuous. She worked year after year hopping tables in a bar.

 I am a blonde. I have a soft musical voice. I have always had high grades. Working as a tutor, I have helped other students to improve their grades.

I have worked as a bookkeeper and assistant personnel manager. Still, some people don't take me seriously because of the way I look and sound. I've been told to put up my hair in a bun, wear glasses, quit wearing makeup, and work to lower the pitch of my voice.

Men are not the only ones doing the stereotyping. I had a female instructor criticize my voice as unprofessional during an oral report critique. I had a female student say in a group endeavor that I should go last because my "Barbie Doll" voice would leave an emotional impression on the audience.

All blonde hair does not come out of a bottle, and the pitch of the voice is determined by the size of the larynx and by how tightly the muscles in it are stretched. Voiceprints, like fingerprints, are highly individual and can be used as a means of identification.

The myth of the beautiful childlike blonde will exist as long as men want to take care of women who need protection. The stereotype will wane when men begin to respect women who take care of themselves.

Writing/Thinking Strategies

What kind of thinking will go into your writing? The more serious you are about a topic, the more your readers will expect you to think the matter through. The kind of thinking that shapes your writing is not divorced from the kind of thinking you do every day. It is merely a more structured kind of thinking that you do on the computer screen or on paper.

When working out the strategy for a paper, you will often be putting thinking strategies to work that help you make sense of experience and that will help your readers find their way. These are not strategies writers take down from a rack; rather, they grow out of an assignment, a situation. They suggest themselves as the logical way to tackle a subject. Here are examples of writing situations and the kinds of thinking they might bring into play:

• Looking back over your personal experience, you may decide that your life has gone through very different *stages*. What were major phases that have left a lasting imprint on your personality? You may decide to mark off three or four major waystations — for instance, going from a happy childhood through a confused adolescence to determined young adulthood.

• Thinking that finds the common denominator in miscellaneous data is one of the major ways your mind processes information. Much thinking finds a *common pattern* or traces a general trend. Trend watchers track incidents and data that seem to point in a similar direction. (At the same time, they try to face up to apparent exceptions or check out countertrends.) Assume that over the course of a week you hear a senator from an oil state squelch ideas for a new energy tax. You watch East Coast senators plead for the preservation of navy bases threatened with closure. A senator from Wyoming is protesting plans for higher grazing fees on public lands. These news items are likely to make you formulate a tentative generalization — or harden a suspicion you already had: Members of the Senate are often advocates of regional interests.

- To sort out confusing data, you may find you need to set up *categories*. For instance, with much antiimmigrant rhetoric in the air, you may early decide that different issues arise for different classes of people. You try to set up a scheme of classification that would allow you to sort out confusing data: illegal immigrants — U.S.-born children of illegal immigrants — legal visitors who have overstayed their visas — legal immigrants not U.S. citizens — U.S.-born children of legal immigrants — naturalized immigrants, now U.S. citizens. Legislators, lawyers, or public agencies are always classifying people, and often much depends on what bin the individual is assigned.

- Has the women's movement stalled? Has there been a loss of momentum? The natural organization for a paper on this topic might be to trace the *contrast* of then and now. The human mind is programmed to follow along when you line up opposites: then and now — earlier enthusiasm and current second thoughts, feminism and the backlash against feminism.

- Much of your thinking and writing is likely to mirror the play of *pro and con*. You go from "on the one hand" to "on the other hand." You listen to two (or more) sides on an issue and try to reach a reasonable conclusion. What are the advantages and disadvantages of a new ballpark? (It might bring much business downtown — but it might also cause horrendous traffic problems and bring rioting fans.) What are the arguments for and against proposed guidelines banning offensive or demeaning language on campus? (If we try to counteract hate speech, is censorship the lesser evil?)

- Much of our thinking leads from *shared assumptions* to logical conclusions. We search for assumptions or values that the audience can be expected to share. Effective writers often argue a case by showing the principles at stake. (Sometimes the audience will accept an assumption "for the sake of the argument," to see where it leads.) Such a paper will often follow a basic *if-then* pattern. Here are some familiar assumptions you might invoke in arguing from principle:

> If students have a right to privacy, school authorities should not search their lockers for illegal substances.

If we object to conflicts of interest, the mayor should not be a partner in a construction firm doing city jobs.
If all human beings are created equal, theories of racial superiority are un-American.

When your writing employs one or more of the major reasoning strategies, you are not asking your readers to accept your conclusions on faith. They are thinking an issue through along with you. You are taking them along on an intellectual journey. You are respecting their judgment. One of the best compliments your readers can pay you is that you have made them think.

Rewriting and Rethinking

I firmly believe that good writers vary from bad writers not in the quality of the first draft — most of those probably look pretty much the same — but in the revising process. I say of my own work, "Only my wastebasket knows for sure!"

SHEILA TOBIAS

How satisfied are you with your first attempt? What needs work? Most writers expect to do several rewrites of an early draft. Time permitting, professionals think of any draft as subject to revision. Many articles, speeches, or books go through several rewrites. Feedback from editors, consultants, or friends can make the writer rethink overall strategy. They may fault the lack of evidence for a key point. They may raise potentially damaging objections. When revising your own writing, be prepared for major adjustments or reshufflings as needed. This is the time for second thoughts. Be prepared for more than cosmetic revision (which covers surface blemishes). If necessary, consider major changes in strategy or approach.

Responding to Feedback   Even well-meant advice can be painful, but using it constructively can strengthen a promising first draft. Look for pointers on how to build on your strengths and shore up your weaknesses.

• In a writing class, **instructor's comments** will vary. For instance, you may find a running commentary in the margin of your paper, or an extended comment at the end, or both. You might also receive feedback on audiocassettes or through e-mail. Writing teachers are quick to point out lack of a clear focus or lack of logical connection between parts. (How did you get from point A to point B?) They will often challenge statements you make. (What makes you think so?)

They will often ask for additional and more detailed examples or for more convincing evidence. Ideally, the comments will help you make clearer in your own mind what you are trying to say and help you say it more effectively.

• In many writing classes, **peer revision** helps student writers strengthen their sense of audience. Oral or written responses from your classmates can answer for you questions like the following: How much of what you tried to do was communicated to your fellow students? What parts of a paper worked well, and what was weak or confusing? The following might be a fellow student's written response to a paper on bilingual education:

> PEER RESPONSE: I learned from this paper that bilingual education has become a very controversial issue. The point is whether bilingual education is really helping students with limited English proficiency or whether it is holding them back. Your examples from personal experience and the case studies of bilingual students (Hector, Maria, Elsa) were very helpful. Maybe some statistics on programs and success rates are needed. I was wondering whether Spanish-speaking students were the only ones affected by bilingual education. And where is the other side of the argument? I think you need to illustrate and disprove the arguments on the other side.

First Draft and Revision Suppose you have finished a first draft for a paper that explores changing attitudes toward the disabled. Perhaps the idea for the paper came from an entry in your thought log in which you repeated a family friend's story about the struggle of a disabled veteran to master simple tasks. In your first draft, you have stayed close to personal observation: You have made your point about society's efforts to improve mobility — improved access to public buildings and restaurants for people in wheelchairs. You have also talked about another important area: efforts to counteract job discrimination. Your first draft might read like this:

> FIRST DRAFT: **Helping the Disabled**
>
> There seem to be signs popping up everywhere: VAN-ACCESSIBLE, WHEELCHAIR-ACCESSIBLE, HANDICAPPED PARKING. Making buildings and public places navigable for people with limited mobility or sight, our society is leaping forward on the road to making our world completely disabled-accessible.
>
> Access has been the big issue for many years for the organizations that aim at enabling the disabled to live a more normal life. Curbs are torn up and rebuilt so that a wheelchair can roll over them. Buildings are made accessible for the disabled everywhere. Blueprints for new public buildings

provide for ramps, elevators, doorways, and walkways that a wheelchair can easily maneuver. A restaurant downtown was forced to build a new and larger restroom with better access because the old one was up a flight of narrow winding stairs.

Another area where progress has been made is the area of work. Job opportunities for the disabled have expanded. Disabled people often say they do not want pity; they want to become independent. I had a literature class taught by a blind teacher who had assignments and papers read to him and who knew many poems by heart. A friend is taking an economics class that is taught by a teacher who was partially paralyzed in a diving accident and who comes to the campus in a specially equipped van. The computer age is making it possible for disabled people to work out of their homes. We hear about people learning to work computer keyboards with their toes or with pointers held between their teeth.

No one wants to raise false hopes. I know about a disabled veteran who was teaching himself to remove his own TV dinner from the freezer. He finally managed to put it in the oven himself, without help.

Even as a first draft, this paper makes the essential point: There has been much consciousness-raising about the needs and rights of people with disabilities. Much of it has translated into action improving the quality of people's lives. We see this change especially in two major areas: access to facilities and wider job opportunities.

How would revision improve this paper? You yourself may have sensed a gap as you finished typing: The second part of the paper brings in the point about job opportunities — which was not included in your initial overview of the progress that has been made. You decide to make it less of an afterthought, giving your readers early notice that this is part of your program. Also, feedback from your instructor and your peers may alert you to a third crucial area: schooling. How the disabled fare in the world of work depends on the training and education they have received. You decide to adjust your general plan to cover three major areas instead of two: facilities, schooling, work. This plan would take the reader from the most visible to the least visible but perhaps most crucial goal:

REVISED PLAN: improved access to facilities (ramps, elevators, bathrooms)
improved access to schooling (mainstreaming the disabled)
improved access to meaningful, well-paying work

In the following rewrite, added or changed passages (including the new title) have been italicized:

SECOND DRAFT: **Building Ramps**

There seem to be signs popping up everywhere: VAN-ACCESSIBLE, WHEELCHAIR-ACCESSIBLE, HANDICAPPED PARKING. *From making buildings accessible through mainstreaming disabled students to providing better jobs,* our society is leaping forward on the road to making our world completely disabled-accessible.

Access has been the big issue for many years for the organizations that aim at enabling the disabled to live *a fuller life.* Curbs are torn up and rebuilt so that a wheelchair can roll over them. Buildings are made accessible for the disabled everywhere. Blueprints for new public buildings provide for ramps, elevators, doorways, and walkways that a wheelchair can easily maneuver. *Restaurants need to build bathrooms that conform to new size requirements, even though such changes can often prove painful and costly for the establishment in question.* A restaurant downtown was forced to build a new and larger restroom with better access because the old one was up a flight of narrow winding stairs. *New rapid transit lines provide equipment that will hoist wheelchairs into the cars.*

Schools have become more responsive to the requirements of students with special needs. Dyslexic students used to be misdiagnosed as having low IQs or suffering from attention deficit disorder. They now can receive instruction geared to their situation. Some institutions have interpreters that can translate lectures or instructions into sign language. Many books are becoming available on audiotape, helping visually impaired students keep up with ordinary readers.

Job opportunities for the disabled have expanded. Disabled people often say they do not want pity; they want to become *as independent as it is possible for them to be.* I had a literature class taught by a blind teacher who had assignments and papers read to him and who knew many poems by heart. A friend is taking an economics class taught by a teacher who was partially paralyzed in a diving accident and who comes to the campus in a specially equipped van. The computer age is making it possible for disabled people to work out of their homes. We hear about people learning to work computer keyboards with their toes or with pointers held between their teeth.

No one wants to raise false hopes. *I remember hearing from a family friend* about a disabled veteran who was learning to remove his own TV dinner from the freezer. He finally managed to put it in the oven himself, without help. *Whatever the limitations of the individual, we should do everything we can to help disabled people to improve their lives.*

You may take your revision a step further in a third draft: As you talk about your paper with classmates, you are reminded that what to *call* the disabled has itself become an issue: *handicapped — disabled — physically challenged? deaf — hearing-impaired?* You decide to dramatize the changes in attitude by highlighting the changes in the language we use to talk about disability. Early in your paper, you will examine changes in labels that outgroup those named, making us see them in a negative light. In the meantime, classmates have alerted you to an article about new technologies that may revolutionize the lives of the disabled: computers that translate ordinary print into Braille, miniature TV cameras that help the vision-impaired "see" by transmitting outlines of shapes to be imprinted and felt on the skin of a person's back.

FINAL REVISED PLAN:
- the changing language of disability
- improved access to facilities (ramps, elevators, bathrooms)
- improved access to schooling (mainstreaming the disabled)
- improved access to meaningful, well-paying work
- the future: revolutionary new technologies

How well has the added information been integrated into the second rewrite? Can you point to improved transitions — logical links that should help the reader move from one point to the next?

THIRD DRAFT: **Building Ramps**

There seem to be signs popping up everywhere: VAN-ACCESSIBLE, WHEELCHAIR-ACCESSIBLE, HANDICAPPED PARKING. From making buildings accessible to integrating the disabled into our schools and in the workplace, our society is leaping forward on the road to making our world completely disabled-accessible.

Our changing language and vocabulary reflect the ways our attitudes toward the disabled have changed. What to call the disabled has itself become an issue. Should we say *handicapped* or *disabled* or *physically challenged?* Should we say *deaf* or *hearing-impaired?* When we change from "wheelchair-bound" or "confined to a wheelchair" to "using a wheelchair," we avoid an emphasis on the person's limitations. Such changes aim at avoiding words that outgroup those named, making us see them in a negative light.

For many years, physical access was the big issue for many organizations that advance the cause of disabled Americans and help them lead a fuller life. In the past, steep stairs and narrow doors kept many disabled people out of office buildings, court rooms, and schools. Buildings were made accessible for the disabled everywhere. Blueprints for new public buildings provided for ramps, elevators, doorways, and walkways that a wheelchair could easily maneuver. New rapid transit lines provided equipment that hoisted wheelchairs into the cars. Restaurants were required to build bathrooms that conformed to new size requirements. Although these changes were costly and painful for some establishments, they helped establish the principle that people with disabilities should be allowed to participate as fully as possible in everyday life.

Although physical access has been much improved, society has also realized that to help the disabled, improved access to education is essential. Schools have generally become more responsive to the requirements of students with special needs. Dyslexic students used to be misdiagnosed as having low IQs or suffering from attention deficit disorder; they now can receive instruction geared to their situation. Some institutions have interpreters that can translate lectures or instructions into sign language. Many books are becoming available on audiotape, helping visually impaired students keep up with ordinary readers.

Better mobility and better education translate into improved chances for integration of the disabled in the labor market. Job opportunities for the disabled have expanded. Colleagues no longer gawk if a wheelchair user pleads a case in court or attends a committee meeting. It is no longer unusual to have literature taught by a blind teacher or to have an economics class taught by a partially paralyzed teacher who comes to the campus in a specially equipped van. The computer age is making it possible for disabled people to work out of their homes. We hear about people learning to work computer keyboards with their toes or with pointers held between their teeth.

We should not raise false shopes. A friend of my family who is married to a disabled Vietnam veteran often talks of the severe limitations many of the disabled face and of their daily struggle. It may be a real achievement if a disabled person can remove a TV dinner from the freezer and put it in the microwave. Even so, breakthroughs in technology are going to improve the lot of many struggling against adversity. Computers now translate ordinary print into Braille and vice versa. Researchers are experimenting with miniature TV cameras that help the vision-impaired "see" by transmitting outlines of shapes to be imprinted and felt on the skin of a person's back. Perhaps in the next century we will spend less money on military technology designed to destroy people and more on peacetime technology designed to improve people's lives.

Self-evaluation   To become a confident and effective writer, you gradually have to become your own critic and editor. You begin to think critically about how you think and write, becoming better at mobilizing your own resources. You start anticipating the reactions of your readers as you internalize the concerns of your writing instructor or your peers. The test of a professional is that professionals can choose among the writer's options and make important decisions about strategy and approach on their own.

A Checklist for Revision

Learn to look at your writing through the reader's eyes. Keep in mind suggestions like the following. These are based on comments that instructors and peer readers frequently make on students' papers.

1 *Dramatize the issue.* Use your introduction to bring the issue to
   life. Make your central question real for your readers by starting
   with a striking example. Use a vivid incident to bring the issue
   into focus. Or start with a startling statistic or a provocative quotation. Rewrite a flat title to make it more inviting.

BEFORE: **Divorce**

   Many young people in our society today come from split homes. They
have lost their families and their sense of belonging. This is one of the
central issues confronting our society today.

AFTER: **A House Divided**

   A friend of mine has been acting strange lately. She was normally cheerful, personable, and helpful — the person to call when the car breaks
down or the Visa card is maxed out. However, lately, when I tried to talk
to her, she had become hostile, saying things like "You only call me when
you want something from me" or "All you want to talk about is your
problems." I became angry and tried to avoid her. Later, I found out that
her parents had just separated. My friend is not alone; she is one of many
young people who have lost their families and their sense of belonging.
The National Center for Health Statistics reported that in a single year
1,175,000 couples were divorced, and 1,045,750 children were involved
in these divorces.

2 *Sharpen your trial thesis.* Spell out more accurately what your
   paper as a whole is designed to show. Avoid two extremes: Scale
   down sweeping generalizations that your paper does not really
   support. At the other extreme, revise statements that are too
   evasive — that merely postpone the point at which you will have
   to take a stand. An opening statement like the following is too
   open to serve as a thesis. It seems to announce a fishing ex-
   pedition rather than pulling together the overall conclusions
   reached by the writer:

TOO OPEN: How can we account for the recent revival of racist attitudes
            in this country? What are the causes? These are the ques-
            tions facing our nation today, each with an infinite number of
            responses.

Thesis statements like the following stake out a definite claim
that a paper as whole could try to support:

TRIAL THESIS: Racism makes a comeback when hard times make people
                blame their hardships on a minority.

TRIAL THESIS: Apparent racism among the young may be a reaction against
                lip-service to liberal ideas by their elders.

3 *Fine-tune your plan.* Check the logical flow of your paper. Do sections follow one another in the most effective or natural order? If necessary, reshuffle sections of your paper. Suppose you are exploring the way young people react to the breakup of their parents' marriage or to the absence of strong home ties. You first show how they compensate by joining gangs or by turning to teenage sex. You then illustrate this point by talking about close friends, who ultimately rethought and reoriented their lives to take care of their baby. You finally show how organizations — your church, the Big Brother program — try to help lost young people develop new ties. To end the paper on a strong personal note, you might want to shift the example of your friends to the end:

REVISED OUTLINE:
- the loss of family ties
- how young people compensate
    - youth gangs
    - teenage sex
- how society compensates
    - church programs
    - Big Brother program
- how one young couple reinvented the family

4 *Fill in missing links.* Make sure the reader sees the waystations of your paper and can follow along as you move from one to the other. Provide necessary **transitions** — missing links like *however, on the other hand, nevertheless.* Show logical connections between paragraphs by filling in links like "Contrary to what the media have led many of us to believe, . . ." or "Serious objections have surfaced to this proposed solution."

5 *Move in for the closer look.* Add detailed examples — or add vivid detail to examples you mentioned in passing. Bring in real-life people, real-life incidents. Show what your ideas mean in the lives of actual people.

BEFORE: Many observers attribute the electorate's shift to the right to the influence of talk radio. People get their ideas from talk show hosts like Rush Limbaugh, who has become a prime spokesperson for conservative ideas. Day after day Limbaugh's listeners are subjected to a barrage of right-wing views.

AFTER: Many observers attribute the electorate's shift to the right to the influence of talk radio. Talk show host Rush Limbaugh, the author of million-copy bestsellers, claims twenty million listeners. Limbaugh, who has been described as a "fat, baldish, old-fashioned middle American guy" who gorges on steak and drinks "adult beverages," promotes a standard conservative agenda, preferring free-market solutions to government programs, preaching individual initiative and denouncing "entitlements."

6 *Feed in supporting quotations from authorities or insiders.* Scan newspapers or newsmagazines for material that can shed light or provide sidelights on your topic. Look for key statistics. Work in quotable quotes, identifying the sources, showing how the quotation fits into your argument:

BEFORE: Racism has made a disturbing comeback among the young.

AFTER: Racism has made a disturbing comeback among the young. Recess at school becomes an opportunity not for making friends but for racial taunts and racially motivated fights. As Jonathan Peters says in an article in *The Daly City Record*, "The way our children have begun to regard kids of a separate race is unbelievably ignorant, old-fashioned, and embarrassing."

7 *Draw on oral as well as printed sources.* Back up your points by quoting what you have heard others say. Informally interview someone informed or concerned about your subject. Or do a mini-survey of interested parties.

8 *Rewrite lame conclusions.* Did you just repeat your main points one more time? Try reinforcing them with a final striking example that points forward to the future. Bring in parallels or precedents to show the issue to be part of a larger picture. Try circling back to a striking image or quotation that you used at the beginning. Rework conclusions that sound like good intentions or pious hopes without any real guidance to how they might be realized.

BEFORE: In the years ahead, questions about immigration are bound to increase. How many immigrants should be allowed into this country, and by what criteria, will continue to be questioned. One thing that is certain is that our nation must tackle these questions head-on and confront the diversity that exists in these United States.

AFTER: We are not the only country where pressure to reverse the tide of immigrants has increased. Countries like France and Germany are passing new legislation to stem the flow of immigration from Africa and Eastern Europe. Everywhere conservative politicians try to use antiimmigration sentiment for their own purposes. Are we going to build Berlin walls or lower new iron curtains to keep out the new migrations?

WRITING WORKSHOP 10

Questions for Peer Review

When you participate in **peer review**, you try to give fellow students feedback that will help them build on the strengths of a promising draft. (Sometimes you will be trying to help a writer salvage a weak paper or start over.) Ask questions like the following when participating in peer review:

• Do you think the writer cared? Why or why not?

• Is the title informative? Is it at the same time in some way different, provocative, or inviting? (Can you suggest a better one?) Does the introduction bring the subject to life?

• Is the paper focused on its subject? What to you is the central issue? Does it come clearly into focus?

• What is the writer's main point? Where is it stated? Does it emerge clearly from the paper?

• Does the writer use detailed, convincing examples? Where does the supporting material seem strongest; where does it seem weakest? Where would you like to see more graphic examples or detailed evidence?

• Is the paper easy or hard to follow? How would you outline the flow of the paper? Do you have suggestions for strengthening or streamlining the overall plan?

• Is there anything unclear or confusing? Are there any striking phrases or sentences that you will remember?

• What questions would you like to ask the writer?

• Did the writer make you think? Did you learn something new? Did you in any way change your mind? Why or why not?

• What would you say in response to what the writer said?

SAMPLE DRAFT FOR PEER REVIEW: **The Race against Prejudice**

Prejudice is the intolerance or hatred of another race. It means a preconceived usually unfavorable idea, an opinion held in disregard of facts that contradict it. All of these definitions combine to form an ignorance that has been around since the beginning of humankind. Are we winning the race against prejudice? When I walk into a grocery store with two black friends, I see people staring at us, unable to handle the fact that not all people look alike. After class, a fellow student talks about his dislike for Texas because of its large Mexican population. However, I do believe that there is hope for the future, as races combine to become more and more cultures and begin to respect one another for who they are.

Coming from a multicultural public high school has made me realize that we can work together and make a difference in society. I understand now that the theory of a "melting pot" is wrong. This phrase implies that we want everyone to be the same. In reality, we should expect to be different in culture, heritage, and beliefs. Not only should we expect this; we should respect this. Rather than a melting pot, we should consider ourselves a salad bowl — each different but thrown into the same mix.

Prejudice remains strong today, and I have seen this at first hand among the students at my own campus. One student claims, "There is a definite separation among the students here. I don't know if it is because people aren't given much choice or they just don't want to be together. I do feel that this is one negative aspect of the school, the segregation."

The topic of prejudice is touched on almost daily by our newspapers, magazines, and authors. There is hope for our future. One cannot turn on MTV these days and watch it for ten minutes without seeing some sort of antiracist message. The only way that we can overcome ignorance is to bring it out into the open and face it. Grammar schools are now beginning to have culture weeks. High schools have multicultural clubs that bring students together and discuss current issues. All of these factors are helping to cure people of fear and ignorance of other races.

However, with all of this helping to bond different races, there is some backsliding. Some exclude themselves, creating a wall that limits them to their own race. Gang violence, for example, is killing people every day, because of not only what color rags they wear but also the color of their skin. The neo-Nazis, or skinheads, exemplify a violent racial organization sweeping the nation. A student here on this campus was affected directly by this violence when his brother was beaten by the skinheads. He claims, "They will only jump you if they have you outnumbered. . . . They hit my brother in the head with a pipe and scarred him for life." During my last year in high school, the same gentlemen that wore "Love sees no color" shirts would shove me in the hallway because I was white.

There is hope for our future. Prejudice can be overcome through eliminating ignorance. Teaching the young, middle-aged, and old that different cultures should be respected and not ignored is one way to stop ignorance. The only time that race does not seem to matter is when we are side by side in the nursery or side by side in the grave. Together we can make a difference. I have seen it happen throughout high school, groups consisting of many cultures and not just one. Prejudice is a learned behavior, and education is the key for stopping it.

Writing Edited English

Writing is a very fabulous occupation because miraculously it can always be made better.

JOHN UPDIKE

Before you submit a finished paper, what final editing or fine-tuning is required? It's time to run a spell-check and do other final editing and polishing. For instance, you may try to find a better word for a key idea, rewrite murky sentences, or pare down passages that sound talky and roundabout. You reword passages that seem too slangy and disrespectful — or too hyperformal and stodgy — for your intended reader. In your early drafts, you may push ahead even when you are not happy with how a sentence reads or what associations a word brings into play. You then attend to such matters in final editing.

Here is a preview of basic editing tasks:

Word Choice You search for the right word to replace a word that blurs your meaning or calls up the wrong associations.

> BLURRED: In order to *diagnose* this claim, we need to listen to the testimony of eyewitnesses. (But a claim is not an illness?)
>
> BETTER: In order to *verify* this claim, we need to listen to the testimony of eyewitnesses. (We can "establish the truth" of a claim.)

Nonsexist Language You are careful to use unisex terms for occupations: *flight attendant, firefighter, police officer, mail carrier.* You avoid condescending terms like *the girls in the office.* You work your way around the **generic** *man (human being)* and *mankind (humanity, humankind).* Men have often said that they were using *man* ("The History of Man") and *mankind* to include both genders, but the terms tend to make readers visualize mainly the male of the species nevertheless.

Sentence Style You reword murky sentences. You rewrite sentences where the words seem to get in the way of the meaning. You ask yourself: "Is this a sentence that my readers will be able to remember and quote?"

> JARGON: Recently it has become explicitly obvious that there has been a resurgence of racism, expecially among young people.
>
> PLAIN ENGLISH: Racism has come back, especially among the young.

You can often strengthen roundabout or unfocused sentences by rewriting them on the "Who-does-what" model.

> ROUNDABOUT: There is one major factor in the outcome of a child in a divorce, and that is the parents. (Who does what?)
>
> DIRECT: *Parents make the difference* in how a child survives the divorce.

Parallel structure lines up sentence elements that go together in similar grammatical form: "red, white, and blue"; "married, single, and divorced." Lack of parallelism can derail a sentence when a latter part snaps out of a pattern that the earlier part seems to have set up:

NOT PARALLEL: The more resilient among the children of divorce make the best of a situation over which they have no control; in others, *the anger and confusion felt is evident* in the moodiness and unpredictability of the person's actions.

PARALLEL: The more resilient among the children of divorce make the best of a situation over which they have no control; *others show their anger and confusion by their moodiness and unpredictable actions.* (Some do this; some do that.)

Proofreading   Text looks deceptively finished on the computer screen. Many editors recommend that you proofread your text first on the screen — and then again as hard copy. If early in your paper you have *facial tension* when you mean *racial tension,* and if you refer to this country as the *Untied States,* your credibility is bound to suffer. No matter how hurried you may be, take time to check spelling and punctuation. Do a final spell-check. It's essential to double-check names.

Many publications — whether a student daily, a company newsletter, or a national magazine — have stylesheets with editorial guidelines for contributors. Such a style sheet may rule on matters ranging from when to use hyphens to whether to use *Afro-American, African American,* or *black.* Traditional handbooks, online handbooks, and various kinds of editing software are available to help you with your editing tasks.

Computer Writing, Collaborative Writing, Interactive Writing

Everybody is a writer. At one time, a would-be author might have bought into the myth of the lonely misunderstood individual whose manuscript is finally discovered and found to be a work of genius. However, rapidly advancing technology and new patterns of communication and networking have greatly broadened the base. Desktop publishing of near-professional quality has enabled a myriad of contributors to newsletters and special-interest publications to become published authors. The world of zines, like another side of the moon to the staid world of establishment publications, has for many provided an outlet for the zany or irreverent side of their personalities. E-mail is for many users replacing the telephone as the medium of instant off-the-top-of-the-head communication.

Computer Writing Writing on the computer has brought our writing process closer to the way we think. The text on the screen is infinitely malleable, like modeling clay. It allows us to reflect instantly our second thoughts and sudden inspirations. Our writing comes to resemble a process of continuous growth rather than a stop-and-go process of unfinished and abandoned drafts.

Our thinking does not go through stages where we stop after Phase 1 to say "Print out half-formed thoughts." Instead, even while driving to school or having coffee, we may be elaborating our half-formed thoughts until they take more definite shape. Writing on the computer allows us to keep up with this process of thinking and rethinking. We can give a statement a slightly different direction in midsentence; we can shift material from a paragraph that is getting top-heavy into a later paragraph. We can feed in material from another document when we become aware of a previously unnoticed connection.

Computers are increasingly linked in networks in classrooms, dorms, or libraries, with students exchanging drafts of papers with peers or with the instructor commenting electronically on student writing.

Collaborative Writing Work in writing classes and other areas of the curriculum increasingly recognizes collaboration as a major dimension of a writer's world. Many studies and reports are the result of teamwork, with assignments farmed out in accordance with the contributors' special areas of interest or expertise. Collaborative writing projects can lead to a fruitful meeting of male and female perspectives, for instance, or of youthful enthusiasm and experienced judgment. A project may involve collaborators in a productive balancing of differing political points of view.

How do collaborating authors interact? How do they communicate? How do they work? What strengths do they bring to a writing task? How can mutual needs actually further the collaboration? Alleen Nilsen Pace, co-author of an article on computer jargon, described the collaboration as follows:

> I had the interest in language but limited expertise in computer science, and my collaborator, a professor of computer science, had the computer expertise but no special background in language. I approached him by phone about collaborating on an article on computer jargon. We then

switched to e-mail and began to pass our ideas back and forth. E-mail allowed us to communicate rapidly. It generated momentum; in the exchange, the idea of one triggered new ideas in the other until there was a snowball effect. Since the article was my idea, I sent him my handful of tentative untechnical ideas on the metaphoric aspects of computer jargon. I reminded him that when hearing him talk to someone also in computers, I had felt left out of the loop. What does it mean to say: "You shake hands with the printer"? To fill in gaps, my coauthor scouted a dictionary of jargon terms, such as "the bleeding edge" (he sees himself on the bleeding edge of computer science) and faxed them to me. I, in turn, made a list of terms I wanted to explore and e-mailed them back to him. He immediately e-mailed back additional ideas which gave me enough substance to write a rough draft. In reading my draft, he was able to provide the sample sentences. By now we were bouncing ideas back and forth, shaping and refining our text. This collaborative process led to a product which gave us both much pleasure.

Guidelines like the following can prepare you for some of the hurdles and opportunities ahead:

• *Be prepared to see the collaboration as a test of group dynamics.* Collaboration requires people with different personalities and sometimes different agendas to work together. You may have to make necessary adjustments in your own thinking and procedures. You may have to do your share to head off possible interpersonal conflicts.

• *Understand how lines of authority will be drawn.*   In a team or group, will everyone be thought of as an equal partner, with disagreements settled by friendly discussion or by vote? Or will someone be chosen as senior partner or project director on the basis of experience and expertise or the special commitment and energy that predispose some people to be leaders? With a larger group, will there be a steering committee coordinating everyone's efforts?

• *Be clear on the nature of the final product.*   Will the final product pool contributions representing different styles or perspectives — but essentially put them side by side? Or will there be an editor (or editorial committee) rewriting the materials to make them conform to a common style — smoothing out differences, making the material seem of one piece?

• *Feel responsible for the success of the project as a whole.*   You will of course hope to be given credit for any outstanding contribution you have made. But often the reality of the situation is that you will share in the success or failure of the collaborative effort as a whole.

- *When asked for a self-evaluation, don't be shy.*   Give an honest accounting of your personal contribution — of ideas and suggestions contributed and of time and effort invested.

Interactive Writing   Online communication is changing our definition of writing. It becomes a kind of speak-write, with one writer thinking out loud, throwing out perhaps preliminary or unfinished ideas. Instant feedback will often help ideas to take shape. Friendly questions may encourage the writer to recover memories or to spell out ideas more frankly or more aggressively. Hostile feedback may change the direction of an argument or perhaps put the writer on the defensive.

A new vocabulary is developing for the electronic give-and-take of interactive computer writing. A topic may "drift" or experience slippage as a participant pushes it in a tangential direction. "Flames" are personal attacks that can short-circuit intelligent discussion. A "screed" is the result of someone getting on a soapbox — and perhaps causing others to log off. A participant not really joining in and perhaps biding his or her time is said to "lurk."

Interactive computer writing is like written conversation. Computer gurus predict that increased participation in and familiarity with interactive online communication will help push conventional writing in the direction of greater spontaneity and flexibility.

OPTIONS FOR WRITING I

Discovering Your Topic

Choose one of the following writing projects. Ask yourself: "Which of these is *my* topic? On which of these do I have something to say?" Choose a topic that you can relate to your own observation, experience, reading, and viewing. Take a stand or make your point of view clear early in your paper. Be sure you back up what you say with specific examples or other supporting material. Make up your own title. Write for the educated general reader — a reader informed about public issues and concerned about the state of our society.

If possible, discuss your interest in a topic and your tentative plans for it in a small group or with your class as a whole.

1 Do you think racism is on the rise among young people? Some observers see (and some polls seem to show) a resurgence of racism among the younger generation. Write to assure or to alarm members of an older generation.

2 Is there too much brutal violence on our movie or television screens? Are media watchers right who accuse the media of being addicted to the sick thrill of violence? Support the claim, or defend the media against the charge. (What if anything can be done about it?)

3 How much progress has our society made toward accepting or integrating the disabled? Write for people of good will who have not however given the challenges of mainstreaming the disabled much thought.

4 Is it true, as the cigarette ad says, that women "have come a long way"? What would you say to the advertisers who use this slogan?

5 Have Americans lost the sense of home? Is it true that as the result of split families many young Americans have lost a sense of belonging?

6 Have you had a chance to observe our endangered wildlife? Have you explored a wildlife refuge or the kind of animal park that tries to provide a quasi-natural habitat for different species? What can you say to alert city dwellers to the danger to our fellow creatures of the animal world?

7 Is it true that as the result of current sexual politics many young males have developed a defensive attitude?

8 Leaders of religious cults often set up their own communities, isolating their followers from the rest of society. Should the government leave them alone?

9 Have you ever observed closely or served as a volunteer at a homeless shelter, a Salvation Army outpost, a soup kitchen, a homeless encampment? What should members of the affluent majority know about your experience?

10 Should court trials be televised? Do the media tend to turn a trial into a media circus? Can justice be done in an atmosphere of sensational reporting?

WRITING WORKSHOP 11

A Planning Report

Which of these possible writing assignments would allow you to say: "This is my topic?" Write a **planning report,** answering questions like the following:

• What has been your previous exposure to or experience with the topic?

• How does the topic relate to your own observation, experience, reading, or viewing? (What is the personal connection?)

• What tentative point or points do you intend to make, or what side would you take, and why? (Where do you think you would take your stand?)

• What might be your tentative strategy for structuring the paper?

• What key evidence or personal experience might you bring in as supporting material?

• Who would be your ideal reader?

The Writer's Tools 1

Starting a Thought Log

Use a thought log for putting into words memories, concerns, and feelings that later might provide material for a paper. At the beginning, you may want to use your log to look back over incidents or issues that have played a role in your past experience. Later you may use your journal mainly for notes and reflections on your current life. What is happening in your life — personal life, schooling, reading, and viewing — that is worth jotting down and thinking about? What new people and what new ideas have you encountered?

Writing in a log or journal is more informal and less pressured than writing for publication. You can put things down in a more spontaneous way, without a reader or an editor looking over your shoulder. Although you may share your writing with your instructor or your classmates, your log is first of all a communication with yourself. It is the writer's equivalent of what people do when they think out loud, so that they can listen to what goes on in their minds. At the same time, however, an entry will often contain the germ of a promising idea for a longer paper.

Make it a habit to write in your journal two or three times a week. Write at least half or two-thirds of a single-spaced page. Although some of your entries may be unsorted or miscellaneous, focus at least some of your entries on a unifying topic. For instance, discuss a photography exhibit at the Art Building, a new television program on the Civil War, a major speaker visiting the campus, or a heated current controversy. Include striking details, quotable quotes. Include questions to yourself.

THOUGHT LOG I

The Personal Résumé

What do you as a person bring to your writing? Use early entries in your thought log for a **personal résumé** — a stock-taking of material that you might be able to draw on in your written work. Who are you? What kind of person are you? What might you be able to contribute to the class? Write a paragraph or two under headings like the following. You might want to answer one or more of the sample questions. These are merely suggestive, meant to stimulate your own thinking and exploration.

• ROOTS: What kind of family life did you experience? Did ethnic origin or an old-country culture play a role in your growing up?

Did you have a religious upbringing? Did you experience any turning points or traumatic events?

• SCHOOLING: Did you enjoy school or hate it? What was the social or racial mix of the students? What teachers made a special impression on you? Did you have favorite subjects or encounter special hurdles? What did you learn from your schooling besides academic subjects?

• FRIENDS: Have you had special friends or enemies? Have you seen a friendship change or develop over the years? Have you been involved in a serious relationship?

• INTERESTS: Have you experienced challenges or disappointments while participating in sports? Are you committed to a cause or political organization? Are you a reader or a nonreader? What are your favorite and least favorite kinds of entertainment?

• WORK: Have you had experience with chores and part-time work? Have you had work that you would call your first real job? How definite are your career interests?

SAMPLE ENTRY 1:   I went to Catholic schools for my education. I don't know if the experience helped me or not. I attended a Catholic grade school for eight years (where discipline was administered by the "Sisters of Mercy"). Then I went to a parochial high school, with reasonably good grades. Going to college has been a new experience for me, because it is the first time I have had so much freedom. Usually there were so many rules that I could hardly breathe without getting into trouble. Now I am free to wear anything I want without having to answer to anyone. I know I am supposed to enjoy my new freedom, but at times I feel I am just floundering.

SAMPLE ENTRY 2:   When I was sixteen years old, I worked for the pope, in a manner of speaking. My first job was that of a part-time receptionist at the St. John rectory. The rectory, a Spanish-style building, white-washed and topped with a red tile roof, was the nerve center of the parish. As one of three part-time receptionists, I needed tact, decent communication skills, and a basically friendly outlook toward the rest of humanity. My duties included answering the telephone and writing messages; stuffing, sealing, and organizing mountains of envelopes; running errands; closing the church at night; and often helping with the dishes. I also had free access to the refrigerator and baked goods. I performed my job with a happy-go-lucky attitude, but I was often troubled and surprised by the number of people who were in need of food and shelter. Before I worked at the rectory, I thought I had been living in a prosperous middle-class parish.

I suppose it was inevitable that as my word base broadened I could for the first time pick up a book and read and now begin to understand what the book was saying. Anyone who has read a great deal can imagine the new world that opened.   MALCOLM X

2

You the Reader

Learning from Your Reading

How good a reader are you? How long is your attention span? How good are you at taking in key data or picking up the thread of an argument? In any writing situation, readers have a headstart over nonreaders or reluctant readers:

• Good readers know there is more to subjects like illegal immigration or the dropout rate than jumps from the headlines. Do you read a newspaper regularly? Do you spend an hour or two a week reading *Time, Newsweek, Ms.* magazine? If you read newspapers, newsmagazines, and books, you will have a headstart for many possible topics. As a regular reader, you can draw on your reading for background, bringing in precedents, key examples, arguments pro and con.

• Experienced readers read not only for the "general idea" but for the ifs and buts. As an experienced reader, you read important clues to the writer's intention. You become better at grasping the major elements in a proposal or at following the steps in an argument. Becoming better at reading between the lines, you notice comments that show a writer to be friendly or hostile to women, to minorities, or to white males.

• Writers learn from other writers. Reading with the writer's eye, you become aware of strategies that have worked for others. You learn from their successes — and sometimes from their failures. You notice how successful authors hook readers into a topic — how they raise an issue, how they dramatize a question. You learn how a good writer leads up to the main point — and then later reinforces it, driving it home. You learn how others lay out a subject — leading you from the easy to the difficult, or from the familiar to the strange.

THOUGHT LOG I

Thinking about Your Reading

Write in your thought log about a special book. Or write about a kind of reading that has taken up much of your time. Do you remember a book that made a special impression on you? Perhaps it opened a window on a world unfamiliar to you. Perhaps it changed your mind about something important. Did you spend much of your time reading science fiction or detective fiction or fantasy fiction? Write about what impressed you about a book or what fascinated you about a kind of reading.

The Ideal Reader

Writer and reader together make up a rich fabric of their mutual weaving.

MELANIE SPERLING

Do you have a system for reading an article or a chapter from a book? Do you give it a first quick reading — and then go over it again slowly point by point? Do you highlight or underline? Do you write notes in the margin, like "How so?" These and similar procedures show that you are serious about your reading. Your first task as a reader is to do justice to what is there. You try to see how the argument shapes up, to take in what a piece of writing says. Suppose you are reading an article on the role of talk shows in the current cultural and political scene. What would an alert reader get out of the following major section of the article? What would a receptive reader take in? The comments in parentheses after each paragraph register the mental notes a receptive reader might make as the passage takes shape:

RICHARD M. LEVINE

I Feel Your Pain

It seems as though everyone famous for more than fifteen minutes has his or her own talk show. . . . Seamlessly the former inter-

viewers and the formerly interviewed join Phil and Oprah and Larry
and David and Jay and Geraldo and Joan and Sally Jessy and Maury
and the hundreds of others in every local TV market who make it
possible for us to celebrate celebrities — or watch them celebrate
themselves, and around the clock from sea to shining sea. To paraphrase our national bard, I hear America talking (and talking and
talking).

> [COMMENT: This author is not just mentioning talk shows in passing but
> is *focusing* on them in earnest. He is serious about their being on every-
> where and around the clock. A long list of names of talk show hosts drives
> home this point. By the end of this paragraph, we already have a strong
> hint of the author's overall attitude toward his subject: The shows already
> sound as if they were just talk — "talking and talking."]

Clearly the talk show fills some crucial need in our national life,
which I think has to do with felt absence of place and power. Talk
shows provide some communal sense in an increasingly fragmented
world. The studio audience — and by extension the television audience — becomes a kind of therapeutic, personal-problem-solving
support group that helps us feel better about ourselves and resolve
to live better, one hour at a time. Talk shows allow us to feel connected to the community of self-improving, self-motivated doers
"empowering" themselves — without affecting in any way the actual circumstances of our lives.

> [COMMENT: Here Levine gives the talk shows some credit for filling
> a "crucial need" in our modern lives. First, people lack a sense of belong-
> ing — they lack a place where they belong. To make up for this lack, the
> shows offer some "communal sense"; they allow people to feel "con-
> nected" to a kind of "community." And, second, the purpose of this
> association is "therapeutic," or healing. It compensates for our lack of
> power — the second key term in this paragraph. The shows seem to offer
> "problem-solving"; they make us "resolve to live better"; they make us
> feel like "self-improving, self-motivating doers" who become "empow-
> ered." But the shows help us feel better about ourselves "without affecting
> in any way the actual circumstances of our lives."]

For even more than the lack of place it is the lack of power in our
lives that has helped turn television into a twenty-four-hour-a-day
talk-show marathon. In a troubled economic time, when people distrust government and feel helpless to affect their fate, talking back
may be the only form of power left to them. (This is particularly true
with the call-in segment of talk shows, where it becomes apparent
that the audience is swollen with the ranks of the un- and under-

employed.) Those of us who can't act ourselves can watch others seeming to act — voyeurs watching exhibitionists in a pantomime of power.

> [COMMENT: Here the writer closes in on the more important of the two factors: the attempt of people who feel "helpless" to compensate for their "lack of power." When calling in to talk shows and "talking back" to the establishment, people who are unemployed or underemployed exercise perhaps the only form of power left to them. However, all this talk is all an illusion — these people are just "seeming to act." They are "exhibitionists" in a "pantomime" — an actor's imitation of real actions. We as viewers are "voyeurs" — people who get their thrills by watching, not doing.]

But the talk show never leads to genuine action, in part because it isn't really about talk at all. The two components of its name bear vastly unequal weight; in terms of what really matters the genre is all show and very little talk, or rather the talk is just the excuse for the show. Words are at best disposable items on television, and the best talk show hosts know this instinctively. . . . Sometimes the talk is interesting or informative; sometimes it's boring or irrelevant. It doesn't matter. Genuine expertise about a subject is a hindrance, almost an embarrassment calling for an apology. When candidate Clinton's media advisors decided to broaden his demographics with an appearance on "Arsenio," Clinton went off by himself to practice his saxophone renditions of "Heartbreak Hotel" and "God Bless the Child."

> [COMMENT: Here is a final touch in the author's denying talk shows a real role in influencing political debate or political action: The basic problem with talk shows is that they are more show than real talk about things that matter. Showmanship, not the issues discussed, is what matters.]

from *Mother Jones*

| WRITING WORKSHOP 1 |

A Student Editorial

The following article appeared on the editorial page of a student daily. Would you make a good reader for the author? Think about questions like the following:

• What is the writer's purpose? What set this editorial in motion — what triggered it?

• What kind of audience did the writer have in mind?

• What is the writer's main point? Where is it stated and echoed in the editorial?

• What is the overall plan? Can you identify and label major stages or sections of the editorial? Does the overall plan make sense?

• What material or detail backs up the author's points? What are its sources?

• What points or what details are especially striking or provocative for you as the reader?

• Did the writer make you rethink the issue or cause you to change your mind? Why or why not?

• Do you think the writer was a man or a woman?

The Fight against Discrimination
Has Gone Too Far

When a woman's self-defense class is canceled because it is considered to be discriminatory against men, something is seriously wrong. In some situations, separation of men and women should be allowed and accepted.

Issues in Self Defense for Women was canceled this quarter at Stanford University because of a complaint of sexual discrimination, according to an article in the *Mercury News*. Originally taught by a feminist organization called Women Defending Ourselves, this class is violating Title IX of the Education Amendments Act by putting men and women in separate classes. Stanford's associate general counsel says that Title IX prohibits educational institutions from teaching classes separated by gender.

We put men and women in separate bathrooms; we group men together with men and women together with women in hospitals; we have all-women shelters; we have men's golf and women's golf. Should we stop doing that too? A spokeswoman for Women Defending Ourselves told the *Mercury News* that having male students in the class would radically change it. She also said the all-woman class created a haven for women to discuss sexual violence.

It is safe to say that the majority of men don't think about using the blue phones on campus to request an escort to their parking lot. They probably don't think twice about walking into a dark apartment or house, wondering if someone could be waiting in a closet or behind a door to attack them. So how could men, the majority of whom were not raped or molested, relate to issues and fears that result from the experience?

This class is not just some underwater basket weaving class for women only. It is a class teaching women to protect themselves from *men*. The class consists of three parts — learning to fight, reading and discussion, and assertiveness training.

Stanford offered an equivalent course for men, but it was canceled because only three people signed up. If you consider that a hundred women signed up for the same course, you might wonder if the class is truly as essential for men as it is for women.

Under Title IX, female athletes are required to have the same opportunities extended to them as men. Spelled out in simpler terms, if female students make up 50 percent of the student population, they must make up 50 percent of the varsity slots. If not, then the school must document efforts that it is at least meeting the level of interest that exists among women athletes. Stanford University attempted to do just that. The school offered a class for men to enroll in, but the effort was unsuccessful because the interest of the male population was not there.

Offering the class to women who are interested in this subject makes sense. Unfortunately, in this particular scenario, the interpretation of Title IX is going too far.

Reading the Clues

We read often with as much talent as we write.

RALPH WALDO EMERSON

How good are you at reading the clues to an author's intentions? As an experienced reader, you see how the author introduces an issue and leads up to the main point. You see the bearing of key examples and start saying to yourself: "I see where all this is headed." You key in on major stages in a process or crucial steps in an argument.

Looking out for elements like the following will help you get more out of your reading:

Focus Where does a key question or central issue come into focus? What is the problem to which the writer will try to provide a solution? Near a logging town in Orgeon, a small stand of original-growth trees remains. Will they survive? A writer may introduce us to two locals with opposing views — one the owner of a small lumber mill and the other an environmentalist. The conflict between the two serves to highlight the central issue: saving jobs or saving trees.

Thesis Does the writer early state his or her answer to the central question? Does the writer give a hint or preview of his or her solution to the central problem? Look for a claim or a charge that the rest of the article will support.

> We need a clearer definition of sexual harassment; we trivialize the issue when we mention an unwanted remark in the same breath as rape.
> The basic reason for the decline of the family is the unwillingness or inability of today's young males to commit.
> Today's recessions are different from those of the past; today when the economy "recovers," you still do not get your job back.

Some writers highlight their central thesis — they lead up to it and announce it emphatically. They *reiterate* it — drive it home — while marshaling the evidence. They may circle back to it in a final paragraph. Sometimes, however, they may decide to lead up to the thesis at the end — after eliminating wrong answers or weighing alternatives.

Key Examples   What key examples help alert you to the drift of an article? Writers often use a key example to bring an issue into focus. What does it prove? Where does it lead? The following might be the opening of an article on office politics:

One Up in the Office

You are in a conference room with several fellow workers, and the executive in charge brings up a project your company is working on. Trying to make a good impression, you say: "We did very well with something like that in the fall quarter of 1993." And one of your colleagues — someone you never liked — looks up and says very calmly: "It wasn't the fall quarter; it was the spring quarter."

Where are we headed? We are already well into a look at one-upmanship — mainly in the office but perhaps also more generally in our society. We can expect to take a good look at people with the knack of correcting others on minor points — to make themselves look good.

Organization   What is the author's plan? The writer may give you an explicit preview: "Imports are surging because imported goods can be more cheaply produced; they are often of better quality; and they give the distributor better profit margins than American goods." If the author is as well-organized as he or she sounds, major sections of the argument are likely to drive home each of these points on the agenda. More often, you may have to look out for a transitional phrase that starts a sequence:

A first key reason . . .
Another reason, often denied by interested parties, is that . . .
A third reason has only recently begun to contribute heavily to the imbalance . . .

Often a crucial *however* or *on the other hand* provides a turning point in an argument. A writer may start by giving a familiar proposal the benefit of the doubt — but then marshal the evidence that shows it to be misguided. Or an author may be presenting alternative solutions in order to find them wanting. The plan may be to eliminate one after the other till only the author's own favorite solution is left.

Related Terms   Does a network of related terms and meanings keep the reader's attention focused on key concerns? The following excerpts are from a historian's discussion of the roots of the traditional work ethic. Note how a network of **synonyms** — of terms with the same or similar meaning — helps keep the reader on track:

Honor Labor

What elements of the national character are attributable to this long-time agrarian environment? First and foremost is the habit of *work*. For the colonial farmer, ceaseless *striving* constituted the price of survival. . . .

The tradition of *toil* so begun found new sustenance as settlers opened up the boundless stretches of the interior. "In the free states," wrote Harriet Martineau in 1837, "*labor* is more really and heartily honored. . . ."

One source of Northern antagonism to the system of human bondage was the fear that it was jeopardizing this basic tenet of the American creed. "Where *labor* is mainly performed by slaves," Daniel Webster told the United States Senate, "it is regarded as . . ."

This worship of *work* has made it difficult for Americans to learn how to play. . . .

The first mitigations of the *daily grind* took the form of hunting, fishing, barnraisings, and logrollings — activities that had no social stigma because they contributed to the basic needs of living. . . .

Arthur M. Schlesinger, *Paths to the Present*

Complications   How does the writer handle objections or complications? Does the author take opposition seriously? What counter-arguments does the writer seem to consider most damaging — and therefore worthy of detailed rebuttal? On a much controverted topic, a writer may spend much time defusing familiar objections, heading off opponents at the pass.

Imaginative Language   What striking imaginative comparisons stand out? A writer may use the term "the sandwich generation" to give you a vivid image of people sandwiched in between the generations. They are caring for their own young children and for their own aging, infirm parents at the same time. Another writer may zero in on the cult of grasping self-interest often identified as the religion of the eighties (the "decade of greed"). The writer may focus your attention by calling it a "beggar-thy-neighbor and pull-up-the-drawbridge" mentality.

WRITING WORKSHOP 2

Writing and Thinking

Some writing shows especially clearly the way the author thought the matter through. Find a short current newspaper or magazine article with an exceptionally clear or definite train of thought. Chart the sequence of ideas for your classmates or members of your group. Point out clues that help the reader follow the author's train of thought.

From Reading to Writing

How do you draw on your reading as input for your own writing? Effective writers relate to current arguments or draw on expert opinion. They draw on reading notes, viewer's logs, clippings, or photocopies. They download data or articles. Here are ways to feed the results of your reading into your writing:

Raising the Issue   You use other writers to help you raise the issue. You may want to show that what concerns you is a concern shared by others. Or you may need to show that a seemingly far-fetched idea enjoys reputable support. For instance, you may decide to start a paper on the revival of the vigilante mentality with a thought-provoking quotation like the following:

Vigilantism Reconsidered

As conventional ways of dealing with violence are seen to be breaking down, our society seems to be developing a new respect for the vigilante not as a scofflaw but as someone filling a vacuum. Historian Daniel Boorstin claims that vigilantism arose "not to circumvent courts, but to provide them; not because the machinery of government had become too complicated, but because there was no machinery at all."

Establishing Your Authority   You use your reading to establish your authority. Well-chosen references to current discussions or studies enhance your credibility. When you write about prison overcrowding or health care reform, you do not want to sound as though you discovered the subject only yesterday. Pointed quotations can show that you are aware of current arguments or that you have kept up with current information. A paragraph like the following effectively bundles several such quotations:

People have long had false teeth, artificial limbs, and pacemakers — why not artificial hearts? For a while, the future looked bright for a major medical breakthrough. However, after the ordeal of several artificial-heart recipients many observers have had second thoughts. As Robert Bazell said in *The New Republic*, "Exotic medical procedures make compelling news stories" but the "trouble is that they are indeed experimental, and often they do not work." The costs are horrendous. In an article in *Business Week*, Kathleen Deremy and Alan Hall estimated that the widespread use of artificial hearts could add up to $3 billion to the nation's health costs.

Supporting Key Points   You draw on your reading for support. Effective writers use **clincher quotes**. Clinching quotations appearing at strategic points bring in the heavy guns: experts, insiders, official reports, eyewitnesses, highly qualified observers. In the following passage, Rachel Carson, a pioneer in the movement to protect the environment, clinches her argument against the indiscriminate use of pesticides by using an authoritative quotation:

> Quarantine and massive chemical campaigns are only extremely expensive ways of buying time. We are faced, according to Dr. Elton, "with a life-and-death need not just to find new technological means of suppressing this plant or that animal"; instead we need the basic knowledge of animal populations and their relations to their surroundings that will "promote an even balance and damp down the explosive power of outbreaks and new invasions."

"Bouncing Off" Others   You take issue with writers with whom you disagree. We often use a quotation to focus attention on a claim we wish to refute. We quote other writers to argue with them, as does the author of the following passage:

> Tuchman draws on examples from Jewish history to remind us that "the good in humanity operates even if the bad secures more attention." The Jews of ancient Palestine repeatedly fought for independence, invoking "the divine right of insurrection" against alien rulers. The defenders of Masada were willing to die rather than be captured, choosing suicide over surrender to the Romans. It is true that the "right to insurrection" occasioned heroic deeds, but at the same time it reminds us of an age-old record of oppression. The story of Masada reminds us of the human capacity for cruelty and violence. People would not have to rise against oppression "time after time" if oppression and exploitation were not constants in human history.

You need to give some thought to *how* to weave material from your reading into your own writing. How will you integrate quoted material so that your text will not simply stitch together quotations? Consider advice like the following:

• *Introduce your quotations.*   Answer questions likely to arise in your reader's mind: Why is this in here? What is the source? (Are you quoting from a book? article? news report?) Who is talking? (What are the person's credentials? Why should your reader listen to this person?) What is the person saying? (What is the point?)

SOURCE: In her essay, "Pornography and the First Amendment," Susan Jacoby describes herself as a "First Amendment junkie."

CREDENTIALS: Elaine Kim, professor of Asian American Studies at the University of California at Berkeley, says: "Historically, Asian Americans as we renamed ourselves, have had no place in the discourse on culture and race in the United States except as 'model minorities' on the one hand or as unassimilable aliens on the other."

POINT: Garrett Hardin, author of articles and books on "human ecology," has used the lifeboat analogy to dramatize our limited capacity for helping the world's poor: "Our survival demands that we govern our actions by the ethics of a lifeboat, harsh though they may be."

• *Keep your credit tags varied and flexible.*   You will often use the basic "So-and-so says such-and-such" pattern. In most cases, a comma will separate your **credit tag** from what you quote. You may use a colon for a more formal or weighty quotation.

Jessica Hagedorn says in introducing her collection *Charlie Chan Is Dead,* "I thought all Americans were blond and freckled and ate apples, and all fairhaired children had dogs like Spot."
In her introduction to *Charlie Chan Is Dead,* Jessica Hagedorn says: "The first *Aiiieeeee!* anthology, published in hardback in 1974 and in paperback in 1975, was an absolute breakthrough for Asian Americans."

Repeated too often, this pattern may sound mechanical. Draw on the full repertory of other credit tags, or introductory phrases, ranging from *according to* or *in the words of* to *as Professor Brown says.*

According to Susan Faludi, author of *Backlash*, the dialogue in these women's films "probes the economic and social inequities of traditional wedlock."
In the words of psychologist Hilda Ignes, "Neurosis is the condition where an individual's emotional elevators go to top floor when least desired."
As Gloria Steinem says in *Revolution from Within*, "many high achievers have come out of female-headed households and beaten the societal odds."
To quote Mark Twain, "The very ink with which history is written is merely fluid prejudice."

A study of police departments in three large cities challenges the assumption that police officers are unwilling to "bear witness against corrupt fellow officers."

WRITING WORKSHOP 3

A Paper for Peer Review

How did the author of the following paper integrate material from firsthand observation and from her reading? Where and why does she turn to authorities? Where and why does she use paraphrase, where direct quotation?

The Fire Seeder

As we drove along the west shore of Yellowstone Lake, we could see the angular island in the middle of the lake to our right. We watched one lodgepole pine after another turn into a flaming orange-red torch, shooting skyward through the black smoke like a fireworks display on a foggy night. The fire swept through the island leaving much of it unscathed before it ran pell-mell into the lake, drawing its last destructive breath in a billowing gasp of steam and black smoke. We were witnessing what to some was the avoidable destruction of an invaluable national treasure and to others a lesson in the renewal or rebirth of ecosystems.

We had entered the burn area mid-afternoon and been told by a park attendant to turn on our lights and not to stop for pictures. About two miles down the road, the first acrid fumes irritated our nostrils and eyes and besmudged what had been a clear blue sky. Around the bend, we encountered the result of the fire's frenetic activity several hours earlier, its erratic path looking like the work of a giant baker run amok with a cookie cutter. Gray ash covered the burnt-out patches of forest, and red-hot coals smouldered in the "snags," the smoking stumps that had been towering lodgepole pines.

We had been afraid our trip would have to be called off. When the great fire broke out in July, television stations covered its daily progress and devastating aftermath in living color. With headlines like "FIRES RAVAGE NATIONAL TREASURE," we were surprised we were still allowed to make a swing through the park. Long before we entered the burn area, we saw the lodgepole pines everywhere. They made a canopy so thick that for miles all we could see were the trees with their limbs wrapped around each other, with the fallen dead trees making artistic patterns on the barren forest floor. When the road wound out of the forest and through a clearing, we could see smoke rising from the top of a grove in the distance.

The devastating fires of which we saw the early stages were the result of the park's natural burn policy, which had actually been in effect for sixteen years, and which allows fires caused by lightning to burn themselves out, except where they threaten towns or park buildings. Before it ended, the inferno had raged over half of Yellowstone's 2.2 million acres. According to newspaper accounts, the tourist industry suffered enormous losses because of the adverse publicity, and the logging interests and tourist industry started their own political firestorm to protest the policies of the Park Service.

Why would the Park Service allow such devastation to our oldest national park and the largest wildlife preserve in the United States? According to Research Biologist Donald Despain, fire plays an essential role in the regeneration of the pine forests. The lodgepole pines require a fire to propagate themselves; their tiny quarter-inch seeds, or "wings," are slowly released from the rock-hard pine cones only after they have been seared by the passing flames. The little wings act like the rotary blades of a helicopter in dispersing the seeds — perhaps one million seeds an acre. It was no coincidence that many of the burnt trees were old, losing their natural resistance to disease and insects. Dead trees fall to the forest floor, joined by others blown over by the winds howling down from the surrounding peaks. The thinning canopy, in turn, lets in more sunlight to the forest floor; dormant grass seeds fill in the open spaces between the trees; the ground clutter thickens; more trees fall. With the help of a prolonged drought, as Despain says, "the old forest creates its own funeral pyre."

In the words of John Varley, Yellowstone's chief of research, "We see what's going on here not as devastation and destruction but rather as rebirth and renewal of these ecosystems."

Revising Papers about Your Reading

A first draft may have good material and cover major points. At the same time, it may have too many undigested quotations — chunks of direct quotation without enough introduction and interpretation. It may not have a clear purpose or a clear enough plan. It may not show clearly enough where the ideas of an author you are discussing stop and where your own reaction or response starts. The following might be a peer response to a first draft you wrote on an article about the "greenhouse effect" and the threat of global warming:

> PEER RESPONSE: You show that the author sounds the familiar warning but also listens to the skeptics. You cover the major dimensions of the issue well — the projected rise of the sea level around the globe, the changes in climate affecting agriculture, and the horrendous costs of trying to deal with these changes. The quotations you select often get my attention, like "famines of biblical proportions." However, when you quote

from the article, your follow-up at times seems weak. You often end up repeating the author's ideas in almost identical words rather than explaining in your own words what the author meant. You give too much repetition of the ideas and not explanation or helpful examples. Did the author explain how fruitful agricultural valleys would turn into deserts? Why would countries like Bangladesh suffer most? I personally was put off by repeated uses of language like *mankind, man-made,* and *man's role.* What about woman's role?

Check whether editorial advice like the following applies to your early draft:

• *Clarify the focus of your discussion.* The following might be the beginning of your review of an article before and after revision:

UNFOCUSED: As the title of her article indicates, Dana Allison in "Whales: Natural Resource or Threatened Wildlife?" gives much information about whales and the current arguments surrounding them. Much public discussion has revolved around the threatened extinction of different whale species. . . .

FOCUSED: As the title of her article indicates, Dana Allison in "Whales: Natural Resource or Threatened Wildlife?" pits the arguments of those who consider the whales a natural resource to be managed and exploited against those who consider them endangered fellow creatures. Although she discusses the arguments of those who talk about "sustainable yields" and "harvesting," her sympathies are clearly with those who feel a special kinship with these majestic creatures as symbols of the mystery of life. . . .

• *Avoid the dumped quotation.* Do not simply dump quotations (and especially long or weighty quotations) on the reader. How does the quotation fit into your argument? Why is your source worth listening to? What do you think the quotation proves?

DUMPED: An article in the *Economist* magazine brings up an interesting point: "What is really happening is merely a mutation in the Darwinian struggle for the survival of white-male supremacy." [Why is this in here? What are the credentials of the author? What does the quotation say?]

WELL USED: In a January 1995 article in the *Economist*, a social science professor at London University reminds us that privileged classes rose to the top in a dog-eat-dog struggle for power and wealth: "What is really happening is merely a mutation in the Darwinian struggle for the survival of white-male supremacy." White males today are fighting off challengers — women, minorities — the way the strong and ruthless always fight back when their dominant position is called into question.

- *Explain technical or unusual terms.*   Help your readers by furnishing an approximate time frame when your source refers to the "Cromagnon people" or the "Wurm glaciation." Provide a capsule definition when needed.

> Were the cave paintings worked over and over by successive generations, producing the "crowded palimpsest-like effect" — like a parchment reused with previous messages scraped out — "suggested by some of the photos"?

- *Do not take a quotation out of context.*   One well-known scientist objected to "half quotations" — selecting only the part of a quotation that seems to *support* the quoting author's own position but leaving out important reservations that point in the opposite direction.

Reading Online

The computer is changing our reading habits — as it is changing our writing habits. Reading online promises instant access to data, news, commentary, and opinion. A reader trying to keep up with current news can punch in key words like PEACE (or PEACE PROCESS) and MIDDLE EAST and call up a range of current coverage, downloading the most relevant material for future use. Visitors to a site like the Whole Earth 'Lectronic Link (WELL) can follow special-interest material tracked by many people. Tasks that used to require hours of fact-grubbing become easy: With classics like Melville's *Moby Dick* available online, a researcher can have instant access to all passages mentioning BLUBBER, for instance, in the great mythic novel about whales and the whaling industry. Readers can work at their home computers, free of the frustrations of dealing with conventional library materials — which may prove to be missing, vandalized, or checked out.

Some readers are already reading the Sunday edition of the *New York Times* (or at any rate much of it) online. Books and articles are beginning to be published simultaneously in hardcover and electronic versions. Encyclopedias and unabridged dictionaries available online save the user the trek to a library. A whole minor growth industry is developing navigational aids that promise to help users find their way on the Internet. Manuals with titles ranging from *How to Use the Internet* or *How the Internet Works* to *Internet for Dummies* guide newcomers in their search for specific resources.

With rich related materials assembled on a CD-ROM, reading becomes part of a multimedia experience. The user may be taking a virtual-reality trip through a museum, stopping in front of a favorite painting, zooming in for a close-up view, clicking on biographical material about the painter or critical discussion of the work.

Like many other users, you may discover the flexibility of working on the computer, which allows you to develop your own personal working style. Articles you have downloaded are yours for future use or reference and do not have to be returned to the library. You can make the print bigger or smaller or change fonts. You can interact with the authors by addressing responses or queries to them. You can print out hard copy for detailed closed reading and annotation.

You may want to keep cautions like the following in mind:

• Articles reproduced online may be digests or abridgements, with the origin of materials or authorship uncertain.

• Cyberspace is clogged with unsorted, unedited material, with great variation in quality. Unlike conventional print publishing, the Internet lacks editors, reviewers, and critics to filter the flow of material. One researcher found that he had to sort out files ranging from expert testimony to an eighth-grader's library paper. "Facts" you have tracked down may be of dubious validity.

• Inexperienced users may miscalculate access or utilization costs. (A librarian may be able to help you estimate costs for accessing research resources.) Newcomers may underestimate delays or interruptions in times of user overload. Waiting for the computer to assemble an image may be like watching paint dry.

• Many unresolved questions of copyright and intellectual property remain. Will original authors receive royalties based on how many users log in? Will most publishing contracts have to be rewritten?

OPTIONS FOR WRITING 2

The Informed Reader

Write a paper based on your careful reading of one or more recent articles from periodicals aimed at the educated general reader. Identify and explain the general drift or unifying thesis as well as major points or steps in an argument. Work key quotations into your text, using different ways of introducing quotations and integrating them with your text.

1 Is there a "new wave" or a new phase of feminism? How is it different from earlier phases of the movement? Find a recent newspaper or magazine article that explores a major trend or charts current directions in the women's movement.

2 Charges of sexual harassment have become common in recent years. Find an article that discusses one or more important test cases. Identify key concerns or key issues for your reader.

3 Who or what is the religious right? How is it different from the religious left or center? Find an informative article that helps you understand the influence of the religious right or the media attention it receives. Share your findings with your reader.

4 Do public figures have a right to privacy? Are the private lives of political leaders or of celebrities fair game for aggressive journalists? Where does the right to privacy end and the public interest or the moral standards of the community begin? Find a recent article that explores the issue.

5 Are children going hungry in our society? Can you find reliable information on this subject? Collate and interpret it for your reader.

6 Examine lead articles in recent issues of a newsmagazine or magazine of opinion. Choose a publication like *Time, New Republic, Harper's, Atlantic, Mother Jones, National Review, Rolling Stone,* or *Ms.* magazine. What assumptions do the editors of the publication seem to make about their audience? Who is the ideal reader?

7 In your reading of newspapers or magazines, do you encounter proposals to stem the flood of illegal immigration? What seem to be key issues or trends? What assumptions do the writers make about the attitude of the citizenry on the subject?

8 What is your community doing about the homeless? Study newspaper reports and editorials on the subject. What assumptions are the writers making about their readers? What attitudes do they expect the citizens of your community to share?

9 "Political correctness" has become a frequently heard charge. Where and how do you find the term used? Why has it become one of the fighting words of the current cultural or political scene?

10 The term *diversity* has become a buzzword frequently used in statements of institutional or national goals. Who uses it? What agenda does it imply?

Reading, Discussion, Writing

The Writer's Purpose

OVERVIEW: What makes writers write? They may set out to share with us consumer information, as Sallie Tisdale does in "Shoe and Tell." They may point directions — as Richard Rodriguez, son of Mexican immigrants, does in charting shifting patterns of immigration and assimilation. They may write to give meaning to a much abused term, as William Stafford does in his poem about freedom.

Shoe and Tell

SALLIE TISDALE

Who cares whether running shoes are manufactured here or abroad? Writers like Sallie Tisdale care. Tisdale is not an industry expert or highly paid consultant but a free-lancing observer of the current scene. She first became known for Harvest Moon, *a book about a nursing home where she worked as a nurse. Her* Stepping Westward: The Long Search for Home in the Pacific Northwest *(1992) pays tribute to the landscape of her native region and deplores the loss of its heritage in an era of "felled forests, trapped-out otters and beaver, mined-out hills and streams" (*Women's Review of Books*). In the following article, Tisdale set out to research an apparently simple question: Is it possible to buy a pair of running shoes made in America? When we buy a pair of sneakers, do we have to buy one that was made in Indonesia, Korea, or Taiwan?*

I live in Portland, Oregon, where Nike has its corporate headquarters and where the first Niketown store was built, but for the last several years I've worn Reeboks. This winter my Reeboks began to give out. It was time to look for new shoes. I started browsing, picking up one spanking clean, aerodynamically designed sneaker after the other and reading the small labels hidden inside: "Made in China." "Made in Korea." "Made in Indonesia." "Made in Thailand." A few years ago Nike's overseas labor practices were publicized, and the small scandal that followed made it clear that the foreign operations of a number of U.S. shoe companies left a lot to be desired. My Reeboks were made in Korea, and I promised myself that my next pair of athletic shoes would be made in America.

I asked clerks about American-made shoes. The ones who weren't bewildered by my request told me there's no such thing as an American-made court shoe, unless you count Chuck Taylors. So I called Nike, and made my way through voice-mail until I reached a customer service representative. When I told him my problem, he replied that the company was "still manufacturing in Indonesia and a lot of other countries in that area."

"Do you know if any of those factories are unionized?" I asked. There was a short silence.

"I don't know if they *have* unions in Indonesia," he finally said.

"Well, are Nike's domestic employees unionized?"

But he'd grown impatient by then. "We're all management here," he answered. "We don't *need* unions."

5

I called the headquarters for L.A. Gear in Santa Monica. "I want to talk to someone about how your shoes are manufactured," I told the young woman in customer service. "Are they made in the United States?"

"Made in the U.S.?" She seemed taken aback. Their shoes are made in Brazil and Asia, she said.

When I called Reebok, I identified myself as a journalist, and this time I was transferred to Corporate Public Relations. "All of our shoes are manufactured outside of the United States," a woman told me. I asked her which countries and she didn't know. She did, however, send me Reebok's Human Rights Standards brochure. Artfully designed, done up in red, white and blue, it uses phrases like "appropriate in light of national practices and conditions" to define acceptable wages and working schedules. It took me several more calls to find out the countries in which Reebok manufactures appropriately — China, Thailand, Indonesia, Korea and the Philippines.

Bill Krenn, a public relations manager for K-Swiss shoes, returned my call but stopped me before I could finish my questions. "We do not talk about our manufacturing," he said. "All I can tell you is that we manufacture offshore." — 10

Saucony does manufacture some shoes domestically; the company was, in fact, frequently suggested to me by shoe clerks. But when I called Saucony and identified myself as a journalist, no one would answer questions unless they were submitted in writing.

I went back to stores and looked at labels — in Filas, Adidas, Avias, Etonics. China, Korea, Indonesia, the Philippines. By now, my Reeboks had a hole in them.

Most shoe workers in Southeast Asia are teenagers and young women. They work fifteen- to sixteen-hour days doing endless piece work. (Even Reebok's space-age brochure mentions sixty-hour work weeks as normal.) Many of these women live away from their families in barracks; in some cases, they are virtual prisoners, forbidden to leave the factory compound without a pass. The minimum wage in Indonesia is now $1.80 per day. And it's not always enforced.

Jeff Ballinger, a labor lawyer specializing in Asian issues, told me that even Indonesia's minimum wage at sixty hours a week fails to meet the local poverty level. He pointed out that Bata, which makes a variety of cheap shoes largely for the Asian market, pays its workers $3.90 per day — quite a bit more than companies producing for the American market.

The woman I spoke with at Reebok hadn't known how much Asian workers making Reeboks were paid. "We don't own the manu- — 15 facturing plants," she'd said — a common practice. According to Jeff Fielder of the AFL-CIO, much of this kind of manufacturing is now done through third parties. American companies contract with Asian entrepreneurs, often South Korean, who buy and run the factories producing shoes for the American market. Fielder calls this "exploitation by proxy."

And then I called Nike one more time, as a journalist. I spoke with Keith Peters, the director of public relations. Our conversation was peppered with Peters's long silences. He told me that it wasn't "economically viable" for Nike to make its shoes in the United States. (This is the same company that considered a serious cash bid for Madison Square Garden, the Knicks and Rangers included). Why was Asia a better choice? "Some of it clearly has to do with the cost of labor," Peters said. Then he brightened, remembering the South Koreans. "Nike owns no factories," he noted. "We contract with people," adding that the company demanded workers be paid "at least the minimum wage mandated by law in the country we manufacture in."

"I would like to know how I, as a consumer, can feel good about buying shoes made under conditions that don't meet American human rights standards," I said. "I would like to buy a homegrown product. Can you help me with that?"

"I might point out that there are 2,500 people who work for Nike right here."

"How many people work for Nike overseas?" I asked. Peters didn't know. Nike has only a few hundred actual employees in Asia, he said, many of them in quality control. But on the other side of the middlemen, about 75,000 people make Nike shoes and clothing.

So I called New Balance and talked to Catherine Shepard in the press relations department. She told me that 70 percent of their shoes are made in the United States, at four plants in Massachusetts and Maine; the rest are made in Europe and Asia. New Balance's plants aren't unionized, but all are run on a modular manufacturing plan — meaning no assembly-line piece work. Employees are paid between $10 and $12 per hour, plus bonuses and benefits. "We're working toward being 100 percent U.S. made," she said. Then Shepard told me the bad news. The women's court shoe that would best meet my needs is one of the few made in China. But a men's court shoe might work, she added, since New Balance shoes come in several different widths. 20

Every time I turn on the television, I see Michael Jordan and Larry Bird, Nancy Kerrigan and Bo Jackson and Charles Barkley — ducking and jumping and running and skating for shoe companies. When I spoke with Keith Peters of Nike, I asked him how much money Nike spends on endorsement contracts.

"That number," he insisted, "is not divulged." It was widely reported that Nike signed Alonzo Mourning to a $16 million contract just last year.

How much does it matter, I wondered, squeaking around the volleyball court in my frayed Reeboks? How easily do principles give way to the pressing need for ankle support? For brand loyalty? For fashion?

Manufacturing in the United States is not economically viable. Can't be done. But New Balance manages to survive, albeit on a scale smaller than Nike. How much would Nike, which had profits of $360 million in 1993, earn if it manufactured shoes here, or simply paid its overseas workers a living wage? Somewhat less, perhaps. But the company would probably stay afloat.

Last week, I bought a pair of New Balance 665s with a little label   25
inside reading "USA." The plain white shoes cost $59.95, and I like the fit. They're comfortable in several different ways.

THE INVOLVED READER

 1 What is Tisdale's answer to the claim that "manufacturing in the United States is not economically viable"? How does she support her conclusions?

 2 Why are spokespersons for American companies reluctant to discuss wages and working conditions in their factories abroad?

READING, THINKING, WRITING

 3 Do you care where the merchandise you buy was made? Do you care who made it? Do you think other people care? Should they?

 4 How much attention do consumers pay to consumer research? How much attention do *you* pay to it?

 5 Do you think this author is antibusiness? Do you share her values or biases? Why or why not?

 6 Are sweatshops in this country a thing of the past?

COLLABORATIVE PROJECTS

 7 Working with a group, you may want to research the following question: What does the label *American-made* mean when applied to cars? Is it true that even in domestic cars engines and many parts are likely to be foreign-made? Working with a group, where would you turn for information on this subject?

Does America Still Exist?

RICHARD RODRIGUEZ

What does it mean to be an American? Writers have asked this question since the beginnings of this country. Today the process of self-definition continues, as conflicting voices direct traffic on the road toward a multicultural future. Richard Rodriguez has been called "one of America's leading essayists, a writer whose life speaks to the nation's controversies over race and culture." Born in Sacramento, California, the son of Mexican immigrants, he became a professor at the University of California at Berkeley and a widely respected media voice. In his much debated Hunger of Memory *(1981), he told the story of joining a class of white middle-class children as the only Mexican American, able to understand "some fifty stray English words." He talked about the price the immigrant child pays for becoming Americanized by gradually becoming alienated from his parents' language and culture. In his* Days of Obligation: An Argument with My Mexican Father *(1993), Rodriguez continued his exploration of the meeting of the two cultures.*

For the children of immigrant parents the knowledge comes easier. America exists everywhere in the city — on billboards, frankly in the smell of French fries and popcorn. It exists in the pace: traffic lights, the assertions of neon, the mysterious bong-bong through atriums of department stores. America exists as the voice of the crowd, a menacing sound — the high nasal accent of American English.

When I was a boy in Sacramento (California, the fifties), people would ask me, "Where you from?" I was born in this country, but I knew the question meant to decipher my darkness, my looks.

My mother once instructed me to say, "I am an American of Mexican descent." By the time I was nine or ten, I wanted to say, but dared not reply, "I am an American."

Immigrants come to America and, against hostility or mere loneliness, they recreate a homeland in the parlor, tacking up postcards or calendars of some impossible blue — lake or sea or sky. Children of immigrant parents are supposed to perch on a hyphen between two countries. Relatives assume the achievement as much as anyone. Relatives are, in any case, surprised when the child begins losing old ways. One day at the family picnic the boy wanders away from their spiced food and faceless stories to watch other boys play baseball in the distance.

There is sorrow in the American memory, guilty sorrow for having   5 left something behind — Portugal, China, Norway. The American story is the story of immigrant children and of their children — children no longer able to speak to grandparents. The memory of exile becomes inarticulate as it passes from generation to generation, along with wedding rings and pocket watches — like some mute stone in a wad of old lace. Europe. Asia. Eden.

But, it needs to be said, if this is a country where one stops being Vietnamese or Italian, this is a country where one begins to be an American. America exists as a culture and a grin, a faith and a shrug. It is clasped in a handshake, called by a first name.

As much as the country is joined in a common culture, however, Americans are reluctant to celebrate the process of assimilation. We pledge allegiance to diversity. America was born Protestant and bred Puritan, and the notion of community we share is derived from a seventeenth-century faith. Presidents and the pages of ninth-grade civics readers yet proclaim the orthodoxy: We are gathered together — but as individuals, with separate pasts, distinct destinies. Our society is as paradoxical as a Puritan congregation: We stand together, alone.

Americans have traditionally defined themselves by what they refused to include. As often, however, Americans have struggled, turned in good conscience at last to assert the great Protestant virtue of tolerance. Despite outbreaks of nativist frenzy, America has remained an immigrant country, open and true to itself.

Against pious emblems of rural America — soda fountain, Elks hall, Protestant church, and now shopping mall — stands the cold-hearted city, crowded with races and ambitions, curious laughter, much that is odd. Nevertheless, it is the city that has most truly represented America. In the city, however, the millions of singular lives have had no richer notion of wholeness to describe them than the idea of pluralism.

"Where you from?" the American asks the immigrant child. "Mexico," the boy learns to say. 10

Mexico, the country of my blood ancestors, offers formal contrast to the American achievement. If the United States was formed by Protestant individualism, Mexico was helped by a medieval Catholic dream of one world. The Spanish journeyed to Mexico to plunder, and they may have gone, in God's name, with an arrogance peculiar to those who intend to convert. But through the conversion, the Indian converted the Spaniard. A new race was born, the *mestizo*, wedding European to Indian. José Vasoncelos, the Mexican philosopher, has celebrated this New World creation, proclaiming it the "cosmic race."

Centuries later, in a San Francisco restaurant, a Mexican-American lawyer of my acquaintance says, in English, over *salade niçoise,* that he does not intend to assimilate into gringo society. His claim is echoed by a chorus of others (Italian-Americans, Greeks, Asians) in this era of ethnic pride. The melting pot has been retired, clanking, into the museum of quaint disgrace, alongside Aunt Jemima and the Katzenjammer Kids. But resistance to assimilation is characteristically American. It only makes clear how inevitable the process of assimilation actually is.

For generations, this has been the pattern. Immigrant parents have sent their children to school (simply, they thought) to acquire the "skills" to survive in the city. The child returned home with a voice his parents barely recognized or understood, couldn't trust, and didn't like.

In Eastern cities — Philadelphia, New York, Boston, Baltimore — class after class gathered immigrant children to women (usually women) who stood in front of rooms full of children, changing children. So also for me in the 1950s. Irish-Catholic nuns. California. The old story. The hyphen tipped to the right, away from Mexico and toward a confusing but true American identity.

I speak now in the chromium American accent of my grammar   15
school classmates — Billy Reckers, Mike Bradley, Carol Schmidt, Kathy O'Grady. . . . I believe I became like my classmates, became German, Polish, and (like my teachers) Irish. And because assimilation is always reciprocal, my classmates got something of me. (I mean sad eyes; belief in the Indian Virgin; a taste for sugar skulls on the Feast of the Dead.) In the blending, we became what our parents could never have been, and we carried America one revolution further.

"Does America still exist?" Americans have been asking the question for so long that to ask it again only proves our continuous link. But perhaps the question deserves to be asked with urgency — now. Since the black civil rights movement of the 1960s, our tenuous notion of a shared public life has deteriorated notably.

The struggle of black men and women did not eradicate racism, but it became the great moment in the life of America's conscience. Water hoses, bulldogs, blood — the images, rendered black, white, rectangular, passed into living rooms.

It is hard to look at a photograph of a crowd taken, say, in 1890 or in 1930 and not notice the absence of blacks. (It becomes an impertinence to wonder if America *still* exists.)

In the sixties, other groups of Americans learned to champion their rights by analogy to the black civil rights movement. But the heroic vision faded. Dr. Martin Luther King Jr. had spoken with Pauline eloquence of a nation that would unite Christian and Jew, old and young, rich and poor. Within a decade, the struggles of the 1960s were reduced to a bureaucratic competition for little more than pieces of a representational pie. The quest for a portion of power became an end in itself. The metaphor for the American city of the 1970s was a committee: one black, one woman, one person under thirty.

If the small town had sinned against America by too neatly defining who could be an American, the city's sin was a romantic secession. One noticed the romanticism in the antiwar movement — certain demonstrators who demonstrated a lack of tact or desire to persuade and seemed content to play secular protestants. One noticed the romanticism in the competition among members of "minority groups" to claim the status of Primary Victim. To Americans unconfident of their common identity, minority standing became a way of asserting individuality. Middle-class Americans — men and women clearly not the primary victims of social oppression — brandished their suffering with exuberance. 20

The dream of a single society probably died with *The Ed Sullivan Show.* The reality of America persists. Teenagers pass through big-city high schools banded in racial groups, their collars turned up to a uniform shrug. But then they graduate to jobs at the phone company or in banks, where they end up working alongside people unlike themselves. Typists and tellers walk out together at lunchtime.

It is easier for us as Americans to believe the obvious fact of our separateness — easier to imagine the black and white Americas prophesied by the Kerner report (broken glass, street fires) — than to recognize the reality of a city street at lunchtime. Americans are wedded by proximity to a common culture. The panhandler at one corner is related to the pamphleteer at the next who is related to the banker who is kin to the Chinese old man wearing an MIT sweatshirt. In any true national history, Thomas Jefferson begets Martin Luther King, Jr. who begets the Gray Panthers. It is because we lack a vision of ourselves entire — the city street is crowded and we are each preoccupied with finding our own way home — that we lack an appropriate hymn.

Under my window now passes a little white girl softly rehearsing to herself a Motown obbligato.

THE INVOLVED READER

1 At the beginning, how does Rodriguez play off the pull of American popular culture for immigrants' children against the old-

country nostalgia of their parents? What makes the contrast real for you?

2 For Rodriguez, how does the heritage from America's past help us understand our common culture? (What for him defines the Puritan tradition? What is "nativism"? What does Rodriguez say about "pluralism"?)

3 What does Rodriguez see as key differences in the history of Mexico and North America? How does Mexico serve as a counterpoint to the North American experience in his essay?

4 What does Rodriguez mean when he says, "assimilation is always reciprocal"?

5 How would you sum up Rodriguez' vision of the American future?

READING, THINKING, WRITING

6 To judge from your own experience, are the forces separating Americans getting stronger? Or are Americans becoming more alike?

7 Rodriguez says that "resistance to assimilation is characteristically American." In a recent interview, he again says that the decision to "de-assimilate" seems to be "a very American way of thinking." What makes these statements paradoxical — contradictory at least on the surface? Do they make sense?

COLLABORATIVE PROJECTS

8 As Rodriguez reminds his readers, Aunt Jemima, the black cook in the white folks' kitchen, at one time was used to advertise pancake mix. The Katzenjammer Kids were cartoon characters who played pranks on immigrant elders with a heavy German accent. What role does ethnic identity play in American advertising or the American comic strip today?

Learning to Love

NELL BERNSTEIN

Does sex education reduce unprotected sex? Or does sex education hasten the onset of sexual activity? Writers face a special challenge when dealing with a subject that brings into play age-old taboos and has become the subject of ugly controversies. Nell Bernstein is the editor of YO! *(Youth Outlook), a regional newspaper produced by Pacific News Service. Her article was part of an issue of* Mother Jones *magazine designed to show the value of sex education in spite of past mistakes and tremendous obstacles. At the same time, the editors quoted with approval an educator who said "parents are the primary sex educators" and "all institutions — families, schools, churches, and social service agencies — should help teenagers become loving, caring, responsible adults."*

> When the University of Chicago released a comprehensive sex survey detailing what Americans are doing in private, one bedroom door remained firmly shut — the one at the end of the hall with the Pearl Jam poster and the "Keep Out" sign.
>
> It's public knowledge that federal funding for the sex survey (which looked at Americans age 18 to 59) had been scratched and that private foundations ended up footing the bill. What's gone unreported, however, is that a comprehensive study of adolescent sexual behavior was also in the works, and it was not revived after the federal funding cut.

The adolescent survey was even more politically unpalatable than its adult counterpart. Dr. Richard Udry, a social scientist at the University of North Carolina, is one of the researchers who planned the five-year, 24,000-teen survey. He recalls that Louis Sullivan, then secretary of Health and Human Services, "said the study might give the wrong message to adolescents, when the official policy of the administration was to encourage abstinence." The researchers talked to a few foundations but concluded that they would not be able to raise enough money to do the study properly.

The final nail in the American Teenage Study's coffin came when the Senate approved a Jesse Helms–sponsored bill and subsequent amendment: the first transferred the original funding for both the adult and adolescent surveys to the abstinence-only Adolescent Family Life program, and the second prohibited the government from ever funding either study in the future. Helms argued that the Senate faced "a clear choice — between support for sexual restraint

among our young people, or, on the other hand, support for homosexuality and sexual decadence."

The death of the American Teenage Study is right in line with the   5
country's unofficial policy on teen sex, which might be described as
"Don't Ask, Tell." As panic over teen pregnancy and AIDS escalates,
adults have defined their role as dispensing warnings and impera-
tives, rather than examining the complexities of young people's lives.

Teen sex, like teen violence, has come to be seen as a national
crisis, both symptom and symbol of a "generation out of control."
But even as it reaches a near-hysterical pitch, the national dialogue
on adolescent sexuality remains painfully abstract. Sex is to the '90s
what drugs were to the '80s: the locus of adult anxiety over what the
kids are doing when we're not around (which is more and more of
the time); something we want desperately to stop but not necessarily
to understand.

Efforts to manage the "crisis" of adolescent sexual activity consistently focus on consequences rather than motivations, and are
driven in great part by political enmities. The left accuses the right
of imposing its own repressive mores on defenseless teens, of driving young girls to back-alley abortions and lives of shame. The right
charges the left with fostering legions of junior Murphy Browns, who
drain the public coffers with their babies and diseases. This ideological battle is reflected back to teenagers in lectures about "values"
and "choices" — sex education buzzwords that are also, not coinci-
dentally, the rallying cries of political movements.

As the chasm widens between the rhetoric of their elders and the
word on the street, young people are left alone with their deepest
questions about relationships, pleasure, and risk. In North Carolina,
educators are training junior high school girls to counsel friends
whose boyfriends assault them, having found that most battered
girls do not discuss it with an adult. A recent study showed that half
of all 15-year-old girls have never discussed birth control or STDs
with a parent, and one-third have never discussed how pregnancy
occurs.

Another study indicates that growing numbers of teenagers are
having sex at home in the afternoon, while their parents are out of
the house — a far cry from the era of backseats and drive-ins, of
sneaking out from under the watchful parental eye. And what are we
offering those kids left all by themselves in the downstairs bedroom?
A "True Love Waits" button, or a condom and a map of their genitals — neither of which addresses the underlying loneliness of a generation raised in empty houses.

Most of the research on adolescent sexual behavior focuses on   10
declining virginity rates and growing social costs. We know, for example, that more than half of American women and three-quarters
of American men have had intercourse by their 18th birthday, compared to a quarter of women in the mid-1950s (they didn't count
men then). We know that 3 million teens acquire a sexually transmitted disease each year, and that 1 million become pregnant, a
third of whom have abortions. And although the number of reported
AIDS cases among teenagers is still very small, we know that 20 percent of AIDS cases are among people in their 20s, many of whom
probably contracted HIV as teenagers.

What we don't know is why young people do what they do, and
how it makes them feel. "There's a tremendous amount of information about a truly small number of questions," says Mindy Thomp-
son Fullilove, associate professor of clinical psychology and public
health at Columbia University. "Anything that is not about contraception is missing. We tend to be very obsessed with counting things.
We don't value asking, 'What do you mean?'"

While teen sexual activity is increasing, condom use among teenagers is also on the rise: among urban adolescent males, it nearly
doubled between 1979 and 1988. Teenage girls are no more likely
than older unmarried women to have multiple partners, and are actually less likely to have an unwanted pregnancy. But if advocates
across the political spectrum agree on one thing, it's that teen sex is
fraught with danger — and they tailor their messages accordingly.
"It's always 'Don't get AIDS,'" points out Dr. Lynn Ponton, a professor of psychiatry at the University of California at San Francisco,
"never 'Have a good time.'"

A study of state guidelines for sexuality education done last year
by the Sexuality Information and Education Council of the United
States found that HIV and other STDs were among the most widely
covered topics; "shared sexual behavior" and "human sexual response," among the least. In other words, young people are learning
in school that sex can hurt or kill them without learning that it can also
bring them pleasure or give them a connection to another person.

"Fear messages never persuade anybody to do anything except
for a very short period of time," says John Gagnon, a sociologist at
the State University of New York at Stony Brook and co-author of the
Chicago sex study. He notes that adults lose credibility when they
feed young people oversimplified warnings instead of trusting them
to understand ambiguous realities. "It's absolutely irresponsible not
to give kids sex ed, including information on condoms, and the pos-

sibility of not having sex. But it's also irresponsible not to mention that many people find sex a great source of pleasure."

Also lost in the "Just Say No" frenzy are ways for young people to   15
say yes — not just to sex, but to love, family, each other. All around them, adults are rewriting the social script: bearing children out of wedlock; introducing kids to stepfathers, ex-wives, casual girlfriends, and other "options"; publicly venting fury at each other in vicious divorce and custody battles. As we struggle to sort things out for ourselves, we are offering fewer and fewer coherent models for conducting and sustaining intimate relationships. Lifelong marriage, whether or not the desirable norm for sexual relationships, at least had the advantage of being imitable.

With our relentless focus on disease and pregnancy, we leave our children without much explicit guidance when it comes to high-risk activities of the heart. We talk to young people as if their genitals were a matter of public concern, while their souls were none of our business. "People say 'Use a condom,'" says Stephanie Brown, who manages the teen clinic at a Planned Parenthood in Northern California, "but not 'Why are you having sex with this person?'"

Those who do ask that question say they often hear surprisingly sentimental answers. "The degree to which adolescents believe in being in love is absolutely extraordinary," says Gagnon. Surveys show that the vast majority of young people want to marry and raise children with a spouse. Unlike the children of the '60s — for whom the fear of ending up like their parents manifested itself as a terror of being old, married, and bored — today's teens fear ending up old and alone.

One of the better-kept secrets about teen pregnancy is that many of the babies born to adolescents are anything but "unwanted." Ask a 15-year-old why she got pregnant and she's more likely to tell you that she wanted company than that she didn't know how to use a condom. One pregnant 18-year-old I know — a girl who spent last Christmas alone in her apartment, while her mother and stepfather went on vacation together — told me she'd always planned to have a baby right after high school, to make a person all her own, who would love her and not leave. Like most of her friends, she had no illusions that the young man she made the baby with — or any man — would fill that role. "Do you think I'm selfish?" she wanted to know.

With responsible adults focusing mainly on the pitfalls of sexual activity, the task of showing young people what sex and love have to offer is left to that trusted family friend, the television. And television — along with movies, music, and advertising — offers up a sexual universe that has little room for either "values" or "choices." In this universe, sex is everything — and the beautiful people, the glamorous people, the people who *matter,* are having it all the time.

"Abstinence makes the heart grow fonder," promise the advocates. Meanwhile the media map out a very different route to love and fulfillment, hammering home the message that — as Woody Allen put it when called upon to explain his own sexual involvement with a teenager — "the heart wants what it wants." 20

Perhaps most dangerously for teenagers, points out Sexuality Information and Education Council of the United States director Debra Haffner, the media reinforce the idea that good sex means being swept away: "It just happens. There's almost no sexual negotiation, no portrayal of sexual communication, no limit setting, very little condom and contraceptive use. What we see on TV is that people kiss and then they have intercourse."

The Chicago study painted a picture of sex in America that was much more moderate and restrained. But when Baltimore-based sex educator Deborah Roffman asked her students what they *thought* the study would find, she says, "They predicted the image of sexual behavior that is presented in the media — that there was a lot of intercourse, that married people were less happy with their sex lives than single people, that Americans are sex bunnies." The effect of the dissonance between the official teachings on sex and what the media dish up, says Roffman, is clear: "Any teacher knows that when students get mixed messages from adults, they test."

Gagnon is even more explicit about the role of adults in convincing young people that they are "ready" for sex. "The 'raging hormones' argument is nonsense," he says. "Society *elicits* sexual behavior in kids." But — as with so many problems that plague our children — we rarely acknowledge our own complicity. We prefer to define adolescent sexuality as a crisis of self-control that we, the responsible (but not culpable) adults, must find ways to manage.

Bombarded with messages telling them both that sex is the ticket to love, glamour, and adulthood — and that it is bad and will kill them, adolescents in America are ultimately left with few models and little guidance in the area where they need it most: human relationships. Busy with their battles over propaganda and prophylactics, adults aren't addressing young people's yearning for intimacy, for contact, for connections that prove they matter. "Adults are so evasive, so unwilling to confront the reality of young people's lives," says Gagnon. "It's a maelstrom. And we've abandoned kids to it."

THE INVOLVED READER

1 What evidence does Bernstein provide that surveys of adolescent sexual behavior are "politically unpalatable" in our society? How does adolescent sexual activity become a pawn in the "political enmities" of the right and the left?

2 What evidence does Bernstein cite of the widening "chasm" between young people and their elders on questions related to sex and sexual relations?

3 According to this article, what do current studies and statistics show about teenage sexuality? What, according to Bernstein, are the limitations of current research?

4 Why does Bernstein criticize current efforts at sex education? What are some of the well-kept "secrets" about teenagers' attitudes that emphasis on the "pitfalls of sexual activity" fails to take into account?

5 What's wrong with the "sexual universe" offered up by the media? For Bernstein, what is the result of the discrepancy between "the official teachings on sex and what the media dish up?"

READING, THINKING, WRITING

6 Do you agree that young people "are left alone with their deepest questions about relationships, pleasure, and risk"?

7 Do you incline to one side or the other in the ideological battles over sex education? How would you explain or defend your position to people representing the other side?

COLLABORATIVE PROJECTS

8 Is it true that sex education amounts to maybe half a dozen hours during a school year — compared with the bombardment of young Americans with sexual messages outside school? Working with a group, you may want to explore what goes on in sex education classes in your area or community.

The Cost of Living Clean

N O R M A N   A T K I N S

Is putting young people in jail our only answer to drug addiction? What happened to treatment programs, substance abuse clinics, or other efforts at rehabilitation? Norman Atkins is an experienced inter- viewer who researched the following article for a special issue of Roll- ing Stone *devoted to the topic of "Drugs in America." The contributors shared the assumption, stated in the lead editorial, that the failure of our drug laws "has created a permanent underclass of unemployable inner-city youths whose lives have become hopelessly interwoven with drug crime and who in turn are becoming parents to another genera- tion of dysfunctional children." Atkins focuses on treatment programs for addicts, asking: What works, and what doesn't? How much does it cost, and can we afford it? For answers to these questions, he turns to authorities close to the situation in the inner cities where society's "war on drugs" is waged. What experts does he consult? What is their background, credibility, expertise? What did he learn from them?*

They appeared from the smoke and the shadows of the city. There had been no newspaper advertisements, not a single poster on a train platform or a public-service announcement on local TV. Yet when a new methadone program opened in Pittsburgh, heroin ad- dicts kept filing in. Michael Dennis, who studies drug treatment there for the Research Triangle Institute, was stunned when he wit- nessed this response. It convinced him of the need for more pro- grams. "Increase the supply of treatment," he says, "and you will increase the demand."

Mathea Falco, president of Drug Strategies, a nonprofit public- policy organization, estimates that there are 6 million Americans with serious drug problems, among whom perhaps 2 million are chronic, "hard-core" addicts. Roughly one-quarter of the addicts are hooked on heroin and three-quarters on cocaine; many are also al- coholic. For most, private rehab centers are prohibitively expensive, and locating an empty bed in a publicly funded facility requires a notoriously long wait.

Despite countless campaign promises of "treatment on demand," President Clinton's anti-drug budget was scarcely a seismic shift. The budget called for 74,000 new treatment slots, and a new crime bill could add 66,000 more, but that's still a far cry from treatment on demand. Experts reckon that as few as one out of four of those who need treatment will be able to get it.

For those few the question is, what kind? What type of treatment works best for different people, and what are the most cost-effective models for the American taxpayers? Unfortunately, in the world of drug rehabilitation, there is no hard science to point the way to guaranteed cures. Programs can last from a few weeks to a few years. Some are led by saints, others by hucksters. Some cost upward of $25,000 a patient; others, like Narcotics Anonymous, cost nothing.

Therapeutic Communities (TCs) are highly structured, one- to two-year residential treatment programs, the largest of which is Phoenix House, which has roughly 15 percent of the nation's 12,000 beds. Phoenix House embodies a military-style, in-your-face, group-encounter approach. New residents scrub toilets and climb an elaborate hierarchy of work responsibilities. Facial hair and sex are *verboten;* using the phone is a privilege to be earned. Rule breakers wear signs around their necks advertising the error of their ways. Naturally, there is a high turnover in the first 60 days. While most of Phoenix House's long-term residents admit that they found it oppressive and weird at first, they now claim it was just what they needed to become drug free.

TCs tend to be best suited for hard-core addicts, or what UCLA researcher Douglas Anglin calls the "dysfunctionally dependent." Phoenix House costs about $15,000 per resident per year; some other programs run between $10,000 and $25,000, much of which comes from government support or charitable dollars. Phoenix House president Mitchell Rosenthal says the nation could plausibly expand TC capacity to 100,000 beds in the next four years, and he calls for converting abandoned military bases into TCs. Meanwhile, Mathea Falco argues that for an additional 10 percent investment on top of the $30,000 to $40,000 it costs to incarcerate a drug addict for a year, a prison-based TC can knock down ghastly recidivism rates.

For heroin injectors, methadone maintenance has been the treatment of choice since it was first introduced three decades ago. Methadone is a legalized synthetic opiate that blocks heroin cravings, causes no harmful side effects and produces no high. A small portion of the approximately 125,000 currently enrolled in methadone programs will use the drug as a bridge to abstinence; many others maintain a crime-free life while on methadone. Some critics worry that the treatment method simply replaces an illegal addiction with a legal one. Others point out that methadone can't neutralize cocaine, which many recovering heroin abusers still snort or smoke. Methadone is occasionally sold on the street when extra doses are dispensed to recovering addicts. It's expected that a new long-acting

5

methadone approved by the Food and Drug Administration last year
will put an end to this practice.

The best methadone programs offer counseling and other rehabilitative services, and studies indicate that the rate of crime commission drops 65 percent for those who stay in the program at least
one year; after three years, there is an 85 percent decrease. Says
Falco: "For heroin addicts who have truly tried over and over again
to kick the habit, methadone may be the only course. It is often a
very effective way of stabilizing their lives."

Chemical dependency (CD) programs offer short-term residential
treatment, usually a monthlong stay, often starting with a period of
detoxification. Ideally, the stay is followed by a year of after care,
meaning anything from placement in a halfway house to attendance
at self-help groups. Based on AA's 12-step model of personal change,
CD programs specialize in treating alcoholics and are less effective,
studies show, at helping drug addicts. But at Hazelden, in Center
City, Minn., the nation's oldest and best regarded CD program,
nearly half the residents abuse some combination of drugs and alcohol. "We think it's dependency and not the drug of choice that
is the issue," says Jerry Spicer, Hazelden's president. At an average
of $9,300 per month, Hazelden might be appropriate for residents
whose private insurance will cover it or whose families can afford it.
Since CD programs are generally not publicly financed, however,
hard-core addicts (the vast majority of those seeking treatment are
poor and uninsured) have to turn elsewhere.

In the 1980s, hospital-based CD programs were notorious for   10
over-treating anyone with dirty urine as a way to suck up a seemingly endless supply of insurance coverage. Since then, with the insurance industry singing the mantra of managed care, half of the
nation's CD programs have dried up, and there are only an estimated
9,000 beds in the country today. Says Dean Gerstein of the National
Opinion Research Center, one of the nation's leading experts on
treatment effectiveness: "The trend seems to be that the only good
patient is an outpatient."

There are roughly 660,000 outpatients in day-treatment programs, ranging from a come-when-you-like drop-in center and
weekly pep talks from a social worker to daily acupuncture sessions.
(Chinese acupuncture techniques are reported to be able to suppress cocaine cravings.) The Matrix Institute, in Los Angeles, runs a
highly structured program that meets four to six hours per week.
Matrix claims that this is a "practical" option for working, functioning cocaine addicts who don't have either the time or the need for
more intensive treatment. Such programs generally are not well-

suited to poverty-stricken hard-core addicts. "Brief interventions for the dysfunctionally dependent and lifetime poor," says Douglas Anglin, "is like pissing upwind."

When tied to mandates from a "drug court," however, day programs may be more promising. That's certainly what Jeffrey Tauber discovered when he suited up as an Oakland, Calif., municipal judge in drug court in 1986. "I kept seeing the same people going in and out of the system like a revolving door," he says, "and their drug problems certainly weren't being treated." So three and a half years ago, Tauber created a program that speedily steers almost everyone who appears in his court to drug treatment. Whereas people lingered in jail for two to three months after arrest, now Tauber disposes of their cases within two days. He gives them two years' probation and a contract that lays out rewards and sanctions and requires them to meet weekly with their probation officer, submit to random urine testing and enter an outpatient treatment program. "It's more important that they are in contact with the court system three or four days a week than what the treatment is," says Tauber.

Not only has the felony-recidivism rate among Tauber's probationers been cut in half, but Oakland earned $1 million last year renting its empty jail cells to neighboring counties. Drug courts in Portland, Ore., and Miami are experiencing similar success. "First-time nonviolent drug offenders should be steered to treatment before prison," says Falco. "It has nothing to do with being soft or tough on drug crime but with putting our resources into more effective alternatives."

Gerstein cautions against expecting scientific proof of some perfect rehabilitative method. Based on his extensive social-science research, however, he estimates that roughly half of those patients entering CD, outpatient or methadone programs will stick with their treatment regimen and one-half to three-quarters of those will recover from their addictions and stabilize their lives; one-quarter of TC residents will gut out the long-term treatment, and of those who do, 80 percent will continue to be drug-free on their own. But Gerstein and others also stress that many recovered addicts will relapse, sometimes many times through the years.

It is this notion that prompts Anglin to advocate a coordinated   15 safety net of rehabilitative services that will catch addicts each time they slip and match them with treatment methods best suited to their needs at that time. Even with modest success rates, Anglin and others are convinced that treatment is a cost-effective strategy for reducing the more than $225 billion that substance abuse costs the United States each year. For those who doubt that addicts will avail themselves of new treatment programs, the lesson that Michael Dennis derives from the Pittsburgh methadone program is very simple: If you build it, they will come.

THE INVOLVED READER

1   How does Atkins dramatize both the need for treatment and its limited availability? Are his statistics early in the article shocking or familiar?

2   What major alternative treatment programs does Atkins survey? How do they work? What are advantages and drawbacks of each?

3   What claims does Atkins make concerning success in lowering addiction and crime rates? On what evidence does he base his claims? Are they convincing, or do they leave you skeptical?

READING, THINKING, WRITING

4   What is Atkins' strategy for enlisting support for his proposals — appeals to compassion? claims of cost-effectiveness? What do *you* think it would take to make voters support treatment programs in the current political climate?

5   What has shaped your own views of drug addiction? Have you observed addiction or treatment programs at first hand?

COLLABORATIVE PROJECTS

6   Working with a group, you may want to investigate programs for combating drug addiction in your community. What is their rationale or justification? What obstacles or roadblocks have they run into, and why? How successful have they been overall?

MAKING CONNECTIONS

7   Tisdale, Rodriguez, Bernstein, and Atkins represent differing points of view — but they all assume an educated reading audience concerned about current issues. What would you include in a composite portrait of the mythical "educated reader" who provides the market for writers like those represented in this chapter?

short story

Mericans

S A N D R A   C I S N E R O S

*When do immigrants or the children of immigrants cease to be for-
eigners in their own country? Born and raised in Chicago, Sandra Cisneros is one of the country's most widely read Chicana — short for*
Mexicana — *authors. (*Chicano *is the corresponding term often used
for male Mexican Americans of the West and Southwest.) Cisneros'
stories in* The House on Mango Street *were vignettes, or snapshots, of
life in this country's Spanish-speaking communities. The following
story is from a later collection,* Woman Hollering Creek *(1991). Like
other short stories, this story takes us to a setting, peoples it with a
limited number of characters, and enacts a short sequence of events.
What we make of what happens is up to us as readers. Like other
writers of imaginative literature, Cisneros tests our ability to read between the lines. Rather than preach or editorialize, poets or writers of
short stories may act out scenarios for us that make us think. A few
references might need to be explained to the outsider: The first PRI
elections installed Mexico's traditional political and economic elite
and left many of the more radical supporters of the Mexican revolution disillusioned.* La Virgen de Guadalupe *is the Virgin Mary of
Guadalupe.*

We're waiting for the awful grandmother who is inside dropping
pesos into *la ofrenda* box before the altar to La Divina Providencia.
Lighting votive candles and genuflecting. Blessing herself and kissing her thumb. Running a crystal rosary between her fingers. Mumbling, mumbling, mumbling.

There are so many prayers and promises and thanks-be-to-God
to be given in the name of the husband and the sons and the only
daughter who never attend mass. It doesn't matter. Like La Virgen
de Guadalupe, the awful grandmother intercedes on their behalf.
For the grandfather who hasn't believed in anything since the first
PRI elections. For my father, El Periquín, so skinny he needs his
sleep. For Auntie Light-skin, who only a few hours before was break-
fasting on brain and goat tacos after dancing all night in the pink
zone. For Uncle Fat-face, the blackest of the black sheep — *Always
remember your Uncle Fat-face in your prayers.* And Uncle Baby — *You
go for me, Mamá — God listens to you.*

The awful grandmother has been gone a long time. She disappeared behind the heavy leather outer curtain and the dusty velvet inner. We must stay near the church entrance. We must not wander over to the balloon and punch-ball vendors. We cannot spend our allowance on fried cookies or Familia Burrón comic books or those clear cone-shaped suckers that make everything look like a rainbow when you look through them. We cannot run off and have our picture taken on the wooden ponies. We must not climb the steps up the hill behind the church and chase each other through the cemetery. We have promised to stay right where the awful grandmother left us until she returns.

There are those walking to church on their knees. Some with fat rags tied around their legs and others with pillows, one to kneel on, and one to flop ahead. There are women with black shawls crossing and uncrossing themselves. There are armies of penitents carrying banners and flowered arches while musicians play tinny trumpets and tinny drums.

La Virgen de Guadalupe is waiting inside behind a plate of thick   5
glass. There's also a gold crucifix bent crooked as a mesquite tree when someone once threw a bomb. La Virgen de Guadalupe on the main altar because she's a big miracle, the crooked crucifix on a side altar because that's a little miracle.

But we're outside in the sun. My big brother Junior hunkered against the wall with his eyes shut. My little brother Keeks running around in circles.

Maybe and most probably my little brother is imagining he's a flying feather dancer, like the ones we saw swinging high up from a pole on the Virgin's birthday. I want to be a flying feather dancer too, but when he circles past me he shouts, "I'm a B-Fifty-two bomber, you're a German," and shoots me with an invisible machine gun. I'd rather play flying feather dancers, but if I tell my brother this, he might not play with me at all.

"*Girl*. We can't play with a *girl*." *Girl*. It's my brothers' favorite insult now instead of "sissy." "You *girl*," they yell at each other. "You throw that ball like a *girl*."

I've already made up my mind to be a German when Keeks swoops past again, this time yelling "I'm Flash Gordon. You're Ming the Merciless and the Mud People." I don't mind being Ming the Merciless, but I don't like being the Mud People. Something wants to come out of the corners of my eyes, but I don't let it. Crying is what *girls* do.

I leave Keeks running around in circles — "I'm the Lone Ranger,   10
you're Tonto." I leave Junior squatting on his ankles and go look for
the awful grandmother.

Why do churches smell like the inside of an ear? Like incense
and the dark and candles in blue glass? And why does holy water
smell of tears? The awful grandmother makes me kneel and fold my
hands. The ceiling high and everyone's prayers bumping up there
like balloons.

If I stare at the eyes of the saints long enough, they move and wink
at me, which makes me a sort of saint too. When I get tired of winking saints, I count the awful grandmother's mustache hairs while she
prays for Uncle Old, sick from the worm, and Auntie Cuca, suffering
from a life of troubles that left half her face crooked and the other
half sad.

There must be a long, long list of relatives who haven't gone to
church. The awful grandmother knits the names of the dead and the
living into one long prayer fringed with the grandchildren born in
that barbaric country with its barbarian ways.

I put my weight on one knee, then the other, and when they both
grow fat as a mattress of pins, I slap them each awake. *Micaela, you
may wait outside with Alfredito and Enrique.* The awful grandmother
says it all in Spanish, which I understand when I'm paying attention.
"What?" I say, though it's neither proper nor polite. "What?" which
the awful grandmother hears as "¿Guat?" But she only gives me a
look and shoves me toward the door.

After all that dust and dark, the light from the plaza makes me   15
squinch my eyes like if I just came out of the movies. My brother
Keeks is drawing squiggly lines on the concrete with a wedge of glass
and the heel of his shoe. My brother Junior squatting against the
entrance, talking to a lady and man.

They're not from here. Ladies don't come to church dressed in
pants. And everybody knows men aren't supposed to wear shorts.

"*¿Quieres chicle?*" the lady asks in a Spanish too big for her mouth.

"*Gracias.*" The lady gives him a whole handful of gum for free,
little cellophane cubes of Chiclets, cinnamon and aqua and the
white ones that don't taste like anything but are good for pretend
buck teeth.

"*Por favor,*" says the lady. "*¿Un foto?*" pointing to her camera.

"*Sí.*"   20

She's so busy taking Junior's picture, she doesn't notice me and
Keeks.

"Hey Michele, Keeks. You guys want gum?"

"But you speak English!"

"Yeah," my brother says, "we're Mericans."

We're Mericans, we're Mericans, and inside the awful grand-   25
mother prays.

THE INVOLVED READER

1 Like much writing about minority experience, this story is in part a story of two generations. What do you learn about the older generation — their history, their values, their way of life?

2 Would you call the younger generation Americanized? What is their relationship with the older generation and the traditional Mexican culture? What is their relation to American popular culture?

3 What does the tourist lady stand for in this story? What to you is the point of the story?

READING, THINKING, WRITING

4 Conservative columnists like George Will talk about the "cult of diversity" as a threat to mainstream American culture. Do you consider this story an example of the "cult of diversity"?

5 Have you ever been in a situation where you felt you were thought of as different? How did you cope with the situation?

poem

Freedom

WILLIAM STAFFORD

*Are we the land of the free? Or are we the land of the hemmed in —
by small-town bigotry, government regulation, peer pressure, or the
corporate mentality? Writers write to restore meaning to important
but abused words, as William Stafford does in this poem about freedom. Stafford (1914–1992) was one of America's most widely read
and admired poets. He grew up in small towns in Kansas, and his
poems often evoke the setting and the traditions of life in the Midwest.
They stay close to the soil and to people suspicious of glib talk. When
his poems touch on important ethical issues, they stay close to what
our large abstractions mean in the everyday experience of actual
people.*

Freedom is not following a river.
Freedom is following a river
    though, if you want to.
It is deciding now by what happens now.
It is knowing that luck makes a difference.   5

No leader is free; no follower is free —
    the rest of us can often be free.
Most of the world are living by
creeds too odd, chancy, and habit-forming
    to be worth arguing about by reason.   10

If you are oppressed, wake up about
four in the morning; most places
you can usually be free some of the time
    if you wake up before other people.

THE INVOLVED READER

  1 What does freedom have to do with following or not following a
     river?
  2 It's easy to see that "followers" would not have much free-
     dom — they obey orders; they tag along. But why does the poet
     say "No leader is free"?
  3 Do you think of creeds as a matter of habit? Or do you think they
     should be "worth arguing about by reason"?

READING, THINKING, WRITING

4 In this poem about freedom, why is there nothing about the flag, patriots, the Statue of Liberty, and "Give me liberty or give me death"?

5 Do you think of yourself as a "follower"?

6 Do you agree that "most places / you can usually be free some of the time"?

The Writer's Tools 2

Quote/Unquote

Experienced writers work material from their reading effectively into their own text. They know how to introduce and identify quotations. Here is a checklist of ways to integrate material from a source into your own writing.

Complete Quote (one or more complete sentences quoted verbatim)

You will often use **direct quotation** — the original author quoted exactly word for word. When you use it, you show that not only *what* was said but also *how* it was said is important. For example, you are likely to use direct quotation when a statement dramatizes the issue or brings it into focus. You may also want to use direct quotation when a statement is provocative or controversial (did the writer actually say this?):

> In the words of a counselor, "infertility rips at the core of a couple's relationship; it affects sexuality, self-image, and self-esteem."

Partial Quote

Your text will often flow more smoothly if you work parts of a quoted sentence into a sentence of your own:

> Barbara Tuchman, in "Humanity's Better Moments," writes to remind us that "the good in humanity operates even if the bad secures more attention."

Paraphrase

You will often **paraphrase** what someone said, putting an author's ideas into your own words. This way you can make them more easily accessible to your reader, and you can condense them, focusing on essentials. You are then using **indirect quotation** — no quotation marks:

> Preschoolers who can speak two languages learn to read more quickly than their monolingual peers, reports Kenji Hakuta, psychology professor at Yale and author of *The Mirror of Language.*

Quoted Phrase

Even when you paraphrase your source, you may want to quote verbatim some words or phrases that are especially telling or memorable:

Koelsch and Jasany, like other advocates of artificial intelligence, tout the potential of expert systems, or "experts in a box."

Block Quotation

If you quote more than four lines of text, set the passage off as a **block quotation.** Indent one inch or ten typewriter spaces — no quotation marks. Unless you use block quotations sparingly, they may give a lumpy quality to your prose. Use them at key points — for instance, when you let the original author spell out an important development or process.

> Robert Bly, in *Iron John,* traces men's discovering of their feminine, or androgynous, side to their rejection of the false image of manhood promoted by advocates of the Vietnam War: "If manhood meant Vietnam, did they want any part of it?" At the same time, the feminist movement forced men to become conscious of women's perspectives and concerns:
>> As men began to examine women's history and women's sensibility, some men began to notice what was called their *feminine* side and pay attention to it. This process continues to this day, and I would say that most contemporary men are involved in it in some way. There is something wonderful about this development — I mean the practice of men welcoming their own "feminine" consciousness and nurturing it.

Quote-within-Quote

Sometimes an author you quote is in turn quoting someone else. You then use **single quotation marks** to set off the quotation-within-a-quotation:

> According to Gloria Steinem, "Adults still need 'unconditional' love . . . that says: 'No matter how the world may judge you, I love you for yourself.'"

A final caution: Will the people you quote feel fairly represented? No one likes to be quoted out of context. No one likes to see a comment made in passing played up as a major commitment. Have you signaled any changes you have made in a quotation? Show omissions when you shorten a quotation to make its main point stand out. Signal an omission or **ellipsis** by three spaced periods — or four if you include a period used as end punctuation. Use **square brackets** to signal anything you have inserted as a comment or correction of your own.

ELLIPSIS: The report questioned the correlation between academic achievement and self-esteem: "White male students who have a high opinion of themselves . . . often rank low on standard academic tests."

A University of Michigan research group studying the academic performance of American students found "that the academic achievement of our students is inferior to that of students in many other societies. . . . The low scores of the American students are distressing."

INSERTION: Emilio Gomez voices a familiar complaint: "The [North] American press pays little attention to the indigenous peoples of South and Central America."

WRITING WORKSHOP 4

Drawing on Printed Sources

In the following paper, the student writer draws on her reading to explore two conflicting views on pornography and censorship. What use does she make of her sources? How does she identify or introduce them? What use does she make of extended direct quotation? Where does she paraphrase? Where does she use selected quoted phrases? Does the student writer do justice to both sides of the argument? Do you agree with her?

Sticks and Stones

Are we willing to do something about pornography and the violence it promotes? Among American women today, opinion is sharply divided between those who feel that drastic action is long overdue and those who feel that we must not let our disapproval of pornography lead us to abridge freedom of speech, our constitutional right to communicate. Gloria Steinem, in her essay "Erotica and Pornography," writes that "the number of pornographic murders, tortures, and woman-hating images is on the increase in both popular culture and real life." She believes that by lumping all types of "nonprocreative sex" together, we let pornography off the hook. She distinguishes between erotica and pornography. Erotica deals with sex in a way that is compatible with love and respect, and with "the yearning for a particular person." Pornography is based on domination over women. Erotica appeals to both sexes, whereas the root word of pornography points to prostitutes or "female captives."

Erotic material celebrates "a mutually pleasurable, sexual expression between people who have enough power to be there by positive choice." On the other hand, pornography is abusive; its message is "violence, dominance, and conquest." It portrays an attitude of "conqueror and victim." Although Steinem does not state outright that she would use the law to restrict pornographic publications, she alerts us to their "lethal confusion of sex with violence."

Susan Jacoby, a widely read writer and feminist like Steinem, takes a quite different stand in her essay, "Pornography and the First Amendment." A journalist, she is a hands-on, self-described "First Amendment junkie." She believes that feminists have inflated the threat pornography actually poses. She refuses to believe that "porn books, magazines, and movies pose a greater threat to women than similarly repulsive exercises of free speech pose to other offended groups" — such as Jewish groups who object to the circulation of neo-Nazi propaganda.

When it comes to the most offensive kind of pornography, "kiddie porn," Jacoby believes that we have obscured the issue. Kiddie porn is not a First Amendment issue, but rather an issue of the "abuse of power." She believes that the irresponsible parents of the children involved should be rounded up and put in jail.

Her classic argument, however, is that feminists cannot agree among themselves on what is "good taste" and what is "harmful pornography." Are all pictures of nude women obscene? Where do we draw the line between the artistic nude and obscenity? Jacoby believes in the democratic process: "We should not shift the responsibility from individuals to institutions." She would have us wait until men decide "they have better uses for $1.95 each month than to spend it on a copy of *Hustler*."

However, it seems to me that democracy requires exactly the kind of soul-searching decision-making that Jacoby feels we are incapable of in the area of pornography. It is true that the courts have often refused to put publishers of pornography or actors in pornographic movies in jail. But as recent court decisions indicate, we are willing to search our souls and draw the line somewhere. As the connections become clear, will we start to hold people and groups accountable for the violence they propagate?

I agree with Steinem. We are not safe as long as our liberal-mindedness condones what should not be condoned. We should not just remain "offended" and yet be afraid to take a stand.

One writes of one thing only — one's own experience. Everything depends on how relentlessly one forces from this experience the last drop, sweet or bitter, it can possibly give.   **JAMES BALDWIN**

I write of one life only: my own. If my story is true, I trust it will reso-nate with significance for other lives.   **RICHARD RODRIGUEZ**

3

The Personal Connection

Drawing on Personal Experience

Do you ask yourself who you are or who you really want to be? Did you grow up in a setting that did much to shape your outlook? Do you remember true friends — or others who were fair-weather friends? Do you have family memories that help explain your personality? On subjects like these, *you* are the expert. You know more about what you have witnessed and felt than anyone else. Much widely read writing is **autobiography**. Successful writers of autobiography relive with us their experiences. They tell us how they make sense of their lives. They share with us their encounters, their discoveries, and their attempts to find their own identity.

What gives writing from personal experience its special power and immediacy?

Mobilizing Your Memory   From the memory bank of your mind, you call up experiences that shaped your outlook or influenced your personal history. Some writers seem to have total recall for the revealing details and telling touches that bring places or people to life. In the following selection, a Chinese American writer remembers characteristic activities of his father. What does this passage tell you about the father's character?

> I know my father like this. I see him working in his white apron, flashing and sharpening his cleaver on the back rim of a white Chinese pottery bowl. Zhap zhap zhap, the gray steel cleaver on the sturdy bowl. After arranging different vegetables on the table, I see him grasping the handle

of the cleaver firmly, then nudging the jade bitter melon under the blade, at a slant, so that the pieces come out in even green crescents, like perfect waves of a green sea, at the same angle, and then the carrots, in thin narrow ovals, cut and dropped to boil lightly in a pot a while, and then the green bell peppers, the seeds and pale green mulch scooped out with a spoon, then cut in quarters and sliced. Then all the vegetables are arranged in neat piles on a large plate, ready to be cooked, the hardest fibrous vegetables to be cooked first in a dash of oil, and then the more delicately flavored ones, with purple and orange-tipped spears of heat, sizzling them in the heart, while all along the rice is boiling on another part of the stove, each white grain destined to be firm and separate from his brother.

My father's hands were always busy preparing food and papers, writing and touching inanimate and ultimately useful things such as pencils and knives. Yet I do not know the real strength of my father's arms. I have never been lifted on his hand, brought up to see any life outside of my own.

Russell C. Leong, "Rough Notes for Mantos"

Giving Voice to Your Feelings In the following childhood reminiscence, Gary Soto, a Mexican American poet, makes us share in what he thought and felt. He does not just put *labels* on feelings — anger, excitement, frustration, longing — but knows how to act them out for the reader. How does he make you share in what he thought and felt?

When I heard the far away sound of a train, I wiped my hands on my pants, set a rock on the tracks, and enjoyed wild thoughts about the train overturning. As the train rumbled closer, a plume of black smoke riding over its back, I felt a rumbling in my chest. The wind stirred dust and litter of candy wrappers. The sparrows on the shiny rails took flight. The gate lowered and a bell clanged to the beat of the red signal.

I hid behind a spidery tumbleweed as the train grew closer, its hypnotic eye of light swirling in its socket. The train was huge and black, and for the first time since my brother and I had tried to burn down our house, I felt something really exciting was going to happen. I held my breath, hands over my ears, as the train met up with its fate, *me*. But I stood up from behind the tumbleweed, again disappointed, when the rock just ricocheted off the tracks. Car after car swaggered past and the man in the caboose just stared when I waved.

A Summer Life

Facing Divided Loyalties At important stages in your life, you may find yourself at the crossroads. Family may pull you one way, school or work the other. You may find yourself outgrowing old friends or old loyalties. You might at first wonder if you want to be open about things that are private and perhaps painful. However, you may decide to write candidly about something important in your life, good or bad — as did the student who wrote the following passage:

> Our parents were always fighting. They would rage at each other's faults for hours on end. My mother's bitterness at having chosen the wrong man to marry eventually destroyed us as a family. My brother tried to intervene, but that merely diverted their rage towards him for a while. I knew that if I got involved I would have to face those bitter, narrowed eyes and the assault of epithets that stung like gravel thrown by bullies. So I went into my room, shut the door, sat cross-legged on my bed, hands clamped over my ears, and read books.

Is anybody going to care? Some personal writing is so private it remains a message we are sending to ourselves. However, most personal writing reaches others. They can relate it in some way to things they have experienced or have witnessed in the experience of people close to them. The columnist Adair Lara says,

> Personal writing, when it works, is a mirror. If I write a column about my dad, and a man comes up to me at a party and starts to talk to me about my old man, the writing has failed. If he comes up to me and starts talking about the last conversation he had with his father, in an airport hangar in Iowa at dawn one summer morning, then it starts to do its work.

| **THOUGHT LOG 3** |

Thinking about People

For an entry in your thought log, think about someone who had a special meaning for you. How much do you remember? Is there a special detail or special image that sticks in your mind? Write a capsule portrait of someone who played a role in your early years or is still playing a role in your life.

The Common Thread

We don't see things as they are; we see things as we are.

ANAIS NIN

Much writing from personal experience traces the connection between things that helped shape your personality. What is the common thread? Events happening over time may seem disjointed at first, but they may eventually fall into place. What is the pattern?

In a personal experience paper, you might be tracing a recurrent theme — something that became an issue or concern and had a serious effect on you. How did you come to terms with it? What did it mean in your life?

Here are two examples of how such a central issue might come into focus:

• Many young Americans experience a change that becomes a turning point in their lives. Perhaps a major event in your life was having to leave the area where you grew up. Perhaps the parent you lived with remarried and moved to a place with new opportunities. Thinking about your uprooted feeling may bring to mind memories of your parents' separation or divorce. It may bring back memories of family talks trying to "make the relationship work." More recently, you went through the breakup of a relationship with someone close to you who stayed behind in your hometown. What is the connecting thread? You may decide to focus your paper on the theme of separation — in spite of good intentions, in spite of the need for caring people in one's life.

• Many young Americans live in two worlds. At home, parents may still speak the language of the old country, upholding values and traditions of the culture into which they were born. However, in your neighborhood, the peer culture may exercise a strong pull. Friends on your home turf or at school may talk and act in ways different from those you were taught. At some point, you begin to ask yourself: What am I? Can I be Puerto Rican and American, or Vietnamese and American, at the same time? Can I be Mormon or Jewish or a born-again Christian and at the same time be one of the in-crowd in school?

Experience papers are by definition personal. More of your own personality will show through than in other kinds of writing. Nevertheless, you are likely to write a stronger paper if you keep major dimensions of personal experience writing in mind:

Pushing toward a Thesis   What is the main point or connecting thread of your paper? What does it all prove? What does it all show? The following trial thesis focuses the paper on the central issue, but it may be too general to hook the reader into the paper. It stays too interchangeable. Many other people could say something similar in the opening paragraphs of a paper:

TRIAL THESIS: Although I grew up in this country and am used to American ways, I am often reminded of the culture of my parents, who came from

south of the border. *Many differences exist between these two cultures —*
in religion, manners, and customs within the family.

What *are* these differences? Try giving your reader a preview of
the differences that concerned you as a person:

STRENGTHENED THESIS: Although I have grown up in this country and am
used to American ways, I am often reminded of the culture of my parents, who came from south of the border. *In their traditional way of life,*
there is a right way to act as a Catholic, as an obedient child, or as an unmar-
ried daughter.

Highlighting the Pattern   What are key stages or turning points in
your paper? Look at the way the opening sentences of three major
sections in the following paper direct the reader's attention:

Two Lives

My friends have a hard time deciding whether I am a cheerful or a
brooding person. The reason may be that I am leading two different lives.
I spend most of my time with my mother and stepfather, who have done
their best to raise me as a serious, responsible, law-abiding young person.
I started winning model citizen awards when I was still in junior high
school. However, I spend many weekends and vacations with my divorced
father's side of the family, where enjoying life has a higher priority.

My mother, it often seems, is still bitter about the divorce that happened
sixteen years ago. There is little storytelling in her house, and most of my
feeble jokes fall flat. It seemed there always was homework or housework
to do when I was really in the mood to go out and play. . . .

My divorced father represents the Italian side of the family, and he has the
gift of enjoying life's limited blessings. Meals at his house are an occasion, even
when the food is basically spaghetti. . . .

My father's parents, my grandparents, provide a kind of bridge between my
two families. My mother was their favorite daughter-in-law, and they still
send Christmas cards. They laugh at my jokes, but they also think that
some of my escapades with my friends were not really funny. . . .

Bringing People and Events to Life   You let down your readers if
you merely *talk* about your Irish parents taking you to Irish fairs and
dances. Your readers are likely to feel: "Take us along! Let us share
in the experience!"

UNDEVELOPED: As the many youth groups assembled for the day's events,
I was caught up in the flow and spectacle of the meeting,
but what impressed me the most was the power of the
religious experience in the lives of so many people.

DEVELOPED: For hours, youth groups from all over France and around
the world wound their way up the street to the square in

front of the cathedral. They carried banners that said "God — Family — Country." They sang, "*Marie, mère de Dieu, priez pour nous* — Mary, mother of God, pray for us." What impressed me most was the power of the religious experience in the lives of so many young people.

Trying to Sound Like Yourself Magazines and talk shows may give you a ready-made vocabulary for talking about relationships, bad parenting, and dysfunctional families. Some popular publications encourage people to find the silver lining, to look at the brighter side, never to give up, and to play ball and become a member of the team. Some of this talk may fit your own experience — however, it may also make what you say sound secondhand. You may want to reexamine passages like the following to see if you can sound more like yourself:

> I experienced a *unique sense of accomplishment*. . . . My experience proved that *you can do anything if you want it badly enough*. . . . I learned to *work with other people as a team*. . . . The experience was an opportunity for *personal growth* that helped me *discover my self-identity*. . . . I learned that above all *communication is essential in a relationship* . . .

WRITING WORKSHOP I

From Notes to Draft

Study the notes from the prewriting stage for the following student paper. What did the writer use or discard? What did she do to bring out the connecting thread or overall point implied in her original notes? How would you chart the overall pattern of the paper? How do you relate to the student writer? Do you think male and female readers will react differently? What do you think is strong or weak about the finished paper?

PREWRITING NOTES: **Mother and Daughter**

"looking nice"
"don't carry the ice chest"
"get good grades in school"
dependence — having to go for rides in the car to get out of the house and my mother being angry and staring out the window, head on her hand and not saying a word the whole time — I always thought that was ridiculous.
My grandmother was an independent woman. In 1928, she sailed from Canada to Manila, by herself, so that my grandfather and she could get married on his next leave from the Navy.

My mother was always concerned with what the neighbors would say, about anything. When I was in high school and went on a protest march, my mother wasn't concerned with the cause, if it was right or wrong, but "what will the neighbors say?"

Independence wasn't on the agenda for my mother's childhood. My grandmother, a woman of the 1920s, used her independence as a way and means. With the War, Depression, alone a lot and moving from base to base, she was outspoken, unconventional and atypical of an officer's wife.

My mother in contrast seemed meek and shy, growing in the shadow of their only other child, a boy. He was the one destined to follow in my grandfather's footsteps (although he never did).

Growing up with uncertainty, my sister seemed to flourish. She set a goal and has stayed with that same goal for 15 years. My brother and I floundered under a dual message. My father was a lightpost. Always there, sturdy, despite his appearance, methodical and self-satisfied with himself. When my mother got furious and started slamming the kitchen cabinets and doors, my father would calmly ride out the storm. Trying to do the best that we could was father's objective for his children.

Thanksgiving dinner was always the same at our house. The women cooked the meal, served the meal and cleaned up after the meal, while the men sat down to watch the football game. Most of the women enjoyed this whole set-up. It was a chance to talk "girl talk": where the best bargains were, who was seeing whom (in terms of marriage), and what was happening on the soaps.

FINAL DRAFT: **Declaration of Independence**

I had a very fuzzy concept of the woman's role in society when I was growing up. My mother was a very dependent woman, relying on my father for everything from basic necessities to entertainment. She had a firm picture in her mind of what women should be. But at the same time I saw the frustration this vision of hers caused her, and I developed opposite tendencies for my benefit.

My mother wanted to be the type of woman that appeared in the *Dick and Jane* readers I grew up with in elementary school. Dick and Jane's mother was always wearing crisp linen dresses with her curly hairdo and hanging the laundry in her well-trimmed yard. Already nicely dressed and made up, she would prepare breakfast for the whole family, kiss her briefcase-carrying husband goodbye as he drove off to his job, and send her immaculately dressed children off on the school bus.

My mother mirrored this blissful picture. She always tried to keep her appearance up with weekly trips to the beauty salon, and she exhausted herself by doing the first fifteen minutes of the daily exercise show. She spent much of her time being concerned with how things looked from the neighbor's viewpoint. She was especially pleased if her daughters were considered popular and her son considered brilliant. When I decided to become involved in a protest march, she didn't ask whether my decision was right or wrong; she asked, "What will the neighbors say?"

I first became confused about my own values when I realized how dependent my mother was on my father. On weekends, my mother expected to be "taken out." This usually meant going for rides, with my father driving, my mother in the other front seat, and the children in the back. I sometimes liked these rides — the warm feeling of being sandwiched between my brother and sister, the familiar smell of our old car, the chance to look at different houses and farms. Often, however, these rides would get off to a bumpy start. My father would be too tired, wanting to relax on the weekend. My mother would get irritated. Getting out of the house on the weekend, she felt, was her reward for taking care of the household during the week. She would start slamming doors and kitchen drawers until my father would say, "All right, let's go for a ride." By this time she would be so angry that she would slump into the car and stare out of the window, head on hand, and we would drive along in silence.

Part of my mother's philosophy was the notion that physical capabilities correlated with a person's sex. When I was thirteen and excited by the idea of a family camping trip, my mother stopped me from carrying a heavy ice chest with my father and had my less-than-average-size brother carry it instead. "She shouldn't be carrying that — she is going to hurt herself!" The only thing that was hurt in the incident was my pride.

I early saw what I did not want for myself by observing my mother's dependence. I had to take responsibility for my own happiness and well-being. I can't blame someone else if my life is not as I expect it to be. It can be frustrating trying to fix a drain or build a shelf, but it is satisfying to discover my own proficiencies. I push myself to the limits — physically in scuba diving and other sports, mentally in going to school while working. Pushing myself to the limit, I am trying to accommodate my own independent nature.

Revising Your Experience Paper

Writing is like a mirror. Whoever goes to the mirror risks a confrontation with the self.

STUDENT PAPER

Much of the feedback you receive on a personal experience paper may amount to readers saying: "Tell us more! Tell us more about the people! Tell us more about how you really felt!" The following is a sampling of more specific comments. Does editorial advice like the following apply to your early draft?

• *Do without empty labels.*   You might want to declare a moratorium on the use of *interesting, fascinating, beautiful, terrific, picturesque, spectacular,* or *cute.* To call something interesting is no substitute for *making* it interesting.

> WEAK: Like other border towns, Juarez is an interesting place to visit.
>
> INFORMATIVE: Unlike other border towns, Juarez is *a large genuine Mexican city.*

• *Move in for the closer look.*   Look for passages that remain too general. If you push them another notch or two toward the specific, your reader may begin to visualize something — see something with the mind's eye.

> COLORLESS: Rodeo artists live a strenuous life, eating poorly, always exposed to injury.
>
> CONCRETE: Rodeo artists live a strenuous life, *living off hot dogs at county fairs and rupturing their intestines while twisting the necks of steers.*

• *Watch your abstraction count.*   Abstractions pull you away from real-life events to a rarified, simplified level. A single paragraph piling up terms like *values, respect, ethics, responsibility, open-mindedness,* and *progressive thinking* is already a danger signal: Readers do look for inspiration, but inspirational words have to become more than words. Passages like the following need to be toned down and fortified with real-life examples of struggle and achievement:

> ABSTRACT: I have always *worked to the best of my ability* when participating in athletics. My *work ethic based upon tremendous effort* could be identified on the playing field when participating in athletics. I continually had the *aspiration to excel.* . . .

• *Steer clear of clichés.*   This is the time to edit out tired phrases like "Mother Nature," "the great outdoors," "the mighty ocean," or "island paradise." Look critically at any phrase that comes to you all glued together ready to type:

> CLICHÉ: At work, there was the usual *hustle and bustle* of a busy construction site.
>
> FRESH: At the construction site, cranes lifted steel beams thirty stories. The wet concrete flowed into huge wooden frames as the laborers shouted and banged their shovels against the chutes.

• *Avoid overwriting.*   Prose can be too colorless, but the color can also become too rich. Your prose turns into **purple prose** when you use too many phrases like "breath-taking sights," "magical moment," "sparkling waters," or "natural beauty of the dense woods." Try to let natural beauty speak for itself rather than smothering it under flowery language:

OVERWRITTEN: Invitingly lured from slumber by the sound of the rhythmic waves gently caressing the black rocks, lying lonely in their salty pools below, I witness the dawn's early morning rays thrust their way through the layer of thick frigid clouds curtaining this uniquely beautiful spot by the sea.

IMPROVED: At low tide the next morning, the black rocks are exposed among the salt-water pools. In the narrow channels between the rocks, incoming waves fill the crevices with foaming spray. Sea snails and small crabs hide among the masses of seaweed. Only yards away, sandpipers trot in and out after receding and returning waves.

WRITING WORKSHOP 2

A Paper with Peer Response

The following first draft focuses on a topic of current concern — how to keep a family together. It brings together good detail from personal experience and observation. However, like other first drafts, it seems to mirror the order in which the material came to mind. Pay special attention to the flow of material. Look at the added editorial notes charting for you the connection between the paragraphs. How do the parts fit into the overall picture? Could the writer have done more to show how the parts are connected and how they add up? Would the paper profit from a reshuffling or rearranging of its major parts?

FIRST DRAFT: **The Endangered Family**

(PARAGRAPH 1: Personal testimony — the broken home)

I vividly remember coming home from school one day to find my parents waiting for me in the living room to announce they were getting divorced. I remember that they seemed more shaken up than I was. I was a senior in high school and was so involved in my own future that I did not really think about what was happening until later. I was getting married myself. My marriage also ended in divorce. I was a single parent at age 18 and felt very much alone in the world.

(PARAGRAPH 2: Contrast — memories of a happy family)

When my sister and I were growing up, we seemed to have a happy storybook home. My mother worked "outside the home," but she would stay up till late into the night to sew our wicked-witch or gorilla costumes for Halloween. She would make homemade soup from carrots we pulled out of the ground in the morning and from other vegetables that made our kitchen smell like the produce section at the supermarket. My father did little around the house but took us bike riding or played baseball with us.

(PARAGRAPH 3: Update — second try at marriage)

I remarried and my husband and I are working hard to make a home and happy family life for ourselves and my son Michael. He started to call his new father "Dad" not long after the wedding. At first the name sounded somewhat forced, but now it seems the most natural thing in the world. He finds it hard to understand why other kids play games with their parents while his are working Saturdays or writing a paper at the library. We try hard to find time together.

(PARAGRAPH 4: The media picture — the family in trouble)

Locally, more than half of all marriages end in divorce. Projections show that more and more Americans will be living alone, shoving a TV dinner into the microwave after a day at the office. Teenage pregnancy is increasing at epidemic rates, usually leading to a kid's growing up in a single-parent family.

(PARAGRAPH 5: A close friend — a troubled marriage)

My friend's daily routine is to get her five-year-old off to school and to take care of a four-month-old daughter. She is trying very hard to keep her marriage together. Her husband has had drug and alcohol problems. His childhood was not happy, but he is trying to make sure his children are loved and taken care of. They are struggling to provide food and shelter. They know it's not going to be easy to keep the pieces together, but they feel it's important to try.

(PARAGRAPH 6: An older brother — a modernized traditional family)

My brother and his wife, however, still think of their family as a traditional family with traditional roles, although she works part-time and helps a great deal around the house and with meals. They have a structured routine and eat dinner every day at five o'clock. They cook together and eat together, and they both clean up. Their two-year-old is already trying to help his father around the yard.

What could be done to strengthen this paper? Fellow students might make the following comments:

PEER RESPONSES:

READER 1   I was puzzled by the dual nature of this paper. First it sounded like a strictly personal story, but the issue concerns not just the writer but society as a whole. Maybe you could make this clear by moving the material in paragraph 4 up front. Maybe also bring in facts and statistics from the media.

READER 2   I would have liked to see more of the people, like the two-year-old helping out in the yard.

READER 3   You tell your personal story, but where are you going with it? I wasn't sure what exactly was the agenda of the paper. Maybe the events should be tied together earlier with a reason or point behind them. Much in this paper points in the same direction. Shouldn't your thesis be something like: "People today have to make a special effort to make a marriage work"?

READER 4   The paper seemed to move back and forth in time. I think I would have followed better if you started with the happy family of childhood days and then went on to divorce and then to the effort to start again. Go from the past to the present and on to the future?

READER 5   The example that stuck in my mind was the marital problems of your friend. This sounded like what some of the people I know are struggling with. I would use this example in the conclusion to remind the reader that this is an ongoing problem.

How have these suggestions for revision been implemented in the following rewrite?

SECOND DRAFT: **Picking Up the Pieces**

Most American marriages are headed for divorce. Projections show that more and more Americans will be living alone, spending an hour at the fitness club before shoving a diet TV dinner into the microwave after a day at the office. Sex education and free condoms notwithstanding, teenage pregnancies are increasing at epidemic rates, usually leading to a kid growing up in a single-parent family. The media statistics only confirm what most Americans know from personal experience: The American family is an endangered species. Americans find it hard to start a family and to hold it together.

I was lucky enough as a child to experience the storybook happy home of the old-fashioned nuclear family. My mother worked outside the home, but she would stay up till late into the night to sew our wicked-witch or gorilla costumes for Halloween. She would make homemade soup from carrots we pulled out of the moist ground in the morning and from other homegrown vegetables that make the kitchen smell like the produce section at the supermarket. My father did little around the house, but he took us bike riding or played baseball with us at the school grounds around the corner.

However, like many in my generation, I eventually found myself one of the "children of divorce." I vividly remember coming home late from school one day in my senior year to find my parents waiting for me in the living room to announce they were getting divorced. I remember that my parents seemed more shaken than I was. My mother would not look at me, and my father used his special solemn, concerned voice, like a minister in church. At the time, I was so involved in my own future that I did not really think about what was happening until later. I was getting married myself. Unfortunately, I soon followed the example of my parents. My own marriage also ended in divorce. I was a single parent at eighteen and felt very much alone in the world.

I am now remarried, and my husband and I are trying hard to "make our marriage work." We are working hard to make a home and happy family life for ourselves and my son Michael. He started to call his new father "Dad" soon after the wedding. At first the name sounded forced, but now it seems the most natural thing in the world. Our main problem is to find time to be with our son — to be there for him. He finds it hard to understand why other kids play games with their parents while his are working on Saturdays or writing a paper at the library.

A lucky few still seem to have the secret of how to build a happy family life. My brother and his wife think of their family as a traditional family, although she works part-time and he helps around the house and with meals. They have a structured life and eat dinner every day at six o'clock. They cook together and eat together, and they both clean up. Their two-year-old is already trying to share in the yardwork, dragging around a child-size shovel and rake. "Start them early" is the parents' attitude.

More typical perhaps is the marriage of a close friend. Her daily routine is to get her five-year-old off to school and take care of a four-month-old daughter. She is trying very hard to keep her marriage together. Her husband has had drug and alcohol problems. His childhood was not happy, but he is trying hard to make sure his children are taken care of and loved. They are struggling to provide food and shelter. They know it's not going to be easy to keep the pieces together, but they feel it's important to try.

Talking to my friend on the phone reminds me of what I have learned from my own experience: Married couples today do not live happily forever after Prince Charming kisses the blushing bride. If they want to succeed, they have to be prepared to work at it. They have to make a deliberate effort to succeed against odds.

OPTIONS FOR WRITING 3

Telling Your Story

Write a paper that will give your reader a sense of who you are. Try to focus on one major strand in your personal experience. Think about something that has helped shape your outlook or your personality. Bring scenes, people, and events to life for your reader.

1 Have you had to choose between conflicting influences in your upbringing? For instance, have you experienced a clash of cultures or the blending of different cultural traditions? Have you experienced the conflict of different customs or ways of looking at the world?

2 Some people embrace tradition; others at some point rebel against what is expected of them. Where do you fit on the spec-

trum that runs from conformity to rebellion? Aim at a reader from your own generation who may be expected to recognize choices you have faced.

3 Have you or has someone close to you been the victim of prejudice or stereotyping? How did you cope? Or have you found yourself in situations where you may have been guilty of prejudice or stereotyping yourself? What did you learn about the workings of prejudice?

4 We hear much about bad parenting or dysfunctional families. Have family problems played a major role in your own private history? Or can you write about your family background as a source of strength? Write for readers who are themselves searching for a definition of what family means in a changing society.

5 Are you one of the children of divorce? How did the experience shape your outlook or your personality? Can you make your experience real for someone from a different family background?

6 An institution is often a world of its own. Has an institution — boarding school, church, the Boy Scouts — played a major formative role in your life? Can you write about being a patient or worker in a hospital, psychiatric ward, convalescent home, or similar institution? Can you give the inside story of life in a highly regulated institutional environment — army barracks, military academy, monastery, juvenile detention center, or jail? How has the experience affected your outlook or personality? Write as the insider trying to give others a sense of what you experienced.

7 Can you write about a turning point in your life? For instance, was your life changed by a serious illness or a major accident? Have you experienced a conversion to or leaving behind of religious faith?

8 How has your life or your outlook been shaped by the setting in which you grew up? Are you a city person? a country person? a suburbanite? Have you experienced a major move from one environment to another? Have you grown up in a border town, fishing town, logging town, reservation, or migrant camp different from Anywhere, USA? How has the experience affected your outlook or your personality?

9 What has been your experience in the world of work? What role has work played in your life? For instance, has your outlook been affected by working in an unusual environment — sweatshop, morgue, sawmill? Or can you introduce your readers to the world of the part-time worker?

10 How do you relate to other people? Do you make friends easily
    or are you a loner? What problems have you had in communi-
    cating with others?

Reading, Discussion, Writing

Other Lives

OVERVIEW: In the following selections, the author tells his or her
story. On what does each author focus? What does the writer select
from the flow of personal experience, and why? How does each author give shape to material from his or her life? What do you learn
from each selection about the person who wrote it?

The Legacy of Emotional Absence

GABRIEL CONSTANS

Is bad parenting more than a buzzword? Do American men tend to make bad fathers? Reruns of fifties' sitcoms and some nostalgic current programs keep alive the memory of the ideal American television family. A caring father and a patient mother steer their wisecracking offspring through the tribulations of adolescence. What we read about the family today usually plays a different tune. Children who experience emotional problems, lack of inner security, or inability to relate to others point the finger at their parents. Fathers especially come in for their share of the blame. City buses in a big American city for a time carried public service posters that gave a telephone number and said " Come Between a Father and His Son. Report Child Abuse." The search is on for deadbeat dads who abandoned their families. We read about family members who become co-dependents when the father turns alcoholic or drug addict. However, none of these descriptions apply to the father who is the subject of the following very personal statement. What is the charge against the writer's father?

My dad was never abusive. He didn't abandon my mother when I was born. Nor did he drink, use drugs or chase other women. Why, then, do I experience such resentment, anger and loss toward this man of good intentions? If my dad was so good, what feels so bad?

What feels so bad can be summarized in two words: emotional absence. He was taught to speak about things, not feelings. If his father had ever said, "I love you" even once, he probably would have dropped dead from the shock.

The men in my family were not alone in this quagmire of male expressive impotence. Millions of the testosterone species inherit this affliction at an early age.

For centuries fathers have learned to stifle their feelings toward their children, especially their sons. The messages that inundate the male psyche are clear, overpowering and consistent. Be strong. Be a man. Don't act like a wimp. Stop crying like a girl. Work hard. Be successful. Who you are depends on your position and income. Keep your feelings under control. Stand up and fight like a man. Show them who's boss.

American men are raised to think and act, not to feel, compromise, accept, share or love.   5

When I was a young boy I idealized my father. He played games with my sister and me, built forts, castles and playhouses in our backyard, and took us on countless outings and trips. I remember waiting in the late afternoon for him to get home from working at the lumber mill. As soon as I saw him I'd run down the street, jump into his arms and give his tired, dirty body a big hug.

It wasn't until my parents divorced and I reached adolescence that I discovered how ineffectual he was in relating to me as a young adult.

When I tried to talk with him about anything other than sports, school or work he would change the subject or nod his head knowingly, without having heard a word I said. This was a crucial time in my life. I had just turned thirteen and my parents were separated. I needed a father who felt confident about himself — he didn't. I needed his acknowledgment and love — he couldn't give it. Our relationship began to erode slowly, until it became a spiritless sequence of superficial exchanges.

Like thousands of men in this country, I had no other male mentor or role model to turn to. More than half of my friends rarely, if ever, saw their fathers. And those who did often wished they hadn't.

My friend Alex's dad worked such long hours that he seldom spent   10
any time with his son. David's father left two months after he was born. And my buddy Andrew longed for his alcoholic and abusive father to drop dead.

Thank God for women. If it hadn't been for the women's movement in the last 25 years and their courage in challenging destructive male attitudes and behavior, we wouldn't have a chance to change our cancerous legacy of emotional absence.

Occasionally I delude myself into believing that men in our society are breaking through these stifling stereotypical father images. Such delusions are quickly shattered when I read the news, listen to men talk at lunch, see a movie or watch television.

There are a few exceptions. I hope I'm one of them. I pray I don't pass on the "sins of our fathers" to my children.

THE INVOLVED READER

1   Do you sympathize with the author? What is the basic problem? Have you or people close to you encountered it?

2   What was the father's role in the lives of the author's friends? (If you had to do a similar accounting of your own friends' fathers, what would you include?)

3   Is Constans too hard on his father?

TALKING, THINKING, WRITING

4 Is "be a man — don't act like a wimp" still the theme song of how boys are brought up in this country?

5 In your own growing up, do you think "male attitudes and behavior" or the influence of women played the stronger role?

6 Did you go through a phase where you idealized an adult who played a major role in your life? Did you go through a phase of disappointment or disillusionment? On balance, what is your view of the person?

COLLABORATIVE PROJECTS

7 Members of your class might each want to write a letter to a parent or other significant person. Or they might choose to write a letter to an imaginary father or mother they would have liked to have had. Help your class collect and edit these letters for a class publication.

Step Forward in the Car, Please

MAYA ANGELOU

*How do people cope with discrimination or overcome prejudice?
Maya Angelou has written several autobiographical volumes focused
on a classic theme: making it against odds. She tells her story in* I
Know Why the Caged Bird Sings *(1970),* Gather Together in My
Name *(1974),* Singin' and Swingin' and Gettin' Merry like Christmas
(1976), The Heart of a Woman *(1981), and* All God's Children Need
Traveling Shoes *(1986). Angelou spent her childhood in Sparks, Arkansas, where her grandmother ran a country store at a time when
black people toiled in the fields for minimal wages and when nightri-
ders terrorized their neighborhoods. She went on to a spectacular career as poet, singer, dancer, actor (she appeared in* Roots*), playwright,
lecturer, and writer-producer. Martin Luther King, Jr., named her the
Northern Coordinator for the Southern Christian Leadership Conference. Millions heard her read her poem "With Hope, Good Morning"
at the inauguration of President Clinton in January 1993. In the
words of one editor, Angelou is outstanding among writers who,
"speaking in the collective voice of African Americans," bear witness
that their rights "as individuals and citizens of this country cannot be
denied."*

My room had all the cheeriness of a dungeon and the appeal of a
tomb. It was going to be impossible to stay there, but leaving held
no attraction for me, either. The answer came to me with the sud-
denness of a collision. I would go to work. Mother wouldn't be difficult to convince; after all, in school I was a year ahead of my grade
and Mother was a firm believer in self-sufficiency. In fact, she'd be
pleased to think that I had that much gumption, that much of her in
my character. (She liked to speak of herself as the original "do-it-
yourself girl.")

Once I had settled on getting a job, all that remained was to decide which kind of job I was most fitted for. My intellectual pride had
kept me from selecting typing, shorthand, or filing as subjects in
school, so office work was ruled out. War plants and shipyards demanded birth certificates, and mine would reveal me to be fifteen,
and ineligible for work. So the well-paying defense jobs were also
out. Women had replaced men on the streetcars as conductors and
motormen, and the thought of sailing up and down the hills of San
Francisco in a dark-blue uniform, with a money changer at my belt,
caught my fancy.

Mother was as easy as I had anticipated. The world was moving so fast, so much money was being made, so many people were dying in Guam, and Germany, that hordes of strangers became good friends overnight. Life was cheap and death entirely free. How could she have the time to think about my academic career?

To her question of what I planned to do, I replied that I would get a job on the streetcars. She rejected the proposal with: "They don't accept colored people on the streetcars."

I would like to claim an immediate fury which was followed by the   5
noble determination to break the restricting tradition. But the truth is, my first reaction was one of disappointment. I'd pictured myself, dressed in a neat blue serge suit, my money changer swinging jauntily at my waist, and a cheery smile for the passengers which would make their own work day brighter.

From disappointment, I gradually ascended the emotional ladder to haughty indignation, and finally to that state of stubbornness where the mind is locked like the jaws of an enraged bulldog.

I would go to work on the streetcars and wear a blue serge suit. Mother gave me her support with one of her usual terse asides, "That's what you want to do? Then nothing beats a trial but a failure. Give it everything you've got. I've told you many times. 'Can't Do is like Don't Care.' Neither of them has a home."

Translated, that meant there was nothing a person can't do, and there should be nothing a human being didn't care about. It was the most positive encouragement I could have hoped for.

In the offices of the Market Street Railway Company, the receptionist seemed as surprised to see me there as I was surprised to find the interior dingy and drab. Somehow I had expected waxed surfaces and carpeted floors. If I had met no resistance, I might have decided against working for such a poor-mouth-looking concern. As it was, I explained that I had come to see about a job. She asked, was I sent by an agency, and when I replied that I was not, she told me they were only accepting applicants from agencies.

The classified pages of the morning papers had listed advertise-   10
ments for motorettes and conductorettes and I reminded her of that. She gave me a face full of astonishment that my suspicious nature would not accept.

"I am applying for the job listed in this morning's *Chronicle* and I'd like to be presented to your personnel manager." While I spoke in supercilious accents, and looked at the room as if I had an oil well in my own backyard, my armpits were being pricked by millions of hot pointed needles. She saw her escape and dived into it.

"He's out. He's out for the day. You might call him tomorrow and if he's in, I'm sure you can see him." Then she swiveled her chair around on its rusty screws and with that I was supposed to be dismissed.

"May I ask his name?"

She half turned, acting surprised to find me still there.

"His name? Whose name?"   15

"Your personnel manager."

We were firmly joined in the hypocrisy to play out the scene.

"The personnel manager? Oh, he's Mr. Cooper, but I'm not sure you'll find him here tomorrow. He's . . . Oh, but you can try."

"Thank you."

"You're welcome."   20

And I was out of the musty room and into the even mustier lobby. In the street I saw the receptionist and myself going faithfully through paces that were stale with familiarity, although I had never encountered that kind of situation before and, probably, neither had she. We were like actors who, knowing the play by heart, were still able to cry afresh over the old tragedies and laugh spontaneously at the comic situations.

The miserable little encounter had nothing to do with me, the me of me, any more than it had to do with that silly clerk. The incident was a recurring dream concocted years before by whites, and it eternally came back to haunt us all. The secretary and I were like people in a scene where, because of harm done by one ancestor to another, we were bound to duel to the death. (Also because the play must end somewhere.)

I went further than forgiving the clerk; I accepted her as a fellow victim of the same puppeteer.

On the streetcar, I put my fare into the box and the conductorette looked at me with the usual hard eyes of white contempt. "Move into the car, please move on in the car." She patted her money changer.

Her Southern nasal accent sliced my meditation and I looked deep   25
into my thoughts. All lies, all comfortable lies. The receptionist was not innocent and neither was I. The whole charade we had played out in that waiting room had to do with me, black, and her, white.

I wouldn't move into the streetcar but stood on the ledge over the conductor, glaring. My mind shouted so energetically that the announcement made my veins stand out, and my mouth tighten into a prune.

I WOULD HAVE THE JOB. I WOULD BE A CONDUCTORETTE AND SLING A FULL MONEY CHANGER FROM MY BELT. I WOULD.

The next three weeks were a honeycomb of determination with apertures for the days to go in and out. The Negro organizations to whom I appealed for support bounced me back and forth like a shuttlecock on a badminton court. Why did I insist on that particular job? Openings were going begging that paid nearly twice the money. The minor officials with whom I was able to win an audience thought me mad. Possibly I was.

Downtown San Francisco became alien and cold, and the streets I had loved in a personal familiarity were unknown lanes that twisted with malicious intent. My trips to the streetcar office were of the frequency of a person on salary. The struggle expanded. I was no longer in conflict only with the Market Street Railway but with the marble lobby of the building which housed its offices, and elevators and their operators.

During this period of strain Mother and I began our first steps on   30
the long path toward mutual adult admiration. She never asked for reports and I didn't offer any details. But every morning she made breakfast, gave me carfare and lunch money, as if I were going to work. She comprehended that in the struggle lies the joy. That I was no glory seeker was obvious to her, and that I had to exhaust every possibility before giving in was also clear.

On my way out of the house one morning she said, "Life is going to give you just what you put in it. Put your whole heart in everything you do, and pray, then you can wait." Another time she reminded me that "God helps those who help themselves." She had a store of aphorisms which she dished out as the occasion demanded. Strangely, as bored as I was with clichés, her inflection gave them something new, and set me thinking for a little while at least. Later when asked how I got my job, I was never able to say exactly. I only knew that one day, which was tiresomely like all the others before it, I sat in the Railway office, waiting to be interviewed. The receptionist called me to her desk and shuffled a bundle of paper to me. They were job application forms. She said they had to be filled out in triplicate. I had little time to wonder if I had won or not, for the standard questions reminded me of the necessity for lying. How old was I? List my previous jobs, starting from the last held and go backward to the first. How much money did I earn, and why did I leave the position? Give two references (not relatives). I kept my face blank (an old art) and wrote quickly the fable of Marguerite Johnson, aged nineteen, former companion and driver for Mrs. Annie Henderson (a White Lady) in Stamps, Arkansas.

I was given blood tests, aptitude tests, and physical coordination tests, then on a blissful day I was hired as the first Negro on the San Francisco streetcars.

Mother gave me the money to have my blue serge suit tailored, and I learned to fill out work cards, operate the money changer and punch transfers. The time crowded together and at an End of Days I was swinging on the back of the rackety trolley, smiling sweetly and persuading my charges to "step forward in the car, please."

For one whole semester the streetcars and I shimmied up and scooted down the sheer hills of San Francisco. I lost some of my need for the black ghetto's shielding-sponge quality, as I clanged and cleared my way down Market Street, with its honky-tonk homes for homeless sailors, past the quiet retreat of Golden Gate Park and along closed undwelled-in-looking dwellings of the Sunset District.

My work shifts were split so haphazardly that it was easy to be-   35 lieve that my superiors had chosen them maliciously. Upon mentioning my suspicions to Mother, she said, "Don't you worry about it. You ask for what you want, and you pay for what you get. And I'm going to show you that it ain't no trouble when you pack double."

She stayed awake to drive me out to the car barn at four-thirty in the mornings, or to pick me up when I was relieved just before dawn. Her awareness of life's perils convinced her that while I would be safe on the public conveyances, she "wasn't about to trust a taxi driver with her baby."

When the spring classes began, I resumed my commitment with formal education. I was so much wiser and older, so much more independent, with a bank account and clothes that I had bought for myself, that I was sure I had learned and earned the magic formula which would make me a part of the life my contemporaries led.

Not a bit of it. Within weeks, I realized that my schoolmates and I were on paths moving away from each other. They were concerned and excited over the approaching football games. They concentrated great interest on who was worthy of being student body president, and when the metal bands would be removed from their teeth, while I remembered conducting a streetcar in the uneven hours of the morning.

THE INVOLVED READER

1 What was Angelou's goal? What was the obstacle — when and how does it surface? How did she overcome?

2 What do you learn from this account about the workings of prejudice? Is prejudice here blatant and overt, or is it subtle and indirect? Does the way it operates here seem unexpected, or does it seem predictable and familiar?

3 In thinking about her encounter with the white receptionist, Angelou moves from one interpretation to another. How does

she explain to herself what happened? Why does she change her mind?

4 What role does the mother play in this account? Is she more than a supporting player? How would you describe the mother-daughter relationship?

TALKING, THINKING, WRITING

5 What experience have you had with screening and testing procedures used by employers? Have you developed any survival skills as a test taker?

6 Does the reader have to be black to identify with the writer? Or more generally, does the reader have to be a member of a minority to identify with the writer?

7 Have the workings of prejudice changed since the time of Angelou's account? If so, how?

8 Have you encountered a major hurdle in your life? Have you come up against a major challenge or obstacle? What was your experience? How did you cope or come to terms with it? How did it affect you as a person?

COLLABORATIVE PROJECTS

9 Working with a group, you may want to interview minority students about their experiences in applying for jobs. Are they apprehensive about discrimination? How do they cope with it?

The Violent Politics of Crime

BRUCE SHAPIRO

Are we looking on helplessly as American cities deteriorate? Many who love city life have watched with helpless anger as our cities continue their downward slide. Can you identify with the author of the following article? How real does the central incident become for you? Do you understand the author's reactions and feelings? Would you have felt the same or differently in his place? Shapiro is an editor and writer for the weekly magazine The Nation, *where this story of his encounter with violent crime first appeared. Whereas much discussion of our violent culture relies on numerous examples and eye-opening statistics, Shapiro presents his personal testimony as a crime victim.*

Alone in my home I am staring at the television screen and shouting. On the local evening news I have unexpectedly encountered video footage, several months old, of myself writhing on an ambulance gurney — skin pale, shirt open and drenched with blood, trying desperately to find relief from pain.

On the evening of August 7, 1994, I was among seven people stabbed and seriously wounded in a café a few blocks from my house. Any televised recollection of this incident would be upsetting. But tonight's anger is quite specific, and political, in origin: My picture is being shown on the news to illustrate why my state's legislature plans to lock up more criminals for a longer time. A picture of my body, contorted and bleeding, has become a propaganda image in the crime war. I had not planned to write about this assault. But for months now the politics of the nation have in large part been the politics of crime, from last year's federal crime bill to the "Taking Back Our Streets" clause of the Contract with America. Among a welter of reactions to my own recent experience, one feeling is clear: I am unwilling to be a silent poster child in this debate.

Here is what happened: At about 9:45 P.M. I arrived at the coffeehouse on Audubon Street with two neighborhood friends, Martin and Anna. We sat at a small table near the front; about fifteen people were scattered around the room. Just before ten, as Martin went over to the counter for a final refill, chaos erupted. I heard him call Anna's name. I looked up and saw his arm raised and a flash of metal and people leaping away from a thin, bearded man with a ponytail. Tables and chairs toppled. Without thinking I shouted to Anna, "Get down!" Clinging to each other, we pulled ourselves along the wall toward the door.

What actually happened I was only tentatively able to reconstruct later. Apparently, as Martin headed toward the counter the thin, bearded man, whose name we later learned was Daniel Silva, asked the time from another patron, who answered and then turned to leave. Without warning, Silva pulled out a hunting knife and began moving about the room with demonic speed, stabbing six people in a matter of seconds. Among these were Martin, stabbed in the thigh and the arm, the woman behind the counter, stabbed in the chest and abdomen while phoning the police, and Anna, stabbed in the side as we pulled each other toward the door.

I had gone no more than a few steps down the sidewalk when I   5 felt a hard punch in my back followed instantly by the unforgettable sensation of skin and muscle tissue parting. Silva had stabbed me about six inches above my waist, just beneath my rib cage. Without thinking, I clapped my hand over the wound before the knife was out, and the exiting blade sliced my palm and two fingers.

"Why are you doing this?" I cried out. I fell, and he leaned over my face, the knife's glittering blade immense. He put the point into my chest. I remember his brown beard, his clear blue-gray eyes looking directly into mine, and the round globe of a streetlamp like a halo above his head.

"You killed my mother," Silva answered. At my own desperate response — "Please don't" — he pulled the knifepoint out of my chest and disappeared. A moment later I saw him flying down the street on a battered bicycle.

I lay on the sidewalk, screaming in pain. Every muscle in my back felt locked and contorted; breathing was excruciating. A woman in a white-and-gray plaid dress was sitting on the curb in a stupor, covered with blood. Up the street I saw a police car's flashing lights, then another's, then an officer with a concerned face and a crackling radio was crouching beside me. I stayed conscious as the medics arrived and I was loaded into an ambulance.

Until August 7 Daniel Silva was a self-employed junk dealer and a homeowner. He lived with his mother and several dogs. He had no arrest record. A police detective who was hospitalized across the hall from me recalled Silva as a socially marginal neighborhood character. He was not, apparently, a drug user. He had told neighbors about much violence in his family — showing one a scar on his thigh he said was from a stab wound.

A week earlier, Silva's seventy-nine-year-old mother had been   10 hospitalized for diabetes. After a few days the hospital moved her to a new room; when Silva saw his mother's empty bed he panicked, but nurses swiftly took him to her new location. Still, something seemed to have snapped. On the day of the stabbings, police say, Silva released his dogs, set fire to his house, and rode away on his bicycle as his home burned. He arrived on Audubon Street evidently convinced that his mother was dead.

While I lay in the hospital, the big story on CNN was the federal crime bill then being debated in Congress. Even fogged by morphine I was aware of the irony. I was flat on my back, with tubes in veins, chest, penis, and abdomen, the result of a particularly violent assault, while Congress was busy passing the anticrime package that I had criticized in print just a few weeks earlier. Night after night, unable to sleep, I watched Republicans and Democrats fall over one another to prove who could be the toughest on crime.

A few days after I returned home, the bill passed. What I found when I finally read its 412-page text was this: Not a single one of those pages would have protected me or Anna or Martin or any of the others from our assailant. Not the extended prison terms, not the forty-four new death-penalty offenses, not the three-strikes-and-you're-out requirements, not the summary deportations of criminal aliens. The even stiffer provisions of the Contract with America, including the proposed abolition of the Fourth Amendment's search-and-seizure protections, still would have offered me no practical protection.

On the other hand, the mental-health and social-welfare safety net shredded during the 1980s might have made a difference in the life of someone like my assailant — and thus in the life of someone like me. Silva's growing distress in the days before August 7 was obvious to his neighbors. He had muttered darkly about relatives planning to burn down his house. A better-funded, more comprehensive social-service infrastructure might have saved me and six others from untold pain and trouble.

In fact, it was in no small measure the institutions of an urban community that saved my life that night. The police officer who found me was joined in a moment by a phalanx of emergency medics, and his backups arrived quickly enough to chase down my assailant three blocks away. In minutes I was taken to nearby Yale–New Haven hospital — built in part with the kind of public funding so hated by the right — where several dozen doctors and nurses descended to handle all the wounded. If my stabbing had taken place in the suburbs, I would have bled to death.

One thing I could not properly appreciate in the hospital was how 15 deeply other people were shaken by the stabbings. The reaction of most was a combination of decent horrified empathy and a clear sense that their own presumption of safety had been undermined.

But some who didn't bother to acquaint themselves with the facts used the stabbings as a sort of Rorschach test on which they projected their own preconceptions. Some present and former Yale students, for instance, were desperate to see in my stabbing evidence of the great dangers of New Haven's inner city. One student newspaper wrote about "New Haven's image as a dangerous town fraught with violence." A student reporter from another Yale paper asked if I didn't think the attack proved that New Haven needs better police protection. Given the random nature of this assault, it's tempting to dismiss such sentiments. But city-hating is central to today's political culture. Newt Gingrich excoriates cities as hopelessly pestilent, crime-ridden, and corrupt. Fear of urban crime is the right's basic fuel, and defunding cities is a central agenda item for the new congressional majority.

"Why didn't anyone try to stop him?" That question was even more common than the reflexive city-bashing. I can't begin to guess the number of times I had to answer it. Each time, I repeated that Silva moved too fast, that it was simply too confusing. And each time, I found the question not just foolish but offensive.

"Why didn't anyone stop him?" To understand that question is to understand, in some measure, why crime is such a potent political issue. To begin with, the question carries not empathy but an implicit burden of blame; it really asks, "Why didn't *you* stop him?" It is asked because no one likes to imagine oneself a victim. It's far easier to imagine assuming the aggressive power of the attacker, to embrace the delusion of oneself as Arnold Schwarzenegger: *If I am tough enough and strong enough, I can take out the bad guys.*

The country is at present suffering from a huge version of this same delusion, a myth nurtured by historical tales of frontier violence and vigilantism and by the action-hero fantasies of film and television. Bolstered by the social Darwinists of the right, who see society as an unfettered marketplace in which the strongest individuals flourish, this delusion frames the crime debate.

To ask, "Why didn't anybody stop him?" is to imply only two choices: Rambo-like heroism or abject victimhood, fight or flight. And people don't want to think of themselves choosing flight. In last year's debate over the crime bill, conservatives successfully portrayed themselves as those who would stand and fight; liberals were portrayed as ineffectual cowards.

But on the receiving end of a violent attack, the fight-or-flight dichotomy didn't apply. Nor did that radically individualized notion of survival. At the coffeehouse that night there were no Schwarzeneggers, no stand-alone heroes. But neither were there abject vic- 20 tims. The woman behind the counter helped one of the wounded out the back window; Anna, Martin, and I clung to one another as we escaped; and two patrons who had never met sought a hiding place together around the corner. In the confusion and panic of life-threatening attack, people reached out to one another. This sounds simple, yet it suggests that there is an instinct for mutual aid that poses a profound challenge to the atomized individualism of the right.

I do understand the rage and frustration behind the crime-victim movement, and see how the right has harnessed it. Anyone trying to deal with the reality of crime, as opposed to the fantasies peddled to win elections, needs to understand the complex suffering of those who are survivors of such traumas, and the suffering and turmoil of their families. I have impressive physical scars, but to me the disruption of my psyche is more significant. For weeks after the attack, I awoke nightly, agitated, drenched with sweat. Any moment of mental repose was instantly flooded with images from that night. Sometimes my mind simply would not tune in at all. My reactions are still out of balance and disproportionate. I shut a door on my finger, not too hard, and my body is suddenly flooded with adrenaline, nearly faint. Walking on the arm of my partner, Margaret, one evening I abruptly shove her to the side of the road because I have seen a tall, lean shadow a block away. An hour after an argument, I find myself quaking with rage, completely unable to restore my sense of calm.

What psychologists call post-traumatic stress disorder is, among other things, a profoundly political state, in which the world has gone wrong, in which you feel isolated from the broader community by the inarticulable extremity of experience. I have spent a lot of time in the past few months thinking about what the world must look like to those who have survived repeated violent attacks — to children battered in their homes and prisoners beaten or tortured behind bars — and to those, like rape victims, whose assaults are rarely granted the public ratification that mine was.

If the use of my picture on television unexpectedly brought me face-to-face with the memory of August 7, some part of the attack is relived for me daily as I watch the gruesome, voyeuristically reported details of the deaths of Nicole Brown Simpson and Ronald Goldman. And throughout the Colin Ferguson trial, as he spoke of falling asleep and having someone else fire his gun, I heard Daniel Silva's calm, secure voice telling me I had killed his mother. When I hear testimony by the survivors of that massacre — on a train as comfortable and familiar to them as my neighborhood coffee bar is to me — I feel a great and incommunicable fellowship.

But the public obsession with these trials, I am convinced, has no more to do with the real experience of crime victims than do the posturings of politicians. I do not know what made my assailant act as he did. Nor do I think crime and violence can be reduced to simple political categories. I do know that the answers will not be found in social Darwinism and individualism, in racism, in dismantling cities and increasing the destitution of the poor. To the contrary: every fragment of my experience suggests that the best protection from crime and the best aid to victims are the very social institutions most derided by the right. As a crime victim and a citizen, what I want is the reality of a safe community — not a politician's fantasyland of restitution and revenge. That is my testimony.

THE INVOLVED READER

1 Why does Shapiro chronicle his traumatic experience in such excruciating detail? How much do you learn about the circumstances? How much do you learn about the assailant?

2 What does Shapiro have to say about "the delusion of oneself as Schwarzenegger" and "Rambo-like heroism"?

3 Confronted with irrational violence, people may turn cynical or despondent. What does Shapiro say about the aftermath of violence for the victims? For Shapiro, were there any redeeming positive or encouraging aspects of his experience?

4 What is "social Darwinism"? Why is it an issue in this essay?

TALKING, THINKING, WRITING

5 What did Shapiro learn from the experience? What do you learn from his account of it? Would your reactions have been similar or different?

6 Was what happened to Shapiro an "isolated incident"? Or do you think what happened to him "could have happened to anybody"? Was he "in the wrong place at the wrong time"?

7 Do you think the media spend too much time on exploiting sensational crimes or refereeing sensational court battles and to little on what the aftermath of crime means for victims or their families?

Coed Prison: Notes from the Country Club

KIMBERLY WOZENCRAFT

Do we think of prisoners in our jails as fellow human beings or as caged animals who are not on our conscience? Many of those incarcerated will eventually rejoin society. Will prison life rehabilitate them and make them more constructive fellow citizens? Or will they emerge from prison more hostile than when they went in? In the following selection, a police officer turned convict tells the inside story of prison life. As a twenty-four-year-old narcotics officer, she participated in an eight-month undercover narcotics investigation that led to the arrest of about a hundred people, many from prominent families, in a small East Texas town. Associating with dealers and users, she developed a serious drug habit of her own, and she narrowly escaped death while her undercover partner and later husband was severely wounded. In the end, she and her partner were convicted of falsifying reports and giving false testimony, and every drug case the two had been involved in was dismissed. She told her story again in fictionalized form in her novel Rush, *published in 1990.*

They had the Haitians up the hill, in the "camp" section where they used to keep the minimum security cases. The authorities were concerned that some of the Haitians might be diseased, so they kept them isolated from the main coed prison population by lodging them in the big square brick building surrounded by eight-foot chain-link with concertina wire on top. We were not yet familiar with the acronym AIDS.

One or two of the Haitians had drums, and in the evenings when the rest of us were in the Big Yard, the drum rhythms carried over the bluegrass to where we were playing gin or tennis or softball or just hanging out waiting for dark. When they really got going some of them would dance and sing. Their music was rhythmic and beautiful, and it made me think of freedom.

There were Cubans loose in the population, spattering their guttural Spanish in streams around the rectangular courtyard, called Central Park, at the center of the prison compound. These were Castro's Boat People, guilty of no crime in this country, but requiring sponsors before they could walk the streets as free people.

Walking around the perimeter of Central Park was like taking a trip in microcosm across the United States. Moving leftward from the main entrance, strolling along under the archway that covers the wide sidewalk, you passed the doorway to the Women's Unit, where I lived, and it was how I imagined Harlem to be. There was a white face here and there, but by far most of them were black. Ghetto blasters thunked out rhythms in the sticky evening air, and folks leaned against the window sills, smoking, drinking Cokes, slinking and nodding. Every once in a while a joint was passed around, and always there was somebody pinning, checking for hacks on patrol.

Past Women's Unit was the metal door to the Big Yard, the main recreation area of three or four acres, two sides blocked by the building, two sides fenced in the usual way — chain-link and concertina wire. It was generally in the Big Yard entrance that you would find people "jumping." Prison sex was fast and furious; even the threat of shipment to a maximum security joint did not entirely subjugate the criminal libido.

Past the Big Yard you entered the Blue Ridge Mountains, a sloping grassy area on the edge of Central Park, where the locals, people from Kentucky, Tennessee, and the surrounding environs, sat around playing guitars and singing, and every once in a while passing around a quart of hooch. They make it from grapefruit juice and a bit of yeast smuggled out of the kitchen. Some of the inmates who worked in Cable would bring out pieces of a black foam rubber substance and wrap it around empty Cremora jars to make thermos jugs of sorts. They would mix the grapefruit juice and yeast in the containers and stash them in some out-of-the-way spot for a few weeks until presto! you had hooch, bitter and tart and sweet all at once, only mildly alcoholic, but entirely suitable for evening cocktails in Central Park.

Next, at the corner, was the Commissary, a tiny store tucked inside the entrance to Veritas, the second women's unit. It wasn't much more than a few shelves behind a wall of Plexiglas, with a constant line of inmates spilling out of the doorway. They sold packaged chips, cookies, pens and writing paper, toiletries, some fresh fruit, and the ever-popular ice cream, sold only in pints. You had to eat the entire pint as soon as you bought it, or else watch it melt, because there weren't any refrigerators. Inmates were assigned one shopping night per week, allowed to buy no more than seventy-five dollars' worth of goods per month, and were permitted to pick up a ten-dollar roll of quarters if they had enough money in their prison account. Quarters were the basic spending unit in the prison; possession of paper money was a shippable offense. There were vending machines stocked with junk food and soda, and they were supposedly what the quarters were to be used for. But we gambled, we bought salami or fried chicken sneaked out by the food service workers, and of course people sold booze and drugs. The beggars stood just outside the Commissary door. Mostly they were Cubans, saying "Oye! Mira! Mira! Hey, Poppy, one quarter for me? One cigarette for me, Poppy?"

There was one Cuban whom I was specially fond of. His name was Shorty. The name said it, he was only about five-two, and he looked just like Mick Jagger. I met him in Segregation, an isolated section of tiny cells where prisoners were locked up for having violated some institutional rule or another. They tossed me in there the day I arrived; again the authorities were concerned, supposedly for my safety. I was a police woman before I became a convict, and they weren't too sure that the other inmates would like that. Shorty saved me a lot of grief when I went into Seg. It didn't matter if you were male or female there, you got stripped and handed a tee shirt, a pair of boxer shorts and a set of Peter Pans — green canvas shoes with thin rubber soles designed to prevent you from running away. As if you could get past three steel doors and a couple of hacks just to start with. When I was marched down the hall between the cells the guys started whistling and hooting and they didn't shut up even after I was locked down. They kept right on screaming until finally I yelled out, "Yo no comprendo!" and then they all moaned and said, "Another fucking Cuban," and finally got quiet. Shorty was directly across from me, I could see his eyes through the rectangular slot in my cell door. He rattled off a paragraph or two of Spanish, all of which was lost on me, and I said quietly. "Yo no comprendo bien español. Yo soy de Texas, you hablo inglés?" I could tell he was smiling by the squint of his eyes, and he just said, "Bueno." When the hacks came around to take us out for our mandatory hour of recreation, which consisted of standing around in the Rec area while two guys shot a game of pool on the balcony above the gym, Shorty slipped his hand into mine and smiled up at me until the hack told him to cut it out. He knew enough English to tell the others in Seg that I was not really Spanish, but he kept quiet about it, and they left me alone.

Beyond the Commissary, near the door to the dining hall, was East St. Louis. The prison had a big portable stereo system which they rolled out a few times a week so that an inmate could play at being a disc jockey. They had a good-sized collection of albums and there was usually some decent jazz blasting out of there. Sometimes people danced, unless there were uptight hacks on duty to tell them not to.

California was next. It was a laid back kind of corner near the 10
doors to two of the men's units. People stood around and smoked hash or grass or did whatever drugs happened to be available and

there was sometimes a sort of slow-motion game of handball going on. If you wanted drugs, this was the place to come.

If you kept walking, you would arrive at the Power Station, the other southern corner where the politicos-gone-wrong congregated. It might seem odd at first to see these middle-aged government mavens standing around in their Lacoste sport shirts and Sans-a-belt slacks, smoking pipes or cigars and waving their arms to emphasize some point or other. They kept pretty much to themselves and ate together at the big round tables in the cafeteria, sipping cherry Kool-Aid and pretending it was Cabernet Sauvignon.

That's something else you had to deal with — the food. It was worse than elementary school steam table fare. By the time they finished cooking it, it was tasteless, colorless, and nutritionless. The first meal I took in the dining room was lunch. As I walked toward the entry, a tubby fellow was walking out, staggering really, rolling his eyes as though he were dizzy. He stopped and leaned over, and I heard someone yell, "Watch you, he's gonna puke!" I ducked inside so as to miss the spectacle. They were serving some rubbery, faint pink slabs that were supposed to be ham, but I didn't even bother to taste mine. I just slapped at it a few times to watch the fork bounce off and then ate my potatoes and went back to the unit.

Shortly after that I claimed that I was Jewish, having gotten the word from a friendly New York lawyer who was in for faking some of his clients' immigration papers. The kosher line was the only way to get a decent meal in there. In fact, for a long time they had a Jewish baker from Philadelphia locked up, and he made some truly delicious cream puffs for dessert. They sold for seventy-five cents on the black market, but once I had established myself in the Jewish community I got them as part of my regular fare. They fed us a great deal of peanut butter on the kosher line; every time the "goyim" got meat, we got peanut butter, but that was all right with me. Eventually I was asked to light the candles at the Friday evening services, since none of the real Jewish women bothered to attend. I have to admit that most of the members of our little prison congregation were genuine *alter kokers,* but some of them were amusing. And I enjoyed learning first hand about Judaism. The services were usually very quiet, and the music, the ancient intoning songs, fortified me against the screeching pop-rock vocal assaults that were a constant in the Women's Unit. I learned to think of myself as the *shabot shiksa,* and before my time was up, even the rabbi seemed to accept me.

At the end of the tour, you would find the jaded New Yorkers, sitting at a picnic table or two in the middle of the park, playing gin or poker and bragging about their days on Madison Avenue and

Wall Street, lamenting the scarcity of good deli, even on the kosher line, and planning where they would take their first real meal upon release.

If you think federal correctional institutions are about the business of rehabilitation, drop by for an orientation session one day. There at the front of the classroom, confronting rows of mostly black faces, will be the warden, or the assistant warden, or the prison shrink, pacing back and forth in front of the blackboard and asking the class, "Why do you think you're here?" This gets a general grumble, a few short, choked laughs. Some well-meaning soul always says it — rehabilitation. 15

"Nonsense!" the lecturer will say. "There are several reasons for locking people up. Number one is incapacitation. If you're in here, you can't be out there doing crime. Secondly, there is deterrence. Other people who are thinking about doing crime see that we lock people up for it and maybe they think twice. But the real reason you are here is to be punished. Plain and simple. You done wrong, now you got to pay for it. Rehabilitation ain't even part of the picture. So don't be looking to us to rehabilitate you. Only person can rehabilitate you is you. If you feel like it, go for it, but leave us out. We don't want to play that game."

So that's it. You're there to do time. I have no misgivings about why I went to prison. I deserved it. I was a cop, I got strung out on cocaine, I violated the rights of a pornographer. My own drug use as an undercover narcotics agent was a significant factor in my crime. But I did it and I deserved to be punished. Most of the people I met in Lexington, though, were in for drugs, and the majority of them hadn't done anything more than sell an ounce of cocaine or a pound of pot to some apostle of the law.

It seems lately that almost every time I look at the *New York Times* op-ed page, there is something about the drug problem. I have arrested people for drugs, and I have had a drug problem myself. I have seen how at least one federal correctional institution functions. It does not appear that the practice of locking people up for possession or distribution of an insignificant quantity of a controlled substance makes any difference at all in the amount of drug use that occurs in the United States. The drug laws are merely another convenient source of political rhetoric for aspiring officeholders. Politicians know that an antidrug stance is an easy way to get votes from parents who are terrified that their children might wind up as addicts. I do not advocate drug use. Yet, having seen the criminal justice system from several angles, as a police officer, a court bailiff, a defendant, and a prisoner, I am convinced that prison is not the answer to the drug problem, or for that matter to many other white-collar crimes. If the taxpayers knew how their dollars were being spent inside some prisons, they might actually scream out loud.

There were roughly 1,800 men and women locked up in Lex, at a ratio of approximately three men to every woman, and it did get warm in the summertime. To keep us tranquil they devised some rather peculiar little amusements. One evening I heard a commotion on the steps at the edge of Central Park and looked over to see a rec specialist with three big cardboard boxes set up on the plaza, marked 1, 2, and 3. There were a couple of hundred inmates sitting at the bottom of the steps. Dennis, the rec specialist, was conducting his own version of the television game show *Let's Make a Deal!* Under one of the boxes was a case of soda, under another was a racquetball glove, and under a third was a fly swatter. The captive contestant picked door number 2, which turned out to contain the fly swatter, to my way of thinking the best prize there. Fly swatters were virtually impossible to get through approved channels, and therefore cost as much as two packs of cigarettes on the black market.

I worked in Landscape, exiting the rear gate of the compound   20 each weekday morning at about nine after getting a half-hearted frisk from one of the hacks on duty. I would climb on my tractor to drive to the staff apartment complex and pull weeds or mow the lawn. Landscape had its prerogatives. We raided the gardens regularly and at least got to taste fresh vegetables from time to time. I had never eaten raw corn before, but it could not have tasted better. We also brought in a goodly supply of real vodka, and a bit of hash now and then, for parties in our rooms after lights out. One guy strapped a six-pack of Budweiser to his arms with masking tape and then put on his prison-issue Army field jacket. When he got to the rear gate, he raised his arms straight out at shoulder level, per instructions, and the hack patted down his torso and legs, never bothering to check his arms. The inmate had been counting on that. He smiled at the hack and walked back to his room, a six-pack richer.

Despite the fact that Lexington is known as a "country club" prison, I must admit that I counted days. From the first moment that I was in, I kept track of how many more times I would have to watch the sun sink behind eight feet of chain-link, of how many more days I would have to spend eating, working, playing and sleeping according to the dictates of a "higher authority." I don't think I can claim that I was rehabilitated. If anything I underwent a process of dehabilitation. What I learned was what Jessica Mitford tried to tell people many years ago in her book *Kind and Usual Punishment*. Prison is a business, no different from manufacturing tires or selling real estate. It keeps people employed and it provides cheap labor for NASA, the U.S. Postal Service, and other governmental or quasi-governmental agencies. For a short time, before I was employed in Landscape, I worked as a finisher of canvas mailbags, lacing white rope through metal eyelets around the top of the bags and attaching clamps to the ropes. I made one dollar and fourteen cents for every one hundred that I did. If I worked very hard, I could do almost two hundred a day.

It's not about justice. If you think it's about justice, look at the newspapers and notice who walks. Not the little guys, the guys doing a tiny bit of dealing, or sniggling a little on their income tax, or the woman who pulls a stunt with welfare checks because her husband has skipped out and she has no other way to feed her kids. I do not say that these things are right. But the process of selective prosecution, the "making" of cases by D.A.s and police departments, and the presence of some largely unenforceable statutes currently on the books (it is the reality of "compliance": no law can be forced on a public which chooses to ignore it, hence, selective prosecution) make for a criminal justice system which cannot realistically function in a fair and equitable manner. Criminal justice — I cannot decide if it is the ultimate oxymoron or a truly accurate description of the law enforcement process in America.

In my police undercover capacity, I have sat across the table from an armed robber who said, "My philosophy of life is slit thy neighbor's throat and pimp his kids." I believe that the human animals who maim and kill people should be dealt with, as they say, swiftly and surely. But this business of locking people up, at enormous cost, for minor, nonviolent offenses does not truly or effectively serve the interest of the people. It serves only to promote the wasteful aspects of the federal prison system, a system that gulps down tax dollars and spews up *Let's Make a Deal!*

I think about Lexington almost daily. I will be walking up Broadway to shop for groceries, or maybe riding my bike in the original Central Park and suddenly I'm wondering who's in there now, at this very moment, and for what inane violations, and what they are doing. Is it chow time, is the Big Yard open, is some inmate on stage in the auditorium singing "As Time Goes By" in a talent show? It is not a fond reminiscence, or a desire to be back in the Land of No Decisions. It is an awareness of the waste. The waste of tax dollars, yes, but taxpayers are used to that. It is the unnecessary trashing of lives that leaves me uneasy. The splitting of families, the enforced monotony, the programs which purport to prepare an inmate for re-entry into society but which actually succeed only in occupying a few more hours of the inmate's time behind the walls. The nonviolent offenders, such as small-time drug dealers and the economically deprived who were driven to crime out of desperation, could remain in society under less costly supervision, still undergoing "punishment" for their crime, but at least contributing to rather than draining the resources of society.

THE INVOLVED READER

1 What expectations concerning prison life did you bring to the reading of this article? What in the article lived up to your expectations? What was different, startling, or surprising?

2 Wozencraft organizes her observations around the idea of a tour for visitors. What are the waystations on her tour of her "country club" prison? What are major stages in this "trip in microcosm across the United States"?

3 What is the author's attitude toward the daily routine of prison life? Where do you think it shows most clearly? What hints on survival skills do you think she might give to future inmates?

4 What did the author learn from her experience? What does she have to say on subjects like rehabilitation, election-year rhetoric, and selective prosecution? What, to you, is her main point or central recommendation?

TALKING, THINKING, WRITING

5 Does the author's status as a police officer turned convict give her a special authority as an insider? Or does her own history make her a biased observer? For you, does her own history invalidate what she says?

6 Many Americans live in a homogenized world of shopping malls, freeways, and parking lots. Can you bring back the inside story on a place that other people seldom see? For instance, what goes on in emergency rooms? in psychiatric wards? in police stations? in soup kitchens? in juvenile detention centers? in special classes for the disabled?

COLLABORATIVE PROJECTS

7 Do you think the purpose of prison should be incapacitation, deterrence, punishment, or rehabilitation? You may want to help set up a panel discussion in which each of the participants chooses and argues the case for one of these alternatives.

MAKING CONNECTIONS

8   Norman Atkins in "The Cost of Living Clean" (in Chapter 2) and
Shapiro and Wozencraft (in this chapter) offer different perspectives on people "in trouble with the law" who help populate
America's rapidly growing Gulag archipelago of overcrowded
prisons. Can you pull together some key observations that voters concerned about crime might do well to keep in mind?

short story

Stockings

TIM O'BRIEN

Do you think of war as something that happens to other people? War, or protest against war, has often been the formative experience for a generation. The loss of the Vietnam War polarized American society and poisoned political discourse for a generation. In the sixties, an army of young Americans was sent to fight in Vietnam, and more than 50,000 died there. Tim O'Brien was a college student when he was drafted in 1968, and he went to Vietnam convinced that the war was wrong, "wrongly conceived and poorly justified." He said of his fellow GIs — those who died there and those who came back maimed or traumatized — "some thought the war was proper and others didn't and most didn't care." He told their story in If I Die in a Combat Zone Box Me Up and Ship Me Home *(1973) and* Going After Cacciato *(1976), the story of a GI who goes AWOL and is hunted down by his buddies as a deserter. His books evoke a conflict in which a highly disciplined Communist guerrilla force fought against poorly trained, demoralized American troops, trapped in a jungle war under constant threat of ambush, their clothes and skin rotting and their ammunition corroding in foxholes filled with mud and water.*

Henry Dobbins was a good man, and a superb soldier, but sophistication was not his strong suit. The ironies went beyond him. In many ways he was like America itself, big and strong, full of good intentions, a roll of fat jiggling at his belly, slow of foot but always plodding along, always there when you needed him, a believer in the virtues of simplicity and directness and hard labor. Like his country, too, Dobbins was drawn toward sentimentality.

Even now, twenty years later, I can see him wrapping his girlfriend's pantyhose around his neck before heading out on ambush.

It was his one eccentricity. The pantyhose, he said, had the properties of a good-luck charm. He liked putting his nose into the nylon and breathing in the scent of his girlfriend's body; he liked the memories this inspired; he sometimes slept with the stockings up against his face, the way an infant sleeps with a magic blanket, secure and peaceful. More than anything, though, the stockings were a talisman for him. They kept him safe. They gave access to a spiritual world, where things were soft and intimate, a place where he might someday take his girlfriend to live. Like many of us in Vietnam, Dobbins felt the pull of superstition, and he believed firmly and absolutely in the protective power of the stockings. They were like body armor, he thought. Whenever we saddled up for a late-night ambush, putting on our helmets and flak jackets, Henry Dobbins would make a ritual out of arranging the nylons around his neck, carefully tying a knot, draping the two leg sections over his left shoulder. There were some jokes, of course, but we came to appreciate the mystery of it all. Dobbins was invulnerable. Never wounded, never a scratch. In August, he tripped a Bouncing Betty, which failed to detonate. And a week later he got caught in the open during a fierce little firefight, no cover at all, but he just slipped the pantyhose over his nose and breathed deep and let the magic do its work.

It turned us into a platoon of believers. You don't dispute facts.

But then, near the end of October, his girlfriend dumped him. It was a hard blow. Dobbins went quiet for a while, staring down at her letter, then after a time he took out the stockings and tied them around his neck as a comforter.   5

"No sweat," he said. "I still love her. The magic doesn't go away."

It was a relief for all of us.

THE INVOLVED READER

1 Do the people in this story seem weird or alien to you? Or do you feel you understand them as if you were a brother or sister?

2 What does O'Brien mean when he says of Henry that "in many ways he was like America itself"?

TALKING, THINKING, WRITING

3 Have you been in situations where superstition played a role? Why would it play a special role in a wartime setting?

4 O'Brien's fiction often echoes the crude humor of his Vietnam buddies. Is there any humor in this story? Is O'Brien making fun of Henry? Does he look down on him?

5 Has war or the aftermath of war played a role in your experience or your family's experience? Or has war for you been something taking place in the media or in books?

poem

The Possessive

SHARON OLDS

Is the generation gap more than a cliché? The breakdown of communication between the generations — between children and their parents and then in turn their own children — has been a recurrent theme in American popular culture. Sharon Olds, who was born in San Francisco and studied at Stanford and Columbia, writes emotional and often startlingly frank poetry about the challenges, joys, and traumas of personal experience. One reviewer said, "Out of private revelations she makes poems of universal truth, of sex, death, fear, love. Her poems are sometimes jarring, unexpected, bold, but always loving and deeply rewarding" (Elizabeth Gaffney). Olds' poems have been published in a wide range of national and regional publications, and she began to be widely anthologized in the eighties as an outstanding representative of a new generation of women poets.

My daughter — as if I
owned her — that girl with the
hair wispy as a frayed bellpull

has been to the barber, that knife grinder,
and had the edge of her hair sharpened.   5

Each strand now cuts
both ways. The blade of new bangs
hangs over her red-brown eyes
like carbon steel.

        All the little   10
spliced ropes are sliced. The curtain of
dark paper-cuts veils the face that
started from next to nothing in my body —

My body. My daughter. I'll have to find
another word. In her bright helmet   15
she looks at me as if across a
great distance. Distant fires can be
glimpsed in the resin light of her eyes:

the watch fires of an enemy, a while before
the war starts.   20

THE INVOLVED READER

1   Poets usually do not use dry, matter-of-fact language but draw on imaginative comparisons instead. Olds speaks the language of metaphor when she calls the daughter's hair a "bright helmet." Why does the daughter's haircut become such a big issue in this poem? What other key metaphors does the mother use to express her feelings about the daughter? What do these metaphors have in common?

2   Imaginative comparisons that are spelled out, signaled by *like* or *as*, are called similes. The simile is a close cousin or a special kind of metaphor. Can you find several similes in this poem?

3   *My* is one of the possessive pronouns (like also *your, his,* and *her*), which show where or to whom something belongs. Why does the use of this pronoun become an issue in this poem?

TALKING, THINKING, WRITING

4   What is it about hair that often makes it a point of contention? Have you seen hair become a symbol or an issue in the conflict between generations or between conflicting values?

5   Does the reader have to be a mother to empathize with the mother speaking in this poem? Why or why not?

6   In your experience, is the generation gap a tired cliché or a major factor in young people's growing up?

MAKING CONNECTIONS

7   How would you compare and contrast the child's point of view in Constans' essay (earlier in this chapter) and the parent's point of view in Olds' poem?

The Writer's Tools 3

Making Your Sentences Count

A writer doesn't look with her eyes; she looks with her words. She doesn't listen with her ears; she listens with her words. She doesn't touch with her fingers; she touches with her words.

ABBY FRUCHT

How can you make each sentence count? Writers with a good eye for detail pack a sentence with the authentic touches that make writing come to life. They give us images to see, sounds to hear, textures to feel.

Snapshot Sentences

Snapshot sentences call up a person or a scene before the reader's eye. How did the student authors pack each of the following sentences with sensory details?

On a hot August afternoon on First Street, I saw a gray-haired woman in a ragged woollen coat and basketball shoes pushing a supermarket wire basket filled with crumpled cans, her head hung low.

In the computer center, the clicking of keyboards, the clatter of teletypes, and the hum of an idle printer bounce off each other in an area where cables snake across the floor.

Details First

In a details-first sentence, you give convincing, authentic details first — to show that you have really looked at what a general label stands for. Study the following examples:

The overpowering aroma of seafood, glazed fisheyes looking up at the customer, the ruffling of butcher paper, the jangle of the cash register: this is a fishmarket.

The sterile white floors and walls; the people pushed in their wheelchairs; the stale smell of overcooked food; the sad, lonely faces of people once young and spirited, now forgotten and left alone: this is a nursing home.

Sentence Stretching

Through sentence workouts, you can expand a bare-minimum sentence until your readers say: "That's quite a sentence!" The original sentence may have little more than a subject and a verb: "A woman (subject) runs (verb)." The expanded sentence would fill in when, where, how, why, or which one or what kind.

BARE-BONES SENTENCE: A woman runs.

EXPANDED: A slim, dark-haired woman runs ten miles each day over back country roads in preparation for the "Heart of America" Marathon, sponsored by the Columbia Track Club each Labor Day in Columbia, Missouri.

Multiple Examples

Effective writers pile up graphic examples until we say: "I see the point!" Multiple-examples sentences fill in the blanks in sentence frames like the following with striking real-life examples.

SENTENCE FRAMES: Messages I tune out include _____.
_____ are part of the constant stream of junk mail.

COMPLETED: Messages I tune out include ads for gold coins ("Valued at ten times the original price!"), Vegematics ("Slice 'em and dice 'em in ten seconds flat!"), Ginsu knives used by real Japanese chefs, and furniture stores that promise instant credit and deliver ugly dinettes.
Applications for credit cards, grocery store coupons, department store sales promotions, and contest literature ("You may already be a winner!") are part of the constant stream of junk mail.

Imaginative Comparisons

Live prose makes telling use of imaginative comparisons. The following sentences call up vivid images, using similes (introduced by *like* or *as*) or metaphors (no signal such as *like* or *as*):

The hang glider, with bright rainbow colors on its back, dove slowly down, looking like a piece of paper floating down from a six-story building.

The marching band changed direction like a school of minnows as the players moved as one on the football field.

His pen moved with the rapid, jerky motions of the needle on a seismograph, charting the flow of his thoughts.

WRITING WORKSHOP 3

The Sentence Workout

1 Write three or four *snapshot* sentences about people and places you have observed. Here is an additional example.

The quiet boy sat angled on the edge of his creaking desk chair, eyes glazed behind his wire-rimmed glasses, nearly kissing the monitor as he tapped away at the keys of his faithful PC.

2   Write three or four *details-first* sentences. Here is an additional example.

The cherry-red color, the sleek design, the original black-pony leather interior, the chrome wheels, and the rebuilt Ford Motorsport engine that gives off the most beautiful shine — my 1965 Ford Mustang.

3   Expand *bare-bones* sentences. Choose three or four of the following:

BARE BONES: A woman runs.
                  Sports attract crowds.
                  Fitness centers cater to customers.
                  Companies pollute.
                  Skiers head for the slopes.
                  Musicians perform.
                  Painters paint.

SAMPLE SENTENCE: Bone-crunching, body-bashing sports attract action-craving beer-drinking crowds in all parts of the country.

4   Write three or four sentences in which you pile on *multiple examples*. Fill in the blanks in the following:

People I dislike include _____.
Sensational trials feature _____.
_____ are part of the constant stream of junk mail.
People who call in to talk shows include _____.
_____ crowd the shelves of my favorite bookstore.

SAMPLE SENTENCE: People I dislike coming to my door include sales reps selling carpet cleaner, pestering children selling chocolate bars, Greenpeace asking for donations to save the environment, and those souls who want to repaint my address on the curb.

5   Write several sentences in which you bring a place or person to life by using a striking *imaginative comparison*. Here is an additional example:

As the car raced down the straight forest road, the sun flashed behind the tall pines, shining a strobe light into our eyes.

We write to find out what we think. Even when doing something as simple as writing in a journal — intellectual doodling — you're figuring out things. Writing is a way of laying things out. You write to find out what you think, what you know, and what you don't know.

LARRY HEINEMANN

Charting the Trend

Writing to Learn

Have you ever tried to make sense of a changing situation — sorting out signs that things were not as they once were? Do you read or listen to trend watchers who ask where we are headed? Much instructive writing is done by writers whose minds are not made up. They write to learn. They look at current trends, trying to see how familiar patterns are changing. They reexamine familiar ideas because they no longer fit the facts. They arrive at tentative generalizations, and they revise and adjust them in the light of new observations.

Trend watchers formulate general conclusions on topics like the following:

• Is student aid drying up?

• Are older students reentering college more mature and productive than their younger counterparts?

• Are the real wages of American workers declining?

• Will the next wave of feminism be women in low-income jobs?

• Do children hold women back in their careers?

• Is the traditional family doomed?

What kind of paper could show your willingness to learn? Suppose you are a member of a group that has been the target of prejudice in the past. What do you know about how prejudice works today? You start jotting down notes like the following:

PREWRITING NOTES:

> A friend talks about why he would just as soon stay away from whites: "They do not necessarily reject me, but they consider me only an acquaintance — not someone to be close to. I find it easier to be friends with people like myself."
>
> My parents advise me against choosing a business major and aiming at a business career. They tell me I have two strikes against me — I am female and I'm not white.
>
> Every time I tell my friend about a job opening that seems right for him, he finds an alibi for failing to apply. "Look at their staff," he says. "They are all white kids from private schools. I don't have a chance."

What do these observations tell you? People from a minority background are used to encountering evidence of prejudice, subtle or crude. Apparently, however, prejudice often does its work even when not applied from the outside. The people who are its targets may have *internalized* it. People live up to the stereotypes that make them different. They stay with "their own kind." They head for jobs traditionally assigned to people like them. Here is a tentative generalization that could become the central idea or thesis for a paper:

TRIAL THESIS: Prejudice works from within as well as from without; we at times conform to damaging stereotypes that we have internalized.

Although your paper will draw mainly on personal experience, you may decide to bolster it by bringing in supporting materials from your reading and from informal interviews:

Drawing on Your Reading To show how aware you are of the role of external prejudice, you may decide to quote an African American writer who wrote that being black in this society is like adding "a hundred extra pounds to your weight."

Drawing on Informal Interviews You may decide to talk to one or two faculty members from minority backgrounds, expecially if they have participated in mentor programs or are actively involved in minority politics. One of them, for instance, may talk about refusing to conform to the natural rhythm stereotype and be his natural bookish self.

The learning experience you went through in exploring this topic may suggest a three-step strategy for your paper:

Living the Stereotype

STEP 1: You give one or two striking examples of prejudice applied to you or someone else from without. (This is what many people know and expect.)

STEP 2:   You then present your claim that prejudice also works from within: People have internalized damaging stereotypes. They may play up to them consciously or unthinkingly. (Here you depart from the familiar emphasis.)

STEP 3:   You give convincing examples of how people live up to damaging stereotypes. (Here you present the evidence that made you reach your conclusion.)

THOUGHT LOG 4

Thinking about Trends

In your thought log, write about trends you have observed on your campus. Try to include colorful convincing examples. The trends you observe might be lifestyle trends. For instance, are there new fashions in clothes, music, parties, television viewing, movies? However, the trends might also be intellectual trends. What topics seem to be popular in discussions, editorials in the student newspaper, public lectures, educational campaigns?

Pushing toward a Thesis

Facts do not speak for themselves, nor do figures add up on their own. Even the most vividly detailed report or computer printout requires someone to make sense of the information it contains.

NANCY R. COMLEY

As a writer, you will often be pushing toward a general conclusion after taking in much detail. Generalizing after a study of examples is a basic way we process information. If you have become interested in race relations on campus, you may over the course of a few weeks make observations pointing in the same direction:

EXAMPLES:
African American students congregate at one particular corner of the inner quad. A black friend reports that black students who spend much of their time with whites are frowned upon or ostracized by others of their group.

Vietnamese students gather together between classes, speaking Vietnamese.

Latino or Hispanic students spend much time together at events with Hispanic cultural or political themes.

Whites congregate with whites; one teacher notes the existence of a "white boys' club" in several of her classes.

Teachers you talk to confirm what you saw and are concerned about students' tendency to stay within their own group. An advisor for foreign students deplores the voluntary segregation of students from other countries. After mulling over what you have seen and heard, you may draw a conclusion that could become the trial thesis of a paper:

TRIAL THESIS: Here and on other campuses, voluntary segregation has replaced the enforced segregation of the past.

As you formulate this conclusion, you may remember evidence of a countertrend: Women's groups on campus make a special effort to involve minority women. You decide to note this countertrend in your introduction or in your conclusion as an encouraging exception.

In your paper, you will often present your general conclusion as the **thesis** or central idea early in your paper. The rest of the paper then backs up the claim you have staked out. The thesis-first approach has several advantages. First, a strong thesis helps focus your paper. It sets directions; it helps chart your course. Second, an effective thesis is a promise to the reader. It keeps you alert to the need to fulfill that promise by delivering detailed, authentic, convincing examples.

WRITING WORKSHOP I

The Common Thread

In recent years, there has been much concern about how to avoid offensive language. The following excerpts are from guidelines first published in *Ms.* magazine. What general conclusion or conclusions can you draw about their intent or impact? What to you seems to be the common denominator of these instructions? Do any seem to point in a different direction — are there exceptions to your general conclusion?

A M O J A   T H R E E   R I V E R S

Cultural Etiquette: A Guide

"Exotic," when applied to human beings, is ethnocentric and racist.

While it is true that most citizens of the U.S.A. are white, at least four fifths of the world's population consists of people of color. Therefore, it is statistically incorrect as well as ethnocentric to refer to us as minorities.

The term "minority" is used to reinforce the idea of people of color as "other."

A cult is a particular system of religious worship. If the religious practices of the Yorubas constitute a cult, then so do those of the Methodists, Catholics, Episcopalians, and so forth.

A large radio/tape player is a boom-box, or a stereo or a box or a large metallic ham sandwich with speakers. It is not a "ghetto blaster."

Asians are not "mysterious," "fatalistic," or "inscrutable."

Native Americans are not stoic, mystical, or vanishing.

Latin people are no more hot-tempered, hot-blooded, or emotional than anyone else. We do not have flashing eyes, teeth, or daggers. We are lovers pretty much like other people. Very few of us deal with any kind of drugs.

Middle Easterners are not fanatics, terrorists, or all oil-rich.

If you are white, don't brag to a person of color about your overseas trip to our homeland. Especially when we cannot afford such a trip. Similarly, don't assume that we are overjoyed to see the expensive artifacts you bought.

Southerners are no less intelligent than anybody else.

It is not a compliment to tell someone: "I don't think of you as Jewish/ Black/Asian/Latina/Middle Eastern/Native American." Or "I think of you as white."

It is not "racism in reverse" or "segregation" for Jews or people of color to come together in affinity groups for mutual support. Sometimes we need some time and space apart from the dominant group just to relax and be ourselves.

"Race" is an arbitrary and meaningless concept. Races among humans don't exist. If there ever was any such thing as race, there has been so much constant crisscrossing of genes for the last 500,000 years that it would have lost all meaning anyway.

WRITING WORKSHOP 2

Working with a Trial Thesis

Each of the following student-written passages points toward a general conclusion that could become the central idea of a paper. Could you help the writer support and develop his or her trial thesis? Can you think of real-life examples, firsthand experiences, or input from viewing and reading that might be used to support the general conclusion? (Can you think of *counterexamples* that the writer may have to take into account?)

1 I found that many students do not like to be classified as "Caucasian" or as "European American." Like the term *Asian*, these labels lump

together people from many different cultures with widely divergent histories.

2 The dragon that every woman, especially Asian women, must slay is the stereotype that makes women subordinate to men. In the workplace, women still bump into the glass ceiling that keeps them from being promoted to management positions along with men. Asians are stereotyped as brainy nerds that do homework all day long and have no social lives; they are expected to be quiet types that are taught to make no waves in society. When I am passed over for an assignment or for a promotion, I always have to ask myself: Is it because I am a woman, or because I am Asian, or both?

3 It is a common sight on television newscasts now to have one of the anchors be a person of color: a white male and an Asian female, or a white female and a black male. When I worked for a telemarketing company, I remember being asked to pose for a picture for the company brochure along with a friend who was Mexican. Naturally our multicultural click was included in the brochure to show the "family atmosphere" of the firm. We both suspected at the time that we had been hired because the corporation needed some "color" for occasions like publicity brochures.

| WRITING WORKSHOP 3 |

A Paper for Peer Review

On what does the writer of the following paper base her general conclusions? Where does she spell them out most clearly or effectively? Does the evidence that she presents justify her generalizations? What is the mix of personal experience, firsthand observation, and expert opinion? How might the writer improve the flow? What shifting of material would you recommend to the writer?

Thin Is Beautiful

Each week brings another fat-to-thin, rags-to-riches story about a woman who was once one hundred pounds overweight but lost it all by following her custom-designed diet plan with an additional fifty hours of hardcore exercise. From Tommy Lasorda's Ultra-Slim Fast Weight Loss powder or Linda Evans' Weight Watcher's 50 Calories Per Meal to Ann Jillian's Nestle's Sweet Success, thousands of Americans buy into the diet insanity. The covers of almost every beauty magazine picture a slim, elegant, 5′8″ woman without bulging thighs or hips. This is how the media see the woman of today — skinny, almost weightless, satisfied, and beautiful. Women's magazines shout such headlines as "Firm Your Thighs and Hips in Just 15 Minutes!" or "4 Easy Summer Exercises So You Can Be Slim in Your Swimsuit." Although being healthy and fit should be everyone's concern, the gimmicks and programs of the diet industry have pushed things too far. Magazine articles and advertisements use supermodels like Cindy Crawford as spokespeople to promote the ideal look that women should strive for. However, somewhere between the diet bars and strenuous workouts is the innocent woman left stranded in no man's land, desperately trying to be victorious in the battle of the bulge.

Millions are invested to lure the customers into investing their paychecks in weight loss programs and diet gimmicks. In the words of Susan Wooley, a psychiatrist at the University of Cincinnati Medical College, "there are hundreds of diet drinks, bars, powders, and meals floating around in the supermarkets. The presence of these diet products is one of many factors which contribute to the paranoia of the public to become overly conscious about their physical appearance." Celebrities, the rich and famous, are enlisted to help promote these products. Such influential spokespeople as Ann Jillian and Kathy Lee Gifford are presented to the viewers as having been diet successes. Sports star Tommy Lasorda makes male viewers want to lose those beer bellies. Media marketing techniques are not only appealing, they are misleading as well. Inside those weight loss packages of diet bars, the fine print says: "WARNING: The use of this product may cause kidney disorders, nausea, cramps, menstrual irregularities, and other medical complications. Consult a physician before following any dietary program." In watching only three hours of daytime television programing, I saw thirty-one commercials pertaining to some kind of weight loss or diet product. Almost half of the advertisements we see in newspapers, in magazines, and on television remind us of the battle to lose weight.

On billboards, we see thin, slender supermodels that make us envy those million-dollar bodies. The television industry feeds the public's notion that to be famous we would first have to be thin, as if being in the limelight added twenty pounds to a person's figure. The obsession with looking like a supermodel goes back to the time when *Vogue* magazine introduced the Twiggy look. Twiggy had a slender body, high cheek bones, and emaciated legs; she looked so fragile that if she were to stand in the wind, she might snap in two. Although women come in all shapes and sizes, models — the women chosen to represent the ideal female form — are thinner now than ever. According to Catherine Cavendor, executive editor of *Seventeen* magazine, the ever-present media images cause our society "to reward underweight women — by making them supermodels, Miss Americas, and other types of sex symbols." Although it is perfectly all right to want to be beautiful and fit, some women are pressured by the calorie counts and exercise tapes to sacrifice their health in order to attain the cover girl look.

One in every hundred adolescent girls develops anorexia. Another two or three out of a hundred develop bulimia. According to a study in *Consumer Research* magazine, one in every 250 American females ages twelve to eighteen develops an eating disorder, and nine percent of these die of starvation. The incidence of these eating disorders has more than doubled in the last two decades. For many young women who develop such disorders, the message has been that "one should strive for perfection; asceticism is superior to self-indulgence; thinness is admirable; fat is disgusting and weight gain means that one is bad or out of control." In an article in *Cosmopolitan*, one former anorexic admits "I thought I was the perfect weight. Then I noticed just how ardently boys looked at those skinny cover girl models. Comparing them to myself, I was haunted by the feeling that they were all more attractive — meaning thinner — than I." The media have brainwashed the women of America to the point that some risk their lives by starving themselves in order to be considered perfect.

I know I always felt guilty each time I took a bite of chocolate. I would see the beautiful models in magazines, and I was obsessed with trying to look thin. I remember a month before my senior prom I wanted to lose twenty pounds so badly that I tried diet drinks and gained more weight than I lost. I finally realized that not everyone can be on the cover of *Vogue*. Too much money is being invested in trying to change the average woman into the ideal cover girl. Instead of focusing our attention on issues such as AIDS, social injustice, and poverty, we waste effort on trying to manufacture the perfect you.

Reworking Your Generalization Paper

When you look back over a first draft, you have a chance to reexamine your general conclusions. You may want to check an early draft against guidelines like the following:

Sweeping Generalization Are you making any unsupported sweeping claims? Are you making charges that apply to *all* men, or *all* women, or the media in general? This is the time to reconsider statements that apply to the whole "white community" or "black community." To avoid charges of **hasty generalization,** word your claims more cautiously, and buttress them with convincing examples.

TOO SWEEPING: Americans have lost faith in the political system.

[COMMENT: But a public figure like Ross Perot was able to start a millions-strong political grass-roots movement. Millions have watched debates on the federal deficit or on international trade agreements. American election campaigns drag on for months and months, with every minor development covered by the media.]

SCALED DOWN: Many Americans say they have lost faith in the political system. For instance, . . . Another striking example . . . A recent case in point. . . .

Oversimplification   Have you recognized exceptions and complications? Perhaps you are setting out to show the damage done by the "beauty myth" — by media images that promote the "waif look" of the thin, half-starved supermodel. At some point, you may want to acknowledge exceptions: Some of the most successful female television personalities — Roseanne, Oprah — have not been stereotypically thin. By making **concessions** like the following, you preempt potential counterarguments:

> *It is true that* political campaigns generate much hoopla and receive extensive media coverage. Issues like abortion or NAFTA (the North American Free Trade Agreement) generate heated controversies. However, *many Americans today are losing faith in the political system.* Even when they make their voices heard, they do not really expect the government to do anything for them or for the political process to resolve the nation's problems. . . .

Representative Sample   Are you using a representative sample? After talking mainly to business majors, you may have written: "Today's generation of students is materialistic, looking only at the bottom line." However, your sample — even of business majors — is probably much too small to warrant such a sweeping indictment. A more **representative sample** should include students majoring in art, music, literature, or comparative religion — but also in areas like engineering, where pride in achievement and competence matter, as well as material incentives.

Case in Point   Have you built up key examples? To support charges of sensationalism in current journalism, you should do more than mention briefly the media coverage of a recent lurid trial. Instead, make it a **case in point**. Give it an in-depth look. Show that you have sat through a day's television coverage of court proceedings or waded through the sordid details in a week's newspaper coverage.

Here is a passage from a media-watching paper before and after revision:

> SKIMPY: Vigilante justice has become a major theme in mainstream Hollywood movies. Whether it is an indignant soldier taking on a corrupt army establishment or a vengeful woman killing the man who raped her, it is hard to find an action film today without this type of violence. *The blockbuster movie* True Romance *was entirely about a vigilante and his killing spree. The movie not only glorified his actions; it made them romantic.*

> BUILT UP: Vigilante justice has become a major theme in mainstream Hollywood movies. Whether it be an indignant soldier taking on a

corrupt army establishment or a vengeful woman killing the man who raped her, it is hard to find an action film today without this type of violence. *The blockbuster movie* True Romance *was entirely about a vigilante and his killing spree. The movie not only glorified his actions; it made them romantic. After falling in love with a prostitute, the hero vows to free her from her pimp. He goes to the pimp's bar and murders five people. Upon hearing the news, the prostitute begins to cry. The hero doesn't understand and asks what is wrong. She replies, "That's the most romantic thing anyone's ever done for me."*

Hypothetical Examples   Real-life cases are more convincing than hypothetical examples. It is too easy to make up an imaginary couple to act out your theories about the breakdown of communication in relationships. It is easy to invent a "typical" business student who illustrates neatly what you are trying to prove. To convince the skeptical reader, you will have to work in authentic real-life cases, genuine real-life situations.

WRITING WORKSHOP 4

Testing Generalizations

How often do you find yourself questioning someone else's generalizations? Which of the following statements would you challenge? On what grounds? What counterexamples or counterarguments could you offer?

1 Journalism is a business like any other. A television station structures its news programs to attract high ratings and well-paying sponsors. A newspaper packages its news so that it will attract buyers for the paper. The network or newspaper executive's job is the same as that of the corner grocer: to attract buying customers.
2 In America, all ethnic groups watch the same TV shows, live in boxes of similar design and decor, wear about the same clothing, and eat the same convenience foods. . . . The nationality-based social club and athletic team, the foreign language newspaper, the church, the Kosher butcher, and the ethnic political organization are all in steep decline.

Martin Mayer

3 On the subject of male nurses: If a man wants to be a nurse, let him find a job in a veterans' hospital. Men should confine their nursing to men only (or they should stay in man's work altogether). Women are by nature caretakers. We take care of family members when they are sick. In the end, we women take care of elderly patients. Men are too self-absorbed to provide care for others; a fair percentage of them are

child molesters, wife beaters, serial murderers, and all-around louses.
4 The TV manipulators of reality have discovered that Americans will
trust anyone who is good-looking.

OPTIONS FOR WRITING 4

Trend Watchers

Start working on a paper in which you report your findings as a
trend watcher. Look for relevant material in newspapers, newsmagazines, television commercials, television shows, or current
movies. Talk to people likely to be concerned; conduct at least one
informal interview. Draw on your own experience and observation.
Choose one of the following:

1 Many voices have denounced the cult of violence on the big and
   small screen. How is violence portrayed in current megahit
   movies? Has television violence become more brutal? (You may
   want to concentrate either on movies or TV, or on one special
   area.) Can anything be said in defense of the current level of
   violence in the media?

2 Do current movies and television shows glorify vigilante justice?
   Do they glamorize people who take the law into their own hands?

3 Is violence on the rise in your community? Study recent newspaper reports. Talk to people in a position to know. Draw on
   personal experience and observation.

4 Americans have often thought of themselves as a "nation of immigrants." Is there a backlash against earlier attitudes welcoming the immigrant? How strong is it? What causes it?

5 Is it true that the media brainwash American women to starve
   themselves? How pervasive is the anorexic look? Are feminists
   right about the "beauty myth"?

6 Is there an anti-male bias in current movie or television entertainment? Are men likely to be portrayed as violent and abusive?
   Are new stereotypes about aggressive males being created?

7 Is it true that the media undermine family values? What family
   values do critics of the media have in mind? How are these values being undermined?

8 Do the media promote the image of a new sensitive male? Is
   there evidence of a new sensitized, politically correct male?

9 How does our society treat the disabled? How has the public image of people with disabilities changed in recent years?

10 Choose one ethnic, racial, or cultural minority in which you have a special interest. Do you think it is fairly represented on TV? Is it represented fairly in terms of either its percentage of the population or its importance in American life?

Reading, Discussion, Writing

Observing the Scene

OVERVIEW: The writers in the following group generalize about trends that are changing our society. The self-images of men and women, the career expectations of Americans, the way the media shape our perception of reality — these are in flux, and these writers try to help us understand our changing lives. Where do they turn for evidence? How sound are their conclusions? Which of them concern you most as a reader?

The Community of Men

ROBERT BLY

We make the path by walking.

ROBERT BLY

Is there a "men's movement" to counterbalance the women's movement in today's world? Robert Bly, American poet and translator, has taught audiences around the country to think of poetry as a performance art. According to Bly, in the words of one of his readers, "women in the last few decades have begun to rediscover what femininity is, while for men — separated from their fathers and from other male models — the concept of masculinity gets progressively blurred" (Mihaly Csikszentmilhalyi).

Bly looks at literature — from fairy tales, legends, and myths to the work of today's poets — as lore providing a rallying point for the defensive, disoriented modern male. Through literature we can explore how to meet new situations, how to develop "new ways of responding that we can adopt when the conventional and current ways wear out." In 1990, Bly published Iron John: A Book about Men, *which Deborah Tannen called "a brilliantly eclectic written meditation on why men today are unhappy, and how they can become happier." Bly has said that today's typical sensitive young man, when called a chauvinist or sexist by his female partner, does not fight back but "opens his shirt so she can see more clearly where to put the lances." A new collection of his poems,* Meditations on the Insatiable Soul, *appeared in 1994.*

We are living at an important and fruitful moment now, for it is clear to men that the images of adult manhood given by the popular culture are worn out; a man can no longer depend on them. By the time a man is thirty-five he knows that the images of the right man, the tough man, the true man which he received in high school do not work in life. Such a man is open to new visions of what a man is or could be.

The hearth and fairy stories have passed, as water through fifty feet of soil, through generations of men and women, and we can trust their images more than, say, those invented by Hans Christian Andersen. The images the old stories give — stealing the key from under the mother's pillow, picking up a golden feather fallen from the burning breast of the Firebird, finding the Wild Man under the lake water, following the tracks of one's own wound through the forest and finding that it resembles the tracks of a god — these are meant to be taken slowly into the body. They continue to unfold, once taken in.

It is in the old myths that we hear, for example, of Zeus energy, that positive leadership energy in men, which popular culture constantly declares does not exist; from King Arthur we learn the value of the male mentor in the lives of young men; we hear from the Iron John story the importance of moving from the mother's realm to the father's realm; and from all initiation stories we learn how essential it is to leave our parental expectations entirely and find a second father or "second King."

The dark side of men is clear. Their mad exploitation of earth resources, devaluation and humiliation of women, and obsession with tribal warfare are undeniable. Genetic inheritance contributes to their obsessions, but also culture and environment. We have defective mythologies that ignore masculine depth of feeling, assign men a place in the sky instead of earth, teach obedience to the wrong powers, work to keep men boys, and entangle both men and women in systems of industrial domination that exclude both matriarchy and patriarchy.

Most of the language in my book speaks to heterosexual men but does not exclude homosexual men. It wasn't until the eighteenth century that people ever used the term homosexual; before that time gay men were understood simply as a part of the large community of men. The mythology as I see it does not make a big distinction between homosexual and heterosexual men. 5

We talk a great deal about "the American man," as if there were some constant quality that remained stable over decades, or even within a single decade.

The men who live today have veered far away from the Saturnian, old-man-minded farmer, proud of his introversion, who arrived in New England in 1630, willing to sit through three services in an unheated church. In the South, an expansive, motherbound cavalier developed, and neither of these two "American men" resembled the greedy railroad entrepreneur that later developed in the Northeast, nor the reckless I-will-do-without culture settlers of the West.

Even in our own era the agreed-on model has changed dramatically. During the fifties, for example, an American character appeared with some consistency that became a model of manhood adopted by many men: the Fifties male.

He got to work early, labored responsibly, supported his wife and children, and admired discipline. Reagan is a sort of mummified version of this dogged type. This sort of man didn't see women's souls well, but he appreciated their bodies; and his view of culture and America's part in it was boyish and optimistic. Many of his qualities were strong and positive, but underneath the charm and bluff there was, and there remains, much isolation, deprivation, and passivity. Unless he has an enemy, he isn't sure that he is alive.

The Fifties man was supposed to like football, be aggressive, stick   10
up for the United States, never cry, and always provide. But receptive space or intimate space was missing in this image of a man. The personality lacked some sense of flow. The psyche lacked compassion in a way that encouraged the unbalanced pursuit of the Vietnam war, just as, later, the lack of what we might call "garden" space inside Reagan's head led to his callousness and brutality toward the powerless in El Salvador, toward old people here, the unemployed, schoolchildren, and poor people in general.

The Fifties male had a clear vision of what a man was, and what male responsibilities were, but the isolation and one-sidedness of his vision were dangerous.

During the sixties, another sort of man appeared. The waste and violence of the Vietnam war made men question whether they knew what an adult male really was. If manhood meant Vietnam, did they want any part of it? Meanwhile, the feminist movement encouraged men to actually look at women, forcing them to become conscious of concerns and sufferings that the Fifties male labored to avoid. As men began to examine women's history and women's sensibility, some men began to notice what was called their *feminine* side and pay attention to it. This process continues to this day, and I would say that most contemporary men are involved in it in some way.

There's something wonderful about this development — I mean the practice of men welcoming their own "feminine" consciousness and nurturing it — this is important — and yet I have the sense that there is something wrong. The male in the past twenty years has become more thoughtful, more gentle. But by this process he has not become more free. He's a nice boy who pleases not only his mother but also the young woman he is living with.

In the seventies I began to see all over the country a phenomenon that we might call the "soft male." Sometimes even today when I look at an audience, perhaps half the young males are what I'd call soft. They're lovely, valuable people — I like them — they're not interested in harming the earth or starting wars. There's a gentle attitude toward life in their whole being and style of living.

But many of these men are not happy. You quickly notice the   15 lack of energy in them. They are life-preserving but not exactly life-giving. Ironically, you often see these men with strong women who positively radiate energy.

Here we have a finely tuned young man, ecologically superior to his father, sympathetic to the whole harmony of the universe, yet he himself has little vitality to offer.

The strong or life-giving women who graduated from the sixties, so to speak, or who have inherited an older spirit, played an important part in producing this life-preserving, but not life-giving, man.

I remember a bumper sticker during the sixties that read "WOMEN SAY YES TO MEN WHO SAY NO." We recognize that it took a lot of courage to resist the draft, go to jail, or move to Canada, just as it took courage to accept the draft and go to Vietnam. But the women of twenty years ago were definitely saying that they preferred the softer receptive male.

So the development of men was affected a little in this preference. Nonreceptive maleness was equated with violence, and receptive maleness was rewarded.

Some energetic women, at that time and now in the nineties, 20 chose and still choose soft men to be their lovers and, in a way, perhaps, to be their sons. The new distribution of "yang" energy among couples didn't happen by accident. Young men for various reasons wanted their harder women, and women began to desire softer men. It seemed like a nice arrangement for a while, but we've lived with it long enough now to see that it isn't working out.

I first learned about the anguish of "soft" men when they told their stories in early men's gatherings. In 1980, the Lama Community in New Mexico asked me to teach a conference for men only, their first, in which about forty men participated. Each day we concentrated on one Greek god and one old story, and then late in the afternoon we gathered to talk. When the younger men spoke it was not uncommon for them to be weeping within five minutes. The amount of grief and anguish in these younger men was astounding to me.

Part of their grief rose out of remoteness from their fathers, which they felt keenly, but partly, too, grief flowed from trouble in their marriages or relationships. They had learned to be receptive, but receptivity wasn't enough to carry their marriages through troubled times. In every relationship something *fierce* is needed once in a while: both the man and the woman need to have it. But at the point when it was needed, often the young man came up short. He was nurturing, but something else was required — for his relationship, and for his life.

The "soft" male was able to say, "I can feel your pain, and I consider your life as important as mine, and I will take care of you and comfort you." But he could not say what he wanted, and stick by it. *Resolve* of that kind was a different matter.

In *The Odyssey*, Hermes instructs Odysseus that when he approaches Circe, who stands for a certain kind of matriarchal energy, he is to lift or show his sword. In these early sessions it was difficult for many of the younger men to distinguish between showing the sword and hurting someone. One man, a kind of incarnation of certain spiritual attitudes of the sixties, a man who had actually lived in a tree for a year outside Santa Cruz, found himself unable to extend his arm when it held a sword. He had learned so well not to hurt anyone that he couldn't lift the steel, even to catch the light of the sun on it. But showing a sword doesn't necessarily mean fighting. It can also suggest a joyful decisiveness.

The journey many American men have taken into softness, or receptivity, or "development of the feminine side," has been an immensely valuable journey, but more travel lies ahead.   25

THE INVOLVED READER

 1 What for you is the keynote in Bly's introduction? What perspective is he establishing? What seems to be his agenda?

 2 What models for the true American does Bly find in the nation's early history? Which of these models do you recognize? (What is the meaning of *Saturnian* and *cavalier*?)

 3 According to Bly, what made the fifties male? What are his strengths? What are his weaknesses? What is his fatal flaw?

 4 What, according to Bly, explains the emergence of the sixties male? What about the sixties male appeals to Bly? What does Bly think is lacking?

 5 Does Bly chart a direction for the future? What is Bly's own vision of the ideal male?

READING, THINKING, WRITING

 6 Is the fifties man extinct? Or has there been a resurgence of his type? Do you identify with or feel attracted to the sixties man?

 7 Bly claims that he is not trying to resuscitate a John Wayne macho image. Nevertheless, feminist reviewers have accused him of rehabilitating the traditional chauvinist, patriarchal male. Are they right?

 8 Do we tend to debunk our leaders — cutting them down to size? (Is it true that our popular culture constantly denies the existence of "positive leadership energy"?)

COLLABORATIVE PROJECTS

9 Can you identify images of the American woman that have played a similar role as the images of manhood identified by Bly? For instance, working with a group, what would you include in capsule portraits of pioneer woman, fifties woman, sixties woman, liberated woman?

Talk TV: Tuning In to Trouble

JEANNE ALBRONDA HEATON AND
NONA LEIGH WILSON

*How do the media shape our perception of reality? How heavily
does our thinking about crime, sexual harassment, skinheads, or inflation depend on images fed to us by the mass media? The authors of
the following article on talk television are concerned about how TV
talk shows have changed from their promising beginnings, when they
gave women an opportunity to air their concerns, to look at issues
from a woman's point of view. How do today's TV talk shows teach
women to think of themselves, of their relations with other women,
and of their relations with the male sex? Heaton is a practicing psychologist who also teaches psychology at Ohio University. Wilson
teaches counseling and human resource development at South Dakota State University. Their essay is adapted from their book* Tuning
In to Trouble: Talk TV's Destructive Impact on Mental Health
(1995).

In 1967, *The Phil Donahue Show* aired in Dayton, Ohio, as a new
daytime talk alternative. Donahue did not offer the customary "wom-
en's fare." On Monday of his first week he interviewed atheist Mad-
alyn Murray O'Hair. Tuesday he featured single men talking about
what they looked for in women. Wednesday he showed a film of a
baby being born from the obstetrician's point of view. Thursday he
sat in a coffin and interviewed a funeral director. And on Friday he
held up "Little Brother," an anatomically correct doll without his
diaper. When Donahue asked viewers to call in response, phone
lines jammed.

For 18 years daytime talk *was* Donahue. His early guests reflected
the issues of the time and included Ralph Nader on consumer rights,
Bella Abzug on feminism, and Jerry Rubin on free speech. Never
before had such socially and personally relevant issues been discussed in such a democratic way with daytime women viewers. But
his most revolutionary contribution was in making the audience an
integral part of the show's format. The women watching Donahue
finally had a place in the conversation, and they were determined to
be heard. The show provided useful information and dialogue that
had largely been unavailable to housebound women, affording them
the opportunity to voice their opinions about everything from politics to sex — and even the politics of sex.

No real competition emerged until 1985, when *The Oprah Winfrey Show* went national. Her appeal for more intimacy was a ratings winner. She did the same topics Donahue had done but with a more therapeutic tone. Donahue seemed driven to uncover and explore. Winfrey came to share and understand. In 1987, Winfrey's show surpassed Donahue's by being ranked among the top 20 syndicated shows. Phil and Oprah made it easier for those who followed; their successors were able to move much more quickly to the top.

At their best, the shows "treated the opinions of women of all classes, races, and educational levels as if they mattered," says Naomi Wolf in her book *Fire with Fire:* "That daily act of listening, whatever its shortcomings, made for a revolution in what women were willing to ask for; the shows daily conditioned otherwise unheard women into the belief that they were entitled to a voice." Both Donahue and Winfrey deserve enormous credit for providing a platform for the voices of so many who needed to be heard, and for raising the nation's consciousness on many important topics, including domestic violence, child abuse, and other crucial problems. But those pioneering days are over. As the number of shows increased and the ratings wars intensified, the manner in which issues are presented has changed. Shows now encourage conflict, name-calling, and fights. Producers set up underhanded tricks and secret revelations. Hosts instruct guests to reveal all. The more dramatic and bizarre the problems the better.

While more air time is given to the problems that women face, 5 the topics are presented in ways that are not likely to yield change. The very same stereotypes that have plagued both women and men for centuries are in full force. Instead of encouraging changes in sex roles, the shows actually solidify them. Women viewers are given a constant supply of the worst images of men, all the way from garden-variety liars, cheats, and con artists to rapists and murderers.

If there is a man for every offense, there is certainly a woman for every trauma. Most women on talk TV are perpetual victims presented as having so little power that not only do they have to contend with real dangers such as sexual or physical abuse, but they are also overcome by bad hair, big thighs, and beautiful but predatory "other" women. The women of talk are almost always upset and in need. The bonding that occurs invariably centers around complaints about men or the worst stereotypes about women. In order to be a part of the "sisterhood," women are required to be angry with men and dissatisfied with themselves. We need look no further than at some of the program titles to recognize the message. Shows about men bring us a steady stream of stalkers, adulterers, chauvinistic sons, abusive fathers, and men who won't commit to women.

The shows provide a forum for women to complain, confront, and cajole, but because there is never any change as a result of the letting loose, this supports the mistaken notion that women's complaints have "no weight," that the only power women have is to complain, and that they cannot effect real changes. By bringing on offensive male guests who do nothing but verify the grounds for complaint, the shows are reinforcing some self-defeating propositions. The idea that women should direct their energies toward men rather than look for solutions in themselves is portrayed daily. And even when the audience chastises such behavior, nothing changes, because only arguments and justifications follow.

On *The Jenny Jones Show* a woman was introduced as someone who no longer had sex with her husband because she saw him with a stripper. Viewers got to hear how the stripper "put her boobs in his face" and then kissed him. The husband predictably defended his actions: "At least I didn't tongue her." The next few minutes proceeded with insult upon insult, to which the audience "oohed" and "aahed" and applauded. To top it all off, viewers were informed that the offense in question occurred at the husband's birthday party, which his wife arranged, *stripper and all.* Then in the last few minutes a psychologist pointed out the couple weren't wearing rings and didn't seem committed. She suggested that their fighting might be related to some other problem. Her comments seemed reasonable enough until she suggested that the wife might really be trying to get her husband to rape her. That comment called up some of the most absurd and destructive ideas imaginable about male and female relationships — yet there was no explanation or discussion.

It is not that women and men don't find lots of ways to disappoint each other, or that some women and some men don't act and think like the women and men on the shows. The problem is talk TV's fixation on gender war, with endless portrayals of vicious acts, overboard retaliations, and outrageous justifications. As a result, viewers are pumped full of the ugliest, nastiest news from the front.

When issues affecting people of color are dealt with, the stereo-   10 types about gender are layered on top of the stereotypes about race. Since most of the shows revolve around issues related to sex, violence, and relationships, they tend to feature people of color who reflect stereotypical images — in a steady stream of guests who have children out of wedlock, live on welfare, fight viciously, and have complicated unsolvable problems. While there are less than flattering depictions of white people on these shows, white viewers have the luxury of belonging to the dominant group, and therefore are more often presented in the media in positive ways.

On a *Ricki Lake* show about women who sleep with their friends' boyfriends, the majority of the guests were African American and Hispanic women who put on a flamboyant display of screaming and fighting. The profanity was so bad that many of the words had to be deleted. The segment had to be stopped because one guest yanked another's wig off. For many white viewers these are the images that form their beliefs about "minority" populations.

The shows set themselves up as reliable sources of information about what's really going on in the nation. And they often cover what sounds like common problems with work, love, and sex, but the information presented is skewed and confusing. Work problems become "fatal office feuds" and "backstabbing coworkers." Problems concerning love, sex, or romance become "marriage with a 14-year-old," "women in love with the men who shoot them," or "man-stealing sisters." TV talk shows suggest that "marrying a rapist" or having a "defiant teen" are catastrophes about to happen to everyone.

Day in and day out, the shows parade all the myriad traumas, betrayals, and afflictions that could possibly befall us. They suggest that certain issues are more common than they actually are, and embellish the symptoms and outcomes. In actuality, relatively few people are likely to be abducted as children, join a Satanic cult in adolescence, fall in love with serial rapists, marry their cousins, hate their own race, or get sex changes in midlife, but when presented over and over again the suggestion is that they are quite likely to occur.

With their incessant focus on individual problems, television talk shows are a major contributor to the recent trend of elevating personal concerns to the level of personal rights and then affording those "rights" more attention than their accompanying responsibilities. Guests are brought on who have committed villainous acts (most often against other guests). The host and audience gratuitously "confront" the offenders about their wrongdoing and responsibilities. The alleged offenders almost always refute their accountability with revelations that they too were "victimized." On *Sally Jessy Raphael,* a man appeared with roses for the daughter he had sexually molested. He then revealed that he had been molested when he was five, and summed it up with "I'm on this show too! I need help, I'll go through therapy."

His sudden turnabout was not unusual. Viewers rarely see guests   15
admit error early in the show, but a reversal often occurs with just a
few minutes remaining. This works well for the shows because they
need the conflict to move steadily to a crescendo before the final "go
to therapy" resolution. But before that viewers are treated to lots of
conflict and a heavy dose of pseudo-psychological explanations that
are really nothing more than excuses, and often lame ones at that.
The guests present their problems, the hosts encourage them to do
so with concerned questions and occasional self-disclosures, and
the audience frequently get in on the act with their own testimonies.
Anything and everything goes.

The reigning motto is "Secrets keep you sick." On a *Jerry Springer*
show about confronting secrets, a husband revealed to his wife that
he had been having an affair. Not only was the unsuspecting wife
humiliated and speechless, but Springer upped the ante by bringing
out the mistress, who kissed the husband and informed the wife that
she loved them both. Conflict predictably ensued, and viewers were
told this was a good idea because now the problem was out in the
open. When Ricki Lake did a similar show, a man explained to his
very surprised roommate that he had "finally" informed the roommate's mother that her son was gay, a secret the roommate had been
hiding from his family.

Referring to these premeditated catastrophes as simply "disclo-
sures" softens their edges and affords them a kind of legitimacy they
do not deserve. On a program about bigamy, Sally Jessy Raphael invited two women who had been married to the same man at the
same time to appear on the show. The man was also on, via satellite
and in disguise. His 19-year-old daughter by one of the wives sat on
the stage while these women and her father tore each other apart.
Sally and the audience encouraged the fight with "oohs" and "aahs"
and rounds of applause at the ever-increasing accusations. A "relationship therapist" was brought on to do the postmortem. Her most
notable warning was that all this turmoil could turn the daughter "to
women," presumably meaning that she could become a lesbian. The
scenario was almost too absurd for words, but it was just one more
show like so many others: founded on stereotypes and capped off
with clichés. From the "catfight" to the "no-good father" to archaic
explanations of homosexuality — cheap thrills and bad advice are
dressed up like information and expertise.

These scenarios are often legitimized by the use of pseudo-
psychological explanations, otherwise known as psychobabble. This
is regularly used as a "disclaimer," or as a prelude to nasty revelations, or as a new and more sophisticated way of reinforcing old ste-

reotypes: "men are cognitive, not emotional," or "abused women draw abusive men to them." This not only leaves viewers with nothing more than platitudes to explain problems and clichés to resolve them, but it fails to offer guests with enormous conflicts and long histories of resentment and betrayals practical methods for changing their circumstances. The "four steps to get rid of your anger" may sound easy enough to implement, but what this kind of ready-made solution fails to acknowledge is that not all anger is the same, and certainly not everyone's anger needs the same treatment. Sometimes anger is a signal to people that they are being hurt, exploited, or taken advantage of, and it can motivate change.

Rather than encouraging discussion, exploration, or further understanding, psychobabble shuts it off. With only a phrase or two, we can believe that we understand all the related "issues." Guests confess that they are "codependents" or "enablers." Hosts encourage "healing," "empowerment," and "reclaiming of the inner spirit." In turn, viewers can nod knowingly without really knowing at all.

Talk TV initially had great potential as a vehicle for disseminating accurate information and as a forum for public debate, although it would be hard to know it from what currently remains. Because most of these talk shows have come to rely on sensational entertainment as the means of increasing ratings, their potential has been lost. We are left with cheap shots, cheap thrills, and sound-bite stereotypes. Taken on its own, this combination is troubling enough, but when considered against the original opportunity for positive outcomes, what talk TV delivers is truly disturbing. [20]

THE INVOLVED READER

1 According to the authors, what was "revolutionary" about the early Phil Donahue show? Was there a general drift in the topics and guests? How was the early Oprah Winfrey show different from Donahue's? What did the two shows have in common?

2 Where in this essay is the crucial turning point from the pioneering early shows to today's fare? What key changes have occurred? What key charges do the authors make?

3 According to the authors, what is wrong with the treatment of men in today's shows? What is wrong with the treatment of women?

4 What is wrong with the way people of color are represented on TV talk shows?

5 According to the authors, what is the role of psychologists and counselors on these shows, and on what grounds do the authors criticize them? What is "psychobabble"?

TALKING, THINKING, WRITING

6 After watching several episodes of current shows, would you tend to agree with the authors or take issue with them? How and why?

7 Do considerations of gender and race tend to get interwined?

COLLABORATIVE PROJECTS

8 Liberal critics charge that radio talk shows are dominated by right-wing talk show hosts and right-wing views. Working with a group, organize a project to investigate the validity of these charges.

Downsizing Hits Home

ROGER E. SWARDSON

What trends or policies create jobs, and which kill jobs? Arguments over massive layoffs and loss of well-paying jobs have grown heated in recent years. Is it true that many workers officially listed as employed have had to settle for part-time work? Is it true that many are "temporary" workers with no health plan, no job security, and no opportunities for advancement? Roger Swardson, a freelance writer, uses his own story as a case in point. He writes about his experience working as a temporary worker for an insurance company in Minnesota. He is a shrewd observer of the ways of management and especially of the slogans and rationalizations management uses in launching new policies. Is what he has experienced in store for many others like him? Is there a temporary or a part-time job in your future?

When I stand and look across the maze of beige cubicles, I see that Linda's is strung with blue and white crepe paper and festooned with balloons. Vera stayed late yesterday and decorated. That's the way it usually works. And Linda most likely brought a box of bagels or doughnuts this morning. That's what you do on your birthday.

Just as the first Friday of the month is Jeans Day, when you wear casual clothes, and Chili Day, when a dozen people bring in their versions in slow-cookers for lunch. A couple of male managers judge the chili and make comments about each other's waistlines, and there is scattered laughter.

These aren't company events so much as they are the inventions of unquenchable women whose life mission seems to be to invent activities to keep the world's chin up. But as I stand here I can't stop thinking, "My God, the bus is going to hit many of these women."

That's the image I have of Gunther, the monolithic computer system that is scheduled to replace the workers who fill this office.

You and I are standing on a curb and a group of women are crossing the street, just as they've been doing for years in the crosswalk, where they're supposed to be, but there's this bus bearing down on them. Many of them don't see it until it's too late.

I'm horrified, but you're not. You are rooting for the bus. Your colleagues are on the bus. So is your future.

I'm a temporary, a transient co-worker of the women in this office, in this crosswalk. You have a promising job here where the company says it is becoming leaner (smaller), healthier (more profitable) and

meaner (more competitive). You see change as exciting and have little patience with whiners who haven't smelled the fresh-ground Co-
lombian of "quality plus" or "service excellence" and terms whose
meaning relies on how often management repeats them.

But here's the other side of it. There isn't just that cluster of
women in this one crosswalk at this one company. There are thousands of others. And not one careening bus but hundreds.

The obsession with boosting productivity has created widely dis-
parate layers of working Americans. One is prosperous, whipping
around chanting slogans and wondering what the hell the problem
is beyond some bad attitudes; another works each day fearful that it
will be the last; and another has fallen through the cracks into dis-
location and a dreadful wage depression with little prospect of improvement. In the meantime, the economy does not produce jobs.
And it will not as long as profit rests on downgrading or eliminating
jobs, rather than creating them.

New workplace technology is wiping out jobs wholesale. That's   10
not news — it's what it was designed to do. But tossing job creation from the foundation of our economic lives is another matter.
Beyond the corporate boardrooms and crumbling union fiefdoms
there is real fear and growing anger with the new social compact
that says, "Hey, isn't this great? We're all on our own now." There's
even a cheerful political philosophy for it, called communitarianism,
which as much as says, "The government can't help you anymore.
So get together and fend for yourselves. You'll love it" — a think-
tank rehash of "I've upped mine. Up yours," the social policy of
the 1980s.

Workers are being cut adrift in the publicized large layoffs, but
more are quietly let go each day as their jobs simply disappear.

Here's one way it happens. This is the story of Gunther, which
could be the bus we were watching but is actually a piece of equipment, a playing piece in the transition game. The game itself is not
all that easy to follow, but the objective is simple: Don't get caught
in the crosswalk.

We are in a service center of a major insurance company. It is the
place where decisions are made on whether and how to insure thousands of clients of independent agents across the country, where
policies are issued and constant updates are processed to keep them
current. It is generally calm unless a woman on maternity leave brings
in the new baby or it's Girl Scout cookie delivery day and blood sugar
is at a seasonal high or it's midwinter and flu is rampant. There are

more than 100 people here occupying almost the whole floor of a downtown office building. Eleven of us are men, one a vice president. Three men are temporaries.

There are four basic job classifications, as well as some specialist and support positions. At the entry level are policy assemblers, who convert stacks of paperwork into individual policies ready for the mail room. One step up are data-entry people pecking streams of instruction from the underwriters and assistants into video display terminals. The underwriters, assistants and, when the call is close, higher-ups consult oracles, odds and company policy and make book on medical practices, buildings, equipment and vehicles.

In my group we service eight Midwestern states. I am one of four policy assemblers. Three of us are temporary, two are men. A temp is brought in when a full-time assembler moves up or out. The job of assembler is being taken over by a machine called Gunther that will do our job automatically. When Gunther is ready, the last temps will be dismissed with a phone call to our agency, and the job of policy assembler, which has existed since this company began, will disappear. 15

Not that it's a great job. You start each day with stacks of paper, and you try to combine them in the right way and get them all the hell gone by day's end. There are light moments when, as a result of software permitting only so many characters per slot, the computer provides collision insurance on a Volkswagen Rabbi or issues a policy to "A Partnership Composed of William," but the job is mostly routine. Some people like it. More to the point, many people need this job. One said, "Hey, we can't all be rocket scientists, but we need some way to make a living."

Policy assembly is the traditional entry level to service-center work. Some underwriters began here. With this job going, the entry-level stakes move higher, and when the data-entry job is upgraded with the advent of the "paperless office," the first rung on the employment ladder will be out of reach for many traditional beginning workers. And the heap of dislocated workers will become steadily bigger.

So here we are, you and I, standing on this curb. The bus had done its work, many of the workers in the crosswalk silently whisked away. You are giving me a quizzical look, as if to say, "So? What did you think was going to happen? Some workers saw the bus coming a long time ago and made plans. Some didn't get wiped out. It's what happens."

Hold that thought.

What really happened was a committee, a task force, perhaps an   20
adept salesperson got a foothold somewhere in the company with a
proposal to improve on the labor-intensive, error-prone and costly
process of using people to assemble thousands of insurance policies each day. The idea was a new system. With a new machine. A
Gunther.

Not a startling notion, really. Just the next step on the long road
that reaches back over a century to when policies were handwritten.
The company was finally ready to buy the whole automation scheme,
which would combine abundant memory for countless policy details, image processing to digitize paperwork, specialized equipment
(such as Gunther) to churn out grunt work, powerful personal computers for super underwriters, and software that reaches out to the
fingertips of far-flung independent agents.

Initial steps appeared routine, even mundane. They involved the
consolidation of service offices scattered across the country into bigger regional centers to form the critical mass needed to satisfy the
new system's voracious appetite. This meant uprooting people, retraining some, letting some go, not replacing others and finding a
way to talk about it to secure cooperation and avoid chaos.

Few people knew the master plan. Nobody was ever told his or her
job was disappearing until the last moment. There was talk of restruc-
turing. New opportunities. The future lies ahead. Banners were run
up. White ones said "quality" or "service," black ones "global competition" and "economic downturn." No widespread layoffs. Just
people leaving here and there. An office moving. A department gone
over time. Not much you could really see.

Of three basic ways to winnow workers, attrition is cheapest.
Some people see what's coming and leave or move on for other reasons. The second winnower is "performance factors." Here stress
identifies who can handle increased complexity and workload and
who can't keep up. Finally, there are transfers for those who hold up
and terminations for those left when time runs out. In the first year
of consolidating the service centers, 234 people, 3 percent of the division's population, were terminated.

Management called this "exciting." Rapidly escalating fringe ben-   25
efit costs, with health care in the lead, made shrinking the work force
even more attractive. The strong motivation of middle-management
women, shouldering ever more work in hopes of hanging on to
their gains and moving even higher, added an unexpected boon for
male senior management. And, finally, the recession-driven flood of
trained temporary workers (often having been laid off from similar
jobs) smoothed out the final phases of the transition plan.

In St. Paul, the last step in that transition began with a job fair. It was a casting call for people with "clerical skills and career motivation." Nearly 500 applicants showed up for full-time policy assembly, data entry and clerical jobs. Implementation of the new system was speeding up.

But by the following summer, a little over a year after being recruited for "career opportunities," 18 full-time assemblers had been cut to six in the first service center where I worked. The rest were temps. It was not a happy place.

You lightened the day by inventing diversions. For example, one day I noticed an unusual stockpile of cat hair on my sport coat. A nap had clearly been taken there. The game of the day then called for including one cat hair in a number of policies selected for maximum geographic coverage. By day's end, a souvenir of a 13-year-old Maine Coon tomcat from Minnesota named Fitzgerald was on its way to policyholders in 19 states.

Pressure in the last days was intense. If it wasn't the work, which was being piled on, it was the uncertainty. Even the temporaries were jumpy. You never know, after all, when your time is up or whether your agency has another job for you. Those stories of lighthearted temps who love the freedom and wouldn't have it any other way are the rare exception. Every temporary I've ever known, except for students, craves a decent, permanent job. We read benefits material like the menus of expensive restaurants that are equally out of reach.

A temporary here gets $7 an hour, a good temp wage in St. Paul. 30 No benefits, of course. The standard work-week, 38 hours and 45 minutes, yields a paycheck of $211.75 after deductions, or just under $850 a month if you are never ill, your job transfers are seamless and you've accrued enough hours to qualify for paid holidays. That's the absolute best you can do, and all those things rarely happen.

More realistically, your monthly expenses must be covered by a variable and unpredictable wage of between $600 and $850. Try it. First single, then married, and then married with children. Now imagine there are millions of us, working, with annual incomes under $10,000.

Around Christmas I was switched over to the medical-industry service center and got through the trial period. This was the office of crepe paper and Chili Days; also of mothers on the shared phone making sure their children were home from school. Because the common phone was near my work area, I frequently answered it and got used to the fact that the departmental children out there expected us to know who they were. They would simply blurt, "Is my mom there?" And after a while you did get to know them, even to the point of responding, "Gee, I don't know, Tommy. Did you clean your room yet?"

The temps, of course, had a special rapport. There was the young guy who had worked his way through the University of Minnesota and graduated last year, never so much as taking out a student loan, and who would show up in a tie now and then because he had yet one more interview. And there was the temp about my age who had been in television production and who brought me a few jars of Dolga Crab Apple jelly. He quit after several months, after the pressure again became unreasonable as Gunther Day neared. When he left, another temp had to do his work and hers, too.

Two weeks before Gunther, the young graduate and I were let go. The next week the last temp, a woman from Ohio who had come to town hoping for work, also went. The last full-time assembler was then reassigned for training, and the job of policy assembly went the way of the buggy whip.

Improved productivity leads to improved profitability, which leads to job creation, right? The first part is working like a charm, judging from record amounts of money that management is shoving into its pockets across the country. But there has been no appreciable job creation. Why?

Strange things happen in corporations. One day while looking for paper clips I found a memorandum that shouldn't have been in my desk. It described the very productivity program that produced my temporary job and would eventually take it back. In this insurance company, each piece of business, even an address change, is called a work unit. When most of the transition game is over, revenues, expressed in terms of gross work units, are projected to have tripled over the four-year transition period. Net work units, after factoring in the impact of the new office technology, are projected to be less than half of what they were in year one. In other words, the business will triple with a service mechanism that will be reduced by half. If it all works, there will never be a need to significantly increase service-center jobs. Ever. The company can even absorb acquisitions into the new service system. Think of the profitability. Think of the people who will be tossed out in those unsuspecting work forces.

So what happens to these leftover people? What happens in a nation filling up with leftover people?

Here we are on the curb, and you're still giving me a look. You've turned sardonic. Change happens, you say. And you believe that the change you're a part of can be predicted by computer model. OK. But how broad is the model? Is the shape of change out here on the street predictable? Manageable? In a nation of such size and diversity? One that is already breaking up into polarized fragments?

Recently I had the chance to ask James Tobin, a Nobel Prize-winning economist at Yale University, how he accounted for the dramatic increase in the nation's working poor and unemployed. Global competition? The terrible residue of trickle-down? A cyclical downturn?

Some of all of that, he said. But something much bigger as well: the final downhill ride into a new era. The information age, or whatever term you prefer. Change on a scale not seen since farmhands were beckoned into the factories. Major upheaval. Mayhem, perhaps. But it will settle down again in a decade or so, he said. Eventually there will be new jobs, even if we don't now know where they will come from. But they will come. They have before. It's what happens, he said. 40

A new era. In a decade or so. And, along the way, new levels of insulated wealth and a new peasantry. Riches in isolation. Idleness and despair in the street. The classic formula for revolution. So how long does the computer model say we have until the rabble go for their pitchforks this time?

So here we stand. The temp whiner and the productivity freak. We could both be wrong, of course. Maybe none of that is happening. Or will happen. After all, I never did see Gunther. It's humming away in another building. Out in the suburbs. All I saw was the crosswalk.

THE INVOLVED READER

1 Swardson early uses the metaphor of the crosswalk and the bus. How does he use it to dramatize the issue? How does he use it to divide the workforce into two different camps? (How does he circle back to it at the end?)

2 What is Swardson's main point, or what are his main points?

3 What details in this account do you think you will especially remember? What about the article had a special impact on you? Why?

4 American corporations today use their own lingo, their own corporate-speak, to justify policy, motivate employees, or placate customers. What do you learn from Swardson about the language of modern management?

TALKING, THINKING, WRITING

5 Does Swardson convince you that the situation at the insurance company is representative — that it is merely one outstanding

example of a national trend? Why or why not? Have you observed or do you know about similar situations?

6 As you read this article, do you find yourself identifying with the "productivity freaks" or the "whining temps"?

COLLABORATIVE PROJECTS

7 Educators used to predict that there would be little work for unskilled labor. Now we hear warnings that educated or skilled workers will have trouble finding jobs. You may want to work as a member of a small-scale task force checking out evidence or counterevidence for this trend.

Age and the Beauty Myth

NAOMI WOLF

Thirty-three thousand American women told researchers that they would rather lose ten to fifteen pounds than achieve any other goal.

NAOMI WOLF

Are American women under the spell of the "beauty myth"? Are they an easy mark for advertisers who play to the fear of fat and the fear of aging? Called by its publisher "a cultural hand grenade for the 90s," Naomi Wolf's The Beauty Myth *(1991) had an impact comparable to that of earlier feminist manifestoes, such as Germaine Greer's* The Female Eunuch *and Betty Friedan's* The Feminine Mystique. *Wolf is a Manhattanite who went from Hebrew School in San Francisco and an early bout with anorexia to Yale and Oxford. In* The Beauty Myth, *she filed an aggressive indictment of the cult of youth and beauty in American society and the way it debilitates women and thwarts their striving for economic and political equality. Her book was hailed as an "impassioned polemic" (Fay Weldon), but whereas much polemical writing leaves facts and figures behind to inflame the reader's passions, Wolf impressed many of her readers with her sharp-eyed observation of the ploys of the multibillion-dollar diet and skin care industries, by her relentless marshaling of statistics, and by her amassing of testimony from insiders and outside experts.*

The following scene plays on television in the United States: A charismatic leader dressed in white addresses an audience, her face aglow. Women listen transfixed: Three steps are to be undertaken in total solitude. "Give this time to yourself . . . Concentrate. Really feel it," she says. "Follow the steps religiously." Women testify: "I wasn't a believer at first either. But look at me now." "I didn't want to commit to it. I'd tried everything and I just didn't believe anything could do it for me — I've never known anything like it. It's changed my life." The camera focuses on their faces. Finally, all are wearing white and clustered around the leader, eyes shining. Cameras pan backward to the sound of a hymn. The source of the shared secret is Collagen Extract Skin Nourishment, $39.95 for a month's supply.

These video conversions only supplement the main cult action in department stores, where 50 percent of holy oil sales are made at "points of purchase." The scheme is pure religion carefully organized.

A woman enters a department store from the street, looking no doubt very mortal, her hair windblown, her own face visible. To reach the cosmetics counter, she must pass a deliberately disorienting prism of mirrors, lights, and scents that combine to submit her to the "sensory overload" used by hypnotists and cults to encourage suggestibility.

On either side of her are ranks of angels — seraphim and cherubim — the "perfect" faces of the models on display. Behind them, across a liminal counter in which is arranged the magic that will permit her to cross over, lit from below, stands the guardian angel. The saleswoman is human, she knows, but "perfected" like the angels around her, from whose ranks the woman sees her own "flawed" face, reflected back and shut out. Disoriented within the man-made heaven of the store, she can't focus on what makes both the live and pictured angels seem similarly "perfect": that they are both lacquered in heavy paint. The lacquer bears little relation to the outer world, as the out-of-place look of a fashion shoot on a city street makes clear. But the mortal world disintegrates in her memory at the shame of feeling so out of place among all the ethereal objects. Put in the wrong, the shopper longs to cross over.

Cosmetics saleswomen are trained with techniques akin to those used by professional cult converters and hypnotists. A former Children of God member says in Willa Appel's *Cults in America: Programmed for Paradise* that she sought out people in shopping malls "who looked lost and vulnerable." The woman making her way down an aisle of divinities is made to look "lost and vulnerable" in her own eyes. If she sits down and agrees to a "make-over," she's a subject for a cultic hard sell.

The saleswoman will move up close into the face of the shopper, ostensibly to apply the substances, but in fact generally much closer than she needs to be do to so. She keeps up a patter that focuses in on a blemish, wrinkles, the bags under the woman's eyes. Cult converters are trained to stand very close to their potential subjects and "stare fixedly in their eyes. . . . You'd look for the weak spots in people." The woman then hears herself convinced of the sins and errors that are putting her in jeopardy: "You use *what* on your face?" "Only twenty-three, and look at those lines." "Well, if you're happy with those pimples." "You're *destroying* the delicate skin under your eyes." "If you don't stop doing what you're doing to it, in ten years your whole face will be a mass of creases." Another cult member interviewed by Appel describes this procedure: "It was the whole thing of exuding confidence, of maintaining direct communication so forceful that you're always in complete control. . . . You have to

5

play up the feeling that all these people have of no sense of real security, no sense of what was going to happen in the future, and the fear of just continuing to repeat old mistakes."

The shopper probably gives in, and accepts Lancôme as her personal savior. Once back in the street, though, the expensive tubes and bottles immediately lose their aura. Those who have escaped from cults feel afterward that they have emerged from something they can only dimly remember.

Advertisements in print must now approach the potential cult member with more sophistication. For two decades they have used a mysterious language the way Catholicism uses Latin, Judaism Hebrew, and Masons secret passwords: as a prestigious Logos that confers magic power on the originators of it. To the lay person, it is a gibberish of science and mock-science. For example: "Phytolyastil," "Phytophyline," "Plurisome™"; "SEI Complex" and "biologically active tissue ceramides" (Chanel); "a syntropic blend of the unique BioDermia™"; "Complex #3" "Reticulin and mucopolysaccharides" (Aloegen); "Tropocollagen and hyaluronic acid" (Charles of the Ritz); "Incellate™" (Terme di Saturnia); "Glycosphingolipids" (GSL, Glycel); "Niosomes and Microsomes and Protectinol" (Shiseido).

"Western societies from the early centuries of the second millennium," writes Rosalind Miles, "all found their own techniques for ensuring that the 'new learning' did not penetrate the great underclass of the female sex." A long history of intellectual exclusion precedes our current intimidation by this battery of mock-authoritative language.

The ads refined this daunting nonsense language to cover the fact   10 that skin creams do not actually do anything. The holy oil industry is a megalith that for forty years has been selling women nothing at all. According to Gerald McKnight's exposé, the industry is "little more than a massive con . . . a sweetly disguised form of commercial robbery" with profit margins of over 50 percent on a revenue of 20 *billion* dollars worldwide; in 1988 skin care grossed 3 billion in the United States alone, 337 million pounds in the United Kingdom, 8.9 trillion lire in Italy, and 69.2 million guilders in the Netherlands, up from 18.3 million in 1978.

For forty years the industry has been making false claims. Before 1987, the Food and Drug Administration just twice made minor objections. In the past two decades, holy oil makers went beyond the outrageous, claiming to retard aging (Revlon Anti-Aging Firmagel), repair the skin (Night Repair), and restructure the cell (Cellular Recovery Complex, G. M. Collin Intensive Cellular Regeneration, Elancyl Restructurant). As women encountered the computerized work force of the 1980s, the ads abandoned the filmy florals of "hope in a bottle" and adopted new imagery of bogus technology, graphs and statistics, to resonate with the authority of the microchip. Imaginary technological "breakthroughs" reinforced women's sense that the beauty index was inflating out of control, its claims reported too fast for the human brain to organize or verify.

Information overload joined new technologies in airbrushing and photo doctoring to give women the sense that scrutiny itself had become superhuman. The eye of the camera, like God's, developed a microscopic judgment that outdid the imperfect human eye, magnifying "flaws" a mortal could not detect: In the early 1980s, says Morris Herstein of Laboratoires Serobiologiques, who characterizes himself as a "pseudo-scientist," "we were then able to see and measure things that had been impossible before. It came about when the technology of the space program was made available, when we were allowed to use their sophisticated analysis techniques, the biotechnological advances which allowed us to see things at the cellular level. Before that we had to touch and feel." What Herstein is saying is that by measuring tissue invisible to the naked eye, beyond "touch and feel," the struggle for beauty was transposed into a focus so minute that the struggle itself became metaphysical. Women were asked to believe that erasing lines so faint as to be nonexistent to the human gaze was now a reasonable moral imperative.

The tenuous link between what the holy oils claimed to do and what they did was finally broken, and no longer meant anything. "The numbers are meaningless until all the tests and rankings are standardized," a women's magazine quotes industry spokesman Dr. Grove, adding that "consumers should always remember that what the machine measures may not be visible to the naked eye."

If the "enemy" is invisible, the "barrier" is invisible, the "eroding effects" are invisible, and the holy oil's results "may not be visible to the naked eye," we are in a dimension of pure faith, where "graphic evidence" is provided of the "visible improvement" in the number of angels that after treatment will dance on the head of a pin. The whole dramatic fiction of the holy oil's fight against age began, by the mid-1980s, to unfold on an entirely make-believe stage, inventing psychic flaws to sell psychic cures. From that point on, the features of their faces and bodies that would make women unhappy would increasingly be those that no one else could see. More alone than ever, women were placed beyond the consolation of reason. Perfection had now to hold up beyond the artist's frame, and survive the microscope.

Even many industry insiders acknowledge that the creams do not   15
work. According to Buddy Wedderburn, a biochemist at Unilever:
"The effect of rubbing collagen onto the skin is negligible. . . . I don't
know of anything that gets into these areas — certainly nothing that
will stop wrinkles." Anita Roddick of The Body Shop, the beauty care
chain, says, "There is *no* application, no topical application, that
will get rid of grief or stress or heavy lines. . . . There's nothing, but
nothing, that's going to make you look younger. Nothing." Anthea
Disney, editor of the women's magazine *Self,* adds, "We all know
there isn't anything that will make you look younger." And as "Sam"
Sugiyama, codirector of Shiseido, concludes, "If you want to avoid
aging, you must live in space. There is no other way to avoid getting
wrinkles, once you are out of the womb."

The professional collegial spirit that has helped keep the fraudu-
lent nature of the industry's claims fairly quiet was belatedly broken
by Professor Albert Kligman of the University of Pennsylvania —
whose whistle-blowing must be put in context: He is the developer
of Retin-A, the one substance that does seem to do something, including subjecting the skin to inflammation, sunlight intolerance,
and continuous heavy peeling. "In the industry today," he wrote
presciently to his colleagues, "fakery is replacing puffery . . . a consumer and FDA crackdown is inevitable and damaging to credibility." He goes further in interviews: "When they make a claim of
anti-aging, of the stuff having deep biological effects, then they have
to be stopped. It's pure bunkum . . . beyond the bounds of reason and truth." And he says that the new products "simply cannot
function as their backers and makers say they do, because it is physically impossible for them to get deep enough into the skin to make
any lasting difference to wrinkles. The same applies to the removal
of lines or wrinkles, or the permanent prevention of the aging of
cells." The hope of anything achieving such effects is, he says, "actually zero."

"Some of my colleagues," Kligman admits, "tell me, 'Women are
so dumb! How can they buy all that grease and stuff? Educated
women, who've been to Radcliffe and Cambridge and Oxford and
the Sorbonne — what gets into them? Why do they go to Blooming-
dale's and pay $250 for that hokum?'"

Women are "so dumb" because the establishment and its watch-
dogs share the cosmetics industry's determination that we are and
must remain "so dumb." The "crackdown" came at last in the United
States in 1987 — but not from concern for women consumers exploited by a $20-billion-a-year fraud. The first straw was when heart
specialist Dr. Christiaan Barnard brought out Glycel ("a fake, a com-

plete fake," says Dr. Kligman). The doctor's fame and superoutrageous claims for his product ('This was the first time in history that we can recall a physician putting his name to a cosmetic line," says Stanley Kohlenberg of Sanofi Beauty Products) provoked envy in the rest of the industry. According to one of Gerald McKnight's sources: "Somebody put it to the Agency that if they did not pull the product off the shelves, the industry would see to it that the FDA's name was dragged through the mire." The Food and Drug Administration then went after the industry as a whole "because we were all doing it, making wild claims." The agency asked twenty-three chief cosmetics executives to account for "claims that they were flagrantly making in magazines, films and every possible area of hype . . . that they had added 'magical' anti-aging and cellular replacement ingredients to their products." The FDA asked for "immediate withdrawal of the claims or submission for testing as drugs." "We are unaware," FDA director Daniel L. Michaels wrote to them, "of any substantial scientific evidence that demonstrates the safety and effectiveness of these articles. Nor are we aware that these drugs are generally recognized as safe and effective for their intended uses." In other words, the agency said, if the creams do what you claim, they are drugs and must be tested. If they don't, you are making false claims.

Is all this proof that anyone really cares about an industry whose targets for religious fraud are women? Morris Herstein points out that "the FDA is only saying, 'Look, we're concerned about what you're *saying,* not what you're doing.' It is a dictionary problem, a lexicon problem, a question of vocabulary." The head of the agency hardly sounds adversarial. "We're not trying to punish anyone," he told Deborah Blumenthal, a reporter for *The New York Times,* in 1988. She believed that the products would stay the same, only the "surrealist nature" of some claims would disappear. Three years later, these "surrealist" claims have reemerged.

Think of the enormity: For twenty years the holy oils made "scientific" claims, using bogus charts and figures, of "proven improvement" and "visible difference" that were subject to no outside verification. Outside the United States, the same manufacturers continue to make false claims. In the United Kingdom, almost all holy oil ads ignore the British Code of Advertising warning not to "contain any claim to provide rejuvenation, that is to prevent, retard or reverse the physiological changes and degenerative conditions brought about by, or associated with, increasing age." The British Department of Trade and Industry finally followed suit in 1989 (as British dermatologist Ronald Marks said, "A lot of this stuff is cosmetic hoo-ha"), but the DTI has not yet committed the time or resources to follow through. In neither country has there been a public move to put pressure on the industry to print retractions or apologies to women; nor in the coverage of the change in regulations has the possibility been raised of financial compensation for the women consumers cheated so thoroughly for so many years.

Is it an overreaction to take such deception so seriously? Isn't women's relation to holy oils as trivial, the pathos of our faith as harmless, even endearing, as it is reflected in popular discourse? Women are poor; poorer than men. What is so important about 20 billion of our dollars a year? It would buy us, trivially enough, *each year,* roughly three times the amount of day care offered by the U.S. government: or 2,000 women's health clinics; or 75,000 women's film, music, literature, or art festivals; or 50 women's universities; or 1 million highly paid home support workers for the housebound elderly; or 1 million highly paid domestic or child care workers; or 33,000 battered-women's shelters; or 2 billion tubes of contraceptive cream; or 200,000 vans for late-night safe transport; or 400,000 full four-year university scholarships for young women who cannot afford further education; or 20 million airplane tickets around the world; or 200 million five-course dinners in four-star French restaurants; or 40 million cases of Veuve Clicquot champagne. Women are poor; poor people need luxuries. Of course women should be free to buy whatever they want, but if we are going to spend our hard-earned cash, the luxuries should deliver what they promise, not simply leech guilt money. No one takes this fraud seriously because the alternative to it is the real social threat: that women will first accept their aging, then admire it, and finally enjoy it. Wasting women's money is the calculable damage; but the damage this fraud does women through its legacy of the dread of aging is incalculable.

THE INVOLVED READER

1   How does Wolf bring the beauty cult to life for her readers? What will you remember about her recreating of a television commercial or of a department store cosmetics counter? What is her comment on the language of cosmetics advertising?

2   Where does Wolf's central thesis emerge? What does she basically claim or charge? Where do you think she sums it up most clearly or forcefully?

3   What kind of authorities does Wolf quote, and what do they say? Which of the quotations do you find most convincing or thought provoking?

4 What is the upshot of Wolf's probing of the role played by government regulation? What evidence does she provide to support her findings?

5 Wolf has been called a muckraker, seizing on and exaggerating everything negative. Does she offer positive alternatives? Does she have a constructive agenda?

TALKING, THINKING, WRITING

6 In our society today, how important are good looks to a woman's success? (As one of Wolf's reviewers put it, "Do women need good looks to get through the door so they play hardball once they get in?")

7 Is cosmetic surgery unnatural and a form of "violence against women"?

COLLABORATIVE PROJECTS

8 Are college women today victims of the beauty myth? Working with your classmates, you may want to organize a study or survey on your campus.

short story

The Lesson

TONI CADE BAMBARA

Is our country becoming two nations — the rich and the poor? Toni Cade Bambara is a writer of fiction who is vividly aware of the widening gap between the privileged and the dispossessed. Bambara is a student of theater, dance, and film who studied at Queens College in New York as well as in Florence, Italy, and in Paris. She has written screenplays for both private and public television. She has taught at a range of universities and colleges and has been much involved in community work, including writers' workshops and work with libraries and prisons. Her writing often draws on sources of pride and solidarity in the African American community. Unlike many of her contemporaries among writers of fiction, Bambara does not hesitate to spell out the point of her stories, often making a character in the story give voice to the author's point of view.

Back in the days when everyone was old and stupid or young and foolish and me and Sugar were the only ones just right, this lady moved on our block with nappy hair and proper speech and no makeup. And quite naturally we laughed at her, laughed the way we did at the junk man who went about his business like he was some big-time president and his sorry-ass horse his secretary. And we kinda hated her too, hated the way we did the winos who cluttered up our parks and pissed on our handball walls and stank up our hallways and stairs so you couldn't halfway play hide-and-seek without a goddamn gas mask. Miss Moore was her name. The only woman on the block with no first name. And she was black as hell, cept for her feet, which were fish-white and spooky. And she was always planning these boring-ass things for us to do, us being my cousin, mostly, who lived on the block cause we all moved North the same time and to the same apartment then spread out gradual to breathe. And our parents would yank our heads into some kinda shape and crisp up our clothes so we'd be presentable for travel with Miss Moore, who always looked like she was going to church, though she never did. Which is just one of the things that grownups talked about when they talked behind her back like a dog. But when she came calling with some sachet she'd sewed up or some gingerbread she'd made or some book, why then they'd all be too embarrassed to turn her down and we'd get handed over all spruced up. She'd been to college and said it was only right that she should take responsibility for the young ones' education, and she not even related by marriage or blood. So they'd go for it. Specially Aunt Gretchen. She was the main gofer in the family. You got some ole dumb shit foolishness you want somebody to go for, you send for Aunt Gretchen. She been screwed into the go-along for so long, it's a blood-deep natural thing with her. Which is how she got saddled with me and Sugar and Junior in the first place while our mothers were in a la-de-da apartment up the block having a good ole time.

So this one day Miss Moore rounds us all up at the mailbox and it's puredee hot and she's knockin herself about arithmetic. And school suppose to let up in summer I heard, but she don't never let up. And the starch in my pinafore scratching the shit outta me and I'm really hating this nappy-head bitch and her goddamn college degree. I'd much rather go to the pool or to the show where it's cool. So me and Sugar leaning on the mailbox being surly, which is a Miss Moore word. And Flyboy checking out what everybody brought for lunch. And Fat Butt already wasting his peanut-butter-and-jelly sandwich like the pig he is. And Junebug punchin on Q.T.'s arm for potato chips. And Rosie Giraffe shifting from one hip to the other waiting for somebody to step on her foot or ask her if she from Georgia so she can kick ass, preferably Mercedes'. And Miss Moore asking us do we know what money is, like we a bunch of retards. I mean real money, she say, like it's only poker chips or monopoly papers we lay on the grocer. So right away I'm tired of this and say so. And would much rather snatch Sugar and go to the Sunset and terrorize the West Indian kids and take their hair ribbons and their money too. And Miss Moore files that remark away for the next week's lesson on brotherhood, I can tell. And finally I say we oughta get to the subway cause it's cooler and besides we might meet some cute boys. Sugar done swiped her mama's lipstick, so we ready.

So we heading down the street and she's boring us silly about what things cost and what our parents make and how much goes for rent and how money ain't divided up right in this country. And then she gets to the part about we all poor and live in the slums, which I don't feature. And I'm ready to speak on that, but she steps out in the street and hails two cabs just like that. Then she hustles half the crew in with her and hands me a five-dollar bill and tells me to calculate 10 percent tip for the driver. And we're off. Me and Sugar and Junebug and Flyboy hangin out the window and hollering to everybody, putting lipstick on each other cause Flyboy a faggot anyway, and making farts with our sweaty armpits. But I'm mostly trying to figure how to spend this money. But they all fascinated with the meter ticking and Junebug starts laying bets as to how much it'll read when Flyboy can't hold his breath no more. Then Sugar lays bets as to how much it'll be when we get there. So I'm stuck. Don't nobody want to go for my plan, which is to jump out at the next light and run off to the first bar-b-que we can find. Then the driver tells us to get the hell out cause we there already. And the meter reads eighty-five cents. And I'm stalling to figure out the tip and Sugar say give him a dime. And I decide he don't need it bad as I do, so later for him. But then he tries to take off with Junebug foot still in the door so we talk about his mama something ferocious. Then we check out that we on Fifth Avenue and everybody dressed up in stockings. One lady in a fur coat, hot as it is. White folks crazy.

"This is the place," Miss Moore say, presenting it to us in the voice she uses at the museum. "Let's look in the windows before we go in."

"Can we steal?" Sugar asks very serious like she's getting the ground rules squared away before she plays. "I beg your pardon," say Miss Moore, and we fall out. So she leads us around the windows of the toy store and me and Sugar screamin, "This is mine, that's mine, I gotta have that, that was made for me, I was born for that," till Big Butt drowns us out. 5

"Hey, I'm goin to buy that there."

"That there? You don't even know what it is, stupid."

"I do so," he say punchin on Rosie Giraffe. "It's a microscope."

"Whatcha gonna do with a microscope, fool?"

"Look at things." 10

"Like what, Ronald?" ask Miss Moore. And Big Butt ain't got the first notion. So here go Miss Moore gabbing about the thousands of bacteria in a drop of water and the somethinorother in a speck of blood and the million and one living things in the air around us is invisible to the naked eye. And what she say that for? Junebug go to town on that "naked" and we rolling. Then Miss Moore ask what it cost. So we all jam into the window smudgin it up and the price tag say $300. So then she ask how long'd take for Big Butt and Junebug to save up their allowances. "Too long," I say. "Yeh," adds Sugar, "outgrown it by that time." And Miss Moore say no, you never out-grow learning instruments. "Why, even medical students and in-terns and," blah, blah, blah. And we ready to choke Big Butt for bringing it up in the first damn place.

"This here costs four hundred eighty dollars," says Rosie Giraffe. So we pile up all over her to see what she pointin out. My eyes tell me it's a chunk of glass cracked with something heavy, and different-color inks dripped into the splits, then the whole thing put into a oven or something. But for $480 it don't make sense.

"That's a paperweight made of semi-precious stones fused to-gether under tremendous pressure," she explains slowly, with her hands doing the mining and all the factory work.

"So what's a paperweight?" asks Rosie Giraffe.

"To weigh paper with, dumbbell," say Flyboy, the wise man from the East.   15

"Not exactly," say Miss Moore, which is what she say when you warm or way off too. "It's to weigh paper down so it won't scatter and make your desk untidy." So right away me and Sugar curtsy to each other and then to Mercedes who is more the tidy type.

"We don't keep paper on top of the desk in my class," say June-bug, figuring Miss Moore crazy or lyin one.

"At home, then," she say. "Don't you have a calendar and pencil case and a blotter and a letter-opener on your desk at home where you do your homework?" And she know damn well what our homes look like cause she nosys around in them every chance she gets.

"I don't even have a desk," say Junebug. "Do we?"

"No. And I don't get no homework neither," says Big Butt.   20

"And I don't even have a home," say Flyboy like he do at school to keep the white folks off his back and sorry for him. Send this poor kid to camp posters, is his specialty.

"I do," says Mercedes. "I have a box of stationery on my desk and a picture of my cat. My godmother bought the stationery and the desk. There's a big rose on each sheet and the envelopes smell like roses."

"Who wants to know about your smelly-ass stationery," say Rosie Giraffe fore I can get my two cents in.

"It's important to have a work area all your own so that . . ."

"Will you look at this sailboat, please," say Flyboy, cuttin her off and pointin to the thing like it was his. So once again we tumble all over each other to gaze at this magnificent thing in the toy store which is just big enough to maybe sail two kittens across the pond if you strap them to the posts tight. We all start reciting the price tag like we in assembly. "Handcrafted sailboat of fiberglass at one thou-sand one hundred ninety-five dollars."   25

"Unbelievable," I hear myself say and am really stunned. I read it again for myself just in case the group recitation put me in a trance. Same thing. For some reason this pisses me off. We look at Miss Moore and she lookin at us, waiting for I dunno what.

"Who'd pay all that when you can buy a sailboat set for a quarter at Pop's, a tube of glue for a dime, and a ball of string for eight cents? It must have a motor and a whole lot else besides," I say. "My sail-boat cost me about fifty cents."

"But will it take water?" say Mercedes with her smart ass.

"Took mine to Alley Pond Park once," say Flyboy. "String broke. Lost it. Pity."

"Sailed mine in Central Park and it keeled over and sank. Had to 30 ask my father for another dollar."

"And you got the strap," laugh Big Butt. "The jerk didn't have a string on it. My old man wailed on his behind."

Little Q. T. was staring hard at the sailboat and you could see he wanted it bad. But he too little and somebody'd just take it from him. So what the hell. "This boat for kids, Miss Moore?"

"Parents silly to buy something like that just to get all broke up," say Rosie Giraffe.

"That much money it should last forever," I figure.

"My father'd buy it for me if I wanted it." 35

"Your father, my ass," say Rosie Giraffe getting a chance to finally push Mercedes.

"Must be rich people shop here," say Q. T.

"You are a very bright boy," say Flyboy. "What was your first clue?" And he rap him on the head with the back of his knuckles, since Q. T. the only one he could get away with. Though Q. T. liable to come up behind you years later and get his licks in when you half expect it.

"What I want to know is," I says to Miss Moore though I never talk to her, I wouldn't give the bitch that satisfaction, "is how much a real boat costs? I figure a thousand'd get you a yacht any day."

"Why don't you check that out," she says, "and report back to the 40 group?" Which really pains my ass. If you gonna mess up a perfectly good swim day least you could do is have some answers. "Let's go in," she say like she got something up her sleeve. Only she don't lead the way. So me and Sugar turn the corner to where the entrance is, but when we get there I kinda hang back. Not that I'm scared, what's there to be afraid of, just a toy store. But I feel funny, shame. But what I got to be shamed about? Got as much right to go in as anybody. But somehow I can't seem to get hold of the door, so I step away from Sugar to lead. But she hangs back too. And I look at her and she looks at me and this is ridiculous. I mean, damn, I have never ever been shy about doing nothing or going nowhere. But then Mercedes steps up and then Rosie Giraffe and Big Butt crowd in behind and shove, and next thing we all stuffed into the doorway with only Mercedes squeezing past us, smoothing out her jumper and walking right down the aisle. Then the rest of us tumble in like a glued-together jigsaw done all wrong. And people lookin at us. And it's like the time me and Sugar crashed into the Catholic church on a dare. But once we got in there and everything so hushed and holy and the candles and the bowin and the handkerchiefs on all the drooping heads, I just couldn't go through with the plan. Which was for me to run up to the altar and do a tap dance while Sugar played the nose flute and messed around in the holy water. And Sugar kept givin me the elbow. Then later teased me so bad I tied her up in the shower and turned it on and locked her in. And she'd be there till this day if Aunt Gretchen hadn't finally figured I was lyin about the boarder takin a shower.

Same thing in the store. We all walkin on tiptoe and hardly touchin the games and puzzles and things. And I watched Miss Moore who is steady watchin us like she waitin for a sign. Like Mama Drewery watches the sky and sniffs the air and takes note of just how much slant is in the bird formation. Then me and Sugar bump smack into each other, so busy gazing at the toys, specially the sailboat. But we don't laugh and go into our fat-lady bump-stomach routine. We just stare at that price tag. Then Sugar run a finger over the whole boat. And I'm jealous and want to hit her. Maybe not her, but I sure want to punch somebody in the mouth.

"Watcha bring us here for, Miss Moore?"

"You sound angry, Sylvia. Are you mad about something?" Givin me one of them grins like she tellin a grown-up joke that never turns out to be funny. And she's lookin very closely at me like maybe she planning to do my portrait from memory. I'm mad, but I won't give her that satisfaction. So I slouch around the store bein very bored and say, "Let's go."

Me and Sugar at the back of the train watchin the tracks whizzin by large then small then getting gobbled up in the dark. I'm thinkin about this tricky toy I saw in the store. A clown that somersaults on a bar then does chin-ups just cause you yank lightly at his leg. Cost $35. I could see me askin my mother for a $35 birthday clown. "You wanna who that costs what?" she'd say, cocking her head to the side to get a better view of the hole in my head. Thirty-five dollars could buy new bunk beds for Junior and Gretchen's boy. Thirty-five dollars and the whole hosehold could go visit Granddaddy Nelson in the country. Thirty-five dollars would pay for the rent and the piano bill too. Who are these people that spend that much for performing clowns and $1000 for toy sailboats? What kinda work they do and how they live and how come we ain't in on it? Where we are is who we are, Miss Moore always pointin out. But it don't necessarily have to be that way, she always adds then waits for somebody to say that poor people have to wake up and demand their share of the pie and don't none of us know what kind of pie she talking about in the first damn place. But she ain't so smart cause I still got her four dollars from the taxi and she sure ain't gettin it. Messin up my day with this shit. Sugar nudges me in my pocket and winks.

Miss Moore lines us up in front of the mailbox where we started from, seem like years ago, and I got a headache for thinkin so hard. And we lean all over each other so we can hold up under the draggy-ass lecture she always finishes us off with at the end before we thank her for borin us to tears. But she just looks at us like she readin tea leaves. Finally she say, "Well, what did you think of F.A.O. Schwarz?"

Rosie Giraffe mumbles, "White folks crazy."

"I'd like to go there again when I get my birthday money," says Mercedes, and we shove her out the pack so she has to lean on the mailbox by herself.

"I'd like a shower. Tiring day," say Flyboy.

Then Sugar surprises me by sayin, "You know, Miss Moore, I don't think all of us here put together eat in a year what that sailboat costs." And Miss Moore lights up like somebody goosed her. "And?" she say, urging Sugar on. Only I'm standin on her foot so she don't continue.

"Imagine for a minute what kind of society it is in which some people can spend on a toy what it would cost to feed a family of six or seven. What do you think?"

"I think," say Sugar pushing me off her feet like she never done before, cause I whip her ass in a minute, "that this is not much of a democracy if you ask me. Equal chance to pursue happiness means an equal crack at the dough, don't it?" Miss Moore is besides herself and I am disgusted with Sugar's treachery. So I stand on her foot one more time to see if she'll shove me. She shuts up, and Miss Moore looks at me, sorrowfully I'm thinkin. And somethin weird is goin on, I can feel it in my chest.

"Anybody else learn anything today?" lookin dead at me. I walk away and Sugar has to run to catch up and don't even seem to notice when I shrug her arm off my shoulder.

"Well, we got four dollars anyway," she says.

"Uh-hunh."

"We could go to Hascombs and get half a chocolate layer and then go to the Sunset and still have plenty money for potato chips and ice cream sodas."

"Un hunh."

"Race you to Hascombs," she say.

We start down the block and she gets ahead which is O.K. by me cause I'm going to the West End and then over to the Drive to think this day through. She can run if she want to and even run faster. But ain't nobody gonna beat me at nuthin.

THE INVOLVED READER

1 Everything in this story is seen through the eyes of the street-smart, tough-talking kids from uptown. What do they have in common? Are they all the same type? What are the relationships or crosscurrents among them? Can you enter into their world of thought and feeling? Why or why not?

2 What is the lesson promised in the title? What is the lesson the uptown kids learn on their trip downtown?

3 What is the role of Miss Moore in the story? Does your perception of her change?

4 What makes the street language of the uptown kids different from the prestige dialect of school and office? (Do you find their use of profanity offensive?)

TALKING, THINKING, WRITING

5 How much can you tell from the way people talk about the kind of people they are?

6 Do you remember a journey, field trip, excursion, or the like that taught you a significant lesson?

7 For you, is the gulf between the rich and the poor just a fact of life? Or do you consider it a challenge to your system of values?

MAKING CONNECTIONS

8 Many critics of American society share the view that rock-bottom economic facts — a person's job, income, position in the class structure — determine the basic realities of people's lives. Much else — like the myths created by advertisers — is window dressing. It serves mainly to distract people from facing up to basic realities. Could you use your reading of Swardson, Wolf, and Bambara to explain or justify this point of view? (If you disagree, how would you challenge or dissent from this point of view?)

poem

Mending Wall

ROBERT FROST

*What made Robert Frost a living legend among American poets?
Poems like "Stopping by Woods on a Snowy Evening" and "Mending
Wall" are among the most widely reprinted in the English language.
At a time when readers expected modern poetry to be difficult or will-
fully obscure, Frost wrote poems about everyday situations in accessible everyday language. Often these poems were set in a rural New
England setting, acting out scenarios of a country life that many of his
readers had long since left behind. Critics have found his poems deceptively simple, taking readers in by a folksy commonsense surface
but leaving them to ponder the true intention of the poet long after
the poet has passed on to other matters.*

Something there is that doesn't love a wall,
That sends the frozen-ground-swell under it
And spills the upper boulders in the sun,
And makes gaps even two can pass abreast.
The work of hunters is another thing: 5
I have come after them and made repair
Where they have left not one stone on a stone,
But they would have the rabbit out of hiding,
To please the yelping dogs. The gaps I mean,
No one has seen them made or heard them made,   10
But at spring mending-time we find them there.
I let my neighbor know beyond the hill;
And on a day we meet to walk the line
And set the wall between us as we go.
To each the boulders that have fallen to each.   15
And some are loaves and some so nearly balls
We have to use a spell to make them balance:
"Stay where you are until our backs are turned!"
We wear our fingers rough with handling them.
Oh, just another kind of outdoor game,   20
One on a side. It comes to little more;
There where it is we do not need the wall:
He is all pine and I am apple orchard.
My apple trees will never get across
And eat the cones under his pines, I tell him.   25

He only says, "Good fences make good neighbors."
Spring is the mischief in me, and I wonder
If I could put a notion in his head:
"Why do they make good neighbors? Isn't it
Where there are cows? But here there are no cows.   30
Before I built a wall I'd ask to know
What I was walling in or walling out,
And to whom I was like to give offense.
Something there is that doesn't love a wall,
That wants it down." I could say "Elves" to him,   35
But it's not elves exactly, and I'd rather
He said it for himself. I see him there,
Bringing a stone grasped firmly by the top
In each hand, like an old-stone savage armed.
He moves in darkness as it seems to me,   40
Not of woods only and the shade of trees.
He will not go behind his father's saying,
And he likes having thought of it so well
He says again, "Good fences make good neighbors."

THE INVOLVED READER

1 According to this poem, what actually happened? What are the
   basic down-to-earth facts? What background or history does the
   poet fill in for his readers?

2 The poem presents two dramatically opposed interpretations of
   what happened. What are they? How and why do the two neighbors disagree?

3 According to this poem, *do* fences make good neighbors? Critics
   reading and rereading this poem have given opposite answers,
   disagreeing on the poet's intention. Which of the two neighbors
   do *you* agree with, and why?

TALKING, THINKING, WRITING

4 Do you tend to idealize simple country living? Do Americans today feel the pull of a simpler rural world as an escape from the
   neuroses of city living?

5 Walls, like gates and towers, have many historical and symboli-
   cal associations. You may want to explore the history or symbolism of one of these.

The Writer's Tools 4

Developing Effective Paragraphs

Most beginning writers underdevelop, underestimating the reader's hunger for information.

DONALD MURRAY

The paragraph is your basic means of linking the general and the specific. The well-developed paragraph makes a general point and then backs it up. It follows through with examples, statistics, or expert testimony — until the reader says: "I see your point!" Suppose an article in a science magazine focuses on the adaptability that helps explain the diversity of life. In key paragraphs, the writer shows the application of the general principle of adaptability to specific instances. In an early paragraph, the writer may have shown that feathers were once scales, making birds distant cousins of reptiles. In a later paragraph, the writer may go on to make a similar point about the leaves of plants. Leaves take many different forms. They undergo many permutations, including many that we no longer recognize as leaves at all:

> As their functions become more and more specialized, leaves take forms that we often no longer recognize as leaves. For example, the spines of cactuses were once leaves. The bulb of an onion is formed of layers and layers of specialized leaves. The needles of pine trees are specially modified leaves, as are the tendrils of climbing plants. The hard woody sheathing around the trunks of palm trees is made up of modified leaves, so large in one plant in the Amazon river basin that local tribes use it to make a makeshift canoe.

In many of your paragraphs, you will be shoring up the general points you make with multiple examples. We call the general point of a paragraph the **topic sentence**. Often the topic sentence comes first, or right after a short introductory statement. As you write your paragraphs, imagine the reader over your shoulder who says: "Such as?" "For instance?" "For example?"

At times, a variation on the multiple-example paragraph will better serve your purpose. Note that in the following sample paragraphs, a **transition** like *for example* or *for instance* often signals the shift from general to specific.

Downshifting

Not all examples in a paragraph are likely to receive equal emphasis. When you **downshift** in a paragraph, you choose one (or more) in a set of examples for more detailed treatment. You slow down for a closer look. The following paragraph moves on three different levels of generalization. It moves from the general through the intermediate to the specific:

GENERAL: *Most commercials succeed by working on the viewer's need to be loved, and most commercials appeal to hidden fears.* For

INTERMEDIATE: example, we have been schooled from early childhood (sociologist David Riesman called the American child a "consumer trainee") that our bodies produce numerous odors which "offend." Those who advertise deodorants, toothpastes, mouthwashes, colognes, and soaps have laid out billions of dollars to convince us that natural odors are un-

SPECIFIC: natural. In an attempt to appeal to the environmentally conscious younger generation, the makers of Gillette Right Guard once announced: "A new anti-perspirant as natural as your clothes and makeup."

David Burmester, "The Myths of Madison Avenue," *English Journal*

One Key Example

Sometimes one vivid detailed example is more eloquent than would be several shorter ones. The extended example then becomes a **case in point**. It gives the reader a chance to take in something new and to think about how it works:

TOPIC SENTENCE: *As more and more clerical workers use computers, they increasingly find that their work is monitored from afar.* For

KEY EXAMPLE: instance, computerization changed the workplace in the accounting department of a large airline: The company hired a computer consultant to observe the work of clerks sifting through flight coupons and tabulating revenues. The consultant then devised a computerized system to keep exact count of how many tickets each clerk was processing each day. The system also identified periods during the day when productivity would dip while workers socialized or took breaks. The system enabled supervisors to set work quotas and to identify electronically those employees who fell short. Like the chickens on a computerized chicken farm, the workers were no longer allowed to waste the company's time.

Point and Explanation

Sometimes you will decide that your topic sentence needs explanation or elaboration before you go on to examples. You may want to take time to define a key term or spell out what is implied in a snappy opening sentence. The following paragraph shows a common pattern of statement — explanation — illustration:

TOPIC SENTENCE:	*I always wished to be famous.* As other people have an
EXPLANATION:	imagination for disaster, I have had an imagination for
	fame. I can remember as a boy of nine or ten returning
ILLUSTRATION:	alone from the playground in the early evening after dinner dodging, cutting, stiff-arming imaginary tacklers on the way to scoring imaginary touchdowns before enormous imaginary crowds who chanted my name. Practicing free throws alone in my backyard I would pretend that I was shooting them at a crucial moment in a big game at Madison Square Garden. Later, as a boy tennis player, before falling off to sleep, I imagined the Duchess of Kent presenting me with the winner's trophy on the center court at Wimbledon.

Aristides, "A Mere Journalist," *The American Scholar*

Citing Statistics

Statistics bundle large numbers of bit facts. Instead of citing individual examples, you may want to show how widely a general pattern applies by citing authoritative statistics. In the following sample paragraph, the general point is sandwiched between statistics that help establish the authority of an insider, someone in the know:

STATISTICS:	Four of the ten hardcover bestsellers in a recent year were fitness books. Americans spent over a billion dollars on exercise devices, and many people have turned
TOPIC SENTENCE:	their homes into private gymnasiums. *Nevertheless, in spite of the fitness craze that has swept the nation, Americans are*
STATISTICS:	*actually less physically fit than they were five years ago.* Between 80 and 90 percent of Americans still do not get enough exercise. (Exercise is defined as any activity that boosts heart and lung performance to 60 percent or more of its capacity for at least twenty minutes three times a week.) According to a study published by the Department of Health and Human Services, American children are fatter today than they were twenty years ago. Only 36 percent of our children can pass minimum fitness standards set by the Amateur Athletic Union.

Quoting Sources

Often you will be able to strengthen a paragraph with well-chosen quotations. Where you can, you quote experts, eyewitnesses, officials, seasoned observers. You draw on their testimony to show that people who are better known or have a better track record than you have reached conclusions similar to yours. The following paragraph uses a mix of striking examples and quotable quotes to back up the general point:

TOPIC SENTENCE: *For decades, Dali, the bizarre Spaniard with the erratic eyes*
                      and the antenna moustache, was the uncontested leader of
                      surrealism, the art movement that expresses the unanalyzed
EXAMPLES: *subconscious.* In their illogical and hallucinatory patterns,
                      his paintings look like the record of extravagant dreams.
                      These paintings bear such titles as "Rotting Mannequin in
                      a Taxi" or "Debris of an Automobile Giving Birth to a
                      Blind Horse Biting a Telephone." Images of ants, snails,
                      melting watches, cauliflowers, lobsters, and women with
                      chests of drawers in their abdomens appear throughout
QUOTATIONS: his work. When he first burst upon the scene with an
                      exhibition of surrealist paintings in Paris, one critic said,
                      "We have here a direct, unmistakable assault on sanity
                      and decency." A French poet called Dali "the great legis-
                      lator of delirium." Dali said of himself, "The only differ-
                      ence between me and a madman is that I am not mad."

                                                            Student editorial

Clincher Sentence

To make sure your reader takes in the key point, you may want
to restate it at the end in a **clincher sentence**. A good clincher sentence does not just repeat the point but drives it home, perhaps reinforcing it with some striking detail, a snappy quoted phrase, or
strategic contrast:

TOPIC SENTENCE: *Most often the male role in advertising is that of the*
                          strong, silent outdoorsman, athlete, or adventurer. The ar-
FIRST EXAMPLE: chetypal male figure in advertising is, of course, the
                          Marlboro man. This famous mythic figure was the
                          product of an intensive campaign that transformed a
                          poorly selling cigarette, originally aimed a women
                          smokers, into the biggest selling filter-tip on the mar-
                          ket. At the same time, it promoted an attitude about
                          male roles still being sold in almost every cigarette ad
SECOND EXAMPLE: currently in print. Commercials for beer also push the
                          take-charge male image, showing men, generally in
                          groups, participating in active, physically demanding
                          sports or jobs and being rewarded with a cool bottle
                          of beer. Rarely are women seen in these commercials
                          other than as silent companions to these he-men. *The*
CLINCHER SENTENCE: *Marlboro man and his descendants exemplify the self-suf-*
                          ficient, highly individualistic male who provides the comple-
                          ment to the sexy, empty-headed female of toiletry
                          commercials.

                      David Burmester, "The Myths of Madison Avenue," *English Journal*

Topic Sentence Last

Usually, a topic sentence early in your paragraph will help your readers find their bearings. But at times you may prefer to reverse the usual order. Your stance may be, "I will show you first what I have in mind — and then tell you what it means."

EXAMPLES:

> It is Friday night at any of ten thousand watering holes of the small towns and crossroad hamlets of the South. The room is a cacophony of the pingpong-dingdingding of the pinball machine, the pop-fizz of another round of Pabst, the refrain of "Red Necks, White Socks, and Blue Ribbon Beer" on the juke box, the insolent roar of a souped-up engine outside,

TOPIC SENTENCE LAST:

> and, above it all, the sound of easy laughter. *The good ole boys have gathered for their fraternal ritual — the aimless diversion that they have elevated into a lifestyle.*

> Bonnie Angelo, "Those Good Ole Boys," *Time*

Just as no two sentences are alike, no two paragraphs are alike. A paragraph might follow a *yes, but* pattern: You might start with an example that is really an exception and that might put the unwary observer on the wrong track. Then the rest of the paragraph might present the counterexamples that will point the reader in the right direction. Another paragraph might be built around a contrast of *then and now.* The key question to ask yourself about your paragraphs is: Am I following through? Am I backing up my general point?

WRITING WORKSHOP 5

What Is the Point?

In each of the following paragraphs, a set of examples points in the same direction. The several instances point to the same general conclusion. For each passage, write the missing topic sentence that would sum up the general point. Compare your own suggested topic sentences with those of your classmates.

1 _____. According to Gloria Steinem, *Ms.* lost a major cosmetics account because it featured Soviet women on its cover who were not, according to the advertiser, wearing enough makeup. Thirty-five thousand dollars worth of advertising was withdrawn from a British magazine the day after an editor, Carol Sarler, was quoted as saying that she found it hard to show women looking

intelligent when they were plastered with makeup. A gray-haired editor for a leading women's magazine told a gray-haired writer, Mary Kay Blakely, that an article about the glories of gray hair cost the magazine the Clairol account for six months. An editor of *New York Woman*, a staff member told me, was informed that for financial reasons she had to put a model on the cover rather than a remarkable woman she wished to profile.

Naomi Wolf, *The Beauty Myth*

2 _____. Magazines like *Savvy* and *Working Woman* offer tips on everything from sex to software, plus the occasional instructive tale about a woman who rises effortlessly from managing a boutique to being the CEO of a multinational corporation. Scores of books have told the aspiring managerial woman what to wear, how to flatter superiors, and when necessary, fire subordinates. Even old-fashioned radicals like myself, for whom "CD" still means civil disobedience rather than an interest rate, can expect to receive a volume of second-class mail inviting them to join their corporate sisters at a "networking brunch" or to share the privileges available to the female frequent flier.

Barbara Ehrenreich, "Strategies of Corporate Women," *The New Republic*

WRITING WORKSHOP 6

Tracking the Paragraph

What is the role of general and specific in each of the following paragraphs? Does the paragraph have a topic sentence? How much is explanation; how much is illustration? Do any of the writers employ downshifting or the clincher sentence? Why do examples appear in the order they do?

1 The action film is a terrible vehicle in which to try to probe anything political, because it has to deliver shocks on schedule. And it colors anything political by its own brand of action politics. The viewer gets the feeling that the world is irredeemably violent: in a Clint Eastwood film, Eastwood can't go into a diner and ask for a glass of water without someone's picking a fight with him. Action movies say that the world is always threatening your manhood every minute of the day. In the forties, action directors used the anti-Nazi theme for hollow and sadistic violence; in the late sixties and early seventies, they used the anti-Vietnam war theme the same way (and we became the Nazis). In recent years, action directors have been using "survival." In other eras, the wilderness was sentimentalized as innocent. Now even nature is malevolent.

Pauline Kael, "The Swamp," *The New Yorker*

2 Greeks enslaved foreigners and other Greeks. Anyone captured in war was dragged back as a slave, even if he was a Greek of a neighboring polis.

In Athens slaves, especially women, were often domestic servants, but of 150,000 adult males, 20,000 were set to work in the silver mines, in ten-hour shifts, in tunnels three-feet high, shackled and lashed; the forehead of a retrieved runaway was branded with a hot iron. Aristotle called slaves "animate tools," forever indispensable, he thought, unless you were a utopian who believed in some future invention of automatic machinery. In Athens it was understood that the most efficient administrator was someone who had himself been born into slavery and then freed; such a man would know, out of his oppressive experience with severity, how to bear down hard.

Cynthia Ozick, "The Moral Necessity of Metaphor," Harper's

3 Examples of Doublespeak — the sometimes unwitting but more often deliberate misuse of words to cover up, rather than explain, reality — are easy to find almost everywhere. Government bureaus, for instance, have been instructed to eliminate the word *poverty* from official documents, replacing it with *low-income*, a term not nearly as alarming as *poverty*. Instead of *prisons*, there are now only correctional facilities. U.S. State Department employees are not *fired* but *selected out*, a term that sounds like an award for excellence. Other government types tend to be terminated. In each instance, the aim is to make things appear better than they are or, in the case of correctional facilities, actually to seem what they decidedly are not. If all this were only a matter of semantics and style, there would be little cause for concern. Unfortunately, the linguistic cosmetics are often used to create the impression that nasty problems have already been solved or were not really too nasty in the first place.

Fred M. Hechinger, "In the End Was the Euphemism," World

Knowledge that is understood by a few can only be acted upon by a few. **GLORIA STEINEM**

5

Mapping the Territory

Writing to Analyze

How good are you at sorting out information and laying it out in an intelligible order? Effective writers analyze the available information and develop the blueprint that makes it accessible. For instance, they trace the stages of a process — whether the manufacturing process in a robotized factory or the life cycle of the salmon. Or they make a set of data fall into place, arranging them under headings that show what goes with what. (For instance, they classify kinds of vegetarians or arrangements for day care.) Or they look at key factors that explain current developments, tracing cause and effect.

To analyze something means to identify its key parts, stages, or causes, and to show what they contribute to the whole. In a history course or introduction to economics, you may be studying the sources of America's envied prosperity, now endangered. After World War II, the United States was the world's leading economic power. You are likely to have some notions of why this was so. You may also have some theories why this country has since slipped from its preeminent position. Much discussion today centers on how this decline should be arrested or reversed. For a better understanding of what is involved, you turn to an analysis of the major facets or key causes of the prosperity of earlier decades. In an article or in a chapter in a textbook, an author might lay out the key factors like this:

The Roots of Prosperity

(most basic and obvious)

At the peak of American prosperity and influence, America had the largest internal market in the world, making possible the efficiencies and economies of mass production — for instance, of automobiles.

(also very important and well recognized)
> While factories and laboratories in Europe and Japan lay in ruins after World War II, America led the world in technology, profiting from the expertise of European scientists who had come here as refugees.

(less obvious but also very important)
> High school education and college education, available in other countries mostly to a small elite, reached millions, providing the country with the best educated and most skilled workforce in the world.

(resulting from and fueled by the first three)
> Spending power of consumers was the highest in the world, with per capita income four times that of Germany and fifteen times that of Japan.

(not always recognized)
> American management was the most experienced in the world, while in other countries the most ambitious still looked for careers in the military or in public service.

A brief overview of the writer's points would look like this:

  I MASS MARKET
 II THE TECHNOLOGICAL EDGE
III BROAD-BASED EDUCATION
 IV MASSIVE SPENDING POWER
  V HIGH-POWERED MANAGEMENT

This strategy takes you from the most to the least obvious. It is likely to put you in an assenting mood, starting with things that make you nod in agreement. Under each of the headings, the writer would fill in the data and striking examples needed to make each point stick. When well done, such an analysis makes us say: "I begin to understand. I see what it was: the mass market, advanced technology, mass education, massive spending power, top management." You may of course want to quarrel with all or part of this account. However, this writer has mapped the territory for you — you can improve the map as necessary.

Writing that analyzes or explains does not have to be dryly analytical. Scientists explaining global warming or desertification are motivated by their concern for our endangered planet. Naturalists studying the life cycles or communication patterns of animal species are moved by their love for fellow creatures. When writing to analyze, try to choose a topic that has a personal meaning for you. For instance, write about something you love to do, or sort out a situation that has stymied you in the past.

	THOUGHT LOG 5

Thinking about Your Writing Process

How conscious are you of your own writing process? How consciously aware are you of how you write? Write freely to answer questions like the following: What helps you most with your writing? Do you suffer from writer's block — and do you have ideas on how to overcome it? What helps you get started? How does a plan for a paper take shape in your mind? Do you write a first draft start to finish — or do you write in chunks and then put them together? What has been your worst or most difficult experience in your career as a writer? What has been your best?

SAMPLE THOUGHT LOG ENTRY: I have, as I always did, a tough time starting my papers, deciding what sort of stance I want to take. I usually gather information from a variety of places and read through it until I find a point of view I can connect with. Once this connection has been made, I find more information on a more focused topic. After reading and highlighting, I can usually sit down and type out my paper. Starting with a personal story or a "picture" description to make the issue real has been an eye-opener for me. I do not think I usually write a separate first draft. I sit at my computer and type — if I get stuck I find a quote in one of the sources I have and am then usually able to continue.

Charting Your Strategy

Writing students think they're supposed to have a completed plan — to know just what the finished product will look like — yet good writers dive in or start to work knowing that they will work out where to go from the inside.

SHEILA TOBIAS

How do you lay out a subject so that your readers can get their bearings? Much information comes to you unsorted. Your task is to piece it together, bringing order out of confusion. To strengthen your own sense of pattern, you can study organizing strategies — strategies that alone or in combination give shape to much effective writing.

Tracing a Process   What is the process that produces the end result? How does one thing lead to another? Readers can follow your account of activities or events when you show them to be part of a process or a cycle. Life forms on our planet move from the seed through the sapling to the mature tree and to the dying tree. They move from conception through the embryo to the infant and adolescent and to the mature and aging individual.

Similarly, many manufacturing and creative activities require us to think in terms of where to start, what to do next, and what steps to go through in what order. For example, how can your readers make their own bread — staying away from preservative-laden, bleached-flour supermarket bread and filling their homes with the aroma of loaves fresh from the oven? What does it take to produce a loaf of bread that is not hard as a rock, flat as a board? Working on your how-to paper, keep advice like the following in mind:

• *Tell your readers why as well as how.* You may want to start by explaining the purpose or the benefits of the process. What is the satisfaction in baking your own bread?

The Natural Way to Eat Bread

Much of the bread we see on supermarket shelves is filled with preservatives so that it can stay on the shelves longer without spoiling. Much of it has an unnaturally pale-white appearance because of the use of bleached flour stripped of much of its natural richness. Often, when unwrapped from the cellophane, the store-bought product has the taste and consistency of a sponge. To reduce the amount of dubious chemicals in our diet we can learn to bake our own bread from natural ingredients.

• *Mark off major stages of the process.* Early in your paper, give your readers a preview or overview of essential steps. Readers get lost in a welter of miscellaneous instructions. Clear division into major tasks lets your readers follow the process with a sense of direction, making them feel at each stage that they know where they are.

Baking bread is one of the oldest and most satisfying human activities. The first step in making natural bread is shopping for organic, natural ingredients. The second is kneading the dough. The next essential step is letting the dough rise. Finally, the loaves will be ready for the oven.

• *Pay patient attention to detail.* Include the details needed to make things work. Include cautions about predictable ways things might go wrong. The following might be your paragraph about one essential stage of the bread-making process:

What makes the dough rise? The difference between flat bread and well-rounded loaves is yeast — minute organisms that grow and make the dough expand when exposed to moisture and heat. After the yeast has been dissolved in hot water and milk, mix it with the other ingredients of the dough. Turn the dough out on a lightly floured pastry cloth and knead it for about five minutes until it is smooth and elastic. The bread is now ready to rise, with the entire process taking about four or five hours. Place the dough in a lightly greased bowl, cover it with a damp cloth, and let it rise to about double its original bulk. Make sure the temperature is about 80 degrees: A higher temperature will produce a dry bread. If the room is too cold, put the dough in the oven with a pan of hot water under it. After the dough has risen to about double bulk, turn the dough out on a lightly floured cloth and knead it again.

Not all processes are linear, moving on a single track toward their destination. For instance, the undercarriage, the engine, and the hull of a car might move along separate feeder lines until they meet to be assembled into the finished car. Different lines of development then feed into a finished product the way tributaries feed into a river. Other processes are cyclical. An article tracing the life cycle of the salmon might start from salmon fighting their way upstream. It might show them reaching the spawning grounds, with the young fish eventually hatching and heading for the sea, until the mature fish move upstream to spawn again, starting the cycle anew.

WRITING WORKSHOP I

Capsule Summaries

Study the following capsule summaries of processes, techniques, or procedures. How do the writers show that they have an eye for essentials? How do they make each process vivid for the reader? Write a similar sentence for each category.

1. (a natural cycle)
    The flower begins as a seed; it takes root; it grows; it blooms; it dies, leaving behind a seed that will begin the process again.

2. (an agricultural or manufacturing process)
    Tomatoes are grown, irrigated, fed, sprayed, now taken, soon to be cooled, squashed, boiled, barreled, and held at the ready, then canned, shipped, sold, bought, and then after being sold and bought a few more times, uncanned and dumped on pizza.

    Mark Kramer

3. (a technique or procedure)
    The Heimlich maneuver involves encircling the victim from behind so that the rescuer's grasped hands press hard into the abdomen, forcing the diaphragm upward and creating a rush of air that expels whatever may be stuck in the windpipe.

4. (a job or task)
    The tree trimmer clinks and clanks climbing up the tree; the chain saw roars as it comes to life; sawdust comes raining down on our heads till

finally there is a loud crack as another huge limb comes down with an earth-shaking thud.

Classification What goes with what? Sorting things out into categories makes them manageable and accessible. Much of the planning that organizes our lives involves informal classification: children, young adults, adults, and seniors; married, single, and divorced; overachievers, average achievers, and underachievers.

Classification fills a special need when changing patterns make old guideposts misleading or when old categories no longer fit. For instance, the traditional think scheme of upper class — middle class — working class worked well for a time. However, the traditional scheme required updating in order to recognize a large new underclass of people permanently dependent on welfare or chronically unemployed.

Here are accounts of two writing projects involving classification:

• Working on a classification paper, you will often start with a comprehensive stock-taking of the material to be charted. For instance, the following might be sample entries in your **viewer's log** for a paper sorting out the appeals used by television advertisers:

> powerful macho truck barrels through rugged country
> panthers or cougars flex their limbs and bare their fangs in car commercials
> headache tablets wipe your headache away
> the American dream family oohs and ahhs over a breakfast cereal
> life insurance gives suit-and-tie young father "peace of mind"
> dashboard of car looks like control panel of Starship Enterprise
> bronzed youngsters playing volleyball drink no-calorie drink
> "nobody can be turned away" for insurance for veterans
> bearded, flannel-shirted beer drinkers work in rugged country,
> then drink with admiring young women in bar
> young woman with the right mouthwash cuddles up with adoring young man
> wide-eyed starving African children look at the viewer in a plea for food for the hungry

What goes with what? After a first rough sorting out, you may conclude that commercials hold out different kinds of promises:

> Appeals to basic needs and desires:
> promises of the magic touch (every chore made easy)
> promises of adventure
> daydreams of power

daydreams of good looks and eternal youth
daydreams of problem-free sex

This first sorting leaves several entries unaccounted for that point in a different direction. They appeal to our anxieties and fears. You decide to set up a second major category. You come up with a two-pronged system of classification — two major categories, each with several subcategories.

Advertising's Magic Kingdom

Appeals to basic needs and desires:
promises of the magic touch (every chore made easy)
promises of adventure
daydreams of power
daydreams of good looks and eternal youth
daydreams of problem-free sex
Appeals to basic fears:
fear of rejection
fear of loneliness
fear of illness and death

This more comprehensive outline still leaves out the occasional public-service message that appeals to our more generous or responsible selves. You may decide to discuss such messages in your introduction (or in your conclusion) as a foil or contrast for the more prevalent type of appeal.

• In trying to sort out the broad range of sports in American life, you may ask: "How do sports mirror the class structure of society?" What is the social status of the participants and the fans? Your first category might be tony upper-class sports such as polo or yachting. Your second category might be middle-class sports like football and baseball. Farther down the social scale, your third category might be lower-class sports like professional wrestling and drag racing. You might discuss a formerly upper-class sport like tennis as an interesting example of a sport moving up or down in the social scale.

However, your interest might be less in the sociology of sports than in the psychology of sports as an arena of competition. Your key question would become: "What is the nature of the competition?" For example, often individual competes against individual, but just as commonly team competes with team. And often the contestant is in a contest not with others but, as in mountain climbing, with the forces of nature. Looking at sports from this angle may help you and your readers better understand the motives and rewards of key sports. The following might be your tentative scheme. Your thesis provides a preview of your major categories:

Meeting the Competition

THESIS: Sports offer us the means of testing ourselves by facing and overcoming opposition, whether human competitors, the forces of nature, animals, or our own human limits.

I Competing with other human competitors
    football
    racquetball
    wrestling

II Competing against the forces of nature
    rock climbing
    skiing
    sailing

III Competing against animals
    rodeos
    bullfights

IV Competing with ourselves
    marathon running
    body building

WRITING WORKSHOP 2

A Paper for Peer Review

Study the following paper. Compare your comments and reactions with those of other members of a small group or your class as a whole. Pay special attention to questions like the following:

• How does the writer set the paper in motion? How does the paper lead up to its thesis? Is there a preview or overview?

• What are the major categories the writer has set up? Do they seem equally important? Does the order in which they appear make sense?

• Which examples are most striking or convincing? Which least?

• Where and why does the writer quote printed sources?

Meeting the Competition

Our word *athlete* is the Greek word for contestant. When we think of sports, we usually think of one contestant competing with another or others for a prize — an Olympic gold medal, a cherished trophy. On the surface, much of the world of sports presents human beings in contest with each other. When we go beyond the surface, however, we see that much of the time human contestants struggle against other kinds of opposition. Sports offer us a means of testing ourselves by facing and overcoming opposition, whether human competitors, natural forces, or animals. Often the adversary we are trying to overcome is our own human limits.

Obviously, many of the spectator sports that attract large crowds feature battles between teams of human competitors, with winners and losers, with victory celebrations and the consequences of defeat. In football, opponents literally face each other, with one player shoving the other down the field. Wrestling is one of the oldest of these symbolic confrontations between human contenders, as one contestant contends with another, trying to pin the opponent's shoulders to the ground.

On the other hand, some sports that seem to be a competition between human contestants really challenge athletes to test their own limits. For example, in marathon running the contest on the surface is between runners competing for first or second place. But many compete who have no chance to win and who are working toward a personal goal. Running the twenty-six miles is their challenge to themselves. An article in the *American Medical News* told the story of a twenty-three-year-old runner in the Triathlon World Championship in Hawaii:

> With only one hundred yards left between her and the finish, Moss fell to her knees. She then rose, ran a few more yards, and collapsed again. As TV cameras rolled, she lost control of her bodily functions. She got up again, ran, fell, and then started crawling. Passed by the second-place runner, she crawled across the finish line, stretched out her arm, and passed out.

This woman was in a race against herself, fighting the limitations of her own body. Other sports that seem competitive in the conventional sense also involve contestants who are basically testing their own limits. A golfer tries to get a lower score than in all previous games. A bowler tries to get a higher score than ever before.

In some sports, participants are pitting their own strength and skill against the forces of nature. In sailing, human beings struggle against the variables of wind and water. In the contest with nature, sports often cease to be play and become deadly serious instead: The mountain climber has to trust in a rope holding to break a fall; handholds and footholds in crevices or on ledges make the difference between life and death. Some three years ago, a brother of a friend of mine, in spite of warnings, went rock climbing alone and fell 150 feet to his death.

The grimly serious nature of the contests is strongest in sports that have their roots in prehistoric contests between human beings and animals. Modern rodeos entertain spectators by having riders try to control broncs and bulls, at danger to life and limb. In bullfighting, the matador kills the bull, and it appears that the animal is the inevitable loser. Yet according to Fodor's *Travel Guide to Spain* (1983),

> A bullfighter's chance of dying in the ring is one in ten. Chance of dying or being crippled is about one in four. They know, usually, what the horn ripping through the flesh feels like; no bullfighters finish their careers completely unscathed.

Wherever we look, the contest seems to be taking place on several levels. A race car driver is competing with other contestants for first place. At the same time, the driver is struggling to assert his or her mastery over a powerful, deadly machine. And the most basic contest is between pride, ambition, determination on the one hand and fear, fatigue, and human fallibility on the other.

Cause and Effect What causes will produce what effects? Analyzing a problem often means probing the causes that produced it and then recommending remedies. Cause-and-effect writing centers on two related questions: First, what are the true causes? The answer to this question can help us understand the past and teach us how to avoid past mistakes. Second, what will be the consequences? The answer can help us predict future developments and help us control the results of our present actions.

A cause-and-effect paper addressing a problem may be structured as follows: problem — obstacles to solution — identifiable causes — remedial action:

Slowing Down Pollution

PROBLEM: A striking example of pollution running wild: A jogger running along a canal encounters a large white truck with a hooded, space-suited individual spraying a white liquid chemical into the air.

OBSTACLES: Two main reasons for our faltering efforts to clean up the environment: First, we are fatalistic about pollution, assuming that it is the price we pay for living in a highly developed industrial society. Second, the causes of ecological disasters like acid rain are hard to pin down and control.

TRACEABLE CAUSES: Many major causes of pollution *can* be exactly traced: strip mining, toxic chemicals dumped into rivers, toxic wastes improperly buried in inadequate sites.

TOWARD SOLUTIONS: The first major step toward stronger remedial action is heightened public awareness. To overcome the feeling that nothing much can be done, we can participate in symbolic acts: We can carry our own refuse out of the wilderness. We can participate in tree-planting campaigns. We can promote recycling efforts at home and in the workplace. We can join in efforts to help save wildlife trapped in oilspills.

WRITING WORKSHOP 3

Tracing Cause and Effect

The following might be a classmate's prewriting notes for a cause-and-effect paper that probes beyond surface symptoms and explores possible remedies. What suggestions would you give the writer for developing this tentative plan? What questions would you like to ask? Which of the causes and suggested remedies seem most plausible or convincing? Which least?

Hotheads and Short Fuses

Symptoms

A teacher drives his car back to campus to pick up papers at the office. He is unable to avoid hitting a jaywalker who suddenly appears in front of the car. The incensed jaywalker drags the driver out of the car while the car careens wildly across the street.

After a narrow victory over a traditional rival in a championship football game, the fans rock and overturn cars of the visiting team; one car is set afire, and dozens of people are injured.

At a local school, vandals spraypaint library books and walls and scatter records, causing $75,000 worth of damage.

A seventeen-year-old gang member is fatally shot after straying onto a neighboring gang's "turf."

Causes

According to zoologists, primates mark their territories by scent or visual display. Humans similarly "leave their mark" on territory they are otherwise unable to control.

Gangs that vandalize public property as a group effort reinforce their sense of mutual loyalty, producing a stronger degree of "social bonding."

Much seemingly unprovoked individual violence expresses pent-up anger at an oppressive or frustrating environment. Angry people lash out at random targets. People who feel thwarted or hemmed in strike at others who are invading their turf.

Traditional Response

Nebuchadnezzar tried to counteract vandalism by issuing edicts against the defacement of temples in Babylon.

In Singapore, an American youth convicted of vandalism was sentenced to a brutal caning.

In our society, we try to curb misbehavior by public outcry and threats of punishment, but we basically seem at a loss when trying to deal with offenders guilty of random violence.

Alternative Approaches

Psychologists ask us to think about the underlying psychological mechanisms that precipitate — or could prevent — violent and destructive behavior. What could help to develop sensitivity in apparently calloused individuals? One landscape architect in Seattle wraps newly planted trees in gauze. The gauze bandage, suggesting something wounded or vulnerable, is designed to produce a caring rather than a destructive response.

Revising Your Analysis Paper

When you look at early drafts, think of them as stages in a process. You have taken a big step in your first draft if you have laid out your subject to your own satisfaction. You can say to yourself: "I am beginning to see how the parts fit together. I have a better sense of what goes with what." The next step is to ask yourself: "Have I hooked my readers into the subject? Have I done enough to help them follow?"

Reread your first draft through the reader's eyes. Consider questions like the following:

• *Is your analysis too impersonal or too dull?* Explaining why young people join gangs or cliques, you may have discussed lack of parental supervision in two-wage-earner or single-parent families, need for peer approval, the pull of group loyalty. However, looking back over your draft, you should ask: "Have I brought the subject to life with dramatic, convincing examples? Have I brought in authentic incidents and actual people — from personal experience, first-hand observation, or current media coverage?"

• *Should you do more to push toward a unifying thesis?* What is the connecting strand or overarching idea? For instance, assume you are discussing three kinds of popular music that captured the imagination of the young: blues, rock and roll, and punk rock. What is their common appeal? Exploitation and racism gave blacks reasons to sing the blues. The rock-and-roll generation was voicing its rebellion against a materialistic lifestyle. Punk rock expresses violent anger and alienation. In your revision, you may want to bring out more strongly the common element:

> THESIS: The most influential musical forms of the youth culture have been rooted in rebellion against established society.

• *In tracing a process, are you taking too many small steps?* Readers lose their way if they lose sight of the large outlines of a procedure or a cycle. Keep them from getting bogged down in an "and then . . . and then" pattern. Group related operations or developments together as one major phase. Identify major turns in the road.

• *Are you giving a strong, inviting preview of your overall scheme?* Early on, are you creating the expectations that the rest of the paper will satisfy? For instance, in reworking a paper on male stereotypes in popular entertainment, you may want to do more to highlight your five basic types:

Macho or Wimp?

I The outdoor macho type (the Marlboro man)
II The male authority figure (doctor, professor, expert)
III The harassed, well-meaning sitcom father
IV The goof-off perennial delayed adolescent
V The wimp

• *Have you settled on striking, memorable labels for major phases or categories?*   When you write about people's attitudes toward work, your readers will remember labels like the workaholic, the climber, the nine-to-fiver, and the shirker (or the call-in-sick-on-Monday).

• *Are you giving adequate coverage to different facets of your subject?*   For what steps or categories do you need a detailed example to serve as a case in point? For instance, as you classify the growing homeless population, you may not need to belabor familiar expected categories: the mentally ill, alcoholics, people with substance abuse problems. You might however need additional real-life examples for another less often recognized category — ordinary people whose safety net was rent by layoff, catastrophic physical illness, or similar misfortune.

WRITING WORKSHOP 4

A Paper for Peer Review

On an issue clouded by tradition, prejudice, or stereotype, readers welcome someone who can map the territory. Study the following student paper. How successfully does the author identify potentially relevant factors? What parts of the papers are strongest or most informative? Which are weakest? For you, what questions does the paper leave unanswered? What questions would you like to ask the author?

Math and the Sexes

When I was a child, school was never a problem. I was never stressed out over grades. I was a straight A student until I started my freshman year of high school and began Algebra One. Algebra was the most difficult subject I have ever had to face. I struggled with that class all year, and while I remained an A student in my other classes, it took all my effort to get a C+ in math. I had never had to work so hard for such a low grade. Prior to taking algebra I had confidence in myself as a student. I felt I was just as intelligent as anyone else. After struggling with math for three years, I lost all confidence in myself as a math and science student. After completing a disastrous year in Algebra Two, I dropped math and made it my goal to avoid math at all costs.

Several of my close female friends have had similar experiences. We were honors students with straight A's until it came to math. Why should this subject produce so much anxiety, particularly for women? Is mathematical ability sex-linked, or are we just conditioned to believe so?

According to Sheila Tobias in her book, *Overcoming Math Anxiety*, it is a common myth that to succeed at math the student needs a mathematical mind. According to Tobias, parents, and especially parents of girls, often expect their children to be nonmathematical. "Parents are either poor at math and had their own sudden death experiences, or, if math came easy to them, they do not know what it feels like to be slow. In either case they unwittingly foster the idea that a mathematical mind is something one either has or does not have."

Tobias asks, "Why should people who can do college-level work in other subjects not be able to do college-level math as well?" Nevertheless, like other women before me, I have fallen into the trap of blaming my struggles with math on my not having mathematical ability. The trend in our society is to tell young men struggling with math that it is time to work harder, whereas a young woman is likely to be told that she is not a math-minded individual and that her talents lie elsewhere. Men are conditioned to think of math as a challenge, whereas women are more readily given permission not to succeed. A woman struggling with math can give up and not feel like a failure or be looked down upon for quitting.

Traditionally math has not been considered a feminine subject. Women are expected to excel in English while math is traditionally male territory. Men who write poetry and women who excel in math are considered odd; they don't fit the norm. A friend of mine dropped out of a third-year calculus class as a high school senior after completing one semester, not because the material was too difficult but because she felt "too weird about the experience." She was the only female student in a class of thirty. She says, "I really didn't want to tell my friends that I was taking the class because I thought they would think I was strange. I also felt that men are intimidated by women who do well in math. They feel that math is their territory, and they don't like women to move in on it."

The kind of conditioning that programs young people for success or failure at math starts in early childhood. As Tobias points out, boys are more likely to get toys they can take apart; they deal with parts that force them to keep count and that train them to think in terms of cause and effect. They engage in sports where measurements and statistics play a major part. By contrast, an informal survey I conducted of a group of college women revealed that their most popular childhood toy was a stuffed animal or doll. Playing with dolls does not provide any mathematical training.

I believe that it is part of our culture to expect women to do poorly at math. Recently a talking Barbie doll was put on the market. Among the things she said was "I hate math. Math is hard." After feminists protested, the doll was pulled off the shelves, but that it could have been produced in the first place makes one wonder.

We need to encourage women to see math as a challenge to be met rather than as an obstacle only a select few can conquer. We need more female mathematicians as role models. We should experiment with all-female math classes, where male–female rivalry or male condescension cannot play a role. Men are not biologically superior in math ability; our culture just fosters that harmful stereotype.

| OPTIONS FOR WRITING 5 |

Charting the Territory

Choose a topic that will make a difficult or challenging subject accessible for your reader. Try to clear up confusion, guide choices, or offer practical instructions or advice. Choose a topic where you can play the role of the insider — where you have relevant experience or special expertise, where you can observe from a special vantage point, or where you can do some detailed investigation.

1 Can you help explain a problem affecting young people? For instance, can you offer your readers some insight into the workings of gangs or cliques? Can you offer parents a perspective on the causes of vandalism, high dropout rates, or high suicide rates among the young?

2 In analyzing pollution we often look for the major institutional culprits. What are major everyday sources of pollution where people like you and us might be to blame?

3 Naturalists write with awe and wonder about the natural world, but they are at the same time patient students and alert observers of the processes at work in nature. Trace a natural process or cycle that you can track through major stages or phases. For instance, explain desertification, the growth cycle of a flower or tree, the life cycle of a butterfly, the life cycle of salmon, or the development of our solar system. Write for city dwellers cut off from nature much of the time.

4 Trace a process that over the years has transformed a neighborhood you know well or an area that has a special meaning for you. For example, have you had a chance to observe urbanization, gentrification, or ghettoization? Can you mark off major stages or identify turning points?

5 Are you tired of being a manipulated, passive consumer in a mass market economy? Initiate readers who share such feelings into a process or skill that will help them become more self-reliant. For instance, you may want to introduce your readers to breadmaking, beer brewing, or organic gardening.

6 Have you ever felt moved to point out important distinctions between things that are often lumped together? For instance, to the outsider, all country music or all rock may be the same. Can you identify important major kinds? Not all vegetarians, not all politicians, and not all teachers are alike. Can you distinguish major different schools or orientations?

7   What are major options today for women in the world of work? Sort out major kinds of work open to women today. Can you help young women sort out job prospects in today's world?

8   Foreign visitors to this country marvel at the role of sports in our society. Can you sort out the major kinds of sports and explain the sources of their popularity? Or can you sort out major kinds of sports that have become popular in recent years?

9   Can you help readers who wish to become more health conscious? For instance, can you put together a consumer's guide ranking types of foods on a scale from best for your health to worst for your health?

10 As more and more channels become available to the viewer, can you serve as a media guide? For instance, can you offer guidance for parents on major types of television shows for children? Or can you sort out different types of crime shows and explain why you approve of some and not of others?

Reading, Discussion, Writing

Writing to Explain

OVERVIEW: The following reading selections explain how things work. The writers are good at sorting out a confusing array of data. They demystify what might be a mystery to outsiders or to casual observers. They give you expert guidance on topics ranging from the language of the computer world to the psychology of disability. How and how well do they lay out their subjects? Which of these pieces do you consider most useful or informative?

The Trouble with Talent

KATHY SEAL

Are we born smart, or do we get smart? Are successful students naturally gifted, or have they been conditioned to apply themselves? Many journalists make a living by answering questions such as these. They focus on a question in their readers' minds. They pull together what is known on the subject, collating observations and data. They explain technical terms, processes, or experiments. In the end, although we may not totally agree with their answers, we know more about the issue. The author of the following article asks a question of concern to students, teachers, parents, administrators, and politicians: What accounts for scholastic success? Why do some students succeed while others fail? Why do children of Vietnamese, Chinese, or Japanese parents do well in American schools? Seal pulls together an array of expert testimony that points toward hard work rather than inborn talent as the clue to high academic performance. How well does she make you understand the issue? How successful is she in analyzing the workings of success?

Jim Stigler was in an awkward position. Fascinated by the fact that Asian students routinely do better than American kids at elementary math, the UCLA psychologist wanted to test whether persistence might be the key factor. So he designed and administered an experiment in which he gave the same insolvable math problem to separate small groups of Japanese and American children.

Sure enough, most American kids attacked the problem, struggled briefly — then gave up. The Japanese kids, however, worked on and on and on. Eventually, Stigler stopped the experiment when it began to feel inhumane: If the Japanese kids were uninterrupted, they seemed willing to plow on indefinitely.

"The Japanese kids assumed that if they kept working, they'd eventually get it," Stigler recalls. "The Americans thought: Either you get it or you don't."

Stigler's work, detailed in his 1992 book *The Learning Gap* (Summit Books/Simon & Schuster), shatters our stereotypical notion that Asian education relies on rote and drill. In fact, Japanese and Chinese elementary schoolteachers believe that their chief task is to stimulate thinking. They tell their students that anyone who thinks long enough about a problem can move toward its solution.

Stigler concludes that the Asian belief in hard work as the key   5
to success is one reason why Asians outperform us academically.

Americans are persuaded that success in school requires inborn talent. "If you believe that achievement is mostly caused by ability," Stigler says, "at some fundamental level you don't believe in education. You believe education is sorting kids, and that kids in some categories can't learn. The Japanese believe *everybody* can master the curriculum if you give them the time."

Stigler and his coauthor, Harold W. Stevenson of the University of Michigan, are among a growing number of educational psychologists who argue that the American fixation on innate ability causes us to waste the potential of many of our children. He says that this national focus on the importance of natural talent is producing kids who give up easily and artful dodgers who would rather look smart than actually learn something.

Cross-cultural achievement tests show how wide the gap is: In a series of studies spanning a ten-year period, Stigler and Stevenson compared math-test scores at more than 75 elementary schools in Sendai, Japan; T'aipei, Taiwan; Beijing, China; Minneapolis; and Chicago. In each study, the scores of fifth graders in the best-performing American school were lower than the scores of their counterparts in the worst-performing Asian school. In other studies, Stigler and Stevenson found significant gaps in reading tests as well.

Respect for hard work pervades Asian culture. Many folk tales make the point that diligence can achieve any goal — for example, the poet Li Po's story of the woman who grinds a piece of iron into a needle, and Mao Tse-tung's recounting of an old man who removes a mountain with just a hoe. The accent on academic effort in Asian countries demonstrates how expectations for children are both higher and more democratic there than in America. "If learning is gradual and proceeds step by step," says Stigler, "anyone can gain knowledge."

To illustrate this emphasis, Stigler videotaped a Japanese teacher at work. The first image on screen is that of a young woman standing in front of a class of fifth graders. She bows quickly. "Today," she says, "we will be studying triangles." The teacher reminds the children that they already know how to find the area of a rectangle. Then she distributes a quantity of large paper triangles — some equilateral, others right or isosceles — and asks the class to think about "the best way to find the area of a triangle." For the next 14½ minutes, 44 children cut, paste, fold, draw, and talk to each other. Eventually nine kids come to the blackboard and take turns explaining how they have arranged the triangles into shapes for which they can find the areas. Finally, the teacher helps the children to see that all nine solutions boil down to the same formula: $a = (b \times h) \div 2$ (the area equals the product of the base multiplied by the height, divided by two).

Stigler says that the snaillike pace of the lesson — 52 minutes from start to finish — allows the brighter students enough time to understand the concept in depth, as they think through nine different ways to find the areas of the three kinds of triangles. Meanwhile, slower students — even learning-disabled students — benefit from hearing one concept explained in many different ways. Thus children of varied abilities have the same learning opportunity, and the result is that a large number of Japanese children advance relatively far in math.

Americans, on the other hand, group children by ability throughout their school careers. Assigning students to curricular tracks according to ability is common, but it happens even in schools where formal tracking is not practiced.

So kids always know who the teacher thinks is "very smart, sorta smart, and kinda dumb," says social psychologist Jeff Howard, president of the Efficacy Institute, a nonprofit consulting firm in Lexington, Massachusetts, that specializes in education issues. "The idea of genetic intellectual inferiority is rampant in [American] society, especially as applied to African-American kids."

A consequence is that many kids face lower expectations and a watered-down curriculum. "A student who is bright is expected just to 'get it,'" Stigler says. "Duller kids are assumed to lack the necessary ability for ever learning certain material."

Our national mania for positive self-esteem too often leads us to puff up kids' confidence, and we may forget to tell them that genius is 98 percent perspiration. In fact, our reverence for innate intelligence has gone so far that many Americans believe people who work hard in school must lack ability. "Our idealization of a gifted person is someone so smart they don't have to try," says Sandra Graham of UCLA's Graduate School of Education.

Columbia University psychologist Carol Dweck has conducted a fascinating series of studies over the past decade documenting the dangers of believing that geniuses are born rather than made. In one study, Dweck and UCLA researcher Valanne Henderson asked 229 seventh graders whether people are "born smart" or "get smart" by working hard. Then they compared the student's sixth and seventh grade achievement scores. The scores of kids with the get-smart beliefs stayed high or improved, and those of the kids subscribing to the born-smart assumption stayed low or declined. Surprisingly, even kids who believed in working hard but who had low confidence in their abilities did very well. And the kids whose scores dropped the most were the born-smart believers with high confidence.

Dweck's conclusion: "If we want our kids to succeed, we should emphasize effort and steer away from praising or blaming intelligence per se."

Psychologist Ellen Leggett, a former student of Dweck's at Harvard, has found that bright girls are more likely than boys to believe that people are born smart. That finding could help to explain why many American girls stop taking high school math and science before boys do.

Seeing intelligence as an inborn trait also turns children into quitters, says Dweck. "Kids who believe you're born smart or not are always worried about their intelligence, so they're afraid to take risks," Dweck explains. "But kids who think you can *get* smart aren't threatened by a difficult task or by failures, and find it kind of exciting to figure out what went wrong and to keep at it." Or, in Jeff Howard's words, "If I know I'm too stupid to learn, why should I bang my head against the wall trying to learn?"

Getting Americans to give up their worship of natural ability and to replace it with the Asian belief in effort seems a mammoth undertaking. But Dweck maintains that it's possible to train kids to believe in hard work. The key to bringing kids around, says Dweck, is for the adults close to them to talk and act upon a conviction that effort is what counts.

The Efficacy Institute is working on exactly that. The institute's work is based on theories that Howard developed as a doctoral candidate at Harvard, as he investigated why black students weren't performing in school as well as whites and Asians. Using the slogan "Think you can; work hard; get smart," the institute conducts a seminar for teachers that weans them from the born-smart belief system. 20

"We tell teachers to talk to kids with the presumption that they can all get A's in their tests," explains project specialist Kim Taylor. Most kids respond immediately to their teachers' changed expectations, Howard says. As proof, he cites achievement-test scores of 137 third grade students from six Detroit public schools who were enrolled in the Efficacy Institute program during 1989 and 1990. The students' scores rose 2.4 grade levels (from 2.8 to 5.2) in one year, compared with a control group of peers whose scores only went up by less than half a grade level.

Institute trainers now work in approximately 55 school districts, from Baltimore to St. Louis to Sacramento. In five cities, they're working to train every teacher and administrator in the school district.

During a talk to the California Teachers Association, U.S. Secretary of Education Richard Riley pledged to work on setting national standards in education. "These standards," he says, "must be for all of our young people, regardless of their economic background. We must convince people that children aren't born smart. They get smart."

THE INVOLVED READER

1   Why does the author describe an experiment first?

2   Where does the author first spell out her main point, or thesis? Where or how does she keep reminding you of it?

3   Are you impressed by the authorities or experts the writer quotes? Which of them do most to make the point clear for you? Which do least?

4   Writers often aim at a clincher effect in the concluding paragraph. How does Seal follow this pattern? How does her essay come full circle?

TALKING, THINKING, WRITING

5   How many of your classmates fully understand the discussion of triangles in this article? How many know what *equilateral* and *isosceles* mean? Who among your classmates can give the clearest explanation of these and other technical terms?

6   Why does the author of *The Learning Gap* claim Americans believe "education is sorting kids"? Have you seen any evidence that "sorting" or classifying students (instead of teaching them) is a major priority of American education?

7   Which of the following options would you choose? How would you argue in support of your choice? Asian students do well in school because (a) they come from a traditional culture that values learning (b) they are afraid to disappoint their parents or teachers (c) they are smarter than other American students.

COLLABORATIVE PROJECTS

8   Working with a group, interview Asian American students about their attitudes toward school, teachers, homework, books, math. Do they have less interest in athletics or their social lives than other students? Do they listen more to parents and teachers than other students?

Linguistic Metaphors and Linguistic Innovations in Computer Language

KELVIN DON NILSEN AND ALLEEN PACE NILSEN

How are computers changing the way we think and talk? Growing numbers of people spend much of their time interacting with their computers. The computer is their electronic door to a buzzing interactive always-open-for-access world. There they talk to friends or colleagues via e-mail, participate in special-interest newsgroups, track down information, transfer files across the country or to other parts of the world, or browse the Internet. The following article focuses on how the electronic revolution is changing the English language. The collaboration that produced this article brought together a computer expert and a language expert: Kelvin Don Nilsen teaches computer science at Iowa State University in Ames. Alleen Pace Nilsen teaches English at Arizona State University. She is a former co-editor of the English Journal, *a professional journal for teachers, with a special focus on current trends and innovation in the teaching of English.*

An important linguistic principle is that when speakers meet new concepts that they don't have words for, they are not likely to create new sets of sounds to arbitrarily attach to the new ideas; instead they will adapt old words to new concepts. Over the last three decades, we've seen this principle illustrated by people working with computers.

These people form a distinctive sub-culture which has developed its own language. We don't mean the language or "codes" that computer programmers use to communicate with their machines but instead the very human kind of language that people use to talk with each other about computers. While this language is based on English sound patterns and grammar and is built for English words (often with adapted spelling, capitalization, and spacing), the end result is nevertheless quite different from mainstream English. As an exploration of how a sub-culture goes about developing its own language, we have gathered examples of names, concepts, and allusions that have been adapted from literature and given new meanings in relation to computers.

Just as speakers who study a foreign language sometimes gain insights about their own language, an examination of aspects of language change brought about by computers will also provide insights. First, both teachers and students will increase their understanding of "computer language," and second, they will come to a greater understanding of how languages change in relation to changing needs.

The creators of "computer talk" come from two different camps. On one end are the *hackers* (see Notes), those individuals who spend inordinate amounts of time at computer terminals as they devise software, create challenges for themselves and their machines, and communicate with each other via electronic or *e-mail.* In the other camp are those the hackers call the *suits* or the *marketroids.* These are the company managers and the sales people who create product names and manage the advertising campaigns. In between is a much larger group of people who use computers as a tool for their daily work but whose primary interest is not in the computer itself as much as in how it can help them accomplish their other goals. Hackers call the most computer-knowledgeable of these people *techies,* while they refer to those who barely get by as *lusers* — a pun on user and loser. Although some interesting product names have been created for both hardware and software, we are looking here at the more creative language bubbling up from computer hackers, some of which makes its way into techie language or even into mainstream English.

While hackers are connected electronically so that they exchange   5
written messages almost instantaneously — either between individuals or with all members of a like-minded group — they are basically strangers to each other in that their messages lack the benefits of eye contact and voice intonation. This means that when a hacker relies on a literary reference, the communication will fail unless the receivers of the message are already familiar with the piece being cited and unless the image being invoked is clearly memorable.

For English teachers, an important point of interest is which literature satisfies these requirements for this cultural subset. Although hackers say that women are welcome and respected members of the community (in faceless and sometimes nameless communication, who's to know?), the literature that has become part of their vocabulary is what used to be labeled as "boys' books." We found no references to Shakespeare or to romances, but lots of references to science fiction and fantasy. *Heavy wizardry* is a term used to talk about the integration and maintenance of components within large, complicated, poorly documented software systems; while *deep magic,* a term borrowed from C. S. Lewis' Narnia books, refers to the implementation of software that is based on difficult-to-understand mathematical principles.

The Internet is respectfully, or fearfully, spoken of as the *Shub-Internet* a reference to H. P. Lovecraft's horror fiction and his evil *Shub-Niggurath,* the Black Goat with a Thousand Young. The definition in *The Jargon File* (see Notes) clarifies this harsh personification as:

> Beast of a Thousand Processes, Eater of Characters, Avatar of Line Noise, and Imp of Call Waiting; the hideous multi-tendriled entity formed of all the manifold connections of the net . . . its purpose is malign and evil, and is the cause of all network slowdown.

A slightly less malevolent reference is to *code police* as a comparison to the *thought police* in George Orwell's *1984.* Code police take upon themselves the responsibility of enforcing idealized styles and standards for programming language codes. The term is generally used pejoratively, and the feeling among the hacker community is that those who are most likely to assume this role are outsiders (management, ivy-tower academics) who rarely participate in the practice of software development. A closely related term is *net police,* which describes members of the network community who assume the role of enforcing protocol and etiquette standards. In public e-mail and electronic bulletin board forums, the net police shame anyone who violates the established rules.

Archaic operating systems that print only uppercase letters are called *Great Runes,* a usage probably influenced by the writings of J. R. R. Tolkien, who has contributed more words to hacker language than has any other author. Hackers talk of the pre-1980s as their *elder days,* while they use *Hobbit* to describe the high-order bit of a byte (see Notes). An infamous 1988 bugging of the Internet was called *The Great Worm,* named after Scatha and Flaurung, Tolkien's powerful and highly feared Middle Earth dragons. Printers, and especially the people who use printers to provide unnecessary paper copies, are called *Tree-killers* based on what Treebeard the Ent called the Orcs. *Elvish,* the name of the fictional language that Tolkien created in *The Lord of the Rings,* was first used to refer to a particularly elegant style of printing, but is now used more generally for any odd or unreadable typeface produced through graphics.

Terms coming from various sources in the genre of science fiction   10 include *hyperspace,* which describes an errant memory access (Valid memory regions include *code* or *text space, static space, stack space,* and *heap space.* Anything else is considered *hyperspace*); *cyberpunk,* which refers to an imagined world in which anthropomorphized computers participate in human interactions as if they were human; and *cyberspace,* which characterizes future human-computer systems in which humans communicate with the computer as if by mental telepathy. In cyberspace, computers display images directly within the user's mind, similar to prophetic visions as described in biblical writings. Similarly, the science fiction term *martian* is used to describe a network packet received from an unidentifiable network node.

Droid, from *android,* a science fiction term since the 1920s, was popularized in the *Star Trek* television series. Computer hackers frequently use droid or the suffix *-oid* in a derogatory way to imply that a person is acting mindlessly, as though programmed. Thus, *market-roids* and *sales droids* promise customers things which can't be delivered, while a *trendoid* is concerned only with being up-to-date with the latest fads.

The term *Vulcan nerve pinch* also comes from the original *Star Trek* television series. It describes the keyboard action of simultaneously pressing on three keys as when rebooting with the control, alternate, and delete keys.

When there is a need for a random number that people will recognize as such, *42* is often used because in *The Hitchhiker's Guide to the Galaxy* (1980, New York: Harmony) that's what Douglas Adams had his computer give as "The Answer to the Ultimate Question of Life, the Universe, and Everything."

Another interesting term is *Twonkie,* a software addition that is essentially useless but nevertheless appealing in some way, perhaps for marketing purposes. Its meaning is made clear by its resemblance to *Twinkie,* which has become almost a generic term for junk food. However, its source is thought to be the title of Lewis Padgett's 1942 short story "The Twonky," which has been frequently anthologized since its original publication in *Astounding Science Fiction.*

Grok, from Robert Heinlein's *Stranger in a Strange Land* (1961, New   15 York: Putnam), is used to mean that a computer program understands or is "one with" a particular idea or capability. Often, older versions of commercial software products can't grok data files produced by newer releases of the same product. In a more playful usage from Heinlein's *The Moon Is a Harsh Mistress* (1966, New York: Putnam), the acronym *TANSTAAFL* has become a quick and socially acceptable way to tell someone "There Ain't No Such Thing As A Free Lunch." Another Heinlein usage is *Waldo,* taken from the title of his 1942 story in which he invented mechanical devices working under the control of a human hand or foot. Computer hackers prefer the term Waldo, but NASA, which hopes to use such devices to manipulate robot arms in space, has chosen the more technological sounding name *telepresence* (see Notes).

Two of the cleverest science fiction references are based on the *Star Wars* movies. *UTSL* is a shorthand way to send someone the message that they should do some research before they send out a network call for help. It is an acronym for "Use The Source, Luke!," a play on the line, "Use the Force, Luke!," (see Notes). An *Obi-Wan error,* a pun on the name of Obi-Wan Kenobi, refers to any computation that is off-by-one, as when a programmer started counting a particular quantity at 1 instead of 0. By analogy, an Obi-Wan code would give the name *HAL* (from the movie *2001,* each letter is one away from the corresponding letter in the original acronym) for IBM. In another *Star Wars* allusion, someone who uses computer skills for devious purposes is called a *dark-side hacker* (as opposed to a *Samurai*), meaning the person is like Darth Vader in having been seduced by the "dark side of the Force."

There are relatively few references to traditional children's literature. However, in the 1960s people spoke of *IBM and the Seven Dwarves* with the dwarves being Burroughs, Control Data, General Electric, Honeywell, NCR, RCA, and Univac. Lewis Carroll's *Snark* is an appropriate name for any unexplained foul-up that programmers have to go hunting for. In a classic computer hacker story about a conflict between Motorola and Xerox, two hackers at Motorola wrote a pair of "bandit" background processes they affectionately named *Robin Hood* and *Friar Tuck.* These two processes took over the Xerox developer's main computer system. The point of this activity was to get the attention of the Xerox team in order to deliver an important message that had been repeatedly ignored during the several months prior to the attack. The *Trojan Horse* legend provides the name for a program that is designed to get around security measures by sneaking into a system while disguised, perhaps as a game or a useful utility. When the program is invoked, it does unexpected and unwanted harm to a computer system, in addition to providing the advertised functionality.

One of the most common references to a piece of traditional literature is *moby,* meaning something immense or huge. Although this comes from Herman Melville's *Moby Dick,* its use was popularized in precomputer days by model train fans and such usages as *Moby Pickle.* Hackers use it in such sentences as "The disk crash resulted in moby data loss," and "Writing a new back-end for the compiler would be a moby undertaking!" Several years ago when the University of California Library System named its library access program *Melvyl* after *Melvyl Dewey,* developer of the Dewey Decimal System, some users assumed a connection to Herman Melville because it was such a moby of a data base.

There's always a lag between the popularization of a term and its being adapted to a new use. However, today's instant communication shortens the lag as shown by two fairly recent references. *Feature Shock* is a play on the title of Alvin Toffler's *Future Shock* (1970, New York: Random House). It describes a user's reaction to a program heavy on features, but light on explanations. The other recent usage is *Sagan* from the name of Carl Sagan, star of the TV series "Cosmos," who is often heard repeating the phrase "billions and billions." His name is used as shorthand for any large number as in "There's a sagan different ways to tweak EMACS."

One thing this discussion shows is the importance of television and movies in contributing to the store of literary images from which hackers take their references. A *Godzillagram*, based on the hero of Japanese monster movies, is a network packet of maximum size or one broadcast to every conceivable receiver. *Dr. Mbogo*, the witch doctor from the old Addams Family television show, has his name memorialized in *Dr. Fred Mbogo* (hackers often use *Fred* as a random name because it's so easy to type) as a humorous identifier for someone with "bogus" skills.

Computer hackers are relatively young (ranging from teenagers to their mid-forties) and they grew up watching *Sesame Street*, hence the name *Cookie Monster* for a hacker who manages to deny computer access to other users of a system, thereby obtaining exclusive access for selfish purposes. *Double Bucky* is a play on the *Sesame Street* "Rubber Duckie" song. It originated as a joke when human-computer interface designers were trying to figure out how to get more characters from the same keyboard. One suggestion was that foot pedals be added to serve as extra shift keys which would allow typists to make more changes without moving their fingers from their home keys.

Real programmers (a reference to the book *Real Men Don't Eat Quiche*) refer to aspiring teenaged programmers as *Munchkins* in memory of the little people in *The Wizard of Oz*. Depending on their behavior, such hackers might also be called *Wabbits*, from cartoon character Elmer Fudd's famous "You wascawwy wabbit!" The specific meaning of the latter term is a trouble-making hacker who programs something so that it will keep repeating itself. In contrast, a protocol that accidentally includes a bug resulting in multiple messages being sent or multiple instances of a particular abstract object being created is described as being in *Sorcerer's Apprentice mode*, a reference to the Walt Disney movie *Fantasia*.

Because computers are such a new part of American culture, students can have the experience of doing original field work. Using a broad definition of metaphor to mean any computer term that is based on a similarity between what is being named and what the base word refers to in standard English, they can search for terms taken from specific semantic areas. Just as we collected computer metaphors related to literature above, different groups of students can collect metaphors related to transportation (*driver, bus, channel, map, information highway, hard drive crash, cruising the Internet*), food and kitchen (*menu, byte, nybble, cooked, raw, fork, filter, fold, stack*), human activities (*handshaking, bootstrapping* or *booting, memory, massage, motherboard, daughtercard, "smart"* and *"dumb" terminals, "second"* and *"third" generations*), architecture (*back door, port, window, screen, pane, desk top, trap door,* and *pipe* or *pipeline*), and pre-computer kinds of writing and printing (*envelope, mail, file, address, clipboard, format, scroll,* and *bulletin board*). This latter set is a good illustration of how new inventions are described with the language of their predecessors — as when cars were called horseless carriages and vans were named after the kinds of caravans that depended on camels and oxens instead of machines.

Computer users purposely "misspell" some of their words to identify them as computer words and to keep them from being confused with similar words. For example, *byte* is spelled with a *y* because it was important to distinguish it from *bit.* The *y* spelling caught on as "computer talk" and is also seen in *nybble. Luser,* as a pun on loser and user, influenced the spelling of *turist* as someone who out of curiosity temporarily joins various groups; *c.f.* TV channel surfing.

In the dinosaur days of computers, some machines printed only capital letters. Ever since, computer users have had a unique attitude toward upper and lower case letters. Bicapitalization describes the practice of inserting caps inside words as with these trademarks: *WordPerfect, NeXt, GEnie, TeX, VisiCalc, dBASE, FrameMaker,* and *CompuServe* (often spelled playfully by hackers as *Compu$erve* because this public network access provider costs so much in comparison with university and employer facilities). Students could clip product names from old catalogs and make a poster to use as part of a discussion of whether the deviant capitalization helps the names to be memorable. (Another reason for the practice is so companies can register them as original trademarks.)

Computer hackers even have acronyms for acronyms. *TLA* stands for Three Letter Acronym while *YABA* stands for Yet Another Bloody Acronym. When new names are chosen, creators check to make sure they are "YABA compatible," meaning the initials can be pronounced easily and won't make a suggestive or unpleasant word. But no matter how carefully acronyms are chosen, hackers will still try to create new meanings as when they say that the true meaning of *LISP* (LISt Processing Language) is "Lots of Irritating Superfluous Parentheses." In discussing acronyms, students can talk about their space saving features as compared to their potential for confusion. What's the difference between the ones that run together in people's minds and the ones like *GIGO* (Garbage In, Garbage Out) that are becoming part of mainstream English?

The name of the television news program *Hard Copy*, which suggests both "hard line" and "hard core," was undoubtedly influenced by the computer term *hard copy* for something printed on paper (i.e., "documented") compared to soft copy for something in the machine. As a comparison to e-mail and Internet, people refer to the U.S. Postal Service as *USnail, snail mail,* or *papernet.* The widespread use of computers has also increased the general use of such words as *glitch, bug* and *debug, user-friendly, protocol, input, zap,* and *programming* or *de-programming* people or things other than computers. Students can collect headlines and news clippings for a display of such new usages. They can then compare their specialized computer meanings with their original and now their new meanings in mainstream English.

Steve Jobs was "into" health foods, and when it came time to choose a name for the new computer he had designed for ordinary people rather than professional computer whizzes, he settled on *Apple* to stand out from other companies' high tech names. Apple included such positive connotations as "an apple for the teacher" and "an apple a day keeps the doctor away." It also provided for a "family tree" with such later names as *Macintosh* and *Newton. Lotus* software has an equally inspired name based on the comparison of a lotus blossom opening out and the creation of a spread sheet. And what could be more persuasive in getting customers to buy a product than the name *WordPerfect?* Another tricky bit of persuasion is that when users want to get into their *Windows* program, they have to type *WIN?*

It's common for people who feel frustrated or out of control to make jokes that release some of the nervousness or hostility they are feeling. For example, the computer building at Stanford is named the Margaret Jacks Hall, but students refer to it as the *Marginal Hacks Hall.* Computer hackers also refer to the IBM 360 as the *IBM Three-Sickly,* to a Macintosh as a *Macintoy* or *Macintrash,* and to programs coming from the University of California at Berkeley as *Berzerkeley.* And frustrated users of newly released technology often lament that they are living on the *bleeding edge* (a play on *leading edge*). Chances are that students in your school have their own share of pejorative jokes related to computing.

Notes

Hackers: In common usage, hacker has several different connotations. Some readers will be more familiar with the following definition of hacker: "A malicious meddler who tries to discover sensitive information by poking around." R. Raymond's *The New Hacker's Dictionary, Second Edition* (1993, Cambridge, MA: MIT Press), written and maintained by the community of friendly hackers (as defined in the main body of this text), suggests that the malicious meddler is more properly titled a *cracker.*

Bits and *Bytes:* Within a computer, all numbers are represented by strings of bits (a bit is a binary digit, each bit representing either a 0 or 1). A byte is a string of exactly eight bits. The least-significant bit represents the 1s, the next bit represents 2s, and the third represents 4s. The most-significant (high-order) bit within a byte represents 128s. Compare this with our base-ten numbering system in which the least-significant digit represents 1s, the next digit represents 10s and so on.

Telepresence: Allows a human user on earth, for example, to manipulate a mechanical arm belonging to a robot walking on the surface of the moon. Visual and sensual feedback are provided to human operators in order to portray the illusion that they are actually present on the moon.

Sources and *Object Codes:* Modern computer software is written in high-level programming languages designed to simplify programming effort. Compilers are programs that translate the high-level programming languages to the machine language required for execution of the program in a particular environment. The high-level program written by the user is called the source code, whereas the program's machine-language translation is called the object code. Most commercial applications are supplied only in object-code form, as the object code hides many of the developer's trade secrets. However, members of the hacker subculture regularly share source codes with one another. When user-level documentation is missing or unintelligible, hackers are encouraged to refer directly to the source code to better understand the program's features and capabilities.

The Jargon File: We could not have written this article without the help of innumerable hackers who over the past 15 years have contributed definitions and examples to *The Jargon File,* most recently edited by Eric Raymond (eric@snark.thyrsus.com). *The Jargon File* can be downloaded by anonymous ftp from prep.ai.mit.edu as pub/ gnu/jarg300.txt.gz. The contents of this file were recently published as *The New Hacker's Dictionary, Second Edition.* Many of the examples presented in this paper were prompted by this resource.

THE INVOLVED READER

1   Word watchers watch words the way bird watchers watch birds. Why was the Apple computer named after the apple? What is a *moby* of a database, and why is it called that? What is meant by "a sagan different ways"? Why do some people call Berkeley *Berzerkeley*?

2   In the world of computer talk, what is the difference between *hackers, suits, techies,* and *lusers*? What is the difference between *cyberpunk* and *cyberspace*? What is wrong with *marketroids* and *trendoids*? What's a *Twonkie*? What's a *Munchkin*?

3   How much of the computer talk discussed here deals with technical issues? Why is it important for software to *grok* with new releases? What is an *Obi-Wan error*?

4   How much do you learn here about the politics and etiquette of electronic communication? Why do hackers talk about the *Shub-Internet,* the *code police,* and the *net police?* What's the objection to *Cookie Monsters* and *Wabbits*?

5   What's an acronym? What are striking examples discussed in this article?

TALKING, THINKING, WRITING

6   How much computer talk is becoming part of general everyday language? What computer terms have become part of your own vocabulary?

7   Is the world of computers a male-dominated field? Does the article offer evidence pro or con?

8   What for you are key differences between electronic communication and other kinds?

The Challenge of Disability

NANCY MAIRS

*What changes have occurred in the way we look at disabling ill-
nesses and conditions? Nancy Mairs became known for frank and disturbing autobiographical essays she wrote about life with chronic illness and collected in volumes like* Plaintext *(1986),* Remembering the
Bone-House *(1989), and* Carnal Acts *(1990). A self-described radical
feminist and pacifist, she has written "Hers" columns for the* New
York Times Magazine. *While chronicling her fight against illness and
depression, she was teaching writing, teaching medical students how
to give neurological examinations, and picking up freelance editing
jobs. When still in graduate school, she had developed the first symptoms of multiple sclerosis, a chronic degenerative disease of the central
nervous system that progressively impaired her mobility. Ten years
later, she said about the disease:*

> *My left leg is now so weak that I walk with the aid of a brace and
> a cane; and for distances I use an Amigo, a variation on the electri-
> cal wheelchair that looks rather like an electrified kiddie car. I no
> longer have much use of my left hand. Now my right side is weak-
> ening as well. I still have the blurred spot in my right eye. Overall,
> though, I've been lucky so far. My world has of necessity been cir-
> cumscribed by my losses, but the terrain left me has been ample
> enough for me to continue many of the activities that absorb me:
> writing, teaching, raising children and cats and plants and snakes,
> reading, speaking publicly about MS and depression, even playing
> bridge with people patient and honorable enough to let me scatter
> cards every which way without sneaking a peek.*

I don't want to think about having MS. I don't want to *have* MS to
think about. Having to speak of it, aloud, to others, forces me to examine what about life-with-MS (about which I have no choice) is
worth having. And celebrating.

In the fall of 1986 I undertook what came to be known in my
family as The Great Los Angeles Adventure, which began on a low
note when I fell onto a concrete floor on my head and knocked myself out cold. This event taught me, as disagreeable events often will,
a number of lessons that I'm glad enough to know but wish I'd been
permitted to learn in some other way. It gave me, for instance, a live-
lier sense than I'd ever had before of the existence of worlds absolutely other than, and perhaps inimical to, the one I occupy and generalize from. During the several hours I lay in the emergency room

at the Brotman Medical Center, a black woman with labor pains but without health insurance was bustled into a taxicab and sent away to another hospital. A black security guard who'd tried to stop a robbery had been kicked and pummeled bloody. The robbery had been completed. "You shouldn't ever try to stop them," said the police officer. "They could have guns, and then where would you be?" "I don't know who did it," a black teenager moaned to his mama and another police officer. "I was just getting something out of the trunk of my girlfriend's car when — *blam!* — right in the ass." After consultation, the doctors decided to leave the bullet where it was, and both they and the police released him.

In a sense, my accident forced me briefly into the helpless and violent world these glimpses suggested. The first thing I remember after being wheeled in from the ambulance was a young doctor's earnest face close to mine: "Who did this to you?" "Why — no one," I said. "I did it to myself. I fell." But I, who have seldom been struck and never beaten, understood with a wholly new immediacy that women like me are carried into these places night after night and, whatever they say, they haven't fallen. When George visited me the following weekend, he was drawn into this vision. Eating lunch in an outdoor café on Venice Boulevard, we gradually became aware of the stares — pitying for me, hostile for him — aroused by my battered face. In spite of our innocence, we shrank in humiliation.

On a happier note, I learned that, even in a city of several million strangers (at least if you're white and well dressed and have health insurance), people will take care of you. The doctors and nurses attended me as carefully as their harried lives permitted; and a couple of young physicists from my apartment building who'd been in the group that gathered around me after my fall adopted me, checking on my progress and driving me home from the hospital after my release. Because I travel a good deal, this confidence in strangers makes my life less anxious than it might be. True, I was once verbally abused by a Providence cabby, who told me people like me had no business traveling but ought to stay home where they belonged, but what's one crank among millions of potential caregivers? . . .

Take it from me, physical disability looms pretty large in one's life. 5
But it doesn't devour one wholly. I'm not, for instance, Ms. MS, a walking, talking embodiment of a chronic incurable degenerative disease. In most ways I'm just like every other woman of my age, nationality, and socioeconomic background. I menstruate, so I have to buy tampons. I worry about smoker's breath, so I buy mouthwash. I smear my wrinkling skin with lotions. I put bleach in the washer so my family's undies won't be dingy. I drive a car, talk on the tele-

phone, get runs in my pantyhose, eat pizza. In most ways, that is, I'm the advertisers' dream: Ms. Great American Consumer. And yet the advertisers, who determine nowadays who will get represented publicly and who will not, deny the existence of me and my kind absolutely.

I once asked a local advertiser why he didn't include disabled people in his spots. His response seemed direct enough: "We don't want to give people the idea that our product is just for the handicapped." But tell me truly now: If you saw me pouring out puppy biscuits, would you think these kibbles were only for the puppies of cripples? If you saw my blind niece ordering a Coke, would you switch to Pepsi lest you be struck sightless? No, I think the advertiser's excuse masked a deeper and more anxious rationale. To depict disabled people in the ordinary activities of daily life is to admit that there is something ordinary about disability itself, that it may enter anybody's life. If it is effaced completely, or at least isolated as a separate "problem," so that it remains at a safe distance from other human issues, then the viewer won't feel threatened by her or his own physical vulnerability.

This kind of effacement or isolation has painful, even dangerous consequences, however. For the disabled person, these include self-degradation and a subtle kind of self-alienation not unlike that experienced by other minorities. Socialized human beings love to conform, to study others and then to mold themselves to the contours of those whose images, for good reasons or bad, they come to love. Imagine a life in which feasible others — others you can hope to be like — don't exist. At the least you might conclude that there is something queer about you, something ugly or foolish or shameful. In the extreme, you might feel as though you don't exist, in any meaningful social sense, at all. Everyone else is "there," sucking breath mints and splashing on cologne and swigging wine coolers. You're "not there." And if not there, nowhere.

But this denial of disability imperils even you who are able-bodied, and not just by shrinking your insight into the physically and emotionally complex world you live in. Some disabled people call you TAPs, or Temporarily Abled Persons. The fact is that ours is the only minority you can join involuntarily, without warning, at any time. And if you live long enough, as you're increasingly likely to do, you may well join it. The transition will probably be difficult from a physical point of view no matter what. But it will be a good bit easier psychologically if you are accustomed to seeing disability as a normal characteristic, one that complicates but does not ruin human existence. Achieving this integration, for disabled and able-bodied people alike, requires that we insert disability daily into our field of vision: quietly, naturally, in the small and common scenes of our ordinary lives.

THE INVOLVED READER

1 What "other world" did Mairs discover after the fall she describes at the beginning of this selection? What "lessons" did she learn? What experiences built up her "confidence in strangers"?

2 How does Mairs convey her basic theme that there is more to disabled people than their disability?

3 Where did Mairs encounter evidence of the exclusion or "isolation" of the disabled? How does she explain the psychology involved? How does it lead to "self-alienation"?

4 How does the "denial of disability" imperil the able-bodied? What warning does Mairs have for them?

TALKING, WRITING, THINKING

5 What has been your personal experience with disability or serious illness or with people with disabilities? How do disabled people cope?

6 How do others act around people with disabilities? Has Mairs changed your own thinking or attitudes concerning disability?

7 Mairs has criticized movies or television programs focusing on disability for excluding "the complexities that round out a character and make her whole." She said about one example, "It's not about a woman who happens to be physically disabled; it's about physical disability as the determining factor of a woman's existence." Does this criticism apply to movies or TV programs you have seen?

COLLABORATIVE PROJECTS

8 Working with a group, study official policies or initiatives designed to improve conditions for the disabled in your community. How successful are they?

Private Lives, Public Values

WILLIAM J. DOHERTY

*What is happening to the American family? Conservative politi-
cians (often divorced themselves) have been calling for a return to
family values, denouncing teenage pregnancy and single mothers. At
the same time, progressive groups have campaigned for legal recognition of new kinds of domestic partnerships, including same-sex marriages. The following essay is based on the assumption that family —
however we define or stretch the term — is "central to human life." At
the same time, changing social realities and evolving lifestyles have
altered traditional patterns of family life beyond recognition. In an
article written for* Psychology Today, *William J. Doherty sorts out for
his readers major kinds of family units and relationships. Do you recognize the major categories he sets up? Do you agree with his analysis
of major phases in the evolution of the family? Do you endorse the
family values he sketches out?*

Settling down after two decades of tumultuous change, families
are painfully caught between their own needs and an indifferent culture. What could help everyone is a dose of reality — a new marriage
of family values and public policy.

Whoever said that death and taxes are the only inevitable things
in life was overlooking an obvious third one: family. No other social
institution surrounds us more intimately from cradle to grave, so
shapes our bodies and minds, remains such an emotional presence
wherever we go, and gives us such generous measures of joy and
frustration. Pretending that family is not important in our lives is like
trying to cheat death: it doesn't work and you end up feeling foolish
for trying.

Because the family is so central to human life, no one can be neutral about its future prospects. In fact, Americans have been wring-
ing their hands about the state of the family for well over 100 years —
with remarkably little change in the tenor of the worries. In the late
19th century, Americans began to focus on the changes wrought by
urbanization and industrialization: smaller families, increased divorce rate, less connection to traditional kin and community networks, more child abuse and neglect, and squalid living conditions
in urban slums. Sound familiar?

Faced with such changes in the American family, 19th-
century professionals and community leaders divided into two

groups, whose descendants are with us still. The "pessimists" believe that the American family is declining alarmingly in its ability to
carry out its functions of child rearing and providing stability for
adult life. The pessimists see the divorce rate — nine times higher
than a century ago — as a key indicator of the deterioration of family
bonds and the fragmentation of American society. They call for a
return to the traditional values of commitment and responsibility,
and are appalled by the proliferation of family types and forms in
the late 20th century — never-married mothers, single-parent families, step-families, cohabiting couples, and gay and lesbian families.

The "optimists," on the other hand, view the family as an institu-   5
tion that is not declining, but rather showing its flexibility and resilience. The optimists believe that traditional family structures are
no longer appropriate for the modern age, and that these structures
were too male-dominated and conformity-oriented to begin with.
Contemporary families may be less stable in the traditional sense,
but most people are still committed to being in a family. It's just
that they need a larger menu of family arrangements to choose from.
The world is now more oriented to individual options, particularly
for women, and the family has changed accordingly. From this point
of view, the main problems faced by contemporary families can be
traced to the failure of society to accept that the "Leave It to Beaver"
family is a dinosaur, and to provide adequate support for the variety
of post-Beaver families that now dominate the landscape.

Depending on whether you are in the optimist or pessimist camp,
the next decade or two of family life will bring either: a) more deterioration, unless a shift in values occurs; b) continued creative change,
troublesome only if other social institutions keep facing backwards
instead of forwards. There is, however, a third orientation emerging,
a both/and approach, and I believe it will become more influential
in our national discourse about family life in the next decade. This
orientation agrees with the pessimists that the family is in trouble
and that a transformation of values is needed. It also agrees with the
optimists that changes in family structures are inevitable and here
to stay, and that both old and new family forms should receive more
community support.

We are at the threshold of a new dialogue about family life in the
United States, one that transcends the tired debates of the past and
that might lead to a workable consensus for the first time in our
history. To understand this emerging consensus on the American
family, let's take a quick tour of the revolution in family forms in the
20th century.

In a breathtaking period of change, the 20th century has witnessed the demise of one standard of family life, the birth of a second, its subsequent decline, and the emergence of a third standard —
one that we are still learning to live with. The first two decades of the
century were dominated by the Institutional Family as the ideal. The
Institutional Family represented the age old-tradition of a family organized around economic production, kinship network, community
connections, the father's authority, and marriage as a functional
partnership rather than a romantic relationship. Family tradition,
loyalty, and solidarity were more important than individual goals
and romantic interest. For the Institutional Family, the chief value
was RESPONSIBILITY.

The Institutional Family was doomed by the spirit of individualism that developed gradually in the Western world since the Renaissance, and that was given a definitive boost by the breakup of rural
communities in the 19th century and the emergence of the modern
state. The modern world is based more on individual responsibility
and achievement than on traditional family land holdings and kinship connections. In the culture of individualism, as Robert Bellah
and his colleagues observed in their book, *Habits of the Heart* (University of California Press; 1985), relationships are based on "contracts" — what people can do for each other, rather than on traditional "covenants" — virtually unbreakable commitments based on
loyalty and responsibility.

In the 1970 movie *Lovers and Other Strangers,* a young man, Tony, 10
tells his traditional Italian father than he and his wife are divorc-
ing because "we don't love each other any more." The befuddled
father asks, "Tony, what's the story?" For the next several minutes,
Tony keeps repeating his explanation, and his father keeps asking,
"But, Tony, what's the story?" To a man from an Institutional Family,
Tony's explanation did not compute as a reason to break up a family. The scene captured the generational shift from one type of family
standard to another.

During the first half of this century, the Institutional Family gave
way to the Psychological Family. In the 1920s, family sociologists began to write about the shift from "institutional marriage" to "com-
ponent marriage." The Psychological Family was a more private affair than its predecessor — more nuclear, more mobile, less tied to
extended-kin networks and the broader community. It aspired to
something unprecedented in human history: a family based on the
personal satisfaction and fulfillment of its individual members in a
nuclear, two-parent arrangement.

Marriage was to be based on continued friendship, love, and attraction, not on economic necessity or the requirements of child rearing. Parents were to nurture their children's personalities, not just socialize them as good citizens. The Psychological Family arose during the time when the media and consumerism provided strong competition for traditional family values. If the chief value of the Institutional Family was RESPONSIBILITY, the chief value of the Psychological Family was SATISFACTION.

Within the Psychological Family lay the seeds of its own demise, as Judith Stacey points out in *Brave New Families* (Basic Books; 1990). Although the ideal Psychological Family was a mutually satisfying, intact, nuclear family, the underlying gender and generational politics were still traditional: male prerogatives were assumed, and the younger generation was to respect the authority of the older.

When the social changes in the 1960s challenged the Psychological Family under the banners of gender equality and personal freedom, the Psychological Family began to give way as a normative ideal in American society. Women began to achieve more independence through paid employment, the sexual revolution made marriage less necessary for sexual fulfillment, adolescents and young adults saw themselves as deserving more and owing less to their families, and men and women alike began opting out of their unhappy marriages in unprecedented numbers. By the late 1980s, the Psychological Family, itself a radical shift from the Institutional Family, had given way to its successor, the Pluralistic Family.

The Pluralistic Family (sometimes called the Postmodern Family)   15
has not broadly accepted an ideal family form. No new single family arrangement has replaced the Psychological nuclear family; instead, a plethora of family types has emerged, including dual-career families, never-married families, and gay and lesbian families, Legislative bodies and courts are beginning to codify the Pluralistic Family by redefining the term to include arrangements considered deviant, non-family forms in the past. Tolerance and diversity, rather than a single family ideal, characterize the Pluralistic Family.

The chaotic proliferation of family types brought about by the disintegration of the Psychological Family has stabilized now around a variety of forms that individuals move in and out of during their lives. In the Pluralistic Family of the immediate future, an average child can expect to grow up in some combination of: a one-parent family, a two-parent family, or a step-family, and will go on in adulthood to cohabitate, marry, divorce, remarry, and perhaps redivorce.

The Pluralistic Family by definition will have room for some lingering Institutional Families, and a larger number of nuclear families representing the Psychological Family. Family forms do not arrive and evaporate overnight; they just become more or less normative over time. In the late 20th century, the Psychological Family hasn't died; it has just become one family type among others. The chief value — satisfaction — continues to be prominent in the Pluralistic Family, but it is now supplemented by a new family value for the postmodern age — FLEXIBILITY.

The near future of the American family lies with the Pluralistic Family. At its best, this completes a century-long trek toward liberation of the individual, particularly women and children, from the oppressive features of the traditional family. The Pluralistic Family offers individuals freedom to create the family forms that fit their changing needs over life's course, with little stigma about failing to conform to a single family structure and value system. And it fits the free-form American social life of the late 20th century, where the pace of life requires quick adjustments and where respect for diversity is a paramount civic virtue.

At its worst, however, the Pluralistic Family is filled with more internal contradictions and ambivalence than were the Institutional Family and the Psychological Family in their heyday. Surveys indicate that most Americans still believe in the traditional family values of responsibility and commitment, and most believe that the stable, two-parent family is the best environment for raising children.

Family sociologist Dennis Orthner makes a distinction between 20 family "values" and family "norms." He notes that the traditional family values, or ideals, have not changed much, according to national surveys, but that norms, or expectations, for actual behavior have changed remarkably. The discrepancy between ideals for stability and permanent commitment, and the reality of instability and provisional commitment, is one of two Achilles heels of the Pluralistic Family. Most Americans simply do not believe that the Pluralistic Family is stable and secure enough, especially for meeting the needs of children; they feel that divorce and other changes that liberate adults do not benefit their children.

The other Achilles heel of the Pluralistic Family is the lack of support from social institutions. The powerful decision makers in America tend to be men who were raised during the transition from the Institutional Family to the Psychological Family and who have lived their adult lives in gender-stereotyped, conformity-oriented Psychological Families. They believe in a "natural" split between the private world of the family and the public world of society —

although such a split did not exist until the Institutional Family began to break down in the late 19th century.

When the umbilical cord connecting the family and the community is severed, both the family and the community become malnourished. Struggling families are left to their own devices. Family violence is seen as a personal failure, not a social and political problem. And the community loses its sense of moral obligation to promote and protect the welfare of children and other vulnerable citizens.

Many business and political leaders are suspicious of the Pluralistic Family, and fear that offering it economic and legal support is tantamount to undermining the American family as they know it — which, of course, is true. On the other hand, as they go through their own divorces and remarriages, and as they see the diversity of their children's families, these men are showing signs of accepting the reality of the Pluralistic Family.

In one sense, the next two decades for the American family are relatively easy to forecast: The Pluralistic Family will be the prevailing norm — and practically nobody will be happy about it. Conservatives will lament the decline of the nuclear Psychological Family, and liberals will decry the lack of community support for alternative family forms. And families will struggle to catch their collective breath following the tumultuous changes of the 1970s and '80s.

As they do so, there is palpable reappraisal about what the family   25
revolution has wrought. The divorce rate has stabilized, and there is evidence that the divorce rate after remarriage is declining. There is growing alarm that the sexual revolution has brought unacceptably high levels of sexual activity among teenagers with an increasing rate of teenage childbirth and a surge of single-parent families. A spate of new books, including Michele Weiner-Davis's *Divorce Busters* (Simon & Schuster, 1992), reflect a popular sentiment that marriage bonds need strengthening — in contrast to books on "creative divorce" of 25 years ago. And best-sellers such as Judith Wallerstein's *Second Chances* (Tichnor & Fields; 1989) tap many Americans' fears that divorce is ruining the lives of our children.

If most Americans are fearful about the family of the future, how have our political leaders responded? They generally don the century-old roles of pessimists and optimists. Pessimistic conservatives decry the lack of traditional family values and call for a values revolution. Optimistic liberals endorse flexibility in family values, although conservatives still seem to be slower to talk about policies.

Critics of this recent trend toward emphasizing family values view it as part of a conservative backlash against women's newfound freedoms and acceptance of alternative family lifestyles. For them, the battlefront for families lies only in the public arena, and the emergence of the "V" word (values) is a rear-guard action that threatens needed social change under the camouflage of conservative rhetoric.

Regardless of the merits of these criticisms, family values will clearly be on the national agenda in the next decade or two, as will family-policy issues such as parental leave, child care, divorce, and child-support laws, and support for families to provide health care for frail members. I predict that the two will become inextricably linked in the future. Family policies will make sense to most Americans only when they are couched in terms of family values such as commitment and care. And espousing values without addressing the policy agenda for families will be seen as posturing rather than helping. What we are approaching, for the first time in our history, is a public discussion about a family ethic to go hand in hand with a family policy.

The outline of this new family ethic underlying family policy is beginning to emerge. A new family ethic for the next decade, I believe, will embrace several timeless values of the Institutional Family and the Psychological Family — but go beyond these to incorporate the newer values of the Pluralistic Family. Here are the elements in such an old and new family ethic that I see emerging in the next decade or two:

• **Commitment** — the sense of "covenant" that binds spouses to each other, parents to children and children to parents, and extended family members to one another. Without turning the clock back to an Institutional Family – era when marriage until death was sometimes psychologically deadly to trapped spouses, there will be a renewed emphasis on finding ways to renew troubled marriages rather than end them, especially when children are involved. After a divorce, there will be stronger expectations that both parents remain faithful to the unbreakable covenant that binds parents to their children.

• **Care** — the physical and emotional support of spouses and family members for one another. As philosopher Nel Noddings writes in her book, *Caring: A Feminine Approach to Ethics and Moral Education* (University of California Press; 1984), care builds on the sense of commitment and requires the ability to empathetically understand one another. To the Institutional Family's emphasis on physical and moral care of children, the Psychological Family added the idea that parents should understand and foster the emotional lives of their children, and that spouses should nurture each other emo-

30

tionally. These values are relatively new in human history and will require support from larger efforts for family-life education in the coming decades.

• **Community** — the importance of the family's ties with its neighborhood, local community, state, nation, and world, with responsibilities going both ways — the family to the community and the community to the family. This value reflects efforts to mend the split between the private world of the family and the public world of the community and its institutions. I believe that community leaders will increasingly see that the family can be no healthier than its community — and that communities can be no healthier than their families.

• **Equality** — the belief that women and men should have equal say in family matters and should stand as equals in the larger community, and that children should be given influence commensurate with their age and developmental abilities. This is the litmus test for the use of the new emphasis on family values. Will they become part of an effort to reverse women's gains towards equality with men, or will they instead become a vehicle for creating something entirely new in human history — namely, a family arrangement that provides commitment, care, and community support within the context of full personhood for men and women. Ultimately, such equality can be achieved only if it is embraced at both family and community levels at the same time.

• **Diversity** — the support for all family forms that embrace the values stated above and provide for the well-being of their members. This is the chief new value underlying the Pluralistic Family, and I see no way to build a new consensus on family values without incorporating the value of diversity. Such family forms as the never-married mother with children and gay and lesbian families are here to stay in a world that accepts the rights of citizens to form nontraditional family arrangements. This does not mean, however, that anything goes; all family forms should be judged by how well they provide commitment, care, and community for their members. Family arrangements that pass this test deserve greater measures of community support in the future.

This emerging family ethic is not a recipe for making complex decisions, such as whether to divorce one's spouse. But it does offer guidelines for responsible, caring, and fair actions when individuals are experiencing a problem such as severe marital distress. It also points the way for communities to support these family values with programs and policies.

Here's how this new family ethic could be applied: It could be considered irresponsible to get a divorce without consulting a marital therapist, especially when there are children involved, just as it is considered irresponsible to let someone die without consulting a physician. Communities, for their part, would ensure that marital-therapy services are available and affordable for couples, and just as important, provide funds for community-based family-life education so that more couples will be equipped to handle the rigors of contemporary marriage.

For families going through the divorce process, the new family ethic would expect parents to put their children's interests and needs first, to treat their ex-spouse fairly, and to support each other as parents. Adults would be expected to act maturely and responsibly for the welfare of their children after a divorce, including providing ongoing financial and emotional support. And the community would back these values by offering mediation services, family therapy, support groups, and a non-adversarial legal process.

In the new family ethic, these "shoulds" about post-divorce families would not be seen just as matters of private values and morality — or as nosegays spouted by public officials. They would be matters of major importance to the community. Fathers who abandon their children financially or emotionally after divorce would be subjected to the same social stigma as drunk drivers. The same would go for mothers who try to break their children's bonds with their fathers. And appropriate laws and policies would provide sanctions against these abuses of family values.

At the level of broad government policies, the best way for the government to support the new family ethic is to ensure adequate living standards for families. Almost all serious family problems are more common when income is lacking. In the lowest-income groups in our cities, marriage itself is threatened as an institution, since the majority of births are to single mothers, and the great majority of couples who do marry eventually divorce. In the face of decades of poverty and terrible living conditions, the values of commitment, care, community, and equality are nearly impossible to sustain. That is why calling for a transformation in family values without an accompanying transformation in public policies is like criticizing people for stumbling in the dark instead of offering them candles.

To echo the line from *Death of a Salesman,* most people agree that 40 if the family is to be viable in the coming decades, "attention must be paid." There is little new about the concerns for families, but there are promising signs that we might be able to move beyond the

stalemate between liberals and conservatives, that we might tran-
scend the split between the private world of the family and the public world of the community.

This is a perfect time for discussion about a new family ethic, because the wave of changes in the family has subsided for the present.
During the years of turbulence, we gained a lot of knowledge from
research on families. We now know what factors contribute to better
(and worse) adjustment for children after divorce. We now know
much more about how to provide educational, therapeutic, and mediation services to families. Marriage and family therapy, for example, has matured in the past decades as a mental-health service
and professional specialty. We have learned that value-free public
policies do not achieve a broad national consensus. We have learned
that both the pessimists and the optimists make good points, but
that the tedious terms of the century-long debate about the American family must be set aside.

The Pluralistic Family is here to stay for an indefinite future. The
forces of gender equality, diversity, and personal freedom may never
again permit a single ideal family structure like the Institutional Family or the Psychological Family. The quality of the Pluralistic Family
of the future depends, however, on whether we can create a new
kind of family ethic that will help establish and maintain healthy
bonds between family members in different living arrangements,
and between families and their communities. Like death and taxes,
some kind of family may be inevitable in human life, but the responsible, satisfying, and flexible family required for the next century —
that is far from inevitable.

THE INVOLVED READER

1 According to Doherty, how do pessimists and optimists differ in
   their perspective on the American family? (Where does he hint
   at a third alternative perspective that would be the basis of a
   new consensus?)

2 For Doherty, what defines the Institutional Family, the Psychological Family, and the Pluralistic Family? What are the
   strengths and weaknesses (or "Achilles heels") of each? What
   options does he include under the heading of the Pluralistic
   Family?

3 What are major points in the "new family ethic" that Doherty
   sketches out? How will it incorporate "timeless values" but also
   go beyond them?

4 Why would the "new family ethic" involve public policy and

community standards as well as individual options or private choice?

TALKING, WRITING, THINKING

5   What is your own personal definition of family? Does the term have positive or negative associations for you? Do you feel there should be more or less emphasis on "family values"?

6   If you were asked to classify them, what for you would be the most significant kinds of family ties or family-type relationships? What would be key features and good examples of each?

7   Do you think that teenage pregnancy, single motherhood, or same-sex relationships are losing their stigma — the way divorce did in an earlier cycle?

COLLABORATIVE PROJECTS

8   Same-sex marriages have been hotly contested in local elections or referendums and in court decisions, including a landmark Supreme Court decision in 1996. Working with a group, you may want to investigate the current status — legal, political — of the issue.

short story

Only Approved Indians Can Play: Made in USA

J ACK   F ORBES

What defines someone as a member of a group? In some periods of history, who was defined as Jewish or other persecuted nationality has been a matter of life and death. Today membership in or exclusion from a tribe can make one eligible or ineligible for benefits under court decisions. Much of what we read in current newspapers and magazines revolves around questions of ethnic or racial identity. Di-versity, pluralism, and separatism have become buzzwords pushing different buttons for different readers. Like the author of the following story, Native American writers have grappled with the question of whether to maintain a separate ethnic cultural identity or assimilate to white society. Jack Forbes is a Californian of Renape, Lenape, and Saponi ancestry. He became a university teacher at the University of California at Davis.

The all-Indian basketball tournament was in its second day. Ex-citement was pretty high, because a lot of the teams were very good or at least eager and hungry to win. Quite a few people had come to watch, mostly Indians. Many were relatives or friends of the players. A lot of people were betting money and tension was pretty great.

A team from the Tucson Inter-Tribal House was set to play against a group from the Great Lakes region. The Tucson players were mostly very dark young men with long black hair. A few had little goatee beards or mustaches though, and one of the Great Lakes fans had started a rumor that they were really Chicanos. This was a big issue since the Indian Sports League had a rule that all players had to be of one-quarter or more Indian blood and that they had to have their BIA roll numbers available if challenged.

And so a big argument started. One of the biggest, darkest Indians on the Tucson team had been singled out as a Chicano, and the crowd wanted him thrown out. The Great Lakes players, most of whom were pretty light, refused to start. They all had their BIA iden-tification cards, encased in plastic. This proved that they were all real Indians, even a blonde-haired guy. He was really only about one-sixteenth but the BIA rolls had been changed for his tribe so legally he was one-fourth. There was no question about the Great Lakes team.

They were all land-based, federally-recognized Indians, although living in a big midwestern city, and they had their cards to prove it.

Anyway, the big, dark Tucson Indian turned out to be a Papago. He didn't have a BIA card but he could talk Papago so they let him alone for the time being. Then they turned towards a lean, very Indian-looking guy who had a pretty big goatee. He seemed to have a Spanish accent, so they demanded to see his card.

Well, he didn't have one either. He said he was a full-blood Tara-   5
humara Indian and he could also speak his language. None of the Great Lakes Indians could talk their languages so they said that was no proof of anything, that you had to have a BIA roll number.

The Tarahumara man was getting pretty angry by then. He said his father and uncle had been killed by the whites in Mexico and that he did not expect to be treated with prejudice by other Indians.

But all that did no good. Someone demanded to know if he had a reservation and if his tribe was recognized. He replied that his people lived high up in the mountains and that they were still resisting the Mexicanos, that the government was trying to steal their land.

"What state do your people live in," they wanted to know. When he said that his people lived free, outside of the control of any state, they only shook their fists at him. "You're not an official Indian. All official Indians are under the whiteman's rule now. We all have a number given to us, to show that we are recognized."

Well, it all came to an end when someone shouted that "Tarahu-   maras don't exist. They're not listed in the BIA dictionary." Another fan yelled, "He's a Mexican. He can't play. This tournament is only for Indians."

The officials of the tournament had been huddling together. One   10
blew his whistle and an announcement was made. "The Tucson team is disqualified. One of its members is a Yaqui. One is a Tarahumara. The rest are Papagos. None of them have BIA enrollment cards. They are not Indians within the meaning of the laws of the government of the United States. The Great Lakes team is declared the winner by default."

A tremendous roar of applause swept through the stands. A white BIA official wiped the tears from his eyes and said to a companion, "God Bless America. I think we've won."

THE INVOLVED READER

1 Why does the author tell this story? What is his purpose? Who or what is his target? Are you surprised by the way he describes fellow Native Americans?

2   What is the point of the ending? Why does the BIA (Bureau of Indian Affairs) official say what he says?

TALKING, THINKING, WRITING

3   Have you encountered situations where someone's being one-quarter or other fraction of some ethnicity or race becomes an issue? Why or to whom would it matter? What portion of "Indian blood" would a person have to have before you would consider the person a Native American?

4   What does it mean to be white? Who is included; who is left out? Who decides? Are there legal definitions? When or where does it matter?

5   When are you ready to call someone an American? Would the person either have to be born in the United States or have to be a naturalized citizen? Can a person who was born and raised in this country be Mexican?

poem

The Seven Deadly Sins: Anger

LINDA PASTAN

Where do you turn for advice on how to cope with stress, anger, or frustration? Would you turn to a psychologist, spiritual advisor — or a poet? A poet laureate of the state of Maryland, Linda Pastan was born in New York City and was a student at Brandeis and Radcliffe. Collections of her poetry include A Perfect Circle of Sun *(1971)*, Five Stages of Grief *(1978)*, AM/PM *(1982)*, Imperfect Paradise *(1988)*, and* Heroes in Disguise *(1991).*

You tell me
that it's all right
to let it out of its cage,
though it may claw someone,
even bite.   5
You say that letting it out
may tame it somehow.
But loose it may
turn on me, maul
my face, draw blood.   10
Ah, you think you know so much,
you whose anger is a pet dog,
its canines dull with disuse.
But mine is a rabid thing, sharpening its teeth
on my very bones,   15
and I will never let it go.

THE INVOLVED READER

1   What does this poem say about the psychology of anger? As seen by the speaker in the poem, how does anger work? What are alternative ways of coping with it?

2   Do you think animal imagery fits the subject of this poem particularly well? Or does it in some ways fail to do justice to the human dimension of anger?

TALKING, THINKING, WRITING

3   Are you one of the people who tend to let anger out of its cage? Or do you tend to keep it caged? Or is your anger a pet dog?

4   Poets often talk about life's problems or choices in images from the world of nature. How does a person's background or occupation color that person's perception of the world? Have you known anyone who tends to see issues or events from the perspective, for instance, of a teacher, butcher, police officer, cook, coach, physician, or nurse? (You may want to try your hand at writing a poem or prose passage looking at anger, stress, frustration, love, or other emotion from one such perspective.)

MAKING CONNECTIONS

5   You may want to look back over essays in this book that deal candidly with personal experience — Constans, Angelou, Shapiro, and Wozencraft in Chapter 3; Swardson in Chapter 4. Do the authors strike you as highly emotional or surprisingly unemotional? Is there a common pattern? (Does our society discourage people from baring their emotions — "losing their cool," letting their anger show, or becoming overly sentimental?)

The Writer's Tools 5

Using Accurate Words

Do you ever feel at a loss for words when explaining a complicated situation? Are you at times tongue-tied when taking a stand on an issue? The first step toward using words more resourcefully is to become a word watcher. Word watchers keep an eye out for how words work, what company they keep, and what images and associations they call up for the reader.

Words in Context

Words seldom carry meaning by themselves alone. Word watchers see how words work in **context**. They read how a word fits into a phrase, sentence, or longer passage. The word *cell* means something different in each of the following sentences:

The Reformation took the monks out of their *cells*.

(A cell was originally the cubicle of a monk.)

Little is known about why the virus attacks some healthy *cells* but not others.

(In this context, cells are the smallest self-reproducing components of an organism.)

Manuel joined a communist party *cell* in Prague.

(In this context, a cell is a small tightly knit local unit of the communist party.)

One way to expand your vocabulary is to extrapolate the meaning of new or difficult words from the context. What is bound to be the meaning of *obliterate* in the following passage?

The talk show is the most democratic of media forms. It is the great equalizer, *obliterating* all distinctions — between truth and falsity, between image and argument, between one guest and another.

(What do we do to distinctions in order to equalize things and make them more "democratic"? We do away with them — to judge from this passage, do away with them completely, not leaving a trace. That's what *obliterate* means: do away with completely, erase.)

Shades of Meaning

What makes one word more accurate or more informative than another? The word with the right shade of meaning seems calibrated for a specific situation or attitude. For example, an *aversion* is more than just a dislike. It is a strong dislike — literally a "being turned off" or away. An *antipathy* is a strong deep-seated, intuitive feeling of dislike for a person — a feeling that might be hard to explain rationally. *Antagonism* is a hostile feeling that at any moment might lead to open hostility.

Words like the following carry special implications beyond their broad general meaning:

realm   *general meaning:* area
            original meaning: a kingdom or domain
            special meaning: an area under the control of those in
                charge, with its own rules and traditions, and able
                to repel intruders or outsiders
ostracize   *general meaning:* to exclude, to cast out
            original meaning: in ancient Greece, to take a vote to
                send someone into exile
            special meaning: a drastic kind of exclusion, totally
                cutting a person off, making any contact with the
                person taboo

Connotations

Words carry attitudes as well as information. The added freight of attitudes, feelings, and value judgments makes up the **connotations** of a word. Words do not just report — they praise or condemn; they glorify or belittle. *Bureaucrat, demagogue, mercenary,* or *career politician* do not simply point to people. They point a finger at them. A demagogue was once a "leader of the people," but the word now fingers a leader who leads us by the nose. Words may **denote**, or point to, the same object or person but carry different connotations. *Dad* is personal and intimate; *father* may sound more distant; *biological father* is likely to sound cold and uncaring.

Effective writers are aware of connotations like the following:

maverick   *literal meaning:* a person who does not go along with
                the crowd; someone who, as one student wrote,
                "goes against the grain"
            connotation: an admirable person, who perhaps has
                more of the courage to be himself or herself than
                we do
intuitive   *literal meaning:* not arrived at by logical reasoning;
                intuitive people are people "who just know"
            connotation: an admirable kind of direct insight that
                is superior to plodding, literal-minded logic

feudalism   *literal meaning:* a hierarchic, layered political system where vassals owe allegiance and service to a warlord, who in turn may be a vassal to a more powerful overlord

                connotation: a splintered political system, prone to constant civil war among competing warlords

Networks of Meaning

Words are related; they have cousins or more distant kin. You will be able to use words like the following more accurately and effectively when you see them as part of a network of meaning:

inimical   the opposite of *amicable* or friendly

anachronism   something out of its proper *chron*ological order; something placed at the wrong time or the wrong point in history; often something that has outlasted its time

homogeneous   the opposite of heterogeneous; a homogeneous population is of one kind, whereas a heterogeneous population brings together many different kinds

Technical Terms

The expert has a word for it. Mechanics need terms like *alternator, differential,* and *catalytic converter* to ply their trade. Computer users need terms like *mainframe, interface, modem, CD-ROM, megabyte,* and *DOS* to communicate. However, insiders need to gauge which terms, and how many at a time, an outsider can handle. The following passage explains a few basic terms in accessible language:

> The disk drive works like a very fast tape recorder, recording information on a magnetic medium, the floppy disk. When the user needs that stored information, she tells the computer to load the information into its own short-term memory (RAM — for "random access memory"), where the data can be examined and revised.

It's a helpful habit to give a quick pointed explanation whenever a new or difficult term is likely to draw a blank in the newcomer's mind.

> During extended mountain climbing expeditions. the climbers **bivouac,** *resting in temporary emcampments in the open, using only tents as an improvised shelter.*

Figurative Language

When ordinary literal language fails them, effective writers turn to **figurative language**. They use imaginative comparisons that convey ideas and feelings hard to put into words. What comparisons are built into sentences like the following? What do the figurative expressions in the following samples add to the bare facts in each statement?

> The sterile white pharmacy was enclosed in glass, *trapping the pharmacist in a cage* walled with bottles of many sizes.
> Her greenhouse looked *like a section of a tropical rain forest* with fiberglass walls enclosing it.
>
> In the far reaches of the cable system, celebrities of years past *float like dead moons.*
>
> Lewis Lapham

These examples show two different kinds of figurative language: The cage is a **metaphor** — an imaginative comparison that comes into a sentence unannounced. There is no signal to alert us that a comparison is coming. The alert reader has to supply the implied "as if." It is *as if* the pharmacist's cubicle were a cage. The tropical rain forest is presented as a **simile**, a close cousin of the metaphor. With a simile, the comparison is signaled by a word such as *like* or *as* or *as if*. (See the editing guidelines in Chapter 12 for mixed or inept metaphors.)

| **WRITING WORKSHOP 5** |

Words in Action

What do the words selected for study below mean to you? What overtones or shades of meanings set related words apart? Where or how would each be the right word?

• *How does the* context *help you understand each italicized word?* What clues does the context provide for a reader not sure of its meaning?

> To *paraphrase* our national bard, I hear America talking (and talking and talking). Clearly, the talk show fills some *crucial* need in our national life, which I think has to do with a felt absence of place and power. The studio audience — and by extension the television audience — becomes a kind of *therapeutic*, personal-problem-solving support group that helps us feel better about ourselves and resolve to live better, one hour at a time. Talk shows allow us to feel *connected* to this community of self-improving, self-

motivated doers "empowering" themselves — without in any way affecting the actual circumstances of their lives. For even more than lack of place it is the lack of power that has helped turn television into a twenty-four-hour-a-day talk-show *marathon*. In a troubled economic time, when people distrust government and feel helpless to *affect* their fate, talking back may be the only form of power left to them. Those of us who can't act ourselves can watch others seeming to act — *voyeurs* watching *exhibitionists* in a *pantomime* of power.

Adapted from Richard M. Levine, "I Feel Your Pain," Mother Jones

• *What* shades of meaning *set apart the near synonyms in the following sets?*

1 agreement — covenant — compromise — appeasement — deal
2 eccentric — crank — maverick — loner
3 female — feminine — womanly — womanish — effeminate
4 idealized — visionary — utopian
5 practical — pragmatic — opportunistic — expedient

• *How does each of the following sentences use* connotative words? What emotions or attitudes do they bring into play?

1 The last of the cyclical postwar recessions was ending, and a quarter century of burgeoning prosperity was on the launch pad.

Laurence Shames

2 Loaded words try to seduce the mind into accepting a prefabricated opinion about the thing described.
3 The advice that most Southern mothers pass on is that men are the enemy — a pack of Yankees.

Shirley Abbott

4 Women started to emancipate themselves from a paternalistic society.
5 Corporate law practice has always been the Rolls-Royce of legal careers.

Fred Graham

• *In one sentence each, how would you make the following technical terms intelligible to the newcomer or outsider?* meltdown, symbiosis, syncopation, black hole, superconductor, digital.

• *How does the writer of the following passage use* figurative expressions? What images and associations does each imaginative comparison bring to mind? Which of the figurative expressions seem familiar; which seem fresh or provocative?

A great many loaded words bring along not only their meanings but some extra freight — a load of judgment or bias that plays upon the emotions instead of lighting up the understanding. These words deserve careful handling — and minding. They are loaded. Such words babble up in all corners of society, wherever anybody is axe-grinding, arm-twisting, back-scratching, sweet-talking. Political blather leans sharply to words (*peace, prosperity*) whose moving powers outweigh exact meanings. Merchandising depends on adjectives (*new, improved*) that must be continually re-charged with notions that entice people to buy. In casual conversation, emotional stuffing is lent to words by inflection and gesture. The innocent phrase, "Thanks a lot," is frequently a vehicle for heaping servings of irritation.

Frank Tippett, "Watching Out for Loaded Words," *Time*

Writing is often sitting there waiting for my brain to make connections that I don't know. **AMY GROSS**

6

Comparing Your Options

Writing to Compare

When you look at a new car, do you notice the features that make it different from last year's model? When you listen to people who wear business suits, do you notice that they talk differently from friends who are artists or musicians? We naturally compare and contrast. Encountering something new, we notice how it is similar to what we know — but also different from it in other ways. We may study new legislation — and note how it changes the law. We look at changes in familiar arrangements — and note what adjustments they would require.

Here are current topics that invite comparison. If you were to sketch out a tentative comparison on one or more of these, what would you include? What key points would you plan to cover?

How does life in the traditional nuclear family compare with life in a single-parent family?
Which diets are damaging crash diets, and which are likely to lead to healthier eating and living?
What makes health foods different?
How does private health insurance perform compared with the government-sponsored plans of other countries?
How does the outlook of reentry students differ from that of students fresh out of high school?
Can public transport compete with the private automobile?
Which is more damaging to the environment — nuclear energy or fossil fuels?

Comparison and contrast can suggest alternatives and guide choices. Much widely read writing focuses on what people do differently who are healthier, more successful, or more popular than we are. Why do Americans run up multibillion-dollar trade deficits with Japan? Why are the Japanesee formidable competitors when it comes to selling VCRs, TVs, cameras, cars, and computer chips? What do the Japanese do differently? In asking Americans to change their ways, you might line up essential contrasts like this.

The Competitive Edge

DECEPTIVE SIMILARITIES — A Shared Civilization
> Japanese businesspeople and politicians do not just wear Western-style suits and ties or get caught up in Western-style scandals and charges of corruption. Japan and the West share a highly developed technology and have similar political and economic systems.

FIRST CONTRAST — Corporate Goals
> Whereas Americans put the emphasis on short-term quarter-by-quarter profit, the Japanese concentrate on the long-range health and growth of a company. Long-range empire building rather than this year's bottom line is what counts.

SECOND CONTRAST — National Mindset
> Whereas the American national mythology glorifies the lone individual (Rambo, the Lone Ranger), the Japanese prize teamwork. They value dedicated collective effort over the American cowboy mentality.

THIRD CONTRAST — Labor Relations
> Whereas turnover in American companies is high (leaving those not fired anxious and insecure), the Japanese have a turnover rate that is one-tenth the American rate (because they prize experienced, loyal workers).

FOURTH CONTRAST — Executive Personnel
> Whereas the highest paid executives in America tend to be money managers or former financial officers ("bean counters"), the Japanese reward expertise in production and labor management.

When supported by an array of striking examples, this comparison should make your readers think: Should Americans change their ways to become team players and empire builders who take more pride than we do now in shared effort?

Writers naturally compare to help us understand. To make us understand conditions on the planet Venus, they tell us which earth elements would liquefy or evaporate in the heat. They tell us why the gases in the atmosphere would be unbreathable for human beings. Writers naturally compare to guide our choices. Discussing two political candidates, they tell us which has the better track record on crime or taxes or the environment.

> **THOUGHT LOG 6**
>
> *Thinking about Contrasts*
>
> Write in your thought log to explore a contrast between before and after, between then and now, or between here and there. For instance, you might write about how your relationship to a parent or someone else close to you has changed as the result of illness, divorce, or remarriage. Or you might compare your life before and after a move to a different part of the country. Or you might write about a place you know well before and after it was changed by urban blight, gentrification, deindustrialization, or changing demographics.

Structuring Your Comparison

How will you lay out your comparison so that your readers see the connections between two sets of data? You may find that a comparison-and-contrast paper tests your ability to organize — things may not naturally fall into a pattern. The key questions you use to help you organize your writing are likely to be: What is alike? What is different?

Similarities First   Your aim may be to go beyond surface impressions to examine underlying causes. You may decide to show surface similarities first. Then you zero in on key differences that do not meet the eye. For instance, your paper about what makes Japan different might start by showing businesspeople in suits and ties and cars with the latest gadgets and sales features. However, the bulk of your paper might then explore not-so-obvious differences that seem to give Japan the competitive edge. For example, the Japanese have a rigorous, demanding educational system. They focus on long-range goals. They have a tradition of teamwork and community effort, and a loyal and relatively stable workforce.

Differences First   You may be worried by increasing divisions in the community, and you may want to write a paper reminding your readers of common goals. You first focus on differences that set people apart — citing speeches by militants or looking at favoritism toward their own on the part of officials or juries. However, you then go beyond differences to remind people of essential common concerns. For instance, ethnic or racial groups in different parts of a city have a common stake in shoring up a weakened industrial base or salvaging the schools. They have a stake in guaranteeing police protection and other essential services.

Point-by-Point Comparison   With some subjects, the best strategy for highlighting connections is a **point-by-point** comparison — taking up major points and showing how two things compare on each. For instance, what are key differences between the typical American diet and an ideal healthful diet? What is the difference between eating a superburger with 935 calories and 61 grams of fat and eating a healthful meal? You may choose to compare the two kinds of diet point by point. You look first at high-calorie versus low-calorie diets, then at high-fat versus low-fat diets. Then you look at meat-centered diets versus diets emphasizing fruits and vegetables.

Suppose you have been reading discussions of the two hemispheres of the brain: the intuitive, synthesizing, emotionally responsive right side and the analytical, linear logical left side. The right side is nonverbal and "holistic" — it is good at grasping wholes or patterns. The left side is verbal and rational — we draw on it when we talk and argue and deal with figures. Here is a rough outline for a point-by-point comparison:

Right Brain, Left Brain

POINT ONE: Appearance

My artist friends wear sandals; they wear paint-spattered jeans and old shirts or sweaters.	My business friends wear dark suits and ties.

POINT TWO: Shop talk

My artist friends talk about design and composition, about lines and textures and paints.	My business friends have graphs, flowcharts, and printouts on the lunch table when they eat.

POINT THREE: Jobs

My artist friends take jobs merely to stay afloat, to earn enough money to take time out for creative work, which is its own reward.	For my business friends, work is the most important thing in life. They are goal oriented, with each job a stepping stone toward the goal of success.

POINT FOUR: Personality

My artist friends are visually oriented and emotional. They respond intuitively to analogies and similarities; they love symbols and metaphors.	My business friends like to analyze and quantify a problem (the "bottom line"). They want the objective facts.

Parallel-Order Comparison In writing about two people, or about two kinds of institutions, you may decide that you have to give a rounded picture of each. In other words, you opt to discuss them separately. So how are you going to make your reader see the connections? The answer is: Each time, you take up roughly the same points in the same order. For instance, you may be writing about what should guide parents' choices when looking for daycare. As you look at contrasting experiences, you arrive at three criteria for evaluating daycare centers that are available: the nature of the staff, the activities offered to children, and the participation of the parents. As you look at two contrasting centers, you each time check off the same criteria in the same order.

Your **parallel-order** comparison would be structured roughly as follows:

It's Your Choice

THESIS: Parents looking for a place to help their children grow should look for a center with a stable staff, the right activities, and an active role for the parents.

TEST CASE ONE

POINT ONE: staff
The staff changed every few months, mainly because workers were paid minimum wage. The teachers who stayed did so because they did not feel qualified to work for a higher salary elsewhere. . . .

POINT TWO: activities
The children's day was as follows: TV — inside play — outside play — lunch — nap — outside play — parents' pickup. The main goal was to make the children follow the rules and keep them quiet. . . .

POINT THREE: participation
Parents were not encouraged to participate; their role was to drop off the children and pick them up. . . .

TEST CASE TWO

POINT ONE: staff
There was a low turnover of staff, with workers who had worked there for years and showed their pride in the work of the center. . . .

POINT TWO: activities
The children's schedule was as follows: play — story time — work time — music — outside play — lunch — nap — independent work or play — story time — outside play — art — parents' pickup. . . .

POINT THREE: participation
The parents joined in all the outside activities and often stopped for lunch with the children. Parents should be wary of any school that does not allow drop-in visits. . . .

WRITING WORKSHOP I

A Paper for Peer Review

In the paper that follows, how has the student writer used or adapted the point-by-point scheme? How effective are the examples? How clear or convincing is this writer's presentation of the left-brain/right-brain theory?

L-Mode, R-Mode

When I picture my artist friends, I see them clustered on grass like a bevy of quail, looking at each other's paintings. Their clothes, as they say, "make a statement": Some wear sandals (and a few are barefoot); most wear paint-spattered jeans and old shirts or sweaters. They are lost in a world of cadmium yellow and veridian green as they talk shop about lines and textures and paints.

When I picture my business friends, I see them sitting around a conference table. They wear the sales manager's uniform: dark suits (in shades of gray and blue and black), with ties or scarves of subdued patterns. In their regulation attaché cases, they carry the graphs, flowcharts, printouts, and statistical tables that link them to the outside world.

Do artists and businesspeople only look different — or do they think differently? To an artist, ordinary prosaic work is only a means to an end; mundane "outside" work may be necessary for survival. What matters is the expression of inner feelings; the reward is in the pleasure of working on whatever current project designed to make a comment on some aspect of life.

For the business-oriented person, work is one of a series of never-ending steps toward the ultimate, unobtainable, nebulous goal of success. Feeling and emotions are likely to get in the way. What matters is not the creative moment now but the goals, the objectives, the projections of tomorrow's campaign, of next year's "bottom line."

Neither the artistic person nor the practical person is right or wrong in his or her perception of and reaction to reality. Each is experiencing life and relating to life from a different perspective. According to one theory, much in these different approaches can be traced to different styles of thinking represented by the right and left hemispheres of the brain. In her book, *Drawing on the Right Side of the Brain*, Betty Edwards quotes Roger Sperry (who pioneered this theory in the late sixties) as saying, "There appear to be two modes of thinking, verbal and nonverbal, represented rather separately in the left and right hemispheres. . . ." Edwards says, "Both hemispheres are involved in higher cognitive functioning, with each half of the brain specialized in complementary fashion for different modes of thinking, both highly complex."

The left hemisphere of the brain is responsible for cognitive mental processes such as math, language, and consecutive reasoning. This L-mode is linear; it analyzes step by step; it keeps track of time by sequencing one thing after another; it verbalizes to describe or define; it draws conclusions based on systematic logical reasoning.

The right hemisphere is responsible for perceptual and visual activity (such as art) and for the emotions. This R-mode is synthetic (it puts things together to form patterns or wholes) rather than analytic. It is without a sense of time. It seizes analogies and similarities (it creates metaphors). It has a nonverbal awareness of things. It is intuitive rather than logical and sees things holistically (as wholes) rather than dissecting them in linear fashion.

We are told that the left hemisphere is usually dominant. It is therefore no surprise that business and science are dominant in our society. By righting the balance, we can broaden our perception and come closer to a well-rounded life.

Revising Your Comparison/Contrast Paper

In working on a comparison/contrast paper, you may have found that it needed a definite blueprint, more so than some other kinds of writing. In revising an early draft, you have a chance to check how clearly you have shown connections, how clearly you have lined up similarities and differences. The following might be mental notes to yourself to guide your revision:

• *Spell out more clearly the point of your comparison.* For instance, when you compare competing designs for a metal sculpture to adorn the space in front of a new city hall, what is really at stake? Should your cash-strapped community lay out $285,000 for a sculpture that to some is a searing indictment of capitalism but to others a pile of scrap?

• *Post better signposts to highlight the structure of your comparison.* Do you need stronger **transitions** — showing essential links in your chain of thought? You may need to add signals like the following:

> **On the one hand,** AIDS spread through contagion like other infectious diseases. The infected blood supply of blood banks both here and abroad was early identified as one link in the transmission of the disease. . . .
>
> **On the other hand,** AIDS turned out to be very different in a number of ways. . . .
>
> **In the first place,** the disease had a long incubation period. People who tested HIV positive might not actually get sick till five years later. . . .
>
> **In the second place,** AIDS was not in itself a killer disease like cholera or tuberculosis. People died from "opportunistic infections" or "AIDS-related diseases." . . .
>
> **In the third place,** testing for AIDS early became a political football

because of deep-rooted social taboos and also because of the apprehen-
sions of the gay community. . . .

    Finally, and perhaps most important, prevention turned out to
be an epidemiologist's nightmare. People who would not dream of drinking cholera-infested water continued to have unprotected sex. . . .

• *Fill in cross references that will help the reader see important connections.* Should you do more to keep the paper from breaking up
into separate mini-essays on two things being compared? Remind
your readers that this is a comparison:

    **Whereas left-brained people tend to pride themselves on lin-
ear one-two-three logic,** right-brained people are more open to intuitive leaps. . . .

• *Strengthen weak links.* Look with suspicion at perfunctory transitions that merely say "also" or "another interesting point is. . . ."
Why is this point interesting at this juncture in your paper?

WEAK LINK: **Another** misleading image created by television is that of the
             working mother. . . .

BETTER: **The gap between image and reality is even wider** in
             television's treatment of the working mother. . . .

OPTIONS FOR WRITING 6

Exploring Alternatives

    Organize a comparison/contrast paper on one of the following
topics. Give serious thought to your general strategy or overall plan.
Draw on a mix of sources: personal experience and observation,
talking to concerned or knowledgeable people, reading of current
publications, your viewing of television programs and movies.

1 How does life in the traditional nuclear family compare with life
with a single parent? Would you criticize or defend the single-
parent family?

2 What are the arguments in favor of preferring private to public
schools? What have been your opportunities to experience or
observe either? What are the strengths and weaknesses of each?

3 How is life in the suburbs different from life in the inner city?
Does city life give people a different outlook? For instance, are
city people tougher, more cynical, more streetwise?

4 How does a system of private health insurance perform compared with the government-operated plans of other countries? How does our health system compare with "socialized
medicine"?

5 How is the outlook of older reentry students different from that of students fresh out of high school? Are older students advantaged or handicapped compared with younger students?

6 What is wrong with the way we eat? What makes health foods different from the ordinary American diet?

7 Is it true that male students are predisposed to do better than female students in math? Do men and women differ in aptitude, attitude, conditioning, or achievement? Are young women held back by "math anxiety"? If so, why?

8 What are the arguments for supporting public transport over private transportation? Does public transport have a chance to compete successfully with the automobile?

9 Are there basic differences between male-dominated sports and "women's sports"? Can sports for women achieve the same level of prominence in our society as sports for men?

10 Is there any difference between addiction to drugs and addiction to alcohol? Or, is there any difference between smoking cigarettes and smoking marijuana?

Reading, Discussion, Writing

Probing Contrasts

OVERVIEW: The authors of the following selections explore significant contrasts and show why they matter. For instance, they alert us to changes for the worse in literature for young girls. They illuminate differences between the way the Japanese and Americans work to explain why the Japanese have the competitive edge. They compare different kinds of intelligence to help us gauge better the full range of human aptitudes.

The Mystery of Nancy Drew

JACKIE VIVELO

Is popular entertainment just that — entertainment? Or does popular entertainment reflect trends in the culture in which we live? Does it in turn help shape our attitudes? Major shifts in the images projected by American popular culture may help us understand forces at work in our society. Jackie Vivelo traces one such shift in adolescent literature for girls. What role models does adolescent fiction provide for young women? How have these role models changed over the years? And have they changed for the better or for worse? Vivelo writes non-fiction for adults and fiction for young readers. The editors of Ms. *magazine, where the following article first appeared, described her Super Sleuth series as featuring "young detectives who solve mysteries through logic."*

For more than 30 years, the Nancy Drew books enlarged horizons for young readers, as Nancy's courage, supported by common sense, saw her through harrowing situations. Unfaltering in the face of skepticism from police officials and her elders, she rejected others' definitions of her and the limitations they placed on her. Young and female, Nancy was a force to be reckoned with.

In *Don't Tell the Grown-Ups: Why Kids Love the Books They Do* (Avon, 1990), Alison Lurie includes the Nancy Drew books among "the sacred texts of childhood, whose authors had not forgotten what it was like to be a child. To read them was to feel a shock of recognition, a rush of liberating energy." Lurie is speaking, of course, of the original texts.

Rewriting of the Nancy Drew books and modifications to Nancy's character began in 1959, and continue to this day. Nancy is no longer the intrepid, independent detective of the original novels. The teen-age detective who was once a symbol of spunky female independence has slowly been replaced by an image of prolonged childhood, currently evolving toward a Barbie doll detective.

The change is indisputable.

The Secret of the Old Clock

In the original version, Nancy is 16, a young adult. Her relation-   5
ship to Hannah Gruen is employer/employee. Nancy leaves a list of instructions for Hannah, who hardly enters the story.

The floor manager of the River Heights department store is a woman. When Nancy gives a lift to a police official, she drives. In a visit to a summer camp, Nancy and her friends are on their own.

In the revised version, Nancy is 18, a teenager, Hannah is clearly Nancy's adviser. The housekeeper gives a list of errands to Nancy. They hug. Hannah warns and counsels her.

The floor manager of that same store is now a man.

This time when the official accepts a ride, Nancy moves over to let him drive her car. At camp, in the new version, Nancy and her friends are supervised by the aunt of one of the girls.

The Clue of The Tapping Heels

Original version: 10

"A stowaway!" gasped the woman.

"This girl is not a stowaway!" George exclaimed indignantly. "She's tied up and gagged!"

Quickly the girls set Nancy free and assisted their chum to her feet.

"I thought help would never come," the girl gasped. "I've been tapping on that door for hours."

"I don't know how you came to be here," said the stewardess, 15 "but you'll have to explain everything to Chief Officer Murray."

"He's the one who must do the explaining!" Nancy cried.

Revised version:

Nancy was quickly lifted into the attic and the gag and bonds removed. Bess flung both arms around her friend, completely blocking off any affectionate hugs the others might have wished to give her.

George's face showed anger. "Who did this to you?" she demanded.

"Two men came up behind me while I was investigating this 20 stairway."

"I'll call the police," Ned said, but Burt said, "You stay with Nancy. I'll do it."

Ned could see that Nancy was pretty shaken. He swooped her up and carried the exhausted girl to the second floor.

In the 1930 edition of *The Hidden Staircase*. Nancy tells her lawyer father, Carson Drew, "You've often said you wanted me to grow up self-reliant and brave," a statement that disappears in the revised edition. In the 1933 *The Sign of the Twisted Candles,* when Nancy's girlfriend George suggests that they need a mechanic to fix their car, Nancy says, "I can repair it myself." In the revised text, the car is stopped by a fallen tree rather than by mechanical failure. The changes provide a real-life mystery. What became of the original Nancy Drew?

"Carolyn Keene," author of the series, was the pseudonym first of Edward L. Stratemeyer and later of his daughter, Harriet S. Adams. Stratemeyer, responsible for dozens of series, created the plucky 16-year-old Nancy Drew as a match for the spirited, already popular Hardy brothers. When Harriet Adams took over managing her father's publishing empire following his death in 1930, she continued his practice of outlining and then assigning story writing to others for most of the series. But the Hardy Boys and the Nancy Drew novels became her personal projects, written entirely by her as they had been by her father. How then can we explain the changes in Nancy Drew?

Despite the immediate and huge success of the series, letters   25
of complaint arrived along with the first fan letters. Taking over from her father, Adams did, to her credit, avoid dialect attributed to ethnic characters, and she eliminated ethnic and racial stereotypes. She deleted Nancy's gun, on the grounds that it was controversial. But she also began a process of constricting Nancy's independence. Nancy, though now two years older, was reduced to the status of clever child. Adams was rewarded by seeing the series, once rejected by public libraries, become accepted — even occasionally recommended — reading. Reacting to public opinion, Adams and her successors chipped away at Nancy's most striking qualities.

Today, the original 56 Nancy Drew titles, many in revised versions, are still available from Grosset & Dunlap. Since Adams' death, however, the series has almost doubled. Continued under the Minstrel Book imprint by Simon & Schuster, the most recent titles have no early counterparts.

While the new additions contain female police officers and female bosses, they no longer depict an autonomous Nancy. The stories are filled with action, but less of it is initiated by Nancy. Along with a degree of self-reliance and confidence, gone is her alert defense of the underdog. What is left is the glamorous life of a teenage detective, a lucky person to whom exciting things happen.

The Nancy Drew Files, a second series published at Simon & Schuster's Archway paperbacks, was launched in 1986 with *Secrets Can Kill*. Written concurrently with the latest volumes of the regular series, these books have young adult appeal. Instead of seeing the world through Nancy's bold eyes, the reader is now constantly checking out Nancy's appearance. Every few pages bring reminders of Nancy's looks, her clothing, her effect on other people.

Both the Archway and Minstrel series are overseen by Anne Greenberg, who makes sure that the books, now written by many different authors, conform to a unified image. According to Greenberg, the authors are chosen for their ability to "deal with the insecurity, the emotions of teens, and how they look at the world."

The first entry in this series carries a description of Nancy: "The tight jeans looked great on her long, slim legs and the green sweater complemented her strawberry-blond hair." Her friend Bess sighs, "You'll make the guys absolutely drool." (In the original series, Nancy's appearance was dismissed with one word: "attractive.")   30

While readers who know the original series may deplore the current trend, the books are enormously popular. Twelve new titles are added each year to the Nancy Drew Files. Three titles a year combine the adventures of Nancy Drew and the Hardy Boys, and new additions continue. After an absence of 33 years, some of the original books are back in facsimile form, reprinted by Applewood Books of Bedford, Massachusetts. Reproduced with the same cover art, type style, and illustrations, the books are popular with nostalgia buffs, selling as well among adults as preteens.

The original Nancy was what she *did;* her looks were taken for granted; she matched her keen intelligence against adult problems. All that, however, was once upon a time. Today, the Nancy who unflinchingly represented female resource, cunning, and ingenuity is gone, replaced by a slick — and highly successful — imposter.

THE INVOLVED READER

1 How does Vivelo describe the original Nancy Drew? What qualities does she stress? (What does *intrepid* mean?)

2 What are striking contrasts between the original and the revised versions of the specific books Vivelo examines? Is there a common denominator in the changes that have been made?

3 How does Vivelo explain the changes that have occurred? What to her are key changes in the editors' perspective? How does she sum up the contrast between the original and the current Nancy Drew?

TALKING, THINKING, WRITING

4 Feminists have promoted greater independence and more "spunk" on the part of young women. How do you explain that in the adolescent fiction examined by Vivelo the trend seems to be in the opposite direction?

5 In your own upbringing, did the image of the strong independent woman or the image of the "weak sister" predominate?

6   In current popular entertainment, do strong or weak images of women have the upper hand?

COLLABORATIVE PROJECTS

7   Working with a group, explore the questions raised by Vivelo's article: What do adolescent girls read? What images of young women are predominant in some of the most popular current adolescent fiction?

The Competitive Edge: Japanese and Americans

WILLIAM OUCHI

What has made Japan the world's leading economic and financial power? Is it better schools? a better trained workforce? better long-range planning? more competent management? a different work ethic? William Ouchi was one of the first students of management to examine the factors giving Japanese industry the edge in world markets. He became known through his book Theory Z: How American Business Can Meet the Japanese Challenge *(1981). In the following excerpt, Ouchi studies cultural patterns that set the two countries apart. He leads his readers to reexamine the relationship between freedom and social responsibility, which he identifies as the central issue in studies of civil society from the Greek philosopher Plato* (The Republic), *through the British seventeenth-century philosopher Thomas Hobbes* (Leviathan), *to the twentieth-century American psychologist B. F. Skinner* (Walden Two). *Ouchi's study was one of the first of a flood of books and articles with titles like* Japan as No. 1: Lessons for America.

Perhaps the most difficult aspect of the Japanese for Westerners to comprehend is the strong orientation to collective values, particularly a collective sense of responsibility. Let me illustrate with an anecdote about a visit to a new factory in Japan owned and operated by an American electronics company. The American company, a particularly creative firm, frequently attracts attention within the business community for its novel approaches to planning, organizational design, and management systems. As a consequence of this corporate style, the parent company determined to make a thorough study of Japanese workers and to design a plant that would combine the best of East and West. In their study they discovered that Japanese firms almost never make use of individual work incentives, such as piecework or even individual performance appraisal tied to salary increases. They concluded that rewarding individual achievement and individual ability is always a good thing.

In the final assembly area of their new plant, long lines of young Japanese women wired together electronic products on a piece-rate system: the more you wired, the more you got paid. About two months after opening, the head foreladies approached the plant manager. "Honorable plant manager," they said humbly as they bowed, "we are embarrassed to be so forward, but we must speak to

you because all of the girls have threatened to quit work this Friday."
(To have this happen, of course, would be a great disaster for all
concerned.) "Why," they wanted to know, "can't our plant have the
same compensation system as other Japanese companies? When
you hire a new girl, her starting wage should be fixed by her age.
An eighteen-year-old should be paid more than a sixteen-year-old.
Every year on her birthday, she should receive an automatic increase
in pay. The idea that any of us can be more productive than another
must be wrong, because none of us in final assembly could make
a thing unless all of the other people in the plant had done their
jobs right first. To single one person out as being more productive
is wrong and is also personally humiliating to us." The company
changed its compensation system to the Japanese model.

Another American company in Japan had installed a suggestion
system much as we have in the United States. Individual workers
were encouraged to place suggestions to improve productivity
into special boxes. For an accepted idea the individual received a
bonus amounting to some fraction of the productivity savings realized from his or her suggestion. After a period of six months, not a
single suggestion had been submitted. The American managers were
puzzled. They had heard many stories of the inventiveness, the commitment, and the loyalty of Japanese workers, yet not one suggestion
to improve productivity had appeared.

The managers approached some of the workers and asked why
the suggestion system had not been used. The answer: "No one can
come up with a work improvement idea alone. We work together,
and any ideas that one of us may have are actually developed by
watching others and talking to others. If one of us was singled out
for being responsible for such an idea, it would embarrass all of us."
The company changed to a group suggestion system, in which workers collectively submitted suggestions. Bonuses were paid to groups
which would save bonus money until the end of the year for a party
at a restaurant, or if there was enough money, for family vacations
together. The suggestions and productivity improvements rained
down on the plant.

One can interpret these examples in two quite different ways. Perhaps the Japanese commitment to collective values is an anachronism that does not fit with modern industrialism but brings economic success despite that collectivism. Collectivism seems to be
inimical to the kind of maverick creativity exemplified in Benjamin
Franklin, Thomas Edison, and John D. Rockefeller. Collectivism does
not seem to provide the individual incentive to excel which has
made a great success of American enterprise. Entirely apart from its

economic effects, collectivism implies a loss of individuality, a loss of the freedom to be different, to hold fundamentally different values from others.

The second interpretation of the examples is that the Japanese collectivism is economically efficient. It causes people to work well together and to encourage one another to better efforts. Industrial life requires interdependence of one person on another. But a less obvious but far-reaching implication of the Japanese collectivism for economic performance has to do with accountability.

In the Japanese mind, collectivism is neither a corporate or individual goal to strive for nor a slogan to pursue. Rather, the nature of things operates so that nothing of consequence occurs as a result of individual effort. Everything important in life happens as a result of teamwork or collective effort. Therefore, to attempt to assign individual credit or blame to results is unfounded. A Japanese professor of accounting, a brilliant scholar trained at Carnegie-Mellon University who teaches now in Tokyo, remarked that the status of accounting systems in Japanese industry is primitive compared to those in the United States. Profit centers, transfer prices, and computerized information systems are barely known even in the largest Japanese companies, whereas they are a commonplace in even small United States organizations. Though not at all surprised at the difference in accounting systems, I was not at all sure that the Japanese were primitive. In fact, I thought their system a good deal more efficient than ours.

Most American companies have basically two accounting systems. One system summarizes the overall financial state to inform stockholders, bankers, and other outsiders. That system is not of interest here. The other system, called the managerial or cost accounting system, exists for an entirely different reason. It measures in detail all of the particulars of transactions between departments, divisions, and key individuals in the organization, for the purpose of untangling the interdependencies between people. When, for example, two departments share one truck for deliveries, the cost accounting system charges each department for part of the cost of maintaining the truck and driver, so that at the end of the year, the performance of each department can be individually assessed, and the better department's manager can receive a larger raise. Of course, all of this information processing costs money, and furthermore may lead to arguments between the departments over whether the costs charged to each are fair.

In a Japanese company a short-run assessment of individual performance is not wanted, so the company can save the considerable expense of collecting and processing all of that information. Companies still keep track of which department uses a truck how often and for what purposes, but like-minded people can interpret some simple numbers for themselves and adjust their behavior accordingly. Those insisting upon clear and precise measurement for the purpose of advancing individual interests must have an elaborate information system. Industrial life, however, is essentially integrated and interdependent. No one builds an automobile alone, no one carries through a banking transaction alone. In a sense the Japanese value of collectivism fits naturally into an industrial setting, whereas the Western individualism provides constant conflicts. The image that comes to mind is of Chaplin's silent film "Modern Times" in which the apparently insignificant hero played by Chaplin successfully fights against the unfeeling machinery of industry. Modern industrial life can be aggravating, even hostile, or natural: all depends on the fit between our culture and our technology.

. . .

The *shinkansen* or "bullet train" speeds across the rural areas of   10
Japan giving a quick view of cluster after cluster of farmhouses surrounded by rice paddies. This particular pattern did not develop purely by chance, but as a consequence of the technology peculiar to the growing of rice, the staple of the Japanese diet. The growing of rice requires the construction and maintenance of an irrigation system, something that takes many hands to build. More importantly, the planting and harvesting of rice can only be done efficiently with the cooperation of twenty or more people. The "bottom line" is that a single family working alone cannot produce enough rice to survive, but a dozen families working together can produce a surplus. Thus the Japanese have had to develop the capacity to work together in harmony, no matter what the forces of disagreement or social disintegration, in order to survive.

Japan is a nation built entirely on the tips of giant, suboceanic volcanoes. Little of the land is flat and suitable for agriculture. Terraced hillsides make use of every available square foot of arable land. Small homes built very close together further conserve the land. Japan also suffers from natural disasters such as earthquakes and hurricanes. Traditionally homes are made of light construction materials, so a house falling down during a disaster will not crush its occupants and also can be quickly and inexpensively rebuilt. During the feudal period until the Meiji restoration of 1868, each feudal lord sought to restrain his subjects from moving from one village to the next for fear that a neighboring lord might amass enough peasants with which to produce a large agricultural surplus, hire an army and pose a threat. Apparently bridges were commonly built across rivers and streams until the late nineteenth century, since bridges increased mobility between villages.

Taken all together, this characteristic style of living paints the picture of a nation of people who are homogeneous with respect to race, history, language, religion, and culture. For centuries and generations these people have lived in the same village next door to the same neighbors. Living in close proximity and in dwellings which gave very little privacy, the Japanese survived through their capacity to work together in harmony. In this situation, it was inevitable that the one most central social value which emerged, the one value without which the society could not continue, was that an individual does not matter.

To the Western soul this is a chilling picture of society. Subordinating individual tastes to the harmony of the group and knowing that individual needs can never take precedence over the interests of all is repellent to the Western citizen. But a frequent theme of Western philosophers and sociologists is that individual freedom exists only when people willingly subordinate their self-interests to the social interest. A society composed entirely of self-interested individuals is a society in which each person is at war with the other, a society which has no freedom. This issue, constantly at the heart of understanding society, comes up in every century, and in every society, whether the writer be Plato, Hobbes, or B. F. Skinner.

In order to complete the comparison of Japanese and American living situations, consider flight over the United States. Looking out of the window high over the state of Kansas, we see a pattern of a single farmhouse surrounded by fields, followed by another single homestead surrounded by fields. In the early 1800s in the state of Kansas there were no automobiles. Your nearest neighbor was perhaps two miles distant; the winters were long, and the snow was deep. Inevitably, the central social values were self-reliance and independence. Those were the realities of that place and age that children had to learn to value.

The key to the industrial revolution was discovering that non-human forms of energy substituted for human forms could increase the wealth of a nation beyond anyone's wildest dreams. But there was a catch. To realize this great wealth, non-human energy needed huge complexes called factories with hundreds, even thousands of workers collected into one factory. Moreover, several factories in one central place made the generation of energy more efficient. Almost overnight, the Western world was transformed from a rural and agricultural country to an urban and industrial state. Our tech-

15

nological advance seems to no longer fit our social structures: in a sense, the Japanese can better cope with modern industrialism. While Americans still busily protect our rather extreme form of individualism, the Japanese hold their individualism in check and emphasize cooperation.

THE INVOLVED READER

1   Where for you does Ouchi best sum up the central contrast between Japanese and American society? What are his key examples? How convincing are they?

2   How do the contrasting histories of the two countries help Ouchi explain their different cultures?

3   What according to Ouchi is outmoded or obsolete about American values or ways of thinking?

TALKING, THINKING, WRITING

4   On the basis of Ouchi's analysis, what recommendations would you make for American management or American political leaders?

5   Do you disagree with Ouchi? What would you say in defense of the "anachronistic" or obsolete American values he criticizes?

6   Can you identify two contrasting areas of American life — one where individualism is strong and another where interdependence or teamwork plays a major role?

COLLABORATIVE PROJECTS

7   In recent years, American observers have noted a slowdown of economic growth in Japan. They have hoped for an improvement of America's competitive position as the Japanese wrestle with economic problems. Where can you turn to check whether this might be wishful thinking?

The EQ Factor

NANCY GIBBS

Do you believe that everyone has a level of intelligence that can be measured like a person's height and weight? Or do you believe that people may be smart in one area and slow in another? In his book Frames of Mind: The Theory of Multiple Intelligences *(1983), the psychologist Howard Gardner attacked "the standard notion of intelligence as a single capacity, with which an individual is born, and which proves difficult, if not impossible, to alter." He distinguished different kinds of intelligence, enabling individuals to deal especially well, for instance, with language, with numbers, with music, or with other people. Psychologists and teachers came to recognize linguistic intelligence and social intelligence rather than a single aptitude that could be measured by a single intelligence test. More recently, psychologists have developed the concept of a measurement of emotional aptitude, the EQ, to supplement the traditional IQ, focused too exclusively on intellectual aptitudes. Nancy Gibbs prepared the following feature article for* Time *magazine, assisted by reporters based in New York, Chicago, and Raleigh.*

It turns out that a scientist can see the future by watching four-year-olds interact with a marshmallow. The researcher invites the children, one by one, into a plain room and begins the gentle torment. You can have this marshmallow right now, he says. But if you wait while I run an errand, you can have two marshmallows when I get back. And then he leaves.

Some children grab for the treat the minute he's out the door. Some last a few minutes before they give in. But others are determined to wait. They cover their eyes; they put their heads down; they sing to themselves; they try to play games or even fall asleep. When the researcher returns, he gives these children their hard-earned marshmallows. And then, science waits for them to grow up.

By the time the children reach high school, something remarkable has happened. A survey of the children's parents and teachers found that those who as four-year-olds had the fortitude to hold out for the second marshmallow generally grew up to be better adjusted, more popular, adventurous, confident and dependable teenagers. The children who gave in to temptation early on were more likely to be lonely, easily frustrated and stubborn. They buckled under stress and shied away from challenges. And when some of the students in the two groups took the Scholastic Aptitude Test, the kids who had held out longer scored an average of 210 points higher.

When we think of brilliance we see Einstein, deep-eyed, woolly haired, a thinking machine with skin and mismatched socks. High achievers, we imagine, were wired for greatness from birth. But then you have to wonder why, over time, natural talent seems to ignite in some people and dim in others. This is where the marshmallows come in. It seems that the ability to delay gratification is a master skill, a triumph of the reasoning brain over the impulsive one. It is a sign, in short, of emotional intelligence. And it doesn't show up on an IQ test.

For most of this century, scientists have worshipped the hardware of the brain and the software of the mind; the messy powers of the heart were left to the poets. But cognitive theory could simply not explain the questions we wonder about most: why some people just seem to have a gift for living well; why the smartest kid in the class will probably not end up the richest; why we like some people virtually on sight and distrust others; why some people remain buoyant in the face of troubles that would sink a less resilient soul. What qualities of the mind or spirit, in short, determine who succeeds?

The phrase "emotional intelligence" was coined by Yale psychologist Peter Salovey and the University of New Hampshire's John Mayer five years ago to describe qualities like understanding one's own feelings, empathy for the feelings of others and "the regulation of emotion in a way that enhances living." Their notion is about to bound into the national conversation, handily shortened to EQ, thanks to a new book, *Emotional Intelligence* (Bantam; $23.95) by Daniel Goleman. Goleman, a Harvard psychology Ph.D. and a *New York Times* science writer with a gift for making even the chewiest scientific theories digestible to lay readers, has brought together a decade's worth of behavioral research into how the mind processes feelings. His goal, he announces on the cover, is to redefine what it means to be smart. His thesis: when it comes to predicting people's success, brainpower as measured by IQ and standardized achievement tests may actually matter less than the qualities of the mind once thought of as "character" before the word began to sound quaint.

At first glance, there would seem to be little that's new here to any close reader of fortune cookies. There may be no less original idea than the notion that our hearts hold dominion over our heads. "I was so angry," we say, "I couldn't think straight." Neither is it surprising that "people skills" are useful, which amounts to saying, it's good to be nice. "It's so true it's trivial," says Dr. Paul McHugh, director of psychiatry at Johns Hopkins University School of Medicine. But if it were that simple, the book would not be quite so interesting or its implications so controversial.

This is no abstract investigation. Goleman is looking for antidotes to restore "civility to our streets and caring to our communal life." He sees practical applications everywhere for how companies should decide whom to hire, how couples can increase the odds that their marriages will last, how parents should raise their children and how schools should teach them. When street gangs substitute for families and schoolyard insults end in stabbings, when more than half of marriages end in divorce, when the majority of the children murdered in this country are killed by parents and stepparents, many of whom say they were trying to discipline the child for behavior like blocking the TV or crying too much, it suggests a demand for remedial emotional education. While children are still young, Goleman argues, there is a "neurological window of opportunity" since the brain's prefrontal circuitry, which regulates how we act on what we feel, probably does not mature until mid-adolescence.

And it is here the arguments will break out. Goleman's highly popularized conclusions, says McHugh, "will chill any veteran scholar of psychotherapy and any neuroscientist who worries about how his research may come to be applied." While many researchers in this relatively new field are glad to see emotional issues finally taken seriously, they fear that a notion as handy as EQ invites misuse. Goleman admits the danger of suggesting that you can assign a numerical yardstick to a person's character as well as his intellect; Goleman never even uses the phrase EQ in his book. But he (begrudgingly) approved an "unscientific" EQ test in *USA Today* with choices like "I am aware of even subtle feelings as I have them," and "I can sense the pulse of a group or relationship and state unspoken feelings."

"You don't want to take an average of your emotional skill," argues Harvard psychology professor Jerome Kagan, a pioneer in child-development research. "That's what's wrong with the concept of intelligence for mental skills too. Some people handle anger well but can't handle fear. Some people can't take joy. So each emotion has to be viewed differently."   10

EQ is not the opposite of IQ. Some people are blessed with a lot of both, some with little of either. What researchers have been trying to understand is how they complement each other; how one's ability to handle stress, for instance, affects the ability to concentrate and put intelligence to use. Among the ingredients for success, researchers now generally agree that IQ counts for about 20%; the rest depends on everything from class to luck to the neural pathways that have developed in the brain over millions of years of human evolution.

It is actually the neuroscientists and evolutionists who do the best job of explaining the reasons behind the most unreasonable behavior. In the past decade or so, scientists have learned enough about the brain to make judgments about where emotion comes from and why we need it. Primitive emotional responses held the keys to survival: fear drives the blood into the large muscles, making it easier to run; surprise triggers the eyebrows to rise, allowing the eyes to widen their view and gather more information about an unexpected event. Disgust wrinkles up the face and closes the nostrils to keep out foul smells.

Emotional life grows out of an area of the brain called the limbic system, specifically the amygdala, whence come delight and disgust and fear and anger. Millions of years ago, the neocortex was added on, enabling humans to plan, learn and remember. Lust grows from the limbic system; love, from the neocortex. Animals like reptiles that have no neocortex cannot experience anything like maternal love; this is why baby snakes have to hide to avoid being eaten by their parents. Humans, with their capacity for love, will protect their offspring, allowing the brains of the young time to develop. The more connections between the limbic system and the neocortex, the more emotional responses are possible.

It was scientists like Joseph LeDoux of New York University who uncovered these cerebral pathways. LeDoux's parents owned a meat market. As a boy in Louisiana, he first learned about his future specialty by cutting up cows' brains for sweetbreads. "I found them the most interesting part of the cow's anatomy," he recalls. "They were visually pleasing — lots of folds, convolutions and patterns. The cerebellum was more interesting to look at than steak." The butchers' son became a neuroscientist, and it was he who discovered the short circuit in the brain that lets emotions drive action before the intellect gets a chance to intervene.

A hiker on a mountain path, for example, sees a long, curved   15
shape in the grass out of the corner of his eye. He leaps out of the way before he realizes it is only a stick that looks like a snake. Then he calms down; his cortex gets the message a few milliseconds after his amygdala and "regulates" its primitive response.

Without these emotional reflexes, rarely conscious but often terribly powerful, we would scarcely be able to function. "Most decisions we make have a vast number of possible outcomes, and any attempt to analyze all of them would never end," says University of Iowa neurologist Antonio Damasio, author of *Descartes' Error: Emo-*

tion, Reason and the Human Brain. "I'd ask you to lunch tomorrow, and when the appointed time arrived, you'd still be thinking about whether you should come." What tips the balance, Damasio contends, is our unconscious assigning of emotional values to some of those choices. Whether we experience a somatic response — a gut feeling of dread or a giddy sense of elation — emotions are helping to limit the field in any choice we have to make. If the prospect of lunch with a neurologist is unnerving or distasteful, Damasio suggests, the invitee will conveniently remember a previous engagement.

When Damasio worked with patients in whom the connection between emotional brain and neocortex had been severed because of damage to the brain, he discovered how central that hidden pathway is to how we live our lives. People who had lost that linkage were just as smart and quick to reason, but their lives often fell apart nonetheless. They could not make decisions because they didn't know how they felt about their choices. They couldn't react to warnings or anger in other people. If they made a mistake, like a bad investment, they felt no regret or shame and so were bound to repeat it.

If there is a cornerstone to emotional intelligence on which most other emotional skills depend, it is a sense of self-awareness, of being smart about what we feel. A person whose day starts badly at home may be grouchy all day at work without quite knowing why. Once an emotional response comes into awareness — or, physiologically, is processed through the neocortex — the chances of handling it appropriately improve. Scientists refer to "metamood," the ability to pull back and recognize that "what I'm feeling is anger," or sorrow, or shame.

Metamood is a difficult skill because emotions so often appear in disguise. A person in mourning may know he is sad, but he may not recognize that he is also angry at the person for dying — because this seems somehow inappropriate. A parent who yells at a child who ran into the street is expressing anger at disobedience, but the degree of anger may owe more to the fear the parent feels at what could have happened.

In Goleman's analysis, self-awareness is perhaps the most crucial 20 ability because it allows us to exercise some self-control. The idea is not to repress feeling (the reaction that has made psychoanalysts rich) but rather to do what Aristotle considered the hard work of the will. "Anyone can become angry — that is easy," he wrote in the *Nicomachean Ethics.* "But to be angry with the right person, to the right degree, at the right time, for the right purpose, and in the right way — this is not easy."

Some impulses seem to be easier to control than others. Anger, not surprisingly, is one of the hardest, perhaps because of its evolutionary value in priming people to action. Researchers believe anger usually arises out of a sense of being trespassed against — the belief that one is being robbed of what is rightfully his. The body's first response is a surge of energy, the release of a cascade of neurotransmitters called catecholamines. If a person is already aroused or under stress, the threshold for release is lower, which helps explain why people's tempers shorten during a hard day.

Scientists are not only discovering where anger comes from; they are also exposing myths about how best to handle it. Popular wisdom argues for "letting it all hang out" and having a good cathartic rage. But Goleman cites studies showing that dwelling on anger actually increases its power; the body needs a chance to process the adrenaline through exercise, relaxation techniques, a well-timed intervention or even the old admonition to count to 10.

Anxiety serves a similar useful purpose, so long as it doesn't spin out of control. Worrying is a rehearsal for danger; the act of fretting focuses the mind on a problem so it can search efficiently for solutions. The danger comes when worrying blocks thinking, becoming an end in itself or a path to resignation instead of perseverance. Overworrying about failing increases the likelihood of failure; a salesman so concerned about his falling sales that he can't bring himself to pick up the phone guarantees that his sales will fall even further.

But why are some people better able to "snap out of it" and get on with the task at hand? Again, given sufficient self-awareness, people develop coping mechanisms. Sadness and discouragement, for instance, are "low arousal" states, and the dispirited salesman who goes out for a run is triggering a high arousal state that is incompatible with staying blue. Relaxation works better for high-energy moods like anger or anxiety. Either way, the idea is to shift to a state of arousal that breaks the destructive cycle of the dominant mood.

The idea of being able to predict which salesmen are most likely to prosper was not an abstraction for Metropolitan Life, which in the mid-'80s was hiring 5,000 salespeople a year and training them at a cost of more than $30,000 each. Half quit the first year, and four out of five within four years. The reason: selling life insurance involves having the door slammed in your face over and over again. Was it possible to identify which people would be better at handling frustration and take each refusal as a challenge rather than a setback?

The head of the company approached psychologist Martin Seligman at the University of Pennsylvania and invited him to test some of his theories about the importance of optimism in people's success. When optimists fail, he has found, they attribute the failure to something they can change, not some innate weakness that they are helpless to overcome. And that confidence in their power to *effect* change is self-reinforcing. Seligman tracked 15,000 new workers who had taken two tests. One was the company's regular screening exam, the other Seligman's test measuring their levels of optimism. Among the new hires was a group who flunked the screening test but scored as "superoptimists" on Seligman's exam. And sure enough, they did the best of all; they outsold the pessimists in the regular group by 21% in the first year and 57% in the second. For years after that, passing Seligman's test was one way to get hired as a MetLife salesperson.

Perhaps the most visible emotional skills, the ones we recognize most readily, are the "people skills" like empathy, graciousness, the ability to read a social situation. Researchers believe that about 90% of emotional communication is nonverbal. Harvard psychologist Robert Rosenthal developed the PONS test (Profile of Nonverbal Sensitivity) to measure people's ability to read emotional cues. He shows subjects a film of a young woman expressing feelings — anger, love, jealousy, gratitude, seduction — edited so that one or another nonverbal cue is blanked out. In some instances the face is visible but not the body, or the woman's eyes are hidden, so that viewers have to judge the feeling by subtle cues. Once again, people with higher PONS scores tend to be more successful in their work and relationships; children who score well are more popular and successful in school, even when their IQs are quite average.

Like other emotional skills, empathy is an innate quality that can be shaped by experience. Infants as young as three months old exhibit empathy when they get upset at the sound of another baby crying. Even very young children learn by imitation; by watching how others act when they see someone in distress, these children acquire a repertoire of sensitive responses. If, on the other hand, the feelings they begin to express are not recognized and reinforced by the adults around them, they not only cease to express those feelings but they also become less able to recognize them in themselves or others.

Empathy too can be seen as a survival skill. Bert Cohler, a University of Chicago psychologist, and Fran Stott, dean of the Erikson Institute for Advanced Study in Child Development in Chicago, have found that children from psychically damaged families frequently become hypervigilant, developing an intense attunement to their parents' moods. One child they studied, Nicholas, had a horrible

habit of approaching other kids in his nursery-school class as if he
were going to kiss them, then would bite them instead. The scientists
went back to study videos of Nicholas at 20 months interacting with
his psychotic mother and found that she had responded to his every
expression of anger or independence with compulsive kisses. The
researchers dubbed them "kisses of death," and their true significance was obvious to Nicholas, who arched his back in horror at her
approaching lips — and passed his own rage on to his classmates
years later.

Empathy also acts as a buffer to cruelty, and it is a quality con-   30
spicuously lacking in child molesters and psychopaths. Goleman
cites some chilling research into brutality by Robert Hare, a psychologist at the University of British Columbia. Hare found that
psychopaths, when hooked up to electrodes and told they are going
to receive a shock, show none of the visceral responses that fear of
pain typically triggers: rapid heartbeat, sweating and so on. How
could the threat of punishment deter such people from committing
crimes?

It is easy to draw the obvious lesson from these test results. How
much happier would we be, how much more successful as individuals and civil as a society, if we were more alert to the importance
of emotional intelligence and more adept at teaching it? From kin-
dergartens to business schools to corporations across the country,
people are taking seriously the idea that a little more time spent
on the "touchy-feely" skills so often derided may in fact pay rich
dividends. . . .

Nowhere is the discussion of emotional intelligence more pressing than in schools, were both the stakes and the opportunities seem
greatest. Instead of constant crisis intervention, or declarations of
war on drug abuse or teen pregnancy or violence, it is time, Goleman
argues, for preventive medicine. "Five years ago, teachers didn't
want to think about this," says principal Roberta Kirshbaum of P.S.
75 in New York City. "But when kids are getting killed in high school,
we have to deal with it." Five years ago, Kirshbaum's school adopted
an emotional literacy program, designed to help children learn to
manage anger, frustration, loneliness. Since then, fights at lunchtime have decreased from two or three a day to almost none.

Educators can point to all sorts of data to support this new direction. Students who are depressed or angry literally cannot learn.
Children who have trouble being accepted by their classmates are 2
to 8 times as likely to drop out. An inability to distinguish distressing
feelings or handle frustration has been linked to eating disorders in
girls.

Many school administrators are completely rethinking the weight they have been giving to traditional lessons and standardized tests. Peter Relic, president of the National Association of Independent Schools, would like to junk the SAT completely. "Yes, it may cost a heck of a lot more money to assess someone's EQ rather than using a machine-scored test to measure IQ," he says. "But if we don't, then, we're saying that a test score is more important to us than who a child is as a human being. That means an immense loss in terms of human potential because we've defined success too narrowly.

This warm embrace by educators has left some scientists in a   35 bind. On one hand, says Yale psychologist Salovey, "I love the idea that we want to teach people a richer understanding of their emotional life, to help them achieve their goals." But, he adds, "what I would oppose is training conformity to social expectations." The danger is that any campaign to hone emotional skills in children will end up teaching that there is a "right" emotional response for any given situation — laugh at parades, cry at funerals, sit still at church. "You can't teach self-control," says Dr. Alvin Poussaint, professor of psychiatry at Harvard Medical School. "You can teach that it's better to talk out your anger and not use violence. But is it good emotional intelligence not to challenge authority?"

THE INVOLVED READER

1 What is the point of the experiment described at the beginning? What sets apart the two contrasting personality types identified there?

2 How is the EQ different from the IQ? What have been traditional ways of talking about the same difference?

3 According to the author, how did our human emotions evolve, and what was their survival value? What are the differing roles of intellect and emotion in the way our minds work?

4 Self-awareness, anxiety, and empathy have become the small change of popular psychology. What role do they play in this discussion of emotional intelligence?

5 What applications for recognizing emotional intelligence does Gibbs see in the business world? What applications does she see in the world of education?

TALKING, THINKING, WRITING

6 Have you observed the difference between intellectual ability and emotional intelligence in your own experience?

7 Do you know people who have trouble trying to control their emotions?

8 Are there differences in the way people from different ethnic or racial backgrounds express emotions?

COLLABORATIVE PROJECTS

9 Do you think ways could be found to test a person's "emotional intelligence"? Working with a group, you may want to design a questionnaire that could be used to measure qualities like empathy or interpersonal skills.

Erotica and Pornography

GLORIA STEINEM

*Where do you draw the line between sexually stimulating material
and pornography? When does a nude cease to be art and become an
offense to community standards? Like other feminists, Gloria Steinem,
granddaughter of a pioneer in the fight for women's rights, has wres-
tled with the definition of pornography and the strategies for dealing
with it in a male-dominated society. Steinem became a leading voice,
organizer, and campaigner for the women's movement as co-founder
of* Ms. *magazine, which has been called "the first national magazine
operated by women for the advancement of women's causes." Although
she became known for the witty, irreverent, trendy style of her early
essays, she had a childhood burdened by poverty and the odyssey of
her mother through the world of mental illness. Her "consciousness-
raising" collection* Outrageous Acts and Everyday Rebellions *(1983),
helped define feminism and major feminist themes for many readers.
In her* Revolution from Within: A Book of Self-Esteem *(1992), she
shifted emphasis from the political arena to the need for mobilizing
women's resources of inner strength.*

Human beings are the only animals that experience the same sex
drive at times when we can — and cannot — conceive.

Just as we developed uniquely human capacities for language,
planning, memory, and invention along our evolutionary path, we
also developed sexuality as a form of expression; a way of communicating that is separable from our need for sex as a way of perpetu-
ating ourselves. For humans alone, sexuality can be and often is primarily a way of bonding, of giving and receiving pleasure, bridging
differentness, discovering sameness, and communicating emotion.

We developed this and other human gifts through our ability to
change our environment, adapt physically, and in the long run, to
affect our own evolution. But as an emotional result of this spiraling
path away from other animals, we seem to alternate between periods of exploring our unique abilities to change new boundaries,
and feelings of loneliness in the unknown that we ourselves have
created; a fear that sometimes sends us back to the comfort of the
animal world by encouraging us to exaggerate our sameness.

The separation of "play" from "work," for instance, is a problem
only in the human world. So is the difference between art and nature, or an intellectual accomplishment and a physical one. As a result, we celebrate play, art, and invention as leaps into the unknown;

but any imbalance can send us back to nostalgia for our primate past and the conviction that the basics of work, nature, and physical labor are somehow more worthwhile or even moral.

In the same way, we have explored our sexuality as separable from conception: a pleasurable, empathetic bridge to strangers of the same species. We have even invented contraception — a skill that has probably existed in some form since our ancestors figured out the process of birth — in order to extend this uniquely human difference. Yet we also have times of atavistic suspicion that sex is not complete — or even legal or intended-by-god — if it cannot end in conception.

No wonder the concepts of "erotica" and "pornography" can be so crucially different, and yet so confused. Both assume that sexuality can be separated from conception, and therefore can be used to carry a personal message. That's a major reason why, even in our current culture, both may be called equally "shocking" or legally "obscene," a word whose Latin derivative means "dirty, containing filth." This gross condemnation of all sexuality that isn't harnessed to childbirth and marriage has been increased by the current backlash against women's progress. Out of fear that the whole patriarchal structure might be upset if women really had the autonomous power to decide our reproductive futures (that is, if we controlled the most basic means of production), right-wing groups are not only denouncing prochoice abortion literature as "pornographic," but are trying to stop the sending of all contraceptive information through the mails by invoking obscenity laws. In fact, Phyllis Schlafly denounced the entire Women's Movement as "obscene."

Not surprisingly, this religious, visceral backlash has a secular, intellectual counterpart that relies heavily on applying the "natural" behavior of the animal world to humans. That is questionable in itself, but these Lionel Tiger-ish studies make their political purpose even more clear in the particular animals they select and the habits they choose to emphasize. The message is that females should accept their "destiny" of being sexually dependent and devote themselves to bearing and rearing their young.

Defending against such reaction in turn leads to another temptation: to merely reverse the terms, and declare that all nonprocreative sex is good. In fact, however, this human activity can be as constructive as destructive, moral or immoral, as any other. Sex as communication can send messages as different as life and death; even the origins of "erotica" and "pornography" reflect that fact. After all, "erotica" is rooted in *eros* or passionate love, and thus in the idea of positive choice, free will, the yearning for a particular person.

(Interestingly, the definition of erotica leaves open the question of gender.) "Pornography" begins with a root meaning "prostitution" or "female captives," thus letting us know that the subject is not mutual love, or love at all, but domination and violence against women. (Though, of course, homosexual pornography may imitate this violence by putting a man in the "feminine" role of victim). It ends with a root meaning "writing about" or "description of" which puts still more distance between subject and object, and replaces a spontaneous yearning for closeness with objectification and a voyeur.

The difference is clear in the words. It becomes even more so by example.

Look at any photo or film of people making love; really making love. The images may be diverse, but there is usually a sensuality and touch and warmth, an acceptance of bodies and nerve endings. There is always a spontaneous sense of people who are there because they *want* to be, out of shared pleasure.

Now look at any depiction of sex in which there is clear force, or an unequal power that spells coercion. It may be very blatant, with weapons or torture or bondage, wounds and bruises, some clear humiliation, or an adult's sexual power being used over a child. It may be much more subtle: a physical attitude of conqueror and victim, the use of race or class difference to imply the same thing, perhaps a very unequal nudity, with one person exposed and vulnerable while the other is clothed. In either case, there is no sense of equal choice or equal power.

The first is erotic: a mutually pleasurable, sexual expression between people who have enough power to be there by positive choice. It may or may not strike a sense-memory in the viewer, or be creative enough to make the unknown seem real; but it doesn't require us to identify with a conqueror or a victim. It is truly sensuous, and may give us a contagion of pleasure.

The second is pornographic: its message is violence, dominance, and conquest. It is sex being used to reinforce some inequality, or to create one, or to tell us the lie that pain and humiliation (ours or someone else's) are really the same as pleasure. If we are to feel anything, we must identify with conqueror or victim. That means we can only experience pleasure through the adoption of some degree of sadism or masochism. It also means that we may feel diminished by the role of conqueror, or enraged, humiliated, and vengeful by sharing identity with the victim.

Perhaps one could simply say that erotica is about sexuality, but pornography is about power and sex-as-weapon — in the same way we have come to understand that rape is about violence, and not really about sexuality at all.

Yes, it's true that there are women who have been forced by violent families and dominating men to confuse love with pain; so much so that they have become masochists. (A fact that in no way excuses those who administer such pain.) But the truth is that, for most women — and for men with enough humanity to imagine themselves into the predicament of women — true pornography could serve as aversion therapy for sex.

Of course, there will always be personal differences about what is and is not erotic, and there may be cultural differences for a long time to come. Many women feel that sex makes them vulnerable and therefore may continue to need more sense of personal connection and safety before allowing any erotic feelings. We now find competence and expertise erotic in men, but that may pass as we develop those qualities in ourselves. Men, on the other hand, may continue to feel less vulnerable, and therefore more open to such potential danger as sex with strangers. As some men replace the need for submission from childlike women with the pleasure of cooperation from equals, they may find a partner's competence to be erotic, too.

Such group changes plus individual differences will continue to be reflected in sexual love between people of the same gender, as well as between women and men. The point is not to dictate sameness, but to discover ourselves and each other through sexuality that is an exploring, pleasurable, empathetic part of our lives; a human sexuality that is unchained both from unwanted pregnancies and from violence.

But that is a hope, not a reality. At the moment, fear of change is increasing both the indiscriminate repression of all nonprocreative sex in the religious and "conservative" male world, and the pornographic vengeance against women's sexuality in the secular world of "liberal" and "radical" men. It's almost futuristic to debate what is and is not truly erotic, when many women are again being forced into compulsory motherhood, and the number of pornographic murders, tortures, and woman-hating images are on the increase in both popular culture and real life.

It's a familiar division: wife or whore, "good" woman who is constantly vulnerable to pregnancy or "bad" woman who is unprotected from violence. *Both* roles would be upset if we were to control our own sexuality. And that's exactly what we must do.

In spite of all our atavistic suspicions and training for the "natural" role of motherhood, we took up the complicated battle for reproductive freedom. Our bodies had borne the health burden of

15

20

endless births and poor abortions, and we had a greater motive for separating sexuality and conception.

Now we have to take up the equally complex burden of explaining that all nonprocreative sex is *not* alike. We have a motive: our right to a uniquely human sexuality, and sometimes even to survival. As it is, our bodies have too rarely been enough our own to develop erotica in our own lives, much less in art and literature. And our bodies have too often been the objects of pornography and the woman-hating, violent practice that it preaches. Consider also our spirits that break a little each time we see ourselves in chains or full labial display for the conquering male viewer, bruised or on our knees, screaming a real or pretended pain to delight the sadist, pretending to enjoy what we don't enjoy, to be blind to the images of our sisters that really haunt us — humiliated often enough ourselves by the truly obscene idea that sex and the domination of women must be combined.

Sexuality *is* human, free, separate — and so are we.

But until we untangle the lethal confusion of sex with violence, there will be more pornography and less erotica. There will be little murders in our beds — and very little love.

THE INVOLVED READER

1 For Steinem, what is the essential contrast between desirable erotic material and unacceptable pornography? Where does she draw the line? Do you think it is possible to draw the line?

2 What evolutionary perspective does Steinem sketch out early in her essay? How is it related to her argument?

3 How does Steinem relate her argument to the sexual politics of the right and the left?

TALKING, THINKING, WRITING

4 Do you think a valid distinction can be made between nudes in art and offensive nudity outside art?

5 Have you observed antipornography initiatives or campaigns? Have there been test cases on your campus or in your community? Who initiates antipornography crusades? How successful are they?

6 Susan Jacoby, a self-described "First Amendment junkie," has said that "most of the people who want to censor girlie magazines are equally opposed to open discussion of issues that are of vital concern to women: rape, abortion, menstruation, conception, lesbianism — in fact, the entire range of sexual experience from a woman's point of view." Is she right?

COLLABORATIVE PROJECTS

7 Gloria Steinem wrote *Marilyn* (1986) as a feminist rebuttal to Norman Mailer's biography of the actress as every male's day-dream of sexual fulfillment. Working with a group, you may want to explore the contrast between different versions of the life story of Marilyn Monroe (Norma Jean).

MAKING CONNECTIONS

8 Vivelo, Ouchi, Gibbs, and Steinem work out detailed comparisons and contrasts. Which of these do you find most helpful or instructive? Which least? Why?

short story

Everyday Use

ALICE WALKER

Does most writing by and about African Americans focus on the interaction between white and black? Alice Walker is a widely honored African American writer who became known especially for her novels The Color Purple *(1982) and* The Temple of My Familar *(1989). She has written passionate poetry and fiction about the need for love and solidarity and about the sources of cruelty and division in the black family. She told an interviewer, "In the black family, love, cohesion, support, and concern are crucial since a racist society constantly acts to destroy the black individual, the black family unit, the black child. In America black people have only themselves and each other." Walker was a student at Spelman College in Atlanta when she was swept up in the sit-ins, rallies, and freedom marches of the Civil Rights movement, which, she said, "broke the pattern of black servitude in this country." In stories like "Everyday Use" and "Roselily," Walker explores crosscurrents within the African American community and issues of choice and identity that ask readers to leave old stereotypes behind.*

I will wait for her in the yard that Maggie and I made so clean and wavy yesterday afternoon. A yard like this is more comfortable than most people know. It is not just a yard. It is like an extended living room. When the hard clay is swept clean as a floor and the fine sand around the edges lined with tiny, irregular grooves, anyone can come and sit and look up into the elm tree and wait for the breezes that never come inside the house.

Maggie will be nervous until after her sister goes: she will stand hopelessly in corners, homely and ashamed of the burn scars down her arms and legs, eying her sister with a mixture of envy and awe. She thinks her sister has held life always in the palm of one hand, that "no" is a word the world never learned to say to her.

You've no doubt seen those TV shows where the child who has "made it" is confronted, as a surprise, by her own mother and father, tottering in weakly from backstage. (A pleasant surprise, of course: What would they do if parent and child came on the show only to curse out and insult each other?) On TV mother and child embrace and smile into each other's faces. Sometimes the mother and father weep, the child wraps them in her arms and leans across the table to tell how she would not have made it without their help. I have seen these programs.

Sometimes I dream a dream in which Dee and I are suddenly brought together on a TV program of this sort. Out of a dark and soft-seated limousine I am ushered into a bright room filled with many people. There I meet a smiling, gray, sporty man like Johnny Carson who shakes my hand and tells me what a fine girl I have. Then we are on the stage and Dee is embracing me with tears in her eyes. She pins on my dress a large orchid, even though she has told me once that she thinks orchids are tacky flowers.

In real life I am a large, big-boned woman with rough, man-working hands. In the winter I wear flannel nightgowns to bed and overalls during the day. I can kill and clean a hog as mercilessly as a man. My fat keeps me hot in zero weather. I can work outside all day, breaking ice to get water for washing; I can eat pork liver cooked over the open fire minutes after it comes steaming from the hog. One winter I knocked a bull calf straight in the brain between the eyes with a sledge hammer and had the meat hung up to chill before nightfall. But of course all this does not show on television. I am the way my daughter would want me to be: a hundred pounds lighter, my skin like an uncooked barley pancake. My hair glistens in the hot bright lights. Johnny Carson has much to do to keep up with my quick and witty tongue.

But that is a mistake. I know even before I wake up. Who ever knew a Johnson with a quick tongue? Who can even imagine me looking a strange white man in the eye? It seems to me I have talked to them always with one foot raised in flight, with my head turned in whichever way is farthest from them. Dee, though. She would always look anyone in the eye. Hesitation was no part of her nature.

"How do I look, Mama?" Maggie says, showing just enough of her thin body enveloped in pink skirt and red blouse for me to know she's there, almost hidden by the door.

"Come out into the yard," I say.

Have you ever seen a lame animal, perhaps a dog run over by some careless person rich enough to own a car, sidle up to someone who is ignorant enough to be kind to them? That is the way my Maggie walks. She has been like this, chin on chest, eyes on ground, feet in shuffle, ever since the fire that burned the other house to the ground.

Dee is lighter than Maggie, with nicer hair and a fuller figure. She's a woman now, though sometimes I forget. How long ago was it that the other house burned? Ten, twelve years? Sometimes I can still hear the flames and feel Maggie's arms sticking to me, her hair smoking and her dress falling off her in little black papery flakes. Her eyes seemed stretched open, blazed open by the flames reflected in them. And Dee. I see her standing off under the sweet gum tree she used to dig gum out of; a look of concentration on her face as she watched the last dingy gray board of the house fall in toward the red-hot brick chimney. Why don't you do a dance around the ashes? I'd wanted to ask her. She had hated the house that much.

I used to think she hated Maggie, too. But that was before we raised the money, the church and me, to send her to Augusta to school. She used to read to us without pity; forcing words, lies, other folks' habits, whole lives upon us two, sitting trapped and ignorant underneath her voice. She washed us in a river of make-believe, burned us with a lot of knowledge we didn't necessarily need to know. Pressed us to her with the serious way she read, to shove us away at just the moment, like dimwits, we seemed about to understand.

Dee wanted nice things. A yellow organdy dress to wear to her graduation from high school; black pumps to match a green suit she'd made from an old suit somebody gave me. She was determined to stare down any disaster in her efforts. Her eyelids would not flicker for minutes at a time. Often I fought off the temptation to shake her. At sixteen she had a style of her own: and knew what style was.

I never had an education myself. After second grade the school was closed down. Don't ask me why: in 1927 colored asked fewer questions than they do now. Sometimes Maggie reads to me. She stumbles along good naturedly but can't see well. She knows she is not bright. Like good looks and money, quickness passed her by. She will marry John Thomas (who has mossy teeth in an earnest face) and then I'll be free to sit here and I guess just sing church songs to myself. Although I never was a good singer. Never could carry a tune. I was always better at a man's job. I used to love to milk till I was hooked in the side in '49. Cows are soothing and slow and don't bother you, unless you try to milk them the wrong way.

I have deliberately turned my back on the house. It is three rooms, just like the one that burned, except the roof is tin; they don't make shingle roofs any more. There are no real windows, just some holes cut in the sides, like the portholes in a ship, but not round and not square, with rawhide holding the shutters up on the outside. This house is in a pasture, too, like the other one. No doubt when Dee

sees it she will want to tear it down. She wrote me once that no matter where we "choose" to live, she will manage to come see us. But
she will never bring her friends. Maggie and I thought about this and
Maggie asked me, "Mama, when did Dee ever *have* any friends?"

She had a few. Furtive boys in pink shirts hanging about on   15
washday after school. Nervous girls who never laughed. Impressed
with her they worshiped the well-turned phrase, the cute shape, the
scalding humor that erupted like bubbles in lye. She read to them.

When she was courting Jimmy T she didn't have much time to pay
to us, but turned all her faultfinding power on him. He *flew* to marry
a cheap girl from a family of ignorant flashy people. She hardly had
time to recompose herself.

When she comes I will meet — but there they are!

Maggie attempts to make a dash for the house, in her shuffling
way, but I stay her with my hand. "Come back here," I say. And she
stops and tries to dig a well in the sand with her toe.

It is hard to see them clearly through the strong sun. But even the
first glimpse of leg out of the car tells me it is Dee. Her feet were
always neat-looking, as if God himself had shaped them with a certain style. From the other side of the car comes a short, stocky man.
Hair is all over his head a foot long and hanging from his chin like a
kinky mule tail. I hear Maggie suck in her breath. "Uhnnnh," is what
it sounds like. Like when you see the wriggling end of a snake just in
front of your foot on the road. "Uhnnnh."

Dee next. A dress down to the ground, in this hot weather. A dress   20
so loud it hurts my eyes. There are yellows and oranges enough to
throw back the light of the sun. I feel my whole face warming from
the heat waves it throws out. Earrings gold, too, and hanging down
to her shoulders. Bracelets dangling and making noises when she
moves her arm up to shake the folds of the dress out of her armpits.
The dress is loose and flows, and as she walks closer, I like it. I hear
Maggie go "Uhnnnh" again. It is her sister's hair. It stands straight
up like the wool on a sheep. It is black as night and around the edges
are two long pigtails that rope about like small lizards disappearing
behind her ears.

"Wa-su-zo-Tean-o!" she says, coming on in that gliding way the
dress makes her move. The short stocky fellow with the hair to his
navel is all grinning and he follows up with "Asalamalakim, my
mother and sister!" He moves to hug Maggie but she falls back, right
up against the back of my chair. I feel her trembling there and when
I look up I see the perspiration falling off her chin.

"Don't get up," says Dee. Since I am stout it takes something of a push. You can see me trying to move a second or two before I make it. She turns, showing white heels through her sandals, and goes back to the car. Out she peeks next with a Polaroid. She stoops down quickly and lines up picture after picture of me sitting there in front of the house with Maggie cowering behind me. She never takes a shot without making sure the house is included. When a cow comes nibbling around the edge of the yard she snaps it and me and Maggie *and* the house. Then she puts the Polaroid in the back seat of the car, and comes up and kisses me on the forehead.

Meanwhile Asalamalakim is going through motions with Maggie's hand. Maggie's hand is as limp as a fish, and probably as cold, despite the sweat, and she keeps trying to pull it back. It looks like Asalamalakim wants to shake hands but wants to do it fancy. Or maybe he don't know how people shake hands. Anyhow, he soon gives up on Maggie.

"Well," I say. "Dee."

"No, Mama," she says. "Not 'Dee,' Wangero Leewanika Kemanjo!"   25

"What happened to 'Dee'?" I wanted to know.

"She's dead," Wangero said. "I couldn't bear it any longer, being named after the people who oppress me."

"You know as well as me you was named after your aunt Dicie," I said. Dicie is my sister. She named Dee. We called her "Big Dee" after Dee was born.

"But who was *she* named after?" asked Wangero.

"I guess after Grandma Dee," I said.   30

"And who was she named after?" asked Wangero.

"Her mother," I said, and saw Wangero was getting tired. "That's about as far back as I can trace it," I said. Though, in fact, I probably could have carried it back beyond the Civil War through the branches.

"Well," said Asalamalakim, "there you are."

"Uhnnnh," I heard Maggie say.

"There I was not," I said, "before 'Dicie' cropped up in our family,   35 so why should I try to trace it that far back?"

He just stood there grinning, looking down on me like somebody inspecting a Model A car. Every once in a while he and Wangero sent eye signals over my head.

"How do you pronounce this name?" I asked.

"You don't have to call me by it if you don't want to," said Wangero.

"Why shouldn't I?" I asked. "If that's what you want us to call you, we'll call you."

"I know it might sound awkward at first," said Wangero.   40

"I'll get used to it," I said. "Ream it out again."

Well, soon we got the name out of the way. Asalamalakim had a name twice as long and three times as hard. After I tripped over it two or three times he told me to just call him Hakim-a-barber. I wanted to ask him was he a barber, but I didn't really think he was, so I didn't ask.

"You must belong to those beef-cattle peoples down the road," I said. They said "Asalamalakim" when they met you, too, but they didn't shake hands. Always too busy: feeding the cattle, fixing the fences, putting up salt-lick shelters, throwing down hay. When the white folks poisoned some of the herd the men stayed up all night with rifles in their hands. I walked a mile and a half just to see the sight.

Hakim-a-barber said, "I accept some of their doctrines, but farming and raising cattle is not my style." (They didn't tell me, and I didn't ask, whether Wangero (Dee) had really gone and married him.)

We sat down to eat and right away he said he didn't eat collards   45
and pork was unclean. Wangero, though, went on through the chitlins and corn bread, and the greens and everything else. She talked a blue streak over the sweet potatoes. Everything delighted her. Even the fact that we still used the benches her daddy made for the table when we couldn't afford to buy chairs.

"Oh, Mama!" she cried. Then turned to Hakim-a-barber. "I never knew how lovely these benches are. You can feel the rump prints," she said, running her hands underneath her and along the bench. Then she gave a sigh and her hand closed over Grandma Dee's butter dish. "That's it!" she said. "I knew there was something I wanted to ask you if I could have." She jumped up from the table and went over in the corner where the churn stood, the milk in it clabber by now. She looked at the churn and looked at it.

"This churn top is what I need," she said. "Didn't Uncle Buddy whittle it out of a tree you all used to have?"

"Yes," I said.

"Uh huh," she said happily. "And I want the dasher, too."

"Uncle Buddy whittle that, too?" asked the barber.   50

Dee (Wangero) looked up at me.

"Aunt Dee's first husband whittled the dash," said Maggie so low you almost couldn't hear her. "His name was Henry, but they called him Stash."

"Maggie's brain is like an elephant's," Wangero said, laughing. "I can use the churn top as a centerpiece for the alcove table," she said, sliding a plate over the churn, "and I'll think of something artistic to do with the dasher."

When she finished wrapping the dasher the handle stuck out. I took it for a moment in my hands. You didn't even have to look close to see where hands pushing the dasher up and down to make butter had left a kind of sink in the wood. In fact, there were a lot of small sinks; you could see where thumbs and fingers had sunk into the wood. It was beautiful light yellow wood, from a tree that grew in the yard where Big Dee and Stash had lived.

After dinner Dee (Wangero) went to the trunk at the foot of my   55
bed and started rifling through it. Maggie hung back in the kitchen over the dishpan. Out came Wangero with two quilts. They had been pieced by Grandma Dee and then Big Dee and me had hung them on the quilt frames on the front porch and quilted them. One was in the Lone Star pattern. The other was Walk Around the Mountain. In both of them were scraps of dresses Grandma Dee had worn fifty and more years ago. Bits and pieces of Grandpa Jarrell's Paisley shirts. And one teeny-faded blue piece, about the size of a penny matchbox, that was from Great Grandpa Ezra's uniform that he wore in the Civil War.

"Mama," Wangero said sweet as a bird. "Can I have these old quilts?"

I heard something fall in the kitchen, and a minute later the kitchen door slammed.

"Why don't you take one or two of the others?" I asked. "These old things was just done by me and Big Dee from some tops your grandma pieced before she died."

"No," said Wangero. "I don't want those. They are stitched around the borders by machine."

"That'll make them last better," I said.   60

"That's not the point," said Wangero. "These are all pieces of dresses Grandma used to wear. She did all this stitching by hand. Imagine!" She held the quilts securely in her arms, stroking them.

"Some of the pieces, like those lavender ones, come from old clothes her mother handed down to her," I said, moving up to touch the quilts. Dee (Wangero) moved back just enough so that I couldn't reach the quilts. They already belonged to her.

"Imagine!" she breathed again, clutching them closely to her bosom.

"The truth is," I said, "I promised to give them quilts to Maggie, for when she marries John Thomas."

She gasped like a bee had stung her.   65

"Maggie can't appreciate these quilts!" she said. "She'd probably be backward enough to put them to everyday use."

"I reckon she would," I said. "God knows I been saving 'em for long enough with nobody using 'em. I hope she will!" I didn't want to bring up how I had offered Dee (Wangero) a quilt when she went away to college. Then she had told me they were old-fashioned, out of style.

"But they're *priceless!*" she was saying now, furiously; for she has a temper. "Maggie would put them on the bed and in five years they'd be in rags. Less than that!"

"She can always make some more," I said. "Maggie knows how to quilt."

Dee (Wangero) looked at me with hatred. "You just will not un-derstand. The point is these quilts, *these* quilts!" 70

"Well," I said, stumped. "What would *you* do with them?"

"Hang them," she said. As if that was the only thing you *could* do with quilts.

Maggie by now was standing in the door. I could almost hear the sound her feet made as they scraped over each other.

"She can have them, Mama," she said, like somebody used to never winning anything, or having anything reserved for her. "I can 'member Grandma Dee without the quilts."

I looked at her hard. She had filled her bottom lip with checker-berry snuff and it gave her face a kind of dopey, hangdog look. It was 75 Grandma Dee and Big Dee who taught her how to quilt herself. She stood there with her scarred hands hidden in the folds of her skirt. She looked at her sister with something like fear but she wasn't mad at her. This was Maggie's portion. This was the way she knew God to work.

When I looked at her like that something hit me in the top of my head and ran down to the soles of my feet. Just like when I'm in church and the spirit of God touches me and I get happy and shout. I did something I never had done before: hugged Maggie to me, then dragged her on into the room, snatched the quilts out of Miss Wan-gero's hands and dumped them into Maggie's lap. Maggie just sat there on my bed with her mouth open.

"Take one or two of the others," I said to Dee.

But she turned without a word and went out to Hakim-a-barber.

"You just don't understand," she said, as Maggie and I came out to the car.

"What don't I understand?" I wanted to know. 80

"Your heritage," she said. And then she turned to Maggie, kissed her, and said, "You ought to try to make something of yourself, too,

Maggie. It's really a new day for us. But from the way you and Mama still live you'd never know it."

She put on some sunglasses that hid everything above the tip of her nose and her chin.

Maggie smiled; maybe at the sunglasses. But a real smile, not scared. After we watched the car dust settle I asked Maggie to bring me a dip of snuff. And then the two of us sat there just enjoying, until it was time to go in the house and go to bed.

THE INVOLVED READER

1 What kind of person is the mother who tells the story? What is the relation between her real self and her daydreams?

2 How did the early experiences of the two daughters shape them and help make them different people?

3 How does the mother see Dee and her companion? What do they represent? What clues do you have as to the mother's attitude?

4 Why are quilts central to this story? What do they stand for or symbolize? How do they bring the underlying conflict in the story to a head? How is the conflict resolved?

TALKING, THINKING, WRITING

5 Do you take sides as you read this story? How would you explain and defend the mother's point of view? What would you say in defense of Dee?

6 Have you observed family members who represented very different attitudes or kinds of behavior? Or, have you observed a striking contrast between members of a group that outsiders might have expected to be alike?

poem

The Other House

DAVID WAGONER

Is it true that our personalities are shaped decisively by early child-hood experiences? It is true that we later devote much conscious or unconscious effort to trying to compensate (or overcompensate) for unfilled needs? David Wagoner was born in Ohio and educated at Penn State and Indiana University before he made his home in Seat-tle. He has come to be associated with the Pacific Northwest and with the struggle to protect the shrinking wilderness. He writes understated poetry, suspicious of heroics, looking for the down-to-earth substra-tum in lofty myths. He has written poems about things that are hard to say and about the threat of "ominous silence." He has worked on retellings of the songs, myths, and legends of Native Americans.

As a boy, I haunted an abandoned house
Whose basement was always full of dark-green water
Or dark-green ice in winter,
Where frogs came back to life and sang each spring.

On broken concrete under the skeleton   5
Of a roof, inside ribbed walls, I listened alone
Where the basement stairs went down
Under the water, down into their music

During storms, our proper house would be flooded too.
The water would spout from drains, through the foundation   10
And climb the basement stairs
But silently, and would go away silently,

As silent as my mother and father were
All day and during dinner and after
And after the radio   15
With hardly a murmur all the way into sleep.

All winter, the frogs had slept in an icy bed,
Remembering how to sing when it melted.
If I made a sound, they stopped
And listened to me sing nothing, singing nothing.   20

But gradually, finally April would come pouring
Out of their green throats in a green chorus
To a chorus me home toward silence.
Theirs was the only house that sang all night.

THE INVOLVED READER

1   What is the keynote in the poet's description of his parents' house
    and of their life? How did he feel about his "proper house"?

2   What is the crucial contrast between the boy's home and his
    "other house"? What is the other house literally like? What did it
    come to mean for the boy? What is the symbolic meaning of the
    frogs?

3   Is it a coincidence that the frogs are green and that the word
    green appears four times in the poem?

READING, THINKING, WRITING

4   Have you ever had a private or separate space that you "haunted"
    and that was different from your ordinary existence? What was
    its appeal? What contrast did it set up with your ordinary life?

5   Do you associate a particular part of the country or ethnic back-
    ground with a tendency to be inarticulate? Have you observed a
    difference between groups in how they give or fail to give ex-
    pression to thoughts and feelings? Does our cultural condition-
    ing affect how we are able to communicate emotions?

The Writer's Tools 6

Using Effective Transitions

As your paper moves through its major stages, you may have to mark the turns in the road. A logical connection is often obvious: Your readers can see that you are going from general point to example, or from cause to effect. However, just as often an effective **transition**, or logical link, can serve as a signpost pointing your reader in the right direction.

Transitions help your reader go from one part of a paragraph to another and from one major section of a paper to the next. They can be essential when you structure a comparison. Links like *similarly, along the same lines,* or *in the same vein* signal similarities. Links like *by contrast* or *on the other hand* alert your readers to differences. Other common transitions signal additional logical relationships. *So, therefore, consequently,* and *evidently* signal that you are drawing a logical conclusion. *But, however,* and *nevertheless* show that you are raising an objection. Expressions like *granted* and *it is true that* show that you are taking an objection into account; you are conceding a point.

In the following paragraph, the writer uses *however* to take us from an official version of a situation to the contrasting reality. He uses *and* to show that details to follow will be more of the same. He uses *but* to signal a contrast between what might be interpreted as hopeful signs and the more discouraging hard facts.

> Newspapers like the *New York Times* and *Washington Post* solemnly insisted that they did not discriminate against an employee on the basis of sexual orientation. In practice, **however**, such papers never hired employees who would openly say they were gay, **and** homosexual reporters at such papers privately maintained that their careers would be stalled if not destroyed once their sexuality became known. Gays were tolerated as drama critics and food reviewers, **but** the hard-news sections of the paper had a difficult time acclimating to women, much less inverts. Few in the business ever talked about this. American journalism was always better at defining others' foibles than its own.

Randy Shilts, And the Band Played On

Here is a rundown of common transitional words and phrases.

CONTINUITY:	and, also, furthermore, in addition, moreover, besides
ILLUSTRATION:	for example, for instance, to illustrate
LOGICAL RESULT:	so, therefore, consequently, accordingly, as a result
OBJECTION:	but, however, nevertheless, on the other hand

CONCESSION: granted, admittedly, to be sure, it is true that

REINFORCEMENT: indeed, in fact, above all, in particular

ENUMERATION: first, in the first place, second, third

CHRONOLOGY: initially, next, soon, later, meanwhile, in the end

SUMMARY: in short, in brief, to sum up

CONCLUSION: finally, eventually, in conclusion, to conclude

These words and phrases provide the connecting tissue in much effective writing. However, longer transitional phrases or sentences often do similar work. In the following paragraph, the first major link introduces an earlier theory that has been left behind. The second major link alerts us to a recent discovery, and the third directs our attention to a crucial point previously neglected.

> Running is one of the primal human acts, and the particular human form it takes, using a bipedal stride in a full upright stance, has played an essential part in shaping our destiny. **It was once believed that** our hominid ancestors were rather pitiable creatures compared with the other animals of the jungles and savannahs; lacking the fangs, claws, and specialized physical abilities of the predators, the hominids supposedly prevailed only because of their large brains and their ability to use tools. **But there is now compelling evidence that** our direct ancestors of some four million years ago had relatively small brains, only about a third the size of ours. **What these hominids *did* have** was a full upright stance with the modern, doubly curved spine that enters the skull at the bottom rather than the back (as is the case with the apes). The upright stance increased the field of vision and freed the forelimbs for use in inspecting and manipulating objects, thus challenging the brain to increase its capacity through the process of natural selection.
>
> John Leonard, *Born to Run*

Transitional words, phrases, and sentences help writers show how one idea relates to another. However, when overused, they may become mechanical, standing out like the pipes that run across the ceiling in a converted basement apartment. A writer may use devices like **parallel structure** instead. Parallel sentences — sentences exceptionally similar in form — often line up for the reader two or more examples of the same thing. They may also line up two statements that are opposites.

PARALLEL: **The family is** the seedbed of economic skills, money habits, attitudes toward the world. . . . **The family is a stronger** agency of educational success **than** the school. **The family is a stronger** teacher of the religious imagination **than** the church.

Michael Novak

PARALLEL: Women feel **just as** men feel; they need exercise for their faculties and a field for their efforts **as much as** their brothers do;
they suffer from too rigid a restraint, too absolute a stagnation,
precisely as men would suffer.

CHARLOTTE BRONTË

| **WRITING WORKSHOP 2** |

The Missing Link

What transitional expressions would help the reader follow the
logic of the following passage? Compare your suggestions for the
missing links with those chosen by your classmates.

> Cheap, shoddy handguns account for a large proportion of the homi-
> cides in the United States. _____, in Birmingham, Alabama, police
> estimated that cheap pistols or "Saturday-night specials" accounted for
> more than half of the murders in the city. _____ an enraged person
> could find other means of inflicting deadly harm if handguns were banned.
> _____ easy access to a cheap, convenient murder weapon cer-
> tainly facilitates bloody violence. We do not allow a person to drive a car
> without brakes or headlights. _____ we should not allow people
> to buy and carry guns without elementary safety training or other safe-
> guards. Poll after poll indicates that a majority of Americans favor stricter
> regulation of firearms. _____ legislators afraid of the powerful gun
> lobby sidetrack or delay gun control legislation. _____ most
> Americans can still buy a lethal weapon over the counter with little more
> formality than that involved in buying a loaf of bread. _____ coun-
> tries like England or Japan make purchasing a gun at least as difficult a
> purchasing a dangerous drug.

| **WRITING WORKSHOP 3** |

Linking Your Paragraphs

In much well-organized writing, the opening sentence of a paragraph points back to what came before and points forward to what
is to follow. How does each paragraph opener in the following excerpted sample take you to the next logical step?

The College of Your Choice

> Grades, SAT scores, and college entrance requirements are not the only
> worries for the high school senior thinking about college. Today's soon-to-
> be high school graduate faces an unprecedented range of choice....
> First of all, consider the question of size. The small campus offers a

close-knit atmosphere, similar to that of a small town or a large family. . . .

However, others feel hemmed in by these very qualities. They welcome the comparative anonymity and impersonality of the big university. They look forward to meeting students from other states and from around the world. . . .

A second familiar question is whether the student should go to a college next door or a thousand miles away. Living at home is cheap and offers the comfort and support of family and friends. . . .

Balanced against these advantages, living far from home teaches independence. . . .

Increasingly, however, financial considerations overrule personal preference. Fees, especially for out-of-state students, have skyrocketed at many schools. . . .

Any time you are writing about a controversial subject, counterarguments structure your argument. If they don't, you leave a hole big enough for a truck to drive through. **SUSAN JACOBY**

7

Weighing Pro and Con

Listening to Both Sides

Have you ever discovered that there was another side to an issue on which you had definite opinions? Have you ever helped someone else see another side of an issue? You will often start thinking when you find there is more than one way to look at a problem. Trying to make up your mind, you find yourself weighing the pro and con. You may lean first to one side and then to the other. In the end, you try to reach a balanced conclusion. You may have weighed the pro and con when facing questions like the following:

Should you go to a two-year or a four-year college?
Should you go to a public institution or try a private school?
Should you live at home or move out?
Should you stay single or get married?
Should you stay married or get divorced?
Should you buy an imported car or "buy American"?
Should you keep using your credit card or break the credit habit?

Many private as well as public occasions make you go from "on the one hand" to "on the other hand." There is something to be said on both sides. Weighing advantages and disadvantages, you try to reach a reasonable conclusion. Here are examples of the thinking you do when you weigh the pro and con:

• Should you buy an imported car? *On the one hand,* Japanese cars have a reputation for reliability. They are said to break down less often than their American counterparts; bills for maintenance and repair are low. *On the other hand*, American automakers have in recent years put much emphasis on quality control. When the yen is high and the dollar low, Japanese cars become more expensive, and they are less of a bargain. By buying an American car, you may help American autoworkers keep their jobs.

• Should admission officers at your school be "color-blind" — judging applicants strictly on merit, regardless of race, gender, or ethnicity? Or should the admissions office compensate for economic deprivation, political disenfranchisement, and inadequate schooling experienced by America's minorities? *On the one hand,* we would like to live in a world where the individual's performance in the only thing that counts. *On the other hand*, we may feel morally obligated to give a break to young Americans less privileged than others. They may have grown up with few or no books, gone to schools disrupted by violence, had parents with limited education, and lacked the money for extracurricular activities and educational travel.

To understand a complex issue, you often need to hear people who come to it from a different point of view. Questions like the following can serve as a guide to better listening and more receptive reading:

What are people who disagree with you saying?
What makes them say what they say?
What arguments do they rely on most heavily, and why?
What information do they have that you may have missed?
What background do they have that may explain their thinking?
How might their statements make sense when you see them in context — when you look at what leads up to them and away from them?

Weighing the pro and con is not the same as polarizing an issue. We polarize an issue when we push divergent views so far apart that one side is no longer willing to learn from the other. Ideally, however, learning from the play of opposites is the purpose of the exercise. The payoff is in the broader, more informed perspective we should attain as the result of listening to both sides. Ideally, we move from statement to counterstatement and from there to a reconciling of the two opposed views. We move from **thesis**, or assertion; to **antithesis**, or counterassertion; and from there to **synthesis** — a broader, more balanced view.

THOUGHT LOG 7

Thinking about Opposites

Have you recently listened to arguments that puzzled you? Have you tried to keep informed on an issue on which you have had conflicting input? Have you heard opposite views on a topic like cutting off welfare, distributing condoms in schools, restricting abortion, or voting for gay rights? Do an informal idea inventory: Without sorting them out right now, jot down the conflicting ideas or arguments that you remember. Write freely, putting down ideas as they come to mind.

Structuring Your Pro and Con Paper

From the beginning it seemed to me that the point was not to make readers think like me. It was to make them think.

ANNA QUINDLEN

Writing a pro and con paper is like recording a debate going on in your own head. You start with an open mind. You are willing to listen to someone else's arguments. You make an effort to listen — rather than calling the person naive, un-American, or uninformed. Ideally, an exploration of the pro and con leads to a balanced conclusion. Or it may lead to a choice that you know is less than ideal but that you make with open eyes. You know the shortcomings or the risks of the solution you have embraced.

To promote pro and con thinking, your class may want to stage a panel discussion or informal debate of a topic that is currently dividing opinion on your campus, in your community, or nationwide. Suppose your classmates are divided on the issue of gun control.

• *On the one hand,* in a recent year, 35,000 people were murdered in the United States, with guns being the murder weapons of choice. In nations with strict gun controls, the murder rate stays in the low hundreds. Proponents of stricter gun controls argue that the millions of guns in circulation make killing cheap and easy. Teenage gang members protect their turf with automatic weapons that leave the police outgunned. Disgruntled employees machine-gun supervisors and co-workers.

• *On the other hand,* opponents of gun control argue that it will not control criminals. It will disarm besieged private citizens and leave them at the mercy of armed lawbreakers. Controls are only the first step toward banning weapons altogether. When guns are out-lawed, only outlaws will have guns.

Both sides quote the Second Amendment but disagree on what it means: "A well-regulated militia being necessary to the security of a free state, the right of the people to keep and bear arms shall not be infringed." An advertisement in the *American Rifleman* says that to "shooters and Americans proud of their independence, the Second Amendment is our greatest freedom." Advocates of gun control counter that gun owners resisting regulation are the opposite of a well-regulated militia, or citizen army, envisioned by our ancestors.

Preparing for a pro and con paper, you will often be lining up of such arguments and counterarguments in two opposing columns. Can you spell out more fully the arguments listed on each side in the following outline? Are important arguments misrepresented or omitted here? Do you see how the writer of this sample outline arrived at a possible balanced conclusion?

Bearing Arms

CON: Arguments against gun control	PRO: Arguments for gun control
constitutional right to "bear arms"	Second Amendment: well-*regulated* militia
traditional lifestyle of hunters	bloodbaths caused by disturbed gun lovers
lawlessness in society	senseless drive-by shootings
right to self-defense	record numbers of gun-related deaths
need to protect family and home	gunplay kills inner-city youth
need to deter rapists	police are outgunned by automatic weapons
inadequate police protection	guns kill more family than intruders
gun control creates huge bureaucracy	guns kept in home are stolen by criminals
regulation leads to police state	children killed playing with guns
criminals disregard regulation	we regulate cars, why not guns
only outlaws will have guns	guns make killing easy

POSSIBLE MIDDLE GROUND:
ban assault weapons
register all firearms (as we do cars)
require background check for gun buyers
regulate gunshops (like liquor stores)
mandate training in firearms safety

How would you sum up the result of this student's exploration of the pro and con? The following might be the thesis of the resulting paper:

THESIS: In spite of fears of government regulation and doubts about the effectiveness of gun control, many Americans seem ready to endorse laws aimed at reducing gun-related violence.

To point clear directions for the reader, the writer might state it early, at the end of a short dramatic introduction. Or the writer might choose to have the paper as a whole lead up to the thesis, taking the reader along to it as a well-earned conclusion.

WRITING WORKSHOP I

A Paper for Peer Review

Study and evaluate the following example of a pro and con paper. Compare your reactions with those of your classmates or members of a small group. Consider questions like the following:

- How and how well does the paper bring the issue into focus?
- Did the writer choose to hear out each side in turn or to line up arguments pro and con point by point? How well does the strategy chosen by the writer work?
- Does the writer give equal time to both sides?
- How and how well does the author use supporting sources?
- Does the paper reach a balanced conclusion? Do you agree with it? Why or why not?

The Right of the People to Own Handguns

The Second Amendment of the Constitution says: "A well-regulated militia being necessary to the security of a free state, the right of the people to keep and bear arms shall not be infringed." This statement has become the cornerstone of two diametrically opposed positions on the subject of gun control. An advertisement for a commemorative revolver in a recent issue of *American Rifleman* says that "to shooters and Americans proud of their independence, the Second Amendment is our greatest freedom." For members of the National Rifle Association, bearing arms is a basic constitutional privilege and a patriotic duty. Advocates of stricter gun control measures, on the other hand, point out that today's "recreational gun users" are not members of a well-regulated militia. They in fact fiercely resist regulation. Our nation is suffering from an epidemic of gun-related violence, with different major cities vying for the title of murder capital of the world. Many local and national initiatives — waiting periods and background checks for gun purchases, the banning of handguns altogether, controls on the imports of automatic and semi-automatic weapons — aim at curbing gun-related violence and changing the climate of fear in our communities.

While the two sides often engage in bitter debate, it is important to realize that their ultimate goals are the same. They both want a society that will be safer for law-abiding citizens and their families. The challenge is to reduce gun-related violence without laws and regulations that do more to restrict law-abiding citizens than to reduce violent crime.

Gun control advocates argue that restrictions on firearms and the outright ban of handguns will greatly reduce their criminal use. An argument that would normally end in a fistfight and at worst a broken jaw becomes lethal when one of the aggrieved parties has easy access to a gun. In most states, a fired coworker or a jealous spouse can buy a gun with a minimum of formalities. According to one recent study among many, "more than 60 percent of all murders are caused by guns, and handguns are involved in more than 70 percent of these." However, opponents of stricter regulation answer that criminals do not get their guns from sporting-goods stores. They easily obtain them on a flourishing black market at cut-rate prices.

Advocates of gun control cite statistics on the number of citizens and especially children who die from handgun-related accidents in the home. According to these statistics, the chances of being accidentally killed by a gun legally owned outweigh the chance of being killed by an armed intruder. In the words of one anti-gun crusader, "scarcely a day goes by without a newspaper in any large city reporting that a child has found a gun . . . and killed himself or a playmate." For supporters of the gun lobby, such accidents do not outweigh cases where a gun in the home has saved lives. The "Armed Citizens" column of the *American Rifleman* prints stories like those of the 92-year-old woman in a wheelchair who shot and killed a threatening intruder. Mike Royko, columnist for the *Chicago Tribune*, said about a woman raped twice on her way home by different assailants, "if that woman had had a pistol in her purse or coat pocket . . . it's doubtful that the first rapist would have been able to get her into his car."

Anti-gun lobbyists argue that regulation is already applied to other lethal weapons, such as the automobile. One student I talked to said, "if we regulate cars, why not regulate guns, which kill just as many people?" Pro-gun lobbyists raise the specter of a huge expensive new bureaucracy and ask us to concentrate on the perpetrator, not the weapon used. They see a big part of the answer in the implementation of harsher penalties for those using handguns for criminal purposes.

Perhaps those arguing for and against gun control are not as far apart as they once were. For instance, gun enthusiasts seem well aware of the clamor concerning young children dying while playing with guns. The NRA advocates educational services for kids. According to an article by Wayne LaPierre, one such program is teaching kindergarten through sixth-grade kids a "life-saving message through fun activity books and videos: If you find a gun, stop! Don't touch. Leave the area. Tell an adult." A fellow student who loves to hunt told me, "when I first started to hunt, I made sure that I knew how to handle shotguns. Today women who buy guns to put in their purses take courses in firearm safety. If you are ignorant, you can get yourself killed, and they realize that."

Education, although no cure-all, is a good start. Even those opposed to extended government regulation might support background checks for a gun buyer's possible criminal record. They should support firearms instruction courses for those who purchase handguns. At the other end of the political spectrum, perhaps the more extreme opponents of guns will give up the goal of abolition or outright bans and settle for a "well-regulated" system. We should keep working toward cracking down on handgun violence without abridging our constitutional rights.

Revising Your Pro and Con Paper

Listening patiently to arguments on opposing sides is a challenge. It is easier to call arguments we don't like ludicrous, ignorant, or insincere. In revising a pro and con argument, you may decide to do the following as needed to turn your first draft into a true pro and con paper:

- *Line up the pro and con more clearly.*   Have you clearly identified advocates, proponents, supporters on the one side and opponents, adversaries, or skeptics on the other? What is the key to the differences between opposing views? Obviously, it would be a nonstarter to tell your reader that proponents and opponents offer "interesting points" pro and con. (*What* interesting points?) You may need to add a summarizing statement like the following. Use it early in your paper as a preview or program for what follows.

> For parade goers and Columbus Day shoppers, Christopher Columbus is the genius navigator who bravely set out to sail the unknown ocean without fear that the world was flat and that his fleet would fall off the edge. For protesters, he is a gold-crazed adventurer disguised as a missionary who advanced his own ends by any means possible — even if it meant the near-extinction of a race.

- *Check for lopsided treatment of opposing sides.*   Have you given equal time to opposite views? Have you taken both sides seriously? Or have you given short shrift to one side? (Are you using the arguments of one side only to trigger your own refutation or rebuttal?) As a rough check, you can total the amount of space devoted to each. Bolster the side that you have slighted — explain, add examples, cite

authorities. For instance, critics of affirmative action have been vocal in recent years, and it may prove easy to marshal the arguments
on the opposing side. You may have to make an additional effort to
feed into your paper material like the following on the affirmative
side:

> Critics of affirmative action complain about preferential treatment for
> minorities, calling it "reverse discrimination." However, as Mary H. Coo-
> per says in an article on "Racial Quotas," preferential treatment has always
> gone on and "the only difference is in who was preferred." . . .
>
> Contrary to popular opinion, even at institutions that support affirma-
> tive action, race or gender alone is not an automatic ticket to admission.
> A friend of mine in high school, who was part Native American, felt all he
> had to do was fill in the race identification part of applications, and he
> would be admitted. Unfortunately, he also filled out the rest of the appli-
> cation and disclosed his 1.8 grade point average. . . .
>
> Writers like Shelby Steele, a conservative African American, claim that
> minority students who *are* accorded preferential treatment experience
> self-doubt and low self-esteem, because they can never be sure that they
> are judged on the basis of achievement. "They hold it against you," Steele
> says of the way others look down on beneficiaries of affirmative action.
> However, as Roger Wilkins, a professor of American culture, has said, "I
> would rather have a guy feel bad with a degree from Berkeley than feel
> bad walking the streets with a high school diploma."

• *Let each side speak for itself.*   You may have to make it clear
when someone you quote is not taking sides but reporting other
people's alleged views. Try not to let opposing views be presented
only as seen through the biased eyes of people who disagree. For
instance, in the debate over conserving the ancient first-growth forests of the Northwest, the endangered spotted owl became a symbol
for both of the opposing factions. What were its defenders actually
saying? The following passage uses the kind of detailed quotation
that helps us understand what people were thinking:

> "If the industry is allowed to keep cutting, some forestry experts say,
> the last ancient forests outside wilderness areas could fall within 30 years,"
> claims Ted Gup in a *Time* article titled "Owl vs. Man." He continues: "The
> owl is not alone in the forest. As an 'indicator species,' its well-being is a
> measure of how other creatures and the ecosystem as a whole are faring.
> There are probably dozens of other species just as threatened as the owl."

• *Add logical links that signal the play of argument and counter-
argument.*   Should you highlight a **turning point**? Sometimes a
pointed pro and con paper hinges on a central "However, . . ." or
"Nevertheless, . . ." that takes the reader from one side of the argument to the other.

TURNING POINT: However, although affirmative action long served as a cornerstone in the credo of the liberal establishment, a groundswell of resentment against "reverse discrimination" and preferential treatment of women and minorities has become a major feature of current backlash politics.

Use transitions like *it is true, granted,* or *admittedly* when conceding a point — when recognizing the validity of an objection or reservation. Use paired transitions like *on the one hand* and *on the other hand* to steer the reader's attention.

> Animal experiments inflict suffering on animals in order to reduce suffering experienced by human beings. **Admittedly,** trying out experimental medications on animals and letting them suffer atrocious unexpected side effects seems revolting. **However,** it seems even more barbaric to try out such untested medications on human beings. **On the one hand,** we believe in humane treatment of defenseless laboratory animals. **On the other hand,** we need to extend our knowledge to save human lives and spare other human beings preventable agony.

• *Stake out reasonable middle ground.*   If you can, spell out more fully what you see as the way out of the dilemma. In a paper on animal experiments, for instance, you may want to stress points on which defenders and critics might be able to agree: preventing unnecessary or thoughtless cruelty, minimizing animal use, stepping up the use of computer simulations.

WRITING WORKSHOP 2

Reponding to Peer Reviews

In a small group (perhaps three to five people), rotate the early draft of each member's pro and con paper. Each member of the group will read and comment on the papers of the other members. When you receive the comments of your fellow students, collate them. Sort out and evaluate the advice given by your readers. Write a brief response. Pull together the readers' criticisms, and explain how you will act on them in your revision.

OPTIONS FOR WRITING 7

Weighing the Pro and Con

Write a pro and con paper to present a position that you have reached after weighing the arguments on both sides. Remember the equal-time principle: Give roughly equal space to arguments for and against. Draw on a mix of representative printed and oral sources.

Avoid brushing off the arguments of the side you tend to oppose. Look at both sides of the issue without personal attacks, belittling, or ridicule. Push toward a balanced conclusion — or at least a conclusion that takes the arguments of both sides into account.

1 What are the arguments for and against affirmative action programs in colleges or universities? What were the original arguments in favor of such programs? What are the objections that have led to a rethinking of the issue?

2 What are the arguments for and against stricter environmental legislation? You may want to concentrate on one or more test cases — such as stricter controls on logging in order to protect the habitats of endangered species, or relaxed control on offshore oil drilling. What are the arguments in favor of more determined efforts to protect the environment? On the other hand, what are the social costs and economic consequences?

3 Is it futile to argue about gun control? What are the arguments in favor of stricter controls or outright bans of certain kinds of guns — or of all guns? What are the arguments of those who support or sympathize with the National Rifle Association? (You may want to focus on the pros and cons of a specific gun control initiative. Or you may want to focus on a particular type of weapon, such as handguns or automatic weapons.)

4 Would you vote to change "Columbus Day" to "Indigenous Peoples Day" (or perhaps "Ethnic Heritage Day")? What are the arguments against honoring Columbus and other European explorers? What are the arguments in their defense?

5 Should colleges adopt speech codes banning hate speech or regulating offensive speech? Do such codes conflict with First Amendment rights?

6 What are current arguments for and against bilingual education? What led to the creation of bilingual education programs? What is behind current efforts to abolish bilingual education programs?

7 Has the abortion debate become too inflamed for the opponents to listen to rational arguments? What for you are the key arguments on the pro-life side? What for you are the key arguments on the pro-choice side? On balance, where do you take your stand?

8 Should schools distribute condoms to help reduce the spread of disease (AIDS) and to help reduce teenage pregnancies? What are the arguments pro and con?

9 What are the arguments for and against having training programs for military officers on college campuses? What are the
   arguments of those who want ROTC programs off campus?
   What are the arguments of those defending such programs?

10 Should voters support initiatives to protect gays and lesbians
   from discrimination?

Reading, Discussion, Writing

Opposing Points of View

OVERVIEW: The writers in this section tackle issues on which
people hold radically opposed views. Should we scuttle affirmative
action programs because they have become counterproductive?
Should we disown America's past? Have women made real strides
toward equality? On these issues, opposing sides engage in heated
controversy. Do these writers succeed in engaging you in the play of
pro and con?

Rethinking the Dream

EVAN THOMAS AND BOB COHN

Is it time for a negative vote on affirmative action? When the authors were writing the following article, the backlash against affirmative action was everywhere gathering momentum. The courts had for some time been moving toward questioning preferences on the basis of race or gender, starting with the pivotal 1978 Bakke case, won by a student who had been passed over for admission to medical school in favor of minority students with lower grades or test scores. Since then, conservative representatives of minorities, like Shelby Steele, have argued that being stereotyped as an affirmative action hire caused self-doubts and low self-esteem. In 1996, the governor of California led his appointees on the Board of Regents in voting to end all affirmative action programs on the campuses of the University of California. At the same time, administrators, faculty, and students overwhelmingly expressed their disapproval of the governor's initiative. Many considered any claim that young Americans from the country's ghettos and barrios would be able to compete on equal terms with the sons and daughters of the affluent white majority a sham. Newsmagazines like Time *and* Newsweek *serve as barometers of the public's mood swings on issues such as these. Writers for the newsweeklies often work into their pieces a sampling of grassroots opinions from local officials and ordinary citizens, giving the appearance of the authors having listened to both sides.*

Few white men have better civil-rights credentials. The old newspapermen who had gathered for an informal reunion at the Atlanta airport Holiday Inn on a recent Saturday night had been thrown in jail and chased out of dusty delta towns during the Movement Days of the 1950s and '60s. During a night of strong drink and reminiscence, the old hands from publications like The New York Times and The Washington Post quietly recalled the clarity of the clash between peaceable black demonstrators and the Bull Connors of the then segregated South. "Hell, everything was clearer then," said Claude Sitton, who covered the region for the Times from 1958 to 1964. "Going to the back of the bus, drinking out of separate water fountains, going to segregated schools — those are the kinds of things that just hit you right between the eyes." But in the morning, the aging veterans puzzled over the current state of the civil-rights struggle — the tedious court battles over formulas and standards. "When it gets down to all of the subtleties and complexities of legal tests, well, that's much harder for the public to understand," said John Popham, a dapper octogenarian who covered the first stirrings of the movement for the Times back in the late 1940s. No one came out and said it, but there was a sense that the revolution they courageously covered may be losing its indisputable moral force.

Conservative politicians have been criticizing affirmative action for years. What's different today is that the once liberal establishment has begun, grudgingly and slowly, to have its own second thoughts. The judges and unelected executive-branch officials who have largely made affirmative-action policy for the past 25 years — and the editorial writers who have supported them — are beginning to back off. They eschew the rhetoric of Republican presidential candidates who want to make affirmative action a "wedge issue." The establishment would like to find a comfortable compromise. That's difficult, as President Clinton discovered. The administration's review of government affirmative action became work in progress, with no end in sight. But over time, the likely effect of such second-guessing will be to largely remove the government from handing out jobs or contracts or school admissions based on race.

In a recent decision the U.S. Supreme Court seemed to scale back the federal government's own affirmative action. By a 5-to-4 vote, the justices fashioned a legal test that will make it very difficult, if not impossible, to preserve government programs that give an edge to minorities and women. The decision in *Adarand Constructors v. Pena* was written in the usual murky legalese. But the point was articulated by the plaintiff, Randy Pech, whose Adarand construction outfit in Colorado had lost out to a Hispanic-owned company under a program that earmarked highway contracts for minorities. The burly Pech asked why he should be discriminated against to make up for discrimination that occurred more than a century ago.

Reaction to the decision was muted. Of course, civil-rights leaders were angry; Jesse Jackson called it a "major setback." But except for The New York Times, there was little protest on op-ed pages. A White House spokesman blandly noted that the administration was "asking many of the questions the court focused on."

The decision signals that the high court is following the election returns. For more than a decade, since it ruled that race could be a "factor" in university admissions in the 1978 Bakke case involving the University of California, the court had basically rebuffed challenges to affirmative action. In recent years, however, the court has shown a growing reluctance to use "race-conscious remedies" — the practice of trying to overcome the effects of past discrimination by helping minorities and women. This has been true not only in affirmative-action cases involving jobs and contracts, but in school desegregation and voting rights as well. On the same day the court handed down the Adarand decision, it also cast strong doubt, in a Kansas City, Mo., case, on whether federal courts can promote integration by requiring the state to fund inner-city "magnet schools." The court is expected to curtail the drawing of racially "gerrymandered" congressional districts designed to elect minority lawmakers.

The animating notion of affirmative action has always been that it is necessary to use race to overcome the effects of racism. In some ways, the policy has worked. Affirmative action's cultural impact is unlikely to be reversed entirely — the search for minorities for jobs is now ingrained, at least informally, in many institutions. On a pocketbook level, a 1995 study by Rutgers professor Alfred Blumrosen found that 5 million minority workers and 6 million women have better jobs today than they would have had without preferences and anti-discrimination laws. Certainly, minority contractors who stand to lose from the court's Adarand decision are understandably anxious. "The reality is that 90 percent of the work that we do is in the public sector," said Nigel Parkinson, president of a Maryland construction company. The decision, he said, will "just kill us."

"Beyond racism": At the same time, affirmative action has engendered tremendous resentment among whites, few of whom have lost jobs to minorities, but many of whom think they have. The policy that was supposed to get "beyond racism" risks creating more racists. Court-ordered busing did not produce integration; whites fled the inner cities, leaving schools more segregated than ever. The Kansas City program challenged in the Supreme Court spent $1.3 billion to lure suburban whites to urban magnet schools. But after a decade, the city schools were still two-thirds black.

The rule of unintended consequences is particularly ironic in the voting-rights area. The Voting Rights Act of 1965 guaranteed minorities the right to vote — but did little to increase the number of minority representatives in Congress. The Justice Department responded by encouraging states to draw some majority-minority districts. By 1993, this led to historic gains for the black and Hispanic caucuses. But the weird, serpentine-shaped districts siphoned off liberal voters from other districts — producing conservative congressmen likely to be unsympathetic to minorities.

Impatient with the important but inevitably slow progress of the courts, GOP leaders vow to eliminate all "racial preferences" from federal hiring and contracting. More telling of the shift in the establishment center was a scene in the Senate Labor Committee, where Nancy Kassebaum of Kansas, a moderate, held hearings to warn that affirmative-action requirements on business can become "harmful and unfair."

Diverse world: The private sector's response to all this? Most For-   10
tune 500 companies say they are committed to affirmative action.
Creating a diverse work force, they say, is good business in an increasingly diverse world. But most of these companies now work
under federal rule that make sure they follow through. And many
companies also have federal contracts that require them to hire minorities and women in rough proportion to the local population.
Even if the Feds go all the way and eliminate their requirements,
some sort of affirmative action, however informal, is likely to remain. But without the standards that grew out of the '60s, affirmative
action's future is a bit hazier — and diversity will depend not on
clear federal action but on corporations, and people, doing the right
thing.

THE INVOLVED READER

1   Does the opening paragraph persuade you that affirmative ac-
    tion was the product of a different time, a different place?

2   Why would conservative politicians be likely to be opposed
    to affirmative action? Why would they be likely to use it as a
    "wedge issue"?

3   Why has the "once liberal establishment" developed second
    thoughts about affirmative action? Why are former supporters
    "beginning to back off"?

4   In this article, what cases in point show that court decisions
    have been "following the election returns"?

5   How do the authors try to show that the "law of unintended
    consequences" applies to affirmative action? Do they have any-
    thing positive to say about affirmative action?

TALKING, THINKING, WRITING

6   Have you had firsthand opportunity to observe the workings of
    affirmative action? How would you argue the pros and cons on
    the basis of your own experience and observation?

7   Do you think the purpose of affirmative action is to "make up
    for discrimination that occurred more than a century ago"?

8   In the absence of legal or governmental requirements, will cor-
    porations and Americans in general be "doing the right thing"?

COLLABORATIVE PROJECTS

9   You may want to help set up a panel where advocates and op-
    ponents argue the pros and cons of affirmative action.

Was America a Mistake?

A R T H U R   S C H L E S I N G E R ,   J R .

Are we wrong to judge the European colonization of the Americas by the standards of our own time? Did Columbus open a new chapter in the history of civilization, or was he guilty of genocide? Actually, Columbus' European contemporaries did not unanimously support those who, like the English poet Edmund Spenser, urged their compatriots not to quail in the conquest of "the lands of gold." The Spanish priest Bartolomeo de las Casas chronicled the atrocities of the conquistadores in the New World. The French philosopher Montaigne deplored the civilizations destroyed, the cities razed, and the populations put to the sword by the Europeans in their greed for gold. In the following article, Arthur Schlesinger tries to balance current perspectives and those of Columbus' time, sorting out what is "useful and necessary" in the current rewriting of history and what he considers excessive. Schlesinger is a Pulitzer Prize–winning historian who participated in the "raw material of history" in government service as a special assistant to Presidents John F. Kennedy and Lyndon Johnson. Published during the Nixon years, Schlesinger's The Imperial Presidency *warned against abuses of presidential power while championing the virtues of the American system. Schlesinger wrote the following article at a time of increasing polarization, when "patriotically correct" intellectuals on the right did battle with "politically correct" intellectuals on the left.*

October 12, 1992, marked the five-hundredth anniversary of the most crucial of all encounters between Europe and the Americas. In the contemporary global mood, however, the quincentennial of Christopher Columbus's landing in the New World — new, anyway, to the European intruders; old and familiar to its inhabitants — seemed an occasion less for celebration than for meditation. Indeed, in some quarters the call was for penitence and remorse.

Christopher Columbus has always been as much a myth as a man, a myth incorporating a succession of triumphs and guilts over what is now five long centuries. The myth has found particular lodgment in the mightiest of the nations to arise in the Western Hemisphere — a nation that may not speak Columbus's language (any of them) but has diligently revered his memory.

Though both the continent and the country bear another's name, Columbus has been surpassed in nomenclatural popularity in the United States only by the great George Washington — and Washing-

ton is itself located in the District of Columbia. I make this observation as a native of Columbus, Ohio, the largest of many municipali-
ties called after the great explorer. The preeminent university in the
city in which I now live is Columbia — not to mention such other
North American institutions as the Columbia Broadcasting System,
the *Columbia Encyclopedia,* Columbia Pictures, and a variety of en-
terprises from banks to space shuttles.

The biography that fixed the nineteenth-century image of Columbus was published in 1828 and written by Washington Irving, Manhattan's first international man of letters, a lover of Spain, the aficio-
nado of Granada and the Alhambra, and in later life the U.S. minister
to Madrid. Half a century after, Irish-Americans named a newly
founded Roman Catholic fraternal organization the Knights of Columbus. A movement to honor the day of landfall culminated in
1934, when President Franklin D. Roosevelt proclaimed October 12
a national holiday. The holiday is observed in most Latin American
countries as well.

The United States also staged the most memorable celebration
of the quadricentennial of what it was then widely acceptable to call
the "discovery" of America. The World's Columbian Exposition took
place in bustling, thrusting, midwestern Chicago, the very heart of
the republic. Reconfiguring the great explorer in images of technology and modernity, the Chicago World's Fair saluted the man
then regarded, in the words of President Benjamin Harrison, as "the
pioneer of progress and enlightenment." In a book especially produced for the fair, the historian Meyer Kayserling summed up the
prevailing assessment of Columbus: "In the just appreciation of his
great services to mankind, all political, religious and social differences have vanished."

How things have changed in a century! Political, religious, and
social differences, far from vanishing, place Columbus today in the
center of a worldwide cultural civil war. The great hero of the nineteenth century seems well on the way to becoming the great villain
of the twenty-first. Columbus, it is now charged, far from being the
pioneer of progress and enlightenment, was in fact the pioneer of
oppression, racism, slavery, rape, theft, vandalism, extermination,
and ecological desolation.

The revisionist reaction, it must be said, has been under way for a
while. As far back as the quadricentennial Justin Winsor, a historian
and bibliographer of early America, published a soberly critical biography, arguing that Columbus had left the New World "a legacy of
devastation and crime." George Santayana soon wrote of Columbus,
in one of his *Odes,*

He gave the world another world, and ruin
Brought upon blameless, river-loving nations,
Cursed Spain with barren gold, and made the Andes
Fiefs of Saint Peter.

Today revisionism is in full flood. Much of it is useful and necessary. "The one duty we owe to history," as Oscar Wilde said, "is to rewrite it." The very phrase "discovery of America" is under a ban. It is pointed out, not unreasonably, that America had been discovered centuries earlier by people trickling across the Bering Strait land bridge from East Asia. To call Columbus's landfall a "discovery" therefore convicts one of Eurocentrism. Certainly it is hard to object to the proposal that the arrival of Columbus be seen from the viewpoint of those who met him as well as from the viewpoint of those who sent him.

It is also well that we begin to see the man Columbus not in the nineteenth-century mode, as Benjamin Harrison's "pioneer of progress and enlightenment," but as he saw himself — as, that is, a God-intoxicated man who, for all his superb practical skills as a navigator, believed himself engaged in a spiritual rather than a geographical quest, the messenger not of rationalism and science but of the Almighty, warning that the world would end in another century and a half, prophesying, as he wrote to an intimate of Queen Isabella's, "the new heaven and the new earth which the Lord made, and of which St. John writes in the Apocalypse." We are right, I think, in beginning to read his messianic *Libro de las profecías* not as a cynical attempt to con the Queen nor as the paranoid outburst of an aging and despairing has-been but as the center of the Columbian dream.

Revisionism redresses the balance up to a point; but, driven by 10 Western guilt, it may verge on masochism. Let me cite the resolution on the quincentennial adopted by the National Council of Churches: "What some historians have termed a 'discovery' in reality was an invasion and colonization with legalized occupation, genocide, economic exploitation and a deep level of institutional racism and moral decadence." The Council of Churches' three-page statement is a stern indictment of the criminal history of the European conquest. The quincentennial, the resolution concludes, should be an occasion not for celebration but for "repentance."

The government of Canada decided not to celebrate the quincentennial at all, on the ground that the arrival of Columbus led to the destruction of the existing American cultures. Russell Means, a leader of the American Indian Movement, opines that Columbus "makes Hitler look like a juvenile delinquent." The novelist Hans Koning finds him "worse than Attila the Hun." Last year on Columbus Day protesters in Washington poured fake blood on the Union Station statue of Columbus. Marlon Brando recently demanded that his name be removed from the credits of a new movie, *Christopher Columbus: The Discovery,* on the ground that the film failed to portray Columbus as "the true villain he was," the man "directly responsible for the first wave of genocidal obliteration of the native peoples of North America." (Brando's role in the film, by the way, was Torquemada.)

In the university town of Berkeley, California, a leaflet charged Columbus with "grand theft; genocide; racism; initiating the destruction of culture; rape, torture and maiming of indigenous people; and [being the] instigator of the Big Lie"; city officials thereafter changed October 12 to Indigenous Peoples Day. When Cristobal Colon, a descendant of the explorer's, was appointed grand marshal of Pasadena's annual New Year's Day parade, the Tournament of Roses, the vice-mayor denounced Colon as "a symbol of greed, slavery, rape, and genocide" and his appointment as an insult to American Indians. The protest was stilled only by the naming of Ben Nighthorse Campbell, a congressman and Cheyenne chief, as co-grand marshal.

Recently, in Havana, I asked Fidel Castro how he looks on the quincentennial. He replied, "We are critical. Columbus brought many bad things." I said, "If it weren't for Columbus, you wouldn't be here." Castro said, "Well, Columbus brought good things as well as bad." This slightly schizophrenic reaction is not untypical. North and south of the border Americans of Spanish descent are torn between pride in their Hispanic heritage and romantic identification with indigenous Indian traditions. In the United States some Latinos join the campaign against the Spanish conquest; others take it as an attack on themselves. "My mother sees it as something that brought us religion and civilization," one told Patricia Duarte, of *Newsday.* "Younger people see it as an atrocity."

Still, the "politically correct" image of Columbus as executioner dominates the current discussion. As the art critic Hilton Kramer sums it up,

> Columbus is now vilified as a Eurocentric genocidal maniac who, in addition to decimating the native population of the Americas, was also responsible for destroying their ecology and bringing to this part of the world the most atrocious of all economic systems, namely, capitalism.

Had Columbus foreseen even a portion of all the sins he would be held accountable for five centuries later, he might never have bothered to discover America.

Why this sea change in attitudes? Obviously the global mood has   15
shifted since the exaltation of Columbus's heroic aspects at the quadricentennial. This change reflects the end of European domination
of the planet. It reflects the revolt of the Third World against economic exploitation, against political control, against cultural despo-
liation, against personal and national humiliation, even, at times,
against modernity itself. It reflects the (belated) bad conscience of
the West and the consequent re-examination of the Western impact
on the rest of humanity.

No one can doubt the arrogance and brutality of the European
invaders, their callous and destructive ways, the human and ecological devastation they left in their trail. Genocide — the calculated
and purposeful murder of a race — may be too harsh a term, at least
for Spanish America; it applies more to British America, which widely
believed that the only good Indian was a dead Indian. Many Span-
iards wanted to keep natives alive, if only as slave labor; some, like
Father Bartolomé de Las Casas, denounced inhuman treatment in
brave and searing language. In both South and North America many
more Amerindians died by accident from European diseases —
smallpox, cholera, measles — than by design from European swords,
harquebuses, and lashes. (And in the transatlantic exchange of diseases, the Europeans apparently received syphilis.)

Revisionists tend to portray pre-Columbian America as an Arca-
dia. The most readable statement of the case is by Kirkpatrick Sale,
in his graceful and passionate book *The Conquest of Paradise* (1990).
Sale envisages a continent where people lived in "balanced and fruitful harmony" with nature and with one another, "an untouched
world, a prelapsarian Eden of astonishing plenitude . . . functioning
to all intents and purposes in its original primal state," green and
pure, until European violence smashed the human and ecological
utopia.

The myth of innocence is an old one. "In the beginning," John
Locke wrote three centuries ago, "all the world was *America,* and
more so than that is now; for no such thing as *Money* was any where
known." Yet the vision of an uncorrupted pre-Columbian America is
in acute conflict with another part of the anti-Columbus campaign:
the contention that pre-Columbian America contained elaborate and
advanced civilizations that were ruthlessly obliterated by the European invasion.

One has only to recall the soaring temples, exact astronomical
calculations, accurate calendars, and complex hieroglyphics of the
Maya in Central America; or the wild surmise with which in 1519
stout Cortes and his tiny Spanish band confronted not the Pacific

from Keats's peak in Darien, but, shimmering in the distance, the Aztec city of Tenochtitlán, a metropolis as impressive as any in sixteenth-century Europe; or the contrast between the brutal Spanish thug Pizarro and the courteous and civilized Inca Emperor Atahualpa; or the wonderful grace, symmetry, and imaginative power of pre-Columbian art.

Yet these empires were also theocratic military collectivisms, quite [20] as arrogant, cruel, and ethnocentric as the Europeans who demolished them. Far from living in harmony with nature, the Maya evidently brought about their own collapse by deforestation and other destructive agricultural practices that upset the rain-forest ecosystem of Central America. Far from living in harmony with one another, the Mayan city-states appear to have been engaged in constant warfare, with prisoners ritually tortured and decapitated.

The anthropologist Louis Faron describes the Mundurucú societies of the Amazon basin, whose approach to prisoners of war "ranged from the exotic mutilation of shrinking heads to eating parts of the corpse." After removing the brain and teeth and closing the eyes with beeswax, the Mundurucús parboiled the head and strung cords through the mouth and out the nostrils. The Tupinambas, along the Atlantic coast, "like the Caribs and Cubeos, considered the eating of human flesh a ritual act, part of their belief in consubstantiation."

These were primitive tribes, but the more developed Aztecs brought the processes of ritual torture and human sacrifice to exalted heights. Thousands of captives won in war or exacted in tribute would line up before the 114 steps of the great pyramid waiting for priests to plunge in the obsidian knife and tear out their bleeding hearts — a ceremony no doubt laudably designed to propitiate the sun god, but not easy to reconcile with the revisionist myth of prelapsarian harmony and innocence. Cortes conquered Mexico with such ease because Indian tribes subjugated and persecuted by the Aztecs embraced him as their liberator from unbearable tyranny. As Carlos Fuentes writes, "It was the victory of the *other Indians* over the Aztec overlord."

Given Aztec customs and methods, what, one wonders, would have become of the hapless inhabitants of Spain and Portugal if the Atlantic crossing had been reversed and the Aztecs had conquered Iberia? And those who insist that Aztecs and Incas, Mundurucús and Tupinambas, should be judged by their own values, not by ours, owe the same indulgence to the *conquistadores.*

The melancholy conclusion is that despite the dramatic clash of cultures, one finds in certain respects, as the historian Hugh Thomas argues, little difference between the Europe and the Mexico of 1492: little difference in the uses of power, in prescriptive inequalities, in coercion and torture, in imperialism and violence and destruction, in (to leap centuries forward to contemporary standards) the suppression of individual freedom and of human rights. The record illustrates less the pitiless annihilation of an idyllic culture by a wrecking crew of aliens than it does the criminality of original sin. Cruelty and destruction are not the monopoly of any single continent or race or culture. As William James reminds us, "The trail of the human serpent is thus over everything."

Christopher Columbus, Mario Vargas Llosa observed at a quin- 25
centennial conference in Seville, has become a historical counter in a contemporary political game, and British America and Spanish America use him for different purposes. In North America, Columbus is just one more pretext for the already thriving assault mounted against the establishment by apostles of political correctness. The Latin American reaction, Vargas Llosa continues, is far more primary and organic. There Columbus serves not as scapegoat but as alibi. Blaming everything on the conquest provides a perpetual excuse for the failure of Latin American countries to achieve humane, stable, and progressive democracies. Latin America, Vargas Llosa says, must begin to accept responsibility for its own fate. So, too, says Carlos Fuentes: Latin Americans, confronting the questions raised by their "balkanized, fractured politics, failed economic systems, and vast social inequalities," must finally recognize that "we could only answer the questions from within ourselves."

THE INVOLVED READER

1 For you, what is striking or instructive in Schlesinger's account of the traditional Columbus myth?

2 According to Schlesinger, what are key points in the current "revisionist reaction"? What revision of the traditional picture of Columbus does he himself accept? Where does he think revisionism goes too far? (What makes it "masochistic"?)

3 According to Schlesinger, why do Americans of Spanish descent experience mixed emotions or divided loyalties in the current Columbus debate?

4 How does Schlesinger describe the current idealizing of the Native American past? How are Native Americans being romanticized? (What makes current accounts "utopian" or "prelapsarian" — taking us to a state before Adam's fall brought sin into the world?)

5 What, on balance, is Schlesinger's verdict on how the European and American civilizations of Columbus' time compare?

TALKING, THINKING, WRITING

6 How does Schlesinger influence or challenge your own views of Columbus, the European discovery of the New World, or the pre-Columbian past?

7 What evidence have you seen of the current romanticizing of the Native American past in the media? In films or on television, have you observed a "utopian" vision of native peoples uncorrupted by Western civilization?

8 Do you think today's Americans should have a "bad conscience" about what happened in America's past?

COLLABORATIVE PROJECTS

9 Schlesinger sees striking parallels between the European and American civilizations of Columbus' time. Working with a group, explore one of these parallels in greater detail.

Diversity and Its Discontents

A R T U R O M A D R I D

*Can we honor diversity while searching for the common center? Or
will our society splinter into separate ethnic or racial groups? Will we
be able to bridge the gap between ourselves and those we perceive as
the "other"? Arturo Madrid looks at these questions from the perspective of Spanish-speaking Americans whose "ancestors' presence in
what is now the United States antedates Plymouth Rock." A native
of New Mexico who studied at the University of New Mexico and
UCLA, Madrid took his first teaching job at Dartmouth, an elitist
New England college, and later became president of the Thomas Ri-
vera Center at the Claremont Graduate School in California. He
speaks for Hispanic or Latino Americans of the Southwest who live
in areas formerly part of Mexico and for whom the Anglos were the
immigrants or new arrivals. The following article is excerpted from a
speech Madrid gave at a national conference of the American Association of Higher Education, urging educators to recognize excellence in
people regardless of class, gender, race, and group affiliation.*

My name is Arturo Madrid. I am a citizen of the United States,
as are my parents and as were my grandparents and my great-
grandparents. My ancestors' presence in what is now the United
States antedates Plymouth Rock, even without taking into account
any American Indian heritage I might have.

I do not, however, fit those mental sets that define America and
Americans. My physical appearance, my speech patterns, my name,
my profession (a professor of Spanish) create a text that confuses the
reader. My normal experience is to be asked, "And where are *you*
from?" My response depends on my mood. Passive-aggressive, I
answer, "From here." Aggressive-passive, I answer, "From here."
Aggressive-passive, I ask, "Do you mean where I am originally from?"
But ultimately my answer to those follow-up questions that will ask
about origins will be that we have always been from here.

Overcoming my resentment I try to educate, knowing that nine
times out of ten my words fall on inattentive ears. I have spent most
of my adult life explaining who I am not. I am exotic, but — as Richard Rodriguez of *Hunger of Memory* fame so painfully found out —
not exotic enough . . . not Peruvian, or Pakistani, or whatever. I am,
however, very clearly the *other*, if only your everyday, garden-variety,
domestic *other*. I will share with you another phenomenon that I

have been a part of, that of being a missing person, and how I came late to that awareness. But I've always known that I was the *other,* even before I knew the vocabulary or understood the significance of otherness.

I grew up in an isolated and historically marginal part of the United States, a small mountain village in the state of New Mexico, the eldest child of parents native to that region, whose ancestors had always lived there. In those vast and empty spaces people who look like me, speak as I do, and have names like mine predominate. But the *americanos* lived among us: the descendants of those nineteenth-century immigrants who dispossessed us of our lands; missionaries who came to convert us and stayed to live among us; artists who became enchanted with our land and humanscape and went native; refugees from unhealthy climes, crowded spaces, unpleasant circumstances; and, of course, the inhabitants of Los Alamos, whose sociocultural distance from us was accentuated by the fact that they occupied a space removed from and proscribed to us. More importantly, however, they — *los americanos* — were omnipresent (and almost exclusively so) in newspapers, newsmagazines, books, on radio, in movies, and, ultimately, on television.

Despite the operating myth of the day, school did not erase my   5
otherness. It did try to deny it, and in doing so only accentuated it. To this day what takes place in schools is more socialization than education, but when I was in elementary school — and given where I was — socialization was everything. School was where one became an American, because there was a pervasive and systematic denial by the society that surrounded us that we were Americans. That denial was both explicit and implicit.

Quite beyond saluting the flag and pledging allegiance to it (a very intense and meaningful action, given that the United States was involved in a war and our brothers, cousins, uncles, and fathers were on the frontlines), becoming American was learning English, and its corollary: not speaking Spanish. Until very recently ours was a proscribed language, either *de jure* — by rule, by policy, by law — or *de facto* — by practice, implicitly if not explicitly, through social and political and economic pressure. I do not argue that learning English was not appropriate. On the contrary. Like it or not, and we had no basis to make any judgments on that matter, we were Americans by virtue of having been born Americans and English was the common language of Americans. And there was a myth, a pervasive myth, to the effect that if only we learned to speak English well — and particularly without an accent — we would be welcomed into the American fellowship.

Sam Hayakawa and the official English movement folks notwith-standing, the true text was not our speech, but rather our names and our appearance, for we would always have an accent, however perfect our pronunciation, however excellent our enunciation, however divine our diction. That accent would be heard in our pigmentation, our physiognomy, our names. We were, in short, the *other.*

Being the *other* involves contradictory phenomena. On the one hand being the *other* frequently means being invisible. Ralph Ellison wrote eloquently about that experience in his magisterial novel, *Invisible Man.* On the other hand, being the *other* sometimes involves sticking out like a sore thumb. What is she/he doing here?

For some of us being the *other* is only annoying; for others it is debilitating; for still others it is damning. Many try to flee otherness by taking on protective colorations that provide invisibility, whether of dress or speech or manner or name. Only a fortunate few succeed. For the majority of us otherness is permanently sealed by physical appearance. For the rest, otherness is betrayed by ways of being, speaking, or doing.

The first half of my life I spent downplaying the significance and 10 consequences of otherness. The second half has seen me wrestling to understand its complex and deeply ingrained realities; striving to fathom why otherness denies us a voice or visibility or validity in American society and its institutions; struggling to make otherness familiar, reasonable, even normal to my fellow Americans.

I spoke earlier of another phenomenon that I am a part of: that of being a missing person. Growing up in northern New Mexico I had only a slight sense of us being missing persons. *Hispanos,* as we called (and call) ourselves in New Mexico, were very much a part of the fabric of the society, and there were *hispano* professionals every-where about me: doctors, lawyers, schoolteachers, and administrators. My people owned businesses, ran organizations, and were both appointed and elected public officials.

My awareness of our absence from the larger institutional life of the society became sharper when I went off to college, but even then it was attenuated by the circumstances of history and geography. The demography of Albuquerque still strongly reflected its historical and cultural origins, despite the influx of Midwesterners and East-erners. Moreover, many of my classmates at the University of New Mexico were *hispanos,* and even some of my professors. I thought that would obtain at UCLA, where I began graduate studies in 1960. Los Angeles had a very large Mexican population and that popula-tion was visible even in and around Westwood and on the campus.

Many of the groundskeepers and food-service personnel at UCLA were Mexican. But Mexican-American students were few and mostly invisible, and I do not recall seeing or knowing a single Mexican-American (or, for that matter, African-American, Asian, or American Indian) professional on the staff or faculty of that institution during the five years I was there. Needless to say, people like me were not present in any capacity at Dartmouth College, the site of my first teaching appointment, and of course were not even part of the institutional or individual mind-set. I knew then that we — a we that had come to encompass American Indians, Asian-Americans, African-Americans, Puerto Ricans, and women — were truly missing persons in American institutional life.

Over the past three decades the *de jure* and *de facto* types of segregation that have historically characterized American institutions have been under assault. As a consequence, minorities and women have become part of American institutional life. Although there are still many areas where we are not to be found, the missing persons phenomenon is not as pervasive as it once was. However, the presence of the *other,* particularly minorities, in institutions and in institutional life resembles what we call in Spanish a *flor de tierra* (a surface phenomenon): we are spare plants whose roots do not go deep, vulnerable to inclemencies of an economic, or political, or social, nature.

Our entrance into and our status in institutional life are not unlike a scenario set forth by my grandmother's pastor when she informed him that she and her family were leaving their mountain village to relocate to the Rio Grande Valley. When he asked her to promise that she would remain true to the faith and continue to involve herself in it, she asked why he thought she would do otherwise. "Doña Trinidad," he told her, "in the Valley there is no Spanish church. There is only an American church." "But," she protested, "I read and speak English and would be able to worship there." The pastor responded, "It is possible that they will not admit you. And that is why I want you to promise me that you are going to go to church. Because if they don't let you in through the front door, I want you to go in through the back door. And if you can't get in through the back door, go in the side door. And if you are unable to enter through the side door I want you to go in through the window. What is important is that you enter and stay."

Some of us entered institutional life through the front door; others through the back door; and still others through side doors. Many, if not most of us, came in through windows, and continue to come in through windows. Of those who entered through the front door, 15 some never made it past the lobby; others were ushered into corners and niches. Those who entered through back and side doors inevitably have remained in back and side rooms. And those who entered through windows found enclosures built around them. For, despite the lip service given to the goal of the integration of minorities into institutional life, what has frequently occurred instead is ghettoization, marginalization, isolation.

Not only have the entry points been limited, but in addition the dynamics have been singularly conflictive. Gaining entry and its corollary, gaining space, have frequently come as a consequence of demands made on institutions and institutional officers. Rather than entering institutions more or less passively, minorities have of necessity entered them actively, even aggressively. Rather than waiting to receive, they have demanded. Institutional relations have thus been adversarial, infused with specific and generalized tensions.

The nature of the entrance and the nature of the space occupied have greatly influenced the view and attitude of the majority population within those institutions. All of us are put into the same box; that is, no matter what the individual reality, the assessment of the individual is inevitably conditioned by a perception that is held of the class. Whatever our history, whatever our record, whatever our validations, whatever our accomplishments, by and large we are perceived unidimensionally and dealt with accordingly. I remember an experience I had in this regard, atypical only in its explicitness. A few years ago I allowed myself to be persuaded to seek the presidency of a well-known state university. I was invited for an interview and presented myself before the selection committee, which included members of the board of trustees. The opening question of that brief but memorable interview was directed at me by a member of that august body. "Dr. Madrid," he asked, "why does a one-dimensional person like you think he can be the president of a multidimensional institution like ours?"

Over the past four decades America's demography has undergone significant changes. Since 1965 the principal demographic growth we have experienced in the United States has been of peoples whose national origins are non-European. This population growth has occurred both through birth and through immigration. A few years ago discussion of the national birthrate had a scare dimension: the high — "inordinately high" — birthrate of the Hispanic population. The popular discourse was informed by words such as "breeding." Several years later, as a consequence of careful tracking by government agencies, we now know that what has happened is that the birthrate of the majority population has decreased. When viewed historically and comparatively, the minority populations (for the most part) have also had a decline in birthrate, but not one as great as that of the majority.

There are additional demographic changes that should give us something to think about. African-Americans are now to be found in significant numbers in every major urban center in the nation. Hispanic-Americans now number over 15 million people, and although they are a regionally concentrated (and highly urbanized) population, there is a Hispanic community in almost every major urban center of the United States. American Indians, heretofore a small and rural population, are increasingly more numerous and urban. The Asian-American population, which has historically consisted of small and concentrated communities of Chinese-, Filipino-, and Japanese-Americans, has doubled over the past decade, its complexion changed by the addition of Cambodians, Koreans, Hmongs, Vietnamese, et al.

Prior to the Immigration Act of 1965, 69 percent of immigration   20 was from Europe. By far the largest number of immigrants to the United States since 1965 have been from the Americas and from Asia: 34 percent are from Asia; another 34 percent are from Central and South America; 16 percent are from Europe; 10 percent are from the Caribbean; the remaining 6 percent are from other continents and Canada. As was the case with previous immigration waves, the current one consists principally of young people: 60 percent are between the ages of 16 and 44. Thus, for the next few decades, we will continue to see a growth in the percentage of non-European-origin Americans as compared to European-Americans.

To sum up, we now live in one of the most demographically diverse nations in the world, and one that is increasingly more so.

During the same period social and economic change seems to have accelerated. Who would have imagined at mid-century that the prototypical middle-class family (working husband, wife as homemaker, two children) would for all intents and purposes disappear? Who could have anticipated the rise in teenage pregnancies, children in poverty, drug use? Who among us understood the implications of an aging population?

We live in an age of continuous and intense change, a world in which what held true yesterday does not today, and certainly will not tomorrow. What change does, moreover, is bring about even more change. The only constant we have at this point in our national development is change. And change is threatening. The older we get the more likely we are to be anxious about change, and the greater our desire to maintain the status quo.

Evident in our public life is a fear of change, whether economic or moral. Some who fear change are responsive to the call of economic protectionism, others to the message of moral protectionism. Parenthetically, I have referred to the movement to require more of students without in turn giving them more as academic protectionism. And the pronouncements of E. D. Hirsch and Allan Bloom are, I believe, informed by intellectual protectionism. Much more serious, however, is the dark side of the populism which underlies this evergoing protectionism — the resentment of the *other*. An excellent and fascinating example of that aspect of populism is the cry for linguistic protectionism — for making English the official language of the United States. And who among us is unaware of the tensions that underlie immigration reform, of the underside of demographic protectionism?

A matter of increasing concern is whether this new protectionism, and the mistrust of the *other* which accompanies it, is not making more significant inroads than we have supposed in higher education. Specifically, I wish to discuss the question of whether a goal (quality) and a reality (demographic diversity) have been erroneously placed in conflict, and, if so, what problems this perception of conflict might present. 25

As part of my scholarship I turn to dictionaries for both origins and meanings of words. Quality, according to the *Oxford English Dictionary,* has multiple meanings. One set defines quality as being an essential character, a distinctive and inherent feature. A second describes it as a degree of excellence, of conformity to standards, as superiority, in kind. A third makes reference to social status, particularly to persons of high social status. A fourth talks about quality as being a special or distinguishing attribute, as being a desirable trait. Quality is highly desirable in both principle and practice. We all aspire to it in our own person, in our experiences, in our acquisitions and products, and of course we all want to be associated with people and operations of quality.

But let us move away from the various dictionary meanings of the word and to our own sense of what it represents and of how we feel about it. First of all we consider quality to be finite; that is, it is limited with respect to quantity; it has very few manifestations; it is not widely distributed. I have it and you have it, but they don't. We associated quality with homogeneity, with uniformity, with standardization, with order, regularity, neatness. All too often we equate it with smoothness, glibness, slickness, elegance. Certainly it is always expensive. We tend to identify it with those who lead, with the rich and famous. And, when you come right down to it, it's inherent. Either you've got it or you ain't.

Diversity, from the Latin *divertere,* meaning to turn aside, to go different ways, to differ, is the condition of being different or having differences, is an instance of being different. Its companion word, diverse, means differing, unlike, distinct; having or capable of having various forms; composed of unlike or distinct elements. Diversity is lack of standardization, of regularity, or orderliness, homogeneity, conformity, uniformity. Diversity introduces complications, is difficult to organize, is troublesome to manage, is problematical. Diversity is irregular, disorderly, uneven, rough. The way we use the word diversity gives us away. Something is too diverse, is extremely diverse. We want a little diversity.

When we talk about diversity, we are talking about the *other,* whatever that other might be: someone of a different gender, race, class, national origin; somebody at a greater or lesser distance from the norm; someone outside the set; someone who possesses a different set of characteristics, features, or attributes; someone who does not fall within the taxonomies we use daily and with which we are comfortable; someone who does not fit into the mental configurations that give our lives order and meaning.

In short, diversity is desirable only in principle, not in practice. 30 Long live diversity . . . as long as it conforms to my standards, my mind set, my view of life, my sense of order. We desire, we like, we admire diversity, not unlike the way the French (and others) appreciate women; that is, *Vive la différence! —* as long as it stays in its place.

What I find paradoxical about and lacking in this debate is that diversity is the natural order of things. Evolution produces diversity. Margaret Visser, writing about food in her latest book, *Much Depends on Dinner,* makes an eloquent statement in this regard:

> Machines like, demand, and produce uniformity. But nature loathes it: her strength lies in multiplicity and in differences. Sameness in biology means fewer possibilities and therefore weakness.

The United States, by its very nature, by its very development, is the essence of diversity. It is diverse in its geography, population, institutions, technology; its social, cultural, and intellectual modes.

It is a society that at its best does not consider quality to be monolithic in form or finite in quantity, or to be inherent in class. Quality in our society proceeds in large measure out of the stimulus of diverse modes of thinking and acting; out of the creativity made possible by the different ways in which we approach things; out of diversion from paths or modes hallowed by tradition.

One of the principal strengths of our society is its ability to address, on a continuing and substantive basis, the real economic, political, and social problems that have faced and continue to face us. What makes the United States so attractive to immigrants is the protections and opportunities it offers; what keeps our society together is tolerance for cultural, religious, social, political, and even linguistic difference; what makes us a unique, dynamic, and extraordinary nation is the power and creativity of our diversity.

The true history of the United States is one of struggle against intolerance, against oppression, against xenophobia, against those forces that have prohibited persons from participating in the larger life of the society on the basis of their race, their gender, their religion, their national origin, their linguistic and cultural background. These phenomena are not consigned to the past. They remain with us and frequently take on virulent dimensions.

If you believe, as I do, that the well-being of a society is directly 35 related to the degree and extent to which all of its citizens participate in its institutions, then you will have to agree that we have a challenge before us. In view of the extraordinary changes that are taking place in our society we need to take up the struggle again, irritating, grating, troublesome, unfashionable, unpleasant as it is. As educated and educator members of this society we have a special responsibility for ensuring that all American institutions, not just our elementary and secondary schools, our juvenile halls, or our jails, reflect the diversity of our society. Not to do so is to risk greater alienation on the part of a growing segment of our society; is to risk increased social tension in an already conflictive world; and, ultimately, is to risk the survival of a range of institutions that, for all their defects and deficiencies, provide us the opportunity and the freedom to improve our individual and collective lot.

Let me urge you to reflect on these two words — quality and diversity — and on the mental sets and behaviors that flow out of them. And let me urge you further to struggle against the notion that quality is finite in quantity, limited in its manifestations, or is restricted by considerations of class, gender, race, or national origin; or that quality manifests itself only in leaders and not in followers, in managers and not in workers, in breeders and not in drones; or that it has to be associated with verbal agility or elegance of personal style; or that it cannot be seeded, nurtured, or developed.

Because diversity — the *other* — is among us, will define and determine our lives in ways that we still do not fully appreciate, whether that other is women (no longer bound by tradition, house, and family); or Asians, African-Americans, Indians, and Hispanics (no longer invisible, regional, or marginal); or our newest immigrants (no longer distant, exotic, alien). Given the changing profile of America, will we come to terms with diversity in our personal and professional lives? Will we begin to recognize the diverse forms that quality can take? If so, we will thus initiate the process of making quality limitless in its manifestations, infinite in quantity, unrestricted with respect to its origins, and more importantly, virulently contagious.

I hope we will. And that we will further join together to expand — not to close — the circle.

THE INVOLVED READER

1 Why does Madrid say he does not "fit those mental sets that define America and Americans"? What sets him apart? What has been Madrid's personal experience with being the "other"?

2 What do you learn about the history of the *americanos* in his part of the country and their relationship with people like Madrid?

3 As seen by Madrid, what was the traditional role of the schools in Americanizing those who are different? What was the dominant "myth"? How did it clash with reality?

4 What contradictory impressions does Madrid report of the movement away from segregation in higher education? To what extent have women and minorities become "part of American institutional life"?

5 What demographic changes does Madrid emphasize in our society? Where does he see evidence of the "fear of change" on the part of the majority? Why does he see diversity as a major strength of this country?

TALKING, THINKING, WRITING

6 Can you empathize with the feelings of the outsider? Have your own experiences taught you something about what it means to be "different"?

7 Do you think our society is moving forward to a true acceptance of diversity? Or do you think we are headed toward increasing retreat into separate groups, "ghettoization," and "isolation"?

COLLABORATIVE PROJECTS

8 What are the pros and cons of making English the official language of the United States? What is involved in the English-only controversy?

MAKING CONNECTIONS

9 Do Schlesinger's and Madrid's perspectives on diversity reflect irreconcilable differences between an establishment and a minority point of view? Do they show a gulf between the insider's and the outsider's point of view?

Backlash: Blame It on Feminism

SUSAN FALUDI

*What progress have women made toward equality? Is backlash
politics reversing gains made by the women's movement? Susan Faludi asked these questions in her widely debated* Backlash: The Undeclared War Against American Women *(1991). Faludi is a Pulitzer
Prize–winning reporter who was the editor of both her high school
and college newspapers. She has written for publications including
the* Wall Street Journal, Ms. *magazine, and* Mother Jones. *At Harvard, she wrote a pioneering article about sexual harassment that
helped establish her reputation as a crusading journalist. In the words
of one reviewer, she buttresses her eye-opening analyses with a "relentless presentation of facts, figures, polls, and interviews" (Walecia
Konrad).* Backlash *abounds with well-documented horror stories of
contemptuous treatment of women by male corporate management,
health authorities, and government officials. Faludi has said that
the book is not about man-hating, but it is "very large, so it can be
thrown at misogynists." The following pages are from Faludi's introduction to her book.*

To be a woman in America at the close of the 20th century — what
good fortune. That's what we keep hearing, anyway. The barricades
have fallen, politicians assure us. Women have "made it," Madison
Avenue cheers. Women's fight for equality has "largely been won,"
Time magazine announces. Enroll at any university, join any law
firm, apply for credit at any bank. Women have so many opportunities now, corporate leaders say, that we don't really need equal opportunity policies. Women are so equal now, lawmakers say, that
we no longer need an Equal Rights Amendment. Women have "so
much," former President Ronald Reagan says, that the White House
no longer needs to appoint them to higher office. Even American
Express ads are saluting a woman's freedom to charge it. At last,
women have received their full citizenship papers.

And yet . . .

Behind this celebration of the American woman's victory, behind
the news, cheerfully and endlessly repeated, that the struggle for
women's rights is won, another message flashes. You may be free
and equal now, it says to women, but you have never been more
miserable.

This bulletin of despair is posted everywhere — at the newsstand, on the TV set, at the movies, in advertisements and doctors' offices and academic journals. Professional women are suffering "burnout" and succumbing to an "infertility epidemic." Single women are grieving from a "man shortage." The *New York Times* reports: Childless women are "depressed and confused" and their ranks are swelling. *Newsweek* says: Unwed women are "hysterical" and crumbling under a "profound crisis of confidence." The health advice manuals inform: High-powered career women are stricken with unprecedented outbreaks of "stress-induced disorders," hair loss, bad nerves, alcoholism, and even heart attacks. The psychology books advise: Independent women's loneliness represents "a major mental health problem today." Even founding feminist Betty Friedan has been spreading the word: she warns that women now suffer from a new identity crisis and "new 'problems that have no name.'"

How can American women be in so much trouble at the same time that they are supposed to be so blessed? If the status of women has never been higher, why is their emotional state so low? If women got what they asked for, what could possibly be the matter now?

The prevailing wisdom of the past decade has supported one, and only one, answer to this riddle: it must be all that equality that's causing all that pain. Women are unhappy precisely *because* they are free. Women are enslaved by their own liberation. They have grabbed at the gold ring of independence, only to miss the one ring that really matters. They have gained control of their fertility, only to destroy it. They have pursued their own professional dreams — and lost out on the greatest female adventure. The women's movement, as we are told time and again, has proved women's own worst enemy.

"In dispensing its spoils, women's liberation has given my generation high incomes, our own cigarette, the option of single parenthood, rape crisis centers, personal lines of credit, free love, and female gynecologists," Mona Charen, a young law student, writes in the *National Review,* in an article titled "The Feminist Mistake." "In return it has effectively robbed us of one thing upon which the happiness of most women rests — men." The *National Review* is a conservative publication, but such charges against the women's movement are not confined to its pages. "Our generation was the human sacrifice" to the women's movement, *Los Angeles Times* feature writer Elizabeth Mehren contends in a *Time* cover story. Baby-boom women like her, she says, have been duped by feminism: "We believed the rhetoric." In *Newsweek,* writer Kay Ebeling dubs feminism "the Great Experiment That Failed" and asserts "women in my generation, its perpetrators, are the casualties." Even the beauty magazines are saying it: *Harper's Bazaar* accuses the women's movement of having "lost us [women] ground instead of gaining it."

In the last decade, publications from the *New York Times* to *Vanity Fair* to the *Nation* have issued a steady stream of indictments against the women's movement, with such headlines as WHEN FEMINISM FAILED or THE AWFUL TRUTH ABOUT WOMEN'S LIB. They hold the campaign for women's equality responsible for nearly every woe besetting women, from mental depression to meager savings accounts, from teenage suicides to eating disorders to bad complexions. The "Today" show says women's liberation is to blame for bag ladies. A guest columnist in the *Baltimore Sun* even proposes that feminists produced the rise in slasher movies. By making the "violence" of abortion more acceptable, the author reasons, women's rights activists made it all right to show graphic murders on screen.

At the same time, other outlets of popular culture have been forging the same connection: in Hollywood films, of which *Fatal Attraction* is only the most famous, emancipated women with condominiums of their own slink wild-eyed between bare walls, paying for their liberty with an empty bed, a barren womb. "My biological clock is ticking so loud it keeps me awake at night," Sally Field cries in the film *Surrender,* as, in an all too common transformation in the cinema of the '80s, an actress who once played scrappy working heroines is now showcased groveling for a groom. In prime-time television shows, from "thirtysomething" to "Family Man," single, professional, and feminist women are humiliated, turned into harpies, or hit by nervous breakdowns; the wise ones recant their independent ways by the closing sequence. In popular novels, from Gail Parent's *A Sign of the Eighties* to Stephen King's *Misery,* unwed women shrink to sniveling spinsters or inflate to fire-breathing she-devils; renouncing all aspirations but marriage, they beg for wedding bands from strangers or swing sledgehammers at reluctant bachelors. We "blew it by waiting," a typically remorseful careerist sobs in Freda Bright's *Singular Women;* she and her sister professionals are "condemned to be childless forever." Even Erica Jong's high-flying independent heroine literally crashes by the end of the decade, as the author supplants *Fear of Flying's* saucy Isadora Wing, a symbol of female sexual emancipation in the '70s, with an embittered careerist-turned-recovering-"co-dependent" in *Any Woman's Blues* — a book that is intended, as the narrator bluntly states, "to demonstrate what a deadend the so-called sexual revolution had become, and how desperate so-called free women were in the last few years of our decadent epoch."

Popular psychology manuals peddle the same diagnosis for con-   10
temporary female distress. "Feminism, having promised her a
stronger sense of her own identity, has given her little more than an
identity *crisis*," the best-selling advice manual *Being a Woman* asserts. The authors of the era's self-help classic *Smart Women/Foolish
Choices* proclaim that women's distress was "an unfortunate consequence of feminism," because "it created a myth among women
that the apex of self-realization could be achieved only through autonomy, independence, and career." . . .

Finally, some "liberated" women themselves have joined the lam-
entations. In confessional accounts, works that invariably receive a
hearty greeting from the publishing industry, "recovering Super-
women" tell all. In *The Cost of Loving: Women and the New Fear of
Intimacy*, Megan Marshall, a Harvard-pedigreed writer, asserts that
the feminist "Myth of Independence" has turned her generation into
unloved and unhappy fast-trackers, "dehumanized" by careers and
"uncertain of their gender identity." Other diaries of mad Super-
women charge that "the hard-core feminist viewpoint," as one of
them put it, has relegated educated executive achievers to solitary
nights of frozen dinners and closet drinking. The triumph of equality,
they report, has merely given women hives, stomach cramps, eye-
twitching disorders, even comas.

But what "equality" are all these authorities talking about?

If American women are so equal, why do they represent two-
thirds of all poor adults? Why are nearly 75 percent of full-time working women making less than $20,000 a year, nearly double the male
rate? Why are they still far more likely than men to live in poor housing and receive no health insurance, and twice as likely to draw no
pension? Why does the average working woman's salary still lag as
far behind the average man's as it did twenty years ago? Why does
the average female college graduate today earn less than a man with
no more than a high school diploma (just as she did in the '50s) —
and why does the average female high school graduate today earn
less than a male high school dropout? Why do American women, in
fact, face one of the worst gender-based pay gaps in the developed
world?

If women have "made it," then why are nearly 80 percent of working women still stuck in traditional "female" jobs — as secretaries,
administrative "support" workers and salesclerks? And, conversely,
why are they less than 8 percent of all federal and state judges, less
than 6 percent of all law partners, and less than one half of 1 percent
of top corporate managers? Why are there only three female state
governors, two female U.S. senators, and two Fortune 500 chief ex-

ecutives? Why are only nineteen of the four thousand corporate
officers and directors women — and why do more than half the
boards of Fortune companies still lack even one female member?

If women "have it all," then why don't they have the most basic   15
requirements to achieve equality in the work force? Unlike virtually
all other industrialized nations, the U.S. government still has no
family-leave and child care programs — and more than 99 percent
of American private employers don't offer child care either. Though
business leaders say they are aware of and deplore sex discrimination, corporate America has yet to make an honest effort toward
eradicating it. In a 1990 national poll of chief executives at Fortune
1000 companies, more than 80 percent acknowledged that discrimination impedes female employees' progress — yet, less than 1 percent of these same companies regarded *remedying* sex discrimination as a goal that their personnel departments should pursue. In
fact, when the companies' human resource officers were asked to rate
their department's priorities, women's advancement ranked last.

If women are so "free," why are their reproductive freedoms in
greater jeopardy today than a decade earlier? Why do women who
want to postpone childbearing now have fewer options than ten
years ago? The availability of different forms of contraception has
declined, research for new birth control has virtually halted, new
laws restricting abortion — or even *information* about abortion —
for young and poor women have been passed, and the U.S. Supreme
Court has shown little ardor in defending the right it granted in 1973.

Nor is women's struggle for equal education over; as a 1989 study
found, three-fourths of all high schools still violate the federal law
banning sex discrimination in education. In colleges, undergraduate
women receive only 70 percent of the aid undergraduate men get in
grants and work-study jobs — and women's sports programs receive
a pittance compared with men's. A review of state equal-education
laws in the late '80s found that only thirteen states had adopted the
minimum provisions required by the federal Title IX law — and only
seven states had anti-discrimination regulations that covered all
education levels.

Nor do women enjoy equality in their own homes, where they still
shoulder 70 percent of the household duties — and the only major
change in the last fifteen years is that now middle-class men *think*
they do more around the house. (In fact, a national poll finds the
ranks of women saying their husbands share equally in child care
shrunk to 31 percent in 1987 from 40 percent three years earlier.)
Furthermore, in thirty states, it is still generally legal for husbands to
rape their wives; and only ten states have laws mandating arrest for

domestic violence — even though battering was the leading cause of injury of women in the late '80s. Women who have no other option but to flee find that isn't much of an alternative either. Federal funding for battered women's shelters has been withheld and one third of the 1 million battered women who seek emergency shelter each year can find none. Blows from men contributed far more to the rising numbers of "bag ladies" than the ill effects of feminism. In the '80s, almost half of all homeless women (the fastest growing segment of the homeless) were refugees of domestic violence.

The word may be that women have been "liberated," but women themselves seem to feel otherwise. Repeatedly in national surveys, majorities of women say they are still far from equality. Nearly 70 percent of women polled by the *New York Times* in 1989 said the movement for women's rights had only just begun. Most women in the 1990 Virginia Slims opinion poll agreed with the statement that conditions for their sex in American society had improved "a little, not a lot." In poll after poll in the decade, overwhelming majorities of women said they needed equal pay and equal job opportunities, they needed an Equal Rights Amendment, they needed the right to an abortion without government interference, they needed a federal law guaranteeing maternity leave, they needed decent child care services. They have none of these. So how exactly how have we "won" the war for women's rights?

Seen against this background, the much ballyhooed claim that 20 feminism is responsible for making women miserable becomes absurd — and irrelevant. As we shall see in the chapters to follow, the afflictions ascribed to feminism are all myths. From "the man shortage" to "the infertility epidemic" to "female burnout" to "toxic day care," these so-called female crises have had their origins not in the actual conditions of women's lives but rather in a closed system that starts and ends in the media, popular culture, and advertising — an endless feedback loop that perpetuates and exaggerates its own false images of womanhood.

Women themselves don't single out the women's movement as the source of their misery. To the contrary, in national surveys 75 to 95 percent of women credit the feminist campaign with *improving* their lives, and a similar proportion say that the women's movement should keep pushing for change. Less than 8 percent think the women's movement might have actually made their lot worse.

What actually is troubling the American female population, then? If the many ponderers of the Woman Question really wanted to know, they might have asked their subjects. In public opinion surveys, women consistently rank their own *inequality,* at work and at home, among their most urgent concerns. Over and over, women complain to pollsters about a lack of economic, not marital, opportunities; they protest that working men, not working women, fail to spend time in the nursery and the kitchen. The Roper Organization's survey analysts find that men's opposition to equality is "a major cause of resentment and stress" and "a major irritant for most women today." It is justice for their gender, not wedding rings and bassinets, that women believe to be in desperately short supply. When the *New York Times* polled women in 1989 about "the most important problem facing women today," job discrimination was the overwhelming winner; none of the crises the media and popular culture had so assiduously promoted even made the charts. In the 1990 Virginia Slims poll, women were most upset by their lack of money, followed by the refusal of their men to shoulder child care and domestic duties. By contrast, when the women were asked where the quest for a husband or the desire to hold a "less pressured" job or to stay at home ranked on their list of concerns, they placed them at the bottom.

As the last decade ran its course, women's unhappiness with inequality only mounted. In national polls, the ranks of women protesting discriminatory treatment in business, political, and personal life climbed sharply. The proportion of women complaining of unequal employment opportunities jumped more than ten points from the '70s, and the number of women complaining of unequal barriers to job advancement climbed even higher. By the end of the decade, 80 percent to 95 percent of women said they suffered from job discrimination and unequal pay. Sex discrimination charges filed with the Equal Employment Opportunity Commission rose nearly 25 percent in the Reagan years, and charges of general harassment directed at working women more than doubled. In the decade, complaints of sexual harassment nearly doubled. At home, a much increased proportion of women complained to pollsters of male mistreatment, unequal relationships, and male efforts to, in the words of the Virginia Slims poll, "keep women down." The share of women in the Roper surveys who agreed that men were "basically kind, gentle, and thoughtful" fell from almost 70 percent in 1970 to 50 percent by 1990. And outside their homes, women felt more threatened, too: in the 1990 Virginia Slims poll, 72 percent of women said they felt "more afraid and uneasy on the streets today" than they did a few years ago. Lest this be attributed only to a general rise in criminal activity, by contrast only 49 percent of men felt this way.

While the women's movement has certainly made women more

cognizant of their own inequality, the rising chorus of female protest shouldn't be written off as feminist-induced "oversensitivity." The monitors that serve to track slippage in women's status have been working overtime since the early '80s. Government and private surveys are showing that women's already vast representation in the lowliest occupations is rising, their tiny presence in higher-paying trade and craft jobs stalled or backsliding, their minuscule representation in upper management posts stagnant or falling, and their pay dropping in the very occupations where they have made the most "progress." . . .

The alarms aren't just going off in the work force. In national politics, the already small numbers of women in both elective posts and political appointments fell during the '80s. In private life, the average amount that a divorced man paid in child support fell by about 25 percent from the late '70s to the mid-'80s (to a mere $140 a month). Domestic-violence shelters recorded a more than 100 percent increase in the numbers of women taking refuge in their quarters between 1983 and 1987. And government records chronicled a spectacular rise in sexual violence against women. Reported rapes more than doubled from the early '70s — at nearly twice the rate of all other violent crimes and four times the overall crime rate in the United States. While the homicide rate declined, sex-related murders rose 160 percent between 1976 and 1984. And these murders weren't simply the random, impersonal by-product of a violent society; at least one-third of the women were killed by their husbands or boyfriends, and the majority of that group were murdered just after declaring their independence in the most intimate manner — by filing for divorce and leaving home.

By the end of the decade, women were starting to tell pollsters that they feared their sex's social status was once again beginning to slip. They believed they were facing an "erosion of respect," as the 1990 Virginia Slims poll summed up the sentiment. After years in which an increasing percentage of women had said their status had improved from a decade earlier, the proportion suddenly shrunk by 5 percent in the last half of the '80s, the Roper Organization reported. And it fell most sharply among women in their thirties — the age group most targeted by the media and advertisers — dropping between about ten percentage points between 1985 and 1990. Some women began to piece the picture together. In the 1989 *New York Times* poll, more than half of black women and one-fourth of white women put it into words. They told pollsters they believed men were now trying to retract the gains women had made in the last twenty

25

years. "I wanted more autonomy," was how one woman, a thirty-seven-year-old nurse, put it. And her estranged husband "wanted to take it away."

The truth is that the last decade has seen a powerful counter-assault on women's rights, a backlash, an attempt to retract the handful of small and hard-won victories that the feminist movement did manage to win for women. This counterassault is largely insidious: in a kind of pop-culture version of the Big Lie, it stands the truth boldly on its head and proclaims that the very steps that have elevated women's position have actually led to their downfall.

The backlash is at once sophisticated and banal, deceptively "progressive" and proudly backward. It deploys both the "new" findings of "scientific research" and the dime-store moralism of yesteryear: it turns into media sound bites both the big pronouncements of pop-psych trend-watchers and the frenzied rhetoric of New Right preachers. The backlash has succeeded in framing virtually the whole issue of women's rights in its own language. Just as Reaganism shifted political discourse far to the right and demonized liberalism, so the backlash convinced the public that women's "liberation" was the true contemporary American scourge — the source of an endless laundry list of personal, social, and economic problems.

But what has made women unhappy in the last decade is not their "equality" — which they don't yet have — but the rising pressure to halt, and even reverse, women's quest for that equality. The "man shortage" and the "infertility epidemic" are not the price of liberation; in fact, they do not even exist. But these chimeras are the chisels of a society-wide backlash. They are part of a relentless whittling-down process — much of it amounting to outright propaganda — that has served to stir women's private anxieties and break their political wills. Identifying feminism as women's enemy only furthers the ends of a backlash against women's equality, simultaneously deflecting attention from the backlash's central role and recruiting women to attack their own cause.

THE INVOLVED READER

1   According to Faludi, what conflicting messages does society send to today's women? What negative images of independent women or single women did Faludi observe in popular culture and pop psychology?

2   What claims does Faludi make about the role of women in the workplace? Has the economic status of women changed?

3   What does Faludi say on issues like reproductive freedom and equality of education?

4 What, according to the author, is the current status of women in the family, in the home, in private life? Has it changed for the better?

5 As contrasted with media "myths," what, according to Faludi, are the actual concerns and opinions of American women?

6 According to Faludi, what are key causes and results of the backlash against women?

TALKING, THINKING, WRITING

7 Where do you agree with Faludi, and why? Where do you disagree with her, and why?

8 Alice Walker said about Faludi's book, "The backlash against women is real. This is the book we need to help us understand it, to struggle through the battle fatigue and to keep going." Do you think there has been a return to old-fashioned sexism in advertising, politics, or popular culture?

COLLABORATIVE PROJECTS

9 You may want to help your group devise a questionnaire or other polling method to chart male and female class members' reactions to key points in Faludi's essay.

short story

Dialectic

SIMA RABINOWITZ

Is being torn between conflicting impulses a sign of immaturity?
Imaginative literature is open to contradictions. It recognizes the
mixed feelings and divided loyalties that complicate human rela-
tionships. It goes beyond the loving sentiments of greeting cards to
explore the love/hate relationships in which we become entangled
with real people. It explores the private doubts of followers committed
officially to a party line or reigning ideology. The following story from
a recent collection of short shorts focuses on the conflicting impulses
that go through the speaker's mind. Do you think the person speaking
to you in the story is exceptionally indecisive or confused?

First there's what you believe. Then there's what you need. You
believe that everyone should share equally, as much as her capacity
allows, in the labor at hand. The same folks should make the decision, write it down, copy, collate, distribute, clean it up. What you
need is not to be the only one in the back with the student interns
and newly-hired secretarial assistant stapling, while your colleagues
chat over coffee in the other room.

First there's what you believe. And then there's what you need.
You believe that assuaging hurt feelings (this is the third time the
story's been rejected) with two-year-old scotch which you find in a
flash behind the baking powder on the second shelf is unhealthy and
unwise. Alcohol is a killer. You are sure of that. What you need is a
short drink, a long sleep, and a memory that rivals either or both.

First there's what you believe. Then, of course, there's what you
need. You believe, are certain, in fact, that air conditioning is harmful to the atmosphere, or stratosphere, or to some layer or other of
the earth, air, sea. It's not natural to change what is naturally hot into
what is unnaturally cold and expect that not to matter somehow,
somewhere among the elements. What you need, are certain, in fact,
you will collapse or nearly without, is cool air, right now, full blast,
because the dew point is seventy percent, and the humidity is seventy percent, and the forecast is one hundred percent miserable.

First there's what you believe. Then there's what you need. You
believe fervently that the lottery, despite good intentions, is wasteful, criminal, politically unacceptable. It isn't right to con and cajole
people who can ill afford it into spending their paltry wages on a

chance as remote as those imaginary millions. And certainly, at the very least, there ought to be more winners, smaller prizes. But what you need is to win that two million, tonight at the latest, so that you can quit your job, buy a better typewriter, and write the great American (feminist) novel before your fortieth birthday.

What you believe, and have always said, is that people should be 5 autonomous, free, separate, whole, independent. You know this is true. What you need is your lover's breath against your neck, her arms around yours.

What you believe is that people should not give too much of themselves away. It's important to be cautious, judicious, even guarded. What you need to say, though, is that for the moment you are sitting at a mediocre typewriter, next to an exquisite, albeit artificial arctic blast, sipping stale scotch, eyeing the stack of unpromising lottery ticket stubs on the nightstand, planning to call your lover in the morning, as soon as enough time has gone by to believe you are autonomous, free, separate, whole, independent and patient. Very patient.

THE INVOLVED READER

1 How does the concept of "dialectic" help the writer organize this short short?

2 Which of the contrasts between intellectual belief and personal need in this story become most real for you? Which to you represent choices that others are likely to encounter? (Which seem most and which least serious?) Argue one or two of the opposites with reasons and illustrations of your own.

TALKING, THINKING, WRITING

3 Do you think that in this story as a whole need wins out over belief?

4 Do you think that emotion is stronger than intellect?

poem

About the Elk and the Coyotes That Killed Her Calf

Stephen Dunn

When Charles Darwin formulated the theory of evolution through natural selection, what were the lessons for human behavior? Social Darwinists have concluded that, in order to ensure the survival of the fittest, human beings, like their animal cousins in the wild, have to be predatory and cunning. We have to be strong and relentless like the wolf and cunning as the fox. Their opponents have countered that the whole point of evolution has been for life to evolve to higher levels. Human beings have evolved to a stage where they can leave their animal ancestry behind. The poet dedicated the following poem to Richard Selzer, who has written extensively about the challenges presented to our usual optimistic view of the world by death and disease.

The coyotes know it's just
    a matter of time,
but the elk will not let them

have her calf. You describe
how they attack   5
and pull back, and how she goes on

repelling them, occasionally licking
    her calf's face,
until exhausted she turns

and gives it all up. So the elk,   10
    with her fierce
and futile resistance in which we

recognize something to admire,
    is held up
against the brilliant, wild   15

cunning of the coyotes.
    I love your sense
that the natural world stinks

and is beautiful and how important it is
    to have favorites.   20
Some part of us we'd like to believe

is essentially us, sides with the elk.
    Ah but tomorrow,
desperate, and night falling fast

and with a different sense of family . . .   25

THE INVOLVED READER

1 Is it true that we as human observers tend to side with the elk? Why? Does it depend? On what — gender, upbringing, world view?

2 Can you see the other side? What would you say in defense of the coyotes?

3 What does the poet mean when talking about the sense "that the natural world stinks / and is beautiful"?

TALKING, THINKING, WRITING

4 How important do you consider our animal heritage — nest building, the maternal instinct, marking off and defending your territory (the territorial imperative) — in human behavior?

5 If you were asked to choose an animal as your personal symbol, which would you choose and why?

The Writer's Tools 7

Using Outlines

Writers are always outlining — in their heads, on scraps of paper, or on the computer screen. They outline to impose some first preliminary order on their material. They outline to see how a project is shaping up. They are always fitting ideas or parts of an argument together the way a plumber fits together lengths of pipe. Outlines reveal the strategy of a paper the way an X-ray machine reveals the skeleton that holds an organism together. A good outline reveals the strengths and weaknesses of a paper, alerting you to apparent detours (or digressions) and blind alleys.

Outlines vary greatly — from a few tentative ideas jotted down to a detailed blueprint. For a major project, you may be expected to provide a formal outline with main divisions and subdivisions (or subsubdivisions) marching down the page.

Working Outlines

Sometimes writers are advised to set up an outline and then stick to it. This is not the way most writers work. They start with a rough plan, and by sketching it out on paper (or on the screen) they have a chance to see what is right with it and what is wrong with it. Until the end, an outline is by definition a **working outline**. It alerts you to what is missing. It allows you to check if major sections appear in the best or most logical order. It helps you do the reshuffling that is often part of meaningful revision.

Perhaps you or some of your friends have been reading promotional material from Greek organizations on your campus. Fraternities and sororities for a time were in decline. They had a reputation for being immature, bourgeois, and politically incorrect. Recently they seem to have made a comeback. Why? The following might be your first scratch outline:

> fraternities — bums or bum rap?
> drunken parties
> charges of date rape
> Greek events
> active social life

After talking to a few more people and reading several issues of your campus newspaper, you expand your outline like this:

> fraternities — bums or bum rap?
> drunken parties

charges of date rape
Greek events
active social life
advantages of group living
future business contacts
social service work

These entries suggest a scheme for a pro and con paper. You re-shuffle some of the entries and line up more clearly disadvantages and advantages, disincentives and incentives. The working outline guiding you in writing your first draft might look like this:

Return to Fraternity Row

fraternities — bums or bum rap?
comeback of Greek organizations
      — Greek events
      — coverage in campus newspaper
bad reputation and stereotypes
      — drunken parties
      — charges of date rape
      — *Animal House* movies
advantages of group living
      — active social life
      — future business contacts
      — social service work

Formal Outlines — Topic Outlines

Formal outlines show the exact structure of a paper, with main ideas and supporting ideas in place. With substantial writing proj-ects — grant proposals, research papers, or research reports — a formal outline may be required. The purpose is to give the reader a quick overview — but also to force the writer to think the organiza-tion of a project or a piece of writing through in every detail.

A widely used scheme for formal outlines uses Roman numerals (I, II, III), Arabic numerals (1, 2, 3), and capital and lowercase letters. For shorter papers, first-level heads (Roman numerals) and second-level subheads (capitals) will often be sufficient. For more elaborate papers, you may have to use third-level and fourth-level subheads as needed. Here is a schematized view of a **topic outline**, which charts each subtopic and subsubtopic of your paper:

Your Title Here

THESIS: Your thesis sentence appears here.

I. Roman numeral for first major division
   A. Capital for first subdivision
      1. Arabic numeral for third-level subhead
      2. Arabic numeral for third-level subhead
   B. Capital for second subdivision
      1. Arabic numeral for third-level subhead
         a. Lowercase for fourth-level subhead (if any)
         b. Lowercase for fourth-level subhead (if any)
      2. Arabic numeral for third-level subhead
II. Roman numeral for second major division
   A. Capital for first subdivision
      1. Arabic numeral for third-level subhead
         a. Lowercase for fourth-level subhead (if any)
         b. Lowercase for fourth-level subhead (if any)
      2. Arabic numeral for third-level subhead
   B. Capital for second subdivision
      1. Arabic numeral for third-level subhead
      2. Arabic numeral for third-level subhead
      3. Arabic numeral for third-level subhead
III. Roman numeral for third major division
     (and so on)

The following outline of a student paper uses third-level but not fourth-level heads:

Oedipus Lives

THESIS: Although the generation gap has become a cliché, the traditional
   conflict between parents and the next generation is as strong as ever.
I. The traditional generation gap
   A. Domineering fathers and rebellious sons
   B. Conformist mothers and independent daughters
II. Current sources of conflict
   A. Symbols of self-assertion
      1. Dress
      2. Hairstyle
      3. Music
   B. Choice of jobs or careers
   C. Choice of lifestyles
      1. Unmarried couples
      2. Single mothers
      3. Gays

Observe a few cautions when writing formal outlines:

• *Avoid single subdivisions.* If you have a subdivision A, you need a subdivision B (and maybe C and D). Otherwise, leave the main heading undivided.

• *Reconsider a long unsorted sequence of subheads.* A miscellaneous listing of "factors" as subheads from A to H may make your readers feel that they are getting lost in a maze of detail. Try to split up the list, maybe grouping together four of the subheads as "advantages," the remaining four as "disadvantages."

• *Consider using parallel wording to point up the connection between related ideas.* In a listing like the following, the reader has to shift grammatical gears in going from one entry to the next:

NONPARALLEL: I. Breaking the ice
   II. How to get acquainted
   III. A lasting relationship

Try making each entry run along similar grammatical lines:

PARALLEL: **A Natural History of Relationships**
   I. Breaking the ice
   II. Getting acquainted
   III. Cementing a relationship
   IV. Cooling off
   V. Drifting away

Formal Outlines — Sentence Outlines

In a **sentence outline,** you sum up in one complete sentence each what you have to say on every topic and subtopic. As a result, a sentence outline requires you to spell out your key ideas more completely than a topic outline does. The following sentence outline states the obstacles that in one writer's view have hindered women in their struggle for equal pay:

Why Women Earn Less Than Men

THESIS: While some traditional obstacles to equal pay are weakening, patterns of professional advancement will have to change before pay equity can be achieved.

I. Some traditional causes for the low earning power of women are weakening.
   A. Traditional assumptions about "men's work" and "woman's work" have been challenged in many fields, including police work, management, and medicine.

   B. Differences in educational opportunities for men and women are slowly disappearing.

   C. Traditional views of women as short-term employees are changing as many women spend most of their adult lives in the labor force.

II. Nevertheless, current patterns of professional advancement continue to work against women.

   A. In most occupations, the years between 25 and 35 are crucial to future success.

      1. Corporations identify promising candidates for management jobs.

      2. Academics and scientists are working toward advanced degrees.

      3. Yuppies try out a variety of jobs and develop networking skills.

   B. For many women, the years between 25 and 35 are still years where they may be absent from the labor force for extended periods or take part-time jobs because of family responsibilities.

III. For women to achieve true equity, society must revise its patterns of promotion and advancement to provide greater opportunities for women leaving and reentering the labor force.

WRITING WORKSHOP 3

The Interest Inventory

    The following interest inventory was adapted from a student paper. Sort out the entries and arrange them in a topic outline. Set up major headings and present them in an order that will seem logical to the reader. You may prefer to structure and outline an interest inventory of your own.

My Interests

volleyball
coffee dates
religious retreats
taking a friend to the movies
work to fight world hunger
long hikes
beach barbecues
vacation trips
fellowship meetings
swimming
social work
student government

I have wondered whether we might legitimately try to introduce some new test for the exclusion of the inessential. Suppose, for example, that we were permitted only to say something that we could grow eloquent about.   **KENNETH BURKE**

8
Persuading Your Reader

Writing to Persuade

How good are you at making others change their minds? How good are you at making them change their ways? When you are bent on persuasion, the effect your writing has on the reader becomes the number one consideration. You use the language of persuasion when you talk someone into giving you a job. You try to be persuasive when asking fellow students for their votes. Working with others, you test your powers of persuasion when you plead with them to do a better job. You may encounter the limits of persuasion when exhorting others to support a cause.

In persuasive writing, targeting the audience becomes the prime consideration. A logical argument can interest a range of people who want to understand an issue. Persuasion takes aim more directly at the people whose vote or support or money counts. Persuasion becomes the issue the more you ask yourself: "Does my writing make a difference? Does what I write have an impact? Do I succeed in making others do my bidding?"

Regardless of your specific agenda, keeping in mind questions like the following will make your writing more persuasive:

• *Do you know your audience?*   Persuasive writers are audience-conscious. They know that attitudes toward police work are likely to differ in an affluent suburb and in a low-income neighborhood. They know that some white Southern college students sport the confederate flag as a symbol of a Southern lifestyle but that many

359

African American students object to it as the symbol of an oppressive past.

• *Have you established your authority?* Persuasive writers find ways to establish their credibility. If you can, try to show that you are writing from inside knowledge or long-standing concern. For example, if you are fighting intolerance toward immigrant groups, you need to make your readers see your credentials. You will be writing with a degree of authority if you have sought out relatives or family friends with an immigrant past, talked to Vietnamese fellow students, interviewed Korean shopkeepers.

• *Have you dramatized the issue?* Persuasive writers know how to shake up the apathetic reader. They use a striking incident or provocative statistics to make the reader care. They bring an issue to life with dramatic images and provocative imaginative comparisons. The *New York Times* columnist who wrote the following passage wanted to make sure his audience, jaded about violence, would care. What did he do to dramatize the issue?

> Last year, 72 police officers were shot to death. Two weeks ago, Los Angeles Police Officer Christy Lynn Hamilton was shot to death by a teenager with an AR-15 semiautomatic rifle. Officer Hamilton died just four days after her police academy graduation exercises. The boy who killed her, Chris Golly, also killed his father and himself.

> Bob Herbert, "Just the Facts," *San Jose Mercury News*

• *Are you ready to keep after your reader?* Persuasive speakers and writers **reiterate** their message — restating the point with added force, driving it home. They aim a barrage of thought-provoking examples, dramatic cases in point, and sobering statistics at the reader.

Persuasion is bound to bring the reader's emotions and values into play. It may bypass objective evidence and logical reasoning altogether to appeal directly to the reader's loyalties or self-interest. Every persuasive writer has to decide where to draw the line between legitimate persuasion and hype or manipulation.

THOUGHT LOG 8

Targeting Your Reader

Do you lend only silent support to good causes? Or do you write begging letters, warning letters, or letters of protest? Use your thought log to draft a letter to the editor that would, for instance,

• encourage support for the arts
• promote job opportunities for the disabled

- plead for financial aid to needy students
- make graffiti artists change their ways
- promote opportunities for women in sports
- protest or defend military recruiters on campus
- help save a landmark — or help demolish it to make way for a modern structure

The Strategies of Persuasion

Raw emotion cannot win the day against opponents who demand factual evidence, yet the dull recitation of statistical facts may be meaningless unless you motivate readers and get them involved.

JAMES D. LESTER

What strategy will you adopt for persuading your readers? How will you get their attention? How will you mobilize the good will or break down the resistance of your audience? When bent on persuasion, you need to give serious thought to your game plan for changing the reader's mind. Strategies like the following, alone or in combination, can help you organize your persuasion paper:

Meeting Needs   A basic question guides many a campaign of persuasion: What will the proposal I champion do *for the reader?* How will what I propose serve the reader's needs? For instance, what will a new shopping center, a library addition, or a new sports arena do for the community?

A classic persuasion paper might document one by one the benefits a new sports arena will have for a decaying downtown: The arena project will provide employment first for contractors and construction crews, then for an army of ticket sellers, ticket takers, and hot dog vendors. It will bring dying downtown restaurants and other small businesses back to life. It should also help create a badly lacking sense of community, a focus for civic pride. Young people who might otherwise be engaged in vandalism or petty crime will be cheering in the stands. Feuding ethnic or racial groups will shelve their mutual hostility as they give one another high-fives in the euphoria of a victory by the home team.

Mobilizing Emotions   Persuasive writers know that to make their readers care, they have to do more than argue logically and present the facts. Persuasive writing, more than other kinds, activates the whole register of human emotions. Hard-nosed propagandists appeal to the lowest common denominator. They play on the voters' fear for their pocketbooks, their love of scandal, their suspicion of foreigners, their resentment of people who are different. More inspirational writers appeal to shared values:

- They may mobilize their readers' indignation at injustice.
- They may stir the readers' compassion or feeling of human solidarity. For instance, they may cause us to think of the homeless as real people, who have things to say about their plight, who were once part of a family, who feel deprivation and humiliation the way people would who still have a roof over their heads.
- They may respond to the readers' hunger for the story of someone who has faced and overcome adversity.
- They may help their readers find role models — believable people who set a good example, who set a standard, who renew our faith in human potential.

Building Assent   If you can get your readers to say "Yes, that is true" several times early in your paper, you are creating a pattern of assent. A basic strategy for persuasive writing is to proceed from the less to the more controversial. It is to establish common ground first and then to move on to new or difficult propositions. If you are arguing for integrating girls into the local Boy Scout troop, you will be well advised to start with an eloquent tribute to the ideals of scouting, regardless of sex. Once your audience regards you as a right-thinking person, they might be more receptive to your new ideas than they would otherwise be.

Defusing Objections   Unanticipated objections can deflate the enthusiast's balloon. Warding off questions raised by the opposition can be as important as championing the merits of your own position. When taking a stand that you expect to be unpopular with your audience, you may decide to organize your paper as a whole around major predictable objections. The author of the following excerpted paper addressed her defense of military service for women to skeptical fellow students. For you, are the objections she anticipates the most serious or predictable ones? How successful is she in answering them?

Women in Uniform

During the first-day "introduce yourself" routine in one of my classes, a young woman announced that she had served a two-year enlistment in the armed forces and that "every kid should have to do it." Most of her classmates balked at the suggestion, but I found myself seriously considering her idea. . . .

Many students feel that enlistment would interfere with their plans for a college education. However, many high school students take a year off before entering college. Six or twelve more months would not make a great difference. For many students, in fact, it's the military that can make a college education possible. The armed forces provide financial incentives that may enable a two-year-college student to go on to a four-year college or a college graduate to go on to graduate work. . . .

Other students feel that enlistment would sidetrack them from their careers by removing them from the "real world." However, high school and college classroom "wombs" may do less than military service to prepare young people for the real world of specific skills and responsibilities . . .

Women students may be apprehensive of the use of women in combat. However, there are dozens of options available to women other than combat or clerical work. When I took the Armed Services Vocational Aptitude Test, at least forty percent of those taking the test were women. Their interests ranged from nursing to flight control or working on a Coast Guard cutter. . . .

Capitalizing on Contradictions   A familiar strategy of persuasion is to find the chinks in other people's armor. You may choose to zero in on inconsistencies in order to undermine an opponent's position. The following excerpts show this strategy at work in a *Harper's* article that went after a basic contradiction in the behavior of its target audience:

Boycott Cocaine

Among trendy young professionals in our major cities, there is no stigma attached to using cocaine. In particular, the hip lawyers, doctors, movie stars and so on who use the drug are not deterred, or even bothered much, by the mere fact that it happens to be illegal. But perhaps they will be receptive to a more fashionable approach. After all, many cocaine consumers are the same sort of people who will boycott a cosmetic because the company tortures rabbits. . . .

Most of the coke sold in America originates in two South American countries whose preeminence in the drug trade is due mainly to the ruthlessness of their native practitioners. Several winters ago, rival gangsters broke in to the New York home of an expatriate who was making a fortune importing coke from his native land. The thugs stole $15,000 in cash, abducted a ten-year-old son and a seventeen-year-old babysitter, and hanged the five-year-old daughter with a length of nylon Christmas wrapping . . .

In a recent year in Miami, the cocaine capital of the Northern Hemisphere, a quarter of the city's 614 murders were committed with machine guns. "Children have been killed in cross fires, and so have innocent adults," says a special agent in the Miami division of the Drug Enforcement Administration. "We've had people riddled with machine-gun bullets as they were waiting for traffic lights." . . .

To buy cocaine is to subsidize a network of death and despair. Snorting cocaine is at least as bad for the planet as wearing a coat made from an endangered species. Join the cause. Boycott cocaine.

David Owen in Harper's

WRITING WORKSHOP I

A Critique of Persuasion

Working alone or with a group, prepare a critique of an exceptionally effective (or ineffective) example of persuasion. For instance, choose a full-page advertisement, a newspaper editorial, an exceptional commercial, a fundraising letter, a campaign pamphlet, or a promotional flyer or brochure. What assumptions did those who created the document make about their target audience? What appeals or strategies did they employ, and with what effect? (If you can, provide a photocopy, tape, or transcript of the original.)

WRITING WORKSHOP 2

A Paper for Peer Review

Is the following student paper persuasive? Does it make you think or change your mind? Why or why not? Consider questions like the following:

• What is the central message of this paper, and where does it come through most strongly?
• What is the student's strategy for tackling a highly controversial subject?
• Does the author succeed in bringing the issue to life?
• What shared values does the writer appeal to, and how?
• Does the writer anticipate objections and deal with them? How?
• What if anything in this paper are you likely to remember? What do you think has a chance to make a lasting impact?
• What would you say in a personal letter to the author of this paper?

Go in Peace

Death has always been a dirty word — a word that most people try to sweep under the carpet. True, it is something very frightening, but it is also inevitable. It has been on my mind in recent months because of my aged grandmother's condition. Death has lingered near her as most of her close friends as well as all of her siblings have died. She told me one day that when it was her time she wanted to "go in peace." She said that she wanted no part of a hospital and tubes and machine. She wanted to die and be done with it. Her words opened up new questions for me. What if there were tubes and machines and a long wait? How could she be spared prolonged agony?

Are we ever justified in shortening a person's suffering? The medical profession opposes mercy killing or euthanasia; it strictly adheres to the preservation of human life. But what do we consider the boundaries of life that is truly living? Should we consider the dignity and the wishes of the person who is dying?

Doctors make their careers saving lives. All lives must come to an end at some point, but now the point of death is often postponed indefinitely as medical technology grows. A comatose person can be kept breathing for an indeterminate length of time. It is only a few years since a family won the first court battle to take a young woman in a coma off the machinery that pumped her lungs full of air. Although her body remained alive for some time afterwards, she was never conscious. Many coma victims do die after being removed from the machines that allow them to go on breathing as they lie motionless in a hospital bed.

The medical profession does its job by keeping the person in a coma alive. That body with the tubes down the throat and the needles in the arm is a living being. It is not the walking, talking person that loved ones have known, but its heart is beating and its lungs are rising thanks to medical technology. But what is the quality of that being's life? What has happened to its right of choice, which makes it a thinking creature?

Human beings notoriously fight for their rights — their rights to speech and liberty as well as their right to make decisions concerning their own bodies. Women can legally terminate unborn babies through abortions with the help of the medical profession. They have control over their future. A dying patient is deprived of that control as the medical profession strives to keep the person alive even if the patient wants to die.

Suppose that a cancer patient feels that life is no longer worth living because of insufferable pain. What can the family do? The dying patient's pain is great, and the available choices are few. People should have the right to make choices concerning their own bodies. The patient has the right to die, enlisting the help of others if the patient chooses.

Suppose a person lies braindead. Is that still a full human being? Where is the dignity of such a patient? The family of the braindead person has the right to fight for the dignity of their loved one. If true living is no longer possible, they should be able to opt for death, not for a life in between.

My grandmother asked me what I would do if it came time for her to die. I told her I would weep for her and be very sad, but I would remember how she lived. For me, this means that I could not let her linger in the life in between with machines and tubes. I must respect her wishes of how she wants to die. She must "go in peace" the way she plans, not the way a doctor plans. She chose the way she lived, and, with my help, she will choose the way she dies.

Revising Your Persuasion Paper

Writing that keeps using the floodlights of emphasis finally reaches the opposite of the intended effect: beside the multitude of things flooded by glaring light, nothing distinctively visible remains, and noisy chaos reigns in language.

DOLF STERNBERGER

What are the limits of persuasion? Persuasive writers use words to exhort, incite, denounce, or indict. They know when to come on strong. However, to be persuasive, you have to know both the strengths and the weaknesses of strong language. You don't persuade your readers by simply turning up the volume. Sometimes the first draft of a would-be persuasive paper turns out too colorless and routine. However, the opposite may prove more often true: If you try too hard, your reader may feel badgered. Consider the following in rewriting a paper whose first draft smacked of hype or the hard sell:

• *Vary your emphasis.*   If you want to give parts of your message special **emphasis**, other parts of it will have to be less emphatic. If at the right point in your paper you show that you can discuss the subject calmly, a strong charge will carry that much more weight. In the following quotation, the label *deadly* is a strong word that stands out. Although it is backed up by strong follow-up, it is not drowned out by a rush of other strong words; it has a chance to sink in:

> Of all the drug problems afflicting the world, heroin is the most deadly and the one that most seriously affects American young people. Once addicted, the user needs cash to maintain the habit. The males steal and rob. The women become shoplifters and prostitutes.
>
> Horace Sutton

• *Guard against exaggeration.*   Skeptical readers discount exaggerated claims — and they may also discount other parts of your argument along with them. Scale back **hyperbole** — a tendency to dramatic, theatrical overstatement ("an unparalleled threat to our quality of life"). Tone down **superlatives**, which push everything to an extreme degree ("the most amazing medical breakthrough of modern times"; "the greatest tax increase in history").

• *Avoid routine fault-finding.* Being consistently negative will make you seem guilty of bias. It will call into question your ability to decide key issues on their merits. Try to give credit where due, so that your readers will not think of you as a naysayer, capable only of kneejerk criticism.

• *Reconsider cheap shots and personal attacks.* Try to focus on the issues instead of discrediting opponents by dwelling on their marital or psychiatric history. Too much dealing in personalities may suggest that you are a mean-spirited person. Watch out for arguments **ad hominem** — attacks directed "at the person" rather than at the point at issue. Sometimes, of course, the moral character or shady dealing of your opposition *is* the issue. However, to persuade fair-minded readers, you should be prepared to word your charges carefully and make them stick.

• *Avoid abusing uplifting abstractions.* Rewrite statements that may seem to be cheapening patriotism, the flag, or motherhood. Avoid the appearance of trivializing shared ideals by making them serve your short-range purpose. Many in your audience will be wary if you invoke the Founding Fathers to support your stand on a passing issue of the day. When you start by writing "I as an American . . . ," you may already be alienating readers by implying that they might be less patriotic than you are.

OPTIONS FOR WRITING 8

Making a Plea

On which of the following topics do you have strong feelings? Which will present a challenge as you try to persuade others? Choose a topic that allows you to write with conviction and to work up the kind of material needed to sway an independent-minded reader. Give some serious thought to your general strategy.

1 Write a letter to the editor in which you support a campaign by civic-minded people in your community. For instance, you might lend your support to a campaign to save a historic building, a theater company, a classics station, an art museum, or a school for students with special needs. Or write a letter dissuading people in your community from supporting a lost or misguided cause.

2 Addressing yourself to the general public, write a defense of an organization or institution whose critics claim its time has passed. You might write "In Defense of . . ." the Boy Scouts, fraternities or sororities, ROTC, the DAR, the Democratic party, labor unions, the nuclear family, or the family farm. Or write to persuade supporters of the institution that the time has come for serious change.

3 Write a paper championing tougher laws — or alternative approaches — to a problem that has recently received much attention, such as drunk driving, graffiti, aggressive panhandling, or secondary smoke inhalation.

4 When new health textbooks were adopted for the public schools in Texas, protesters insisted on extensive revision to play down frank discussion of condoms and safe sex for adolescents. Write to persuade parents, schoolboards, or legislators to allow frank discussion of this kind of topic. Or write a paper urging them to respect the wishes of the groups who raised the objections.

5 Do you favor, or do you disapprove of, campaigns to label or otherwise restrict offensive rock lyrics, violent movies, violent children's programming, or "adult" programs on television? Write a paper persuading the ordinary voter or newspaper reader.

6 On some topics, the minds of people on opposing sides seem to be fully made up. Do you think there is nevertheless a point in trying to change the minds of readers with strong views? For instance, try to change the minds of people with strong pro-abortion or anti-abortion views, or of those who favor or oppose school prayer.

7 Much publicity has swirled around campus speech codes or codes regulating student behavior. Write a paper persuading doubting fellow students to support or to fight dating guidelines, ordinances regulating hate speech, or similar campus codes.

8 Write a paper in which you target attitudes that have recently made for conflict or community strife. What would it take to make an effective plea for tolerance or understanding? For instance, try to change (or to defend) the attitudes of some in the black community toward Jews or Koreans, or the attitudes of some native born Americans toward immigrants.

9 Do you believe in a cause that some refuse to take seriously? What would it take to gain converts to the cause? You may want to speak up for vegetarianism, pacifism, Zen, or animal rights.

10 Has the general public become jaded about appeals in support of humanitarian causes? What would it take to counteract public apathy? You may want to make a plea for stronger support for a cause like famine relief, drug treatment programs, battered women's shelters, school lunch programs, or medical care for the poor.

Reading, Discussion, Writing

Swaying the Audience

OVERVIEW: The authors of the following selections use their writing to make a strong plea. They sound a warning, address a need, or ask for support. Who is the reader each writer has in mind? How effective is each writer in changing the reader's mind? (Do they change yours?)

The Government Cannot Protect You

JOAN BECK

Can persuasion change ingrained habits or ways of thinking?
People need little persuasion to accept extra paid vacation time or a
free lunch. Persuasion becomes a challenge when it asks readers to ac-
cept responsibilities that they would prefer to avoid. A columnist for
the Chicago Tribune *wrote the following column after a major inter-*
national scientific conference on AIDS. Ten years after Randy Shilts
wrote And the Band Played On *on the disastrous delays in society's*
recognition of the AIDS epidemic as a major threat, AIDS continues
to spread unchecked, especially among minorities and the young.
How persuasive is Beck's plea? Do you think it will change anyone's
mind or anyone's behavior? Why or why not?

There's a *life-death message* in the final report of the National
Commission on AIDS. But the report concentrates so hard on blaming political leaders for not doing more about the epidemic the message is lost between the lines of anger and frustration.

No cure for AIDS is in sight, the commission's report notes. A vaccine is years away. HIV continues to be a slow, inexorable killer,
mostly of adults in the prime of *life*.

But, as the report should have stressed in language strong enough
to burn into the brains of us all, you can generally protect yourself
from getting AIDS.

The government isn't going to guard you from getting AIDS. It
can't. President Bush couldn't. President Clinton can't. The White
House's new AIDS coordinator, Kristine Gebbie, can't either, no matter how urgently AIDS groups pushed for that post to be created.
Neither can the governors, mayors, members of Congress, corporate
executives or community and religious leaders the commission's report blames for not doing more.

Most AIDS activist groups are much more concerned about people   5
who already have AIDS than about preventing others from becoming infected. Most laws dealing with AIDS are intended to help and
shield the HIV-positive, not to safeguard others. Protecting yourself
from getting AIDS is something you have to do for yourself.

Doctors can't cure you if you get AIDS. They can only postpone
your death, treat some associated illnesses and keep you feeling a
little better as you slowly die. All the politically correct attitudes, all
the anti-discrimination laws, all the political activism, all the red

AIDS ribbons, all the support groups, all the finger-pointing can't change the basic facts about this epidemic.

The same sober assessment about the lack of substantial progress against the AIDS epidemic was sounded repeatedly in Berlin in June, when thousands of scientists met at the annual international conference on AIDS. The lack of encouraging scientific news included studies pointing up the limited benefits of AZT, the primary drug used to treat HIV infections and AIDS.

Prevention is now the only way to stop the epidemic from continuing to spread widely and rapidly throughout the world, scientists repeatedly emphasized at the Berlin conference.

HIV does not infect humans easily, like the common cold. It is not genetic, the result of an unlucky mistake in DNA coding. Its cause is known, unlike most forms of cancer. AIDS, like it or not, is an infection acquired by having sex with an infected partner (anal-receptive sex is particularly risky) or sharing a needle with an infected intravenous drug user.

Exceptions include babies of HIV-positive mothers, people inadvertently transfused with HIV-positive blood, accidentally infected health care workers and a few cases for which the cause has not been established. 10

The hard fact is that those who want to protect themselves against HIV infection and AIDS can almost certainly do so by not sharing intravenous drug needles with an infected person and by having sex only within an established monogamous relationship with a partner who is free of HIV.

Why is it so hard to push this message clearly and explicitly?

For one reason, it's widely assumed that changes in sexual behavior in the last three decades have made the message of premarital abstinence and marital fidelity naive and obsolete. Never mind that two generations ago, it was considered the social norm (whatever the exceptions in practice).

So those who are trying to prevent the spread of AIDS are relying on messages about "safe sex," which generally means condoms. Condoms can substantially reduce the risk of acquiring HIV from an infected partner — as well as the chances of getting other sexually transmitted diseases, which in turn increase susceptibility to HIV. But condoms have a high failure rate as a contraceptive, and the AIDS virus can much more easily slip through microscopic holes in a condom than can a much larger sperm. A woman can usually become pregnant only about two days a month. The sexual partner of a person with HIV is always at risk.

Even so, an increasing number of schools are making condoms   15
available to students, sometimes over the strenuous objections of
parents who feel the implicit message is that sex is okay and expected of teenagers and that more immature young people — not
fewer — will be at risk.

It is also difficult to shape messages about sexual behavior so they
will be acceptable to minorities and to gays who are at higher risk of
AIDS than the population as a whole. But excessive sensitivity, exaggerated political correctness and concern about seeming to blame
the victims can sometimes dilute the cautions too much.

We do need much more scientific research about AIDS — and
more money to pay for it, even though AIDS research is now better
funded than work on other diseases which claim many more lives.
We do need support and good care for persons with AIDS and HIV.
We do need an end to residual prejudice, discrimination and unjustified fears of infected people.

We do need more treatment facilities for drug abusers, although
the high rate of recidivism is discouraging. Needle exchange programs have ardent backers, although critics are concerned about
supporting what is self-destructive behavior regardless of the risk
of AIDS.

We do need more empowerment for women, in the United States
and especially in many Third World cultures, so they can protect
themselves from the sexual demands of high-risk men and from
dangerous sexual practices.

But while we are working on all these difficult things, it would   20
help to broadcast clearly and loudly the message of individual responsibility for avoiding HIV and individual power to do so, instead
of blaming the government for not doing more.

THE INVOLVED READER

1   What assumptions does Beck make about her readers? What
    kind of reader would be her ideal audience? (What kind of per-
    son might be a hostile or an unsympathetic reader?)

2   How or how well does she establish her credibility? Does she
    seem to have an axe to grind? Do you accept her as an authority
    on the subject?

3   What if anything does she do to dramatize the issue?

4   What is Beck's basic message? How does she drive it home?

TALKING, THINKING, WRITING

5   What would you say in reply in a letter to the editor of the *Trib-
    une* or in a guest editorial for a student newspaper?

existence we enjoy — when, for example, we rent or purchase one of those restored townhouses that once provided shelter for people now huddled in the street.

But there may be another reason to assign labels to the destitute. Terming economic victims "psychotic" or "disordered" helps to place them at a distance. It says that they aren't quite like us — and, more important, that we could not be like them. The plight of homeless families is a nightmare. It may not seem natural to try to banish human beings from our midst, but it *is* natural to try to banish nightmares from our minds.

So the rituals of clinical contamination proceed uninterrupted by the economic facts described above. Research that addresses homelessness as an *injustice* rather than as a medical *misfortune* does not win the funding of foundations. And the research which *is* funded, defining the narrowed borders of permissible debate, diverts our attention from the antecedent to the secondary cause of homelessness. Thus it is that perfectly ordinary women whom I know in New York City — people whose depression or anxiety is a realistic consequence of months and even years in crowded shelters or the streets — are interrogated by invasive research scholars in an effort to decode their poverty, to find clinical categories for their despair and terror, to identify the secret failing that lies hidden in their psyche.

Many pregnant women without homes are denied prenatal care because they constantly travel from one shelter to another. Many are anemic. Many are denied essential dietary supplements by recent federal cuts. As a consequence, some of their children do not live to see their second year of life. Do these mothers sometimes show signs of stress? Do they appear disorganized, depressed, disordered? Frequently. They are immobilized by pain, traumatized by fear. So it is no surprise that when researchers enter the scene to ask them how they "feel," the resulting reports tell us that the homeless are emotionally unwell. The reports do not tell us we have *made* these people ill. They do not tell us that illness is a natural response to intolerable conditions. Nor do they tell us of the strength and the resilience that so many of these people still retain despite the miseries they must endure. They set these men and women apart in capsules labeled "personality disorder" or "psychotic," where they no longer threaten our complacence.

Manhattan Borough President David Dinkins made the following observation on the basis of a study commissioned in 1986: "No facts support the belief that addiction or behavioral problems occur with more frequency in the homeless family population than in a similar

socioeconomic population. Homeless families are not demographically different from other public assistance families when they enter
the shelter system. . . . Family homelessness is typically a housing
and income problem: the unavailability of affordable housing and
the inadequacy of public assistance income."

In a "hypothetical world," write James Wright and Julie Lam of
the University of Massachusetts, "where there were no alcoholics,
no drug addicts, no mentally ill, no deinstitutionalization, . . . indeed, no personal social pathologies at all, there would still be a
formidable homelessness problem, simply because at this stage in
American history, there is not enough low-income housing" to accommodate the poor.

New York State's respected Commissioner of Social Services, Cesar
Perales, makes the point in fewer words: "Homelessness is less and
less a result of personal failure, and more and more is caused by
larger forces. There is no longer affordable housing in New York City
for people of poor and modest means."

Even the words of medical practitioners who care for homeless   15
people have been curiously ignored. A study published by the Massachusetts Medical Society, for instance, has noted that the most frequent illnesses among a sample of the homeless population, after
alcohol and drug use, are trauma (31 percent), upper respiratory disorders (28 percent), limb disorders (19 percent), mental illness (16
percent), skin diseases (15 percent), hypertension (14 percent), and
neurological illnesses (12 percent). (Excluded from this tabulation
are lead poisoning, malnutrition, acute diarrhea, and other illnesses
especially common among homeless infants and small children.)
Why, we may ask, of all these calamities, does mental illness com-
mand so much political and press attention? The answer may be that
the label of mental illness places the destitute outside the sphere of
ordinary life. It personalizes an anguish that is public in its genesis;
it individualizes a misery that is both general in cause and general in
application.

The rate of tuberculosis among the homeless is believed to be ten
times that of the general population. Asthma, I have learned in
countless interviews, is one of the most common causes of discomfort in the shelters. Compulsive smoking, exacerbated by the crowd-
ing and the tension, is more common in the shelters than in any
place that I have visited except prison. Infected and untreated sores,
scabies, diarrhea, poorly set limbs, protruding elbows, awkwardly
distorted wrists, bleeding gums, impacted teeth, and other untreated
dental problems are so common among children in the shelters that
one rapidly forgets their presence. Hunger and emaciation are ev-

erywhere. Children as well as adults can bring to mind the photographs of people found in camps for refugees of war in 1945. But these miseries bear no stigma, and mental illness does.

Last summer, some twenty-eight thousand homeless people were afforded shelter by the city of New York. Of this number, twelve thousand were children and six thousand were parents living together in families. The average child was six years old, the average parent twenty-seven. A typical homeless family included a mother with two or three children, but in about one-fifth of these families two parents were present. Roughly ten thousand single persons, then, made up the remainder of the population of the city's shelters.

These proportions vary somewhat from one area of the nation to another. In all areas, however, families are the fastest-growing sector of the homeless population, and in the Northeast they are by far the largest sector already. In Massachusetts, three-fourths of the homeless now are families with children; in certain parts of Massachusetts — Attleboro and Northhampton, for example — the proportion reaches ninety percent. Two-thirds of the homeless children studied recently in Boston were less than five years old.

Of an estimated two to three million homeless people nationwide, about 500,000 are dependent children, according to Robert Hayes, counsel to the National Coalition for the Homeless. Including their parents, at least 750,000 homeless people in America are family members.

What is to be made, then, of the supposition that the homeless are primarily the former residents of mental hospitals, persons who were carelessly released during the 1970s? Many of them are, to be sure. Among the older men and women in the streets and shelters, as many as one-third (some believe as many as one-half) may be chronically disturbed, and a number of these people were deinstitutionalized during the 1970s. But in a city like New York, where nearly half the homeless are small children with an average age of six, to operate on the basis of such a supposition makes no sense. Their parents, with an average age of twenty-seven, are not likely to have been hospitalized in the 1970s, either.

Nor is it easy to assume, as was once the case, that single men — those who come closer to fitting the stereotype of the homeless vagrant, the drifting alcoholic of an earlier age — are the former residents of mental hospitals. The age of homeless men has dropped in recent years; many of them are only twenty-one to twenty-eight years old. Fifty percent of homeless men in New York City shelters in 1984 were there for the first time. Most had previously had homes and jobs. Many had never before needed public aid.

A writer in the *New York Times* describes a homeless woman standing on a traffic island in Manhattan. "She was evicted from her small room in the hotel just across the street," and she is determined to get revenge. Until she does, "nothing will move her from that spot. . . . Her argumentativeness and her angry fixation on revenge, along with the apparent absence of hallucinations, mark her as a paranoid." Most physicians, I imagine, would be more reserved in passing judgment with so little evidence, but this author makes his diagnosis without hesitation. "The paranoids of the street," he says, "are among the most difficult to help."

Perhaps so. But does it depend on who is offering the help? Is anyone offering to help this woman get back her home? Is it crazy to seek vengeance for being thrown into the street? The absence of anger, some psychiatrists believe, might indicate much greater illness.

The same observer sees additional symptoms of pathology ("negative symptoms," he calls them) in the fact that many homeless persons demonstrate a "gross deterioration in their personal hygiene" and grooming, leading to "indifference" and "apathy." Having just identified one woman as unhealthy because she is so far from being "indifferent" as to seek revenge, he now sees apathy as evidence of illness; so consistency is not what we are looking for in this account. But how much less indifferent might the homeless be if those who decide their fate were less indifferent themselves? How might their grooming and hygiene be improved if they were permitted access to a public toilet?

In New York City, as in many cities, homeless people are denied   25
the right to wash in public bathrooms, to store their few belongings in a public locker, or, in certain cases, to make use of public toilets altogether. Shaving, cleaning of clothes, and other forms of hygiene are prohibited in the men's room of Grand Central Station. The terminal's three hundred lockers, used in former times by homeless people to secure their goods, were removed in 1986 as "a threat to public safety," according to a study made by the New York City Council.

At one-thirty every morning, homeless people are ejected from the station. Many once attempted to take refuge on the ramp that leads to Forty-second Street because it was protected from the street by wooden doors and thus provided some degree of warmth. But the station management responded to this challenge in two ways. The ramp was mopped with a strong mixture of ammonia to produce a noxious smell, and when the people sleeping there brought cardboard boxes and newspapers to protect them from the fumes, the entrance doors were chained wide open. Temperatures dropped some nights to ten degrees. Having driven these people to the streets, city officials subsequently determined that their willingness to risk exposure to cold weather could be taken as further evidence of mental illness.

At Pennsylvania Station in New York, homeless women are denied the use of toilets. Amtrak police come by and herd them off each hour on the hour. In July 1985, Amtrak officials issued this directive to police: "It is the policy of Amtrak to not allow the homeless and undesirables to remain. . . . Officers are encouraged to eject all undesirables. . . . Now is the time to train and educate them that their presence will not be tolerated as cold weather sets in." In an internal memo, according to CBS, an Amtrak official asked flatly: "Can't we get rid of this trash?"

I have spent many nights in conversation with the women who are huddled in the corridors and near the doorway of the public toilets in Penn Station. Many are young. Most are cogent. Few are dressed in the familiar rags suggested by the term *bag ladies*. Unable to bathe or use the toilets in the station, almost all are in conditions of intolerable physical distress. The sight of clusters of police officers, mostly male, guarding a toilet from use by homeless women speaks volumes about the public conscience of New York.

A young man who had lost his job, then his family, then his home, all in the summer of 1986, spoke with me for several hours in Grand Central Station on the weekend following Thanksgiving. "A year ago," he said, "I never thought that somebody like me would end up in a shelter. Nothing you've ever undergone prepares you. You walk into the place [a shelter on the Bowery] — the smell of sweat and urine hits you like a wall. Unwashed bodies and the look of absolute despair on many, many faces there would make you think you were in Dante's Hell. . . . What you fear is that you will be here forever. You do not know if it is ever going to end. You think to yourself: it is a dream and I will awake. Sometimes I think: it's an experiment. They are watching you to find out how much you can take. . . . I was a pretty stable man. Now I tremble when I meet somebody in the ordinary world. I'm trembling right now. . . . For me, the loss of work and loss of wife had left me rocking. Then the welfare regulations hit me. I began to feel that I would be reduced to trash. . . . Half the people that I know are suffering from chest infections and sleep deprivation. The lack of sleep leaves you debilitated, shaky. You exaggerate your fears. If a psychiatrist came along he'd say that I was crazy. But I was an ordinary man. There was nothing wrong with me. I lost my kids. I lost my home. Now would you say that I was crazy if I told you I was feeling sad?"

THE INVOLVED READER

1   What misconceptions does Kozol set out to challenge? What stereotypes does he attack? How does he account for the popular misunderstandings he attacks?

2   Where does Kozol turn for support? How does he use numbers to dramatize the issue? What authorities does he turn to to support his position?

3   How does Kozol deal with the widespread perception that people with mental illnesses make up a large part of the homeless population?

4   Much of Kozol's writing records his personal contacts with society's rejects. What for you is striking or provocative about his personal testimony? How does he use the contrast between official attitudes and his firsthand knowledge of the homeless?

TALKING, THINKING, WRITING

5   Do you think Kozol's kind of indictment of a callous society does any good? Why or why not?

6   In Kozol's *Amazing Grace*, a pastor ministering to the poor in her parish in the South Bronx comments on a society where "social blindness is accepted as the normal state of mind." Do you think you or the people you know best suffer from "social blindness"? Is having a social conscience passé in today's America?

7   One city council passed an ordinance making it illegal for the homeless to sleep outdoors within the city limits. Another city, after repeated warnings, had a woman who regularly fed the homeless jailed for failure to meet the city's standards for food handling or food distribution. Write a letter to the editor in which you react to one of these actions or a similar more recent local initiative.

COLLABORATIVE PROJECTS

8   Is anything being done in your community or area to help the homeless? Working with a group, check out any local initiatives or programs.

A Peaceful Woman Explains Why She Carries a Gun

LINDA M. HASSELSTROM

Should women train for self-defense? Has the current concern been successful in improving women's safety? The following essay was excerpted from High Country News, *a regional Rocky Mountain publication, for the* Utne Reader. *Linda M. Hasselstrom has played a variety of roles: poet, environmental activist, and cattle rancher on the arid grasslands of western South Dakota near the Black Hills. Her family, originally from Sweden, started ranching on the South Dakota prairie in the late 1800s, along with other Swedes and Norwegians who "crossed the plains and homesteaded close together in what must have seemed a vast emptiness." For many years, she operated her own small press, Lame Johnny, named after a horse thief. She has said about cattle ranching that "someone who pays attention to the messages the natural world sends can bring cattle home the day before a blizzard nine times out of ten." Her books include* Windbreak *and* Going Over East.

I am a peace-loving woman. But several events in the past 10 years have convinced me I'm safer when I carry a pistol. This was a personal decision, but because handgun possession is a controversial subject, perhaps my reasoning will interest others.

I live in western South Dakota on a ranch 25 miles from the nearest town: for several years I spent winters alone here. As a free-lance writer, I travel alone a lot — more than 100,000 miles by car in the last four years. With women freer than ever before to travel alone, the odds of our encountering trouble seem to have risen. Distances are great, roads are deserted, and the terrain is often too exposed to offer hiding places.

A woman who travels alone is advised, usually by men, to protect herself by avoiding bars and other "dangerous situations," by approaching her car like an Indian scout, by locking doors and windows. But these precautions aren't always enough. I spent years following them and still found myself in dangerous situations. I began to resent the idea that just because I am female, I have to be extra careful.

A few years ago, with another woman, I camped for several weeks in the West. We discussed self-defense, but neither of us had taken a course in it. She was against firearms, and local police told us Mace was illegal. So we armed ourselves with spray cans of deodorant tucked into our sleeping bags. We never used our improvised Mace because we were lucky enough to camp beside people who came to our aid when men harassed us. But on one occasion we visited a national park where our assigned space was less than 15 feet from other campers. When we returned from a walk, we found our closest neighbors were two young men. As we gathered our cooking gear, they drank beer and loudly discussed what they would do to us after dark. Nearby campers, even families, ignored them: rangers strolled past, unconcerned. When we asked the rangers point-blank if they would protect us, one of them patted my shoulder and said, "Don't worry, girls. They're just kidding." At dusk we drove out of the park and hid our camp in the woods a few miles away. The illegal spot was lovely, but our enjoyment of that park was ruined. I returned from the trip determined to reconsider the options available for protecting myself.

At that time, I lived alone on the ranch and taught night classes in   5
town. Along a city street I often traveled, a woman had a flat tire, called for help on her CB radio, and got a rapist who left her beaten. She was afraid to call for help again and stayed in her car until morning. For that reason, as well as because CBs work best along line-of-sight, which wouldn't help much in the rolling hills where I live, I ruled out a CB.

As I drove home one night, a car followed me. It passed me on a narrow bridge while a passenger flashed a blinding spotlight in my face. I braked sharply. The car stopped, angled across the bridge, and four men jumped out. I realized the locked doors were useless if they broke the windows of my pickup. I started forward, hoping to knock their car aside so I could pass. Just then another car appeared, and the men hastily got back in their car. They continued to follow me, passing and repassing. I dared not go home because no one else was there. I passed no lighted houses. Finally they pulled over to the roadside, and I decided to use their tactic: fear. Speeding, the pickup horn blaring, I swerved as close to them as I dared as I roared past. It worked: they turned off the highway. But I was frightened and angry. Even in my vehicle I was too vulnerable.

Other incidents occurred over the years. One day I glanced out a field below my house and saw a man with a shotgun walking toward a pond full of ducks. I drove down and explained that the land was posted. I politely asked him to leave. He stared at me, and the muzzle of the shotgun began to rise. In a moment of utter clarity I realized that I was alone on the ranch, and that he could shoot me and simply drive away. The moment passed: the man left.

One night, I returned home from teaching a class to find deep tire ruts in the wet ground of my yard, garbage in the driveway, and a large gas tank empty. A light shone in the house: I couldn't remember leaving it on. I was too embarrassed to drive to a neighboring ranch and wake someone up. An hour of cautious exploration convinced me the house was safe, but once inside, with the doors locked, I was still afraid. I kept thinking of how vulnerable I felt, prowling around my own house in the dark.

My first positive step was to take a kung fu class, which teaches evasive or protective action when someone enters your space without permission. I learned to move confidently, scanning for possible attackers. I learned how to assess danger and techniques for avoiding it without combat.

I also learned that one must practice several hours every day to be   10
good at kung fu. By that time I had married George: when I practiced with him, I learned how *close* you must be to your attacker to use martial arts, and decided a 120-pound woman dare not let a six-foot, 220-pound attacker get that close unless she is very, very good at self-defense. I have since read articles by several women who were extremely well trained in the martial arts, but were raped and beaten anyway.

I thought back over the times in my life when I had been attacked or threatened and tried to be realistic about my own behavior, searching for anything that had allowed me to become a victim. Overall, I was convinced that I had not been at fault. I don't believe myself to be either paranoid or a risk-taker, but I wanted more protection.

With some reluctance I decided to try carrying a pistol. George had always carried one, despite his size and his training in martial arts. I practiced shooting until I was sure I could hit an attacker who moved close enough to endanger me. Then I bought a license from the county sheriff, making it legal for me to carry the gun concealed.

But I was not yet ready to defend myself. George taught me that the most important preparation was mental: convincing myself I could actually *shoot a person.* Few of us wish to hurt or kill another human being. But there is no point in having a gun; in fact, gun possession might increase your danger unless you know you can use it. I got in the habit of rehearsing, as I drove or walked, the precise conditions that would be required before I would shoot someone.

People who have not grown up with the idea that they are capable of protecting themselves — ther words, most women — might have to work hard to convince themselves of their ability, and of the necessity. Handgun ownership need not turn us into gunslingers, but it can be part of believing in, and relying on, *ourselves* for protection.

To be useful, a pistol has to be available. In my car, it's within 15 instant reach. When I enter a deserted rest stop at night, it's in my purse, with my hand on the grip. When I walk from a dark parking lot into a motel, it's in my hand, under a coat. At home, it's on the headboard. In short, I take it with me almost everywhere I go alone.

Just carrying a pistol is not protection; avoidance is still the best approach to trouble. Subconsciously watching for signs of danger, I believe I've become more alert. Handgun use, not unlike driving, becomes instinctive. Each time I've drawn my gun — I have never fired it at another human being — I've simply found it in my hand.

I was driving the half-mile to the highway mailbox one day when I saw a vehicle parked about midway down the road. Several men were standing in the ditch, relieving themselves. I have no objection to emergency urination, but I noticed they'd dumped several dozen beer cans in the road. Besides being ugly, cans can slash a cow's feet or stomach.

The men noticed me before they finished and made quite a performance out of zipping their trousers while walking toward me. All four of them gathered around my small foreign car, and one of them demanded what the hell I wanted.

"This is private land. I'd appreciate it if you'd pick up the beer cans."

"What beer cans?" said the belligerent one, putting both hands 20 on the car door and leaning in my window. His face was inches from mine, and the beer fumes were strong. The others laughed. One tried the passenger door, locked; another put his foot on the hood and rocked the car. They circled, lightly thumping the roof, discussing my good fortune in meeting them and the benefits they were likely to bestow upon me. I felt very small and very trapped and they knew it.

"The ones you just threw out," I said politely.

"I don't see no beer cans. Why don't you get out here and show them to me, honey?" said the belligerent one, reaching for the handle inside my door.

"Right over there," I said, still being polite. "— there, and over there." I pointed with the pistol, which I'd slipped under my thigh. Within one minute the cans and the men were back in the car and headed down the road.

I believe this incident illustrates several important principles. The men were trespassing and knew it: their judgment may have been impaired by alcohol. Their response to the polite request of a woman alone was to use their size, numbers, and sex to inspire fear. The pistol was a response in the same language. Politeness didn't work: I couldn't match them in size or number. Out of the car, I'd have been more vulnerable. The pistol just changed the balance of power. It worked again recently when I was driving in a desolate part of Wyoming. A man played cat-and-mouse with me for 30 miles, ultimately trying to run me off the road. When his car passed mine with only two inches to spare, I showed him my pistol, and he disappeared.

When I got my pistol, I told my husband, revising the old Colt slogan, "God made men *and women,* but Sam Colt made them equal." Recently I have seen a gunmaker's ad with a similar sentiment. Perhaps this is an idea whose time has come, though the pacifist inside me will be saddened if the only way women can achieve equality is by carrying weapons. 25

We must treat a firearm's power with caution. "Power tends to corrupt, and absolute power corrupts absolutely," as a man (Lord Acton) once said. A pistol is not the only way to avoid being raped or murdered in today's world, but, intelligently wielded, it can shift the balance of power and provide a measure of safety.

THE INVOLVED READER

1 What traditional advice for avoiding danger had Hasselstrom received? What did she feel were its shortcomings? What alternatives did she explore before she turned to guns?

2 What about her situation or living conditions put her especially at risk? What incidents drove home the risks she was running?

3 According to Hasselstrom, what does it take to use a gun successfully for protection? What are the pitfalls? Why does she go into such detail?

4 Do you think the louts Hasselstrom describes in her final paragraphs were exceptions? Or are they typical? Can anything be done about such individuals?

TALKING, THINKING, WRITING

5 Does Hasselstrom persuade you that a pistol, "intelligently wielded," can "shift the balance of power and provide a measure of safety" for women? Why or why not?

6 Do we tend to think that women who are victims of rape or violence are partly to blame?

7 Can women count on men to help protect them from violence or abuse?

8 The cross was the symbol of the European Middle Ages in the time of the crusades. The barbed wire of the camps became the symbol of the totalitarian societies of the twentieth century. At the end of the century, do you think the gun would be a fitting symbol for today's America?

COLLABORATIVE PROJECTS

9 What safety advice does local law enforcement give to women? How useful or how useless is it? Where would you and your classmates turn to find out?

We're in the Army Now

DAVID FRANCE

Is it possible to change deeply ingrained attitudes, perhaps rooted in hostilities or taboos of long standing? Homophobia — the fear or hatred of gays — is one such seemingly deep-rooted attitude. David France wrote the following article when the election of a liberal president had reopened the issue of gays in the military. Traditional policies designed to separate gay men and lesbians from the military (with dishonorable discharges) were being widely questioned. During his campaign for president, Bill Clinton had promised to lift the ban on gays in the armed services, but he seemed ready to settle for a compromise position of quiet acceptance or toleration, summed up as "don't ask, don't tell, don't pursue." At the same time, incidents of brutal "gay-bashing" were being widely reported. Do you think the following article persuasive enough to change the minds of hostile readers?

I was paying scant attention when Bill Clinton first backed the notion of allowing gays in the military. Pundits called it evidence of a lurking homosexual lobby; the truth was, few gay people were very interested. Ask us to rank the various humiliations we regularly endure and we'd list Army purges pretty far from the top. While candidate Clinton was firming up his platform, my lover, Doug, was getting sicker — the chemo he was taking for his AIDS-related cancer was eating away at his strength and at his bone marrow. Every other week he needed transfusions; twice a day he was being injected with a bioengineered substance that was supposed to keep his blood cells reproducing. We administered the injections at home, storing the spent syringes in a mayonnaise jar filled with bleach.

In September, we were battling AIDS-phobic neighbors; in October, antigay nurses. On November 3, on the way back from our polling station, Doug seemed exuberant. But it wasn't about the military issue. It was about the possibility of improved health care. "Tax and spend, tax and spend," he hummed. "I can't wait!" And indeed he couldn't; he died 15 days later, on November 18, at 3:30 A.M., six weeks before his 34th birthday.

When December came and Clinton asserted that the first act of his administration would be to lift the ban, I received the good news listlessly. My life was a petri dish of more acute needs.

In February, I withdrew a bit more than usual and quietly marked what would have been my fifth anniversary with Doug. I didn't go to the two memorial services for friends that month, and barely noted Clinton's trip aboard the *U.S.S. Theodore Roosevelt* until the news reports came out. Apparently, he had peered into the triple-decker sleeping berths and had experienced a terrible vision of unsuspecting young men bending and clambering into their steely bunks while homosexuals brushed up against them wantonly. This apparition, his aides said, made him consider "compromise" on the controversial issue, such as limiting assignments of gay soldiers and segregating troops.

I felt sucker-punched. After propelling the issue of homosexuality   5
to the forefront of his presidency, supposedly in the name of decency, Clinton then provided the kicker to all the national tittering. Just what extremes would gay men go to, given the opportunity and proximity? Clinton may have avoided the service himself, but he must have heard the one about the soldier who dropped the soap in the communal shower — and stooped to retrieve it, against prevailing wisdom and good sense. The bigots were thrilled, of course, and I began to take it personally.

Are the same straight men in the military who've tormented women soldiers for years suddenly convinced they'll find themselves on the receiving end of such harassment?

Obviously, homosexuality hasn't always been a priority for Clinton — in his years as governor of Arkansas, not one law that protected gay men and women was passed. He never fought for the repeal of the state's sodomy proscriptions, which means gay intimacy there remains illegal. And the gays-in-the-military proposal wasn't elevated to the top of the agenda so much by Clinton's conviction as by Republican goading. The GOP persecuted gays, so Clinton had to take a stance; the party pressed the point, and his support became clearer. *Even in the Army? Well, sure, why not?*

As he steadies himself to follow through on a campaign pledge, I hope he's reviewing the facts:

The average age for heeding Uncle Sam's call is between 19 and 20, an age that predates many firm declarations of sexual identity. Hence, many of the men and women who acknowledge their homosexuality in the military are, I'm sure, as surprised by their predicament as their superiors are.

And how many gay troops there are. A 1988 Pentagon study found   10
some 200,000 gay men and lesbians in the service, making the military the number one employer of gays in the world. So we're there already, and everybody knows it — except the chairman of the Joint Chiefs of Staff. "The presence of homosexuals in the force would be detrimental to good order and discipline," General Colin Powell as-

serted. The 1988 statistics were so inconsistent with that view that they were deleted from the final report; they became public at a congressional hearing just this spring. ("You covered an area I don't want you to cover," a Pentagon functionary remembers being told. "Throw this stuff away.")

Homosexuals, then, have remained in the service at the pleasure of their superiors — the purges limited to ones and twos, when it has suited the force.

Still, despite the agreement to look the other way, some people find they must declare their homosexuality to protect their lives. Lieutenant Dirk Selland, a Navy officer, disclosed his sexual orientation to superiors last winter because, he said, the jokes and rumors about his homosexuality — including those from his commanding officer — had become threatening. When Allen Schindler made his disclosure to his Navy commanders, it was with the hope that he'd be transferred off a hostile ship. Instead, he was killed in a men's room by fellow sailors, who so brutally disfigured him that his mother recognized his remains only by the tattoos on his forearms.

Which proves a final fact: Anybody hunting for a homosexual can easily find one. This I know from personal experience.

One warm summer evening, I was accosted by a neighborhood kid so young he hadn't yet grown hair under his arms. His voice, high and discomforting spat, "AIDS fag," and he pressed angry fists into those hairless armpits as though he were holstering two pistols. Who taught him to discern a homosexual, I wondered, and from where did he summon his right to intimidate me? No doubt from the same place as another young man a year or two before, who beckoned me to the passenger-side window of his powder-blue van and offered similar words to describe me. His face was pale and smooth, twitching slightly at the perimeters, especially near his eyes, which were wide and full of ebullient anticipation. A face just like the ones worn by the men who have pinned me to the ground, or hurled objects at me, or surrounded me and doused me in beer and epithets.

Was it gait, attire, comportment, that gave me away? Did they employ updated codes like the rule from junior high (gays clutch their notebooks to their chest *like girls,* instead of dangling them at the end of one arm) or that dreaded fifth grade trap (ask them to look at their nails and straight men make a gentle fist, while the gays fling their hands up like the Supremes)? And who taught them to look for these clues? Was it passed man-to-boy in institutions I had assiduously avoided, like the Boy Scouts, the school locker room, the military?

And how do they decide, once they've identified a homosexual, to launch an assault? Crae Pridgen, a civilian, says he was leaving a North Carolina gay bar when Marines from a nearby base entered, grabbed him, dragged him into the parking lot, and fractured his skull, shouting: "Clinton must pay. All you faggots will die." At his trial in April, Lance Corporal Patrick Cardone said he fought in self-defense. He said he entered the bar with the others and a woman friend and proclaimed to all who could hear him: "I don't want nothing to do with you faggots. We're just waiting for the girl to use the bathroom and we're out of here." Then, he said, he was surrounded by patrons making sexual overtures — giving him no choice but battle. I find that explanation less than convincing, but then Judge Jacqueline Morris-Goodson didn't consult with me before she threw out the charges against the soldiers.

On my list of humiliations, her ruling ranks pretty high.

Can I be the only one to see the irony in the comments made to a reporter by an Army captain trained in the sciences of war, of military invasions and nuclear preparations, rehearsed in missile firing and sharpshooting and annihilating? "If I were to see two male officers dancing together," he said, "it would be difficult for me to accept that." If he can witness death, he can witness dancing.

And so can Clinton. Let him do it so that we can get on with the real gay issues — issues like health care, AIDS research, civil rights, education, civility. None of us can wait too much longer.

THE INVOLVED READER

1   How does the author establish his relationship with his readers? What does he accomplish by making the opening paragraphs very personal? How do they make you feel toward him?

2   How does France use public sources — authorities, news reports, or the like? What claim does he make about the official use or misuse of statistics? Does he convince you that he has a case?

3   Where does the author later in the essay draw on incidents from his own personal experience? How does he use them, and what effect do they have on you as the reader? How effective is the mix of private and public sources in this article?

4   What is the irony that the author wants his readers to see in his conclusion?

TALKING, THINKING, WRITING

5   How would you sum up France's persuasive strategy? What values does he invoke?

6 Who would be the ideal reader for this article? It was originally published in *Lear's*, read widely by success-oriented women. Do you think women would respond to the article better than men?

7 Should gay men and lesbians be allowed to serve in the military without discrimination?

COLLABORATIVE PROJECTS

8 How would you measure the tolerance level in your institution or community? Working with a group, you may want to participate in a survey asking questions like the following: Should gays be allowed to serve in the military? Should women be assigned to combat duty? Should pregnant high school students be allowed to stay in school? Should priests be allowed to marry?

short story

The Zoo Is Not the Zoo

KATHLEEN LYNCH

Are psychologists right when they stress the traumatic impact of childhood experiences on the adult's personality? The following story is a classic short story in the modern tradition. The story is tightly focused on a moment in time: A father and his daughter take a trip to the garbage dump, stop at a friends' trailer on the way back, and return home. Everything is seen from a limited point of view — the perspective of the child in the story. This perspective sets up an ironic contrast between what the child understands and what the adult reader does, who knows more than the child and is likely to apply different standards of judgment. The author does not intrude into the story — there is no editorializing, no preaching. For some readers, though, this story is likely to have a stronger impact than words of condemnation or warning could. The reader lives through the experience, which is allowed to speak for itself.

Cynthia thought going to the dump with her father was an honor, a thrill. Tom Conlan would elect one of his four daughters to accompany him on this mission, and most often he chose Cynthia. Perhaps he chose her because she did not complain about smells, the oily, sickly-sweet stench of garbage baking in the sun. Cynthia pretended she didn't mind being seen in their hulking, beat up station wagon, the wooden sides peeling and scarred, the back down to accommodate the stinking heap of her family's refuse.

Trash accumulated in their narrow side yard and seemed to grow with a force of its own. When it crept around the side of the house, up the little cement stoop and into the service porch, it was Dump Time. Always a Saturday. Always a morning with her father swearing and grumbling, her sisters' stifled whimpers, "icks" and "P.U.s." The girls helped Tom load the car with sodden newspapers, bags of decaying plant cuttings, and kitchen garbage that never made it into the battered, overstuffed can.

Cynthia took to the task energetically, without complaint. She left the easy things for her sisters, recent papers that still looked dry and clean, bags of countless crushed Lucky Lager cans. She chose more sickening things, sopping bags that had become habitats for snails, slugs, maggots. She chose heavy and dirty things, and bore them proudly in the procession from yard to car, hoping to catch her father's eye. Hoping he would see what she was willing to do for him. That he would choose her.

And when he did, they pulled away from the house, two six-packs and a can opener on the seat between them. Cynthia waved to the shadow of her mother, who stood behind the screen door, arms knotted across her chest.

Their journey always started with her father winking at her and saying, "Okey dokey, kiddo, pop one for Poppa." She opened the cold, sweating can and passed it to him, knowing that in minutes his face would slacken, become sweeter and playful, the sense of relief in the car almost as tangible as the smell of garbage. 5

Once on the road, her father sang, his voice deep, loud, lusty. Cynthia loved listening to him, even though he did not sound very tuneful or melodious. He had a wide repertoire: nursery rhymes, navy songs, jingles, love songs, Christmas carols. Even on a 103 degree Saturday in July he might burst into "Deck the Halls," and Cynthia joined in, her own flat little fa-la-las rising in the hot breeze and mingling with her father's.

Frawley's was the last gas stop before the long drive out past McClellan Air Force base to the county dump. Tom wheeled the stuffed, reeking station wagon up to the pump, leaned out the window and hollered, "Hey Sarge. Filler-up with gas-n-oil, okey-dokey?"

He called all gas station attendants Sarge. Cynthia thought he did so because they wore uniforms. The attendants seemed to like being called Sarge, and they definitely liked her father. Tom got out and followed the man around the car as he ministered to it. He asked "Sarge" about his family, his work, which team he wanted to win the ball game. As they huddled in front of the gaping hood, Cynthia heard the rumble of their conversation, punctuated by her father's occasional "Gee whiz," "No foolin" or "Son-of-a-bitch, Sarge." By the time they circled the car, Tom had always made the attendant laugh. Tom thumped the man heartily on the back and shook his hand.

Her father dwarfed most other men. He stood a beefy six-four. The gas station man beamed up at her father as Tom fished out his dollar bills.

"Take care, Mr. Conlan. Stop in again. Don't be a stranger." 10

Cynthia studied the expression on the attendant's face. He looked transformed, as if something good had happened to him. As if he had heard great news or just had a stroke of real luck.

Back in the car, her father tugged one of her dark braids and asked, "What say, little Cricket, wanna go dump some junk?"

Cynthia knew this was the cue for his next question.

"Afterward, does my gorgeous little girl want to go to the zoo?"

Cynthia wished he wouldn't call her a little girl and she knew she   15
wasn't gorgeous. She also knew the zoo was not the zoo. They had a
secret, she and her father. A pact. A sacred trust.

Gulls shrieked and criss-crossed, rising from and alighting on
steaming hills of trash at the Sacramento County Dump. Cynthia
wondered why they didn't seem to mind the putrefying smells of human garbage. They fought over slimy scraps and shreds of rotted
food.

Cynthia helped her father unload the car, sliding bag after bag
across the floor of the wagon onto the back door tipped-down like a
ramp. Tom flung the bags, called "Heave-Ho!" with each toss. Between bags he took a swig of Lucky from the can perched on the roof.
Cynthia watched his face to gauge his mood. This time was good. He
looked like a happy man.

As they pulled back onto the main road in front of the dump site,
Cynthia could tell right away where they were going. If they turned
right, they were going straight home. If they turned left, they headed
toward the river, to the house-boat people. But they crossed onto the
two-lane road that seemed to make an endless cut through miles of
flat farm land, on the way to visit Slim and Dag, in their little trailer
out in the middle of nowhere.

Tom tooted the horn in short, cheery blasts as the station wagon
crunched up the long gravel path to the trailer. All three of Dag's
dogs charged out barking and wagging and loping around the car.
Cynthia and Tom waited in the car until one of the women came out
and herded the goose, "Gander," into his chicken-wire pen. Slim
had warned Cynthia, "You won't catch any grief from those pooches,
kid, but that bird'd make mincemeat out of you. There's only two
humans he'll allow on this planet, and that's me and Dag."

Cynthia had never heard of a guard-goose before. She tried to   20
make friends with it on the first visit by sticking some fresh green
field grass into the pen, but the goose hissed and shrieked and
charged the flimsy-looking wire so fiercely that Cynthia nearly cried.
She gave up the idea that she could be friends with that creature,
and never approached the pen again.

Slim and Dag seemed like they could be sisters, but they weren't.
They looked about the same age, clearly older than Cynthia's mother.
Once Dag said, "Shoot, kid, this old gal's seen more than half a century." They both dressed alike, in tight corduroy Levis, with neatly
ironed, well-tucked-in tailored shirts. They had similar short-
cropped haircuts, too, though Dag's was shorter in front and on top.

Slim let her bangs and hair near the temples grow longer. Usually, when Cynthia and her father visited on a Saturday, Slim had a neat row of curlers rolled from ear to ear over her forehead, like a wreath of small metal flowers.

One time Cynthia asked Slim why people called her Slim when Dag was the thinner one. Slim laughed and smacked her belly with both hands. "Oh honey, I used to be a stick, a real Olive Oyl, I tell ya, 'til I moved out here with Dag. Too many brewskies, I guess. Too much good food." She rubbed her hands up and down her sausagey middle.

Dag told Cynthia that her real name was Dagmar. "Dagmar Dolby. Can you imagine a parent saddling a kid with that? A little girl kid? And then expect her to turn out right?"

Cynthia loved the inside of their trailer. Everything looked so cozy and cute and clean. Even though their whole dwelling was barely bigger than the Conlans' living and dining room combined, it looked neat, gleaming, cheerful.

The windows all had bright yellow curtains edged with orange rick-rack. Except in the bedroom, where pale pink dotted swiss curtains with ruffles covered the window. They matched the spread on the double bed that nearly filled the tiny room. 25

On the wall hung gold-framed pictures of Slim and Dag in their Air Force uniforms, and many snapshots were tucked into the frame around the mirror. One showed the women together at a picnic holding their beer cans aloft and laughing hard, leaning against each other. Another, taken indoors in a dark, crowded place, showed six people at a round table holding up gold filled mugs and stubby glasses of dark liquid. All their eyes glowed red from the flash. Cynthia knew only three of the people in the picture — Slim, Dag, and her father.

Cynthia liked visiting them because Slim fussed over her, called her Doll-face and Doll-buttons, made her salami sandwiches on rye. For a treat, Slim gave her Hershey Kisses or a gooey popcorn ball she made herself. Sometimes they all sat outside on folding chairs, the grownups drinking beer, Cynthia sipping a tall Coke with a lemon wedge squeezed in it.

Cynthia listened as Dag and Tom did most of the talking. They swapped stories about being in the service. Tom's Navy stories and Dag's Air Force tales were as familiar and soothing to Cynthia as the whoosh of summer air through surrounding fields, the clack of cicadas, the rustle of small creatures in the grass.

They laughed a lot. Her father's great booming holler and Dag's loud staccato honking rose and fell in the afternoon air. Cynthia giggled when they were funny like that, and Slim smiled broadly, shaking her head back and forth in little tsk-tsk movements.

Sometimes Slim unbraided Cynthia's hair and brushed it over and over, with long, gentle, rhythmic strokes until it shone and the hair rose up of its own accord to greet the brush. "I always wanted me a little girl like you, Cyn, someone I could dress up, fix real pretty, show off to people."   30

Cynthia wanted to ask Slim why she didn't get married then, and have a little girl if she wanted one, but she felt funny about asking, and never did.

When they stayed inside the trailer, Tom and Dag scooted onto the bench around the table. Her father looked huge in the little booth, like a giant in a dollhouse. Slim puttered nearby, or, when she smoked, stood at the door with her cigarette arm outside, every now and then poking her face out the crack to take a puff, hold it, and let it out.

After an hour or so of sipping beer, Dag said to Slim, "Hey hon, let's crack some of the good stuff." Slim took the whiskey bottle down from the high cupboard and got three wide short glasses from the one below. Cynthia liked the clunk and chink of ice in the glasses and the way the dark shellac-colored liquid swirled when Slim poured it in. She poured less in her glass than the others. "Just a dash," she winked at Cynthia, adding water to fill it to the brim.

As the afternoon wore on, Cynthia wandered around outside, threw sticks for the dogs, walked down the long pebbly drive and onto the road to see how far she could go before she felt too scared, too alone, and had to turn back. Very few cars passed her. Once she went so far down the road that when she turned to see the trailer she couldn't find it at first. A sick feeling rose in her belly and she thought she might cry. Then at last she sighted the trailer, so far away it looked like a bread box in the grasses, the sharp sun glinting on its aluminum roof.

When she returned, she found Dag and her father huddled low over the table, talking deeper, slower, their voices sloshy and trailing off. Slim got a concerned look on her face and said, "Okay, Chief, you better get this Doll-baby home before dark. Now come on, up-'n'-at-'em Tom."   35

As they turned back onto the road headed home, Tom stepped on the gas and drove real fast, fields streaking by, windows down to air out the car. Over the sound of wind and engine, he hollered to Cynthia, "Let's dance, honey, wanta hula?" and the car swerved and careened across both lanes, her father singing, "Oh we're going to a hukilau, a huki-huki-huki-huki-hukilau . . ." and Cynthia slammed into the door, then against her father, then the door, laughing, terrified, tears in her eyes, trying to find something to hold on to.

They did the cha-cha, her father jabbing the brakes then jamming the gas pedal, Cynthia jolting back against the seat then up to the dashboard, her hands held forward to thrust her back. After a while he slowed down, both hands up high on the wheel, leaning forward like he was concentrating on driving right, staying on his side of the road as they got closer to town, to traffic, to home.

"Don't tell your mom we went visiting, okay kiddo?"

Cynthia nodded. "Okay Dad, I won't. I won't tell."

"That's my girl, Cyn. My special girl." 40

They arrived home many hours late, as the purplish dusk darkened and cooled their small home. Her mother stood at the door watching for them, twisting her apron in her fists, her face pulled tight as if she had decided not to breathe anymore.

Tom approached carefully, his hefty hand braced on Cynthia's shoulder, trying to walk without keeling over against the stucco wall. "Sorry so late, Mar. Took my little helper to the zoo." He tried to sound lighthearted but his voice came out too high and tight, as if he, too, couldn't get enough air.

Her mother pushed the screen door open slowly and looked directly into Cynthia's eyes. "Did you go to the zoo, young lady?"

Cynthia tried not to look away from her mother's gaze. Her own eyes suddenly felt too big, like they were bugging out and starting to get dry. "Yes, Mama. We went to the zoo. I had lots of fun."

Marla looked steadily at Cynthia, held her stare until Cynthia 45 looked away, then turned her eyes up to her husband's face and stepped back, admitting them into their home.

As Cynthia ran for the kitchen or the backyard, looking for her sisters, Marla turned and walked resolutely down the hallway to the back bedroom, Tom trailing after her, saying "Hey, Mar, you mad at me? You mad at me, hon? You mad at ole Tom?"

THE INVOLVED READER

1 What lifelike detail does the author use to create the illusion of reality? What details — whether about the garbage, the trailer, the goose — help bring the story to life for you?

2 Instead of pronouncing right-or-wrong judgments, the story allows us to share in the ambivalent feelings of the girl about her father. What are some of the things that are positive or attractive

about the father? At what point in the story do you become
aware of another side of his personality?

3   Is there an implied judgment on the mother? On the two women
in the trailer?

4   Why did the author choose the title? Does it help you focus on a
major theme or concern in the story?

TALKING, THINKING, WRITING

5   In this story, seen through the eyes of the child, where are com-
ments left out that an adult observer would be likely to make?
How would you sum up the feelings of the girl about her father?
How do you think the author wants you to judge the father?

6   Do you read this story as a comment on or warning against alcoholism? How would you compare its effectiveness with more
direct warnings against alcoholism or drunk driving?

7   Can you recount an experience or tell the story of an incident
that raises an issue important to you? Can you tell it in such a
way that it might prove more persuasive than a lecture on the
subject?

poem

The Mutes

DENISE LEVERTOV

Have feminists raised public consciousness about the harassment of women in the streets and public places — by the wolf whistles of construction workers, for instance? Descended from a Jewish mystic on her father's side, Denise Levertov grew up in England "in a house full of books" and of visitors from the rest of Europe — Jewish booksellers, German theologians, Russian priests, and Viennese opera singers. Her earlier poems reflect her experience in England during World War II, when she worked in a hospital helping rehabilitate wounded veterans. Since coming to America, she has published numerous volumes of often provocative and intense poetry, writing about the turbulent undercurrents of the human mind, about the need to fight bitterness, and about the ache and joy of human relationships. She has written searing politically engaged poetry about the Vietnam War.

Those groans men use
passing a woman on the street
or on the steps of the subway

to tell her she is a female
and their flesh knows it,   5

are they a sort of tune,
an ugly enough song, sung
by a bird with a slit tongue

but meant for music?

Or are they the muffled roaring   10
of deafmutes trapped in a building that is
slowly filling with smoke?

Perhaps both.

Such men most often
look as if groan were all they could do,   15
yet a woman, in spite of herself,

knows it's a tribute:
if she were lacking all grace
they'd pass her in silence;

so it's not only to say she's   20
a warm hole. It's a word

in grief-language, nothing to do with
primitive, not an ur-language;*   *Earliest human language*
language stricken, sickened, cast down

in decripitude.* She wants to   *deterioration*   25
throw the tribute away, dis-
gusted, and can't,

it goes on buzzing in her ear,
it changes the pace of her walk,
the torn posters in echoing corridors   30

spell it out, it
quakes and gnashes as the train comes in.
Her pulse sullenly

had picked up speed,
but the cars slow down and   35
jar to a stop while her understanding

keeps on translating:
"Life after life after life goes by
without poetry
without seemliness   40
without love."

THE INVOLVED READER

1 What picture of men does Levertov conjure up in the first dozen
   lines of the poem? What attitudes and emotions does she bring
   into play?

2 In this poem, what contradictory feelings are going through the
   woman's mind? Are they different from what you might have
   expected?

3   Is there any connection between the way the poet describes the arrival of the train in the subway station and the rest of the poem?

4   Do you think the theme that the poet spells out in the concluding lines is justified by the poem as a whole?

TALKING, THINKING, WRITING

5   Do you think this poem is aimed primarily at other women? Do you think it could make men reconsider their behavior in streets and public places?

6   Would you call this poet hostile to men? Would you call her negative about sex?

7   What would you say (or write) to make men understand a woman's point of view on sexual harassment? Or, what would you say or write to make women understand how men react to charges of sexual harassment?

COLLABORATIVE PROJECTS

8   Is the image of men in current women's magazines predominantly negative?

The Writer's Tools 8

Editing for Offensive Language

Many publications and institutions insist that you edit for **offensive language** — language that intentionally or unintentionally demeans others. Many organizations have guidelines or style sheets specifying what is acceptable and unacceptable in references to individuals and groups. Writers today routinely edit for offensive language in references to gender, race, ethnicity, age, disability, and sexual preference.

Name-Calling

Some labels denigrate a whole class of people: *bureaucrat, union boss, young punk, shyster lawyer.* When you use terms like *gun-nut, do-gooder,* or *fem-libber,* you may lose readers who object to mudslinging. *Demagogue, corruption, fascist, racist, Uncle Tom* — these are fighting words, and responsible writers do not use them lightly.

Ethnic or Racial References

Responsible writing has zero tolerance for inscrutable Orientals, dumb Swedes, drunken Irishmen, or other ethnic and racial slurs too ugly to mention. New preferred labels are less likely to carry with them the prejudices or stereotypes of the past: *Oriental* became *Asian, Eskimo* became *Inuit* or *people of the North, American Indian* became *Native American, Negro* became *black* or *African American.* Some Spanish-speaking Americans use *Hispanic* but others now prefer *Latino* (for a male), *Latina* (for a woman). References to ethnicity or race in discussions of welfare or violence are often prejudicial. Identify ethnicity or race even-handedly — and preferably only when it is relevant to the issue at hand.

> BIASED: The police stopped several Mexican American youths for curfew violations.

> RELEVANT: The neighborhood association complained that Mexican American youths were more likely than Anglos to be stopped for curfew violations.

Sexist Language

Most organizations and publications have guidelines for avoiding **sexist language** — language that demeans women or locks them into traditional female roles. Such guidelines ask you to use *young woman* instead of *girl, office staff* instead of *the girls in the office,* and *female student* instead of *coed.* Pay special attention to the following:

• *Avoid gender bias in occupational labels.*   English has many uni-sex, gender-neutral terms for occupations: *senator, physician, scientist, carpenter, professor, mechanic.* But watch out for gender-specific words, especially those ending with *-man* or *-ess*. When you say that we need more *policemen* walking our streets, you make it sound as though in your mental universe police officers are male.

GENDER-SPECIFIC	GENDER-NEUTRAL
policeman	police officer
congressman	representative
mailman	mail carrier
fireman	firefighter
foreman	supervisor
chairman	chair, chairperson
businessman	merchant, businessperson
spokesman	voice, spokesperson
stewardess	flight attendant
waitress	server

• *Be wary of generic labels.*   *Mankind* and the *family of man* theoretically stood for both men and women, but *humanity* and *humankind* are more clearly gender-neutral. *Manpower* has become *labor force* or *workforce*.

• *Use references to gender or marital status not at all or in even-handed fashion.*   Use *Ms. Karen Tigue* instead of *Mrs.* or *Miss* in addressing correspondence unless you know that a woman prefers to be addressed as *Mrs.*

ASKEW: Gerald Grund, local builder, and June Moreno, mother of three, are running for City Council.

BALANCED: Gerald Grund, father of two, and June Moreno, mother of three, are regulars in the cheering section at the Junior Hockey League.

• *Become sensitive to overtones and implications.*   Emily Dickinson was not a "poetess" but America's greatest poet. *Lady Ph.D.* and *male secretary* make it sound as though you marvel that a woman should have an advanced degree or a man know how to type. *Working mother* makes it sound as if mothers not working outside the home are not working.

POOR: The department had a male secretary who explained the forms to me.

IMPROVED: I talked to the department secretary, and he explained the forms to me.

• *Deal with the pronoun dilemma.*   English does not have a gender-neutral, unisex pronoun for *he/she*. Avoid using pronouns that make it sound as if senators, doctors, professors, bosses, managers, and owners were always male and the people who work for them (nurses, assistants, secretaries) always female. A statement like the following sorts out the people involved according to gender and assigns traditional sex roles to physicians and nurses: "When a doctor entrusts *his* patients to a nurse, *he* expects *her* to follow *his* instructions."

GENDER-NEUTRAL: When entrusting patients to a nurse, doctors expect the nurse to follow their instructions.

How can you compensate for the lack of a generally accepted *(s)he* pronoun? Remember two alternatives: Use the double pronouns *he or she.* Or talk about *several* typical people instead of one typical person, changing a whole sentence from singular to plural. This last choice is usually the best option when several uses of *he or she* or *him or her* would make a passage sound awkward or roundabout.

SEXIST: A true leader cannot always please *his* constituents.

DOUBLE PRONOUN: A true leader cannot always please *his or her* constituents.

PLURAL PRONOUN: *True leaders* cannot always please *their* constituents.

Sometimes you can sidestep the pronoun dilemma altogether:

NO PRONOUN: A true leader cannot always please the voters.

Referring to Disability

The media and the general public are learning to protect people with disabilities from slighting remarks. Whether intentionally or not, familiar ways of referring to people with disabilities accentuated their limitations. Style sheets of many publications now require *hearing-impaired* instead of *deaf*; they require *wheelchair user* instead of *wheelchair bound* or *confined to a wheelchair.* They recommend alternatives to expressions that seem to define people by their illness or disability, as if it were the only thing about them that mattered. Instead of "the mentally ill," try "people with a mental illness."

WRITING WORKSHOP 5

Using Strong Language

What is the role of strong, emotionally charged language in the following passage from a student editorial? Where and with what effect does the writer use strong emotional, connotative language? Where and how effectively does he criticize the use of strong language by the other side?

S T E V E N   C H A E

Throwing Stones

The brazen shooting of a doctor by an abortion protester outside a Florida clinic was shocking in its brutality: shocking, but not really surprising. Michael Griffin, who was charged with the murder of Dr. David Gunn, apparently was sick of all the talk. Unlike those milquetoasts who sit around all day jawing about the semantics of conception, Griffin actually did something. Witnesses said Griffin chased Gunn and shot him several times in the back, point-blank, shouting, "Don't kill any more babies!"

This quote reveals the terrifying, twisted reasoning that drove Griffin to kill a husband and father of two. To Griffin, Gunn wasn't a man; he was a despicable murderer of children. Murderers must be stopped. Death mills must be closed — at all costs. Who would argue with that reasoning?

Similar reasons were given to draw support for the war against Hitler.

No one would suggest that everyone who opposes abortion is an intolerant, Bible-thumping zealot. Yet leaders of militant anti-abortion groups were less than mournful after the shooting. Operation Rescue Executive Director Keith Tucci told the Associated Press, "Because we are Christians, we do what we do because we believe that we are commanded by God. When we do what we are commanded to do, we are successful." And Rev. Joseph Foreman, spokesman for something called "Missionaries to the Preborn," told the AP, "Michael Griffin's actions, however motivated, will result in children's lives being saved." And Operation Rescue leader Randall Terry cryptically hinted that today's violence may be only the "tip of the iceberg."

The rhetoric must cool down. When doctors are labeled killers and clinics become mills of death obvious battle lines are being drawn.

When you strike the first blow, you admit you have lost the argument.

CHINESE PROVERB

Rethinking Argument

Writing to Convince

Have you participated in arguments that you remember as intelligent discussion and not as shouting matches? Have you ever felt that a subject was too serious for casual exploration or partisan sniping? When writers present a serious argument, they are asking their readers to listen to reason. They have thought the matter through, and they trust their readers to do the same. In much of the writing you have done, you have obviously already reasoned with your readers. In a structured argument, however, you present your thinking on a subject in an exceptionally systematic manner. Ideally, after weighing the points you make, your readers will reach a conclusion similar to yours.

Current treatments of argument map out roughly three dimensions: First, there is the claim you make — the point you are trying to prove. Second, there are the data you have accumulated, the evidence you have gathered. But, third, there is the real core of your argument: the logical steps that connect your claim and your data and thus warrant your conclusion.

In charting a logical argument, modern logicians, following the lead of Stephen Toulmin and others, have moved beyond traditional logic books in several ways:

• Books on thinking straight used to focus on *two basic thinking strategies*. They focused on induction and deduction as two sides of the same coin. Inductive thinking is the generalizing kind of thinking that makes researchers conclude that high cholesterol puts you at risk for heart disease. They go from specific data to general conclusions; they crunch numbers and find a pattern. Deduction reverses the procedure: It applies general knowledge to specific instances. If high cholesterol puts you at risk for heart disease, then the two-eggs-plus-bacon breakfast is not the best choice. In retrospect, the inductive/deductive scheme did not pay sufficient attention to other thinking strategies, like pro and con thinking. For instance, some researchers have challenged the conventional wisdom about cholesterol. Some of the people still eating eggs for breakfast have gone through a stage where they reviewed conflicting evidence, going from "on the one hand" to "on the other hand."

• Books on thinking straight used to focus on arguments leading to *a necessarily true conclusion*. If A is true, and if B is also true, then C *must* be true. If all human beings are mortal, and if Socrates is a human being, then Socrates *must* be mortal. However, most of the arguments in the real world lead up, not to a certainty, but to a probability. If smoking correlates with a high incidence of emphysema, then there is a strong likelihood that you will develop emphysema if you smoke a pack a day. If workers blame the loss of high-paying factory jobs on cheap immigrant labor, there is a strong chance that they will vote for flag-waving nativist candidates.

• Books on thinking straight had little *hands-on advice for writers.* What are the *uses* of logical reasoning? How do writers use familiar thinking strategies to structure a convincing, cogent argument? What lines of reasoning have often proved effective? The major writing/thinking strategies often shape a key section of a paper or a paper as a whole:

Induction You often show a pattern or a trend by presenting data that all point in the same direction. You marshal facts and figures that bear out your point. If your readers feel that you have given a fair sampling of the evidence, they may accept your conclusions. Perhaps you have documented that highly skilled immigrants have proved an asset in areas like medicine or computer programming. (In fact, the countries of origin of such highly skilled newcomers often complain about a "brain drain.") Your conclusion, even though you will typically present it at the beginning, is the result of the generalizing process, of **inductive** thinking.

Dialectic You often play off opposing views, weighing their merits. You look for common ground, trying to settle for a balanced conclusion. Ideally, from the play of **pro and con**, a less one-sided, better informed position emerges. Your readers can feel that they have looked at both sides of the argument. They have given due weight to different facets of the issue and arrived at a responsible conclusion. Do sports keep primitive aggressive instincts alive, contributing to the escalation of violence in our world? Or do they channel our inherited aggressive and competitive instincts into peaceful rituals that are incomparably preferable to war? Something is to be said on both sides, and a well-balanced paper will make your readers think. Perhaps you can encourage them to lend more support to sports that foster peaceful competition (like women's volleyball) and less to boxing or to races where drivers crash and burn.

Deduction   You will often argue from principle. You start from assumptions that you expect to be accepted by your intended readers. You establish shared assumptions and build an argument on them that has the force of logic. The basic logical pattern is "If A is true, and if B is true, then C will also be true." For example, if only A students are eligible for the honor society, and if you are a B student, then it follows that you are not eligible. The same basic pattern underlies many arguments on public issues:

> IF: The U.S. Constitution separates church and state, religion and government.
>
> AND IF: The nativity scene is a religious symbol.
>
> THEN: The nativity scene should not be displayed on government property, for example, at city hall.

Such arguments draw out conclusions already implied in the premises. They are examples of **deductive** thinking. The shared assumptions are your **premises** — they provide the foundation on which the rest of the argument rests. A successful argument takes the reader from accepted premises through a chain of logical reasoning to a valid conclusion. In much effective writing, deductive thinking applies a general rule or a general principle to specific instances. It guides us when we try to implement general laws or regulations:

• How do current regulations requiring gender equity in college athletics apply to college football? If it is true that the football budget far exceeds the combined outlay for women's sports, is your school in violation of federal guidelines?

• If federal guidelines forbid excluding students from a college because of gender, does this mean the end not only of traditional all-male but also all-women colleges?

- If equal opportunity requires that we do not consider a person's race or gender in applications for employment, then are affirmative action programs a contradiction?

THOUGHT LOG 9

Thinking about Assumptions

Spirited exchanges during debates or on programs like *Crossfire* result when controversial issues are approached by people with different assumptions. Listen to a campus debate or a program that confronts speakers with different views. Try to chart assumptions that underlie the speakers' arguments. What do they assume or take for granted? What attitudes or beliefs are implied in what they say? They are arguing from different premises — what are the premises?

Structuring Your Argument

I think; therefore, I am.

RENÉ DESCARTES

The purpose of a logical argument is to move the discussion of an issue beyond personal preference, beyond likes and dislikes. If statistics show a correlation between smoking and heart disease, and if I am a smoker, I may still decide to smoke, but I don't have the option of denying the risk to my health. When you take your readers through the steps in a structured argument, you try to show that your position has the force of logic on its side.

Arguing from Principle   Traditionally, logicians have charted a deductive argument as a three-step pattern. Such a three-step argument, moving from two accepted premises to a justified conclusion, is called a **syllogism**:

FIRST PREMISE:	All full-time students are eligible for the loan program.
SECOND PREMISE:	You are a full-time student.
CONCLUSION:	Therefore, you are eligible.
FIRST PREMISE:	No illegal aliens will be hired.
SECOND PREMISE:	I am an illegal alien.
CONCLUSION:	Therefore, I need not apply.

FIRST PREMISE: No illegal aliens will be hired.

SECOND PREMISE: I am *not* an illegal alien!

CONCLUSION: Therefore, I am eligible.

There is no arguing with arguments like these: In each of these syllogisms, the first premise specifies what it includes or rules out. The conclusion necessarily follows because the premise includes or rules out *all* members of a group. In practice, many arguments are not true syllogisms. Arguments that use *some* or *many* instead of *all* or *no* in the first premise are less airtight. They lead to a *probable* conclusion:

IF: Most members of the Achievement Club are business majors.

AND IF: Cecily is a member of the Achievement Club.

THEN: Cecily is likely to be a business major.

An argument is only as good as the premises on which it is based. It may be technically valid, proceeding according to the rules. But if it is built on shaky premises, the results will still be untrue. When you present an argument like the following, your readers may challenge your premises rather than your conclusions:

IF: Students learn best in a relaxed, supportive atmosphere.

AND IF: The present system of exams makes for tension and anxiety.

THEN: Exams work against true learning.
           (But do not at least some students perform better under pressure?)

Deductive reasoning sets up the underlying logical structure for many papers that argue from principle or appeal to the reader's basic values. An argument like the following brings widely accepted assumptions about justice to bear on the current controversy about capital punishment:

IF: A basic principle of justice requires that the justice system be willing to correct its mistakes.

AND IF: Capital punishment makes it impossible for the justice system to correct judicial error, since it has literally already buried its mistakes.

THEN: Capital punishment violates a basic principle of justice.

WRITING WORKSHOP I

A Paper for Peer Review

What assumptions underlie the following paper? Can you chart the student writer's arguments according to the *if-and if-then* pattern? If a pollster came to your door and asked you whether you believed in them, would you answer yea or nay? Are you prepared to follow the argument from the principles invoked to the logical conclusion?

Justice Denied

"On the subject of crime, all politicians are demagogues," says a columnist in a recent issue of the *New Republic*. Playing to the public fear of violent crime, legislators everywhere are advocating stiffer sentencing laws and more and bigger prisons. The death penalty, which was in abeyance in the seventies and eighties, has made a comeback. The courts are shortening the appeals process that has kept many convicted criminals on death row for ten, twelve, or fourteen years. However, in spite of the strong grassroots support for the revival of the death penalty, capital punishment violates several basic principles underlying the American system of justice.

The weakness of passionate last-minute appeals for clemency is that they tend to focus on the special circumstances of the individual case. A murderer was the victim of child abuse. A rapist suffered brain damage. By focusing on the individual histories of those waiting on death row, we run the danger of losing sight of the principles at stake when a civilized society reinstitutes capital punishment.

Most basic to our legal system is the commitment to even-handed justice. We believe that equal crimes should receive equal punishment. However, the death penalty has always been notorious for its "freakish unfairness." In the words of one study, "judicial safeguards for preventing the arbitrary administration of capital punishment are not working." Some murderers walk the streets again after three or five or seven years, whereas others — because of ineffectual legal counsel, an ambitious prosecutor, or a hanging judge — join the inmates waiting out their appeals on death row. Judges and juries apply widely different standards. In one celebrated case, two partners in crime were convicted of the same capital crime on identical charges. One was executed; the other is in prison and will soon be eligible for parole.

We believe that all citizens are equal before the law. Justice should be blind to wealth, race, or ethnic origin. However, poor defendants are many times more likely to receive the death penalty than wealthy ones. Rich defendants are protected by highly paid teams of lawyers whose maneuvers stymie the prosecution. Defendants with millions to spend bring in an array of experts who baffle the jury. Minority defendants convicted of capital crimes have a much higher statistical chance of being executed than white defendants. . . .

Finally, fairness demands that the judicial system correct its own mistakes. If someone has been unjustly convicted there should be a mechanism for reversing the verdict and setting the person free. No one doubts that there are miscarriages of justice. Witnesses admit to mistaken identification of suspects. A convict confesses on his deathbed to a crime for which someone else was convicted. A woman withdraws a rape charge years after the accused was sent to prison. However, in the case of the death penalty, any such correction of error is aborted. The judicial system buries its mistakes. We are left with futile regrets, like the prosecutor who said: "Horrible as it is to contemplate, we may have executed the wrong man."

Eliminating Alternatives   Many decisions are the result of a process of elimination. When you examine two proposed solutions to a problem and reject them, your readers will look with hope at proposed solution number three or four.

In a classic essay on sexual harassment in the workplace, the American anthropologist Margaret Mead first identified the problem: physical familiarities around the water cooler, pressuring female subordinates for sexual favors, belittling of a female co-worker's suggestions. She then examined two familiar remedies and found them wanting. First, she looked at the trend to issue regulations and guidelines — which, like other well-meant paper rules, may be no match for deeply ingrained attitudes. Second, she looked at litigation as a familiar recourse — which however puts what may be an unfair burden on the woman bringing suit. The shortcomings of the first two alternatives prepared her readers to see the need for a more basic long-range remedy: education that will bring about basic changes in the attitudes and expectations of the next generation.

This same line of argument often works well in papers weighing other kinds of options:

PHASE ONE: first alternative examined and rejected

PHASE TWO: second alternative examined and rejected

PHASE THREE: third alternative examined and embraced

WRITING WORKSHOP 2

Joining the Argument

What do you think of the logic in the following excerpt? Would you accept or quarrel with the writer's assumptions?

My first premise would be that *half* of everything taught should be about women. This is about the most radical demand that one could make; and there is no way it could currently be met, because the curriculum materials simply have not been constructed to provide students with such a balance.

Gender equity demands nothing less than half the curriculum space; women comprise half the population, have half the human experiences, and have contributed half of the energies to our society, so reason demands that they constitute half the knowledge base. This means that half the authors taught should be women, half the mathematics examples should relate to females, and half the mathematical models should be women as well. Half the science should relate to females, and the increasing prestige of biology, ecological studies, and environmental science makes this a very realistic proposition. Half the sociology, politics, and geography/anthropology disciplines should be concerned with women's lives. And of course, half the history should be about women.

Whenever I teach such information to young women, countering the misinformation they are given, there is no problem about "feminism." Offered an alternative to Madonna, they seize on it with excitement.

Dale Spender, "An Alternative to Madonna," *Ms.*

Checking for Logical Fallacies

Reasoning, like piloting a plane, is subject to human error. Books on straight thinking sound warnings against **fallacies** — predictable ways reasoning goes wrong. For instance, it is human to look for a simple answer to a complicated question — hoping for a quick fix or a quick cure. It is human to place the blame on others rather than ourselves. Some people incline toward an overoptimistic and others toward an overpessimistic hypothesis.

Check your writing for examples of shortcut thinking. Here is a sampling of fallacies that will undermine your credibility with your readers.

Ad Hominem An *ad hominem* argument is directed "at the person." Instead of arguing an issue on its merits, you attack your opponent as corrupt, incompetent, or oversexed. You drag in an opponent's divorce or sexual orientation. Sometimes the moral character or behavior of the opponent *is* the issue, but even then personal attacks put a special burden of proof on you as the writer. And even if you win the argument, readers may think of you as a mean-spirited person.

Circular Arguments Some arguments seem to move forward from premise to conclusion, but in fact they merely circle back to the initial assumption. An argument like the following merely repeats the same assumption in somewhat different words:

CIRCULAR: True ability will always assert itself.
People of true ability see to it that their talents are recognized.
Therefore, true ability will not want for recognition.

Circular Definition   You merely postpone tackling an important term if you start with a circular definition like "Islam is the religion of Muslims." So what *are* the religious beliefs that make them Muslims?

False Analogy   An analogy is a detailed, systematic comparison between two things that are parallel in several ways. You employ a false analogy when you stretch the similarities between two things too far. For instance, it is true that the federal budget is in some ways like a family budget. But the analogy holds only up to a point — and then it breaks down. Like a family, the government has to remember that at some point bills become due. However, unlike the government, a family cannot manipulate interest rates, raise taxes, or print money.

False Dilemma   A true dilemma puts us in a tight spot and leaves us only two ways out — both bad. A true dilemma faces medical researchers conducting animal experiments. Should they heed advocates of animal rights and abandon experiments that torture animals? Or should they continue experiments that benefit suffering human beings? A *false* dilemma narrows your choices to two — so that you will shun the obviously bad one and opt for the one favored by the writer. A false dilemma sets up an either-or choice: Either let a downtown area deteriorate, or raze the area and rebuild. A third alternative, hidden from view here, might be to restore and renovate, preserving much of the original architecture.

Faulty Syllogism   An argument may look like a syllogism and yet march toward a wrong inference. For instance, when the first premise starts with the word *all*, it is easy to draw a wrong conclusion. The word *all* includes everyone in a group — but it does not exclude others. It often means "all these — and maybe others." When you forget this nonexclusive nature of the word, you may engage in shortcut thinking:

FIRST PREMISE: All Marxists admire Karl Marx.

SECOND PREMISE: Professor Walters admires Karl Marx.

WRONG: Therefore, Professor Walters must be a Marxist.

FIRST PREMISE: All pigeons have feathers.

SECOND PREMISE: My canary has feathers.

WRONG: Therefore, my canary is a pigeon.

In the first example, the first premise does not rule out the possibility that, in addition to all Marxists, many *non*-Marxists also admire Karl Marx — while disagreeing with many of his conclusions. Professor Walters may not be a Marxist but merely a person who is knowledgeable about Marx and Marxism. When you label him a Marxist, you are drawing an unjustified conclusion.

Hasty Generalization Have you heard sweeping generalizations about sales clerks, liberals, welfare mothers, or African nations? We often have to rethink hasty generalizations and scale them down as needed, taking both affirmative and contrary evidence into account.

Hidden Premises Your readers may be reluctant to go along with your argument because they sense there are unstated assumptions, or hidden premises. When you bring these out into the open, you have a chance to reexamine them, and to revise them if necessary.

PREMISE:	My economics teacher is from a middle-class background.
CONCLUSION:	She cannot be expected to sympathize with the poor.
HIDDEN PREMISE:	(People cannot sympathize with someone from a different class?)

Innuendo Innuendo makes accusations that are hard to defend against — because no overt accusation has been made. People who use innuendo do not make charges; they hint, whisper, and insinuate. To pledge support for the "truly needy" or the "deserving poor" is to imply that many receive support who aren't. A current variation of innuendo is to say that "questions have been raised" or that "questions remain" — insinuating that the answers might be damaging, whatever they are.

Post Hoc *Fallacy* *Post hoc ergo proper hoc* is Latin for "after this, therefore because of this." When two things happen in succession, it is natural to speculate that one caused the other. However, it is fallacious to rule out other causes. A young man develops schizophrenia after working at a stressful job — did the stress cause the illness? A driver smashes into a concrete pillar of a freeway overpass after drinking two beers — did the drinking cause the accident, or did the driver have a heart attack?

Reductio Ad Absurdum When we "reduce an argument to absurdity," we push it to ridiculous extreme. We discredit a theory by applying it to the most unlikely situation. For instance, a writer may be objecting to advocates "inventing" new rights, such as the right of homeless people to a home, or the right of sick people to a doctor. To discredit such claims, he may start quoting people who claimed a right to become grandparents. While we chuckle at this absurdity, we have been diverted from the point at issue — for instance, whether sick, old, or jobless people have a right to a roof over their heads.

Rationalization   You rationalize when you choose the least damaging or most flattering explanation. You may be rationalizing when you blame a low grade not on missing an important deadline but on your teacher's being prejudiced against white males, black males, women, Southerners, Mexicans, or Jews.

Scapegoating   In good times, we bring in foreign migrant workers to do stoop labor for us in the fields. In bad times, we blame the state's budget deficit on immigrant workers' being on welfare and using state services. Teachers are made scapegoats for the public's neglect and underfunding of education.

Slanting   Slanting is the practice of selecting only evidence that supports your side of the argument — and sweeping contrary evidence under the carpet. If tobacco companies play up studies questioning the health risks of smoking but ignore studies pointing to serious health hazards, they are loading the dice.

Wishful Thinking   People find reasons to believe what they want to believe. If they want to believe that their neighborhood will be safer, they grasp at statistics that seem to show a decline in crime. What if the statistics really show that people *report* fewer crimes — because they don't expect the authorities to do much about them?

| **WRITING WORKSHOP 3** |

Checking for Sound Logic

Which of the following arguments are logical? Which illustrate common fallacies? How would you argue in support of the writer? On what grounds would you take issue with the writer?

1 Carl Losinger disappeared from the city a few days after the police started a crackdown on drug pushers. Losinger must have been involved in the narcotics trade.
2 The main argument for the existence of extraterrestrial civilizations is statistical. There are billions of suns. Some of these suns must have planets. The statistical chances are that some of these places are habitable.

3 Alcoholism is an addiction, like a heroin habit. Therefore, beer should not be sold on college campuses.

4 Students study because they hope for good grades or fear bad ones. When there is no tough grading system to offer reward or punishment, students have no incentive to learn.

5 A law has to be approved by a majority of the people before it becomes the law; therefore, everyone should obey the law.

6 Scholarships awarded at this college will no longer be allowed to be limited to students of a specific ethnic origin. Therefore, special scholarships for African American students will be a thing of the past.

7 Since the airstrikes on suspected guerilla positions, six weeks have passed without renewed terrorist attacks. This proves that terrorists respect the language of force.

8 The police department continues to enforce a minimum height requirement for new hires. As with other species, the human female tends to be less bulky (and less tall) than the human male. Therefore, the police department policy discriminates against women.

9 The holocaust is indelibly engraved on the memory of the Jewish people. My history teacher spent four consecutive class hours on the holocaust. She must be Jewish.

OPTIONS FOR WRITING 9

A Matter of Principle

Choose a topic that for you is a matter of principle. What is the principle involved? What does it mean in practice? What precedents or parallels might you be able to cite? What objections or complications might you have to face?

1 Should schools be able to regulate the appearance of students? For instance, are schools justified in imposing dress codes, issuing regulations concerning hairstyle, or banning gang paraphernalia? Write for an audience that might include administrators, parents, and students.

2 Should parents of a public school student have the right to veto reading materials that they object to on religious or moral grounds? Write for an audience of potential voters in school board elections.

3 Should communities be allowed to have religious displays on public property — at Christmas time, for instance? Try to explain the principles at stake to an audience puzzled by the controversy.

4 Should college football be exempt from laws requiring gender equity — that is, equal recognition and funding for women

sports? Write for an audience including alumni and football fans among others.

5   Should society have laws requiring affirmative action to correct the injustices of the past? Try to argue the issues involved for an audience including both advocates and opponents of affirmative action.

6   Should our laws require equal pay for work of comparable value? Assume you are writing for a predominantly male audience. Can you make your readers see the principle at stake?

7   Should our laws and institutions recognize marriage between domestic partners of the same sex? Write for voters whose vote could affect decisions concerning this issue.

8   Should churches admit women to the ministry or priesthood? Write for readers who were raised in a setting where traditional views on this issue prevailed.

9   Should animal experiments be banned?

10 Should college students be able to choose their own courses in an all-elective curriculum? Write for an audience including administrators and teachers as well as students.

Reading, Discussion, Writing

The Committed Writer

OVERVIEW: The authors of the following selections write from strong commitment or conviction. They take a stand, and they demonstrate what their principles mean in practice. They ask you to rethink your assumptions — whether on censorship, crime and punishment, abortion, or assisted suicide. They try to deal with the complications or obstacles in their path. Do you share their convictions? Or would you argue from different premises?

Whose Lathe?

URSULA K. LE GUIN

*Is censorship on the rise in the United States? In the words of
Ursula Le Guin, "Any author who boasts about freedom of the press
in the United States should, perhaps, make certain that none of his
or her books has been banned, dropped from a reading list as immoral or anti-religious or 'secular humanist' . . . or weeded out or
locked away by a public librarian or school librarian under pressure."
Le Guin, a native of Berkeley who studied at Radcliffe and Columbia,
is best known as a writer of science fiction. Her work, including the
Earth Sea Trilogy, does not focus on space age technology or monsters
from another galaxy but instead takes her readers on voyages through
the inner space of the human mind. Le Guin is a politically active author who writes about the American heartland, about women's issues,
about world hunger, about protecting the environment, and about
the heritage of the Native American past. She included the following
selection in a collection of her talks and essays called* Dancing at the
Edge of the World *(1989). In introducing this essay about censorship,
she said: "The arguments made are local and specific; the problem addressed is national and general."*

In a small town near Portland late this spring, a novel, *The Lathe
of Heaven,* was the subject of a hearing concerning its suitability for
use in a senior-high-school literature class. I took a lively interest in
the outcome, because I wrote the novel.

The case against the book was presented first. The man who was
asking that it be withdrawn stated his objections to the following
elements in the book: fuzzy thinking and poor sentence structure; a
mention of homosexuality; a character who keeps a flask of brandy
in her purse, and who remarks that her mother did not love her. (It
seemed curious to me that he did not mention the fact that this same
character is a Black woman whose lover/husband is a White man. I
had the feeling that this was really what he hated in the book, and
that he was afraid to say so; but that was only my feeling.)

He also took exception to what he described as the author's
advocacy of non-Christian religions and/or of non-separation of
Church and State (his arguments on this point, or these points, were
not clear to me).

Finally, during discussion, he compared the book to junk food,
apparently because it was science fiction.

The English Department of the school then presented a carefully   5
prepared, spirited defense of the book, including statements by students who had read it. Some liked it, some didn't like it, most objected to having it, or any other book, banned.

In discussion, teachers pointed out that since it is the policy of the
Washougal School District to assign an alternative book to any student who objects on any grounds to reading an assigned one, the
attempt to prevent a whole class from reading a book was an attempt
to change policy, replacing free choice by censorship.

When the Instructional Materials Committee of the district voted
on the motion to ban the book, the motion was defeated twenty
votes to five. The hearing was public and was conducted in the most
open and democratic fashion. I did not speak, as I felt the teachers
and students had spoken eloquently for me.

Crankish attacks on the freedom to read are common at present.
When backed and coordinated by organized groups, they become
sinister: In this case, I saw something going on that worried me a
good deal because it did not seem to be coming from an outside
pressure group, but from elements of the educational establishment
itself: this was the movement to change policy radically by instituting, or "clarifying," guidelines or criteria for the selection/elimina-
tion of books used in the schools. The motion on which this committee of the school district voted was actually that the book be
withdrawn *"while guidelines and policies for the district are worked
out."* Those guidelines and policies were the real goal, I think, of the
motion.

Guidelines? That sounds dull. Innocent. Useful. Of course we
have to be sure about the kinds of books we want our kids to read in
school. Don't we?

Well, do we? The dangerous vagueness of the term "guidelines   10
and policies for the district" slides right past such questions as: Who
are "we"? Who decides what the children read? Does "we" include
you? Me? Teachers? Librarians? Students? Are fifteen-to-eighteen-
year-olds ever "we," or are they always "they"?

And what are the guidelines to be? On what criteria or doctrines
are they to be based?

The people concerned with schools in Oregon try, with ever decreasing budgets, to provide good, sound food in the school cafete-
rias, knowing that for some students that's the only real meal they
get. They try, with ever decreasing budgets, to provide beautiful, intelligent books in classes and school libraries, knowing that for many
students those are the only books they read. To provide the best:

everyone agrees on that (even the people who vote against school levies). But we don't and we can't agree on what books are the best. And therefore what is vital is that we provide variety, abundance, plenty — not books that reflect one body of opinion or doctrine, not books that one group or sect thinks good, but the broadest, richest range of intellectual and artistic material possible.

Nobody is forced to read any of it. There is that very important right to refuse and choose an alternative.

When a bad apple turns up, it can be taken out of the barrel on a case-by-case, book-by-book basis — investigated, defended, prose-cuted, and judged, as in the hearing on my *Lathe of Heaven*.* But this can't be done wholesale by using "guidelines," instructions for cen-sorship. There is no such thing as a moral filter that lets good books through and keeps bad books out. Such criteria of "goodness" and "badness" are a moralist's dream but a democrat's nightmare.

Censorship, here or in Russia or wherever, is absolutely anti- 15 democratic and elitist. The censor says: You don't know enough to choose, but we do, so you will read what we choose for you and nothing else. The democrat says: The process of learning is that of learning how to choose. Freedom isn't given, it's earned. Read, learn, and earn it.

I fear censorship in this Uriah Heepish guise of "protecting our children," "stricter criteria," "moral guidance," "a more definite policy," and so on. I hope administrators, teachers, librarians, par-ents, and students will resist it. Its advocates are people willing to treat others not only as if they were not free but were not even wor-thy of freedom.

* Currently (1987) a textbook written for Oregon schools called *Let's Oregon-ize* is going through this process on the state level. The arguments against it were brought by environmentalists and others who found it tendentious and biased towards certain industries and interests. From my point of view it certainly sounds like a rather bad apple. But it is getting a scrupulously fair hearing. [Author's note]

THE INVOLVED READER

1 What is the gist of Le Guin's account of the censorship case in-volving her own book? What makes her account low-key? Do you think it is strange that her account is unemotional when she says elsewhere about censorship, "there is nothing I can do about it except protest against it whenever and wherever I can"?

2 Why does Le Guin object to the setting up of guidelines and cri-teria to guide librarians or teachers in the selection of books?

3 What "guidelines" do you think Le Guin would set up for school districts or libraries under pressure? On what principles does she take her stand?

4 Why is freedom of the press basic to Le Guin's definition of democracy and freedom?

TALKING, THINKING, WRITING

5 Have you observed or experienced censorship at first hand? When and where? Have there been recent censorship controversies on your campus or in your community?

6 Le Guin says that of the students going on record concerning her book "most objected to having it, or any other book, banned." Would you have been on these students' side? Do you think banning books is wrong on principle? Or are there cases when it is justified?

COLLABORATIVE PROJECTS

7 Is censorhip on the rise? Working with a group, check out recent statistics or case histories recorded by librarians' groups or organizations like the National Council of Teachers of English (NCTE).

The Conservative Case for Abortion

JERRY Z. MULLER

Is the choice between "pro-choice" and "pro-life" a false dilemma? Liberals have long fought for abortion rights, with traditionally Catholic countries like Italy and Ireland finally granting women the right to decide whether and when to have a child. In the United States, a strong fundamentalist backlash has called the right to choose into question, with state legislatures debating whether or not to force a woman to bear a rapist's child. Jerry Z. Muller's essay on abortion delineates a third position as an out from the confrontation of pro-choice and pro-life factions. Muller's most recent book, Adam Smith in His Time and Ours, *was published in 1995 in paperback by Princeton University Press. He wrote the following article for the* New Republic, *whose contributors range over the ideological landscape, forcing readers to rethink cherished assumptions.*

In contemporary American political debate, struggles over abortion are usually treated as conflicts between rival interpretations of individual rights. Those who favor abortion most often invoke the "right to choose" of the woman who has conceived the fetus. Those who oppose abortion focus on the "right to life" of the fetus. But there is a third position that is largely overlooked. Essentially conservative and "pro-family," it favors abortion as the right choice to promote healthy family life under certain circumstances.

This argument, which emphasizes the social function of the family over the rights of the individual, begins with the assumption that the possibility of choice matters less than the choices made. It argues that the choice to give birth to a child isn't always the right one. In fact, under some conditions, choosing to give birth may be socially dysfunctional, morally irresponsible or even cruel: inimical to the forces of stability and bourgeois responsibility conservatives cherish.

Supporters of middle-class family values may agree with many Christian Coalition positions. They may advocate raising the income-tax deduction for dependent children, question the legitimation of homosexuality and condemn violence and sex in the cultural marketplace. But the right-to-life position undermines their fundamentally conservative effort to strengthen purposeful families. For the right-to-life position requires massive government intrusion into the most intimate of realms, removes decisions about whether to bear children from those who are to raise them and threatens what many conservatives regard as the most significant mediating institution in modern capitalist society, the family. The success of the right-to-life position would lead almost inevitably to an increase in the number of children born into socially dysfunctional settings.

The prime obstacle to the right-to-life movement is not feminism. It is the millions of more or less conservative middle-class parents who know that, if their teenage daughters were to become pregnant, they would advise her to get an abortion rather than marry out of necessity or go through the trauma of giving birth and then placing the child up for adoption. Many people — young, unmarried, pregnant women loath to bring a child into a family-less environment; parents of a fetus known to be afflicted by a disease such as Tay-Sachs that will make its life painful and short; parents whose children are likely to be born with severe genetic defects, who know that the birth of the fetus will mean pain for them and for their other children — all choose abortion, not because they fetishize choice but because they value the family. Many couples who know that their offspring will be at risk for genetic diseases and other birth defects owe their actual families to abortion: were it not for the possibility of detecting these diseases in utero and of aborting stricken fetuses, such couples would not risk having children at all.

The right-to-life movement regards human "life" as a good — a   5
claim most of us are broadly inclined to accept. But the right-to-life movement goes further. It regards *all* human life as a good, regardless of the mental, emotional or intellectual capacities of the individual. To right-to-lifers, keeping alive anencephalic infants (children missing all or most of their brains) is a moral imperative. The right-to-life movement regards every degree of human life as equal to the most complete development of human life: that is why the moral status of a fetus two weeks into its development is the same as that of children and adults.

For the right-to-life movement, then, human life is not only a good, it is the highest good, and it is always the highest good. The movement's strategic aim is to extend state power to preserve and protect every fetus that is conceived, regardless of the circumstances under which it is conceived, regardless of the condition of the fetus and regardless of the will of the fetus's parents.

The right-to-life movement has done our society a service by insisting upon the humanity and moral worth of the unborn child. But opponents of abortion have turned a legitimate moral concern into a moral absolute. They have made biological life not one good to be fought for, but the only good, to which all others must be subordinated. For this reason, anti-abortion activists insist that abortion be forbidden in cases of rape or incest; to suggest there are moral considerations other than those of the life of the fetus is to question the fundamental premises of the right-to-life movement.

One of those considerations is the creation and preservation of families. The pro-life movement is at odds with the assumptions of middle-class family formation. These families believe that the bearing and rearing of children is not an inexorable fate but a voluntary vocation, and that, like any other vocation, it is to be pursued methodically using the most effective means available. Such a conception of the family includes planning when children are to be born and how many are to be born. It seeks to increase the chances of successfully socializing and educating children in order to help them find fulfilling work and spiritual lives. The number of children is kept low in part because the amount of parental time and resources devoted to raising them is expected to be high.

This depiction of the middle-class family as a vocation borrows from the characterization of economic activity as a vocation in Weber's *The Protestant Ethic and the Spirit of Capitalism*. Weber argued that a key element in the rise of capitalism was a notion of economic activity as purposeful. This notion motivated those most active in capitalist economic activity, providing an alternative to traditional, fatalistic conceptions of economic life. Just as older patterns of economic traditionalism and fatalism persist within advanced industrial societies, fatalistic conceptions of family life remain as well, in which families are not consciously "made" but "happen" because fate has so decreed.

Declining fertility is universal among advanced industrial societies. Beginning in the European bourgeois family, fertility was consciously curtailed by contraception or abortion when the desired and limited number of children was reached. By the late nineteenth century, marriage in Europe was increasingly postponed until a decade or more after puberty, and one or another form of contraception allowed greater control over the timing and spacing of births. 10

The technological repertoire of today's family planning includes abortion to prevent out-of-wedlock childbirth, artificial contraception within marriage and voluntary sterilization when families have reached their desired size. This activist conception of family formation also suggests that artificial reproductive technology should be used to reverse infertility. Prenatal screening is part of the package: potential children known to carry debilitating diseases may be aborted to make possible the birth of children more likely to grow into healthy, productive adulthood. Given the assumptions of middle-class family formation, ignoring such technological possibilities can even be regarded as a form of child neglect.

This middle-class vision of the family is linked to other elements of modern life. It is a conception that those who seek to conserve modern society ought to fortify rather than undermine. It is under attack from many quarters, including the individualism and hedonism of much of our popular and elite culture and the emphasis on career advancement among both men and women. But it is also threatened from another direction by the right-to-life movement.

The struggle between the ideals of middle-class family formation and more fatalistic conceptions of family life is in part a struggle between groups in our society with divergent conceptions of rational, purposeful behavior. Members of the upper middle class are usually either the product of families with a rational, purposeful, planned view of domestic life or have adopted such behavior on their own. It is no coincidence that the Evangelical Protestant denominations that most vociferously oppose abortion draw disproportionately from the lower middle and working classes, emphasize faith as the antidote to fate and stress redemption through divine grace rather than through a lifetime of purposeful activity.

The ideology of middle-class family formation maintains that families are not just another lifestyle option but an essential part of a modern society. Illegitimacy is stigmatized because it is socially dysfunctional. Conservatives have long assured that government should promote those social norms that encourage the creation of decent men and women and discourage those that experience has shown to be harmful. This logic lies at the heart of conservative debates on public policy, including recent proposals to reform welfare to discourage out-of-wedlock births.

The right-to-life movement stands as a barrier to such reform.   15
The removal of government subsidies for the bearing of out-of-wedlock children, it is said, will create an incentive for pregnant teenagers and other pregnant unmarried women to resort more frequently to abortion. Though the claim is most often articulated by pro-life opponents of welfare reform, it is also an unarticulated premise of many who favor the elimination of welfare payments to unwed mothers.

Is it more important to minimize abortion or to minimize the birth of children to women who are unprepared to provide the familial structure needed for children to become stable and responsible adults? A growing consensus holds that unsocialized children are at the heart of our social deterioration, not only because they are more likely to engage in violent and criminal activity, but because they lack the discipline needed to learn in school and to function in the workplace. The socializing influence of the family — comprising husbands and wives in ongoing union and with a commitment to child-rearing — appears to be an essential element of any solution. If these assumptions are correct, as conservatives and many liberals now believe, the trade-off is more biological lives at the cost of more unsocialized children — making people versus making people moral.

Opposition to the elimination of welfare payments of out-of-wedlock children comes from two quarters: the pro-choice movement and the right-to-life movement. The former condemns "welfare caps" because they reduce the choices facing women, and all choices are to be protected. In the words of liberal feminist Iris Young, "A liberal society that claims to respect the autonomy of all its citizens equally should affirm the freedom of all its citizens to bear and rear children, whether they are married or not, whether they have high incomes or not." For the right-to-life movement, of course, no fact about the potentially miserable outcome of the fetus's birth affects the imperative that it be born. Beginning from different commitments, therefore, feminists and pro-lifers converge in rejecting the conservative assumption that the troubling social effects of out-of-wedlock births justify government attempts to limit them.

The current right-to-life strategy calls for "chipping away" at the liberal abortion culture to "save" as many babies as possible under the political circumstances. Because pro-lifers can have the greatest impact on legislation affecting the poor, the socially marginal and those dependent on governmental funding for medical procedures, among their first targets have been, for example, Medicaid recipients. As a result, the success of the pro-life movement is now measured in the lives of poor children born out of wedlock. Most abortions in the U.S. occur to avoid the birth of children out of wedlock. Of the roughly 1.5 million abortions in 1991, only 271,000 were performed upon married women. Among married women, there were eight abortions for every ninety births; among unmarried women, there were forty-eight abortions for every forty-five births. All else being equal, then, eliminating the possibility of abortion would hike the number of out-of-wedlock births from its already disastrous level of 30 percent to 49 percent.

Indeed, the anti-abortion movement may already have helped increase the number of children born out of wedlock. The percentage of out-of-wedlock births in the United States rose from 18.4 percent in 1980 to 30.1 percent of all births in 1992, according to recent reports from the National Center for Health Statistics. During the same period, the proportion of non-marital pregnancies ending in abortion declined, from 60 percent in 1980 to 46 percent in 1991, and the abortion rate among married women fell by 12 percent. Thirty percent of these mothers were teenagers. The statistics on all potential mothers aged 15 to 17, those least able to care adequately for their children, are more alarming still. In the years from 1986 to 1991 the pregnancy rate for this group rose by 7 percent, but the abortion rate dropped by 19 percent, so that the rate of out-of-wedlock births among these very young mothers increased by 27 percent. This trend toward out-of-wedlock births rather than abortion may be due either to the increased difficulty of obtaining abortions or to increased preference for carrying babies to term. Either way, it marks a partial victory for the pro-life movement.

The second thrust of the current right-to-life strategy is the prohibition of abortion late in pregnancy, on the plausible assumption that even those with doubts about prohibiting abortion entirely regard the fetus as subject to ever greater respect as it develops. Here, too, the effect is tragic. Late-term abortions are rare, and, when they do occur, it is frequently because the parents have discovered late that their prospective child suffers from a serious birth defect or malformation. Yet it is these fetuses whom the pro-life movement now aims to "save." A bill now before Congress tries to force women to give birth to such babies. Titled the Partial-Birth Abortion Ban Act by its sponsors, it would be better dubbed the Cruelty to Families Act.

The public is genuinely ambivalent on the question of abortion. It adheres to the tenets of middle-class family life, yet without hearing those tenets articulated. To focus on the conflict between the right-to-life movement and middle-class family values is to call into question the terms in which the abortion debate is usually cast in our political culture. The abortion struggle should be understood as a three-way debate: among liberals, who believe that to let each of us do as we like will work out for the best; pro-lifers, who cling to one ultimate good at the expense of all others; and those committed to conserving middle-class families, sometimes at the expense of "choice," sometimes at the expense of "life." The third group lays best claim to the title "conservative."

20

THE INVOLVED READER

1 According to Muller, why does the right-to-life position threaten the family? To what extent does he sympathize with the right-to-life movement? Where or why does he part company with right-to-life thinking?

2 How does the traditional middle-class belief in "purposeful" activity (as against fatalistic acceptance) become a major point in Muller's argument? How does he relate bourgeois, capitalistic values and family planning?

3 How, according to Muller, does adherence to an extreme pro-life position correlate with social class? Why would opinions on the abortion issue vary with lower-class, middle-class, or upper-class status?

4 Why does Muller see a strange convergence of extreme liberal and conservative positions on the subject of illegitimate children or out-of-wedlock births? Why does he disagree with both factions?

5 As he approaches his conclusion, what does Muller stress as the major social effects of right-to-life legislation — on the poor, on middle-class families?

TALKING, THINKING, WRITING

6 Does Muller convince you that the controversy over abortion should be a "three-way debate"? Do you think he is a "true conservative"?

7 Do you think it is futile to argue about extremely emotionally charged issues like abortion? Is everyone's opinion "set in cement"?

8 What do you think should be the principal means of family planning or population control — abstinence? contraception? abortion?

COLLABORATIVE PROJECTS

9 Is it true that abortion legislation now differs from state to state? Working with a group, investigate the geography of a pregnant woman's legal rights.

Their Dilemma and Mine

BARBARA EHRENREICH

What gives men the right to legislate on the subject of abortion? Barbara Ehrenreich has long been one of the most effective voices of the women's movement. Old enough "to recall when the stereotype of a 'liberated woman' was a disheveled radical, notoriously braless, and usually hoarse from denouncing the twin evils of capitalism and patriarchy," she has seen the advent of the new stereotype of the career woman, carrying an attaché case and "skilled in discussing market shares and leveraged buy-outs." She has published widely in opinion makers' publications ranging from Ms. *and* Mother Jones *to the* New York Times, *the* New Republic, *the* Nation, *and the* Atlantic Monthly. *She has ranged over topics from the alleged "man shortage" to the need for raising the feminist consciousness of working class women. Many of her articles were collected in* The Worst Years of Our Lives *(1990), her irreverent account of the Reagan years and the "Decade of Greed."*

   Quite apart from blowing up clinics and terrorizing patients, the antiabortion movement can take credit for a more subtle and lasting kind of damage: it has succeeded in getting even prochoice people to think of abortion as a "moral dilemma," an "agonizing decision," and related code phrases for something murky and compromising, like the traffic in infant formula mix. In liberal circles, it has become unstylish to discuss abortion without using words like "complex," "painful," and the rest of the mealy-mouthed vocabulary of evasion. Regrets are also fashionable, and one otherwise feminist author writes recently of mourning, each year following her abortion, the putative birthday of her discarded fetus.

   I cannot speak for other women, of course, but the one regret I have about my own abortions is that they cost money that might otherwise have been spent on something more pleasurable, like taking the kids to movies and theme parks. Yes, that is abortions, plural (two in my case) — a possibility that is not confined to the promiscuous, the disorderly, or the ignorant. In fact, my credentials for dealing with the technology of contraception are first rate: I have a Ph.D. in biology that is now a bit obsolescent but still good for conjuring up vivid mental pictures of zygotes and ova, and I was actually paid, at one point in my life, to teach other women about the mysteries of reproductive biology.

. . .

Yet, as every party to the abortion debate should know, those methods of contraception that are truly safe are not absolutely reliable no matter how reliably they are used. Many women, like myself, have felt free to choose the safest methods because legal abortion is available as a backup to contraception. Anyone who finds that a thoughtless, immoral choice should speak to the orphans of women whose wombs were perforated by Dalkon shields or whose strokes were brought on by high-estrogen birth-control pills.

I refer you to the orphans only because it no longer seems to be good form to mention women themselves in discussions of abortion. In most of the antiabortion literature I have seen, women are so invisible that an uninformed reader might conclude that fetuses reside in artificially warmed tissue culture flasks or similar containers. It must be enormously difficult for the antiabortionist to face up to the fact that real fetuses can only survive inside women, who, unlike any kind of laboratory apparatus, have thoughts, feelings, aspirations, responsibilities, and, very often, checkbooks. Anyone who thinks for a moment about women's role in reproductive biology could never blithely recommend "adoption, not abortion," because women have to go through something unknown to fetuses or men, and that is pregnancy.

From the point of view of a fetus, pregnancy is no doubt a good deal. But consider it for a moment from the point of view of the pregnant person (if "woman" is too incendiary and feminist a term) and without reference to its potential issue. We are talking about a nine-month bout of symptoms of varying severity, often including nausea, skin discolorations, extreme bloating and swelling, insomnia, narcolepsy, hair loss, varicose veins, hemorrhoids, indigestion, and irreversible weight gain, and culminating in a physiological crisis which is occasionally fatal and almost always excruciatingly painful. If men were equally at risk for this condition — if they knew that their bellies might swell as if they were suffering from end-stage cirrhosis, that they would have to go for nearly a year without a stiff drink, a cigarette, or even an aspirin, that they would be subject to fainting spells and unable to fight their way onto commuter trains — then I am sure that pregnancy would be classified as a sexually transmitted disease and abortions would be no more controversial than emergency appendectomies.

Adding babies to the picture does not make it all that much prettier, even if you are, as I am, a fool for short, dimpled people with drool on their chins. For no matter how charming the outcome of a pregnancy that is allowed to go to term, no one is likely to come forth and offer to finance its Pampers or pay its college tuition. Nor are the

5

opponents of abortion promising a guaranteed annual income, sub-
sidized housing, national health insurance, and other measures that
might take some of the terror out of parenthood. We all seem to expect the individual parents to shoulder the entire burden of supporting any offspring that can be traced to them, and, in the all-too-
common event that the father cannot be identified or has skipped
town to avoid child-support payments, "parent" means mother.

When society does step in to help out a poor woman attempting
to raise children on her own, all that it customarily has to offer is
some government-surplus cheese, a monthly allowance so small it
would barely keep an adult male in running shoes, and the contemptuous epithet "welfare cheat." It would be far more reasonable
to honor the survivors of pregnancy and childbirth with at least the
same respect and special benefits that we give, without a second
thought, to veterans of foreign wars.

But, you will object, I have greatly exaggerated the discomforts of
pregnancy and the hazards of childbearing, which many women undergo quite cheerfully. This is true, at least to an extent. In my own
case, the case of my planned and wanted pregnancies, I managed to
interpret morning sickness as a sign of fetal tenacity and to find, in
the hypertrophy of my belly, a voluptuousness ordinarily unknown
to the skinny. But this only proves my point: a society that is able to
make a good thing out of pregnancy is certainly free to choose how
to regard abortion. We can treat it as a necessary adjunct to contraception, or as a vexing moral dilemma, or as a form of homicide —
and whichever we choose, that is how we will tend to experience it.

So I will admit that I might not have been so calm and determined
about my abortions if I had had to cross a picket line of earnest
people yelling "baby-killer," or if I felt that I might be blown to bits
in the middle of a vacuum aspiration. Conversely, though, we would
be hearing a lot less about ambivalence and regrets if there were not
so much liberal head-scratching going on. Abortions will surely continue, as they have through human history, whether we approve or
disapprove or hem and haw. The question that worries me is: How
is, say, a sixteen-year-old girl going to feel after an abortion? Like a
convicted sex offender, a murderess on parole? Or like a young
woman who is capable, as the guidance counselors say, of taking
charge of her life?

This is our choice, for biology will never have an answer to that   10
strange and cabalistic question of when a fetus becomes a person.
Potential persons are lost every day as a result of miscarriage, contraception, or someone's simple failure to respond to a friendly

wink. What we can answer, with a minimum of throat clearing and moral agonizing, is the question of when women themselves will finally achieve full personhood: and that is when we have the right, unquestioned and unabrogated, to *choose* not to be pregnant when we decide not to be pregnant.

THE INVOLVED READER

1 Ehrenreich starts by taking issue, not with her conservative opposition, but with her fellow liberals. Why and how?

2 What are Ehrenreich's credentials for discussing the abortion issue? How and with what effect does she bring in her personal experience?

3 Is Ehrenreich right when she claims that in the abortion debate concern for the unborn fetus eclipses concern for the mother? How does she try to correct the imbalance?

4 Does Ehrenreich convince you that abortion looks very different from a woman's and a man's perspective?

5 Ehrenreich feels that concern for the unborn child often abruptly ceases once the child is born. How does she drive this point home?

6 As she approaches the end of her essay, what for Ehrenreich is the central, crucial question in the abortion debate? How does she redefine choice?

TALKING, THINKING, WRITING

7 Do you think that the anti-abortion movement shows more concern for the unborn than for the living?

8 The anti-abortion activists' equivalent of "waving the bloody shirt" is to wave pictures of aborted fetuses. Does Ehrenreich have anything comparable in her arsenal?

MAKING CONNECTIONS

9 For you, do Muller's "The Conservative Case for Abortion" and Ehrenreich's "Their Dilemma and Mine" show the difference between a man's and a woman's point of view?

Going Gentle into That Good Night

ELIZABETH MARTÍNEZ

Do not go gentle into that good night.
Rage, rage against the passing of the light.

DYLAN THOMAS

Has the technology of dying outpaced our ability to deal with the ethical choices it presents? A 1995 study found that many terminal patients were kept alive by expensive medical technology, often in severe pain, contrary to their express wishes, the wishes of their families, or the concerns of the nursing staff. Authorities in Michigan were prosecuting a physician who assisted patients in voluntarily ending insufferable pain or unbearable lives. At the same time, voters in countries like Holland or Australia were inching toward legalizing voluntary termination of life. Elizabeth (Betita) Martínez is a Mexican American author and university instructor in women's studies and Chicano studies. She has written on Latino issues for Z magazine. In the following article, she pleads the case for "death with dignity" rather than reliance on "desperate last-minute technology." Her aim is to provide inspiration for those who look for something better than the "hospital horror stories, courtroom setbacks, and pain" we usually hear or see. She says about her mother's passing, "I am grateful to have known the unexpected beauty of a rightful death."

Since 1987 my mother had been in "a persistent vegetative state," as they say, kept alive by artificial means. In building machines that can breathe, feed, and clean out wastes for people, we have generated a host of anguishing questions: When should life-support measures be taken? If a person's mind and spirit are gone, should these measures be abandoned? If so, when, and who decides? Today we also hear nationwide debate about doctor-induced death, largely as a result of Dr. Jack Kevorkian's suicide devices.

Whether the issue is refusing to prolong life mechanically, facilitating suicide, or more active euthanasia — in Greek, the "easy death" — we eventually confront this society's attitude toward death itself. The dominant U.S. culture breeds fear (and with it, dread of aging). To recognize a timely death as part of planet life, as nature, and sometimes as a friend, does not come easy for most of the Western world.

Defining medical care as a mystery only they can fathom, many physicians disempower patients who might otherwise decide their own life-or-death treatment. Health professionals may also act out ageist attitudes toward the elderly. At the same time patients and their relatives, conditioned by paternalism or perhaps fear of guilt, may *want* the physician to make crucial decisions. Since U.S. doctors tend to be men, who often regard female patients as "immature," "overemotional," or even "hysterical," sexism can play a crucial role. This is a major reason why the National Organization for Women supports death with dignity as a feminist issue. NOW notes that the courts have upheld 60 percent of the male requests to die and only 14 percent of the female requests.

Issues of class, race, and culture further complicate the debate. If you live in a violence-ridden urban area, the right to die must seem a ludicrous middle-class hang-up. When you have no health insurance (up to 36 million Americans in 1992), you're not likely to worry about excessive use of life-support technology. People of color, especially if they have recently immigrated, may consider "the right to die" strange or untrustworthy. There is a sinister side to the picture, too: the right to die may be supported for very wrong reasons by government cost-cutters who note the millions put out for care of the indigent, and by hospital administrators worried about making money under Medicare's reimbursement system.

I knew nothing of such debates when my mother suffered a series 5 of strokes in the early 1980s that left her almost comatose and requiring total care around the clock. Eventually her house had to be sold to pay the nursing home bills. Packing up her papers, I found a one-page typed living will written on her birthday in 1967 and renewed 12 years later. In fact, copies surfaced all over the house. The paper said: "If a time should come when my body can be kept alive only by artificial means which preserve the *breath* of life, but in no way preserve life's *spirit*, I do not want artificial stimuli used. This is my strict direction and my request."

It was no surprise: she had watched her own mother die that way and hated it. The paper also signaled how she had often been ahead of her time. She was an innovative high school teacher of Spanish, a tennis champion without professional training, an astute social critic and supporter of liberal causes, amateur pianist, world traveler, short story writer, and bridge enthusiast. She took special pleasure in dancing with my father until his death and later with a 78-year-old boyfriend who wrote poetry at 3 A.M. and then called her to read it over the telephone ("Do you think it's all right for me to be seeing a younger man?" she asked at the age of 83). She liked to be around hustle and bustle, young people, the unpredictable, anything that seized her imagination. Few people love life more than she did.

This was the person we had seen over recent years grow progressively incontinent and unable to walk, eat, talk, or see. When she turned 90, still semialert, we celebrated in the nursing home with a big lunch on the sunny veranda, other relatives, and a mariachi band. On her next birthday she lay in bed diapered and with a feeding tube, speechless and staring open-eyed at the ceiling. Could she possibly want such an existence?

Yet even after finding her living will, I snatched at the most fragile sign of "life." If she uttered two words, as happened every few weeks, I was thrilled. The desire for her to "stay alive" tugged at one end of my feelings; at the other stood the knowledge of her desire to die with dignity. Visiting her became an encounter with reprimand, real or imagined; her face seemed to ask me crossly, Why haven't you done what I requested? Didn't you notice that it was my *strict* direction? And I asked myself: Am I afraid of what people will think?

In recent years public opinion has been both liberal and cautious about the right to die. A 1990 Gallup poll found that 84 percent of U.S. residents would want treatment withheld if they were on life-support systems with no hope of recovering. The poll also found that 66 percent believe someone in great and hopeless pain had a moral right to commit suicide. Another 1990 poll showed that 53 percent favor allowing a doctor's help in committing suicide.

At the same time voters rejected a 1991 Washington State initiative that would have allowed doctors to end a person's life if two gave written opinions that death would naturally occur within six months. Last year a California "Death with Dignity" initiative would have given mentally competent, terminally ill adults the right to issue a directive requesting physician-aid-in-dying; it too was voted down, by a 54–46 margin. In both cases most voters apparently saw the act as lacking adequate safeguards against abuse or too vague on key requirements. On the other hand, many — like this writer — voted for the California initiative as being basically sound. Many "no" votes in that state must have stemmed from uninformed fear; the Catholic church and the medical establishment waged an almost $4 million opposition campaign against the initiative's $700,000. Future initiative-makers need to draw lessons from the weaknesses of these two.

Antiabortion forces have argued that "*Roe v. Wade* was a precedent for killing people," and from there it's a "slippery slope" down-

10

hill to euthanasia. Thus they negate the right to control one's own body in matters of dying as in birthing. According to a 1990 New York *Times* report, antiabortion groups have blocked legislation in at least three states that would allow withholding of nutrients, which they see as "forced starvation" (they do not usually oppose disconnecting respirators).

Opposition has sometimes come from members of the disabled community, who hear echoes of genocide in the idea that life may not be worth living for the so-called unfit. African Americans and Latinos have supported the right to die much less enthusiastically than other sectors of the population. History, of course, gives all people of color reason to suspect any law that grants power over their lives to mostly white strangers. Advocates of death with dignity as a right respond that the rich have usually been able to have it by virtue of their influence over doctors and their ability to travel if necessary. The poor — which includes so many people of color — should be guaranteed the same right to choose. Death with dignity is the final civil right.

In time it did become clear that I wasn't worried about disapproval from friends or relatives if I ended my mother's life. The battle lay within, between two kinds of love — one that wanted her still on this planet, for me, and one that affirmed respect for her personhood, from me. When she contracted pneumonia after a year of being inert, her doctor said: "It's the old folks' friend, a quick and easy way to go. If you want the antibiotics stopped, let me know." Three long days passed of articulating the decision as: "Today I have to decide whether to kill my mother or not." I finally gave the order, but she had already taken enough medication to recover.

More months passed and the living will would not go away. After another consultation the doctor reduced her fluids, as this might diminish her physical resistance. She showed no effects. The battle resumed in my head: Perhaps she doesn't want to die, after all. Or, in better moments: Is she just laughing at me? The doctor refused to do any more. I assumed, based on reading newspaper stories about such cases, that the law gave him no choice.

Struggles for the legal right to die present a long, sad, and often 15 surreal parade of cases like that of Karen Ann Quinlan, the young New Jersey woman in a coma whose parents finally got her respirator turned off by a historic court order. The parents of Nancy Cruzan, who existed on a feeding tube, went all the way to the U.S. Supreme Court. In 1990 the court issued a double-edged ruling. On one hand it upheld an individual's constitutional right to the discontinuance of life-support treatment. On the other hand the court maintained the right of a state — in this case, Missouri — to demand "clear and convincing evidence" of a patient's desire to avoid life-support measures. As a result the Cruzan family had to produce new witnesses before Nancy could finally die.

Galvanized into action by the court decision, Congress passed the Patient Self-Determination Act. It requires health care facilities that receive Medicare or Medicaid funds (95 percent of such centers) to inform new patients about their legal right to write a living will or choose a proxy to represent their wishes about medical treatment. The Supreme Court's decision also made thousands of people put their wishes in writing to evidence them.

Today all 50 states authorize some form of advance directive from a patient — either a living will or a durable power of attorney, which is the preferred method. (Doing both is best, some say: the first establishes your wishes, the second facilitates their implementation.) Legal uncertainty or conflict continues where the patient has given no directive and where the procedure contemplated — for instance, feeding tube removal — is not authorized. Only one state, Kentucky, specifically prohibits termination of tube-feeding. Others stand silent on the issue and therefore implicitly allow it. It's a legal crazy quilt.

Not knowing California was one of those states that implicitly allowed feeding tube removal at the time, I continued to do nothing about my mother. But the feeling became inescapable: it isn't right to be waiting for the easy or legal way out.

One Sunday, walking on the beach alongside the Pacific with a friend, we talked about my paralysis. She was a nurse, and over the afternoon hours she demystified the steps to be taken and their physical consequences. By sunset I could see the decision — huge and relentless, like the waves rolling in. But also quieting. That evening I talked with a woman who had helped her own mother to die, and she told me what I might expect to feel along with the practical problems. Then she commented, "Perhaps you can think of this as an opportunity."

Until that moment I had thought of having accepted a painful [20] necessity at last. But here was a chance to make my mother a gift: something worthy of the boundless devotion she had given me and my daughter for so many years, something I knew she wanted, something only I could give. Thinking this way, the weight of double guilt — for not carrying out my mother's will and then for wanting to carry it out — floated away. In its place rose an enormous and simple gratitude that she had endowed us with certainty about her wishes.

One large problem remained: no doctor to remove the feeding tube.

The American Hospital Association estimates that 70 percent of the deaths in the United States are somehow negotiated with patients, family, and doctors quietly agreeing not to use life-support technology. In 1986 the American Medical Association declared that all life-prolonging medical treatment could be ethically disconnected when a patient's coma is irreversible. Nevertheless, my mother's doctor had refused to do anything active.

In retrospect I imagine his position then was a matter of personal preference or morality. Health policy expert and practicing physician Dr. Thomas Bodenheimer of San Francisco spoke to me about why doctors sometimes encourage life-support measures. "It is uncomfortable and time-consuming to talk to the family or patient about death. Also, docs may fear malpractice suits, if we don't 'do everything.' And we are trained to save life, not assist death — it's not easy to change our ways. A few unscrupulous doctors think about the fees they don't collect on a dead body, but mostly I think it is a matter of benign neglect. Docs will automatically put more time and thought into acutely ill patients."

An old friend, a doctor, agreed to remove the tube. "I agree with what you're doing," he said immediately. We wanted it done in the nursing home where my mother had received exceptional care for five years. But the social worker there told me, "They think you are doing the right thing, they just couldn't handle it emotionally after taking care of her so long."

Without my asking, she quickly found another facility. The nursing director there, Jane — I have changed her name like others in this story — assured me that the staff would relieve any discomfort that lack of food caused my mother. They were required to offer nourishment and fluids by hand; if somehow my mother took them, this could prolong her life.

But that was the only legal issue that Jane mentioned; her time and heart went into other matters. "In cases like this," she explained, "I call a special meeting of the whole staff and explain the situation to them. I have to be sure that they feel clear about it and some will disagree with what you're doing. Then I ask for volunteers to take care of the person." Jane spoke without hesitation; it would never occur to her just to assign workers, as if they had no feelings. I nodded, wordless. "One more thing," Jane told me. "You should tell your mother what's going to happen. It doesn't matter if she seems not to hear you or understand, I think she will."

On the day of the transfer from the old nursing home to the new one, I sat down by her bed and said that the tube would be taken out in a few hours. That I was doing what she wished, at last. For all my belief in the rightness of this act, I couldn't make my words more direct than that. Nothing showed in her face and her eyes stared straight ahead.

At the new place, after she was settled, my daughter and I stood outside in the sun waiting for the doctor who would remove the tube. Last-minute doubts and fears started to batter me: Was this really what she wanted? Why didn't she refer specifically to feeding tubes in her living will? Maybe she only meant to reject a respirator?

The doctor arrived, listened to my worries. "You know her, you know how she lived, what she wanted," he said. "In the end, what you are doing is right not just because of the living will but because you know what kind of person she is." Then he went in and, with Jane's help, removed the tube. When he came back, he smiled and just said, "This is an amazing nursing home."

The next day, returning to visit, I found my mother asleep in bed.   30 On the pillow next to her head lay the miniature teddy bear that I had left on the bedside cabinet, and a fresh flower perched in her hair. The nurse walked in then, a woman named Frances, who looked at me and explained, "I always sleep with my teddy bear so I thought she might like it too, bless her heart."

Five days later my mother died. "Five days — so quick for such a strong person," friends and relatives commented. "She must have been ready." A few asked, "Why did it take you so long to do what she wanted?" I had no answer to that except it took both of us a long, long time — but then we did meet.

THE INVOLVED READER

1   What associations does the term *euthanasia* bring to mind? Has the issue of withdrawing life support or shortening the suffering of the dying come up in your family or among your friends?

2   What were the circumstances of the mother's death? Do you think they were typical or unusual?

3   The physician is a key player in the drama of a patient's final days. What role do the physicians play in this essay? What role do the nurses play? Is the author hostile toward the medical es-

tablishment? How does she analyze the thinking and the responsibilities of physicians?

TALKING, THINKING, WRITING

4 What decision would you have made if you had been in the daughter's place? How would you have defended your choice to those who might disagree with you?

5 Where would you draw the line between allowing a patient to die a natural death and assisted suicide? Do you think people assisting in the suicide of the desperately ill should be prosecuted?

COLLABORATIVE PROJECTS

6 Widely read authors who have written about witnessing the death of someone close and trying to ease the final days include Simone De Beauvoir (*Une Mort Très Douce*) and Elizabeth Kuebler-Ross. Working with a group, explore major themes in books by authors writing on "death with dignity."

short story

The One Sitting There

JOANNA H. WOŚ

Should we feel guilty about throwing away food? Ours is sometimes called a throwaway society, with Americans wasting food and resources that could sustain a whole Third World nation. The following short short focuses on an argument going on in the narrator's mind. Joanna H. Woś published the story in Malahat Review; *it was reprinted in a collection of minimalist narratives called* Flash Fiction *(1992). The early nineties saw the publication of a number of anthologies with titles like* Sudden Fiction *and* Short Shorts.

I threw away the meat. The dollar ninety-eight a pound ground beef, the boneless chicken, the spareribs, the hamsteak. I threw the soggy vegetables into the trashcan — the carrots, broccoli, peas, the Brussels sprouts. I poured the milk down the drain of the stainless steel sink. The cheddar cheese I ground up in the disposal. The ice cream, now liquid, followed. All the groceries in the refrigerator had to be thrown away. The voice on the radio hinted of germs thriving on the food after the hours without power. Throwing the food away was rational and reasonable.

In our house, growing up, you were never allowed to throw food away. There was a reason. My mother saved peelings and spoiled things to put on the compost heap. That would go back into the garden to grow more vegetables. You could leave meat or potatoes to be used again in soup. But you were never allowed to throw food away.

I threw the bread away. The bread had gotten wet. I once saw my father pick up a piece of Wonder Bread he had dropped on the ground. He brushed his hand over the slice to remove the dirt and then kissed the bread. Even at six I knew why he did that. My sister was the reason. I was born after the war. She lived in a time before. I do not know much about her. My mother never talked about her. There are no pictures. The only time my father talked about her was when he described how she clutched the bread so tightly in her baby fist that the bread squeezed out between her fingers. She sucked at the bread that way.

So I threw the bread away last. I threw the bread away for all the times I sat crying over a bowl of cabbage soup my father said I had to eat. Because eating would not bring her back. Because I would still be the one sitting there. Now I had the bread. I had gotten it. I had bought it. I had put it in the refrigerator. I had earned it. It was mine to throw away.

So I threw the bread away for my sister. I threw the bread away   5
and brought her back. She was twenty-one and had just come home from Christmas shopping. She had bought me a doll. She put the package on my dining room table and hung her coat smelling of perfume and the late fall air on the back of one of the chairs. I welcomed her as an honored guest. As if she were a Polish bride returning to her home, I greeted her with a plate of bread and salt. The bread, for prosperity, was wrapped in a white linen cloth. The salt, for tears, was in a small blue bowl. We sat down together and shared a piece of bread.

In a kitchen, where such an act was an ordinary thing, I threw away the bread. Because I could.

THE INVOLVED READER

1   How much of the family history can you reconstruct? What clues does Woś provide? What is the significance of the title?
2   Why does throwing away the bread become such a big issue in this very short story?
3   What is going on in the last two paragraphs of the story?

TALKING, THINKING, WRITING

4   In a world where many go hungry, should we feel guilty about throwing away food? Why or why not?
5   Do you have qualms like those experienced by the person telling the story? On what subject or in what connection?

poem

Sonnet on the Death of the Man Who Invented Plastic Roses

PETER MEINKE

Are Americans obsessed with trying to find a synthetic substitute for everything natural or organic: plastic imitation leather, fake plastic wood, fake crabmeat, and plastic smiles? Peter Meinke is a widely published poet who revels in the texture, the sights and sounds, of authentic down-to-earth experience. In his poem "Sunday at the Apple Market," he makes readers share in the "miraculous profusion" of apples yellow and green and red, carried away by the cartload by a happy laughing crowd rolling around the cool applechunks in their mouths while dogs bark and the smell of apples is everywhere. In another poem, he advises his son to plant peonies and roses but also squash and spinach, turnips and tomatoes. The following poem appeared in his collection Liquid Paper: New and Selected Poems *(1991). The poem uses some of the features of the traditional sonnet form: a first set of eight lines with alternating rhymes, followed by a second set of six lines that concludes with two rhyming lines — a couplet.*

The man who invented the plastic rose
is dead. Behold his mark:
his undying flawless blossoms never close
but guard his grave unbending through the dark.
He understood neither beauty nor flowers,   5
which catch our hearts in nets as soft as sky
and bind us with a thread of fragile hours:
flowers are beautiful because they die.

Beauty without the perishable pulse
is dry and sterile, an abandoned stage   10
with false forests. But the results
support this man's invention; he knew his age:
a vision of our tearless time discloses
artificial men sniffing plastic roses.

THE INVOLVED READER

1   According to this poem, what did the inventor of the plastic rose
    fail to understand about beauty or flowers?

2   Is there a hint in the poem why he was nevertheless successful?

3   In the traditional sonnet, the concluding couplet often sums up a major theme or thought underlying the poem. Is that true in this modern sonnet?

TALKING, THINKING, WRITING

4   Have you encountered evidence of the tendency toward synthetic substitutes? Should something be said in defense of plastic?

5   If you were to nominate an object, a material, or a practice that could serve as a symbol for contemporary American culture, what would you choose? How would you defend your choice?

6   Is the movement to promote organic or natural foods a fad?

The Writer's Tools 9

Using Definitions

Arguments are fruitless when key words do not mean the same to writer and reader. When you define an important term, you "draw the line." You stake out the territory it covers — or that it *should* cover. When will key words in your writing need definition?

• Key terms change their meanings when traditional boundaries shift or perceptions change. When does intimacy become *date rape*? When does flirtation become *sexual harassment*? When does aggressive law enforcement become *police brutality*?

• We hear and read much about *diversity, multiculturalism, openness, sensitivity*. What's behind the buzzword? For example, why did the word *nurturing* become fashionable? What are good examples of nurturing behavior? Are all women naturally nurturing? Can men be nurturing?

• The language of politics is shot through with large abstractions like *involvement, compassion, the national interest,* or *human rights.* What do such terms mean in the lives of real people? For instance, what does the "right to privacy" protect? Does it protect you against phone solicitations? Does it protect your private history, your credit record, or your personal locker at school?

You will often inject a short definition into an ongoing argument in order to clarify a key term. The following are **capsule definitions** offered in the course of discussion:

> People with Type A personalities — *those uptight, compulsive, competitive, aggressive, sometimes hostile, insecure overachievers* — can greatly reduce their chances for a heart attack by modifying their behavior.

> Black writers such as Alice Walker, Toni Morrison, and ntozake shange . . . talked about a term I had not heard before: role models. A role model is *someone we could relate to, "one of us," someone who demonstrated either through writing or through his or her life, the possibility of greatness.*
>
> Ronald D. White

However, when using a changing and provocative term, you may decide to offer an **extended definition**. For instance, when you use the term *feminism*, what associations does the term have for you? You may decide to use a discovery frame like the following:

What's a Feminist?

PERSONAL EXPERIENCE   Where have you encountered traditional gender roles or feminist rethinking of them in your own life?

I grew up with girls whose parents were leading them down the road to housewifery, motherhood, or low-paying jobs by not urging them on to excel in the way they did their sons. The brother went out for varsity sports; the sister became a cheerleader. I remember being one of only a few girls in a trigonometry class. Two of them dropped, with little effort on the part of the teacher to change their minds. My own attitudes began to change when a black woman teacher said to me: "Every woman should be a feminist because she is a woman."

THE RANGE OF MEANINGS   What is a common denominator in current discussions of future directions in the women's movement?

Much current discussion within the women's movement concerns the unsolved issue of how to reconcile the demands of a career with a commitment to family. As a recent letter-to-the-editor put it, "If a man wants to be totally devoted to his career and not take on the responsibility of children, does he get lectured about family values? Then why should a woman?" On the other hand, a contributor to the same newspaper said in her column, "If feminism represents women who hate men, either as sexual partners or as human beings sharing the planet, it doesn't represent the vast majority of women. . . . I believe most women want a feminism that represents women who want to marry, raise children, balance family and work, balance personal fulfillment with commitment."

HISTORICAL PERSPECTIVE   What is the history of the women's movement? What famous names are associated with it, and what did these people stand for?

The early role models of the feminist movement encouraged women to stretch the boundaries, to go where no woman had gone before. The women's suffrage movement campaigned for women's right to vote at a time when men alone decided the destiny of the nation. Sojourner Truth said at the Women's Rights Convention in 1851: "I think that between the Negroes of the South and the women at the North all talking about rights, the white men will be in a fix pretty soon." Amelia Earhart was the first woman to pilot a plane across the Atlantic. She said, "Women must try to do things as men have tried. When they fail, their failure must be but a challenge to others."

MEDIA COVERAGE   How do current movies, TV shows, and advertising reflect changing images of women?

The feminist movement is designed to help women discover their own powers and their own self-worth. In their own cynical and exploitative way, the media reflect these changing expectations. Advertisers increasingly cater to the image of the woman who is in control of her life. In currently popular movies, women appear as fearless detectives or squad leaders dealing with male wimps. In trendy television shows, angry women take revenge on abusive males.

RELATED OR CONTRASTING TERMS   What similar terms or near-synonyms come up in discussions of feminism? What opposite terms, or antonyms, can help clarify the term?

The women's movement, or women's liberation movement, aimed at the emancipation of women — a setting free from slavery or restraints. It challenged the tradition of patriarchy, a society or way of life where the male father figure rules.

Remembering advice like the following will help you make your definitions more useful or persuasive:

• *Avoid routine use of dictionary definitions.*   A dictionary defini-tion often merely delays the moment when you have to do your own thinking: "Justice, according to the *Ninth Collegiate*, is the quality of being just, impartial, or fair." Use a dictionary definition only if you decide it will be thought provoking or help dramatize the issue: "According to the *New Collegiate*, genocide is 'the delib-erate and systematic destruction of a racial, political, or cultural group.'"

• *Recognize a possible range of meanings.*   Some writers make it clear that they are using a **stipulated** definition. They show that their definition reflects their own perspective or fits a specific context:

> a market economy *as defined here* . . .
> honesty *for many of my generation* means . . .
> *for conservatives like myself in the current culture wars*, political correct-ness has come to mean . . .

• *Sharpen your definition.*   You may want to sum up your find-ings in a **formal definition.** The traditional formal definition first places a term to be defined in a larger class and then narrows it down by specifying distinctive features: "A sorority [term] is a pri-vate association [class] that provides separate dormitory facilities with a distinct Greek letter name for selected female college students [features]."

TERM	CLASS	FEATURES
To double-cross	is to betray someone	whom we have deliberately impressed with our trust-worthiness or loyalty.
Liberation theology	is militant religion	in the service of social re-form or revolution.

WRITING WORKSHOP 3

Checking Out Buzzwords

Help organize a panel discussion in which members of your class or group try to clarify the meaning of a contested term like *date rape, reverse discrimination, welfare dependency, white backlash, human rights, liberation theology,* or *the cultural elite.*

Language is what makes people human, and it is the primary way we have of knowing who other people are.   **JANET MALCOLM**

10

Expanding Your Range

The Personal Voice

How do we recognize a writer's personal voice? What makes the difference between writing that is plodding and dull and writing that is imaginative and alive? Style is a catchall label for how writers write, for how they use language. Here are some questions to ask yourself about your own writing style:

Sentence Style   Do your sentences hit home? For instance, does your writing sum up key ideas in pointed sentences? Do your papers include sentences that will make the reader say "well put!" or "well said"? What makes the following student-written sentences easy to remember and quote?

> Painting is the art of bringing colors to life.
> Mutual trust is more important to me than anything else.
> In Washington, DC, our nation's capital, there are more abortions than live births.

Lifelike Detail   Does your writing remain colorless for lack of authentic real-life detail? How do the following sample sentences show that the student writer has a quick eye for telling details and revealing facts?

> Stacks of neatly folded towels were piled against a wall; a wooden basket was placed next to the stack for used towels to be tossed into; directly across were two gigantic mirrors for use by the daily aerobics class; and a poster behind the juice bar said: "Exercise does a body good."
> Sullen patrons were still jostling in front of the windows where overwhelmed ticket vendors were trying to make change while inside the

arena the leather-clad, tattooed, crotch-grabbing musicians were already warming up in front of a wired crowd.

Vivid Imagery   How imaginative is your writing? Does your writing call up memorable images that will stay in the reader's mind? In the following sentence, do you recognize an imaginative touch that helps bring the writing to life?

> The snow storm was so short-lived it was as if God were playing with one of those Christmas toys that snow when shaken.

Personal Commitment   Will your writing convince readers that you care? Will it get them emotionally involved? In the following student-written passages, do you recognize a personal commitment?

> First-time computer users are often overwhelmed by the multiple thick manuals, tricky system-glitch precautions, the different ways to store and retrieve information, and warnings about how to shut down the computer without harming the program or losing the day's work.
>
> People show their disapproval of abortion by various means: letters of protest, picketing, boycotting, speeches, demonstrations, arson, and murder.

The Lighter Touch   Are you uniformly solemn about matters big and small? An occasional lighter touch reassures us that the writer is human. What makes student sentences like the following a pleasure to read?

> In *On the Road*, Jack Kerouac and two acquaintances travel around the world in search of the perfect party.
>
> People who call in to talk shows include the typical loud-mouthed sexist, the woman who will not let go, the couch potato who calls just to harass the host, and the average all-American male who exercises once a year and wants to kill his mother-in-law.

THOUGHT LOG 10

Using Your Imagination

In your thought log, work on writing that brings your feelings and your imagination into play. For instance, write about the role a recurrent emotion — fear, anxiety, resentment, love — plays in your life. Or write about an image that haunts you or symbolizes something important in your experience. Or write about a recurrent dream. How do you react to the following example of imaginative writing by a student writer?

The House of Fear

Fear knows the corners of our house, where to hide and wait. Fear stuffs the mattress of my bed; it wakes me often with creaks and moans. I reach out for comfort, but touch only the black-grey walls beyond, until I find my way out. I creep past the drowsy ghosts that guard my parents' bedroom door. Fear stands watch with me as I swallow breath after breath studying my mother's sleep-slack face, counting the steady rise and fall of my father's shoulders, listening for my brother's soft night noises from down the hall.

Fear filters through the wisps of my mother's cigarette smoke — weightless, acrid. She loses an hour in the black and white mid-day tragedies — poor Joann, poor Bert. The newspaper delivery man knocks at the door. My mother's laugh snaps like rubber bands, "I'm a little short this month, Bill, can you stop back?" Bill nods and my mother closes the door, slides the lock. Ashes sift from her cigarette as she soundlessly drifts back toward the television and buries herself in a chair.

Fear curls and purrs beneath our kitchen table in the evening. It rises up in rage and pounds the kitchen walls at night; it matches in volume word for word my father's angry howls. He hates his boss, the bastard; his brother, the son-of-a-bitch; his father; his mother; his wife; his son; his daughter — anyone who will not affirm that he is right, he is good, he is worthy. His pain explodes with every dish that shatters against the wall; his dreams bleed night after night under his fist. In the morning fear crawls away to nurse the bruises. My father makes amends.

Fear stings my brother's skinny behind like swats from a thin paddle. He runs and doesn't look back. He runs from house to house along our street chasing trouble, ignoring the chorus and their prophesy songs: he's an imp, he's stupid, what a temper, it's his fault. He runs intent across a summer afternoon to answer the ice cream man's taunting bell. I turn and look up from my popsicle, my mother turns from the television, my father turns the corner onto our street just in time to see my brother bounce against the bumper of a slow moving car, to hear the small thud as he drops to the pavement. Fear pulls us into a circle and whispers just below the ambulance wail, "This is what happens to people like you."

Formal or Informal

How formal or informal is your writing, and what difference does it make? Your level of formality helps shape the personality of your writing. It shows how seriously you take your subject. It shows how respectful or chummy you are toward your audience. To participate effectively in the public dialogue, you have to learn to shift gears from the informality of everyday talk to the more formal style of public discussion. At the same time, you try to keep a personal human touch to prevent your writing from turning hyperformal or stuffy.

Serious Written English Prose grappling with issues and ideas is more **formal** than casual conversation. Formal here does not mean stiff. The best modern prose is serious but not humorless, objective but not impersonal. The following passage, from a discussion of Western movies, assumes a reader willing to take a serious look at what is happening in society, in private life, in the media. The writer seriously explores the contradictory reactions of a viewer who is in turn repelled by and attracted to the tough, silent, swaggering Western hero:

> FORMAL: The Western, a genre that in many ways exists in order to fill its audience's need to be reunited with nature, is also engaged in suppressing and curtailing and in some cases extinguishing the very life source it so eagerly seeks to repossess. Through the cruel treatment of the hero and of animals, through the "drive," the spontaneous, exuberant, fleshly, and passionate part of human beings is a continual object of punishment, manipulation, and control.
>
> Jane Tomkins, *West of Everything: The Inner Life of Westerns*

Genre instead of "kind of film," *curtailing* instead of "cutting back" — words like these raise the level of formality beyond ordinary talk. *Life source, repossess, spontaneous, exuberant* — these are not bookish words, but we do not frequently hear them in casual conversation. The sentences are complex enough to do justice to complications (the Western takes us back to nature *but also* shows people and animals being abused). They are complex enough to do justice to different aspects of the same thing ("spontaneous, exuberant, fleshly, and passionate"; "punishment, manipulation, and control").

The Informal Touch Informal prose moves toward the unbuttoned, casual style of ordinary conversation. It uses conversational tags like *a lot, a couple of, lots*. It takes shortcuts like *won't* and *can't* for *will not* and *cannot*. It may call youngsters *kids* and parents *mom* and *dad*, and the police officer a *cop*. It is likely to use *get across* instead of *convey, put down* instead of *denigrate, end up* instead of *finish*.

Informal English easily becomes *too* informal for serious discussion. Nevertheless, much current prose uses the occasional informal touch. It employs informal touches to keep serious prose from turning deadly serious. The following passage is by a widely published writer who prides herself on not being an ivory tower intellectual but speaking for "the gals in data entry" and "your average office wit."

She is talking to her reader as if to a friend — to someone she can take into her confidence. What informal touches can you point out?

> INFORMAL: Probably it all started when Louise — or was it Thelma? — dispatched that scumball would-be rapist in the parking lot of a bar. In fact, we can't get enough of warrior-woman flicks: Sigourney Weaver in *Alien*, Linda Hamilton in *Terminator II*, Sharon Stone in *Basic Instinct*. . . . In the real world, the new mood was manifested by all the women flocking to gun stores and subscribing to *Women & Guns*, the magazine that tells you how to accessorize a neat little sidearm. And, without any prompting from NOW, thousands of women are sporting bumper stickers identifying themselves as BEYOND BITCH and buying T shirts that say TOUGH ENOUGH or make un-flattering comparisons between cucumbers and men. The new grass-roots female militancy is not something that a women's studies professor would judge p.c. In fact, it looks a lot like your standard conservative backlash, but with a key difference: crime in this case is defined as what men have been getting away with for centuries.

> Barbara Ehrenreich, "Feminism Confronts Bobbittry," *Time*

The Range of Reference   Where a writer turns for comparison and precedent affects the level of formality of the writing. For precedents or parallels, formal writing is likely to turn to the library or to history rather than the football field or the kitchen. A pundit like George Will will raise the level of formality by quoting from Plato's account of an ideal republic or from a letter by Thomas Jefferson. In keeping with a more informal style, a popular culture buff may mention recent sightings of Elvis or allude to the nth farewell tour of the Rolling Stones. A writer's frame of reference helps define the intended audience. For instance, in an article on socially responsible investing, the writer may aim at readers who listen to consumer advocates like Ralph Nader, or who will listen to arguments of whether a coastal bird whose habitat is threatened is actually an endangered breed or only a subspecies of a more numerous inland species.

A Note on Slang   Extremely informal language shades over into **slang**. Slang is free-wheeling, slung about by people who are irreverent toward the restraints of convention. It uses brash getting-to-the-point terms like *wino, junkie, deadbeat, uptight, off the wall*, and *grossed out*, not to mention *barf* and *pig out*. Teacher becomes *teach*, doctor becomes *doc*. Because it tends to be flip, it appeals to the young, who *split* instead of leave, *flip off* people they dislike, and *vegg* *out* on days off. Slang flourishes in subcultures outside the main-stream, among *potheads, deadheads,* and *punks.*

Slang comes and goes; however, sometimes — as in the case of *skinhead* — it crosses over into more more formal speech and writing. In serious prose, slang may on occasion appear when the writer *wants* to be disrespectful. (Referring to noisy beer-drinking fans at the Indianapolis 500, one writer called them *"blotto* on beer.")

WRITING WORKSHOP I

Formal and Informal

Peg the level of formality in the following sample passages. Rank them on a scale from most formal to most informal. Be prepared to discuss the clues that guided your choices. Pay special attention to word choice: What expressions are clearly formal or informal?

1 It's not often I talk to a management guru. All my life, I've tried to stay as far away from corporate culture as I can. Why? A basic distrust, I guess. The last corporate culture tome I read was William Whyte's *The Organization Man* in high school. I've spent the following one hundred years attempting to duck any situation where any of the parties involved were expected to wear a coat and tie. I was talking to Stephen R. Covey because I had written a column about him years ago. It centered on his bestseller, *The Seven Habits of Highly Effective People.* This was a title just asking to be parodied. I took my predictable cheap shot and wrote a little ditty about the seven habits of marginally effective people. . . . Covey has a new book out called *Principle-Centered Leadership.* I tried to get the nutshell version from him before he had to dash off.

D. G. Fulford, "Corporations' Future Assured," *Los Angeles Daily News*

2 Ever since Frederick Douglass forged the story of his escape from slavery into a powerful abolitionist message, black writers such as W. E. B. Du Bois, Richard Wright, and Malcolm X have wielded their autobiographies like emancipating swords. Now that weapon has been taken up by two black journalists, Nathan McCall and Brent Staples, each of whom provides a soul-searing account of his uneasy journey from the segregated world of blacks to the token-integrated fringe of the white world. Together, these life stories provide an unsettling account of the consequences of an American tragedy: the widening division between blacks and whites during the turbulent aftermath of the civil rights movement.

Jack E. White, "Between Two Worlds," *Time*

3 The gender system catches the heroes of the Western in a trap. The free, wild prairie promises liberation from stuffy interiors and bad family scenarios, but the type of heroism it seems to legitimize doesn't produce a very viable person, a person who enjoys living with himself and other

people. Silence, the will to dominate, and unacknowledged suffering aren't a good recipe for happiness and companionability. The model of heroism Westerns provide may help men to make a killing in the stock market, but it doesn't provide much assistance when they go home for dinner at night.

Jane Tomkins, *West of Everything: The Inner Life of Westerns*

A Range of Stylistic Options

What features give writing personality? When your writing seems plodding or uninspired, you may experiment with stylistic options available to every writer. Writing runs the gamut from simple to complex, from impersonal to personal, from low-key to dramatic, and from literal to imaginative.

Simple and Complex   Much of the variety of a live prose style results from the play of short and long. Some sentences are very brief. A writer may rely on sentences that catch us up short. We can then focus on one thing at a time. In a passage like the following, each short sentence says to us: "Take this in. This is important."

> The buzzard turned his head and looked at me. *He stood up on his big yellow legs. His head was snow white. His eyes were gold. He wasn't a buzzard. He was a bald eagle.* Then, not until after I had brought the car to a full stop, he spread his wings and with a slow swoop lifted himself into the air. He turned his head and gave me a long look through the car windshield with his level yellow eyes. Then he slowly wheeled up into the sky until he was just a black dot against the blue.
>
> Bailey White, *Mama Makes Up Her Mind*

Writers may keep a sentence short to make us remember a key idea. A statement that sums up something worth remembering and does so in pointed fashion is called an **aphorism**.

> POINTED: We have just enough religion to make us hate but not to make us love one another.
>
> Jonathan Swift

> We've changed the world just enough in the last twenty years to make it radically different, but not enough to make it work.
>
> Anna Quindlen

At the other extreme, sentences go on, piling up details, drawing in additional examples, reassuring us that the writer is doing justice to the rich variety of things as they really are. **Loose** sentences are open-ended sentences that read as if the writer kept adding material to an expandable sentence frame:

LOOSE: Look at *Bad Lieutenant,* frequently cited as a thunderhead-maker in the climate of violence. In the unrated version, Harvey Keitel engaged in drug abuse, paranoia, statutory rape, extortion, dereliction of duty, blasphemy, disturbing the peace, consorting wih prostitutes and addicts, poor parenting, shaky communication skills, wagering on sporting events, nonpayment of debts, misappropriation of funds, pride, self-pity, petty theft, shoplifting, moral confusion, frontal nudity, and many other colorful personality flaws that made his lieutenant bad — and the movie the feel-good experience of the year.

Ian Shoales

Not all longer sentences are simply cumulative, adding on more of same. Many long elaborate sentences are carefully crafted, putting related ideas in their place, making subordinate ideas fall into line:

ELABORATE: Few themes have gripped the imagination of Americans so intensely as the discovery of talent in unexpected places — the slum child who shows scientific genius, the frail youngster who develops athletic ability, the poor child who becomes a captain of industry.

John Gardner

When your sentences become too plodding or monotonous, you may want to try an occasional one-two pattern: A short pointed sentence sums up a key idea. One or two longer sentences provide explanation, furnish examples, or fill in details:

Most of Wyoming has a "lean-to" look. Instead of big roomy barns and Victorian houses, there are dugouts, low sheds, log cabins, sheep camps, and fence lines that look like driftwood haphazardly blown into place.

Gretel Ehrlich

Games are supposed to bring out the highest standards of sportsmanship in people. *They often bring out the worst.*

Glenn Dickey

Impersonal and Personal   How impersonal or how personal is effective writing? Writing ranges from **objective** writing, minimizing personal preference and emotion, to **subjective** writing that frankly brings personal feelings, agendas, and commitments into play. In some situations, such as when assembling an entertainment center made in Indonesia, we want hands-on objective information. Similarly, much scientific prose *has* to be impersonal. For instance, other researchers have to be able to replicate an experiment without regard for the personal agendas or emotional problems of the original writer. This does not mean, however, that scientists will write neutral, objective prose when discussing, say, the dangers of deteriorating, poorly maintained nuclear reactors in the former Soviet Union.

Writers aim at an objective style when they sense that readers will first of all want information — reliable data so that they can form their own judgment. When you are checking on the fate of precedent-setting school reform initiatives, you may welcome informative writing like the following. What makes the passage an example of relatively objective writing? Do you think it is totally neutral? Or do the authors' sympathies shine through?

> The reform movement is already producing some results. In 1989 Kentucky's supreme court ruled that the state's school-finance system was unconstitutional; the richest schools were allocated as much as $4,200 a year for each pupil, while poorer ones received only $1,700 per student. Under a plan that is in its second year, virtually every school district now has at least $3,200 to spend per student; over the years the gap between rich and poor districts will be further narrowed. Children from low-income families now have new preschool programs, and there is a wide range of Saturday and after-school projects for students with special needs.
>
> Deborah Fowler and Lisa H. Towle, "School Reform and the Courts," *Time*

Journalists like to think of themselves as impartial observers — who leave editorializing to the editorial page and give "just the facts." But a news report like the following, though giving essential facts, is not impersonal or unemotional. Where and how does the following example go beyond the dry facts?

> Two policemen shot to death in a brazen attack at a busy intersection were apparently taken by surprise and didn't fire their weapons at gunmen shooting from a pickup truck, investigators said Tuesday. The mortally-wounded officers were sprawled near their patrol car when backup police units arrived shortly after the Monday 11:20 P.M. shooting. Reserve Officer James Wayne MacDonald, 23, of Santa Rosa and Officer Kevin Michael Burrell, 29, of Compton were each shot several times at close range after pulling over the pickup, said Lt. Joe Flores.

The personal dimension of committed writing becomes obvious when the writer starts speaking in the first person, saying, "I experienced," "I saw," "I witnessed." In much serious discussion, the writer will at some point turn to personal experience for authenticity and credibility. Here is a passage from a discussion of how women today juggle child-rearing and careers:

> Middle-class mothers change their expectations and the way they handle their kids in a relatively short period of time. *I'll use myself as an example.* With my first kid . . . I ground up baby food in a little food mill and mixed it with yogurt. I was always clean and neat and wonderful. By the time I got my third, I had her at seven months sitting at the table with moo shu pork in front of her. My husband's saying, "Should she have that?" and I'm saying "She's got to get with the program. It's a busy household here." I honestly believe that middle-class kids growing up in this environment will be able to cope with the future because, one way or another, they're being "raised."
>
> Anna Quindlen, "What It Means to Be a Woman," Lear's

Low-Key and Dramatic   Much effective prose is businesslike and to the point without being dull. Your own temperament is likely to affect how low or how high you turn the emotional thermostat. The following passage is an introduction to the topic of health care reform. However, even though it mentions the fear "of being ruined by sickness," it may be too low-key to sound any alarms or scare many readers:

> Nearly everyone in favor of health care reform agrees on the two basic problems that must be tackled: the large number of uninsured people and the escalation of health care costs. This is not an ideological matter. The desire to solve the first problem comes from a simple humanitarian impulse — it's wrong that an American should live in fear of not receiving decent medical care, or of being financially ruined by sickness. The desire to solve the second problem comes from an economic worry. . . .
>
> New Republic editorial

The opposite of understatement is pushing everything toward superlatives, toward extremes. A writer may throw understatement to the winds in order to involve, excite, or dazzle the reader. In the following passage, a writer legendary for a jazzed-up style takes us on a roller-coaster ride toward the "right stuff," as he dramatizes a carrier landing that Air Force trainees experienced on their way to becoming astronauts. Italics and exclamation marks help this writer signal: "This is important! This is exciting!" What other features —

graphic details, vivid wording, imaginative comparisons — keep this passage from being dull?

> As the aircraft came closer and the carrier heaved on into the waves and the plane's speed did not diminish and the deck did not grow steady — indeed, it pitched up and down five or ten feet per greasy heave — one experienced a neural alarm that no lecture could have prepared him for: This is not an *airplane* coming toward me, it is a brick with some poor sonofabitch riding it (*someone much like myself!*), and it is not *gliding*, it is *falling*, a fifty-thousand-pound brick, headed not for a stripe on the deck but for *me* — and with a horrible *smash!* it hits the skillet, and with a blur of momentum as big as a freight train's it hurtles toward the far end of the deck — another blinding storm! — another roar as the pilot pushes the throttle up to full military power and another smear of rubber screams out over the skillet — and this is nominal! — quite okay! — for a wire stretched across the deck has grabbed the hook on the end of the plane as it hit the deck tail down, and the smash was the rest of the fifteen-ton brute slamming onto the deck, as it tripped up, so that it is now straining against the wire at full throttle, in case it hadn't held and the plane had "boltered" off the end of the deck and had to struggle up into the air again.
>
> Thomas Wolfe, *The Right Stuff*

Literal and Figurative   Imaginative language helps us translate ideas into images. We call language that helps us translate ideas into vivid images **figurative** language. Effective writers draw on the figurative expressions that add color to the black and white of literal language: *whistleblower, hiring freeze, insurance crunch, deep pockets, brain drain, meltdown.* Two major kinds of figurative language work somewhat differently: A **simile** signals the imaginative comparison by *like* or *as*: "Health benefits for employees, which consume one-fourth of corporate net income, have become *like cement shoes on the feet of American enterprise*" (Barbara Ehrenreich). A **metaphor** arrives unmarked or unannounced; we simply talk as if one thing were the other: "If the new industrial robots have become the *arms and eyes* of our factories, computers have become the *brains.*"

SIMILE: In many of the author's stories, language is *like signals from a vessel in distress,* telling us of desperate needs.

In much modern fiction, happiness is found only briefly and in unexpected places, *like a flower growing in the crack of a sidewalk.*

METAPHOR: Everyone who is born *holds dual citizenship, in the kingdom of the well and in the kingdom of the sick.*

Susan Sontag

> The health insurance industry has been languishing because demand for its product keeps shrinking while prices *shoot through the roof.*

Figurative language can make the reader look at something familiar from a new or provocative perspective. It can help a writer do justice to the emotional side of issues and to deal with human drives and emotional overtones.

The Lighter Touch   Humor is the antidote to dutiful prose. Even in small doses, it has a leavening effect. It can defuse hostility, reassuring others that we are human.

> EARNEST: Much Canadian literature tells the tale of those who made it back from a terrible experience: the frozen North, the snowstorm, the sinking ship.
>
> HUMOROUS: Many Westerns tell the tale of those who survived terrible hardships: saddle sores, warm beer, and bad chili.

You may want to experiment with two uses of humor, each with serious undertones. A writer with a lively sense of the ridiculous can amuse us by highlighting foibles and quirks. **Parody** is comic imitation. It heightens the ridiculous to counteract what is cranky or pretentious. The student author of the following passage pokes fun at the snobbery in yuppie cooking. Like most effective parody, these lines stay close enough to the original to sound at times almost like the real thing:

> The old cookbooks gave recipes for tuna noodle casserole and beanie-weanie surprise. Today, cookbooks give recipes for how to concoct blackened calf's liver grilled over mesquite in a sauce of vermouth, saddle of venison wrapped in blue corn tortillas sauteed with green peppercorns, and terrine of free-range chicken steamed in parchment and graced with green tomatoes.

When humor is methodically used as a weapon, it becomes **satire**. Satire can become cruel and aggressive as it attacks its targets — whether ignorance, callousness, hypocrisy, self-pity, or pretense. The satirist may point up ironic discrepancies between theory and practice, or between promise and result. Satire delights in exposing ulterior motives behind pious talk. When a prominent politician spoke at the Commonwealth Club about the decline of family values among low-income groups, a columnist wrote that the occasion was well chosen, because the business and professional people in attendance could pass the word on to their maids.

WRITING WORKSHOP 2

Language in Action

A What role does figurative language play in the following passage? Which figurative expressions are particularly fresh or striking? What images, feelings, or associations do they bring into play?

> Among the obstacles confronting health care reform, none is more serious than the fog of confusion and doubt surrounding how it is financed. . . . Some of the fog is due to the interests that stand to lose from change and are thus stoking the embers of public anxiety. Insurance brokers oppose reforms that eliminate their role in buying health coverage for small and mid-sized companies. Insurance companies that sell indemnity policies don't want to confront large regional purchasing alliances that will make it impossible to cherrypick the healthy. These interests are the unavoidable purveyors of panic in the crowded theater of health care reform.
>
> Paul Starr, "Against a Myriad of Misconceptions," New Republic

B The author of the following passage finds worthy targets for her barbed wit. What are telling satirical touches here? How does her use of informal language serve her satirical purpose?

> Maybe you didn't buy a racehorse last year. You were worried about what it would do to the lawn, or perhaps you just didn't realize that the IRS regards racehorses as a tax-deductible part of the "farming business," along with cattle or pigs. But that's all right. Next year you can always pick up a hefty deduction simply by changing your name, or you can incorporate yourself in the Cayman Islands and start racking up impressive business losses by issuing yourself big dividends. Maybe you'll even "lose" so much that the IRS will give you refunds going back for years.
>
> Well, probably not *you*, of course. The message of the new book *America: Who Really Pays the Taxes?* by Pulitzer-prize-winning reporters Donald L. Barlett and James B. Steele, is that slippery moves like these are available only to corporations and millionaires, many of whom are already taxed at rates far lower than the rest of us. . . .
>
> One of the great bipartisan axioms of our times is that if you irritate the rich and the corporations — for example, by insisting that they cough up some tax revenue — they'll get all huffy and will refuse to create any jobs for the rest of us. So we solemnly nod our heads when the politicians assure us that cutting the taxes of the wealthy constitutes "tax reform," while increasing them would be a suicidal form of "class warfare."
>
> Unfortunately, however, tax coddling doesn't necessarily put the over-

class in the mood to generate decent employment. Barlett and Steele offer the case of Buster Brown shoes, which managed, by means of some cunning detours through the Caymans, to reduce its 1987 tax rate to 1.7% of sales. Meanwhile, the company was laying off hundreds of stateside employees, who for their part had no choice but to pay taxes on their unemployment benefits.

Barbara Ehrenreich, "Helping the Rich Stay That Way," Time

WRITING WORKSHOP 3

A Paper for Peer Review

The following student paper responded to an assignment that asked student writers to bring their personality, imagination, or sense of humor into play. What makes the paper different from more straightforward prose? How do you react to the piece?

A Matter of the Heart

I usually shy away from giving advice. I read somewhere early in my career as a reader that Lonely Hearts columns or advice columns signed "Aunt Sue" are likely to be written by someone on the newspaper staff who is not trusted with reporting hard news. However, there is a subject on which it is hard to withhold advice that might save an innocent or inexperienced person unnecessary grief.

The subject is ending a love relationship with someone. (This was previously known as "breaking up.") I'm referring specifically to being "dumped." It seems that in our modern civilized society, we need to be guided through how to do things that used to come naturally. I have noted that one of the prices we've paid for being an educated, intellectual society is that we tend to approach everything from a very cerebral standpoint and cover up real feelings. We can be heard telling friends and family variations of the following clichés: "I've ended my relationship with so-and-so." "I realize it's a good thing, a positive thing, the best thing for me." "I've learned a lesson about myself." "I'm putting myself first from now on." "I've grown from this experience." "I'm learning to let go and not be possessive." "Love is a neurotic need." "If you truly love someone, then you let them go." "I think it was karma." "We weren't meant for one another." "There's something better out there for me." "I was addicted to love." "I love too much." "He was afraid of commitment." "She was insecure." "I'm working this through with my therapist," and blah, blah, blah, and so on.

When a couple breaks up, for whatever reasons and whoever initiates it, each person experiences a myriad of conflicting emotions, often negative. This turbulence is unavoidable. The period after a break-up is a confusing time, an emotionally exhausting time. Many modern folk are quite often overwhelmed. They don't know what to do or how to react. Phil Donahue and Oprah Winfrey spend hours with featured psychologists and authors who attempt to teach people how to cope with these feelings. Personally, I say just feel them — the feelings. Go for the high drama. Feel lovesick. Mope around the house and feel sorry for yourself for a while. Cry your eyes out. Tell your story to anyone who wants to listen and even those who don't. Fantasize about terrible things that will happen to your ex. Make him/her out to be the "bad guy." Save your money. Don't go to talk to a therapist. All he/she will do is charge $85 and give you permission to feel what you're feeling — to grieve or be angry or feel hurt. Don't try to talk yourself into feeling better prematurely. Go through the cycle and get it out of your system. Punch walls (pillows are less painful), slam doors, throw things. Most importantly, throw your ideas of controlling your emotions and dealing with this tumult in a mature, civilized intelligent way right out the window.

This is not a time for theories. This is a matter of the heart. Denying feelings only causes ulcers and prolongs the pain of loss.

OPTIONS FOR WRITING 10

Branching Out

Choose a topic that will allow you to experiment with a style different from that of straightforward, businesslike prose. Choose a topic that will allow you to bring your imagination or sense of humor into play.

1 Use the lighter touch in an essay on a neglected sidelight of cultural history. For instance, write a history of the penny — or of poodles. Try to make your paper both informative and amusing.

2 Write an exposé on a topic that makes you angry. Try to arouse the indignation of (but not alienate) the reader. Possible targets might range from the cosmetics industry to drunk drivers.

3 Try to make your readers share in the excitement of some adventurous undertaking that you know well from firsthand experience, whether mountain climbing, bungee jumping, solo flying, or sheep shearing.

4 For an audience of your fellow students, write a satirical paper on some aspect of American popular culture. For instance, satirize rappers, diet fads, beauty contests, soap operas, or movie or TV rating systems.

5 Write a parody of a kind of communication that you find especially annoying. For instance, focus on beer commercials, telephone soliciting, or commencement speeches.

6 Write an imaginary letter home by a visitor to the United States from another country — or another planet. Seen from the visitor's point of view, what would seem strange or funny?

7 Do you belong to a group that is able to laugh at its own quirks or foibles? Research and write about humor that is aimed at members of your own group (ethnic, racial, religious, social, occupational, or ideological) and that you find amusing, revealing, or affectionate rather than offensive.

8 Working with a group, script a witty or lively imaginary dialogue between two people on different sides of the fence. For instance, imagine a dialogue between an immigrant and an opponent of immigration, or between a pro-union worker and an antiunion executive, or between a moviegoer looking for uplift and one looking for light entertainment.

9 Working with a group, help write a script for a lively skit teaching adolescents about contraception or a public health issue.

10 Alone or with a group, script a scene for a parody of a Schwarzenegger, Eastwood, or Madonna movie (or for some other kind of movie that invites parody).

Reading, Discussion, Writing

The Range of Styles

OVERVIEW: The authors of the following selections demonstrate the richness of our stylistic options. The style in these readings ranges from laid-back informality to the formal style of the pundit. It ranges from caustic satire to eloquent tribute and to zany dark humor.

LA Laugh Tracks

PAULA POUNDSTONE

Can a writer be entertaining while getting in some serious points about the annoyances of every day? Many readers follow a favorite columnist, looking forward to the writer's commentary on recent events, often savoring a familiar mix of the serious and the chatty. Columnists like Paula Poundstone write in a nonthreatening, informal style, taking their readers into their confidence the way a friend might. They articulate likes and dislikes that the reader might normally consider too frivolous or personal to be quoted in public. They are unawed by the important and the rich, allowing readers to feel disrespectful and superior to people to whom they may have to be more respectful from nine to five. (Poundstone uses slangy labels that take self-important people down a peg — an editor becomes the "editor guy" and a big executive becomes a "bigwig.")

The editor guy of this magazine asked me the other day if Hollywood has morals. Gee, I certainly don't think so. He seems like such a bright man; why would he ask a question like that? Hollywood uses the TV laugh track, the very soul of dishonesty. In the years before I understood that they couldn't possibly have performed before a live audience, I thought the Flintstones were funny to adults. I assumed the jokes were just over my head and that, when I matured, the elephant who said, "It's a living," while his trunk was used as the spray nozzle for washing dishes would be a knee-slapper.

I can't tell if I'm becoming paranoid or wise, but it feels like no one is honest anymore. I've spent the last month in negotiation over a contract with a TV network, and at the same time contractors have been building a room on the back of my house. In the span of a few short hours I talk to plumbers, electricians, GTE, alarm technicians, construction workers, agents, lawyers, and network executives. They have much in common.

I made the mistake of reading *Outfoxed,* a book about the making of the Fox Broadcasting Company, during all of this. I'm embarrassed to have read it in a page-turning fever, unable to focus on anything else, carrying it with me everywhere I went, underlining passages about Barry Diller's philosophy, and quoting from the book while talking with perfectly intelligent adults.

I've never negotiated a contract before, and there was story after story in the book about big experienced Hollywood types making deals at Fox, getting screwed, and having breakdowns. There's no way I could predict every bad thing that might happen and protect myself contractually. When producer Sherry Lansing was a bigwig at Fox Television and all over magazine covers as the woman with everything, her boss kept calling her "dollface" and asking her to work on a sequel to *The Sound of Music.* Eventually she had to leave. My hair stood on end. Even had Sherry been clever enough to include the unprecedented "no dollface" clause, the odds are good she would have let her guard down only to find the bossman calling her "cupcake" as the ink dried on the signed contract.

I was told my agents would protect me in dealing with the network and that I needed a lawyer to protect me in dealing with my agents. At my house, the construction workers broke the sprinklers, the cable, and the hot-water heater, and then said they didn't. My phone lines had static for months. I called GTE, who promised to come out between noon and midnight one day to fix the lines. Although they didn't fix them, they did screw up the security system. They said they didn't. The toilet, shower, and bathtub backed up. The plumber said I had to have all my sewer pipes replaced, because tree roots had grown through them. I didn't ask the tree. Who wants to be lied to by a tree?

Almost every day some worker set off the burglar alarm or car alarm while I was out, though no one admitted doing it. Criminals couldn't have gotten a turn. I get furious when I think of all of the time and energy I could save if everyone would just be honest. I wouldn't need an alarm to prevent thieves from breaking into my car. I wouldn't have to return to the house ten minutes after I leave, to make double sure I put the alarm on. I wouldn't need agents to protect me from network people, nor lawyers to protect me from agents.

I got to the distressing point in reading the Fox book where I realized there's no protecting yourself from a big company anyway. When Joan Rivers tried to sue Fox for breaching their contractual promises, they just said to go ahead and try and they would keep her tied up in court for a long time. She settled for settling out of court.

I've wanted to work in television as long as I can remember, but I never knew about this part. It actually makes you realize what incredible actors television stars have been. "The Waltons" actress Michael Learned may have been having a screaming fight with some executive about marketing an inflatable doll with her face on it without her permission, just seconds before she played Olivia Walton walking peacefully to Ike Godsey's mercantile, in the dappled glow of the afternoon sun and the quiet, loving company of Elizabeth and Mary Ellen. Now that I know the awful possibilities, I may even be in awe of Suzanne Somers.

Just as I had begun to be stripped of all naiveté in these matters, my negotiation with the network had gotten to a place where I'd ask for something and they'd say, "We won't give it to you in writing, but we will do it," and my agent would say, "Well, if they say they will, they will." This seemed particularly odd, because I hadn't read anything in the trade papers about a prominent agent being kicked in the head by a horse. It was time for another quick chat with the lawyer.

I finally had to hire a private contractor to fix the phone lines. (He said he used to work at GTE and they shouldn't be trusted. Doy.) It took ten hours on a Saturday. Monday the guys doing the drywalling knocked some of the lines loose again. They said they didn't.

Joan Rivers said in an interview in *Outfoxed* that Fox had lied, cheated, and been dishonorable. Fox President Jamie Kellner denied this and said it had just been business. Apparently "business" looks, feels, and sounds so much like lying, cheating, and being dishonorable that even Joan Rivers was fooled.

THE INVOLVED READER

1 What informal or slangy expressions here assure you that the columnist is not a stuffed shirt? What humorous touches contribute to the informal, half-serious tone?

2 What is the connection between the author's misadventures with repair people and her digs at business practices? Do you think she is effective in aiming her barbs at the morals of the media world?

3 Why does the laugh track become a central symbol in this column?

TALKING, THINKING, WRITING

4 Do you think you could become a faithful reader of a columnist like Poundstone? Why or why not?

5 Can you keep your sense of humor when dealing with annoying or conniving people? Try your hand at writing a short half-humorous, half-serious column in the Poundstone style.

6 Do you know a columnist, cartoonist, or talk show host who combines a lighter touch with occasional serious points? Prepare a critique of the person's style, identifying key features and providing striking examples.

The Barbarity of Boxing

GEORGE WILL

Are highbrow critics inevitably at war with popular culture? Or is boxing a sport that makes even friends of popular culture draw the line? George Will cultivates the image of the pundit who discusses serious issues in a formal style, with references to the Greek philosopher Plato and quotations from scholars in think tanks. Hailed by the New York Times *as "the most widely read and heard political commentator in America," Will has for many years written columns for the* Washington Post *and* Newsweek. *Will, who was born in the Midwest but studied at Oxford and Princeton, became a quintessential representative of the East Coast establishment. He traces the roots of his cultural conservatism to English thinkers like Edmund Burke (who denounced the French Revolution), Cardinal Newman (the nineteenth-century Protestant leader who converted to Catholicism), and Benjamin Disraeli (legendary chieftain of the British conservative or Tory party). In recent years, George Will has increasingly used his column to do battle against multiculturalism, political correctness, and other movements he sees as threats to Western civilization.*

For 150 years people have been savoring Macaulay's judgment that the Puritans hated bearbaiting not because it gave pain to the bear but because it gave pleasure to the spectators. However, there are moments, and this is one, for blurting out the truth: The Puritans were right. The pain to the bear was not a matter of moral indifference, but the pleasure of the spectators was sufficient reason for abolishing that entertainment.

Now another boxer has been beaten to death. The brain injury he suffered was more than the injury the loser in a boxing match is supposed to suffer. It is hard to calibrate such things — how hard an opponent's brain should be banged against the side of his cranium — in the heat of battle.

From time immemorial, in immemorial ways, men have been fighting for the entertainment of other men. Perhaps in a serene, temperate society boxing would be banned along with other blood sports — if, in such a society, the question would even arise. But a step toward the extinction of boxing is understandably why that is desirable. One reason is the physical injury done to young men. But a sufficient reason is the quality of the pleasure boxing often gives to spectators.

There is no denying that boxing, like other, better sports, can exemplify excellence. Boxing demands bravery and, when done well, is beautiful in the way that any exercise of finely honed physical talents is. Furthermore, many sports are dangerous. But boxing is the sport that has as its object the infliction of pain and injury. Its crowning achievement is the infliction of serious trauma on the brain. The euphemism for boxing is "the art of self-defense." No. A rose is a rose is a rose, and a user fee is a revenue enhancer is a tax increase, and boxing is aggression.

It is probable that there will be a rising rate of spinal cord injuries and deaths in football. The force of defense players (a function of weight and speed) is increasing even faster than the force of ball carriers and receivers. As a coach once said, football is not a contact sport — dancing is a contact sport — football is a collision sport. The human body, especially the knee and spine, is not suited to that. But football can be made safer by equipment improvements and rules changes such as those proscribing certain kinds of blocks. Boxing is fundamentally impervious to reform.

It will be said that if two consenting adults want to batter each other for the amusement of paying adults, the essential niceties have been satisfied, "consent" being almost the only nicety of a liberal society. But from Plato on, political philosophers have taken entertainments seriously and have believed the law should, too. They have because a society is judged by the kind of citizens it produces, and some entertainments are coarsening. Good government and the good life depend on good values and passions, and some entertainments are inimical to these.

Such an argument cuts no ice in a society where the decayed public philosophy teaches that the pursuit of happiness is a right sovereign over all other considerations; that "happiness" and "pleasure" are synonyms, and that there is no hierarchy of values against which to measure particular appetites. Besides, some persons will say, with reason, that a society in which the entertainment menu includes topless lady mud wrestlers is a society past worrying about.

Sports besides boxing attract persons who want their unworthy passions stirred, including a lust for blood. I remember Memorial Day in the Middle West in the 1950s, when all roads led to the Indianapolis Speedway, where too many fans went to drink Falstaff beer and hope for a crash. But boxing is in a class by itself.

Richard Hoffer of the *Los Angeles Times* remembers the death of Johnny Owen, a young 118-pound bantamweight who died before he had fulfilled his modest ambition of buying a hardware store back home in Wales. Hoffman remembers that "Owen was put in a coma

5

by a single punch, carried out of the Olympic (arena) under a hail of beer cups, some of which were filled with urine."

The law cannot prudently move far in advance of mass taste, so boxing cannot be outlawed. But in a world in which many barbarities are unavoidable, perhaps it is not too much to hope that some of the optional sorts will be outgrown. [10]

THE INVOLVED READER

1 What general perspective on American popular culture underlies this column? What examples other than boxing does Will bring in?

2 What would a reader have to know about Puritans and about bearbaiting to understand Will's allusion to them? Where would you turn to find out who Macaulay was?

3 Along with life and liberty, the pursuit of happiness is among the inalienable human rights enumerated in the Declaration of Independence. What is Will's commentary on this concept? What role does it play in this column?

4 The opening paragraphs use the formal *savor, calibrate,* and *impervious* but also plain everyday words like *blurt* and *bang.* What additional examples of both kinds can you find in the rest of the column? Which kind predominates?

TALKING, THINKING, WRITING

5 How would you sum up Will's objection to boxing? What would you say in support of his position — or in defense of the sport?

6 In 1990, Will published *Men at Work,* a book in praise of American baseball. To judge from the column you have just read, why do you think baseball would be his favorite sport?

7 Are you critical of "mass taste"? Prepare an attack on or defense of another sport or popular entertainment that might be criticized as "coarsening" or offensive.

MAKING CONNECTIONS

8 By temperament or personality, would you make an ideal reader for an informal columnist like Paula Poundstone or for a more formal writer like George Will?

Love It or Leave It

M ICHAEL   K INSLEY

Is ridicule a more potent weapon than earnest exhortation? Satire uses humor to do battle against abusive or antisocial behavior. In the following piece, Michael Kinsley aims his satirical barbs at a new wrinkle in tax evasion — wealthy Americans giving up their citizenship and moving to offshore tax havens beyond the reach of the Internal Revenue Service. A frequent contributor to the New Republic, *Kinsley represents the progressive end of the magazine's editorial spectrum. He has frequently criticized current business ethics and the role of business in American politics. In the following guest column for* Time *magazine, he uses familiar weapons in the satirist's arsenal. For instance, he employs irony when he uses mock-sympathy in recounting the "heart-wrenching" story of the poor wealthy victims of America's tax laws. He turns familiar clichés (like "love it or leave it") against those who are fond of using them.*

Surely the most heart-wrenching human-interest story in the press recently was a cover article in *Forbes* magazine titled "The New Refugees." These miserable souls are not fleeing conventional forms of oppression, such as the famine, dictatorship, torture and murder that have caused millions to seek haven in the U.S. through the generations. These are rich folks who, according to *Forbes,* are giving up their American citizenship — the very status boat people by the thousands are risking their lives for even today — because (according to one quoted legal expert) they "can't pay the federal tax rate and live in the style they want."

Poor babies! To be sure, these are not exactly your classic "huddled masses." Whether they are "wretched refuse," though, is a different question.

As a "trend" story, "The New Refugees" is a bit of a stretch. It turns out that only 306 Americans gave up their citizenship last year. Somewhat desperately, *Forbes* characterizes the number of expatriates as enough to "practically fill a Boeing 747." But out of 260 million citizens, the number is pretty small.

Nevertheless, *Forbes* — a conservative publication, ordinarily not averse to a bit of flag waving — brings enormous sympathy to this tale of Americans abandoning their country. It seems that "victim chic," ordinarily decried as a left-wing phenomenon, knows no bounds of reason or ideology. These people, after all, are less like traditional refugees than they are like the Americans who went to Canada during the Vietnam War. They are fleeing the draft — of their wallets, not their bodies. It's a smaller imposition, some might think. Those who fled in the 1960s were motivated, at best, by principled opposition to a government policy and, at worst, by a desire to save their own lives. The "new refugees" merely want to save money. And these financial draft evaders are not even barred completely from our shores. Under the rules, they are allowed to spend 120 days a year in the country they decline to support.

The "new refugees" aren't going to Canada. Nor are they going to 5 Britain, France, Germany or Japan. These grown-up nations all have tax rates roughly equivalent to those in the U.S., or higher. Mostly the "new refugees" are going to island pseudo countries with names like St. Kitts and Nevis or Turks and Caicos. The U.S. says, "Give me your tired, your poor." These tax havens say the opposite. They are places of Third World poverty where the well-to-do, in exchange for some investment, are invited to shed the normal obligations of citizenship in the developed world.

One of those obligations is the defense of freedom. *Forbes* notes, without irony, that "the end of the cold war means wealthy Americans can live in many developing nations safely." How long would that be true if it weren't for the American defense structure, paid for by the American taxpayer: The Turks and Caicos Islands, freedom loving though they may be, are not exactly in the forefront of the protection of that freedom.

In predominantly middle-class nations like the U.S., taxes also support a level of shared infrastructure (roads, sewers), and social services (police, schools) that poorer countries simply cannot afford. In those countries, the rich provide such services, more cheaply, for themselves alone, and the poor do without. One of the pleasures of membership in an advanced society like ours is precisely the knowledge that certain mundane aspects of life are shared by all. This gives a daily reality to the otherwise abstract democratic ideal. We all drink the same water, walk the same sidewalks, are guarded by the same cops. If 306 rich people derive no such democratic pleasure from life in America, maybe they really do belong someplace else.

True, American taxes serve a third function: outright redistribution that supports even the poorest citizens at levels that would seem luxurious by Third World standards. That too is a price of membership in an advanced democratic society that either you think is worth it or you don't. Of course we argue endlessly here in America about whether tax rates are too high and whether the government should be spending money on this or that. But the U.S. will never be able to compete with Third World backwaters for the allegiance of the mobile rich if tax rates are the only criterion.

Would-be refugees from the U.S. — "yacht people"? — might want to wait, though, before burning their passports. The good news is that in some ways, this country is becoming more like the Turks and the Caicos Islands every day. As noted by thinkers from Clinton's Labor Secretary Robert Reich on the left to IQ-obsessive Charles Murray on the right, technology and global trade are increasing the gap between rich and poor (even as they make us all richer on average). Increasingly, as well, affluent Americans do provide their own social services, such as schools and security and even roads in gated communities, while the general level of such services in society is allowed to deteriorate.

So don't give up on America yet, yacht people. You needn't move   10
to the Third World. The Third World is coming to you.

THE INVOLVED READER

1   Kinsley delights in wordplay and word games. What is the usual context of the phrase "love it or leave it"? How does Kinsley stand it on its head? What verbal games is he playing when using phrases like "huddled masses," "wretched refuse," "victim chic," "fleeing the draft," "Give me your tired, your poor," or "yacht people"? What other clever or barbed uses of language can you point out?

2   What ideal of a democratic society and responsible citizenship emerges from this column? Do you think Kinsley is an effective advocate for it?

TALKING, THINKING, WRITING

3   What is the gist of Kinsley's indictment of the "financial draft evaders"? Do you think they are guilty as charged? Or can you say something in their defense?

4   Representatives of American business have often charged that educators and the media tend to be hostile to business. To judge from your own experience and observation, are these charges justified?

Sister from Another Planet Probes the Soaps

ANDREA FREUD LOEWENSTEIN

Do feminists lack a sense of humor? Do readers expect magazines like Ms. *to be Puritanical? Books like* Women's Glibber: State-of-the-Art Women's Humor *(1993) are counteracting the stereotype of the humorless feminist.* Ms., *where the following piece first appeared, is increasingly providing a forum for women's satire. A time-honored satirist's ploy is to adopt the stance of the naive observer — the visitor from an alien land who sees everything as if for the first time. In the following piece, a visitor from outer space marvels at the weird customs of the natives the way Mark Twain's Huckleberry Finn marvels at ignorance, violence, and treachery as if they had just been invented. Andrea Freud Loewenstein adopts the identity of a space alien voyaging to the universe of the soaps, beaming back to her home base her wide-eyed observations of the pecking order and courtship rituals of the species* Homo soapoid Americanus. *Loewenstein became known for* The Worry Girl, *a collection of stories with echoes of an Austrian Jewish past and the Holocaust, and for her study* Loathsome Jews and Engulfing Women.

> Dear Professor:
> Enclosed is my research paper. As you may remember, I attended every one of your lectures (I float at a right angle in the front row; last Thursday I was an iridescent green with ocher spots) on that most fascinating subject, the human species North Americanus Soapus. For my research project, I viewed several weeks' worth of documentary videotapes from four different "Soaps," chosen because they were among the most widely watched programs in the Earthling year 1993, with some 50 million viewers combined. I will hereafter refer to the humanoids whose acquaintance I made in "The Young and the Restless," "The Bold and the Beautiful," "All My Children," and "General Hospital," as "Soapoids."
> The name "Soaps," by the way, appears to derive from the obsessional recurrence of the cleanliness theme in the "commercials," which occur at rhythmic intervals throughout the tapes. These are short, ritualized hymns of thanksgiving and praise to selected objects of worship, such as toilet bowl cleaners and vaginal deodorants.

I must admit that during the first week of viewing, in which I used all 17 of my sensors, I was unable to distinguish one Soapoid from another. The only distinction I was immediately able to make was between male and female — the Soapoids' preoccupation with ritual ownership of the opposite sex causes them to go to amazing lengths to signal gender distinction. These signals include the compulsory arrangement and selective removal of facial and head hair, distinctive body coverings, and (for the adult female) symbolic facial markings and mutilations.

This species, in contrast to our own, is subdivided into a mere two fixed gender groupings: male and female. Contrary to the lecture in which you informed us that occasionally both male and female choose to couple with their own kind and that those humanoids tend to be ostracized by the majority, I observed no variation in gender identity or object choice. On the contrary, all of my sample were hostile toward their own gender, whom they perceived as rivals in their never-ending fight to possess the opposite sex. Although this goal appears to be the Soapoids' overwhelming motivational force, the humans in my sample spent almost no time actually copulating. Instead, their main behavior consisted of endless discussions of, preparations for, and references to the act.

Nevertheless, copulation, when it does occur, often leads to   5
trouble and confusion, even for the viewer. I spent a great deal of time attempting to determine the name of the young woman from *All My Children* who works in a police station, is the daughter of one of the two possible fathers of Mimi's unborn child, and nosily looked up information to determine the date of conception. Since the records revealed that she had copulated with both men during the same week, Mimi was forced to confess and call off her wedding the day it was scheduled. I never did get the young woman's name.

Copulation does allow the females to exert ownership over the males. You had informed us that males are the dominant gender, and that their inability to express their feelings verbally leads to frequent acts of violence. I regret to inform you that this conclusion is no longer valid. Soapoid males are quite gentle and verbally expressive. Their preferred behavior consists of lengthy expositions on their feelings toward the females. The male is especially prone to elaborate courtship rituals in preparation for copulation. These include the repetition of such submissive phrases as: "I love you so much," "You're my whole life," and "You were amazing last night, darling!" In one typical behavior, a male in *The Bold and the Beautiful* prepared for intercourse by placing at least 20 floating water lilies containing small lit candles in a pool of water upon which floated an inflatable rubber raft, the intended scene of sexual activity.

The far more complex females are the actual aggressors. In a lecture, you had mentioned that some women, referred to as "feminists," join with one another toward a common goal. No such movement was evident in this sample. In fact, the females' most favored posture was the standoff, a highly aggressive position in which two women position themselves from one to two feet apart and emit such statements as "I hated you the first time I saw you." This is accompanied by a full range of physical expressions, including crossing of the arms, curling of the lip, and advancing in a menacing manner.

Unlike the male, the female can be classified into several subtypes, all arranged around the notions of "good" and "evil." These inborn tendencies emerge at puberty, apparently along with the mammary glands. The Good Female mitigates her natural dominance by an exaggerated concern for the welfare and nourishment of "her" male. She is especially solicitous of his title — Writer, Actor, Businessman, Doctor, Lawyer, or Policeman — and is always ready to abandon her own title to have more time to support his efforts. In *The Young and the Restless*, for example, Nikki, a Businesswoman, repeatedly interrupts her own work to service Cole, a Writer who is also a Groomer of Horses. Attired in a series of low-cut red evening gowns, she waits on him at his workplace in the horse stable, serving him champagne and caviar, assuring him that publishers from the mythical city of New York will turn his novel into a "best-seller."

It is important to note, however, that these work titles are symbolic. Soapoids, who possess a limited will to action and often require several hours of "processing" conversation to accomplish a simple task, must limit themselves to the all-important Preparation for Copulation. They have neither the time nor the energy to engage in actual "work." (The now meaningless title *General Hospital* indicates that Soapoids did work at one time.)

Good Females can be recognized by their wide-open, forward-gazing eyes, modest demeanor, and light pink lip-paint. In old age they become wrinkled. Evil Females, on the other hand, remain slim, highly polished, and brightly painted throughout life, a certain tautness of the facial skin being the only visible sign of aging. The Evil Females' characteristics include unfaithfulness, sexual rapacity, and the need to manipulate others. Most Evil Females confine their ambition to collecting a large number of men, but a few exhibit a further will to power through the ownership of Titles, Land, Factories, Businesses, or Patents. These women, whom I call Controllers, have destroyed the lives of generations of Soapoids. 10

In your lecture on racial and ethnic diversity, you brought us almost to jellification with your tale of the oppression of darker-hued or "African American" humanoids at the hands of the lighter ones whom you labeled the subspecies "European American." I am happy to inform you that no such oppression exists among modern-day

Soapoids. In fact, there seems to be no difference between the darker and lighter types. All hues mix and converse on terms of perfect equality and good-will and hold titles of equal symbolic significance. Dark-skinned females (who exhibit a wide range of coloration, unlike the more muted light-skinned humanoids) wear their head hair in the same fashion as all other females — raised two or three inches from the head, then flowing to the shoulders. Darker and lighter humanoids do not mate, and appear to have no desire to do so. Whether this is because of the force of taboo or physical incompatibility cannot be determined at this juncture. It should be noted, however, that none of the African American females had attained the status of Controller, perhaps because they lack the necessary icy blue eyes.

Saul, an elderly male from *The Bold and the Beautiful* speaks with an accent, wears a pink shirt, highly ornamented necktie, and thick spectacles; he appears to be a eunuch. My ethnosensor identified him as a member of the subspecies "Jew." Whether these characteristics are an honest reflection of this identity is hard for me to determine — he was the only member of the group in this sample. Maria from *All My Children* was identified as a member of the subspecies "Latina"; as far as I can tell from my viewing, this group is notable for wavy head hair and the ability to ride a Horse without a saddle. Unlike African Americans, these Latinas appear able to mate with the "European Americans."

The photographs you showed us of the unsavory dwelling places (known as "Ghettos") of some humanoids also appear to be out of date. As of now, all Soapoids inhabit spacious, carefully color-coordinated cubes, filled with plastic flowers and bright modular furniture, in which they engage in their activities of arguing, preparing for copulation, and discussing their feelings for one another. Since eating, cleaning, and evacuation are not part of these sequences (being reserved for the "commercials"), no rooms are provided for these activities. It is unclear whether this is by choice or necessity (perhaps the atmosphere outside these cubes is not pure enough to breathe).

No analysis of Soapoid society would be complete without a mention of the interlacing "commercials." These mini-documentaries demonstrate the Soapoids' unique ability to encapsulate and split off areas of behavior and their need to control their errant bodies. The mini-docs also provide a neat solution for any scholars who may, thus far in my narrative, have been puzzled by the absence of ingestion and excretion in the lives of these living organisms. All such functions are reserved for the mini-docs, during which Soap-oids frantically ingest prepackaged slimness-controlling nourish-ments and rid their cubes, their eating utensils, their garments, and their bodies of all superfluous liquids and imperfections. "Dirty on the outside!" exclaims a voice-over as a female handles her mate's garment in horror. "Uh oh, what about the inside!" A typical hour in the lives of Soapoids contains countless mini-docs that utilize not only a cleaning fluid that will purify garments on the inside, but also: a garment that can absorb the excretions of even the most wiggly of infant young; a tablet that cleans the excreting instrument by pro-viding 2,000 flushes; another tablet to be ingested by the enemy spe-cies Cockroach; and yet another to be taken by the female Soapoid in order to soften her stools and ease excretion.

The lower body of the female seems to be especially in need of such devices. A sequence that begins with the frightening words "Out of control!" introduces tablets that will "take control" of diar-rhea in one day. The vaginal area is serviced by a pellet that cures yeast infections, a deodorant designed to "intercede" between the female's odor and her undergarments, and — for those who would seem to have the opposite problem — an ointment for vaginal dry-ness. Is it because the female Soapoid's vagina is the seat of her dominance over the male, and thus the location of her power, that it requires such constant servicing? Or is the female's verbal aggres-sion yet another mark of her need to "stay in control" of her way-ward body? 15

I end this paper with a confession: I entered my research project with a certain amount of bias against humanoids, whom I had been taught to regard as primitive, quarrelsome creatures, frozen in their limited natures and bodily forms, unable to regulate their own lives and affairs. But slowly, I grew increasingly susceptible to the charm of these beings. Before long, I found myself growing impatient with the time spent in my ordinary occupations. As I went about my daily tasks, I couldn't wait to join those beings who, never challenging, always predictable, asked nothing more from me than to watch them. Now that the viewing is over, I feel empty.

As I beam this paper to your neurotransmitters and project it into the ozone, it is with both fondness and regret that, amid the busy whirl of my life, I pause to remember the Soapoids, a matriarchal people whose lives drag out in long luxurious segments lived within color-coordinated cubes, and who relegate the more messy business of life to quick one-minute segments, thus freeing themselves for a stress-free, germ-free, moisture-controlled existence.

THE INVOLVED READER

1   Parody apes a characteristic style or manner — often in order to make fun of its weaknesses or pretensions. What touches or details make this piece a parody of academic research and of science fiction?

2   What stands out in the space traveler's observation of gender roles, courtship, and sex in the soaps? (Does Loewenstein exaggerate?)

3   What does an episode like the one about Mimi's planned marriage and unborn child show about the moral universe of the soaps? What does it show about the tastes, preferences, or standards of their audience?

4   Much current social criticism focuses on issues of gender, race, and class. What role does race and class play in Loewenstein's satire? What are her targets?

5   Where and why does the space traveler correct mistaken theories she was taught?

TALKING, THINKING, WRITING

6   How would you sum up Loewenstein's criticism of the soaps? Where do you agree with her? Where do you take issue with her? Do you think she is too negative?

7   Do you think of the soap operas as fantasy or wish-fulfillment? Or do they in some way hold up the mirror to real life? Do you think they help shape the thinking, feelings, or behavior of viewers?

COLLABORATIVE PROJECTS

8   Working with a group, script a mini-episode that would serve as a parody of favorite soap operas or a current soap.

MAKING CONNECTIONS

9   Women writers noted for their biting, caustic wit include Sallie Tisdale (Chapter 2), Naomi Wolf (Chapter 4), and Susan Faludi (Chapter 7). Do they live up to their reputations in the selections reprinted in this book?

short story

The School

DONALD BARTHELME

*What is laughable about evil and calamity? Dark humor is often a
reaction against a goody-goody, sentimentalized version of life. Barthelme's fiction projects the zany humor of a writer who has given up
trying to fit reality into rational conventional categories. Like much
twentieth-century art and literature, his stories reflect a lively sense of
the absurd — the feeling that we cannot make sense of life; we can
only laugh at it. Barthelme is a master of parody, mimicking the way
people act and talk. He started writing poetry and fiction while still in
high school; in the seventies and eighties, his stories in the* New Yorker
*gained him a loyal following among readers for whom conventional
ways of storytelling had gone stale. Much current postmodern fiction
abandons traditional elements like plot, characterization, and symbol
to play sophisticated games with the conventions of storytelling and
with the reader.*

Well, we had all these children out planting trees, see, because we
figured that . . . that was part of their education, to see how, you
know, the root systems . . . and also the sense of responsibility, taking
care of things, being individually responsible. You know what I mean.
And the trees all died. They were orange trees. I don't know why they
died, they just died. Something wrong with the soil possibly or maybe
the stuff we got from the nursery wasn't the best. We complained
about it. So we've got thirty kids there, each kid had his or her own
little tree to plant, and we've got these thirty dead trees. All these
kids looking at these little brown sticks, it was depressing.

It wouldn't have been so bad except that just a couple of weeks
before the thing with the trees, the snakes all died. But I think that
the snakes — well, the reason that the snakes kicked off was that . . .
you remember, the boiler was shut off for four days because of the
strike, and that was explicable. It was something you could explain
to the kids because of the strike. I mean, none of their parents would
let them cross the picket line and they knew there was a strike going
on and what it meant. So when things got started up again and we
found the snakes they weren't too disturbed.

With the herb gardens it was probably a case of overwatering, and
at least now they know not to overwater. The children were very conscientious with the herb gardens and some of them probably . . . you
know, slipped them a little extra water when we weren't looking. Or

maybe . . . well, I don't like to think about sabotage, although it did occur to us. I mean, it was something that crossed our minds. We were thinking that way probably because before that the gerbils had died, and the white mice had died, and the salamander . . . well, now they know not to carry them around in plastic bags.

Of course we *expected* the tropical fish to die, that was no surprise. Those numbers, you look at them crooked and they're belly-up on the surface. But the lesson plan called for a tropical-fish input at that point, there was nothing we could do, it happens every year, you just have to hurry past it.

We weren't even supposed to have a puppy.   5

We weren't even supposed to have one, it was just a puppy the Murdoch girl found under a Gristede's truck one day and she was afraid the truck would run over it when the driver had finished making his delivery, so she stuck it in her knapsack and brought it to school with her. So we had this puppy. As soon as I saw the puppy I thought, Oh Christ, I bet it will live for about two weeks and then . . . And that's what it did. It wasn't supposed to be in the classroom at all, there's some kind of regulation about it, but you can't tell them they can't have a puppy when the puppy is already there, right in front of them, running around on the floor and yap yap yapping. They named it Edgar — that is, they named it after me. They had a lot of fun running after it and yelling, "Here, Edgar! Nice Edgar!" Then they'd laugh like hell. They enjoyed the ambiguity. I enjoyed it myself. I don't mind being kidded. They made a little house for it in the supply closet and all that. I don't know what it died of. Distemper, I guess. It probably hadn't had any shots. I got it out of there before the kids got to school. I checked the supply closet each morning, routinely, because I knew what was going to happen. I gave it to the custodian.

And then there was this Korean orphan that the class adopted through the Help the Children program, all the kids brought in a quarter a month, that was the idea. It was an unfortunate thing, the kid's name was Kim and maybe we adopted him too late or something. The cause of death was not stated in the letter we got, they suggested we adopt another child instead and sent us some interesting case histories, but we didn't have the heart. The class took it pretty hard, they began (I think, nobody ever said anything to me directly) to feel that maybe there was something wrong with the school. But I don't think there's anything wrong with the school, particularly, I've seen better and I've seen worse. It was just a run of bad luck. We had an extraordinary number of parents passing away, for instance. There were I think two heart attacks and two suicides, one drowning, and four killed together in a car accident. One stroke. And we had the usual heavy mortality rate among the grandparents, or maybe it was heavier this year, it seemed so. And finally the tragedy.

The tragedy occurred when Matthew Wein and Tony Mavrogordo were playing over where they're excavating for the new federal office building. There were all these big wooden beams stacked, you know, at the edge of the excavation. There's a court case coming out of that, the parents are claiming that the beams were poorly stacked. I don't know what's true and what's not. It's been a strange year.

I forgot to mention Billy Brandt's father, who was knifed fatally when he grappled with a masked intruder in his home.

One day, we had a discussion in class. They asked me, where did   10
they go? The trees, the salamander, the tropical fish, Edgar, the pop-pas and mommas, Matthew and Tony, where did they go? And I said, I don't know, I don't know. And they said, who knows? and I said, nobody knows. And they said, is death that which gives meaning to life? And I said, no, life is that which gives meaning to life. Then they said, but isn't death, considered as a fundamental datum, the means by which the taken-for-granted mundanity of the everyday may be transcended in the direction of —

I said, yes, maybe.

They said, we don't like it.

I said, that's sound.

They said, it's a bloody shame!

I said, it is.

They said, will you make love now with Helen (our teaching assis-   15
tant) so that we can see how it is done? We know you like Helen.

I do like Helen but I said that I would not.

We've heard so much about it, they said, but we've never seen it.

I said I would be fired and it was never, or almost never, done as a demonstration. Helen looked out of the window.

They said, please, please make love with Helen, we require an as-   20
sertion of value, we are frightened.

I said that they shouldn't be frightened (although I am often frightened) and that there was value everywhere. Helen came and embraced me. I kissed her a few times on the brow. We held each other. The children were excited. Then there was a knock on the door, I opened the door, and the new gerbil walked in. The children cheered wildly.

THE INVOLVED READER

1   What makes the narrator sound like a real teacher? When or why do you realize that schools and teachers here are being sent up?

2   What are examples of the narrator's trying to explain everything in a rational, matter-of-fact manner? What makes his explanations comical?

3   Is there a pattern in the way the story develops? What is the connecting thread? Is there a turning point where the story ceases to be mildly humorous and begins to turn truly grotesque — mixing horror and comedy?

4   Is the author satirizing biology lessons, class discussions, sex education? How and why?

TALKING, THINKING, WRITING

5   How do you react to the author's brand of humor? Are you offended by anything in the story? Do you think death and calamity are too serious to be treated in a humorous fashion?

6   Some critics claim that the absurd universe of many modern writers is truer to life than the artificially ordered world and fake optimism of more conventional literature. What's real in this story and what is imaginary? Does the teacher act in some ways like a real teacher? Do the students act in some ways like real students? Does the story have a point?

7   Where do you personally draw the line between offensive and nonoffensive humor?

poem

The House That Fear Built: Warsaw, 1943

JANE FLANDERS

Should poetry be kept a world of its own, with a language of its own? Or should poets be engaged in the struggle for human dignity and justice? Jane Flanders taught in high school and college and became a poet-in-residence at Clark College. She has published her poems in publications including Poetry, Nation, American Poetry Review, New Republic, Atlantic, *and* Massachusetts Review. *She became known for low-key poems about nature and about school days in her native Pennsylvania. However, in the following poem she evokes memories of the Holocaust, the murder of millions of Jews after the Nazi conquest of Poland and large parts of Western Russia in World War II. Fifty years after the war, people were still pondering the haunting photographs of Jewish men, women, and children rounded up after the crushing of a desperate uprising in the Warsaw ghetto.*

> The purpose of poetry is to remind us
> how difficult it is to remain just one person,
> for our house is open, there are no keys in the doors.
>
> —Czeslaw Milosz

I am the boy with his hands raised over his head
in Warsaw.

I am the soldier whose rifle is trained
on the boy with his hands raised over his head
in Warsaw.   5

I am the woman with lowered gaze
who fears the soldier whose rifle is trained
on the boy with his hands raised over his head
in Warsaw.

I am the man in the overcoat   10
who loves the woman with lowered gaze
who fears the soldier whose rifle is trained
on the boy with his hands raised over his head
in Warsaw.

I am the stranger who photographs   15
the man in the overcoat
who loves the woman with lowered gaze
who fears the soldier whose rifle is trained
on the boy with his hands raised over his head
in Warsaw.   20

The crowd, of which I am each part, moves on
beneath my window, for I am the crone too
who shakes her sheets
over every street in the world
muttering   25
What's this? What's this?

THE INVOLVED READER

1 On what nursery rhyme did Flanders model her poem? Why did
   she choose the language of a childhood verse? Why isn't she using the language of passionate indictment of a horrible crime?
2 How could the person speaking in the poem be in turn first the
   boy and then the soldier and so on? How is the speaker part of
   the crowd and at the same time watching it from her window?
3 What is the meaning of the crone's cryptic last words?

TALKING, THINKING, WRITING

4 What do you think went through the minds of each of the persons mentioned in the successive stanzas of the poem? Choose
   one of them and script a brief monologue; then pool your contribution with those by other members of your class for a choral
   reading.

COLLABORATIVE PROJECTS

5 Much debate has swirled about how to commemorate the victims of the Holocaust. What kind of memorial would not seem
   flawed or frivolous considering the enormity of the crimes and
   the suffering of the victims? Working with a group, investigate
   the history and rationale of the Holocaust Museum in Washington, DC, of the memorial at Auschwitz, or of other memorials.

The Writer's Tools 10

Working on Sentence Style

Effective writers draw on the full range of sentence resources. They write sentences readers can remember and quote. They write sentences that make readers want to write in the margin: "Well said! That's a good sentence!"

The Pointed Sentence

Some sentences catch us up short. The following sentences head straight for the point. They are memorable — we remember them after murkier sentences are forgotten:

> Economy is the art of making the most of life.
>
> George Bernard Shaw

> Loneliness is the poverty of the self.
>
> May Sarton

The Mature Sentence

When it is time to fill in explanation and support, effective writers know how to use the fully developed mature sentence, drawing on the full range of our sentence resources. Contrast minimal sentences with those a writer might write who has the gift of words.

MINIMAL: A homegrown orange is much superior to store-bought fruit.

MATURE: An appetizing ripe homegrown juicy navel orange is worth a sackful of greenish dry tasteless supermarket fruit.

MINIMAL: Americans work out frequently.

MATURE: Every day Americans work out on specialized equipment in their local health clubs to rejuvenate their deteriorating bodies in hopes of preventing heart disease, strokes, and arthritis.

MINIMAL: I think I can say I am a fairly good baseball player.

MATURE: As a basketball player, I am fast, quick, patient, smooth, sharp, sensible, magnificent, great, unbeatable, outstanding, outgoing, fantastic, marvelous, and humble.

Jesse E. Kingsberry

General and Specific

Many sentences mirror the one-two rhythm of prose that backs up the general with the specific. Sentences like the following are mini-compositions. They make a point, and they follow through with a striking illustration or example:

> The phrase "mass culture" conveys emotional overtones of passivity; *it suggests someone eating peanuts at a baseball game.*
>
> Northrop Frye

> Many young people today are always in a hurry; *they are on the go so much that their answering machines answer the phone more often than they do.*

Often the same play of general and specific structures the short-and-long of a *pair* of sentences:

> Good families are hospitable. *Knowing that hosts need guests as much as guests need hosts, they are generous with honorary memberships for friends, whom they urge to come early and often and to stay late.*
>
> Jane Howard

Varied Sentence Structure

Two-part statements like the following represent the bare-minimum English sentence: "The condors (subject) survived (verb)." "Wolves (subject) have come back (verb)." In many basic sentences, however, a third part is needed after the verb to complete the statement: "Ecologists are saving *the Everglades*." "Bald eagles may become *extinct*." The basic who-does-what or what-is-what structure provides the underpinnings for many of the workaday sentences of ordinary prose. Many sentences follow this pattern with only a few added essential details:

> STANDARD: The Siberian tiger may soon survive only in zoos.
>   Noise has ruined many a recording.

In a sentence like the following, we still see the basic what-is-what pattern although it has been much amplified:

> *My* various *forays* into the workforce *have been* generally unproductive *attempts* on my parents' part to build some character into their oddly distracted son.
>
> Student paper

When too many of your sentences follow this subject–verb pattern, your writing may become monotonous. You can start varying the pattern by *interrupting* a sentence, for instance, to inject added detail between subject and verb:

> ADDED DETAIL: The Siberian tiger, *an endangered species,* may survive only in zoos.
>   Noise — *hums, hisses, rumbles, pops, clicks, and the like* — has ruined many a recording.

You may vary your sentence beginnings by inserting material *before* you reach the who-does-what:

INTRODUCTORY MODIFIER: *In recent years,* faith in activist government has declined.

Charles Krauthammer

Once roaming the steppes in large numbers, the Siberian tiger may soon survive only in zoos.

Using their dreams, creative people have produced fiction, inventions, scientific discoveries and solutions of complex problems.

Jean Houston

As your sentences become more elaborate, the introductory material may be an additional subject–verb unit, or **clause**, preceding the main clause:

INTRODUCTORY CLAUSE: *Whereas* most science-fiction *writers spend their time* predicting, say, the discovery of planets ruled by angry, invisible dogs, *Clarke has* largely *confined himself* to predicting things that actually come to pass.

David Owen

By manipulating word order, you can make different parts of a sentence stand out. For instance, you may vary **emphasis** by pulling the most important part of the sentence to the beginning. Many typical English sentences go from the subject to the verb and on to the target of the action or a description of the subject. You can bring life and variety into your sentences by occasionally pulling this third element out front:

STANDARD: I will never do that.

VARIED: *That* I will never do.

STANDARD: Most poems of Sappho are *lost in the mists of antiquity.*

VARIED: *Lost in the mists of antiquity are* most poems of Sappho and what the priestess Diotima really said to her disciples.

Parallel Structure

Intentional repetition helps us set up sentence rhythm. In the following sentence, **parallel** sentence parts — parts following the same grammatical pattern — reinforce the basic message:

It is about time we realize that many women make *better teachers than mothers, better actresses than wives, better diplomats than cooks.*

Marya Mannes

In the following example, a writer lines up two related ideas in a well-balanced sentence:

The attempt to suppress the use of drugs is as futile as *the wish to teach cooking to an ape.*

Lewis H. Lapham

In the following example, a writer sets up an **antithetical** pattern — playing off opposites:

Earth dwellers now have the choice of making their world into *a neighborhood or a crematorium.*

Norman Cousins

WRITING WORKSHOP 4

Creative Sentence Work

A Try your hand at what a writing teacher called *fabulous realities.* Write several sentences that each sum up astonishing bit facts on the fringe of the news. Here are some sample sentences:

At Arizona State University, middle-aged pigs on polysaturated and polyunsaturated diets are forced to go jogging.
A U.S. district judge ruled that Colorado prison officials must provide an incarcerated Satanist with a black robe, incense, and a gong, or will otherwise violate his civil rights.

B Write several *pointed sayings* modeled on the following examples. Each time, sum up an idea in a single short crisp sentence.

I ORIGINAL: Economy is the art of making the most of life.

George Bernard Shaw

IMITATION: Cooking is the art of making the most of food.

2 ORIGINAL: Stealing has always been a means of redistributing the wealth.

John Conyers

3 ORIGINAL: Curiosity, like other desires, produces pain as well as pleasure.

Samuel Johnson

C Write several *capsule classics* (one single sentence each) that sum up the plot of a well-known book, movie, or television program. Pack each sentence with detail. Here are some sample student sentences:

> The seasoned crew of the *Pequod,* driven by its insane captain, faces the danger of the sea and an enormous white whale in Herman Melville's classic *Moby Dick.*
>
> A team of specially trained combat marines lands on a desolate planet to investigate the mysterious disappearance of a colony of space pioneers and battles it out with hideous insect-like monsters that need human hosts in which to gestate.

D Write several sentences, or pairs of sentences, that go from *general to specific.* First state a general point and then follow up with a brief example or explanation. Here are some sample sentences:

> Productivity was the paramount concern of the company; each and every second was counted, monitored, and evaluated by the master computer.
>
> We are more interested in success than in failure. We are more interested in the exploits of upwardly mobile young entrepreneurs than in the stories of people who spend their nights sleeping on heating grates.

E Write several sentences that fill in *rich detail.* Here are some sample sentences:

> Sports that promise violence and controversy — boxing, football, soccer, hockey — attract large crowds.
>
> Reactions to involuntary retirement cover a wide spectrum: dismay, shock, resignation, bitterness, hopelessness, impotence, fury, resentment, shame, embarrassment, confusion, frustration, or any combination of the above.

> Garson Kanin

F Each of the following sentences illustrates *varied word order.* For each, write a sentence of your own that follows the same or a very similar pattern.

1 Stronger than the mighty sea is almighty God.

SAMPLE IMITATIONS: Bleaker than a misspent youth is life without experience.
> More precious than a rare gem is a moment alone.
> Heavier than a ton of bricks is a depressed heart.

2 To describe with precision even the simplest object is extremely difficult.

> Aldous Huxley

3   What I call my self-respect is more important to me than anything else.

Doris Lessing

G Try your hand at a *sentence-stretching* exercise. Start with a sentence frame like "_____ is a mistake." Fill in the blank: "*Walking in the desert without a snakebite kit* is a mistake." "*Cheating on a test and copying the wrong answers* is a mistake." For each frame, write three or four sentences filling in the blanks. Each time try to stretch the sentence further, using more elaborate detail.

SENTENCE FRAMES: _____ is a pleasure.
                      _____ is a mistake.
                      _____ is discouraging.

SAMPLE SET: Eating out is a pleasure.
                  To see an old hound dog lying on a dusty porch on a hot summer afternoon in the mountains is a pleasure.
                  To watch as the motorist who had tailgated my car and honked wildly when passing me is stopped by the Highway Patrol for speeding is a pleasure.

H Write several sentences that use *parallel structure* to line up related or contrasting ideas. Use the following as model sentences. Make your own sentence follow a similar pattern as the model sentence.

1   I wanted more than anything the one thing of which there was never enough time: time to think, time to write.

Adrienne Rich

2   We have exchanged being known in small communities for being anonymous in huge populations.

Ellen Goodman

3   Women feel just as men feel; they need exercise for their faculties and a field for their efforts as much as their brothers do; they suffer from too rigid a restraint, too absolute a stagnation, precisely as men would suffer.

Charlotte Brontë

Research of any sort is an activity fundamental to education and, in fact, to all learning, whether it occurs inside or outside of school.

MARY TRACHSEL

Researching Your Topic

The Need for Research

Do you remember occasions when the information you had was incomplete or misleading? How often do you feel the need to check things out? You research a topic when what you already know is not enough. Often what you know comes from casual exposure, or hearsay, or special pleading. When you do serious research, you start becoming an expert on the subject — you may be able to inform or advise others. Research may help you and your readers make decisions: You research a subject so you can base a decision — whether to switch to a new diet supplement or where to go to school — on more than hearsay and the testimony of interested parties.

Some *in*formal research — background reading, talking to resource persons — goes into most writing you do. How does a formal research paper differ?

Synthesis *You integrate material from a wide range of sources.* You bring together relevant testimony from a full range of authorities. Your aim is to give your reader the best available information and thinking on your subject. You try to look at the subject from different perspectives — weighing differing views and reconciling discrepancies.

Documentation *You identify fully the sources of the material you have used.* In a formal research paper, you provide full **documentation** — complete publication data. Who said what, when, and where? Who developed your data, your statistics? Who provided you with valuable background information or stimulating ideas?

493

Objectivity *You stay close to the evidence you present.* A formal research paper allows less leeway than other kinds of writing for casual impressions and subjective preferences, not to mention outright bias. You will want to formulate your conclusions cautiously and support them well. A good stance toward the audience is: "This is the evidence. This is where I found it. This is where it leads."

Writing a research paper is like taking a crash course in how to become an authority on a subject. Ideally, you will be writing on a subject that has intrigued or puzzled you before but that you have not studied in depth. You will already have some sense of what the issues are and where to turn for promising leads. However, you may also be branching out into an area new to you. In either case, you will be a traveler in only partially charted territory. If you are not deterred by false starts or wrong turns in the road, you will be in for the excitement of discovery.

THOUGHT LOG 11

Thinking about Research

What does the idea of research mean to you? Write about one area of research with which you are familiar. For instance, what do you know about the ozone layer or the search for the AIDS virus? What do you know about research in genetic engineering or new medications for mental illness? What does research mean in areas like anthropology, psychology, or sociology? Have you ever been part of a survey or research project?

Choosing Your Topic

The writing process, as I encounter it, begins with an agonizing block of time spent hemming and hawing over the selection of a topic. I firmly believe that the strength of a paper depends on the interest of the writer in that topic.

NICHOLAS WALSH

To do justice to your topic, you have to carve out a limited part of a general subject, limiting your scope to an area that you can explore in depth. For example, the threat to wildlife on our endangered planet is a large general subject. To arrive at a workable topic, you may decide to close in on attempts to save one species that for many has become a symbol of threatened animal life: the condor, the whooping crane, the bald eagle, or the whale. Or you may choose to sift the pros and cons of the movement to rehabilitate the predators: the wolf, the mountain lion, or the coyote. Or you may focus on a key question: Are there any real success stories in the struggle to protect endangered species?

As you mull over possible topics, ask yourself: What question could focus my search and keep me from stitching together bit facts? Remember that the question or issue you focus on will have to hold your interest during weeks of gathering, drafting, and polishing. It will have to motivate your readers to read a lengthy paper. Ideally, a key question like the following will come up as you do your preliminary exploring, reading, and thinking:

> Are there any success stories in the fight to save endangered species?
> Is the threat of AIDS to heterosexual youths sensationalized or exaggerated by the media?
> Is the idea of the model minority a racial stereotype?
> Has the movement toward gender equity in college sports stalled?
> Is "Buy American" an obsolete slogan in the days of the global economy?

Here are some general areas for research. You, your classmates, or your instructor may suggest others. Choose a research topic that confronts you with unanswered questions worth answering. Narrow your topic to the point where you can reach conclusions based on a detailed examination of the best available evidence.

1 Animal and plant species that have evolved over millions of years are disappearing from our planet. Can or should anything be done to reverse this trend? (If you were to focus on one endangered species as a symbol of our endangered wildlife, which would you choose?)

2 How far have we moved toward gender equity in American sports? What has been the impact of Title IX on collegiate athletics? (Is college football as we know it doomed?)

3 In recent years, Native American tribes have asked the courts to reexamine broken treaties or restore rights that had lapsed or been usurped. What has been the result of such litigation? Is there a general trend? What case histories are instructive?

4 What technological breakthroughs for the disabled are becoming reality? For instance, how close are we to developing equipment that will help the blind see or the deaf hear? What is the story of computers that translate ordinary writing into Braille or vice versa?

5 What health care does our nation offer to the economically dis-

advantaged? What happens to the poor when they or their children get sick?

6 What is happening to America's last wild rivers? For instance, what battles are being fought between dam builders and conservationists, and what is the likely outcome?

7 What's behind the buzzword of the "model minority"? Is it true that Asian students tend to exceed others in performance? In what areas? For what reasons? How do Asian immigrants fare compared with others?

8 There has been much agitation against research relying on animal experiments. What are the key issues? What is the merit of charges and countercharges?

9 Prospective car buyers concerned about buying American (and saving American jobs) are sometimes told that the traditional distinction between domestic and imported cars has become meaningless. American companies sell cars made abroad or using a large proportion of foreign-made parts. Japanese and German companies make cars in the United States, and so forth. What are the facts? What should a concerned consumer know?

10 What hope do advances in medical science hold out for people with a mental illness? Is it true that new medications are allowing many former patients to lead normal lives? Are our attitudes changing as we learn more about the biochemistry of the brain?

WRITING WORKSHOP I

Starting a Research Log

You may find it useful to keep a **research log** or search diary. Use the research log to write notes to yourself. Jot down reminders of things accomplished and things to do. Start by writing about why you chose your topic. Why does it interest you? Is there a personal connection? What background or previous exposure do you bring to it? Where or how do you think you might find promising source material? How are you going to narrow the general area — what key question or questions do you think you will explore?

Suppose you have worked as a volunteer in a senior citizen center and have become interested in changing attitudes toward aging. Have we become less prone to think of the elderly as useless and senile? If we overcome our prejudices and stereotypes, will we give many more older people a chance to lead active, meaningful lives? The following might be sample entries from your log as you develop your strategy for researching this topic:

CHARTING DIRECTIONS

The baby boom generation is getting older. (Find statistics on this?) Is society changing from a glorification of youth to more sympathy with the feelings of older people? (Find material from business publications on marketing strategies aimed at older people?)

Are the elderly becoming more assertive and better organized? Do more older people try to lead independent lives?

CHECKLIST OF QUESTIONS

American Assoc. of Retired Persons (AARP) — current membership?
periodicals: <u>Gerontologist</u>, <u>50 plus</u>, other?
What happened to the Gray Panthers?
"fountain of youth" drugs — current research?
image of older people in TV drama and news coverage
     (Channel 7 had special on Senior Olympics — check out?)
interview director of Senior Citizens center

PROMISING SOURCES

check Eliz. Kuebler-Ross, Maggie Kuhn, Simone de Beauvoir (book on aging?)
<u>Sociological Abstracts</u>
     Ageds' status change M3697
     Aged, popular culture centers M2680
     Aging news, no longer negative image M5180
     Attitudes toward age S 15182
     Alex Comfort M5513
<u>Social Sciences Citation Index</u>
     Mehlinger, L. J., "Intergenerational Programs — The Changing Faces
     of Aging," <u>Gerontologist</u> 23: 227
article in February <u>Money</u> on executive fighting forced retirement —
author? title?

As you start following up promising leads, your log may include notes on which sources seem useful and why. You may begin to enter trial outlines and tentative conclusions. In addition to keeping your log, you will soon be taking more formal notes and registering complete information on your sources. Use your log for an *informal* record of progress and for reminders of things to be done.

Going to the Sources

Human beings naturally desire to know.

ARISTOTLE

Pundits talk about the knowledge explosion. Print media, electronic networks, and computerized data banks proliferate. Traveling the information highway, you can track down a wealth of material in a fraction of the time previously needed. For your research paper, your sources may include articles from newspapers and periodicals, material from full-length books, information from computerized reference works, material published online, and input from various nonprint sources.

Evaluating Your Sources   For reliable information and convincing evidence, you will try to draw on authoritative sources. What are the credentials of an author you are quoting or whose statistics you trust? How much of a commitment does the author have to the field or to the subject? Test questions like the following help you evaluate possible sources:

• *Is the source an authority on the subject?*   What is the author's track record? Does the author you are checking out draw on first-hand experience and observation? Has the author written or lectured on the subject previously or since? Is the author associated with a prestigious institution? Is the author quoted or consulted by others?

• *Is the work a thorough study of the subject?*   For instance, does it pay attention to the historical background? Does it look in depth at case histories or key examples? Does it seriously explore possible causes and effects? Does it take the opinions of others seriously, weighing the pro and con on debated issues?

• *Does the author turn to primary sources?*   Reliable authorities do not simply accept secondhand accounts. They often settle important questions by turning to **primary sources** — legal documents, diaries and letters, transcripts of speeches, interviews with eyewitnesses, reports on experiments, or statistical surveys.

• *Is the source up to date?*   Has it profited from recent research or newly discovered facts? If it was first published ten or twenty years ago, has the author updated the findings — perhaps in a more recent article or in a revised edition of a book? In areas like electronics and biochemistry, but also in fields like economics and foreign affairs, an older study may have been left behind by new findings and new thinking.

• *Who paid the piper?*   Was research on the safety record of the coal mining industry funded by the industry or by an outside source? Do unemployment statistics or data on executive salaries come from business sources, labor union sources, or government sources?

Searching Newspapers and Periodicals For many subjects, you will be able to track relevant articles in daily newspapers and in periodicals — publications that may appear on a weekly, monthly, or quarterly basis.

• For a paper focused on a current issue, you may find material — news reports, background studies, editorials — in leading newspapers like the *New York Times, Washington Post, Wall Street Journal, Christian Science Monitor,* or *Los Angeles Times.*

• You may draw on newsmagazines and journals of commentary and opinion. Ranging from the conservative to the progressive, these include *U.S. News and World Report, Time, Newsweek, Harper's, Atlantic, Commentary, New Republic, Mother Jones, Nation,* or *Ms.* magazine.

• Often you will want to go beyond journalistic sources to the work of the experts, scholars, scientists, or theorists on whose work journalists feed. You may draw on material in technical or scholarly journals in areas like psychology, archeology, medicine, history, or art. For instance, for a paper on women's progress toward equity in sports, your sources might range from an article on the last Winter Olympics in the *New York Times* ("The Women of Winter Save U.S.") to an article on "Sex Differences in Performance-Matched Marathon Runners" in the *European Journal of Applied Physiology.*

Computerized databases greatly facilitate your search for relevant and up-to-date material. Systems like INFOTRAC provide an instant listing of current newspaper and magazine articles from hundreds of publications. (Check years covered — INFOTRAC, for instance, started comprehensive indexing only in 1991.) By typing in keywords or **retrieval codes**, you call up a wide range of sources on subjects like divorce, global warming, free trade zones, or men's fashions. You can call up book reviews, articles by or about a person, or information about a company or business.

Here are key words, or **descriptors**, you might try in searching for material on progress toward gender equity in collegiate athletics. The computer will call up articles whose titles include the words you have typed in as key words or as possible subject headings:

women and athletics
women and sports
sports equity
women's physical education
women and college sports

funding for college sports
gender equality in sports

Other large umbrella systems enable you to tap into specialized databases in areas like sociology, public policy, medicine, or education. These databases will direct you to articles published by experts and professionals. For a paper on how schools try to deal with the threat of AIDS, for instance, you may want to check a specialized education database. You will be able to tap into a statistics database providing access to government statistics, like those published by the Center for Disease Control.

A student researcher obtained the following printout from the newspaper index that is part of INFOTRAC when looking for newspaper coverage of the progress women have made toward equity in sports. Study the format:

• After the title, this database often includes a brief parenthetical note on the drift of the article.

• It then tracks the exact location of the item: publication, volume number, section and page, column (with length of article in column inches).

• It then gives the author's name and possible subject headings under which the item can be cataloged.

Database: National Newspaper Index
Subject: sports for women

Women athletes deserve a chance at college scholarships, too. (males get disproportionate share of funds)

Los Angeles Times, March 21, 1993 v112 pM3 col 1 (14 col in).

Author: Heather Willens

Subjects: Sports for women — Finance
Scholarships — Demographic aspects
Sex discrimination against women — Laws, regulations, etc.

AN: 13645169

Database: National Newspaper Index
Subject: sports for women

The girls against the boys; women have played pro ball before. But never against men. Is this exploitation, or feminism . . . or both? (Coors Silver Bullets; the first women's professional baseball team)

The Washington Post, April 24, 1994 v117 pF1 col 3 (82 col in).

Author: Laura Blumenfeld

Subjects: Baseball (Professional) — Analysis
Women athletes — Competitions

Features: illustration; photograph

AN: 15207085

Database: National Newspaper Index
Subject: sports for women

Women's sports are scoring despite a tilted playing field; male athletes still dominate, but women's programs are gaining money and access.

The Christian Science Monitor, Nov 12, 1993 v85 n243 p10 col 3 (19 col in).

Author: Ron Scherer

Subjects: College sports — Finance
Olympic athletes — finance
Sex discrimination against women — Surveys
Women athletes — Attitudes
College athletes — Attitudes

Organizations: NCAA — Reports

Features: illustration; photograph

AN: 14653777

Source information is especially useful if it includes an **abstract** — a summary of the findings or claims presented in an article. The following printout from a sports-centered database first gives the usual information: title of the item, author's name, and name of the journal or other source. But it then includes an abstract to help the researcher decide whether the source is worth following up.

SilverPlatter 3.11   SPORT Discus 1975 — June 1994

TI: Sport and the maintenance of masculine hegemony
AU: Bryson,-L
JN: Womens-studies-international-forum-(Elmsford,-N.Y.); 10(4), 1987, 349 – 360
Refs:37
PY: 1987
AB: Discusses two fundamental dimensions of the support that sport provides for masculine hegemony: 1) it links maleness with highly valued and visible skills, and 2) it links maleness with the positively sanctioned use of aggression/force/violence. Examines four social processes through which women are effectively marginalized in their sport participation — definition, direct control, ignoring, and trivialization — using examples from the sports scene in Australia. Concludes that women need to challenge the definition of sport, take control of women's sports, persistently provide information and reject attempts to ignore women's sport, and attack the trivialization of women in sport.
AN: 213623

For articles published before the 1990s, you may have to search the printed multivolume periodical indexes in your library. One of the most widely used is the *Readers' Guide to Periodical Literature,* which indexes magazines for the general reader, from *Time* and *Newsweek* to *Working Woman, Science Digest,* and *Technology Review.* In the *Readers' Guide,* articles are listed twice — once under the author's name and once under a subject heading. Compare two entries for the same article:

AUTHOR ENTRY: **Harris, Michael**
          Junk in outer space. il Progressive 42:16-19 N '78

SUBJECT ENTRY: **SPACE pollution**
          Junk in outer space. M. Harris. il Progressive 42:16-19
          N '78

The author entry begins with the full name of the author; the subject entry begins with the general subject: space pollution. The title of the article is "Junk in Outer Space." (The *il* shows that the article is illustrated.) The name of the magazine comes next: *Progressive.* Note the kind of data that you will need later when identifying your sources in your finished paper: The *volume number* for

the magazine is 42. *Page numbers* for the article follow after the colon: 16 through 19. (Sometimes the symbol + appears after the last
page number; it shows that the article is concluded later in the
magazine.) The *date of publication* was November 1978. (For magazines published more than once a month, the exact date is given. For
example, N 10 '78 means "November 10, 1978.")

Other guides to periodicals intended for a general audience:

Essay and General Literature Index
Popular Periodicals Index
Applied Science and Technology Index
Art Index
Biological and Agricultural Index
Business Periodicals Index
Education Index
Engineering Index
General Science Index
Humanities Index
Social Sciences Index

Several special reference guides are useful for papers on a political subject or on current events: *Facts on File* is a weekly digest of
world news, with an annual index. *The New York Times Index* is a
guide to news stories published in the *New York Times*. The annual
index to the *Monthly Catalog of the United States Government Publications* lists reports and documents published by all branches of the
federal government.

As you identify promising sources, start a card file or computer
file recording a complete description of each item: author's name,
complete title of articles, name of periodical, date, and page numbers. (Note the section of a newspaper or volume number of a magazine.) Include brief **annotation** as a reminder. A source record annotated by you might look like this:

| periodical | Guterson, David. "Moneyball! On the Relentless |
| room | Promotion of Pro Sports." *Harper's Magazine* Sept. 1994: 37–46 |

The author is a contributing editor of *Harper's Magazine*. "I was not always so
disgusted with sport; I was not always an aging crank," Guterson pleads before
launching into a litany of the excesses of today's sports.

WRITING WORKSHOP 2

Searching for Articles

Do a computer search for articles on AIDS education for young people. Try key words or headings like *safe sex education, safe sex teaching, AIDS education, AIDS prevention, AIDS and schools, AIDS and adolescents, AIDS and high school, AIDS and young adults, AIDS and youth.* (Follow instructions for making sure that the database you use will search for variant forms: *adolescents* and *adolescence* as well as *adolescent.*) Prepare a listing of the six most promising items, with complete description of each.

Locating Books   Most libraries have converted from traditional card catalogs to computerized indexes listing books in the library. The information on traditional index cards and on computer listings is similar, although it may be laid out differently. When you are aware of an important source, you can look for a book under the author's name or under the title. For instance, you would look under *Hughes* or *Culture of Complaint* for Robert Hughes' *Culture of Complaint.* However, when still trolling for possibly relevant sources, you will look under subject headings. For instance, if you were not aware of the book by Hughes, you might be looking for books with a similar focus under subject headings like CULTURE WARS, CULTURAL POLITICS, POLITICAL CORRECTNESS, or BACKLASH.

Computer entries may look like the following **author cards.** Note that the **call number** will direct you or a librarian to the right section and the right shelf in the library.

Call #:	LB 2343.32 F54 1991
Author:	Figler, Stephen K.
Title:	Going the distance: the college athlete's guide to excellence on the field and in the classroom / by Stephen K. Figler. Princeton, N.J.: Peterson's Guides, 1991. xi, 208 p.: illus; 23 cm.
Notes:	Includes bibliography: p. 203–208.
Subjects:	College student orientation — United States College athletes — United States.
Add Author:	Figler, Howard E.

Call #:   HQ1075 B36 1986

Author: Basow, Susan A.

Title: Gender stereotypes: traditions and alternatives by
              Susan A. Basow. 2nd ed. Monterey, Calif: Brooks/Cole
              Pub. Co., 1986. xi, 399p: illus; 23 cm.

Notes: Rev. ed. of: Sex-role stereotypes, 1980.
              Includes indexes and bibliography: p. 319–381.

Subjects: Sex role
              Stereotype (Psychology).

If you remember the title of a book but not the author, you should be able to find a **title card** like the following:

          The American sporting experience
GV
583   Riess, Steven A.
R53   The American sporting experience / Steven A. Riess.
      New York: Leisure Press, 1984.
          400 p.; 23 cm.

          Bibliography: p. 398–400
          ISBN 0-88011-210-7

          1. Sports — United States — History — Addresses,
      essays, lectures. I. Title

      GV583.R53   796.0973
                                             84–7188

When you have no definite leads, you may be looking at **subject cards** like the following:

GV
709   SEX DISCRIMINATION IN SPORTS
N44
             Nelson, Mariah Burton

             Are we winning yet?: how women are changing sports
             and how sports are changing women, by Mariah Burton Nelson.
             1st ed. New York: Random House, 1991

             238 p.

             Bibliography: pp. 215–225, and index

GV
706   OLYMPICS
35
V56   Vinokur, Martin Barry, 1942–
             More than a game: sports and politics, by Martin
             Barry Vinokur. New York: Greenwood Press, 1988.

             155 p. illus. 24 cm (Political Science series)

             Bibliography: pp. 1139–145, and index

As with articles, you will want to prepare **source cards** or source
entries giving complete publishing information for your list of promising sources:

HQ
1426   Faludi, Susan. *Backlash: The Undeclared War*
F35   *Against American Women.* New York: Crown,
             1991.

HQ
1426   Wolf, Naomi. *Fire With Fire: The New Female*
W565   *Power and How It Will Change the 21st*
             Century. New York: Random House, 1993.

To narrow your research to the most promising of available book-length treatments, you may turn for help to **book reviews** or abstracts. For instance, the *Book Review Digest* excerpts book reviews written shortly after publication of a book. Book review sections are a regular feature of many professional publications. The following is an example of a book review from the *Library Journal:*

Heimel, Cynthia. *Get Your Tongue Out of My Mouth, I'm Kissing You Good-Bye!* Atlantic Monthly. Jun. 1993. c.192p. ISBN 0-87113-538-8.
$20.   HUMOR
It's no surprise that the author of *If You Can't Live Without Me, Why Aren't You Dead Yet?* (*LJ* 4/15/91), *Sex Tips for Girls* (*LJ* 6/15/83), and *But Enough About You* (S. & S., 1986) has come up with another snappy eyebrow-raising title. Her brief essays here reflect the same satirical feminist wit that graces the pages of the *Village Voice* and *Playboy* magazine. Among the weighty issues Heimel tackles are boyfriends ("a woman needs a man like a fish needs a net"), dysfunctional family values ("PBS would be bankrupt if its fund-raisers didn't feature hours of John Bradshaw explaining to sobbing audiences how our families fill us with toxic shame and make it impossible for us to have anything other than lives of agony"), and living in L.A. ("Out here I have a car, and I don't know if anyone in Manhattan knows this, but a car is just a moving, giant handbag!"). Brash, hip, and very, very funny, Heimel is essential for all humor collections. [Previewed in Prepub Alert, *LJ* 2/1/93.] — Wilda Williams, "Library Journal"

For many subjects of general interest, you will be able to find a printed or computerized **bibliography** — an inventory of important books and other sources of information. Shorter bibliographical listings often appear at the end of an entry in an encyclopedia or a chapter in a textbook. Especially helpful are **annotated bibliographies** that give a capsule description of each source. The following sample entry is from *An Annotated Bibliography of California Fiction 1864–1970* by Newton D. Baird and Robert Greenwood, 1971. Note that it lists two reviews written upon publication of the book:

1371   [Kerouac, John.]
ON THE ROAD. By Jack Kerouac. New York: Viking Press, 1957. 310 pp.
Two romantic anarchists, Sal Paradise and Dean Moriarty, pursue a vaguely defined notion of purpose on the roads up and down the North American continent, in stolen cars, in buses, airplanes, and by hitch-hiking. California, in part.
Commonweal 66:595 S 13 '57
San Francisco Chronicle p. 18 S 1 '57

WRITING WORKSHOP 3

Searching for Books

Search the main catalog of your library for books on the destruction of the world's forests. Check subject headings like *deforestation, rain forests, acid rain, logging.* Provide a listing of the six most promising sources, with complete publishing information on each.

Using Reference Works   Reference works range from weighty multivolume sets to handy manuals and guides. Many of them, including the *Encyclopedia Britannica,* are now available online and are thus at your fingertips while you work at the computer. You will find specialized reference works in a guide like Eugene P. Sheehy's *Guide to Reference Books,* published by the American Library Association. Here is a sampling of reference works that are often consulted:

Encyclopedias

• *The New Encyclopedia Britannica* (an American publication), brought up to date each year by the *Britannica Book of the Year*
• The *Encyclopedia Americana* with its annual supplement, the *Americana Annual*
• *Columbia Encyclopedia* (one volume)

Biography

• *Who's Who in America,* a biographical dictionary with capsule biographies of outstanding living men and women
• *Who's Who of American Women*
• *The Dictionary of American Biography (DAB)*
• The *Biography Index,* a guide to biographical material in books and magazines

Specialized Reference Guides

• *American Universities and Colleges* and *American Junior Colleges*
• *Harper's Dictionary of Classical Literature and Antiquities*
• *The McGraw-Hill Encyclopedia of Science and Technology,* kept up to date by the *McGraw-Hill Yearbook of Science and Technology*
• *The Encyclopedia of Computer Science and Technology*
• The *Dictionary of American History* by J. T. Adams (six volumes)
• Langer's *Encyclopedia of World History* (one volume)

- The *International Encyclopedia of the Social Sciences*
- *Grove's Dictionary of Music and Musicians*
- The *McGraw-Hill Encyclopedia of World Art* (fifteen volumes)
- The *Funk and Wagnalls Standard Dictionary of Folklore*
- *Vital Speeches of the Day*

WRITING WORKSHOP 4

Using Reference Tools

Study one of the following often-mentioned reference tools. Prepare a brief report on its scope, format, and usefulness. Try to provide useful advice to prospective users; include some interesting sidelights.

1 *Books in Print*
2 *National Union Catalog (NUC)*
3 *Library of Congress Subject Headings*
4 *Sociological Abstracts*
5 *Contemporary Authors*
6 *Who's Who of American Women*
7 *Wall Street Journal Index*
8 *Historical Abstracts*
9 *Dictionary of Scientific Biography*
10 *Comprehensive Dictionary of Psychological and Psychoanalytic Terms*
11 *McGraw-Hill Dictionary of Art*
12 *Concise Encyclopedia of Living Faiths*

Taking Notes

Are you becoming a good note taker? Do you have an eye for material that will prove useful later? As you identify promising sources, you may be making photocopies of whole articles or key pages, circling or bracketing key passages. You may be downloading or obtaining printouts of useful articles, writing notes in the margin as you give them a quick preliminary reading. You may at first spend time browsing, but soon you will be taking notes, recording material that you might be able to use. Accurate and usable notes provide the essential supply line for your paper.

Questions like the following can help you decide whether to note or not to note:

- Am I learning something here about my topic?
- Does this raise a question that I should try to answer?
- Could this serve as evidence or support for a working hypothesis or tentative conclusion?
- Does this provide an additional example, reinforcing material I already have?
- Does this raise an objection that I will have to address?
- Does this help me define a key term related to my topic?

Using or adapting the following procedure will save you time and grief:

Heading   Include a heading — first perhaps only a specific identifier, but later also the tentative subdivision of your paper — with each entry. You may want to use a code like WS for "women in sports," followed by a specific identifier (like "track coach interview" or "women's Olympic marathon"). You can refine your code later as subdivisions of your paper take shape (for instance, WS — hst for "Women in Sports — history"). Some researchers use a numerical code for tentative subdivisions — for instance, 1 for "whaling ships," 2 for "estimates of numbers," 3 for "international agreements on whaling," 4 for "volunteer initiatives."

Attribution   Make sure that later your notes will tell you clearly who said what and where. At the end, include the author and title of your source (in shortened form if you have recorded the full information elsewhere), along with exact page numbers.

Focus   Focus each entry on related information or on a limited point. This precaution will enable you to shuffle your information as the pattern of your paper takes shape. You will not have to disentangle material later for use at different points in your grand design.

Quotation   Use quotation marks to identify all quoted phrases, parts of sentences, or whole sentences. Be sure to transcribe material accurately when recording material verbatim.

In taking notes, when will you copy chunks of material — and when will you already adapt the material to suit your purposes? Here is a note that is all **direct quotation** — it records the author's exact words on an important point. It includes the heading for a tentative subsection of the paper where the material might fit in.

SINGLE MOTHERS

"The numbers of single women with managerial and professional jobs who have elected to bear children nearly tripled between 1982 and 1992. The number among never-married mothers who have completed one year of college and those who have earned a bachelor's degree doubled.

Although the reasons vary, most women, rich and poor, young and old, choose to bear children whom they can love and be loved by. Many older affluent women, facing the prospect of not finding a mate during their fertile years, choose not to forgo the joys of parenthood, and they have the resources to make that possible."

"New Families, Old Values." Editorial in the *Boston Globe,* 19 July 1993, p. 10

Here is a note that is all **paraphrase** — it reproduces statistics from the same newspaper source — without direct quotation. The material has been put in the notetaker's own words.

SINGLE MOTHERS — cost

The nuclear arms buildup of the 1980s cost the taxpayer approximately $350 billion. The money was spent on projects including the B-1 bomber and the MX missile. By contrast, in 1990 the federal contribution to Aid to Families with Dependent Children, the main welfare program for the support of single mothers, totaled $11 billion, about the same as the cost of five state-of-the-art bombers.

"Cold War Tall Tales." Editorial in the *Boston Globe,* 19 July 1993, p. 10

The following note is a mix of **paraphrase and quotation.** In this kind of note, you are already digesting the material, adapting it for use in your actual paper.

DISNEY — negative criticism

In what the reviewer calls a "slash-and-burn biography," Walt Disney appears not as "a pure-of-heart cartoon hero, but pathetic flesh and blood." The reviewer describes the book as an exposé that points out every flaw, "without a trace of compassion, nuance, or, in some areas, credibility." According to the review, this biography makes Disney appear "haunted by family tensions, addled by drink and pills, intermittently impotent, highhanded with employees, cozy with the Federal Bureau of Investigation, a booster of the Hollywood blacklist, an anti-Semite," and much more.

Patrick McGilligan, Review of *Walt Disney: Hollywood's Dark Prince* by Marc Eliot, in *The New York Times Book Review*, 18 July 1993, p. 2

Here is a note that is a **summary** — it condenses several pages of introductory information in John G. Neihardt's book *Black Elk Speaks.*

LAST BATTLES

In the fall of 1930, a field agent helped Neihardt meet Black Elk, a holy man of the Oglala Sioux who was a second cousin to Chief Crazy Horse. Black Elk was nearly blind and knew no English. Neihardt, speaking to him through an interpreter, gained his confidence partly by respecting the holy man's long silences. In the spring of 1931, Black Elk took many days to tell his life story, including the story of his share in the defeat of General Custer, which Black Elk witnessed as a young warrior.

Neihardt, *Black Elk* vii-xi

WRITING WORKSHOP 5

Preparing Sample Notes

Prepare half a dozen note cards or computer entries recording material from your most promising sources. Try to cover the range of direct quotation, paraphrase, partial quotation, and summary. Include headings and identification of sources.

Writing Your First Draft

A research paper is a writing project. As you struggle with the logistics of research or the limitations of libraries, you may at times lose sight of your basic task — to funnel much diverse material into a paper with clear purpose and direction. Questions like the following can help keep you on track:

- What will be the central focus of your paper?
- As the evidence accumulates, what conclusions does it justify?
- What will be a good strategy for laying out the material?
- How will you work material from your sources into your text?
- What will be your mix of direct quotation and paraphrase, and of full-length quotation and partial quotation?

Shaping Your Strategy Early in the course of your project, you need to start thinking ahead: What is going to be your strategy for organizing your material? You need to develop a plan — rough at first, but more definite and detailed as you go along. Unless you get your material under control, both you and your reader may be lost in a maze of unsorted facts and quotations. Even while you are building a rich base of data and ideas, you will be sorting and classifying your notes. You will be pushing toward the general conclusion (or conclusions) that your paper as a whole is going to support.

Often the subject or its history will suggest tentative categories. Suppose you are researching the current state of the controversy over bilingual education. What should we do for students who enter school with limited proficiency in English? Can we afford to let them fall behind as reading, math, or geography is taught in a language they understand poorly or not at all? Should we teach them basic subjects in their own first language — while helping them improve their English to the point where they can profit from subject-matter instruction in English?

Taking your cue from heated public controversies, you may at first sort your notes roughly on a pro and con basis. On the pro side, you will put material from articles with titles like "Progress in Bilingual Education" or "Honoring Language Diversity." On the con side, you will put broadsides from the English-only movement and material from articles titled "Other Nations Do Not Encourage Bilingualism" or "In Defense of the Mother Tongue."

However, as you read more, you may start arranging your material under *three* rather than two main headings. Some advocates of bilingual education seem to aim at preserving the student's separate cultural identity. They stress pride in the student's heritage. Others seem to aim at providing bilingual education mainly as a transition. They see it as a stage toward full integration in the mainstream culture. Finally, opponents of bilingualism invoke the model of earlier immigrant children who learned English on a sink-or-swim basis in schools run on the English-only model.

As you refine your plan, you come closer to a blueprint for your paper. Writing an early draft, you may use a **working outline** like the following:

WORKING OUTLINE: **Does Bilingual Education Have a Future?**

the politics of bilingual education:
    English-only vs. diversity

the conflicting goals of bilingual education:
    bilingual education as transition
    maintaining the student's cultural heritage

the obstacles to effective bilingual education:
    shortage of bilingual teachers
    proliferation of languages
    lack of intensive English instruction

the future of bilingual education

In writing your first draft for a mini-research paper on prison reform, you might be using an outline like the following. This outline already shows the traditional outline form that is required when your instructor asks you to submit a formal outline with your finished paper. Notice the natural flow of topics from old-style jails that stressed punishment, through a liberal phase aimed at rehabilitation and reintegration of convicts into society, to the current conservative backlash — with reformers nevertheless continuing to seek an answer to crime other than retribution.

Dead-End Prisons: Throwing the Key Away

THESIS: Although popular opinion has swung back to a "lock-them-up" mentality, reformers continue to seek for ways to keep prisons from being a dead end.

   I. Punitive old-style penitentiaries
  II. The liberal ideal of rehabilitation
 III. Backlash: the failure of reform
 IV. Promising new experiments
     A. Experiments abroad
     B. Experiments in the U.S.

What is the flow of topics and subtopics in the following outline for the full-length research paper at the end of this chapter? Can you see the logic that will take the reader from one section of the paper to the next?

FORMAL OUTLINE: **Sports Equity: The Long Road**

THESIS: Although enormous changes have already occurred, the revolution in women's sports is far from complete.

   I. Today's highly visible women athletes
  II. Progress toward equality in sports
     A. Challenging traditional restrictions
     B. Making progress: the 50s and 60s
        1. The Sputnik effect
        2. The spirit of political activism
     C. Breakthroughs
        1. Commercial sponsorship
        2. Title IX and its aftermath
        3. Moving into the 21st century
 III. Sports and the changing self-image of women
     A. Fitness: body and mind
     B. Testing the limits
     C. The benefits of sports: self-esteem and confidence
 IV. Women's athletics and traditional sports
     A. Competition v. participation
     B. De-emphasizing violence
  V. A new concept of sport

WRITING WORKSHOP 6

Preparing the Trial Outline

Try to formulate your tentative plan for organizing your material as a four-point or five-point program. (For some papers, the master plan will cover perhaps only three or as many as six or seven key topics.) Include your main points in a working outline, and present it to a group or to the class. Be prepared to explain the rationale or logic guiding your arrangement of the main topics to be covered in your paper. Be prepared to answer oral or written questions from classmates. Does the feedback from your peers make you rethink all or part of your plan?

Integrating Different Sources   In a research paper, you make extensive use of quoted material. You know that you cannot just stitch different notes together or lay material from different note cards end to end. What are effective ways of integrating material from your notes in your paper? How do you combine different notes in a coherent paragraph, using them to explain or support a point? Study the following three sample notes from note cards or computer files:

Endangered Species — Counts

The bald eagle became the national symbol in 1782, and there were nesting pairs in all the lower 48 states. The current bald eagle population has been estimated at 5,000 in the lower 48 states. As of 1975, only 627 nests remained active, and they produced approximately 500 young.

Graham, "Will the Bald Eagle Survive?" 99

Endangered Species — Counts

"In 1948, the wild whooping crane population was up by just two from a decade earlier — to 31. The count sank to 21 in the winter of 1951–52, then rose gradually to an encouraging 74 in 1978–79. Last spring there were six yearlings to join the flight north. . . . The wild whooping crane count now stands at 76, an improvement deriving in large measure from protective practices at Arkansas."

Wilson and Hayden, "Where Oil and Wildlife Mix" 37–38

Endangered Species — Counts

"Whooping cranes, the largest cranes inhabiting North America, are on the U.S. endangered species list. The big birds' population dwindled to 14 in the late 1930s but is now estimated at 95."

Freedman, "Whooping Cranes" 89

How has this material been integrated in the following finished paragraph?

    For years, nature lovers have been keeping an anxious count of such endangered species as the bald eagle and the whooping crane. When the bald eagle became the national symbol soon after Independence, there were nesting pairs everywhere in what is now the continental United

States. Two hundred years later, Frank Graham, Jr., writing in *Audubon* magazine, reported a current estimate of 5,000 bald eagles left in the lower forty-eight states. According to his figures, only 627 nests remained active, and they produced approximately 500 young (99). In 1981, Steven C. Wilson and Karen C. Hayden, writing in the *National Geographic*, reported a count of 76 for wild whooping cranes left in the United States, up from a dismal count of 21 thirty years earlier (37–38). A recent estimate puts the current population at 95 (Freedman 89).

Using Quoted Material   For a seamless flow of your paper, you need to be flexible in adapting quoted material. Much of the time, you will use direct quotation, enclosing phrases and whole sentences quoted verbatim in quotation marks. Where the exact wording or the authentic voice of the original author is less important, you will paraphrase or summarize material, putting data and ideas in your own words. Set off quotations of more than *four typed lines* as **block quotations** — double-spaced, double indentation (indented one inch or *ten* typewriter spaces), with *no* quotation marks.

Here are major possibilities:

> **1 Block Quotation**—to be used sparingly. It is best to use block quotations only for key passages. A series of long block quotations will make your paper lumpy (and may tempt your reader to skip some of them).

> In her biography of President Johnson, Doris Kearns summed up the factors that weakened the role of the traditional political party:

>> The organization of unions, the development of the Civil Service, and the rise of the welfare state deprived the party of its capacity to provide jobs, food, and services to loyal constituents, thus severing its connection with the daily lives and needs of the people. . . . Technology provided access to new forms of amusement and recreation, such as movies and television, which were more diverting than party-sponsored dances and made it unlikely that people would attend political meetings and speeches for their entertainment value. During the 1960s, more and more people declined to affiliate themselves with a party and identified themselves as independents. (162)

COMMENT: The introductory sentence sums up the point of the quotation. The excerpt is set off as a block quotation — *double indentation, no quotation marks.* The introductory sentence gives credit to the original author; the full title of her book will appear after her name in the final listing of "Works Cited." The number in parentheses at the end of the quotation directs the reader to the exact page.

Note: Use no additional paragraph indentation with block quotations unless the quotation runs to more than one paragraph. An additional *three* spaces then shows the beginning of each actual paragraph in the original source.

2   Part Paraphrase, Part Direct Quotation—worked closely into the text. This is the most flexible and effective way of working an author's ideas into your own text.

> In her biography of President Johnson, Doris Kearns traces the changes that weakened the role of our political parties. The growing labor unions, the expanding Civil Service, and the welfare state began to provide the jobs, the favors, and the free food that the old-style party had provided for the party faithful. These changes cut off the party's close "connection with the daily lives and needs of the people." Movies and television made the old-style party-sponsored dances and rousing political speeches obsolete as entertainment. During the 1960s, voters more and more "declined to affiliate themselves with a party and identified themselves as independents" (162).

COMMENT: The adapter explains the main points but at the same time keeps some of the authentic flavor of the original. Direct quotation is limited to characteristic phrases and key points.

3   Legitimate Paraphrase—attributed to the original author. The paraphrase allows you to highlight and explain key ideas.

> As Doris Kearns reminds us, major changes in our society weakened the traditional political party. The old-style party had provided jobs, favors, and even free food to the party faithful, but the unions, the Civil Service, or the welfare state took over many of these functions. People no longer depended on social events sponsored by the party or on rousing political speeches for entertainment; they had movies and television instead. During the 1960s, fewer and fewer people declared a party affiliation; many listed themselves as independents (162).

COMMENT: This paraphrase (followed by the page reference) keeps the essential meaning of the original. But the information is given to us in the adapter's own words, sometimes with added touches that help make the point clear or vivid: "the party faithful," "rousing political speeches."

4 **Plagiarized Version**—illegitimate, unacknowledged paraphrase.

> The political party no longer plays its traditional role. The growth of the unions and the welfare state deprived the party of its capacity to provide jobs, food, and services to people. New forms of amusement and recreation, such as movies and television, were more diverting than party-sponsored dances and made it unlikely that people would attend political meetings for their entertainment value. More and more people declined to affiliate themselves with a party and became independents instead.

COMMENT: The passage takes over someone else's words in a slightly shortened, less accurate form — and without acknowledgment. Even if the source were identified, this adaptation of the material would be unacceptable: Too much of the original author's way of putting things has been copied without the use of direct quotation: "deprived the party of its capacity," "more diverting than party-sponsored dances."

5 **Legitimate Summary**—for preview or overview.

> Doris Kearns shows how the unions, the Civil Service, the welfare state, and the mass media all helped weaken party affiliation. They provided the jobs, the favors, and the entertainment for which voters once turned to the traditional party organizations (162).

COMMENT: This summary, getting at the gist of the passage, could serve as an overview of major points.

WRITING WORKSHOP 7

Using Quoted Material

Alice Walker wrote the following excerpt in her first published essay, "The Civil Rights Movement: What Good Was It?" (*The American Scholar*, Autumn 1967). Prepare several different versions of a passage that would use material from this excerpt:

- a passage introducing an excerpted *block quotation*
- a passage using an extended *paraphrase* of much of the material
- a passage combining paraphrase and *direct quotation*
- a passage using only a brief *summary*

In each version, identify author and source. Introduce the material; make the reader see its point or significance.

The life of Dr. King, seeming bigger and more miraculous than the man himself, because of all he had done and suffered, offered a pattern of strength and sincerity I felt I could trust. He had suffered much because of his simple belief in nonviolence, love, and brotherhood. Perhaps the majority of men could not be reached through these beliefs, but because Dr. King kept trying to reach them in spite of danger to himself and his family, I saw in him the hero for whom I had waited so long.

What Dr. King promised was not a ranch-style house and an acre of manicured lawn for every black man, but jail and finally freedom. He did not promise two cars for every family, but the courage one day for all families everywhere to walk without shame and unafraid on their own feet. He did not say that one day it will be us chasing prospective buyers out of our prosperous well-kept neighborhoods, or in other ways exhibiting our snobbery and ignorance as all other ethnic groups before us have done; what he said was that we had a right to live anywhere in this country we chose, and a right to a meaningful well-paying job to provide us with the upkeep of our homes. He did not say we had to become carbon copies of the white American middle class; but he did say we had the right to become whatever we wanted to become.

Revising Your First Draft

A day or two after finishing your first draft, you may be ready to look at it with the reader's eye. How close to being finished is your paper? How well has your overall plan worked out? How well have you integrated your material? Often you will be able to profit from reactions to your draft from your instructor or from a group of your peers. The following might be an instructor's comment on a first draft documenting the role of the crack epidemic both in a lower-class and a middle-class social setting:

INSTRUCTOR'S COMMENT: This is an eye-opening paper. The paper starts well, except that you need a more focused, informative, and less interchangeable title. The opening scene provides a dramatic lead, immediately followed up by thought-provoking, well-selected statistics. Your main point — that crack is a problem not just in minority neighborhoods but also among high-stress middle-class workaholics — comes through strongly and is well supported by convincing backup from authoritative sources. I like your mix of expert opinion and of personal testimony from people who have the inside information. One weak part is the account of the "six stages" of what happens in a crack house — the authors sound pedantic and uninvolved? Also, since some of your sources are from outside the U.S., I was confused about what part of your information applies to other countries and perhaps not the same way here. Toward the end, your paper seems hurried just when the reader needs a glimmer of hope after your analysis of the depressing facts. You should give your readers more details on the promising treatments and other "ways out" that you mention only briefly, as if you were running out of time.

Depending on previous experience and the pressure of time, writers vary in how close they come to a strong effective paper in the first draft stage. Consult the following checklist as a guide to revision. Which of the following suggestions might help you strengthen your paper?

1 *Bring the issue more clearly into focus.* Did your first draft sketch out a "let's-see-what-we-find" program? Perhaps you should do more to pinpoint the issue, to sum up key findings, to summarize the pro and con. Can you identify a sentence or a passage that sums up what you are trying to prove? Does a strong **thesis** appear in a strategic position — at the beginning or at the end?

   TOO OPEN: We hear many conflicting voices on the use of animal experiments in medical research. Magazines regularly print articles on animal experiments and the controversies they bring about. Protesters at times seem to want to ban all research involving animals.

   FOCUSED: Conflicting voices on the use of animal experiments in medical research leave us unsure of which side to take. Our hearts tell us to listen to often-inflated news reports of cruelty and abuse. Our brains tell us that if it weren't for research involving other living creatures, many of the lifesaving techniques that are common today would not exist.

2 *Strengthen support for key points.* For example, in reading your first draft on the subject of the "Graying of America," you may decide that your statistics on forced retirement are too skimpy and too dated. Revision is your chance to bring in updated information or to use a recognized authority to bolster your point.

3 *Rethink your organization if necessary.* Do you need to check the flow of your paper and perhaps rechannel it? Suppose you are writing your paper on the conflict between ideal and reality faced by many career women today. In your first draft, you have followed this outline:

The New Woman

   I. The media image of the New Woman
   II. Unresolved conflicts
    A. The homemaker stereotype
    B. "Femininity" versus being a professional
    C. Career and motherhood

   III. The realities of the workplace
      A. Predominantly female occupations
      B. Disparity in pay
   IV. The price of progress
      A. Health problems and stress
      B. Difficult personal relationships

On second thought, you may decide that your part II delves too early into material colored by personal grievances. You decide to start with a "let's-look-at-the-cold-facts" approach instead. In your second draft, you reverse the order of parts II and III. You also plug in some material from the history of women's work to add perspective:

The New Woman

   I. The media image of the New Woman
   II. The working woman then
   III. The working woman now
      A. Predominantly female occupations
      B. Disparity in pay
   IV. Unresolved conflicts
      A. The homemaker stereotype
      B. "Femininity" versus being a professional
      C. Career and motherhood
   V. The price of progress
      A. Health problems and stress
      B. Difficult personal relationships

4 *Avoid the dumped quotation.* Do you do enough to lead *into* key quotations? Prepare the ground; sum up who says what and why. Check for clear attribution: Can the reader tell throughout where your information came from or whose judgment you have trusted?

DUMPED: Susan Jacoby is a "First Amendment junkie."

REVISED: Susan Jacoby, who has written widely on women's issues, disagrees with the feminists on the issue of pornography. She is first and foremost a journalist who believes in free speech and the protection of the First Amendment. She is unequivocally a "First Amendment junkie."

5 *Balance quotation and interpretation.* Do weighty quotations need more explanation and follow-up than you have provided? Are there too many undigested quotations?

UNDIGESTED: The arrival of the Europeans did not merely drastically transform the New World but enriched and altered the

Old World from which they came: "It altered science, geography, philosophy, agriculture, law, religion, ethics, government — the sum, in other words, of what passed at the time as Western culture."

FOLLOWED UP: The arrival of the Europeans did not merely drastically transform the New World but enriched and altered the Old World from which they came: "It altered science, geography, philosophy, agriculture, law, religion, ethics, government — the sum, in other words, of what passed at the time as Western culture." *Europeans began to live in a world with vastly extended horizons and new continents. Such New World transplants as the potato and maize forever changed European agriculture. The self-assertion of New World colonists prepared the way for the downfall of the old aristocratic class structure at home.*

6 *Bundle related quotations effectively.* You may need to add a lead sentence that shows what a set of quotations is supposed to prove:

Infertility, now affecting one in five couples, has many causes. J. H. Guenero, writing in *Science News*, identifies familiar medical problems: failure to ovulate, inflammatory disorders, blockage of the fallopian tubes. Hilary Rose, a professor of Social Policy at Bradford University, points to modern birth control methods as a more recent culprit. The prolonged use of the pill, damage due to badly fitted coils, and poorly performed abortions all help explain the rising incidence of infertility.

7 *Review your mix of quoted material.* Are there too many undigested block quotations? Should there be a better mix of sentence-length quotations and brief quoted phrases, worked organically into your text?

8 *Strengthen weak links.* Check for lame transitions using *also* or *another.* Is the additional point you are introducing a confirmation of what went before? Is it an objection that is often raised? Is it a rebuttal of a charge someone made? Help the reader who wonders, "Why is this in here at this point?"

WEAK: Another expert on the dinosaur puzzle is Janice Rotha, who writes in the *American Scientist.* . . .

BETTER: An expert who disagrees strongly with the sudden-extinction theory is Janice Rotha. She writes in the *American Scientist.* . . .

9 *Strengthen the personal connection.* Should you work in material from a personal interview or from personal observation to show your personal involvement with the topic?

WRITING WORKSHOP 8

Participating in Peer Response

Working in a small group, rotate early drafts for peer response. (Your class may want to set up groups so that each writer is furnished feedback from a range of perspectives — with readers differing in gender, ethnicity, social background, or political orientation.) As your turn comes to study a paper, fill in a response sheet in which you answer questions like the following:

1   What did the writer set out to accomplish? Does the paper as a whole have a point or an agenda?
2   What did you learn from this paper?
3   What puzzled or confused you?
4   What supporting material or quoted material seemed particularly strong or helpful?
5   Where was supporting material weak or missing?
6   How would you summarize the overall plan? (Do you think it could be strengthened or improved?)
7   Did you find the writing too technical, too informal, too awkward, or too dull? Or did you find it clear, lively, imaginative? (Try to pinpoint one or two sample passages.)
8   What kind of reader would be the ideal audience for this paper?

WRITING WORKSHOP 9

Preparing a Self-Evaluation

Answer all or most of the following questions about your experience in writing your research paper:

- What did your topic mean to you? Was there anything about it that especially puzzled or interested you? Did you have any special background for your topic? Was there a "personal connection"?
- What leads if any did you have when you started your investigation? What promising leads developed as you got started? What obstacles or frustrations did you encounter? How did you cope with them?
- What did you learn about the range of opinion or perspectives on your topic? Was there much disagreement — and what seemed to account for it? Was there a common center or latent consensus?
- How did you develop your thesis and your overall strategy? Did you start with a key question? Or did a key issue gradually come into focus? Did you change your mind or change direction as you went along?

- What, briefly, was your overall plan or general outline for your paper? Did you have to revise or adjust it as you went along?
- What assumptions did you make about your audience? What reactions did you expect?

Documenting Your Sources (MLA)

Someone who appropriates my work doesn't just appropriate part of my identity; she abdicates part of her own. Students who plagiarize in order to write their papers don't learn to think for themselves.

WENDY KAMINER

What has been your previous experience with writing documented papers? How good are you at following exact detailed instructions concerning format and documentation style? Documentation gives a full accounting of your sources. You enable your readers to track down an article or book you have used and turn to the right page. If they are puzzled or perturbed, they can check the accuracy of your work or see quoted material in its larger context. They can find additional information. Detailed documentation shows that you respect other people's intellectual property: You give a source when you quote word for word but also when you paraphrase or summarize. You show the sources of facts, figures, or ideas that represent someone else's effort or inspiration.

You may already have encountered styles of documentation for different areas of study. Different areas — English, social science, biology — use their own slightly different systems of coding information about sources. For papers in English classes, you will usually follow the documentation style of the Modern Language Association, outlined in the *MLA Handbook for Writers of Research Papers* (Fourth Edition, 1995). For papers in the social sciences, you will usually follow the APA style, outlined in the *Publication Manual of the American Psychological Association* (Fourth Edition, 1994).

Steering Clear of Plagiarism When you are documenting your sources, full disclosure is the best policy. Working on research papers, you will sooner or later hear warnings about plagiarism. Writers plagiarize when they take over other writers' ideas, data, or exact words without acknowledgment. Plagiarism can ruin a grade, an academic record, or a career. Sometimes a writer copies whole pages or a whole article and, with perhaps only minor changes, passes them off as his or her own. More often, plagiarism results from slipshod record keeping, with chunks of material of uncertain origin finding their way into a paper.

What precautions can you take against any suspicion of plagiarism?

- While taking notes, include a *source tag* for all information or ideas you copy. Keep track of the source even when you paraphrase — when you put material into your own words.
- Put in *quotation marks* all material you take over word for word.
- When you paraphrase, change the wording enough so that readers cannot point to a sentence or a phrase and say: "This does not sound like you — this sounds like someone else."
- Give credit to your source whenever you pass on someone else's *data or ideas* — new statistics, recently discovered facts, new theories, or a personal point of view.
- Do not take over someone else's *plan* — someone's outline of key points — without acknowledgment.

It helps to imagine a reader over your shoulder who asks: Who said this? Who found this out? Who conducted this survey? Who developed this theory? As you work material from your sources into your paper, keep providing the **credit tags** that remind your readers of the source of information and ideas you present:

> As a probation officer for the District of Columbia, Edward Read knows the crack culture from close firsthand observation. *In his article,* "Euphoria on the Rocks: Understanding Crack Addiction," in *Federal Probation, Read explains* the history of crack and how it is made. It is virtually impossible to smoke cocaine, so "free basing" was developed to free the basic cocaine alkaloid from its hydrochloric base through a simple chemical conversion using ether, water, and heat. Crack is a freebase ready for smoking. *Read describes it* as "instant expresso." Instead of ether, baking soda is used in the crack-making process. The process produces "rocks" resembling ivory-colored soap shavings that have a hardened texture, much like porcelain. Users put the rocky flakes into a glass water pipe, heat it, and inhale the fumes for an instant "rush" that lasts not longer than ten minutes. *According to Read,* crack may be sold for a mere $5 to $20 a vial (56).

Parenthetical Documentation (MLA)   When you follow the MLA style, you use **parenthetical documentation** in your paper and then give a final listing of **Works Cited**. Here is the MLA style in brief:

- You identify your sources briefly in your text.

- You include page references in parentheses in your text (but you may also need to include the author's name and sometimes a shortened title).

- You give a complete description of each source in a final alphabetical listing of Works Cited.

Here is a preview of how you would identify a source in the body of your documented paper, with page numbers in parentheses:

AUTHOR IN TEXT: In his article "The Warming of the World," Carl Sagan says, "Oceans will drown coastal cities; fertile plains will turn into deserts" (73).

AUTHOR IN PARENS.:   As a leading scientist says in an article on global warming, "Oceans will drown coastal cities; fertile plains will turn into deserts" (Sagan 73).

SOURCE IN PARENS.:   As a leading scientist says in one of his articles on global warming, "Oceans will drown coastal cities; fertile plains will turn into deserts" (Sagan, "Warming" 73).

Here are examples of how you would give full publishing information on an article and on a book in a final alphabetized list of sources — your list of Works Cited:

Sagan, Carl. "The Warming of the World." News from the Future 12 Feb. 1987: 71-74.
Traggart, Joan. Our Overheating Planet. New York: Orion, 1993.

When using parenthetical documentation, you put page references and needed identification in parentheses in the text of your paper (not in separate notes or on a separate page). Here are some possibilities:

1 Simple Page Reference   You will often name the author or the publication (or both) in your running text. You will then use your parenthetical page reference to direct the reader to the right page. Put page number (or page numbers) in parentheses after a closing quotation mark but before a final period:

For Gwendolyn Brooks, the "biggest news" about the events in Little Rock was that the people there "are like people everywhere" (332).

2 Identification by Author   You include the author's last name with the page reference if you have *not* mentioned author and work in your text (and if you cite only one source by this author):

In the eyes of disillusioned observers, funding for bilingual education became a "political football" (Simones 21, 27-29).

3 **Identification by Title**   You include a shortened form of the title if you are using more than one source by the same author. Enclose the title of an article or other *part* of a publication in quotation marks. Underline (italicize) the title of a book or other *whole* publication.

> Alex Comfort has frequently told us that the blunting of abilities in the aged results at least in part from "put-downs, boredom, and exasperation" ("Old Age" 45); the changes we see in old people, according to him, "are not biological effects of aging" (*Good Age* 11).

EDITOR'S TIP: If you shorten a title, keep the *first word* (other than *The, A,* or *An*) the same in the shortened title, so that your readers can find the source in alphabetical order in your Works Cited.

4 **Identification by Author and Title**   You include author's name and a short title if you use more than one source by an author not identified in your text. (Put a comma between author and title, *no* comma between title and page number.)

> In France, Islamic immigrants from North Africa are "increasingly resisting assimilation and integration" (Belvedere, *The Rise of Islam* 187, 207-10).

5 **Reference within a Sentence**   You put page reference and identification where needed for clarity part way through a sentence.

> As Finley (18) had predicted, recent surveys show that many who were laid off as the result of corporate restructuring were not rehired when production picked up again (Gutierrez 211).

6 **More Than One Author**   You include names of several authors with your page reference if you have not specified authors in your text. For more than three authors, give name of first author and then put et al. (unitalicized), Latin for "and others."

> Tests and more tests have often been a substitute for adequate funding for our schools (Hirsenrath and Briggers 198). When not clamoring for more tests for students, legislators clamor for tests designed to check "if the teachers know anything themselves" (Rathjens et al. 112).

7 **Reference with Block Quotation**   Although a parenthetical reference usually comes before a comma or a period, you put it *after* final punctuation that concludes a block quotation.

> Moeller in *Myths about Aging* tries to counteract familiar stereotypes:
>> Older people seem mentally slow or disoriented when we deprive them of intellectual stimulus and active involvement with other people. Provided they remain active and are not isolated or cast off, the majority of older people remain mentally alert. Few of them show signs of mental deterioration or senility, and only a small proportion become mentally ill. (114)

8 Reference to One of Several Volumes You use an Arabic numeral followed by a colon for one volume of a work if in your Works Cited you list several volumes:

> According to Trevelyan, the isolationist movement in America and the pacifist movement in Britain between them "handed the world over to its fate" (3: 301).

9 Reference to a Preface You use lowercase Roman numerals if you find them used in a book for the preface or other introductory material:

> In his preface to The Great Mother, Erich Neumann refers to the "onesidedly patriarchal development of the male intellectual consciousness" (xiii).

10 Reference to a Literary Classic You use Arabic numerals separated by periods for such divisions of literary works as act, scene, and line (*Hamlet* 3.2.73–76). However, some authors prefer the more traditional use of capital and lowercase Roman numerals (*Hamlet* III.ii.73–76).

> In Shakespeare's *Tempest*, Gonzalo, who would prefer to "die a dry death," fits this archetype (1.1.66).

11 Reference to the Bible You use Arabic numerals for chapter and verse (Luke 2.1) although some authors prefer to use a traditional style (Luke ii.1).

12 Quotation at Second Hand You show that you are quoting not from the original source but at second hand. Your Works Cited will list only the secondhand source. (But quote from and cite the original source if you can.)

> William Archer reported in a letter to his brother Charles that the actor playing Pastor Manders never really entered "into the skin of the character" (qtd. in Ibsen 135).

13 Reference to Nonprint Materials When you refer to an interview, a radio or television program, or a movie, you should make sure your text highlights the name of the interviewer, person being interviewed, director or producer, or scriptwriter whose name appears in alphabetical order in your Works Cited list. Sometimes you may name a production or movie in parentheses to direct your reader to the right entry:

> In an interview in 1988, Silveira discussed the roots of his work in *Aztec and Inca art.*

> A news special by a local station fanned the long-smouldering controversy into bright flames (*Poisoned Planet*).

14   Reference to More Than One Source   When mentioning several sources in the same parenthetical reference, you separate them by a semicolon:

> After decades of vitriolic charges and denials, information about Soviet spies working for the American government became available to scholars with access to archives of the former Soviet Union (Kaunas 128; Jablonski 24).

Works Cited — General Guidelines (MLA)   At the end of your research paper, you will furnish an alphabetical listing of your sources. This listing of Works Cited guides the reader to the sources you have used during your search. It will often be more than a **bibliography** (a "book list" or list of printed materials), because it may include non-print sources — interviews, videotapes, software.

You may already have computer software to help you format your Works Cited list, or more likely you will still be doing the keyboarding in accordance with the current MLA style. You start your page with the centered heading "Works Cited." Then you type your first entry, with *no* indentation for the first line. However, you indent the second line one half inch (or five typewriter spaces). The following are general guidelines for preparing individual entries:

1   *Put the last name of the author first.* This order applies only to the first author when you list several authors.

Gaylin, Willard. <u>The Male Ego</u>. New York: Viking, 1992.

Himstreet, William C., and Wayne Murlin Baty. <u>Business Communications: Principles and Methods</u>. 7th ed. Boston: Kent, 1984.

If no name of *author or editor* is known to you, list the publication alphabetically by the first letter of the title, not counting *The, A,* or *An.*

2   <u>Underline</u> (or italicize) *the title of a complete publication; enclose the title of a part in quotation marks.* <u>Underline</u> (or italicize) titles of books, collections, newspapers, or magazines: <u>A Brief Guide to Vegetarian Cooking</u>. Put in quotation marks titles of

articles, reports, stories, or poems that were part of a larger publication: "How to Deep-Freeze Bait." <u>Angler's Monthly</u>. Remember: <u>Underlining</u> (or italics) for the whole; quotation marks for the part.

EDITOR'S TIP: When your typewriter has no italics (or when ordinary type and italics are not sufficiently distinct), underlining tells the printer to use italicized print. Your instructor or editor may require you to use underlining throughout to signal italics. However, the advantage of using italics in preparation of manuscript is that copy will be print-ready for purposes of local or desktop publication.

3 *Show major breaks by periods.* Separate the name of the author or editor from what follows by a period. Set off the facts of publication for a book from what precedes and what follows by periods. (Leave *one* space after periods separating blocks of information.)

Silverberg, Robert, ed. <u>Science Fiction Hall of Fame</u>. London: Sphere Books, 1972.

4 *Include complete page number for an article.* Give the inclusive page numbers for articles in periodicals or for parts of a collection. (If part of an article spills over onto later pages after intervening pages (or page), use a plus sign to show that there is more later.)

Miller, JoAnn. "The Sandwich Generation." <u>Working Mother</u> Jan. 1987: 47-48.

Kaplan, Janice. "Politics of Sports." <u>Vogue</u> July 1984: 219+.

When a periodical uses continuous page numbering through several issues of an annual volume, include the *volume number* as an Arabic numeral. Use a colon before the inclusive page numbers: *PMLA* 96 (1981): 351–62.

5 *If you list several publications by the same author, do not repeat the author's name.* In the second and later entries, use a line made of three hyphens instead.

Comfort, Alex. <u>A Good Age</u>. New York: Simon, 1976.

---. "Old Age: Facts and Fancies." <u>Saturday Evening Post</u> Mar. 1977: 45.

A NOTE ON NOTES: Even though you are not using footnotes or end notes to identify sources, you may be including **content notes**. These can provide backup to satisfy an interested reader. For instance, your text may have mentioned books with titles like *Aging: Continuity and Change* or *Aging and Society.* For the interested reader, you may decide to provide a more extended listing in a note. You put such notes on a separate page headed "Notes" at the end of your paper before your Works Cited. You number the notes consecutively. You put a raised note number (superscript) outside whatever punctuation goes with the sentence or paragraph, as in this example.[2] Sample note:

[2] Books on aging from the publication list of a single publisher include <u>The Social Forces in Later Life</u>, <u>Social Problems of the Aging</u>, <u>Biology of Aging</u>, <u>Human Services for Older Adults</u>, <u>Families in Later Life</u>, <u>The Later Years</u>, <u>Working with the Elderly</u>, <u>Late Adulthood</u>, and <u>Aging: Politics and Policies</u>, among others.

Abbreviations Found in Scholarly Writing

©	copyright (© 1995 by Jonathan Kozol)
c. or ca.	Latin *circa*, "approximately"; used for approximate dates and figures (c. 1852)
et al.	Latin *et alii*, "and others"; used in references to books by several authors (T. V. Hudson et al.)
f., ff.	"and the following page (or pages)"
Ibid.	an abbreviation of Latin *ibidem*, "in the same place." (When used by itself, without a page reference, it means "in the last publication cited, on the page indicated.")
n.d.	"no date," date of publication unknown
op. cit.	short for *opere citato*, "in the work already cited"
passim	Latin for "throughout"; "in various places in the work under discussion" (See pp. 54–56 et passim.)
rev.	"review" or "revised"
rpt.	"reprint"; a reprinting of a book or article

Works Cited Directory: MLA 1995

The following directory will help you code information accurately for your final list of Works Cited. Each model entry comes with a sample reference for parenthetical documentation. Most of the time you will identify author and source in your running text ("Isaac Asimov says in *The Age of Robots*..."). Your parenthetical references will then give *page numbers* only. The sample references in this directory show what you have to do if your text has *not* already identified author or source.

A. Articles in Periodicals

B. Books (and Other Whole Publications)

C.   Electronic Sources

33 Online Publication

34 Database on CD-ROM

D.   Nonprint Sources

35 Personal Interview

36 Broadcast or Published Interview

37 Personal Letter

38 Talk or Lecture

39 Printed Speech

40 Television or Radio Program

41 Movies

42 Videotapes and Other Visuals

43 Audio Recording

A. Articles in Periodicals

1 Standard Entry for Newspaper Article   Start with the last name of the author. Put the title of the *article* in quotation marks. Underline (or italicize) the name of the *newspaper*. Go on to the date, separated from the *complete page numbers* by a colon. Abbreviate most months: Nov. 1990: 23–31. (But do not abbreviate months in the text of your paper.)

If appropriate, specify the edition of the newspaper — early or late, east or west: Wall Street Journal 28 July 1994, eastern ed.: A3. Sections of a newspaper are often identified by letters (B34) or by numbers (late ed., sec. 3:7):

> Lipsyte, Robert. "An Immovable Barrier in the Fight for Equity: Weeks of Women's Sports Stories Don't Add Up to a Day of Football Coverage." New York Times 24 Sept. 1993, B11.
>
> SAMPLE REFERENCE: No page number necessary for one-page article. (Lipsyte)

If an article is interrupted and continued later in the publication, use a plus sign to show that after the initial pages there is more later:

> Vartabedian, Ralph. "Chronic Joblessness after Aerospace Layoffs." Los Angeles Times 8 June 1993: A1+.

EDITOR'S TIP: Leave off the article *The* in names of newspapers like *The Wall Street Journal* or *The New York Times* when you include them in your Works Cited list.

2 **Standard Entry for Magazine Article**   Start with the last name of the author. Put the title of the *article* in quotation marks. Italicize (underline) the name of the *magazine*. Go on to the date (or month), separated from the *complete page numbers* by a colon.

> Norman Atkins. "The Cost of Living Clean." Rolling Stone 5 May 1994: 41-42.
>
> Kirby, Douglas. "Sex Miseducation." Mother Jones Jan./Feb. 1995: 48.
>
> SAMPLE REFERENCES: (Atkins 41)   (Kirby)

3 **Article by Several Authors**   Give the full names of co-authors. If there are more than three, put et al. (Latin for "and others") after the name of the first author instead. (Or you may list all of the authors.)

> Gale, Noel H., and Zofia Stos-Gale. "Lead and Silver in the Ancient Aegean." Scientific American June 1981: 176-77.
>
> Martz, Larry, et al. "A Tide of Drug Killings." Newsweek 16 Jan. 1989: 44-45.
>
> SAMPLE REFERENCES: (Gale and Stos-Gale 176)   (Martz et al. 45)

4 **Unsigned or Anonymous Article**   If the author of an article is unnamed, begin your entry with the title.

> "The Women of Winter Save U.S." New York Times 23 Feb. 1992, late ed., sec. 1: 23.
>
> SAMPLE REFERENCE: ("Women")

5 **Article with Subtitle**   Use a colon to separate title and subtitle. Enclose both in the same set of quotation marks.

> Claflin, Terrie. "Monumental Achievement: Twenty Years after Vietnam, Invisible Vets Get Their Memorial." Ms. Nov./Dec. 1993: 83-88.
>
> SAMPLE REFERENCE: (Claflin 86)

6 **Article with Volume Number**   For scholarly or professional journals, you will typically include the volume number, followed by the year in parentheses. (Usually page numbers are consecutive for the whole volume covering the issues for a year — the second issue will start with page 90 or page 137, for instance.)

> Santley, Robert S. "The Political Economy of the Aztec Empire." Journal of Anthropological Research 41 (1985): 327-37.
>
> SAMPLE REFERENCE: (Santley 327)

7 **Article with Number of Volume and Issue**   If page numbers are not continuous for the whole volume (each new issue starts with page 1), you may have to include the number of the issue. Add it after the volume number, separating the two numbers by a period (no space): 13.4.

> Winks, Robin W. "The Sinister Oriental Thriller: Fiction and the Asian Scene." <u>Journal of Popular Culture</u> 19.2 (1985): 49-61.

If there is no volume number but only the number of the issue, treat it as if it were the volume number:

> Bowering, George. "Baseball and the Canadian Imagination." <u>Canadian Literature</u> 108 (1986): 115-24.
>
> SAMPLE REFERENCES: (Winks 51-53)   (Bowering 117)

8 Signed or Unsigned Editorial   After the title, add the label: Editorial (no italics or quotation marks). If the editorial is unsigned, begin with the title.

> Hernandez, Carlos. "Immigrants Are Not Aliens." Editorial. <u>Harristown News</u> 27 Sept. 1994: 7.
>
> "Giving Women a Sporting Chance." Editorial. <u>Los Angeles Times</u> 23 Oct. 1993: B7.
>
> SAMPLE REFERENCES: (Hernandez)   ("Giving Women")

9 Letter to the Editor   After the name of the author, add the right label: Letter (no italics or quotation marks).

> Nguyen, Long. Letter. <u>Los Angeles Times</u> 7 July 1993, part II: 8.
>
> SAMPLE REFERENCE: (Nguyen)

10 Titled or Untitled Review   Use the abbreviation Rev. before the title of the work being reviewed. For unsigned reviews, start with the title of the review (if any) or the description of the review.

> Harlan, Arvin C. Rev. of <u>A Short Guide to German Humor</u>, by Frederick Hagen. <u>Brownsville Herald</u> 12 Nov. 1994: 89-90.
>
> Rev. of <u>The Penguin Book of Women Poets</u>, ed. Carol Cosman, Joan Keefe, and Kathleen Weaver. <u>Arts and Books Forum</u> May 1990: 17-19.
>
> SAMPLE REFERENCES: (Harlan 89)   (Rev. of <u>Women Poets</u> 17)

B. Books (and Other Whole Publications)

11 Standard Entry for a Book   Start with the *last* name of the author. Underline (italicize) the title. Give place of publication, publisher's name, and date of publication. (Leave one space after periods.)

> Kramer, Peter D. <u>Listening to Prozac</u>. New York: Viking, 1993.
>
> SAMPLE REFERENCE: (Kramer 89)

EDITOR's TIP: Identification of publishers is heavily abbreviated: NAL (New American Library); Harcourt (Harcourt Brace, Inc.); Oxford UP (Oxford University Press); Acad. for Educ. Dev. (Academy for Educational Development).

> Gates, Henry Louis, Jr. Loose Canons: Notes on the Culture Wars. New York: Oxford UP, 1992.
>
> SAMPLE REFERENCE: (Gates 32)

12 Book with Subtitle Use a colon between title and subtitle. Italicize (underline) both the title and subtitle of the book.

> Steinem, Gloria. Revolution from Within: A Book of Self-Esteem. Boston: Little, 1992.
>
> Kozol, Jonathan. Savage Inequalities: Children in American Schools. New York: HarperCollins, 1991.
>
> SAMPLE REFERENCES: (Steinem 87)   (Kozol 24)

13 Book by Two or Three Authors For the first author, put last name first. Then give full names of co-authors in normal order. With three authors, use commas between authors' names.

> Gilbert, Sandra M., and Susan Guber. The Madwoman in the Attic: The Woman Writer and the Nineteenth-Century Literary Imagination. New Haven: Yale UP, 1979.
>
> Wresch, William, Donald Pattow, and James Gifford. Writing for the Twenty-First Century: Computers and Research Writing. New York: McGraw, 1988.
>
> SAMPLE REFERENCES: (Gilbert and Guber 114)   (Wresch, Pattow, and Gifford 67)

14 Book by More Than Three Authors Give the first author's name, followed by a comma and the abbreviation et al. (Latin for "and others"). Do not put a period after et, and do not underline or italicize.

> Stewart, Marie M., et al. Business English and Communication. 5th ed. New York: McGraw, 1978.
>
> SAMPLE REFERENCE: (Stewart et al. 34)

15 Later Edition of a Book If you have used a book revised or brought up to date by the author, identify the new edition the way it is labeled on its title page. After the title of the book, put 2nd ed. for second edition, for instance, or rev. ed. for revised edition.

> Zettl, Herbert. Television Production Handbook. 6th ed. Belmont: Wadsworth, 1997.
>
> SAMPLE REFERENCE: (Zettl 39)

16   Reprinting or Reissue of a Book   If a work has been republished unchanged (perhaps as a paperback reprint), include the date of the original edition before full publishing data for the reprinting. If new material (like an introduction) has been added, include a note to that effect.

> Wharton, Edith. <u>The House of Mirth</u>. 1905. Introd. Cynthia Griffin Wolf. New York: Penguin, 1986.
>
> SAMPLE REFERENCE: (Wharton 7)

17   Book with Editor's Name First   If an editor has assembled or arranged the materials in the book, use ed. after the editor's name or eds. if there are several editors.

> Erdrich, Louise, ed. <u>The Best American Short Stories 1993</u>. Boston: Houghton, 1993.
>
> Kiernan, Kathy, and Michael M. Moore, eds. <u>First Fiction: An Anthology of the First Published Stories by Famous Writers</u>. Boston: Little, 1994.
>
> SAMPLE REFERENCES: (Erdrich 367)   (Kiernan and Moore ix)

18   Book with Editor's Name Later   If an editor has edited the work of a single author, put the original author's name first if you focus on the *author's* work. Add Ed. (for "edited by") and the editor's or several editors' names after the title. (Do not use Eds.) However, put the editor's name first and the author's name later (after *By*) if the editor's work is particularly important to your project.

> Mencken, H. L. <u>The Vintage Mencken</u>. Ed. Alistair Cooke. New York: Vintage, 1956.
>
> SAMPLE REFERENCES: Identify by person mentioned first. (Mencken 98)

19   Book with Translator's Name   Put Trans. followed by the translator's name (or translators' names) after the title. But put the translator's name first if the translator's work matters to your project.

> Freire, Paulo. <u>Pedagogy of the Oppressed</u>. Trans. Myra Bergman Ramos. New York: Seabury, 1970.
>
> Wilson, Marjorie Kerr, trans. <u>On Aggression</u>. By Konrad Lorenz. New York: Harcourt, 1966.
>
> SAMPLE REFERENCES: Identify by person mentioned first. (Freire 34) (Wilson 13)

20   Special Imprint   A line of paperbacks, for instance, may be published and promoted separately by a publishing house. Put the name of the line of books first, joined by a hyphen to the publisher's name: Laurel Leaf-Dell, Mentor-NAL.

Hsu, Kau-yu, ed. and trans. <u>Twentieth-Century Chinese Poetry</u>. Garden City: Anchor-Doubleday, 1964.

SAMPLE REFERENCE: (Hsu 45)

21 Unspecified or Institutional Authorship Reports issued by an organization and major reference books may list a group as the author or not specify authorship:

Carnegie Council on Policy Studies in Higher Education. <u>Giving Youth a Better Chance: Options for Education, Work, and Service</u>. San Francisco: Jossey, 1980.

<u>Literary Market Place: The Directory of American Book Publishing</u>. 1984 ed. New York: Bowker, 1983.

SAMPLE REFERENCES: (Carnegie Council 29)   (<u>Literary Market</u> 178)

22 Work with Several Volumes If you have used *one* volume of a multivolume work, add Vol. followed by an Arabic numeral for the number of the volume: Vol. 3. (You may add the total number of volumes and inclusive dates at the end.) If the separate volumes have their own titles, include the volume title as well as the title of the whole multivolume work.

Woolf, Virginia. <u>The Diary of Virginia Woolf</u>. Ed. Anne Olivier Bell. New York: Harcourt, 1977. Vol. 1.

Churchill, Winston S. <u>The Age of Revolution</u>. New York: Dodd, 1957. Vol. 3 of <u>A History of the English-Speaking Peoples</u>. 4 vols. 1956-58.

SAMPLE REFERENCES: (Woolf 67)   (Churchill 115-16)

If you have used *more than one* volume, list the whole multivolume work, giving the total number of volumes: 3 vols.

Trevelyan, G. M. <u>History of England</u>. 3rd ed. 3 vols. Garden City: Anchor-Doubleday, 1952.

SAMPLE REFERENCES: Include volume number as well as page number(s).

23 Part of Collection or Anthology Identify both the article or other short piece (poem, short story) and the collection. Put the part title in quotation marks; underline (italicize) the title of the whole. Then give publishing data for the collection and inclusive page numbers for the part.

Rogers, Carl R. "Two Divergent Trends." <u>Existential Psychology</u>. Ed. Rollo May. New York: Random, 1969. 87-92.

SAMPLE REFERENCE: (Rogers 87)

24 Several Articles from Same Collection Enter the whole collection in your Works Cited list, giving full publishing data. With each individual article, include the last name(s) of the collection editor(s) to direct the reader to the entry for the whole collection. Include complete page numbers, but do not repeat the full publishing information each time.

> O'Dair, Sharon. "Vestments and Vested Interests: Academia, the Working Class, and Affirmative Action." Tokarczyk and Fay 239-50.
>
> Tokarczyk, Michelle M. "By the Rivers of Babylon." Tokarczyk and Fay 311-22.
>
> Tokarczyk, Michelle M., and Elizabeth A. Fay, eds. <u>Working-Class Women in the Academy: Laborers in the Knowledge Factory</u>. Amherst: U of Massachusetts P, 1993.

25 Encyclopedia Entry   Put titles of entries in quotation marks. Page numbers and facts of publication may be unnecessary for entries appearing in alphabetical order in well-known encyclopedias or other reference books. Date or number of the edition used, however, should be included because of the frequent revisions of major encyclopedias. (Include author's name for signed entries. If only initials are given, you may find the full name in an index or guide.)

> Politis, M. J. "Greek Music." <u>Encyclopedia Americana</u>. 1965 ed.
>
> "Aging." <u>Encyclopaedia Britannica: Macropaedia</u>. 1983.
>
> "Graham, Martha." <u>Who's Who of American Women</u>. 14th ed. 1985-86.
>
> SAMPLE REFERENCES: No page numbers are needed for alphabetical entries. (Politis)   ("Aging")   ("Graham")

26 Introduction, Foreword, or Afterword   If you cite introductory material or an afterword by someone *other than the author* of the book, start with the contributor's name, followed by the appropriate description (*un*italicized, *not* in quotation marks): Introduction. Preface. Foreword. Afterword. Sometimes the introductory material has separate page numbers, given as lowercase Roman numerals: v-ix or ii-xvi.

> Bellow, Saul. Foreword. <u>The Closing of the American Mind</u>. By Allan Bloom. New York: Simon, 1987. 11-18.
>
> DeMott, Robert. Introduction. <u>Working Days: The Journals of</u> The Grapes of Wrath 1938-1941. By John Steinbeck. Ed. Robert DeMott. New York: Viking, 1989. xxi-lvii.

27 Government Publication   References to entries in the *Congressional Record* require only the date and page numbers. For other government publications, identify the government and the appropriate branch or subdivision. Use appropriate abbreviations: S. Res. for Senate Resolution, H. Rept. for House Report, and GPO for Government Printing Office.

Cong. Rec. 7 Feb. 1973: 3831-51.

California. Dept. of Viticulture. Beyond Pesticides. Sacramento: State Printing Office, 1995.

United States. Cong. Senate. Subcommittee on Constitutional Amendments of the Committee on the Judiciary. Hearings on the "Equal Rights" Amendment. 91st Cong., 2nd sess. S. Res. 61. Washington: GPO, 1970.

SAMPLE REFERENCE: (California. Dept. of Viticulture 18-20)

28 **Pamphlet or Brochure**   Treat a pamphlet or brochure like a book, but note that author (and sometimes place or date) may not be specified.

A Guide to Supplements. Boston: Inst. for Better Living, 1994.

SAMPLE REFERENCE: (Guide 12)

29 **Part of a Series**   If the front matter of a book shows it was published as part of a series, include the name of the series (no italics, no quotation marks) before the publishing data.

Rose, Mike. Writer's Block: The Cognitive Dimension. Studies in Writing and Rhetoric. Carbondale: Southern Illinois UP, 1984.

SAMPLE REFERENCE: (Rose 78)

30 **Bible or Literary Classic**   Specify the edition you have used, especially if different versions of the text are important, as with different Bible translations or different editions of a Shakespeare play. Put the editor's name first if you want to highlight the editor's contribution.

The Holy Bible. Revised Standard Version. 2nd ed. Nashville: Nelson, 1971.

Hubler, Edward, ed. The Tragedy of Hamlet. By William Shakespeare. New York: NAL, 1963.

SAMPLE REFERENCES: For chapter and verse: (Job 2.8)   For act and scene: (Hamlet 3.2) or (Hamlet III.ii)

Note: Even when using specific page numbers for an edition you have used, you can help your reader find the passage in a different edition by adding the number of the chapter or of act and scene after a semicolon: (34; ch. 2).

31 **Quotation at Second Hand**   List only the work where the quotation appeared:

Ibsen, Henrik. Ghosts. Ed. Kai Jurgensen and Robert Schenkkan. New York: Avon, 1965.

SAMPLE REFERENCE: (qtd. in Ibsen 48)

32 **Title within a Title**   An italicized (underlined) book title may include the name of another book. Shift back to roman (*not* underlined) for the title-within-a-title: *A Guide to James Joyce's* Ulysses.

> Gordon, Jean. A Guide to Huckleberry Finn. New York: Logos, 1984.

C. Electronic Sources

33 **Online Publication**   For material accessed through a computer service, add Online, name of the system, and date of access. If the material has been previously published elsewhere, start with standard publishing information. If no printed source is specified, treat the material as a complete publication published by the service:

> Angier, Natalie. "Chemists Learn Why Vegetables Are Good for You." New York Times 13 Apr. 1993, late ed.: C1. New York Times Online. Online. Nexis. 10 Feb. 1994.
>
> Glicken, Morley D. "A Five-Step Plan to Renew Your Creativity." National Business Employment Weekly. Online. Dow Jones News Retrieval. 10 Nov. 1992.
>
> SAMPLE REFERENCES: (Angier)   (Glicken)

34 **Database on CD-ROM**   Add the label CD-ROM to access information. Because of frequent updatings, you may have to specify the version: Vers. 1.4.

> Shearson Brothers, Inc. "Reebok: Company Report." 29 July 1993. General Business File. CD-ROM. Information Access. Dec. 1993.
>
> Russo, Michelle Cash. "Recovering from Bibliographic Instruction Blahs." RQ: Reference Quarterly 32 (1992): 178-83. Infotrac: Magazine Index Plus. CD-ROM. Information Access. Dec. 1993.
>
> "Bronte, Emily." Discovering Authors. Vers. 1.0. CD-ROM. Detroit: Gale, 1992.
>
> SAMPLE REFERENCES: (Shearson)   (Russo 179)   ("Bronte")

D. Nonprint Sources

35 **Personal Interview**   Start with the name of the person you interviewed. Use the right label — *un*italicized, *not* in quotation marks.

> Silveira, Gene. Personal interview. 12 Oct. 1995.
>
> Duong, Tran. Telephone interview. 22 Jan. 1994.
>
> SAMPLE REFERENCE: (Duong) No parenthetical reference is necessary if your text names the person you interviewed.

36 **Broadcast or Published Interview**   Identify the person interviewed and label the material as an interview.

> Asimov, Isaac. Interview. <u>Science Watch</u>. With Dorothy Brett. KFOM, San Bruno. 19 Mar. 1986.

If an interview appeared in print, identify it as an interview, and then give standard publishing information about the printed source.

> Asimov, Isaac. Interview. <u>Scientists Talk about Science</u>. By Anne Harrison and Webster Freid. Los Angeles: Acme, 1987. 94-101.

> SAMPLE REFERENCE: (Asimov)   For printed source: (Asimov 98)

37 Personal Letter   For a letter you have received, name the letter writer and label the material as a letter or e-mail. Give the date. For a published letter, use the name of the *recipient* as the title and then give full publishing data, with inclusive page numbers.

> Magnusson, Diane. Letter to the author. 15 Jan. 1995.

> Velasquez, Alberto. E-mail to the author. 8 Apr. 1997.

> Hemingway, Ernest. "To Lillian Ross." 28 July 1948. <u>Ernest Hemingway: Selected Letters. 1917-1961</u>. Ed. Carlos Baker. New York: Scribner's, 1981. 646-49.

38 Talk or Lecture   Name the speaker and give an appropriate label: Lecture. Keynote Speech. Address (no italics or quotation marks). If the talk had a title, use the title (in quotation marks) instead.

> Kernan, Dorothy. Keynote Speech. Opening General Sess. New World Forum. Dallas. 8 June 1995.

> Jacobi, Jean. "Television News: News from Nowhere." Valley Lecture Series. Santa Clara. 29 Oct. 1994.

> SAMPLE REFERENCE: (Kernan) No parenthetical reference is necessary if your text names the speaker.

39 Printed Speech   If you had access to a printed version of a speech, add full publishing data to the usual information about a talk.

> Partlet, Basil. "Yuppies and the Art of Cooking." Western Chefs' Forum. Phoenix. 19 Aug. 1989. Rpt. <u>West Coast Review</u> Spring 1990: 76-82.

> SAMPLE REFERENCE: (Partlet 77)

40 Television or Radio Program   Underline (italicize) the title of a program. The title may be preceded by the name of a specific episode (in quotation marks) and followed by the name of the series (no italics or quotation marks): "The Young Stravinsky." <u>The Great Composers</u>. Musical Masterpieces. Identify network (if any), station, and city (with the last two separated by a comma: KPFA, Berkeley). Pull a name out in front to highlight a person's contribution.

The Poisoned Planet. Narr. Jean Laidlaw. Writ. and prod. Pat Verstrom. WXRV, Seattle. 12 Feb. 1996.

Rostow, Jacob, dir. "The Last Bridge." A Forgotten War. With Eric Seibert, Joan Ash, and Fred Minton. KMBC, Sacramento. 12 Dec. 1987.

SAMPLE REFERENCE: (Poisoned Planet) No parenthetical reference is necessary if your text names the program.

41 Movies   Underline (italicize) the title. Identify the director and the production company, and give the date. Include further information as you wish about performers, scriptwriters, and other contributors. Pull a name out in front to highlight a person's contribution.

It's a Wonderful Life. Dir. Frank Capra. With James Stewart, Donna Reed, Lionel Barrymore, and Thomas Mitchell. RKO, 1946.

Zeffirelli, Franco, dir. Romeo and Juliet. By William Shakespeare. With Olivia Hussey, Leonard Whiting, and Michael York. Paramount, 1968. 138 min.

SAMPLE REFERENCE: (Zeffirelli)

42 Videotapes and Other Visuals   Label the medium: Videocassette. Filmstrip. Slide program (no italics or quotation marks).

Creation vs. Evolution: Battle of the Classrooms. Videocassette. Dir. Ryall Wilson. PBS Video, 1982. 58 min.

SAMPLE REFERENCE: (Creation)

43 Audio Recording   Specify label of the recording company, followed by order number and date. (Use n.d. for "no date" if date is unknown.) Identify references to jacket notes or the like.

Holiday, Billie. The Essential Billie Holiday: Carnegie Hall Concert. Audiocassette. Verve, UCV2600, 1969.

Rifkin, Joshua. Jacket notes. Renaissance Vocal Music. Nonesuch, H-71097, n.d.

SAMPLE REFERENCE: (Rifkin)

A Sample Research Paper (MLA)

As you study the following sample research paper, do justice to three major dimensions:

Larger Elements   How has the author tackled her subject, guided the reader, and maintained the reader's interest? For instance, in the early pages, study the way she introduces her subject and leads up to her thesis. Study the "then-and-now" contrast that provides the basic historical perspective for the paper.

Using Sources How has the author used and identified her sources? How does she introduce quoted material? What is the mix of short direct quotation, paraphrase, and longer block quotations?

Documentation Study the author's use of parenthetical references and her final list of Works Cited. Where did she have to deal with special problems? How did she handle unusual or unconventional sources?

A note on format:

• Your paper does not need a separate title page. The first page starts with the **author block** (author, instructor, course, and date). Note *double-spacing* throughout the sample paper, including author block, title, block quotations, and list of Works Cited.

• **Running heads,** starting on page 1, give the student writer's last name followed by the number of the page (plain numeral — no punctuation or abbreviation).

• The **title** is *not* italicized (underlined), put in quotation marks, or typed as all capitals. Use italics or quotation marks only if your title quotes someone else's title: *Star Trek* and the Myth of Innocence.

• A separate **outline**, when required by the instructor, is double-spaced throughout and follows conventional outline format.

Sondra Gordon Delones

Professor Dobrek

English 2A

November 6, 1996

Sports Equity: The Long Road

THESIS: Although enormous changes have already occurred, the revolution in women's sports is far from complete.

  I. Today's highly visible women athletes

 II. Progress toward equality in sports

    A. Challenging traditional restrictions

    B. Making progress: the 50s and 60s

      1. The Sputnik effect

      2. The spirit of political activism

    C. Breakthroughs

      1. Commercial sponsorship

      2. Title IX and its aftermath

      3. Moving into the 21st century

III. Sports and the changing self-image of women

    A. Fitness: body and mind

    B. Testing the limits

    C. The benefits of sports: self-esteem and confidence

IV. Women's athletics and traditional sports

    A. Competition v. participation

    B. De-emphasizing violence

  V. A new concept of sport

Delones 1

Sondra Gordon Delones

Professor Dobrek

English 2A

November 6, 1996

Sports Equity: The Long Road

The events were sold out. Each time the home teams scored, there was a roar, followed by the hush of anticipation that magnified the slap of a hand on the ball or the squeak of rubber on wood. In the 1994 National Collegiate Athletic Association's (NCAA) basketball final four, the usual big names were present — North Carolina and Purdue and Alabama and Louisiana Tech — and screaming sell-out crowds exhorted the extraordinary athletes and network television recorded each thrilling moment. It was the usual college basketball spring madness with one interesting variation. North Carolina and Purdue had already sent their men's teams home. It was now the women's basketball championship competition.

Twenty years ago, such a scene would have been unlikely. Then women who enjoyed sports had two choices: They could join the Girls' Athletic Association (GAA) and play intramurals, or they could participate vicariously as cheerleaders on the sidelines. Today, in addition to the highly publicized women tennis players, runners, ice skaters, and basketball players, there are women cyclists, swimmers, volleyball players, rowing crews, mountain climbers, fencers, soccer players — and a professional women's baseball team called "The Colorado Silver Bullets." What has happened? Although the revolution in women's sports is unfinished, it has already

Delones 2

changed both what women expect of themselves and what we expect of
athletics.

For years, progress toward equality of the sexes in sports has been
slow. Women were free to participate in genteel games like tennis or golf as
long as they did not perspire too freely or appear too intent on winning.
From the beginning, women athletes had to reckon with the traditional
ideal of the ladylike woman, who was not allowed to appear tough or assertive. Outstanding athletes like the swimmer Esther Williams or the ice
skater Sonja Henie were praised for their beauty and grace rather than for
their athletic achievement. In 1936, the editor of <u>Sportsman</u> magazine
wrote, "As swimmers and divers, girls are as beautiful and adroit as they
are ineffective and unpleasing on the track" (qtd. in Hart 66). Stephen K.
Figler and Gail Whitaker in <u>Sport and Play in American Life</u> concur: "Until
fairly recently, a widespread belief held that strenuous sports activity was
not only beyond the capacity of women but physically harmful to them."
Strenuous sports activity was, "in a word, unladylike" (307). In 1971, Marie
Hart, in an article titled "Sport: Women Sit in the Back of the Bus," concluded that "the emphasis in periodicals is still largely on women as attractive objects rather than as skilled and effective athletes" (66).

By contrast, by the nineties women's athleticism has begun to be acknowledged and encouraged. A <u>Time</u> article describing Martina Navratilova's final Wimbledon appearance celebrated her extraordinary abilities:
"She elevated serve and volley tactics to a higher level on the women's tour
and made it fashionable for women to display muscle tone" (Witteman 61).
Along with Navratilova, athletes like heptathlon world record holder Jackie

Delones 3

Joyner-Kersee and six-time Olympic medal winner Bonnie Blair have indisputably established the power of the female athlete.

The road to today's limited recognition of female sports and female sports figures was long, with setbacks and detours. In the 1950s and 1960s, opportunities for women in sports slowly began to open up, partly as the result of political pressure. Phyllis Bailey, Assistant Director of Athletics at Ohio State University, describes a kind of athletic "Sputnik effect":

> The international scene of the 1950s and 60s had put pressure on
> the government to take women's college sports more seriously.
> The Olympics had become a political battlefield, and our men
> were getting medals, but our women weren't. We had to do something to protect our standing in the world and get American
> women on a par with others. (qtd. in Kaplan 59)

At the same time, the climate of political activism in the 60s and the growing agitation for individual rights encouraged women to knock on doors previously closed. In 1967, Kathrine Switzer crashed the then male-only Boston Marathon. She filled out the entrant's application as K. Switzer, and "was nearly shouldered off the course by officials when they noticed she was, in fact, female." The attempted ouster and resulting controversy "infuriated Switzer and galvanized her into action to change the system," making her a major force in the movement that led to the inclusion of the first women's marathon in the 1984 Olympics (Ullyot 44, 50–51). Joan Benoit Samuelson, who won the gold medal at the 1984 Olympics, went on to establish the U.S. women's marathon record of 2:21:21 the following year in Chicago. Considering that women were not even allowed to run the marathon until the seventies, Samuelson's closeness to the men's world record of 2:06:50 is remarkable.

Delones 4

The major breakthrough for women's sports occurred in the seventies. First, a few major companies gingerly invested in women's professional sports and soon realized that they had discovered a gold mine. Colgate-Palmolive became the controlling dollar behind women's golf, skiing, and tennis. The company decided to put its advertising money into the women's pro circuit instead of afternoon soap operas, and the gamble paid off. Another company to place a lucky bet was Philip Morris. The Virginia Slims tennis tour put women's tennis on the map. The effect of the Slims tour with its lucrative prize money was to establish for the first time the role model of the well-paid, well-respected female athlete.

As women took their first steps into professional, non-team sports, Congress passed the 1972 Education Amendment Act, which was to boost greatly women's participation in amateur athletics. An amendment of the 1964 Civil Rights Act, the Education Amendment Act is comprised of sections or titles, the ninth of which states: "No person in the United States shall on the basis of sex be excluded from participation in, be denied the benefits of, or be subjected to discrimination under any educational program or activity receiving Federal financial assistance" (Figler 311). Title IX as applied to women's athletics meant that immediate adjustments needed to be made so that women athletes would receive a fair, proportionate amount of athletic scholarship money and so that women's sports would receive an equal share of the money devoted to sports overall. Without making such adjustments, institutions stood to lose federal funding. Needless to say, the new legislation received much hostile attention, beginning with the NCAA's unsuccessful attempt "to have revenue-producing sports,

Delones 5

i.e., men's team sports, in particular football and basketball, made exempt from the law" (Figler 312).

Nonetheless, the initial effect of the new law was to focus attention on and promote new growth in women's athletics. Headlines like "The Cardinal Rules" no longer applied exclusively to Stanford's male athletes. Before Title IX, Division I colleges spent two percent of their athletic budgets on women's sports (Guttmann 221); by 1991 the figure for Division I colleges was 26.6 percent (NCAA 4). Before Title IX, there were virtually no athletic scholarships for university-bound women (Guttmann 213); by 1991 just over 16 percent of all scholarship money for division I schools went to female athletes (NCAA 4). In 1972 when Title IX was enacted, there were 32,000 women participating in NCAA athletics (Guttmann 214); by 1991 there were 67,659 (NCAA 4, 21, 25). After the 1994 Winter Olympics, an editorial titled "One for Nancy, Six for Bonnie" noted:

> A generation ago, few American women aspired to excel in sports that demanded speed, strength and endurance rather than the more aesthetic virtues that characterize some of the other Olympic events. But the growth of opportunity for women in scholastic sports — thanks in large measure to federal legislation . . . have had an impact. (A24)

However, in 1984 Title IX suffered a temporary setback which, although soon reversed, has had a permanent effect. In Grove City College v. Bell, the Supreme Court ruled that Title IX banned sex discrimination only in specific programs that received federal funds (Figler 313). Thus a discriminatory athletic department no longer jeopardized federal aid for a college or university as a whole. And since athletic departments receive very

Delones 6

little federal aid, the impetus toward parity was considerably slowed.[1] Although in 1988 the Civil Rights Restoration Act reaffirmed that Title IX did in fact apply to athletic programs, the more permanent aspect of the 1984 setback is that the dispute has moved into the courts as on-going court battles attempt to counteract the glacial pace of change after <u>Grove</u>.

An article in <u>U.S. News & World Report</u> summed up: "Four years later [1988] the law was restored, but it had become apparent that overburdened federal agencies lacked the resources to make inspections or enforce the law" (Schrof 52). As a result women have seized the initiative and attempted to persuade the courts to enforce the law: "At least 35 lawsuits have been filed, and those that have been decided have nearly always favored female athletes and coaches" (Schrof 53). In July of 1993, the <u>Christian Science Monitor</u> reported on lawsuits at Howard, Brown, and Auburn universities, and concluded:

> Nearly a dozen other cases are in various stages of discovery or trial. Among the institutions being taken to court are the California State University System, Colorado State University, University of Texas, Indiana University, and State University of New York, Oswego. (Henderson 12)

Ithaca College President James J. Whalen, who co-chaired the NCAA task force on gender equity, is quoted in the Henderson article: "It looks to me like people are going to have to get their acts together, or the courts, or Congress, will do it for them" (12).

Although the move toward equality seemed to proceed in fits and starts, the achievement of recent women athletes and the accolades awarded to them have been partial compensation. In Albertville in 1992

Delones 7

women brought home nine of the eleven medals awarded to U.S. athletes; a spokesperson for the U.S. Olympic Committee described the games as "a U.S. women's Olympics" (Brennan A1). In Barcelona over 2,800 women from 35 countries competed in the 1992 Summer Olympics. It was at Barcelona that Jackie Joyner-Kersee received her second straight gold medal in the heptathlon as well as a bronze medal in the long jump, and Bruce Jenner (a decathlon gold medalist in 1976) told her, "You're the greatest athlete ever" (qtd. in Boswell A7).

What have the advances in women's sports done for the self-image of women? When the doors to free participation in sports swing open, so do other doors, many of them psychological. The grassroots movement toward greater fitness among women affects both body and mind. In Marathon Mom, Linda Schreiber writes about how running helped to increase her energy and change her outlook, how she experienced the sharpened physical and mental acuity which comes with physical fitness:

> The more I ran, the easier hauling groceries and carrying babies became. I found I had more pep, needed less sleep. Running also seemed to allow me to see things in a more mellow perspective. . . . I didn't feel so narrow and confined, because my day had at least included a run. Somehow I didn't feel so "small" and events at home so petty. (8)

In addition to the joy of physical fitness, there is for many the extra dimension of testing limits. Every athlete can experience pushing at the barrier of his or her own limitations, and many experience the satisfaction felt when the barrier yields to persistent effort. A case in point, from Janice Kaplan's classic Women and Sports, is long-distance running for women:

Delones 8

Women runners were always assumed to lack endurance. The 1928 Olympics were the first games where women were allowed to run anything
longer than a sprint. Eleven women that year entered an 800-meter race. Officials predicted disaster and were correct. Five women dropped out, five
collapsed at the finish line, and the strongest collapsed in the dressing room
afterwards. Kaplan believes that these women failed because they were expected to fail: "None of them had ever trained for long distances, and they
were psyched out by the adumbrations of doom and the ambulance waiting at the finish line" (37).

Ironically, today women are thought to exceed men in their physical
potential for endurance because of a superior ability to metabolize fat.[2]
"The closure of the performance gap in the marathon was spectacular,"
says Allen Guttmann in his history of women's sports. "Between 1972 and
1982, women's records improved by 16.2 percent (to 2 hours, 26 minutes, 11
seconds). For every other distance from 200 to 10,000 meters, the women's
records improved far more rapidly than the men's." In addition, women
have made impressive gains in swimming:

> For fifteen swimming events, the difference between the men's and
> women's records was 12.41 percent in 1936, 11.36 percent in 1956,
> and 9.27 percent in 1976. By 1980, the difference in the 400-meter
> crawl had diminished to only 5.2 percent (Guttmann 252).

Physiological differences between men and women render most such
comparisons moot; what is noteworthy is that women's successes are directly related to Title IX, and are occurring in an atmosphere now significantly more receptive to women in athletics.

Delones 9

Overcoming physical and mental barriers in sports gives women increased confidence and self-esteem. Women athletes experience their efforts
and achievements with pride. Donna Lopiano, head of the Women's Sports
Foundation (WSF), is presented in a <u>Los Angeles Times</u> article as believing
that "sports have always been an essential training ground for boys, helping to develop confidence and self-esteem" (Garcia F6). By providing over
one million dollars in grants and scholarships to girls and women in athletics, the WSF seeks to provide the same essential training ground for the female athlete. It would be difficult to disprove a connection between early
development of confident self-esteem and later successes in a fulfilling
adult life. Courtland Milloy says, "Competitive sports condition minds and
bodies, introduce the concept of teamwork and offer countless other lessons
about life. You don't have to be at risk, or a boy, to be in need of that" (K3).

Benefits derived from participating in athletics occur irrespective of the
sport chosen. From solitary timed contests like running and swimming to
team sports like soccer and basketball, and from expensive pursuits like
equestrian competition to playing stickball in the street, women stand to
benefit from sport.

Much testimony from women athletes indicates that self-confidence
and determination carry over from athletics into other areas of life. Lopiano, described by <u>New York Times</u> sportswriter Robert Lipsyte as "one of
her generation's best softball players," is quoted in his article "Equity, Plus
or Minus": "Your daughter <u>must</u> play sports. It's not fun and games. Sports
is essential for successful people" (30). Sally Ride, first American woman in
space, said, "Athletics teaches endurance and the value of pursuing beyond

Delones 10

one's perceived limits to achieve higher levels of ability" ("A Winning
Combination" 1–2).

   The fact that women are participating in sports in unprecedented numbers is obviously having a strong impact on women. In turn, what impact,
if any, are the women having on sports? Although the extent of actual
change is difficult to assess, women's athletics is challenging two features of
traditional sports: excessive competition and violence.

   Figler cites studies which conclude that insofar as competitiveness and
aggression are measurable, "psychological research" has shown "men and
women to be equally competitive," and that aggression in men is the "result of cultural expectations and conditioning, perpetuated by aggressive
role models." Nonetheless, in situations "where aggression is considered
allowable behavior, sex differences usually disappear" (320). While Guttmann (251) observes that the male hormone testosterone "seems to account
for some of the difference in men's as compared to women's aggressiveness," Figler concludes otherwise: "females with high levels of testosterone
do not display unusually high aggressiveness" (320). What women's sports
needs to strive for is a healthy and spontaneous display of competition and
aggression, without any tendency to resort to the corrupt, win-at-any-cost,
violent philosophy that permeates men's sports. This is especially critical if
women have the same potential for excessive aggression and
competitiveness.

   Women's sports traditionally stressed participation. Because athletic
programs for women tended to be recreational and low-budget, the "every-
one-can-play" ethic prevailed. Today, dazzled by the rewards of increased

Delones 11

money and prestige, women's athletics is in danger of losing sight of the ideal of sports-for-all. Competition systematically narrows the field of participants to only those who are good enough to compete. When there are limited recreational facilities or team berths, some get to play and others become spectators. If winning is the only thing that counts, then a select few battle it out while the many watch. Recruiting and training of top performers become the overriding priorities.

From the beginning of the current expansion of women's sports, there have been voices warning against an imitation of the "male model." George R. LaNoue, in an article in <u>Change</u>, said in 1976:

> Among the leaders of women's athletics there is strong opposition to turning women's sports into an imitation of men's. They do not want to engage in wide-spread off-campus recruiting. They would prefer to remain teachers instead of becoming win-at-any-cost sports promoters. (30)

Fifteen years after LaNoue, Figler writes:

> Furthermore, the large scale adoption of the business model by women's athletic programs appears to have destroyed any hope of reviving the broad-based, educational philosophy of earlier decades of women's sport. In their eagerness to achieve equity with men's programs, women have adopted practices which promote elitism and invite abuses. Scholarships, letters of intent, competitive recruiting, slick publicity, and an emphasis on winning over all else are legacies of men's athletic history whose consequences already bring into question women's judgment in embracing them. (313)

Delones 12

While Figler is right to condemn women's emulation of male athletics, it is not fair to "question women's judgment" alone. On the very next page Figler acknowledges, "women have lost much of the control they previously held over women's programs." To wit, in 1972, "over 90 percent of women's teams and programs were coached and administered by women"; by 1988 the figures had declined to 48.3 percent of women's teams coached by women and 16 percent of women's programs administered by women (314).

While the idea of sport-for-all has become endangered, it has not disappeared entirely. The court battles in process over real implementation of Title IX clearly foster an environment of reflection and discussion. As universities are forced to award proportional scholarships and funding to women's athletics, the larger questions of equal participation can at least be addressed. If universities substitute a number of team sports (like soccer, volleyball, basketball) for women and men, instead of the expensive behemoth that is university football, far greater numbers of athletes should find themselves playing less violent sports in a more collegial environment. As Donna Lopiano once summed up: "My feeling is that equity for women in sports may be the salvation of intercollegiate athletics because it creates a need for reform" (qtd. in Moran 2).

Excessive competition and glory-for-the-few is not the only idea being challenged by the women's sports movement. Another area of traditional athletics to come under attack is the notion that violence is an inescapable element of sport. Traditional male sports are routinely described "as a substitute for war by providing a relatively safe outlet for innate antisocial aggression"; Figler introduces this concept by calling it a "reactive folk belief"

Delones 13

(249). Some of the most popular men's sports — football, ice hockey, boxing — are extremely violent. Don Atyeo, in <u>Violence in Sports</u>, says of football: "Each year it kills on average twenty-eight players and maims
thousands more. It leaves everyone who reaches its higher levels with some
form of lasting injury" (219). He quotes a former player for the Los Angeles
Rams: "People who play for any length of time carry the scars for the rest of
their lives." These may not "be showing on the outside, but they'll have
knees that are worn out, shoulders that don't work right, fingers that point
in a different direction" (220). Part of the code of the male athlete is that a
man must stoically endure the pain to prove his manliness. Atyeo reports:
"It has been estimated that 4 out of every 22 players on the [football] field
are playing with a serious injury, and 5 out of every 22 are playing with an
injury which would prevent any 'normal' person from continuing his
job" (222).

The growth of women's sports will not eliminate violence in sport, but
it will help to temper it. Women's sports are not burdened with the tradition of violence linked to the idea of sport as a proving ground for sexual
identity. Nor are women as caught up in the vicious cycle of sacrificing
one's physical self in order to demonstrate one's toughness. This is not to
say that the risk of pain and injury are not part of the challenge of sports for
many women athletes. Figler, for example, presents basketball as a game
that "can no longer be considered a noncontact sport for either men or
women" (239).

Increasingly, women are competing in tests of endurance that were
once male-only events. In 1985, Libby Riddles became the first woman to
win the Iditarod, a 1,000-mile dogsled race from Anchorage to Nome,

Delones 14

Alaska. By 1990 Susan Butcher had won the race four times, three of them consecutively. In September of 1994 Seana Hogan set a new women's record in the 2,900-mile cycling endurance contest, Race Across America.

Women's sports help society move away from the glorification of violence. When media time is devoted to women's sports like tennis and golf, the focus is entirely upon the healthy athleticism of participants in nonviolent sports. Both the airing of women's athletics and increased participation in sports by women are creating a wider audience of female spectators, which in turn creates greater demand on the networks for coverage of women's events.

In conclusion, the struggle for the acceptance of women's sports is not a battle between men and women. The real enemies of sport for women are the same as they are for men: the trap of passive spectatorship, the philosophy that winning is the only thing, and the idea of violence as a normal, inescapable part of sport. What is needed is a new concept of sport that sees the purpose of sport as lifelong enjoyment and pleasure, increased fitness for life, and a feeling of well-being and joy.

Delones 15

Notes

[1] The negative impact of court decisions and institutional backsliding is chronicled in G. Ann Uhlir's article on "Athletics and the University: The Post-Woman's Era" in <u>Academe</u> for July-August 1987 (25–29).

[2] A more complete examination of fat metabolism and myths about female physiology can be found in Kaplan's chapter on "Physiology" in <u>Women and Sports</u>.

Delones 16

Works Cited

Atyeo, Don. <u>Violence in Sports</u>. New York: Paddington, 1979.

Boswell, Thomas. "Joyner-Kersee Alone atop Olympus." <u>Washington Post</u> 3
    Aug. 1992, final ed.: A1+.

Brennan, Christine. "A U.S. Women's Olympics." <u>Washington Post</u> 24 Feb.
    1992, final ed.: A1+.

"The Cardinal Rules." <u>Sports Illustrated</u>. 9 Apr. 1990: 48.

Figler, Stephen K., and Gail Whitaker. <u>Sport and Play in American Life</u>. 2nd
    ed. Dubuque, Iowa: Wm. C. Brown, 1991.

Garcia, Irene. "Pitching Equality on the Nation's Athletic Fields." <u>Los Angeles Times</u> 18 Apr. 1993, final ed.: F6.

Guttmann, Allen. <u>Women's Sports: A History</u>. New York: Columbia UP,
    1991.

Hart, Marie. "Sport: Women Sit in the Back of the Bus." <u>Psychology Today</u>
    Oct. 1971: 64-66.

Henderson, Keith. "Women Pressure Colleges on Sport." <u>Christian Science
Monitor</u> 19 July 1993: 12.

Kaplan, Janice. <u>Women and Sports</u>. New York: Viking, 1979.

LaNoue, George R. "Athletics and Equality: How to Comply with Title IX
    without Tearing Down the Stadium." <u>Change</u> Nov. 1976: 27+.

Lipsyte, Robert. "Equity, Plus or Minus." <u>New York Times</u> 15 Nov. 1992,
    late ed.: 30.

Milloy, Courtland. "Inspiring Girls Through Sports." <u>Washington Post</u> 14
    Apr. 1991, final ed.: K3.

Moran, Malcolm. "Title IX Is Now an Irresistible Force." <u>New York Times</u>
    21 June 1992, late ed.: 25+.

Delones 17

National Collegiate Athletic Association. "NCAA Gender-Equity Study
     Summary of Results." Overland Park, Kansas: March, 1992.

"One for Nancy, Six for Bonnie." Editorial. <u>Washington Post</u> 11 Feb. 1994,
     final ed.: A24.

Schreiber, Linda, and JoAnne Stang. <u>Marathon Mom</u>. Boston: Houghton,
     1980.

Schrof, Joannie M. "A Sporting Chance?" <u>U.S. News & World Report</u> 11
     Apr. 1994: 51-53.

Ullyot, Joan. "Forcing the Pace." <u>Runner's World</u> Jan. 1986: 43-51.

"A Winning Combination." Cardinal Club Brochure. Stanford, CA: Stan-
     ford U Dept. of Athletics, 1986.

Witteman, Paul A. "Last Waltz at Wimbledon." <u>Time</u> 11 July 1994: 61.

Alternate Documentation Styles (APA)

Many publications in the social sciences follow the APA style of documentation, outlined in the *Publication Manual of the American Psychological Association.* You will enounter this style (with some variations) in periodicals and books in areas like psychology, linguistics, or education.

For identification of sources in the text of a paper, the APA style uses the **author-and-date** method. When using this style, include the date of publication with the author's name: (Garcia, 1996). Do not repeat the author's name between parentheses if you have mentioned it in your text (1996). Often, the APA style identifies an authority and the publication date of research without a page reference. Interested readers are expected to familiarize themselves with the relevant research and consider its findings in context. However, include an exact page reference with all direct quotation.

Parenthetical Citation   Study the following possibilities. Note use of commas, of p. or pp. for "page" or "pages," of the symbol & for *and*, and of similar distinctive features.

1   Author and Date Only

> Anorexia nervosa is a condition of extreme weight loss that results when young women compulsively starve themselves (Grayfield, 1993).

2   Date Only   Author's name in your own text:

> As defined by Grayfield, anorexia nervosa is a condition of extreme weight loss that results when young women compulsively starve themselves (1993).

3   Page Reference   For direct quotation or specific reference:

> Anorexia nervosa is "not really true loss of appetite" but "a condition of emaciation resulting from self-inflicted starvation" (Huebner, 1982, p. 143).

4   Work by Several Authors   Name the several authors. Use et al. (for "and others") only in second or later reference.

> Much advertising promotes miracle diets promising young women beauty and success (Bennings, Vasquez, & Theroux, 1994).

> The harmful effects of crash diets have been well documented (Bennings et al., 1994).

5 Same Author   For several publications in the same year, use *a, b, c,* and so on, in order of publication:

> Menassis has conducted experiments yielding very different results (1993, 1994a, 1994b).

6 Reference to Several Sources   List in alphabetical order, divided by semicolons:

> Official statistics have tended to underreport or underestimate the true extent of homelessness (Bettinger, 1994; Cisneros & Verroux, 1993).

7 Unknown or Unlisted Author   Identify source by shortened title:

> The media pay much attention to the noisy extremes and not much to the quiet plodding middle ("The Culture Commissars," 1995).

8 Institutional Authorship   In general, use acronyms or abbreviations only in second or subsequent citation:

> Many promising drugs proved to have disastrous side effects (National Institute of Mental Health [NIMH], 1994).

> Research into the biochemistry of the brain has led to genuine breakthroughs in the treatment of emotional disorders (NIMH, 1994).

9 Personal Communications   Cite letters, memos, e-mail, or telephone interviews as personal communications. Include the date. Since they cannot be consulted or verified by the reader, do not include personal communications in your list of References.

> Police officers tend to feel that the media tend to give a negative slant to police work (Victor Gomez, personal communication, March 17, 1995).

References List Directory: APA 1994

Use the heading "References" for your final alphabetical listing of works quoted or consulted. Note the author-and-date sequence in parentheses at the beginning of the entry. Study the use of initials with authors' names, lowercase letters in titles, and the abbreviations p. or pp. for page numbers. Indent first line of each entry one half inch (or five typewriter spaces).

A. Articles in Periodicals

 1 Newspaper Article
 2 Magazine Article
 3 Article with Volume Number
 4 Article by Several Authors
 5 Unsigned or Anonymous Article
 6 Article with Subtitle
 7 Article with Number of Volume and Issue
 8 Signed or Unsigned Editorial
 9 Letter to the Editor
10 Review of a Book

B. Books (and Other Whole Publications)

11 Standard Entry for a Book
12 Book with Subtitle
13 Book by Several Authors
14 Later Edition of a Book
15 Book with Editor's Name
16 Book with Translator's Name
17 Several Works by Same Author
18 Part of a Collection or Anthology
19 One of Several Volumes
20 Part of a Book
21 Unspecified or Institutional Authorship
22 Encyclopedia Entry

C. Electronic and Nonprint Sources

23 Computer Service
24 Online Publication
25 Information Service
26 CD-ROM
27 Nonprint Media

A. Articles in Periodicals

1 Newspaper Article   Start with the last name of the author, followed by initials. Enclose the date in parentheses — do not abbreviate months: (1995, November 16). Do not put titles of articles in quotation marks. After the first word of title or subtitle, use lowercase letters except for words you would normally capitalize in your text. Italicize (underline) the name of the newspaper with normal capitalization for words in titles of publications.

Use p. or pp. for "page" or "pages." If appropriate, specify the edition of the newspaper — early or late, east or west: <u>The Wall Street Journal,</u> eastern ed., p. A3. If page numbers for the article are not continuous, use a comma to separate the numbers: pp. 7, 9–10.

> Lipsyte, R. (1993, September 24). An immovable barrier in the fight for equity: Weeks of women's sports stories don't add up to a day of football coverage. <u>The New York Times,</u> p. B11.

EDITOR'S TIP: Keep the article *The* in the names of newspapers like *The Wall Street Journal* or *The New York Times.*

2 Magazine Article Start with the last name of the author. Go on to date, title of article, and name of publication.

> Kirby, D. (1995, January/February). Sex miseducation. <u>Mother Jones,</u> 48.

3 Article with Volume Number Underline (italicize) the volume number for a periodical, with inclusive page numbers following after a comma: <u>6,</u> 152–169. (Do not use p. or pp. after a volume number.)

> Santley, R. S. (1985). The political economy of the Aztec empire. <u>Journal of Anthropological Research, 41,</u> 327-337.

If an article is concluded later in the issue, use a comma between the discontinuous page numbers.

> Miller, G. (1969, December). On turning psychology over to the unwashed. <u>Psychology Today, 2,</u> 53-54, 66-74.

4 Article by Several Authors List the names of all co-authors, last names first. Put the *and*-sign, or ampersand (&), before the last author's name.

> Gale, N. H., & Stos-Gale, S. (1981, June). Lead and silver in the ancient Aegean. <u>Scientific American, 258,</u> 176-177.

5 Unsigned or Anonymous Article If the author of an article is unnamed, begin your entry with the title. Alphabetize by the first word of the title, not counting *The, A,* or *An.*

> The blood business. (1972, September 11). <u>Time,</u> 47-48.

6 Article with Subtitle Use a colon to separate title and subtitle.

> Claflin, T. (1993, November/December). Monumental achievement: Twenty years after Vietnam, invisible vets get their memorial. <u>Ms., 4,</u> 83-88.

7 Article with Number of Volume and Issue   If page numbers are not continuous for the whole volume (each new issue starts with page 1), you may have to include the number of the issue. Put it in parentheses between the volume number and the page numbers: 6(3), 152–169.

> Steinhausen, H., & Glenville, K. (1983). Follow-up studies of anorexia nervosa: A review of research findings. Psychological Medicine: Abstracts in English, 13(2), 239-245.

8 Signed or Unsigned Editorial   After the title, add the label Editorial in square brackets. If the editorial is unsigned, begin with the title.

> Hernandez, C. (1994, September 27). Immigrants are not aliens [Editorial]. Harristown News, p. 7.

> Giving women a sporting chance. (1993, October 23). [Editorial.] The Los Angeles Times, p. B7.

9 Letter to the Editor   After the title, add the right label in square brackets.

> Nguyen, Frank. (1995, November 24). Managed care [Letter to the Editor.] The Los Angeles Times, p. 8.

10 Review of a Book   Start with author and title of review. Include title of book reviewed in square brackets.

> Sheaffer, R. (1995, November). Truth abducted [Review of the book Close encounters of the fourth kind: Alien abduction, UFOs, and the conference at MIT]. Scientific American, 273 (5),102-103.

B. Books (and Other Whole Publications)

11 Standard Entry for a Book   Use initials instead of author's first name and middle name. Capitalize only the first word of title or subtitle (but capitalize proper names that are part of a title as you would in ordinary prose).

> Gaylin, W. (1992). The male ego. New York: Penguin.

Use the full names of publishers, omitting only tags like Inc. or Co.: Cambridge, MA: Harvard University Press.

12 Book with Subtitle   Use a colon between title and subtitle.

> Bruch, H. (1973). Eating disorders: Obesity, anorexia nervosa, and the person within. New York: Basic Books.

13 Book by Several Authors   Put last name first for each of several authors. Use the *and*-symbol & (ampersand) instead of the word *and*.

Minuchin, S., Rosman, B., & Baker, L. (1978). <u>Psychosomatic families: Anorexia nervosa in context.</u> Cambridge, MA: Harvard University Press.

14 **Later Edition of a Book** If you have used a book revised or brought up to date by the author, identify the new edition the way it is labeled on its title page. After the title of the book, put 2nd ed. for second edition, for instance, or Rev. ed. for revised edition.

Zettl, H. (1997). *Television production handbook* (6th ed.). Belmont, CA: Wadsworth.

Rosenthal, R. (1987). Meta-analytic procedures for social research (Rev. ed.). Newbury Park, CA: Sage.

15 **Book with Editor's Name** Put abbreviation for "editor" (Ed. or Eds.) in parentheses.

Hartman, F. (Ed.). (1973). <u>World in crisis: Readings in international relations</u> (4th ed.). New York: Macmillan.

Popkewitz, T. S., & Tabachnick, B. R. (Eds.). (1981). <u>The study of schooling: Field based methodologies in educational research and evaluation.</u> New York: Praeger.

16 **Book with Translator's Name** Put the translator's name (or translators' names) followed by Trans. after the title.

Freire, P. (1970). <u>Pedagogy of the oppressed</u> (M. B. Ramos, Trans.). New York: Seabury Press.

17 **Several Works by Same Author** Repeat the author's name with each title; put works in chronological order.

Bruch, H. (1973). <u>Eating disorders: Obesity, anorexia nervosa, and the person within.</u> New York: Basic Books.

Bruch, H. (1978). <u>The golden cage: The enigma of anorexia nervosa.</u> Cambridge, MA: Harvard University Press.

18 **Part of a Collection or Anthology** Identify both the article or other short piece (poem, short story) and the collection of which it is a part. Reverse initial and last name only for author or editor of the part, not of the collection.

Rogers, C. R. (1969). Two divergent trends. In R. May (Ed.), <u>Existential psychology</u> (pp. 87-92). New York: Random House.

19 **One of Several Volumes** Include volume number.

Davis, S. P. (1984). <u>History of Nevada.</u> Vol 2. Las Vegas: Nevada Publications.

20 **Part of a Book** Use the appropriate label for a preface, introduction, afterword, or other front matter or end matter of a book.

Aufderheide, P. (1992). Preface. In P. Aufderheide (Ed.), Beyond PC: Toward a politics of understanding (pp. 1-4). Saint Paul, MN: Graywolf Press.

21 Unspecified or Institutional Authorship Reports issued by an organization and major reference books may list a group as the author or not specify authorship:

American Psychological Association. (1982). Ethical principles in the conduct of research with human participants. Washington, DC: Author.

22 Encyclopedia Entry List an unsigned entry in an encyclopedia or other reference work under first word of entry. If the author of the entry is identified, include the name.

Russia. (1994). In The new encyclopaedia Britannica (15th ed.) (Vol. 10, pp. 253-255). Chicago: Encyclopaedia Britannica.

C. Electronic and Nonprint Sources

23 Computer Service For material first published elsewhere but obtained through a computer service, include the name of the system and retrieval path (for instance, name of file and item number). Do *not* put a period after retrieval numbers or access numbers.

Schomer, H. (1983, May-June.) South Africa: Beyond fair employment. [On-line]. Harvard Business Review pp. 145, 156. DIALOG File 122, Item 119425 83316

24 Online Publication An availability statement replaces the publisher's name and location provided for print publications. The data needed may be a simple document number but may also be more extensive. For an article by Bridgeman published in the online journal *Psycholoquy* and accessed through the File Transfer Protocol (FTP), the full availability statement after author, date, and title may read as follows:

Available FTP: 128.112.128.1 Directory: pub/harnad File: psych.92.3.26. consciousness.11.bridgeman

25 Information Service If the material had been previously published elsewhere, provide original publishing data, followed by identification of the service and an item number. If the material had not been previously published, cite it as a complete publication published by the service:

Kurth, R. J., & Stromberg, L. J. (1984). Using word processing in composition instruction [On-line]. ERIC, ED 251 850

26 CD-ROM Include source and retrieval number or similar information.

> Croft, F. S. (1995). Cruising in cyberspace. [CD-ROM]. VocEd File: Item 875623

27 Nonprint Media Include label for medium used (in square brackets). Do not list personal communications, such as unpublished letters, telephone interviews, e-mail messages, and similar materials that are not a matter of public record. Identify source and date in your parenthetical citation in your text, for instance (S. Kosinki, personal communication, May 27, 1996).

> Maas, J. B. (Producer), & Gluck, D. H. (Director). (1979). Deeper into hypnosis [Film]. Englewood Cliffs, NJ: Prentice-Hall.
>
> Clark, K. B. (Speaker). (1976). Problems of freedom and behavior modification [Cassette Recording 022-46]. Washington, DC: American Psychological Association.
>
> DiSanto, F. Alienation [Art work]. San Jose, CA: Institute of Mexican American Art.
>
> Vitale, K. (Interviewer). (1996, May 6). Interview with C. Lobos. Behind the news. [Radio program]. Washington, DC: Public Broadcasting Service.

Sample Research Paper Pages (APA)

The following pages are the four opening pages of a research paper observing the APA style. The sample pages are followed by the complete list of References. Note the use of the author-date style both in the brief parenthetical references in the texts and in the detailed list of References at the end. Note the use of specific page references for direct quotations.

Child Criminals 1

James Perry

Professor Guth

English 176

21 November 1995

Child Criminals in Adult Courts — A Crime in Itself?

In August 1993, at a day camp in Savona, New York, Eric Smith, a 13-year-old, brutally murdered a 4-year-old. Eric grabbed the younger boy in a headlock, smashed his head three times with a rock, stuffed a napkin and a plastic bag in his mouth, pummeled his body with a rock, shoved a stick up his rectum, and poured a drink over his body. His trial began on August 1 in Bath, New York. Despite his young age, Eric was tried as an adult, due to the severity of his crime and also due to a law allowing children as young as 13 to be tried as adults when accused of murder (Nordheimer, 1994, p. B5). His act was indicative of some frightening trends in America — an increase in the severity of juvenile crime, and a decrease in the age at which children commit crimes. His trial also shows a current trend in American juvenile justice — children are being tried in adult courts in more cases and at younger ages. Experts, elected representatives, and the general public have been grappling with the issue of how to deal with juvenile crime, and treating youths as adults is currently a popular solution. Many issues are relevant in the debate over whether to try children as adults — how major a problem is juvenile crime; is being harsh with juvenile criminals in the best interest of the defendants and in society's best interest, in terms of rehabilitating criminals, deterring and reducing crime, and justice; is treating child criminals as adults the most effective and most cost-

Child Criminals 2

efficient way of dealing with them; and so on. The alternative to treating juveniles as adults I intend to treat in this paper is a more rehabilitative approach — some experts advocate more preventive efforts, as opposed to more punishment-oriented programs such as trying youths in adult courtrooms. In this paper, I intend to show the causes for the current sentiment towards trying youths as adults. Then I intend to argue that while juvenile crime is a problem, it may not be the epidemic that it has been made out to be, and that although it is necessary to be firm in dealing with juvenile criminals, the best way to deal with them may not necessarily be through adult courts and strictly "getting tough."

In a way, the American justice system seems to be coming full circle. The nation's first juvenile court was established in 1899 in Cook County, Illinois, as a way to deal with young offenders in a more rehabilitative style, as opposed to the harsher justice found in adult courts (Andrews, 1994). However, by the 1960s, the public became more concerned about juvenile crime, as the youth population was growing and becoming more violent. Americans have begun to question the principles and effectiveness of the current juvenile justice systems, and have argued in favor of harsher, firmer alternatives. The 1966 U.S. Supreme Court case *Kent* vs. *United States* established guidelines for the transfer of young offenders to adult courts. The youths' threat to the safety of the public and amenability to treatments within the juvenile justice system were to be considered (Houghtalin & Mays, 1991). Since this time, more and more laws have been proposed and implemented to make it easier, and in some cases mandatory, for youths to be sent to adult courts for certain crimes, both violent and non-violent. The

Child Criminals 3

public seems to want young criminals to be held responsible for their crimes and to be punished, and they believe that this can best be done in adult courts, where child criminals presumably will face harsher sentencing, often including time in adult prisons.

Measures to treat juvenile offenders as adults have been proposed and supported for several reasons in recent years. While some experts advocate and have implemented more preventive measures, these are difficult to implement and would have more of a long-term effect, leaving Americans wondering "what we are supposed to do in the meantime" (Methvin, 1994, p. 95). Bob Herbert argues that attempts to rehabilitate young offenders and treat them lightly are "well-intentioned" but "out of touch with the increasingly violent reality of juvenile crime" (1994, p. E15). Other measures have failed to reduce juvenile crime; for instance, gun control laws are not believed to have a significant effect on violent crime by youths, since they tend to obtain the guns through illegal means anyway (Witkin, 1991, p. 28). Although experts disagree as to the extent and seriousness of current juvenile crime, the fact is that the public feels that juvenile crime is a major problem, and they support measures to deal with it. An assistant Maryland public defender feels that the public's focus on juvenile crime created the "political climate" that exists supporting anti-juvenile crime measures (Stepp, 1994, p. A12).

Many officials within the justice system feel that some young criminals should be treated as adults and tried in adult courts. A study published in August 1994 showed that many judges in the juvenile justice system feel that "the criminal justice system should deal with young criminals more in the way it deals with adults." For instance, two out of five judges surveyed

Child Criminals 4

feel child offenders should be eligible to receive the death penalty in some

situations, and a majority felt that the minimum age for facing murder

charges should be lowered ("Tougher Treatment," 1994, p. A16). Former

administrator of the Office of Juvenile Justice and Delinquency Prevention

Ira Schwartz feels that "juvenile court judges and youth probation workers

are among the staunchest supporters of jailing for juveniles" (1989, p. 18).

Many legislators, and a large portion of the general public, share the

sentiments of these justice authorities. Maryland Delegate Joseph F. Vallario

Jr. feels that "if [youths] want to do adult-type crimes, we're going to treat

them like adults" (Stepp, 1994, p. A12). Another Maryland Delegate, Ulys-

ses Curie, writes that due to the increasing violence and youth of juvenile

offenders, "the juvenile system must be changed to respond to this reality"

by treating youths more like adults (1994, p. C8). Both Democrats and Re-

publicans support measures to treat young criminals more like adults; both

of the Maryland delegates quoted above are Democrats, and a major part of

the Republicans' "Contract with America" was the "Taking Back Our

Streets Act," which supported harsher punishment of crime ("Youth and

Crime," p. 18). In recent years, many states have added legislation that low-

ered the ages at which youths can be tried as adults for certain crimes,

added new crimes to those for which a juvenile may or must be tried as an

adult, implemented mandatory sentencing for children convicted of certain

crimes, and so on. For instance, in 1993, Louisiana added attempted mur-

der and aggravated battery to the list of offenses for which a juvenile may

be tried as an adult. Few politicians feel they can afford to be viewed as

"soft on crime" after speaking out against punitive treatment of troubled

youth.

Child Criminals 12

References

Andrews, J. H. (1994, March 7). Criminals, but still children. <u>Christian Science Monitor,</u> p. 17.

Armstrong, S. (1994, March 7). Colorado tries more carrot and less stick in punishing juvenile crime. <u>Christian Science Monitor,</u> pp. 1, 4.

Bayh, B. (1989). [Foreword]. In I. M. Schwartz, <u>(In)justice for juveniles: Rethinking the best interests of the child</u> (pp. xi-xiii). Lexington, MA: Heath-Lexington.

Curie, U. (1994, February 6). Reality requires tougher responses to juvenile crime. <u>The Washington Post,</u> p. C8.

Fiagone, C. (1995, February 13). Jacksonville's tough answer to problem of youth crimes. <u>Christian Science Monitor,</u> pp. 1, 14.

Herbert, B. (1994, July 24). Little criminals, big crimes. <u>The New York Times,</u> late ed., p. E15.

Houghtalin, M., & Mays, G. L. (1991). Criminal dispositions of New Mexico juveniles transferred to adult court. <u>Crime and Delinquency, 37,</u> 393-407.

Kotlowitz, A. (1994, February 13). Their crimes don't make them adults. <u>The New York Times Magazine,</u> pp. 40-41.

McLean, G. (1986, December 12). Adult prison is no place for a kid. <u>Christianity Today,</u> p. 13.

Methvin, E. H. (1994, April). Behind Florida's tourist murders. <u>Reader's Digest,</u> pp. 92-96.

Nordheimer, J. (1994, August 2). Murder trial begins for teen-ager. <u>The New York Times,</u> late ed., p. B5.

Child Criminals 13

Schwartz, I. M. (1989). (In)justice for juveniles: Rethinking the best interests of the child. Lexington, MA: Heath-Lexington.

Stefan, L. B. (1991). Youth and the law: Getting tough on juvenile crime. Boston: Benchmark Books.

Stepp, L. S. (1994, October 15). The crackdown on juvenile crime — Do stricter laws deter youths? The Washington Post, pp. A1, A12.

Tougher treatment urged for juveniles. (1994, August 2). The New York Times, late ed., p. A16.

Witkin, G. (1991, April 8). Kids who kill. U.S. News and World Report, pp. 26-32.

Youth and crime. (1995, January 10). [Editorial]. Christian Science Monitor, p. 18.

12

Editing Your Writing

The following guide covers editing needs that an editor or teacher may bring to your attention. Many of these become an issue when you shift gears from informal speech to the more formal written word. Educated written English has over the years become less conservative, less formal. For instance, much published prose has moved toward more open punctuation — for instance no commas to set off expressions like *for instance*. Nevertheless, much of your editing will focus on expressions or constructions still widely considered too informal for written English. Editing software will typically alert you to *potential* problems — you as the writer will have to make the right choice for the intended meaning or the context of the sentence.

Editing tasks are here listed under four major headings: WORDS — SENTENCES — MECHANICS — LARGER ELEMENTS.

Words

E1	red	Wordiness and Redundancy
E2	ww	Wrong Word
E3	inf, sl	Informal English and Slang
E4	cn	Concrete Words
E5	cl	Clichés and Buzzwords
E6	jrg	Jargon
E7	euph	Euphemisms
E8	MM	Mixed or Distracting Metaphor
E9	sx, off	Sexist or Offensive Language

Sentences

E10	s	Sentence Review
E11	frag	Complete Sentences and Fragments
E12	agr	Agreement
E13	vb	Problem Verbs
E14	ref	Pronoun Reference
E15	ca	Pronoun Case
E16	adv	Adverb Forms
E17	awk	Awkward Sentences
E18	pass	Weak Passive

E19	FP	Faulty Parallelism
E20	DM	Dangling Modifier
E21	sf	Shifts
E22	std	Standard English

Mechanics

E23	CS	Comma Splice
E24	cm/no cm	Restrictive/Nonrestrictive
E25	cm/no cm	Internal Commas
E26	ap	Missing or Misused Apostrophe
E27	cap	Capitals
E28	hy	Hyphens
E29	sp	Spelling Demons
E30	sp	*Its/it's*
E31	nb/ab	Numbers and Abbreviations

Larger Elements

E32	tl	Ineffective Title
E33	intro	Weak Introduction
E34	ths	Unfocused Thesis
E35	concl	Lame Conclusion
E36	¶/no¶	Weak Paragraphing
E37	dev	Undeveloped Point

Words

E1 red **Wordiness and Redundancy** Effective writers make their words count. They watch out for padding, filler, or deadwood. "The inflation *situation* was *kind of* getting out of hand" says no more than "Inflation was getting out of hand." "Admittedly this is *a* true *and logical fact*" says no more than "Admittedly this is true." Look out for roundabout expressions used where a single word would do:

WORDY	BRIEF
because of the fact that	because
at the present time	now
at a period of time when	when
in the not too distant future	soon
in this time and age	today
ask the question whether	ask whether

Look for roundabout transitions that could be replaced by a simple *therefore* or *however*:

WORDY: *In considering the situation, we must also take into account the fact that* many local residents do not share the city council's enthusiasm for large-scale development.

EDITED: Many local residents, **however**, do not share the city council's enthusiasm for large-scale development.

Wordiness caused by direct duplication is called **redundancy**. Intentional repetition helps you reinforce ideas, helping them sink in. However, *un*intentional, unnecessary repetition causes the piling up of unneeded words. Phrases like *basic fundamentals* are redundant — aren't all fundamentals basic? A *consensus of opinion* is redundant because that's what a consensus is — a meeting of minds, a reconciling of different opinions. Other redundant phrases are *important essentials, true facts, newly renovated, anticipate in advance, necessary prerequisite,* and *free gift*.

REDUNDANT: *As a rule* the media *usually* pay less attention to women's sports.

EDITED: **As a rule** the media pay less attention to women's sports.

REDUNDANT: This common *misconception* is completely *wrong*.

EDITED: This common **perception** is completely **wrong**.

E2 ww   Wrong Word   Some words are similar enough to be confused — like two mustachioed men of similar stature in a police lineup. An instructor, peer reviewer, or collaborator may alert you to slips like the following: "A basic *tenant* [**tenet**] of our country is mututal tolerance and respect." "The construction company had been a *benefactor* [**beneficiary**] of affirmative action policies."

ORIGINAL: With the *implication* of three-strikes-and-out laws, the prison population is expected to double over a period of twenty to thirty years.

EDITED: With the **implementation** of three-strikes-and-out laws, the prison population is expected to double over a period of twenty to thirty years.

E3 inf, sl   Informal English and Slang   You may have to shift gears from the chatty, personal style of informal everyday talk to a more objective academic style. (At the same time, you need to avoid a *hyper*formal style that would make your writing pompous or dull.) Telltale signs of informal English are tags like "Well, . . ." and "Yes, . . ."; the informal *you* (for people in general rather than strictly "you the reader"); folksy references to people as *kids, folks, guys,* or *gals;* abbreviations like *doc* and *prof;* overuse of contractions like *can't, won't,* and *couldn't;* expressions like *could care less, rub it in, cut it out.* Extremely informal English shades over into slang: *gyp the customers, shaft the voters.*

INFORMAL: When *you are* in kindergarten *your* teachers never tell you that some people think Columbus was a *bad guy.* When one of my friends made a comment about not celebrating Columbus Day *it finally dawned on me. I guess* when I *got to* college I learned about the things Columbus did. *I guess* one might say, *better late than never.*

MORE FORMAL: Teachers do not tell their students in kindergarten that Columbus has been charged with spearheading a bloody European invasion. I first became aware of the controversy when one of my friends made a comment about not celebrating Columbus Day. In college, I learned more about the charges against Columbus as a symbol of European domination and conquest.

E4 cn   Concrete Words   General words — all-purpose words — can make your writing flat or colorless. Try to draw on a wider range of words for specific contours, movements, or colors. Birds don't just fly; they *soar, swoop, wheel, glide, flap, flutter,* and *dive.* Water doesn't just flow; it *eddies, swirls, spurts, cascades, oozes,* and *drips.* Prizefighters don't just punch; they *jab, duck, feint, slug,* and *pound.* Consider going for the more **concrete** word — the word that calls up a vivid image in your reader's mind or brings the other senses into play.

What does each of the following more concrete words add to the meaning of the colorless all-purpose word it might replace? What does it make you see or hear or feel?

ALL-PURPOSE	CONCRETE
look	gaze, stare, peer, squint, ogle, pore
walk	stride, march, slink, trot, shuffle, prance, strut, scurry
sit	slump, squat, lounge, hunch, crouch
throw	hurl, pitch, toss, dump, flip
cry	weep, sob, sigh, bawl, whine, sniffle

E5 cl   Clichés and Buzzwords   **Clichés** are tired expressions, overused like a commercial that has been run too many times. We write clichés, or trite phrases, without thinking, and the reader reads them without paying attention. They come to mind ready-made, all glued together: *believe it or not, the last straw, off the beaten track, a shot in the arm, sink or swim.* They practically type themselves: "better late . . . than never"; "last but . . . not least"; "easier said . . . than done"; "few and . . . far between." At one point, the cliché may have been imaginative or witty ("only the tip of the iceberg"). However, most such expressions have long since lost the flavor, like stale bread.

While many clichés are *as old as the hills,* many **buzzwords,** or fashionable current clichés, are of more recent coinage. Everyone *looks at the big picture*, waits for *the window of opportunity* to open, and asks you to look at *the bottom line*. Everything has to be *cost-effective*, not to mention *user-friendly*. Expressions such as these may make you sound as if you had no ideas of your own. Look for fresh and attention-getting ways of saying what you want to say:

TRITE: The dean let us have it, *straight from the shoulder.*

FRESH: The dean spoke to us directly and urgently, **like a scout just re-turned from the enemy camp.**

TRITE: You will never rise to the top of the heap if every setback makes you *throw in the sponge.*

FRESH: You will never be truly successful if every setback makes you **think of defeat as inevitable, like the rain.**

E6 jrg **Jargon** Jargon is the unnecessary use of technical or scientific-sounding words in order to impress the reader. It tries to make the ordinary seem important: "Mandatory verification of your attendance record is required as you exit the work area." (Punch your time card when you leave.) To avoid jargon, watch for overuse of technical-sounding Greek and Latin words like *factors, phases, aspects, facets, phenomena, parameters, concomitants,* and *strata.* Check your writing for overuse of "heavy-duty" words ending in *-otion, -ation, -ition,* like *conceptualization* or *beautification.* Reconsider new-fangled *-ize* words like *maximize* (develop fully) or *prioritize* (rank). Watch out for impersonal constructions, like the **passive**, which often fails to tell us who does what. (On the passive, see also E18.)

PASSIVE: Procedures *were instituted* [by whom?] with a view toward imple-menting the new theoretical framework.

ACTIVE: The new superintendent **started to put** her ideas into practice.

Not all technical-sounding words are jargon. Terms like *gentrifi-cation* or *desertification* efficiently label processes of current con-cern. Jargon results when writers use their jargon generators to blow simple words up to a larger size. Although some of the more verbose words in the following pairs have legitimate uses, a high density of them is a danger signal, warning of dense prose ahead:

PLAIN	JARGON	PLAIN	JARGON
size	magnitude	relation	interrelationship
home	residence	methods	methodology
childhood	preadolescence	planned	preplanned

Look for opportunities to translate inflated prose into plain English:

JARGON: The new director was instrumental in instituting a new dramaturgy.

PLAIN ENGLISH: The new director **helped initiate a new way of doing theater.**

JARGON: Continued monetary support will be contingent upon a re-alization of desired outcomes.

PLAIN ENGLISH: Continued **funding will hinge upon your producing the right results**.

EDITOR'S TIP: Research reports in the sciences often require a more formal and impersonal style than prose of opinion and ideas. Even then, overuse of phrases like the following produces a wooden effect. You will usually want to avoid them in ordinary prose.

WOODEN	PLAIN
reference was made	I mentioned
careful consideration is imperative	we should study carefully
the hypothesis suggests itself	we can tentatively conclude

E7 euph **Euphemisms** Euphemisms are "beautiful" words — words more beautiful than the reality. Verbal upgrading turns gar-bage disposal into *waste management,* jails into *correctional facilities,* and physical education departments into *departments of human performance.* Verbal upgrading of job descriptions gives people improved status without a raise in salary: *sanitary engineer* for plumber, *language facilitator* for translator. Many euphemisms are **circumlocutions** — they "take the long way around": *immoderate use of intoxicants* for heavy drinking, *below the poverty line* for poor.

Effective writers know when to be blunt and direct. There are times when *substance abuse* is best, but there are also times when *drug addiction* may sound a clearer warning. When euphemisms are used with intent to deceive, they become **doublespeak**: The bomb-ing of civilians becomes *collateral damage*. Turning decent jobs into part-time jobs without benefits becomes *flexible scheduling*.

E8 MM **Mixed or Distracting Metaphor** Although figurative lan-guage can light up a whole passage, it can also entangle the reader in images that don't mesh. Watch out for the **mixed metaphor**, which at first *sails smoothly along* but then suddenly *jumps the tracks* (hard to do on the trackless sea).

MIXED METAPHOR: *Lacking the ignition of* advertising, our economic engine would *run at a slower pace.* (Without an ignition, the engine wouldn't just run more slowly; it wouldn't start.)

BETTER: Lacking the stimulus of advertising, our economy **would be sluggish, like a commuter deprived of the early morning cup of coffee.**

MIXED METAPHOR: Enriched programs give a student a chance to *dig deeper* into the *sea of knowledge.* (Digging is usually done on land, not at sea.)

BETTER: Enriched programs give a student a chance **to mine additional layers of knowledge.**

A special subspecies of mixed metaphor is the mixed cliché: "That's the whole kettle of fish in a nutshell." "Rome wasn't burnt in a day." "You can't stop an idea whose time has passed."

EDITOR'S TIP: Some figurative expressions, rather than making the reader's imagination soar, may cause it to nosedive. They are too strained or distracting.

DISTRACTING: Helplessly, the night clerk watched from his desk *while his stomach tied itself into knots.*

BETTER: As the night clerk helplessly watched the event from his desk, he experienced a sick, tense feeling in the pit of his stomach.

Sometimes dead metaphors come back to life when placed in the wrong context:

DISTRACTING: There are several million alcoholics in the world. *This is a staggering number.*

E9 sx, off   Sexist or Offensive Language   Edit for expressions that intentionally or unintentionally diminish other people or lock them into stereotypical roles. See Writer's Tools 8 for detailed guidelines on editing for sexist and offensive language.

SEXIST PRONOUNS: A doctor should give *his* nurse specific guidelines for *her* work. (assumes that doctors are male, nurses female)

GENDER-NEUTRAL: A doctor should give **his or her** nurse specific guidelines for **the nurse's** work.
Doctors should give **nurses** specific guidelines for **their** work.

STEREOTYPED: Health insurance companies discriminate against the *mentally ill.* (makes it sound as if these people are defined by their illness; the illness is all that matters about these people)

UNBIASED: Health insurance companies discriminate against **people with a mental illness.**

Sentences

E10s Sentence Review   To understand editorial comments or editing suggestions, a writer has to have some basic understanding of the building blocks of a complete English sentence. The following brief review should remind you of some of the most essential or most functional terminology. (Many other terms known to traditional grammarians are not included here.)

The most essential building blocks of the complete English sentence are the **subject** and a **verb**. The subject brings something into focus — then a verb starts to make a statement about it. Sometimes a verb alone completes the sentence: Speed *kills*. An **intransitive** verb "is not going anywhere"; it can tell the whole story.

S-V: Accidents **happen**. Experiments **fail**. The license **had expired.**

The core of the subject is usually a noun: *speed, accident, nation.* Some key features help you recognize nouns: You can change most nouns from one to several (singular to plural) by adding a plural ending: *car/cars, application/applications, child/children.* Often an article (*the* car, *an* application) or other noun marker (*this* child, *my* turn) signals that a noun is ahead. Verbs are different: A verb can show a change in time (**tense**) by a simple change in the word itself: *kills* (now)/*killed* (then); *agree* (now)/*agreed* (then). Often helping verbs (auxiliaries) help signal changing relationships in time: *has* agreed, *had* promised, *will* arrive, *are* waiting, *has been* circling, *would have* succeeded, *might have been* killed.

The verb often sets the subject in motion: Somebody *acts.* Something *happens.* To complete the sentence, you often have to go on after the verb. For instance you go on to fill in the target or the result of the action. A **transitive** verb carries the action across to an **object**: Coyotes kill *sheep.* Developments endanger *wildlife.* (Here the sheep and the wildlife are targeted; the action in the sentence is aimed at them.) With verbs like *give* or *send*, the sentence may take a detour to show the receiver or destination (**indirect object**): A friend had sold *the suspect* a gun. (We are told not only *what* was sold but also *to whom*.)

S-V-O: Officers write **tickets**. Engineers build **dams**. Booth shot **Lincoln**.

S-V-IO-O: The class wrote **the president a letter**. The agent gave **the motorist directions.** The association had awarded **the poet a prize.**

Note that **pronouns** (*I, he, we, us, them; this, that; nobody, every-one*) can substitute for a noun in a sentence: *We* despised *him. He* had sold *her* a gun. *Everybody* agreed. **Verbal nouns** (verbs turned into nouns) are a different kind of noun substitute; they also can take the place of a noun: *Meditating* reduces stress (S-V-O). The customers stopped *talking* (S-V-O).

Not all verbs signal actions or events. **Linking verbs** pin a label on the subject. They include *be (is, am, are, was, were, has been), become*, and *turn*: Gorillas are *apes*. Friends became *enemies*. The label is often a noun, but it can also be an adjective: The weather turned *cold*. Most adjectives can show degree: *fast/faster/fastest; dangerous/ more dangerous/most dangerous* (they fit in after *very*: very fast, very dangerous). The following are all complete English sentences:

S-LV-N: Whales are **mammals**. The operation had become **a liability**.

S-LV-ADJ: The audience was **hostile**. Our equipment became **obsolete**.

In two other common sentence patterns, a verb like *call* or *consider* pins a label on the object. We first go on to an object or target — and then attach a label.

S-V-O-N: The judge called **the accused a menace.** I consider **you my friend.**

S-V-O-ADJ: His lawyer called **the charges ridiculous**. He drives **me crazy.**

Additional sentence parts come into a sentence to fill in details or modify its meaning. Such **modifiers** answer questions like when? where? how? which one? what kind?

MODIFIERS: **Each year**, our equipment became obsolete **more quickly.**
             The judge **pronouncing sentence** called the accused a menace.
             Engineers build dams **to prevent floods.**

Many of the modifiers answering questions like which one or what kind are **adjectives**: *blue, sweet, heavy, obvious, wonderful.* Many modifiers answering questions like when, where, and how are **adverbs**: *quickly, obviously, reluctantly.* Many modifiers answering either kind of question are **prepositional phrases** — starting with a preposition like *at, on, in, by, with, for, without, about,* and *around:* (What kind?) Students *with green passes* may register late. (When?) Registration resumes *in the morning.*

ADJECTIVES: Their **small** tree produced **marvelous sweet juicy** oranges.

ADVERBS:	The **surprisingly** small gadget worked **incredibly well**.
PREPOSITIONAL PHRASES:	The car **with the three students from Ohio** got involved **in a head-on collision on a country road**.

(For more on phrases used as modifiers see E11 as well as E24 and E25.)

E11 frag **Complete Sentences and Fragments** Periods mark off complete sentences. They become a problem when they mark off **sentence fragments** — sentence parts that have been split off. Do not carry over into your writing the fragmentary sentences of casual conversation: "Everyone was wearing baggy pants. *Usually a size too big.*"

Most fragments come into your writing as an afterthought — after you have closed off the sentence of which they should be a part. If you have trouble with fragments, you need to study different kinds and learn how to link them to the preceding sentence:

• Fragments result when a possible subject, a possible verb, or *part* of the complete verb is missing. (*Was flying* and *had written* are complete verbs, but *flying* and *written* alone are not.)

NO SUBJECT:	The rig spun out of control. *Hit the center divider.* (What did?)
COMPLETE:	The rig spun out of control. **It** hit the center divider.
NO VERB:	Kathryn was working in Boston. *A systems analyst.*
COMPLETE:	Kathryn was working in Boston **as a systems analyst**.
NO COMPLETE VERB:	Commuters spend hours on the road. *Fighting the traffic.*
COMPLETE:	Commuters spend hours on the road **fighting the traffic**.

Groups of words without a subject and verb of their own are called **phrases**. Here are several kinds that cause fragments. (See E24 and E25 for more on appositives and participles.)

PREPOSITIONAL PHRASE:	You can hike to the canyon floor. *At your own risk.*
COMPLETE:	You can hike to the canyon floor **at your own risk**.
APPOSITIVE:	An extremist assassinated Rabin. *The prime minister of Israel.*

COMPLETE:	An extremist assassinated Rabin, **the prime minister of Israel.**
PARTICIPLE:	The company finally shut down its nuclear reactor. *First built in 1976.*
COMPLETE:	The company finally shut down its nuclear reactor, **first built in 1976**.

• Sentence units with a subject and verb of their own are called **clauses**. Fragments result when you set off **dependent** clauses, which need to be tied to the main statement (main clause). Many of these start with a **subordinator** (subordinating conjunction) like *when, if, unless, because, while,* or *whereas*. Other dependent clauses start with a **relative pronoun** like *who, whose, which,* or *that*. (See E24 for more on how to punctuate dependent clauses.)

FRAGMENT:	The country may go into default. *Unless Congress passes a budget.*
COMPLETE:	The country may go into default **unless Congress passes a budget**.
FRAGMENT:	Businesses tend to use IBM. *Whereas schools often use Macs.*
COMPLETE:	Businesses tend to use IBM, **whereas schools often use Macs.**
FRAGMENT:	The team wanted a new stadium. *Which the taxpayers would finance.*
COMPLETE:	The team wanted a new stadium, **which the taxpayers would finance**.

EDITOR'S TIP: Fragments may be a combination of several of the above types — for instance, an appositive followed by a relative clause:

FRAGMENT:	The new book attacked Margaret Mead. *The anthropologist who wrote pioneering books about non-Western cultures.*
COMPLETE:	The new book attacked Margaret Mead, **the anthropologist who wrote pioneering books about non-Western cultures.**

E12 agr **Agreement**   Agreement requires matching forms of subject and verb: "*Silence is* golden" (both singular); "*Words are* cheap" (both plural). "*A new factory creates* employment" (singular subject and verb); "*new factories create* employment" (plural subject and verb). Agreement may break down when a wedge comes between the subject and the verb:

FAULTY AGREEMENT: Racial tensions *among today's youth* has increased at an alarming rate. (What has increased? *Tensions have.*)

AGREEMENT: Racial **tensions** among today's youth **have** increased at an alarming rate.

FAULTY AGREEMENT: Deterioration *of poorly maintained and supervised Russian nuclear plants* frighten experts in the West. (What frightens them? *Deterioration frightens* them.)

AGREEMENT: **Deterioration** of poorly maintained and supervised Russian nuclear plants **frightens** experts in the West.

EDITOR'S TIP: Watch for sentences on the "I am not *one of those who believes* . . ." pattern. There are *several* of those who *believe* — and the speaker is one of them: "I am not one of those who *believe* in conspiracies."

AGREEMENT: Marcia is not one of **those women** who **expect** a man to change **their** tires for **them**.

E13 vb Problem Verbs Vacationers who are reclining *lie* or *are lying* in the sun; in the past, they *lay* or have *lain* in the sun. When we place something, we *lay* it down or, in the past, *laid* it down (or have *laid* it down). We *sit* somewhere (or *sat* in the past); we *set* something down (or *set* it down in the past). Written English keeps the hypothetical *were* (**subjunctive**) for remote possibility or wishful thinking:

SUBJUNCTIVE: If I **were** [not *was*] a senator, I would have to humor rich constituents. We all wish the election **were** [not *was*] over.

E14 ref Pronoun Reference Pronouns are shortcut words — *he* may stand for *the President of the United States*; *she* may stand for *the Supreme Court Justice*. To avoid confusion, make pronouns like *he, she, it, they,* or *this* point clearly to what they stand for.

AMBIGUOUS: When the *doctor* refused to treat the *patient*, she immediately consulted a lawyer. (*Who* turned to a lawyer?)

CLEAR: Immediately after **she** refused to treat the patient, **the doctor** consulted a lawyer.

Avoid the informal plural pronouns used in everyday speech in sentences like the following: "Everybody had to revise *their* schedules." Informal English here uses a plural pronoun — *they, their, themselves* — to point back to expressions that are singular in edited English: *everyone, everybody, anyone, anybody, no one, nobody.* Treat these **impersonal pronouns** (also *one* and *a person*) as if you were looking at everybody or anybody *one* at a time. Use the nonsexist double pronouns *he and she, his and her.* Or change the whole sentence to a plural:

> INFORMAL: *Everybody* in the police department had to reexamine *their* assumptions.
>
> NONSEXIST: **Everybody** in the police department had to reexamine **his or her** assumptions.
>
> ALL PLURAL: **All members** of the police department had to reexamine **their** assumptions.

EDITOR'S TIP: The pronoun *one* singles out *one* representative person — so *they* or *their* is the wrong pronoun to point back to it. (The very formal *one's* would technically be correct: "*One* should watch *one's* language.") Use the nonsexist *his or her* — or change the *one* to several: for instance, use *people* or *we* instead.

> FAULTY: Cliques become harmful when *one* loses *their* individuality and becomes a mindless member of the group. (mixed singular and plural)
>
> IMPROVED: Cliques become harmful when **people lose their** individuality and **become mindless members** of the group. (all plural)

E15 ca   **Pronoun Case**   Use the right pronoun forms for different positions in a sentence. Use the **subject form** — *I, he, she, we, they* — as the subject of a verb. Ask: *Who* did what? *He* signed the application. *She* initialed the contract. Use these subject forms especially when there is a double subject:

> SUBJECTS: **He and I** attended the conference (not: *Him and me* attended). **We and they** tend to disagree. **The manager and she** had a falling out.

Use the **object form** — *me, him, her, us, them* — as the object of a verb: None of the designs pleased *him*. The governor appointed *her* to the commission. We owe *them* a letter. Use these object forms especially when there is a double object:

> OBJECTS: The judge awarded **my partner and me** first prize (not: *my partner and I*). Nobody invited **him and her** to the same party.

Use the object form also as the object of a preposition — a word like *of, to, at, in, into, by, for, with, without, under, before, between*: for *me*, after *her*, without *him*, by *them*.

> OBJECTS: This is strictly **between you and me** (not: *between you and I*). The memo was addressed **to him and me.** The will made no mention **of her mother and her.**

EDITOR'S TIP: Use *whom* as the object form: *Whom* will they nominate? (*they* is the subject; *whom* is the object of *nominate*). Do not ask *for whom* the bell tolls. (*whom* is the object of the preposition *for*.)

SUBJECT: The man **who** I thought **was** the butler was really the owner. (I thought *he* was the butler.)

OBJECT: The candidate **whom** we thought they would **hire** backed out. (We thought they would *hire her*.)

E16 adv **Adverb Forms** Use distinctive adverb forms when you have a choice: repeat it *slowly;* spoke more *loudly*. Adjectives tell us what kind: *considerable success, has been admirable, good grades*. Adverbs tell us how: *aged considerably, performed admirably, scored well*. Some adjectives have no distinct adverb form: *fast track* and *running fast*. Adverbs come before adjectives to show degree: *really loud, awfully cold, mildly amusing*.

ADVERBS: Their assumptions differed **considerably**, but they **finally** worked **together really well.**

E17 awk **Awkward Sentences** Some garbled sentences result when the writer is aiming at the right idea but misses. In the following sentence, who does what?

GARBLED: A posthumous book is a book written by an author after he died.

ACCURATE: A posthumous book is a book **published** after its author died.

Other sentences become entangled in their own grammatical machinery, like runners tripping over their own feet. Try rewriting on the who-does-what model. For instance, many roundabout sentences use unnecessary grammatical props. Many *there-is* or *there-are* sentences take the long way around:

ROUNDABOUT: *There has been a tendency on the part of the voters* to blame bureaucrats for everything from inflation to potholes and littered neighborhood parks.

DIRECT: **The voters have tended** to blame bureaucrats for everything from inflation to potholes and littered neighborhood parks.

Look at the unnecessary props in a sentence like the following:

WORDY: This year *has been a* discouraging *one* for those *who are* committed to *the issue of* keeping steroids from skewing athletic competition in the sports arena.

TRIMMED: This year has been discouraging for those committed to keeping steroids from skewing athletic competition.

Many static sentences use too many nouns that *label* an action or procedure (*reconsideration*), rather than verbs, which put events in motion (somebody *reconsidered*). Look especially for *-ation, -otion, -ition* words that could be reactivated and turned into verbs:

STATIC: Frequent *disagreements* occurred among the partners concerning the *distribution* of funds.

ACTIVE: The partners frequently **argued** about how **to distribute** the funds.

STATIC: *Reconsideration* of the traditional goal of *rehabilitation* as against mere *warehousing* is becoming necessary.

ACTIVE: We need to **reconsider** whether to **rehabilitate** or merely **warehouse** criminals.

EDITOR'S TIP: Editors and style-checking software alert authors when too many sentences follow a "Such and such *is* . . ." rather than a "Somebody *does* . . ." pattern. They flag overuse of the linking verb *be (is, was, has been,* and so on) — which can become a weak link.

STATIC: *An important asset of any company is* the willingness to rethink its organizational structure.

DYNAMIC: **Any company will profit** from its willingness to rethink its organizational structure.

E18 pass   **Weak Passive**   Unnecessary passives can make for weak, roundabout sentences. Most English verbs have two sets of forms, depending on how we look at an action or event. Dogs *bark* (they are doing it), but dogs *are trained* (this is happening to them). Forms like *barks, barked, is barking, have barked, or will bark* are **active** forms of a verb. Forms like *is trained, are trained, is being trained, had been trained,* and *will be trained* are **passive** forms of a verb. When you change a sentence to the passive, the original subject moves and then follows the verb after *by*. Or it may disappear from the sentence altogether.

ACTIVE: *Health insurance companies* prefer healthy customers.

FULL PASSIVE: Healthy customers are preferred *by health insurance companies.*

ACTIVE: *Companies* have canceled policies after the customer got sick.

SHORT PASSIVE: Policies have been canceled after the customer got sick.

An active sentence looks at an action from the point of view of the agent or doer. Whoever or whatever is active in the sentence is the subject of the sentence: *Companies are cutting* costs. The **passive** reverses this usual doer — action — target perspective. It looks at an action from the point of view of the recipient or the target. In passive sentences like the following, the person at the receiving end becomes the subject of the sentence. The passive works well when you want to focus attention on the target, the receiver, the result:

> EFFECTIVE PASSIVE: **Workers are laid off** in the name of "flexible scheduling." Over two hundred thousand **students were pushed out** of college in California.

However, the passive is lame or roundabout when the doer or agent in a sentence is important but is buried after a passive verb.

> AWKWARD: After each simplification of the tax laws, longer and more impenetrable *instructions must be puzzled out* by the taxpayer.
>
> ACTIVE: After each simplification of the tax laws, **the taxpayer must puzzle out** longer and more impenetrable instructions.

Do not use the passive because you think that it will make your writing sound impressive:

> PRETENTIOUS: *My experiences* at writing *were greatly increased* because of two long essays due each week.
>
> ACTIVE: **I wrote** more than ever, having to turn in two long essays each week.

E19 FP **Faulty Parallelism** Sentences read smoothly when *and, or,* and *but* link sentence parts that are **parallel** — that fit into the same grammatical category. *Body and soul* is parallel (two nouns); *red, white, and blue* is parallel (three adjectives); *to be or not to be* is parallel (two infinitives, or *to* forms). Sentences like the following are well-balanced because they line up identical sentence parts:

> INFINITIVES: Two things that a successful advertisement must accomplish are **to be noticed** and **to be remembered.** (two *to*-forms)
>
> CLAUSES: The young people **who brood** in their rooms, **who forget** to come down to the dining hall, or **who burst** out in fits of irrationality are not worrying about who will win the big game.

Faulty parallelism results when a part of your sentence snaps out of the expected pattern. To improve parallelism, change *race and ethnic quotas* to *racial and ethnic quotas.* Change *personal and society needs* to *personal and social needs.* Edit sentences like the following to make the mismatched sentence parts parallel:

NONPARALLEL: My friends loved *the wilderness* and *to backpack* to solitary lakes.

PARALLEL: My friends loved **to explore** the wilderness and **to backpack** to solitary lakes.

NONPARALLEL: He told us about his marital *problems*, his *loss* of his job, and *what he was going to do next.*

PARALLEL: He told us about his marital **problems**, his **loss** of his job, and his **plans** for the future.

NONPARALLEL: Reporters wondered whether *to believe* her or *should they try* to verify her story.

PARALLEL: Reporters wondered whether they should **believe** her or **try** to verify her story.

EDITOR'S TIP: Repeating structural links like prepositions (*for, to, by, at, with*) or subordinators (*if, when, whether, because*) will sometimes help you realign mismatched sentence parts:

NONPARALLEL: The story focuses on whether *the old man will capture* the large fish or *will the fish* elude him.

PARALLEL: The story focuses on **whether the old man will capture** the large fish or **whether the fish will elude** him.

E20 DM   Dangling Modifier   Modifiers like *losing a job* need to point clearly to *who* is losing a job. Otherwise, the modifier is left dangling:

DANGLING: *Losing a job,* feelings of self-doubt are natural. (*Who* is losing the job?)

IMPROVED: **Losing a job, we** naturally experience self-doubt.

DANGLING: *Upon interviewing her,* she explained that she had suffered from anorexia. (*Who* was interviewing her?)

IMPROVED: **When I interviewed** her, she explained that she had suffered from anorexia.
Upon interviewing her, I learned that she had suffered from anorexia.

DANGLING: *Left in the parking lot for a week, car thieves* quickly stripped her Toyota. (The thieves were left in the lot?)

IMPROVED: **Left in the parking lot for a week, her Toyota** was quickly stripped by car thieves.

A **misplaced** modifier will point to the wrong part of the sentence:

MISPLACED: *At three years old, his grandparents* placed him in an orphanage.

IMPROVED: His grandparents placed **him** in an orphanage **at three years old.**

When **he was** three years old, his grandparents placed him in an orphanage.

E21 sf   Shifts   Look out for shifts in perspective that may distract or confuse the reader. For instance, do not shift from a third party to the informal *you*. Similarly, do not jump from past to present. Do not shift from a factual to a more hypothetical mode, or vice versa. The following sentences show first a common kind of shift and then (boldfaced) the more consistent form.

Once *a singer* becomes a celebrity, *you*/**she** can write *your*/**her** own ticket.

As the plane *lifted* off the runway, we *hear*/**heard** a terrible grating sound.

If the refugees *come* here, they *would*/**will** be refused asylum.

If the refugees *came* here, they *will*/**would** be refused asylum.

EDITOR'S TIP: Sometimes you have to adjust time relationships (tense) to prevent confusion:

The mayor visited the office where she *worked*/**had worked** as a supervisor.

E22 std   Standard English   The **nonstandard** English many Americans hear in the neighborhood or on the job differs from the standard English of school and office. *He don't, she don't,* and *the government don't* are nonstandard for *he doesn't, she doesn't,* and *the government doesn't. Hisself* and *theirself* are nonstandard for *himself* and *themselves. Knowed* and *growed* are nonstandard for *knew* and *grew. These kind* is nonstandard for *this kind* or *these kinds.*

The following sentences show first a common nonstandard form (in italics) and then the corrected standard form.

Our pious neighbors *had went*/**had gone** to church.

An overeager reporter *had already wrote*/**had already written** his obituary.

He *could have took*/**could have taken** early retirement but turned it down.

The fish *is froze*/**is frozen** and then shipped by plane.

Nonstandard English uses **double negatives**, which say no twice. (In standard English the double negative is a "no-no.")

Nobody uses snail mail *no more/***anymore**.
The official-looking envelopes don't fool *no one/***anyone**.
I *can't/***can** hardly wait.

EDITOR'S TIP: Use *a* only before a consonant that is actually pronounced: *a house, a chair, a C, a proposal.* Use *an* before vowels and unheard consonants: *an accident, an omission, an A, an F, an honest mistake, an unnecessary precaution* (but *a useful distinction*).

Mechanics

E23 CS   Comma Splice   Use the **semicolon** to link independent clauses, that is, complete subject–verb statements: "Somebody does one thing; someone else does another." "Something happens here; something else happens there." A period could separate the two statements if you wanted a stronger separation. The semicolon serves as a kind of semi-period:

PERIOD:	One of our senators voted for the bill. The other voted against it.
SEMICOLON:	One of our senators voted for the bill; the other voted against it.

A **comma splice** results when only a comma holds together two such complete statements — statements that *could* appear independently, kept separate. Change the comma to a semicolon:

COMMA SPLICE:	Prejudice is making a comeback, hate crimes are on the increase.
SEMICOLON:	Prejudice is making a comeback; hate crimes are on the increase.
COMMA SPLICE:	Manuel was despondent, he had lost a friend.
SEMICOLON:	Manuel was despondent; he had lost a friend.

• Use the semicolon also when links of the *however* type join two complete statements. These **conjunctive adverbs** include familiar logical links like *therefore, consequently, nevertheless, besides, moreover, similarly, indeed, in fact,* and *on the other hand.* These are movable words; they may move to the middle or the end of the second statement. Their relative freedom of movement is a trait they share with other adverbs. Note that the semicolon stays put where the two statements join.

COMMA SPLICE:	Math is the language of science, *however,* too few students master it.
SEMICOLON:	Math is the language of science; **however,** too few students master it.

> Math is the language of science; too few students, **however,** master it.
>
> Math is the language of science; too few students master it, **however.**

• The comma is right when the two complete statements are joined by a word like *and* or *but*. There are seven such **coordinators** (or coordinating conjunctions): *and, but, so, for, or, nor,* and *yet.* Use the comma when they join two complete statements. Use no comma when they join words or phrases (groups of words without both a subject and a verb of their own).

    COMMA: She slammed on the brakes, **and** the car screeched to a halt.
                   Many are called, **but** few place an order.
                   It was a holiday, **so** the stores were closed.

    NO COMMA: The car swerved **and** turned over.

E24 cm/no cm **Restrictive/Nonrestrictive** Many comma rules hinge on the distinction between restrictive and nonrestrictive. **Restrictive** material brings in essential specifications or conditions. Without them, the point made in the original statement does not apply. **Nonrestrictive** material adds extra information that does not affect the main point; the main statement is true regardless.

• Much essential information comes into a sentence after **subordinators** (subordinating conjunctions) like *if, when, where, before, after, while, until, since,* and *unless*: Use *no* comma when these introduce essential specifications or conditions:

    RESTRICTIVE: My problems will be solved **if** I win in the lottery. (only if)
    (NO COMMA)   You will be evicted **unless** you pay now. (then you are ok)
                   We will consider your application **after** you provide a transcript. (only then)

Nonrestrictive material added in a second statement might be good to know, but it does not change or invalidate the main point. The main point is true regardless. Much nonessential information comes into a sentence after subordinators like *though, although, whereas,* or *no matter how.* It is set off by a comma:

    NONRESTRICTIVE: He graduated with honors, **although** he had done battle
    (COMMA)   with dyslexia. (true regardless)
                       Switzerland stayed neutral, **whereas** countless other countries were drawn into the war. (true regardless)

Subordinators like *because* illustrate the restrictive/nonrestrictive distinction well. Sometimes the reason for something is the main point of the sentence (no comma). At other times you may consider it merely optional, add-on information (comma).

NO COMMA: They left the country **because** they lived in poverty without hope.

COMMA: Many immigrants went to Canada first, **because** visas were easier to get.

When a subordinator adds material to the main statement, the new material may *come before* the original statement, reversing the usual order. Regardless of whether the added material is restrictive or not, use a comma then to show where the main clause starts.

SUBORDINATOR FIRST: **If** I win in the lottery, my problems will be solved.
Although he had done battle with dyslexia, he graduated with honors.

• The restrictive/nonrestrictive distinction applies equally when information is brought into a sentence by the **relative pronouns**: *who (whom, whose), which,* and *that.* Use no comma when the added clause specifies which one or what kind — when it is needed to single out one from a group, or a group among other groups.

NO COMMA: Students **who use racist language** may be expelled. (which students?)
Whales are marine animals **that need to surface to breathe**. (what kind of animals are they?)

Use the comma (or commas) when the person or the group is already sufficiently identified. A *who*-clause or *which*-clause then adds optional extra information:

COMMAS: Gorbachev, **who presided over the dissolution of the Soviet empire,** became a sought-after speaker in the West.

COMMA: Marina's relatives returned to the Ukraine, **which had become an independent nation**.

• The comma rules for restrictive and nonrestrictive apply to **participles** (or participial phrases). Present participles use the *-ing* ending (*repeating, investigating, being sought, having been outlawed*). Many past participles end in *-d* or *-n* (*used, terminated, taken*).

NO COMMAS: Fishing fleets **using sophisticated technology** are decimating a limited natural resource. (Traditional methods were less destructive.)
Fishing communities fight legislation **designed to protect endangered species of fish**. (They fight those particular laws.)

COMMAS: Cod, **almost fished out in some locations,** has made a comeback. (This applies to the whole species.)

Use a comma to set off any *introductory* participial phrase, restrictive or not:

COMMA: **Squeezed by dwindling supplies and strict new regulations,** many operators sold their boats.

Set off participial phrases that seem to carry their own subject with them (absolute constructions):

COMMA: **Its canneries shuttered,** the town faced a grim future.
Other things being equal, the company likes to hire local people.

Punctuate adjective phrases (with the key word an adjective) the same as participial phrases:

NO COMMA: Developers **aware of the new regulations** modified their plans. (only those who were aware)

COMMA: Developers, **aware of the new regulations,** modified their plans. (all were aware)

E25 cm/no cm   Internal Commas   Edit out unnecessary commas. Follow these rules for commas setting off added elements:

• An **appositive**, a second noun putting a label on the first, is usually set off by commas: Jonas Salk, *the discoverer of the polio vaccine.* Use no comma when the second noun helps readers tell two people of the same name apart: Oliver Wendell Holmes *the Supreme Court Justice* [not the writer].

APPOSITIVE: Charles Darwin, **the pioneering naturalist,** avoided photographers.

• Include the last comma in a **series** (three or more of one kind) that follows the a, b, and c pattern: *red, white, and blue; single, married, or divorced.*

SERIES: Charles Darwin avoided **lectures, dinner parties, and photography sessions.**

• Set off introductory **prepositional phrases** with three or more words. Prepositional phrases start with prepositions — words like *at, in, on, for, with, without, before, after, during,* or *despite.*

PREP. PHRASE: **Despite Darwin's reluctance,** a few photographers captured his image.
For Darwin's followers, acknowledging our kinship with the apes did not seem demeaning.

- Set off the contrasting item in the **"this, not that"** pattern:

  CONTRAST: Huxley, **not Darwin,** was the most articulate defender of
  evolution.

- Use a comma to separate **city and state** (and the state from the
rest of a sentence): *Austin, Texas.*

  CITY AND STATE: The company moved its operations from **Detroit, Michigan,** to **Memphis, Tennessee.**

E26 ap   Missing or Misused Apostrophe   The apostrophe is a writing convention with no equivalent in speech. A missing or misused
apostrophe is a telltale sign that can make an intelligent person
seem uneducated. The apostrophe signals the **possessive**, which
shows that one thing belongs to or is related to another: *the singer's
voice, the president's advisors, this fall's fashions, this morning's paper.*
The rules are simple:

- SINGULAR: apostrophe and added -*s* for singular (one owner)

  the mayor's office, the youngest brother's bicycle, a single parent's needs,
  her husband's guns, the Pope's visit

- *S*-PLURAL: apostrophe *only* for plurals that already have an -*s*
(several owners)

  both parents' responsibilities, the boys' locker room, their husbands' guns,
  the girls' voices

- UNMARKED PLURAL: apostrophe and added -*s* for plurals that
have no plural -*s* (like *men, women, people, children*)

  all women's rights, both men's records, people's memories, the children's
  hour

- SPECIAL PROBLEMS: Singular/plural pairs like *man/men,
woman/women, family/families,* or *city/cities* cause special spelling
problems:

  a man's world *but* the men's room; this woman's pay *but* most women's
  salaries; one family's memories *but* both families' memories; a city's
  problems *but* many cities' problems

The same basic rules apply to expressions specifying time or
amount:

  TIME/AMOUNT — SINGULAR: today's paper, tomorrow's meeting, yesterday's
  accident; a week's wage, a month's salary, a dol-
  lar's worth

TIME/AMOUNT — PLURAL: two weeks' pay, three months' salary, ten dollars' worth

Watch for correct placement of the apostrophe in shortened forms, or **contractions.** Check correct spelling of *don't, can't, doesn't, won't,* or *shouldn't. You're* is short for *you are* (*your* means belonging to you). *They're* is short for *they are* (*their* means belonging to them).

Note: Possessive pronouns (*hers, ours, yours, theirs, its*) do *not* use the apostrophe:

NO APOSTROPHE: We thought the painting and **its** frame were **yours** and not **theirs.**

E27 cap Capitals Capitalize proper names — for instance, the names of individual people (including their titles), publications, institutions, vessels, holidays: *John F. Kennedy, General Colin Powell, the Washington Post, the Department of Defense, the Titanic, the Fourth of July.* Capitalize both individual names and labels derived from them: *Marxist economics, Freudian psychology.* In particular, capitalize the names of countries, nationalities, languages, and religions: *England, Great Britain, Spain, Brazil; English, Spanish, German, Portuguese; Christian virtues, the Greek Orthodox tradition, Buddhist priests, a Methodist chapel.* Capitalize the names of months and days of the week but not of the seasons: *the first Monday in September; in the spring of 1995.* Capitalize specific courses but not general subjects: *General Education 32* and *Biology 2A* but *a general education requirement in biology.*

With titles of written work or creative work of all kinds, capitalize first and last words (also first word of a subtitle). Within the title, capitalize all words except articles (*the, a, an*), coordinators like *and* or *or*, and prepositions (words like *at, for, by, in, with, without,* and *among*): *A New Guide to Organic Gardening.*

EDITOR'S TIP: Some general labels, usually lowercase, are capitalized when they are used as proper names: *we drove due west* but *the West and Southwest; democratic institutions* but *the Democratic candidate.*

E28 hy Hyphens Hyphenate combinations like *in-laws, great-grandparents, self-conscious, cost-effective, one-dimensional, cancer-causing, drive-in,* and *write-off.* (Check an up-to-date dictionary when in doubt.) Hyphenate double numbers: *twenty-four, seventy-three.* Hyphenate combinations like *up to date* and *word of mouth* when they appear *before* a noun to show what kind: *up-to-date information, word-of-mouth publicity.* (But write: The information was *up to date.*)

Ethnic labels are now often used without a hyphen: *Irish American, African American, Mexican American:*

NO HYPHEN: Sandra Cisneros became an effective voice for the **Mexican American community.**

E29 sp   Spelling Demons   Poor spelling will damage your credibility, no matter how intelligent or hard-working you are. About two dozen familiar spelling demons cause the most noticeable spelling errors in student writing. Check for the unforgivables.

definite, definitely	(think *finish)*
receive	(think *ceiling)*
separate	(think *parade)*
perform	(think *perfume)*
environment	(think *iron)*
achieve	(think *chief)*
surprise	(think *surplus)*

Watch for problem pairs like *refer* but *referred* (and *referring), prefer* (and *preference*) but *preferred, occur* but *occurring* (and *occurrence).* Spell *a lot* as two words, *nowadays* as one. Watch for confusing doubles:

affect/effect	Absences *affect* (influence) your grades; new regulations *effect* (produce) changes.
accept/except	We *accept* (take *in*) money for dues; we *except* (take *out*) seniors over 65.
conscious/conscience	We are *conscious* or *unconscious*; we have a good or bad *conscience.*
to/too	We travel *to* Chicago (direction), and we start *to* run (action), but we are *too* tired (excess), and someone else is, *too* (also).

Here are other spelling demons to watch for in your proofreading or in running a spell-check.

accommodate	conscience	possible
athlete, athletic	dependent, independent	probably
basically	existence	similar
believe	government	studying
business	library	villain

E30 sp   Its/It's   Avoid the *it's* trap. Use *it's* only when you mean *it is* or *it has*: *it's* been raining, *it's* happened before. Better yet, don't use *it's* at all — since half of the time it's wrong. Use *it is* or *it has* if that's what you mean. Use *its* (*without* the apostrophe) to show where something belongs. (*Its* is a possessive pronoun.)

the band and *its* leader   the corporation and *its* officers
the government and *its* representatives   America and *its* neighbors

E31 nb/ab **Numbers and Abbreviations**   In ordinary prose (rather than in tables, summaries of statistics, and the like) spell out single-digit numbers and round numbers with no more than two words: *at age seven; about two thousand people attended.* Use numerals for most other uses of figures: *only 23 applied.* Use numerals for dates, street numbers, and page numbers: *January 1, 1997; 2789 Blueberry Street; page 173.* Use numerals for exact figures, exact sums, measurements, and technical data: *two dollars* but *$18.59.* Use numerals with A.M. and P.M.: *four o'clock* but *4:35 P.M.* Avoid numerals at the beginning of a sentence: *Fifteen out of 23 applied* or *Of the first sample, 15 out of 23 applied.*

Avoid overusing abbreviations. Use *Mr., Ms., Dr.,* and *M.D.,* but use *Prof., Rev., St.,* and *Ave.* only in addresses. In ordinary prose, spell out the names of states (but write *Washington, DC*). In ordinary prose (rather than invoices or the like) spell out foot, inch, pound, ounce, and percent: *two inches short, 85 percent.* Examples of acceptable abbreviations include: *65 mph, 200 rpm.*

Larger Elements

E32 tl **Ineffective Title**   Good titles are at the same time informative and inviting. Stake out the territory. Include a keyword or descriptor that a computer search could track:

UNTRACEABLE: Unanswered Questions

TRACEABLE: **Unanswered Questions about Cave Art**

At the same time, use the title to challenge or intrigue the reader. Try to make your reader say: "This I want to read!"

ROUTINE: Gun Control

BETTER: **Shooting Straight on Gun Control**
                  Biting the Bullet: America and Gun Control

ROUTINE: Affirmative Action

BETTER: **Affirmative Action Evens Things Out**
                  Affirmative Action: Making or Destroying Dreams

EDITOR'S TIP: No underscoring or quote marks with your title (unless it *is* a quotation). Do not use all caps. Capitalize all major words, with lowercase for articles (*a, an, the*), prepositions (*in, on, at, for, with, without, about*), and coordinators (*and, or, but*). Capitalize the first and last word of your title.

E33 intro   **Weak Introduction**   What is your lead or hook? Use a brief pointed introduction to bring your subject to life. Use your dramatic opening to lead up to your central question or key point. Routine introductions (often merely restating the assignment) are a poor strategy. Readers have short attention spans and are easily distracted by other claims on their time. Here are suggestions for rewriting introductions that are too general and colorless:

• Start with a striking *example* or *incident* that will dramatize the issue.

COLORLESS: **Gun Control**

The issue of gun control has been a major concern for some time now. There have been many biased and unbiased studies published on both sides of the coin. . . .

IMPROVED: **Crime Control, Not Gun Control**

An eighteen-year-old Asian male has no need for a gun unless he is pressured by his friend to have one so that he can officially be "one of them." This is the reason that Kim pulled a gun on my friend when a drink was accidentally spilled. The gun was then pointed straight at my head as I tried to prevent any outbreak, with the words: "Get the f — k out of my way, or I'll shoot you too, bitch."

• Open with startling *statistics.*

COLORLESS: **Smog Control**

Smog has long been a hot topic of debate between environmentalists and conservatives who oppose environmental legislation. . . .

IMPROVED: **The Air We Breathe**

When serious efforts to fight smog first started, according to the Environmental Quality Laboratory at Caltech, Los Angeles County had air that did not meet state air quality standards for photochemical oxidants (such as ozone) on 65 percent of the days, for carbon monoxide on 55 percent of the days, and for nitrogen dioxide on 31 percent of the days.

Many measures were undertaken to rectify this problem, including imposing strict emission controls through smog control devices for automobiles. However, in a recent year California state air quality standards for the Los Angeles Basin were still being exceeded on 110 days during the course of the year.

• Use a thought-provoking *quotation* (or quotations) that will make the issue real for your reader and lead directly into your thesis:

COLORLESS: **White Males**

The problem of discrimination and unfairness to white males may seem absurd to many Americans; however, this is presently a legitimate problem in American society that affects more facets of life than one would originally be led to believe. The discrimination claim, although mostly subjective in nature, is open to a variety of interpretations and affects such parts of society as the job market and the university campus. Investigating the causes, effects, and extent of the situation is the only way to understand and provide solutions to this controversy. There is presently a growing trend among American white males who consider themselves discriminated against. *In American society the white male who was traditionally in authority is under pressure.*

IMPROVED: **Angry White America**

Observers of American society today tell us that "the emotional landscape for the white male is changing." White men are feeling "frustrated, resentful, and most of all afraid," says Michele Galen in her *Business Week* cover story entitled "White, Male, and Worried." John Leo of *U.S. News and World Report* defines the problem as "the demonizing of white men," viewed as "a relentlessly rape-minded and harassing oppressor." In an informal survey of 15 young white males in the freshman dormitory on a university campus, 66 percent believed that they had been discriminated against in one way or another because of their race and sex. *In American society today, the white male, who was traditionally in a position of authority, feels he is under pressure.*

EDITOR'S TIP: You may want to experiment with a *provocative opening statement* to get the attention of the jaded reader. (How might you expect each writer to follow up?)

> Californians are afraid of the future.
> People like killers.
> Today, when a man falls among thieves, the people walking by on the other side of the road call the Good Samaritan a bleeding-heart.

E34 ths   **Unfocused Thesis**   A focused thesis statement shows that the writer has asked: "What is the central point I am making in this paper? How does all the material I have brought together add up?" An unfocused thesis makes it seem as if the writer has taken the easy way out, postponing any hard thinking about the issue till later.

UNFOCUSED: Mandatory life imprisonment of third-time offenders raises interesting points.
              (It probably does. But what *are* they?)

FOCUSED: Mandatory life imprisonment of third-time offenders appeals to voters fed up with crime, but it has its flaws — financial and human costs that most of its supporters do not realize.

E35 concl   **Lame Conclusion**   What can you do to give added punch to your paper by adding a strong conclusion? Do not just let your paper run down. Avoid a tired conclusion that dutifully repeats your main points one more time. Rewrite endings that offer no more than a pious hope, requiring no thought or action of writer or reader: "In the end the good sense of the American people will prevail."

Leave your reader with a strong final impression or a thought to remember. End on a strong note; try giving the reader a memorable punchline:

PARTING SHOT: Taxpayers have pumped so much money into pushing young people in trouble into jail that they can no longer afford to push them into a classroom, into a life of opportunity.

EDITOR'S TIP: Experiment with *circling back* to an opening image, quotation, or incident.

E36 ¶/no ¶   **Weak Paragraphing**   When lengthy passages run on without division into paragraphs, the reader needs a break. Find a logical place to start a new paragraph, so that your reader can follow your account or your argument one step at a time. At the opposite extreme, if several choppy paragraphs appear in a row, your thinking may seem to proceed by fits and starts. Reconsider when several consecutive two-sentence or three-sentence paragraphs seem to raise issues or suggest ideas without following through.

You may occasionally want to use a strategically placed short (one-sentence or two-sentence) paragraph for emphasis:

For decades, environmentalists and concerned citizens have fought the battle to bring contaminated dead lakes and rivers back to life. When toxic effluents from saw mills and manufacturing plants are kept out of rivers, fish and other aquatic life forms return. When sewage plants are modernized, lakes again become places to wade in and to swim in. Human beings starved for fresh air and fresh water can again feel a part of their natural environment. People doing cost-effectiveness analyses of the cleanup of our lakes and rivers need to factor in the returns in improved mental health.

Clean water exhilarates and relaxes.

E37 dev   **Undeveloped Point**   Often a point you have made needs follow-up — an explanation, an example, or authoritative support.

UNDEVELOPED: Gerrymandering is an old American tradition.

DEVELOPED: Gerrymandering is an old American tradition. Politicians in control of drawing up election districts have often designed districts of weird shape (like a salamander) to give candidates of their own party a better chance of being elected. More recently, districts have been set up with enough of a concentration of minority voters to give minority candidates a chance of getting elected.

David Wagoner, "The Other House" from *First Light*. First appeared in *The Slackwater Review*. Copyright © 1983 by David Wagoner. Reprinted by permission of Little, Brown and Company.

Alice Walker, "Everyday Use" from *In Love & Trouble, Stories of Black Women*. Copyright © 1973 by Alice Walker. Reprinted by permission of Harcourt Brace & Company.

Rebecca Walker, "A Day in the Life." Originally appeared in *Ms.* Magazine, July/August 1991. Copyright © 1991 by Rebecca Walker. Reprinted by permission of the author.

George F. Will, "The Barbarity of Boxing" from *The Washington Post*, November 21, 1982. Copyright © 1982 by the Washington Post Writers Group. Reprinted by permission.

Naomi Wolf, "Age and the Beauty Myth" from *The Beauty Myth*. Copyright © 1991 by Naomi Wolf. Reprinted by permission of William Morrow & Company, Inc.

Joanna H. Woś, "The One Sitting There." Originally appeared in *Flash Fiction*, edited by Thomas/Thomas/Hazuka (Norton 1992). Every attempt has been made to locate the rights holder of this selection. If the rights holder should read this notice, please contact Houghton Mifflin Company, College Permissions, 222 Berkeley Street, Boston, MA 02116-3764.

Kim Wozencraft, Excerpts from *Notes from the Country Club*. Copyright © 1993 by Code 3 Communications, Inc. Reprinted by permission of Houghton Mifflin Co. All rights reserved.